Charles J. Ellicott

A critical and Grammatical Commentary

on St. Paul's epistles to the Philippians, Colossians, and to Philemon, with a revised translation

Charles J. Ellicott

A critical and Grammatical Commentary
on St. Paul's epistles to the Philippians, Colossians, and to Philemon, with a revised translation

ISBN/EAN: 9783337378387

Printed in Europe, USA, Canada, Australia, Japan

Cover: Foto ©Lupo / pixelio.de

More available books at **www.hansebooks.com**

A CRITICAL AND GRAMMATICAL COMMENTARY

ON

ST. PAUL'S EPISTLES

TO THE

PHILIPPIANS, COLOSSIANS,

AND TO

PHILEMON,

WITH A REVISED TRANSLATION.

BY

RT. REV. CHAS. J. ELLICOTT, D.D.,

LORD BISHOP OF GLOUCESTER AND BRISTOL.

Andover:
WARREN F. DRAPER.
BOSTON: W. H. HALLIDAY AND COMPANY,
NOS. 58 AND 60 CORNHILL.
PHILADELPHIA: SMITH, ENGLISH, AND CO.
1872.

PREFACE TO THE FIRST EDITION.

THE present volume forms the fourth portion of my Commentary on St. Paul's Epistles, and contains an exposition of the important Epistles to the Philippians and Colossians, and of the graceful and touching Epistle to Philemon.

The notes will be found to reflect the same critical and grammatical characteristics, and to recognize the same principles of interpretation as those which I endeavored to follow in the earlier portions of this work, and on which the experiences slowly and laboriously acquired during this undertaking have taught me year by year more confidently to rely. There is, however, a slight amount of additional matter which it is perhaps desirable briefly to specify.

In the first place, I have been enabled to carry out more fully and completely a system of reference to the great versions of antiquity, and have spared no pains to approach a little more nearly to those fresh and clear, yet somewhat remote, well-heads of Christian interpretation. In the notes on the Pastoral Epistles it was my endeavor to place before the reader, in all more important passages, the interpretations adopted by the Syriac, Old Latin,[1] and Gothic Versions. To these in the present volume I have added references to the Coptic (Memphitic) and Ethiopic Versions; to the former as found in the convenient and accessible edition of Bötticher, to the latter as found in Walton's Polyglott, but more especially and exclusively to the excellent edition of the Ethiopic New Testament by the late Mr. Pell Platt (1830), published by the Bible Society. These have been honestly and laboriously compared with the original; but, as in the preface to the Pastoral Epistles, so here again would I earnestly remind the reader that though I

---

[1] I have now adopted this term, feeling convinced that the term 'Italic' is likely to mislead. The latter I retained in the previous Epistles, as sanctioned by common usage; I was, however, fully aware that the term 'vetus Itala' really belonged to a recension, and not to an independent version. In the present Epistles I have derived the Old Latin from the translation in that language as found in the Codex Claromontanus.

have labored unflinchingly, and have spared no pains faithfully to elicit the exact opinion of these ancient translators, I still am painfully conscious how very limited is my present knowledge, and many must needs be my errors and misconceptions in languages where literary help is scanty, and in applications of them where I find myself at present unaided and alone. Poor, however, and insufficient as my contributions are, I still deem it necessary to offer them; for I have been not a little startled to find that even *critical* editors of the stamp of Tischendorf,[1] have apparently not acquired even a rudimentary knowledge of several of the leading versions which they conspicuously quote: nay more, that in many instances they have positively misrepresented the very readings which have been followed, and have allowed themselves to be misled by Latin translations, which, as my notes will passingly testify, are often sadly and even perversely incorrect. I fear, indeed, that I am bound to say that on the Latin translations attached to the now antiquated edition of the Coptic New Testament by Wilkins, from which Tischendorf appears to have derived his readings, little reliance can be placed; and on that attached to the Ethiopic Version in Walton's Polyglott even less, because not only as a translation is it inexact, but as a representative of the Ethiopic Version, worse than useless, as the text was derived from the valueless edition of 1548 (Rome), which in its transfer to the Polyglott was recruited with a fresh stock of inaccuracies.

It is fair to say that in this latter version Tischendorf appears to have also used the amended translation of Bode, but even thus he is only able to place before the reader results derived from an approximately accurate translation of a careless reprint of a poor original; and thus to give only inadequately and inaccurately the testimony of the ancient Ethiopic Church. The really good and valuable edition of Pell Platt has lain unnoticed and unused, because it has not the convenient appendage of a Latin translation. The same remark applies to the edition of the Coptic Version by Schwartze and Bötticher, which, though differing considerably less from that of Wilkins than the Ethiopic of Platt from the Ethiopic of the Polyglott, is similarly devoid of a Latin translation, and has, in consequence, I fear, received proportionately little attention.

Under these circumstances, when our knowledge even of the true *readings* of these two versions is still so very limited, I do not shrink from offering my scanty contributions, which, though intentionally *exegetical* in character, may be found to some extent useful even to a critical editor. Gladly, most gladly,

---

[1] The fourth volume of the new edition of Horne's *Introduction* will show how conscientiously our countryman Dr. Tregelles has acted in this respect, and what pains he has taken to secure an accurate knowledge of versions in languages with which he himself did not happen to be acquainted.

should I welcome other laborers into the same field, nor can I point out to students in these somewhat intractable languages a more really useful undertaking than a correct Latin translation of Platt's Ethiopic Version, and a similar translation of the portions of the Coptic New Testament published by Schwartze and his less competent successor.

I will here add, for the sake of those who may feel attracted towards these fields of labor, a few bibliographical notices, and a few records of my own limited experiences, as these may be of some passing aid to novices, and may serve as temporary finger-posts over tracks where the paths are not well-trodden, and the travellers but few.

In Coptic, I have used with great advantage the grammar of Archdeacon Tattam, and the lexicon of the same learned editor. The more recent Lexicon of Peyron has, I believe, secured a greater reputation, and as a philological work seems deservedly to rank higher, but after using both, I have found that of Tattam more generally useful, and more practically available for elementary reading, and for arriving at the current meaning of words. The very valuable Coptic grammar of Schwartze cannot be dispensed with by any student who desires to penetrate into the philological recesses of that singular language, but as a grammar to be put into the hands of a beginner, it is of more than doubtful value.

In Ethiopic, the old grammar of Ludolph still maintains its ground. The author was a perfect Ethiopic enthusiast, and has zealously striven, by the most minute grammatical subdivisions, to leave no peculiarities in the Ethiopic language unnoticed and unexplained; the student, however, must not fail to exercise his judgment in a first reading, and be careful to confine himself to the general principles of the language, without embarrassing himself too much with the many exceptional characteristics which this difficult[1] language presents. These leading principles, especially in the second edition, are sufficiently well-defined, and will easily be extracted by any reader of moderate sagacity and grammatical experience. The recent Ethiopic grammar of Dillmann has passed through my hands, but my acquaintance with it is far too limited to pronounce on it any opinion. As far as I could judge, it seems to be very similar to that of Schwartze in Coptic, and only calculated for the more mature and scientific student. With regard to lexicons, there is, I believe, no better one than that of Ludolph (2d ed.). That of Castell, alluded to in the preface to the *Pastoral Epistles*, I have since found to be decidedly inferior.

I do venture then to express a humble hope, that even with no better

---

[1] This epithet must be considered as used subjectively. To me, who am unfortunately unacquainted with Arabic, this language has presented many difficulties. The Arabic scholar would very likely entirely reverse my judgment.

literary appliances than these, earnest men and thoughtful scholars may be induced to investigate patiently and carefully the interpretations of these ancient witnesses of the truth. Surely the opinion of men, who lived in such early ages of the Church as those to which the chief ancient versions may all be referred, cannot be deemed unworthy of attention. Surely a version like the old Syriac, parts of which might almost have been in the hands of the last of the apostles, a venerable monument of almost equal antiquity like the Old Latin, a version so generally accurate as that of Ulfilas,[1] a version so distinctive as that of the Coptic, and so laborious as Platt's Ethiopic,[2] cannot safely be disregarded in the exposition of a Divine Revelation, where antiquity has a just and reasonable claim on our attention, and where novelty and private interpretation can never be indulged in without some degree of uncertainty and peril.

With these three *earthly* aids, first, an accurate knowledge of Hellenic Greek; secondly, the Greek commentators, and thirdly, the five or six principal ancient versions, we may (with humble prayer for the illuminating grace of the Eternal Spirit) address ourselves to the task of a critical exposition of the Covenant of Mercy; we may trust that, though often with clouded and holden eyes, we may yet be permitted to see and to recognize some sure and certain outlines of Divine Truth: but without any of these, or with one, or even two, to the exclusion of what remain, dare we hope that our interpretations will always be found free from uncertainties and inconsistencies, and will never exhibit the tinges of individual opinion, and the often estimable, but **ever precarious, subjectivity** of religious predilections?

I fear indeed that these remarks are but little in unison with popular views and popular aspirations; I fear that the patient labor necessary to perform faithfully the duty of an interpreter is unwelcome to many of the forward spirits of our own times. To be referred to Greek Fathers when suasive annotations of a supposed freer spirit, and a more flexible theology claim from us a hearing; to be bidden to toil on amid ancient versions, when a rough and ready scholarship is vaunting its own independence and sufficiency; to weigh in the balance, to mark and to record the verging scale while religious prejudice is ever struggling to kick the beam, — all seems savorless, unnecessary, and impracticable. I fear such is the prevailing spirit of our own times; yet, amid all, I seem to myself to descry a spirit of graver

---

[1] Some tinges of Arianism have been detected in this Version, *e. g.* Phil. ii. 8, 'ni vulva rahnida visan sik *galeiko* [surely not a correct translation of ἴσα] guþa,' but are not sufficiently strong to detract seriously from the general faithfulness of the Version.

[2] I regret that I cannot in any way agree with my valued acquaintance Dr. Tregelles, in his judgment on the Ethiopic Version: in St. Paul's Epistles I have found it anything but 'the dreary paraphrase' which he terms it in his remarks in Horne. *Introduction*, Vol. IV. p. 319.

search winning its way among us, a more determined allegiance to the truth, a greater tendency to snap the chains of sectarian bondage, and it is to those who feel themselves animated by this spirit, who are quickened by the desire at every cost to search out and to proclaim the truth, who think that there is no sacrifice too great, no labor too relentless, in the exposition of the word of God, — to them, and to such as them, I would fain, with all humility, commend the imperfect and initial efforts to elicit the testimony of the ancient versions which these pages contain, and it is from them that I hopefully look for corrections of the errors and inaccuracies into which my inexperience will, I fear, be often found to have betrayed me.

Another addition which I have striven to make, and which the profound importance of the subject has seemed to require, consists in the introduction of a few *doctrinal* comments upon the passages in these Epistles which relate to our Saviour's divinity; and this I trust no one will deem supererogatory. The strongly developed tendencies of our own times towards humanitarian conceptions of the nature and work of our divine Master, — tendencies often associated with great depth of feeling and tenderness of sympathy, — seem now to demand the serious attention of every thoughtful man. The signs of the times are very noticeable. The divinity of the Eternal Son is not now so much assailed by avowed heretical teaching, as diluted by more plausible, perhaps even more excusable, but certainly no less destructive and pernicious, developments of human error. The turmoil of Arian and semi-Arian strife has comparatively ceased, to be succeeded, however, by a more delusive calm, and a more dangerous and enervating repose. In the popular theology of the present day, the Eternal Son is presented to us under aspects by no means calculated to rouse any active hostility or provoke any earnest antagonism. All is suasive and seductive: our Lord is claimed as united to us by human affinities of touching yet precarious application; He is the prince of sufferers, the champion of dependence and depression, the representative of contested principles of social union; His crucifixion becomes the apotheosis of self-denial, the atonement the master work of a pure and sublimated sympathy, — all principles and aspects the more dangerous from involving admixtures of partial truth, the more harmful from their seeming harmlessness. It is against this more specious and subtle form of error that we have now to contend; it is this plausible and versatile theosophy that seeks to ensnare us by its appeal to our better feelings and warmer sympathies, that seems to edify while it perverts, that attracts while it ruins, that it is now the duty of every true servant of Jesus Christ to seek to expose and to countervail. And this can be done in no way more charitably, yet more effectually, than by simply setting forth with all sincerity, faithfulness, and truth, those portions of the word of life which declare the true nature of the Eternal Son in language that no exegetical artifice can successfully explain away, and against which Arian, semi-Arian, Deist, and Pantheist, have beaten out their strength in vain.

Under these feelings, then, in the important doctrinal passages in these Epistles which relate to our Lord's divinity, I have spared no pains in the endeavor candidly and truthfully to state the meaning of every word, and to put before the younger reader, in the form of synopsis or quotation, the great dogmatical principles and deductions which the early Greek and Latin Fathers, and more especially our own Divines of the seventeenth and early part of the eighteenth century have unfolded with such meek learning, such perspicuity, and such truth. I need scarcely remark that here I have had to rely solely on my own reading; for in the works of the best German commentators sound dogmatical theology will I fear too often be sought for in vain, and even in the more recent productions of our own country, subjective explanation and an inexact and somewhat diffluent theology have been allowed to displace the more accurate and profound deductions of an earlier day. On this portion of my labors more than on any other may the Father of Lights be pleased to vouchsafe His blessing, and to overrule these efforts to issues beyond their own proper efficacy, and to uses which my earnest aspirations, but not my sense of their realization, have presumed to contemplate.

A few additions will be found in what may be termed the *philological* portion of this Commentary. Wherever the derivation of a word has seemed obscure, and an exact knowledge of its fundamental meaning has seemed of importance to the passage, I have noted in brackets its probable philological affinities, and stated, with all possible brevity, the opinions of modern investigators in this recently explored domain of literature. Gladly would I have found this done to my hand in the current lexicons of England or Germany, as it would have saved me not only much labor, but many unwelcome interruptions; but upon the philology of modern lexicons I regret to say very little reliance can be placed. Even in the otherwise admirable lexicon of Rost and Palm, which, I may here remark, is now brought to a completion, it is vexatious to observe how much philology has been neglected by its compilers, and how uncertain and precarious are the derivations of all the more difficult words.

With regard to references to former notes, which, now that my work has extended to eight Epistles, have necessarily become somewhat numerous, I have endeavored to observe the following rule. Where the reference has appeared of less moment, I have contented myself with a simple allusion to the former note. Where the reference has seemed of greater moment, and the note referred to contains any critical or grammatical investigations, I have generally endeavored to embody briefly in the note before the reader the principles previously discussed, leaving the fuller detail to be sought for in the note referred to. My desire is thus to make each portion of this work as much as possible an independent whole, and while avoiding repetition still to obviate, as far as is compatible with the nature of a continuous work, the necessity of the purchase or perusal of foregoing portions.

A few concluding words on the Translation. I have more than once had my attention called to passages in former commentaries, where the translation in the notes has not appeared in perfect unison with that in the Revised Version. In a few cases I fear this may have arisen from an omission to correct the copy of the Authorized Version which lay beside me, but I believe in most instances these seeming discrepancies have arisen from the fact that the fixed principles on which I venture to revise the Authorized Version do not always admit of an exact identity of language in the version and in the note. In a word, the translation in the note presents what has been considered the most exact rendering of the words taken *per se*; the Revised Version preserves that rendering as far as is compatible with the *lex operis*, the context, the idioms of our language, or lastly, that grave and archaic tone of our admirable version which, even in a revised form of it designed only *for the closet*, it seemed a kind of sacrilege to displace for the possibly more precise, yet often really less expressive, phraseology of modern diction. Needlessly to divorce the original and that version with which our ears are so familiar, and often our highest associations and purest sympathies so intimately bound, is an ill-considered course, which more than anything else may tend to foster an unyoked spirit of scriptural study and translation, alike unfilial and presumptuous, and to which a modern reviser may hereafter bitterly repent to have lent his example or his contributions.

I desire in the last place to record a few of my many obligations. These, however, are somewhat less than in earlier portions of this work, as the great and unintermitting labor expended in the examination of the ancient versions, especially the Coptic and Ethiopic, has left me little time, and, perhaps I might say little need, for consulting commentaries of a secondary character. These it is not necessary to specify, but the student who may miss their names on my present pages will, I truly believe, have gained far more from the ancient versions that have been adduced, than lost by the writers that have been left unnoticed.

Of the larger commentaries, I have carefully and thoughtfully perused the excellent commentary of my friend, Dean Alford. From it I have not derived much directly, as I deemed it best for the cause of that truth which we both humbly strive to advance, to consult for myself the original authorities and various exegetical subsidies that were alike accessible to us both, that so my adhesion to the opinions of my able predecessor, or my departure from them, might be the result of my own deliberate investigations. At the same time I have been particularly benefited by the admirable perspicuity of his notes, and have felt rejoiced when our opinions coincide, and unfeignedly sorry when I have deemed myself compelled to take a contrary or antagonistic side.

To the commentaries of De Wette and Meyer, but especially to those of the latter, I am, as heretofore, greatly indebted for grammatical and exegetical details, but in the dogmatical portions I have neither sought for nor derived any assistance whatever. To German commentaries the faithful and candid expositor of Scripture is under great obligations, but for theology, he must turn to the great doctrinal treatises of the Divines of our own country.

Of separate commentaries on the *Philippians*, the learned and laborious production of Van Hengel has been on many occasions extremely useful from its affluence of grammatical examples; but it is rather deficient in that brevity and perspicuity of critical discussion which is nowhere more indispensable than in the aggregation of parallel passages, and the comparison of supposed, but perhaps illusory, similarities of structure.

The commentary of Wiesinger is thoughtful and sensible, and not unfrequently distinguished by a sound and persuasive exegesis. Those of Rilliet and Hölemann, but especially the former, deserve consideration, but have been still so far superseded by more modern expositions, that it will in all cases be advisable for the student to read them with some degree of caution and suspended judgment.

Of commentaries on the *Colossians*, I must first specify the learned and exhaustive work of Bishop Davenant, which has certainly not received that attention from modern expositors which it so fully deserves. Its usefulness is somewhat interfered with by the scholastic form in which the notes are drawn up, nor is it free from the tinge of theological prejudice; but there is a thoroughness and completeness of exegetical investigation, which render it an exposition which no student of this profound Epistle will be wise to overlook.

Of modern commentaries, that of Huther will well repay the trouble of perusal, but both this work and that of Bähr have been so thoroughly examined by De Wette and Meyer, and in many passages so assimilated and incorporated, that a separate study of them is rendered somewhat less necessary. They will, however, always be referred to with advantage, but this should not be apart from a consideration of the opinions of their successors, and of the various rectifications which a more accurate scholarship has occasionally been found to suggest.

The commentary of Professor Eadie has been of occasional service to me; but, as in the commentary on the *Ephesians*, so here also I fear I am compelled in candor to say, that the grammatical comments do not always appear quite exact, nor are the doctrinal passages always discussed with that calm precision and dignified simplicity of language which these subjects seem to require and suggest; still most of the exegetical portion is extremely good, nor will any reader rise from the study of this learned, earnest, and not unfrequently eloquent volume, unimproved either in head or in heart.

Notices of the other and larger commentaries on the New Testament, or on St. Paul's Epistles, to which I have been in the habit of referring, will be found in the prefaces to the preceding portions of this work.

It now only remains for me to commit this volume to the reader, with the earnest prayer to Almighty God that he, who has so mercifully sustained me with health and strength during the anxieties of continued research and the pressure of protracted labor, may be pleased to grant that this research may not prove wholly fruitless, this labor not utterly in vain.

ΤΡΙΑΣ, ΜΟΝΑΣ, 'ΕΛΕΗΣΟΝ.

CAMBRIDGE, OCTOBER 20, 1857.

PREFACE TO THE SECOND EDITION.

The second edition of this portion of my labors is now at length presented to the reader. Like the second edition of the portion which preceded, the Pastoral Epistles, it has been delayed till time could be found for calmly and deliberately reviewing and reconsidering the whole work.

This duty has now been performed. Every portion of the commentary has been read over; every interpretation has been tested; and, I might almost add, every citation of Scripture has been examined and verified anew. For this labor, which has occupied a considerable portion of the past summer, there is but little to show. The book remains nearly in all its details as well as in its larger features exactly what it was. A very few readings, and those unimportant, have been changed; a certain number of alterations have been introduced in the Revised Translation; a small number of references to standard sermons, which had been either overlooked or not known when the commentary was written, are now added; and lastly, a short introduction has been prefixed to each one of the three Epistles that are included in this volume.

This I fear is all that I have to show for the time spent in preparing this edition. Yet perhaps that time has not been spent wholly in vain. It now enables me, with all humility, and with a thorough consciousness of my own imperfections and shortcomings, yet with some measures of chastened confidence, to commend to the reader the interpretations of the many great doctrinal passages,—especially those bearing on the Majesty and Divinity of our adorable Lord,—which he will find in the first two of the portions of Holy Scripture contained in this volume. Those interpretations (which, let it be observed, are nearly in every case those of the early versions or Greek commentators, stated only in a little more precise and technical language) have been again carefully tested. The accuracies of modern scholarship have been anew brought to bear upon them, the finesse and ingenuity of modern exegesis have been freely applied to the passages which they expound to us; and the result is that these ancient interpretations appear to have as strong claim upon our attention as ever, and, in an age of unlicensed criticism and sadly deceitful dealings with the word of God, to stand forth as examples of what the meek wisdom of earlier days regarded as the true and accurate method of expounding the message of salvation.

If such be the result of these present labors,—if the renewed testimony of one humble witness may be permitted in any degree effectually to warn the young and the earnest from rash and unblest modes of Scriptural interpretation; if these pages may be thought in some measure to show that the deductions of rigorous scholarship and of catholic truth stand ever in the truest union,—then I shall humbly and devoutly rejoice, and bless God that amid many recent hinderances and distractions I have been thus enabled carefully to revise and calmly to reconsider a very important portion of my labors, and thus to commend it with renewed confidence to the Christian student.

May the blessing of the Father of Lights rest on all readers and expounders of his inspired Word, and move us all, in these proud and dangerous days, to yield up our high thoughts unto him who 'of God is made unto us wisdom,' and to determine, even as an inspired apostle determined amid the sceptical disputants of his own times, 'not to know anything save Jesus Christ and Him crucified.'

C. J. ELLICOTT.

Exeter, September, 1861.

INTRODUCTION.

This fervent, affectionate, and, in parts, pathetic Epistle was written by the apostle to his liberal and warmhearted converts in the Roman colony of Philippi, towards the close of his *first* captivity at Rome (see *Introd. to* 1 *Tim.*), and at a time when, it would seem, his imprisonment was of a closer and harsher character, and his earthly prospects, though not by any means without hope (ch. i. 25, 26 ; ii. 24), yet, in many respects, cheerless and depressing (ch. i. 20 sq., ii. 17, 28). It has thus been supposed, with some probability, to have been written after the death of the Prætorian Prefect (Burrus) to whom the apostle had been at first entrusted (Acts xxviii. 16), and by whom, as we may infer from Acts *l. c.*, he had been treated with leniency and consideration.

As the death of Burrus took place in A. D. 62 (Clinton, *Fasti Rom.* Vol. I. p. 44), and as there are some expressions in the Epistle that seem distinctly to imply that the captivity had been of some duration (ch. i. 13 sq., comp. ii. 26), we may fix the date of the Epistle towards the close of, or more probably about the middle of, A. D. 63, and may thus place it as the last in order of the *four* Epistles written during the first captivity at Rome : see Davidson, *Introd.* Vol. II. p. 373.

The circumstances that gave rise to the Epistle appear to have been simply the fact of Epaphroditus having come from the Church of Philippi with contributions to alleviate the necessities of the captive apostle, — contributions which, as we learn from the Epistle itself (ch. iv. 15, 16 ; compare 2 Cor. xi. 9), this liberal Church had promptly sent on other and earlier occasions. Moved by this fresh proof of love evinced by his dearly-beloved Philippians, — his 'joy and crown' as he affectionately terms them (ch. iv. 1), the apostle avails himself of the return of Epaphroditus, who now, after a dangerous illness (ch. ii. 27), was on his way back to Philippi, to send to that Church *and* its chief officers (ch. i. 1; see notes *in loc.*) by the hand of their own messenger, his warm and affectionate thanks, mingled with personal notices relative to his own state, earnest commendations, pointed but kindly warnings, and varied expressions of consolation and encouragement. No Epistle written by the inspired apostle is pervaded with a loftier tone of cheering exhortation (see notes on ch. iii. 1); none in which the pressing forward for 'the prize of the high calling of God in Christ Jesus' is set forth in language of greater animation; none in which imitation of his own love of his Master is urged upon his converts in strains of holier incentive (compare ch. iii. 17–21). The supposition that there were definite parties and factions in the Church of Philippi, and that the Epistle was designed to expose their errors, and especially those of the Judaists, does not seem tenable. It is clear that Judaizing teachers had intruded into the Church of Philippi (ch. iii. 2), but it seems also clear that their teaching had at present met with but little reception.

The *genuineness* and *authenticity* of the Epistle are very convincingly demonstrated by external testimony (Polycarp, *ad Philipp.* cap. 3, Irenæus, *Hær.* IV. 34, ed. Grabe, Clem.-Alex. *Pædag.* I. p. 129, ed. Pott., Tertull. *de Resurr. Carn.* cap. 23), and even more so by the individuality of tone and language. Doubts have been urged by a few modern writers, but they have been justly pronounced by all competent critics as wholly unworthy of attention. The same may be said of the doubts as to the unity of the Epistle: see Davidson, *Introd.* Vol. II. p. 387 sq.

THE EPISTLE TO THE PHILIPPIANS.

CHAPTER I.

Apostolic address and salutation.

ΠΑΥΛΟΣ καὶ Τιμόθεος δοῦλοι Χριστοῦ Ἰησοῦ, πᾶσιν τοῖς ἁγίοις ἐν Χριστῷ

1. καὶ Τιμόθεος] Timothy is here associated with the apostle (as in 2 Cor. i. 1, Col. i. 1, 1 and 2 Thess. i. 1), being known to, and probably esteemed by, the Philippians (Grot.), whom he had already twice visited; once in company with St. Paul (Acts xvi. 1, 12), and once alone (Acts xix. 22). The association seems similar to that with Sosthenes, 1 Cor. i. 1; Timothy being neither the joint author of the Epistle (Menoch.), nor the 'comprobator' of its contents (Zanch.; comp. notes *on Gal.* i. 2), nor again the mere transcriber of it (comp. Rom. xvi. 22), but simply the 'socius salutationis,' Est. Two verses lower the apostle proceeds in his own person, and in ch. ii. 19, when Timothy reappears, it is simply in the third person. It may be remarked that it is only in this Ep., 1 and 2 Thess., and, as we might expect, Philem., that St. Paul omits his official designation, ἀπόστολος κ. τ. λ. (Gal. i. 1), or ἀπόστ. Ἰησ. Χρ. (remaining Epp.). This seems due, not to 'modestia' in the choice of a title common to himself and Tim. (Grot.), for see 2 Cor. i. 1, Col. i. 1, but simply to the terms of affection and familiarity on which he stood with the churches both of Thessalonica (ch. ii. 19, 20, iii. 6 —

10) and Philippi: he was their apostle, and he knew from their acts (Phil. v. 14 sq.) and their wishes (1 Thess. iii. 6) that they regarded him as such. On the modes of salutation adopted by St. Paul, see Rückert *on Gal.* i. 1, and compare notes *on Eph.* i. 1, and *on Col.* i. 1.

δοῦλοι Χ. Ἰ.] '*bondservants of Jesus Christ:*' 'servi proprie erant qui toti obstricti erant Domino in perpetuum,' Zanch. ap. Pol. *Syn.*; so Rom. i. 1; compare Gal. i. 10, and also James i. 1, 2 Pet i. 1, Jude 1. The interpretation of Fritzsche (*Rom.* i. 1), 'Jesu Christi cultor,' scil. 'homo Christianus,' is tenable (compare Dan. iii. 26), but like so many of that commentator's interpretations, hopelessly frigid; comp. Gal. i. 10, where to translate Χρ. δοῦλος οὐκ ἂν ἤμην, 'non essem homo Christianus,' is to impair all the vigor of the passage. The term is used in its *ethical*, rather than mere *historical* sense, 'an apostle,' etc. (see Meyer *on Gal. l. c.*), and the genitive is strongly *possessive*: they belonged to Christ as to a master, comp. 1 Cor. vii. 22: His they were; yea, His very marks they bore on their bodies; compare Gal. vi. 17, and see notes *i. loc.* The formula δοῦλος Θεοῦ (comp. עֶבֶד יְהוָה Ps. cxiii. 1, al.) is naturally in re-

3

Ἰησοῦ τοῖς οὖσιν ἐν Φιλίπποις σὺν ἐπισκόποις καὶ διακόνοις.

general; δοῦλος Χριστοῦ, somewhat more personal and special: compare notes on *Tit* i. 1. πᾶσιν τοῖς ἁγίοις κ.τ.λ.] '*to all the saints*,' etc., ' to all that form part of the visible and spiritual community at Philippi;' ἅγιοι being used in these salutations in its most inclusive sense: see notes *on Eph.* i. 1. Though ἅγιος in these sorts of addresses does not necessarily imply any special degree of moral perfection, being applied by the apostle to all his converts, except the Gal. (and apparently Thess., ἁγίοις in ch. v. 27 being very doubtful), yet still the remark of Olsh. (*on Rom.* i. 7) is probably true, that it always hints at the idea of a higher moral life imparted by Christ. This in the present case is made still more apparent by the addition ἐν Χριστῷ: it was '*in Him*' (not for διά, Est., Rheinw.), in union with Him, and Him alone, that the ἁγιότης was true and real; οἱ γὰρ ἐν Χρ. Ἰησ. ἅγιοι ὄντως εἰσίν, Theophyl.: compare Koch on *Thessalon.* i. 1, p. 59. The inclusive πᾶσιν, repeated several times in this Ep., ch. i. 4, 7, 8, 25, ii 17, 26, iv. 23 (*Rec.*), well expresses the warmth and expansiveness of the apostle's love.

Φιλίπποις] Philippi, now Filibah or Filibejih, and anciently Κρηνίδες (not Δᾶτος, Van Heng. after Appian, *Bell. Civ.* IV 106, which was the ancient name of the *port*, Neapolis), was raised to a position of importance by Philip of Macedon about B. C. 358, and called after his name. In later times it was memorable as overlooking the scene of the battle between Antony and Octavius against Brutus and Cassius, when the cause of the republic was finally lost (Merivale, *Hist.* Vol. III. p. 208): soon afterwards it became a Roman colony (Colon. August. Julia Philippensis) and received the '*Jus Italicum*.' It was, however, still more memorable as being the first city in our continent of Europe in which the gospel was preached, Acts xvi. 9. A few ruins are said still to remain; see Forbiger, *Alt. Geogr.* Vol. III. p. 1070, and the article by the same author in Pauly, *Encycl.* Vol. v. p. 1477; compare also Leake, *N. Greece*, Vol. III. p. 216. σὺν ἐπισκ. καὶ διακ.] '*together with the bishops and deacons;*' not merely ' in company with' (μετά), but 'together with' ('una cum,' Beza), — specially included in the same friendly greeting; compare notes *on Eph.* vi. 23. Various reasons have been assigned why special mention is made of these church-officers. The two most plausible seem, (*a*) because there were tendencies to division and disunion even among the Philippians, which rendered a notice of formally constituted church-officers not unsuitable (Wiesinger, al.); (*b*) because the ἐπίσκ. and διάκ. had naturally been the principal instruments in collecting the alms (Chrys., Theoph., and recently Meyer, Bisping). The latter seems most probable; at any rate the date of the Epistle is not enough to account for the addition (Alf.), nor does the position of the clause warrant any contrast with ' the hierarchical views' (ib.) of the Apost. Ff. (now by no means critically certain); for compare Ignatius (?) *Philad.* 1: — the shepherds naturally follow the sheep. On the meaning of the title of *office*, ἐπίσκοπος, here appy. perfectly interchangeable with the title of *age* and *dignity*, πρεσβύτερος (Acts xx. 17, 28, 1 Pet. v. 1), see especially notes *on* 1 *Tim.* iii. 1; and on διάκ. see notes *on ib.* iii. 8. The reading of B³D³; 39, 67, συνεπισκόποις, retained and noticed by Chrys., seems meaningless and indefensible, and arose probably from the epistolary style of later times; comp. Chrys. *in loc.*

2. χάρις ὑμῖν κ.τ.λ.] On the spiritual significance of this blended form of

² χάρις ὑμῖν καὶ εἰρήνη ἀπὸ Θεοῦ πατρὸς ἡμῶν καὶ Κυρίου Ἰησοῦ Χριστοῦ.

³ Εὐχαριστῶ τῷ Θεῷ μου ἐπὶ πάσῃ τῇ μνείᾳ

Occidental and Oriental salutation, see notes *on Gal.* i. 2, and *on Ephes.* i. 2: comp. also Koch *on* 1 *Thess.* p. 60. The formula is substantially the same in all St. Paul's Epistles, except in Col. i. 2, and 1 Thess. i. 1, where the reading is doubtful. In the former, καὶ Κυρ. Ἰησ Χρ. seems certainly an insertion, and in the latter (the apostle's earliest Epistle) it may be doubted whether the simple χάρις καὶ εἰρήνη, without any further addition, may not be the more probable reading; see, however, Tisch. *in loc.*

καὶ Κυρίου] Scil. καὶ ἀπὸ Κυρίου κ.τ.λ. The Socinian interpr. καὶ (πατρὸς) Κυρίου, found also in Erasm. *on Rom.* i. 7, is rendered highly improbable by the use of the same formula without ἡμῶν, 2 Tim. i. 2, Tit. i. 4, most probably 1 Tim. i. 2, and perhaps 2 Thess. i. 2: compare 1 Thess. iii. 11, 2 Thess. ii. 16.

3. εὐχαριστῶ κ.τ.λ.] A closely similar form of commencement occurs in Rom. i. 9, 1 Cor. i. 4, Philem. 4; compare also Eph. i. 16, Col. i. 3, 1 Thess. i. 2. Indeed in all his Epp. to churches, with the single and sad exception of that to the Galat., the apostle either returns thanks to God, or blesses Him, for the spiritual state of his converts: τοῦτο δὲ ποιεῖ ἐκ τοῦ πολλὰ αὐτοῖς συνειδέναι ἀγαθά, Chrys. The present use of εὐχαριστεῖν ('quod pro *gratias agere* ante Polybium usurpavit nemo,' Lobeck) is condemned by the Atticists: see Lobeck. *Phryn* p. 18, Thom. M. p. 913 (ed Bern) Herodian, p. 400 (ed Koch), but consider Demosth. *de Cor.* p. 257. Pollux (*Onom.* v. 141) admits it for διδόναι χάριν, but condemns it for εἰδέναι χάριν; see, however, Boeckh, *Corp. Inscr.* Vol. 1. p. 52, and notes on *Col.* i. 12.

τῷ Θεῷ μου] So Rom. i. 8; compare Acts xxvii. 23, οὗ εἰμὶ ᾧ καὶ λατρεύω 'Signiti at Paulus quanta fiducia vero Deo adhaereat. Sunt enim qui volunt Deum mis ericord am quidem esse per Christum Sanctis donum Justus ob Justitiam non autem se trust Deum it sis esse misericordam,' Calv.

ἐπὶ πάσῃ τῇ μνείᾳ] 'on the whole of my remembrance of you,' not 'every remembrance,' Auth. (but not the older English Vv.), Bloomf., Conyb., and others,— a translation incompatible with the use of the art.; comp. Winer, *Gr.* § 18. 4. p. 101. The prep. ἐπί with the dative (which we can hardly say 'answers to the same prep. with a gen.; Rom. i. 10, Eph. i. 16,' Alf.) is not here temporal (Heb. ix. 26), ὁσάκις ὑμῶν ἀναμνησθῶ, Chrys., Winer, *Gr.* p. 350,— a in anou favored by the ine rrect interpr. of πάσῃ τῇ μν., but *semissual*, and correctly expresses the idea of 'close and complete connection, 'my giving thanks is based upon my remembrance of you.' 'remembrance and gratitude are bound up together' (comp. Isaiah xxvi. 8), the primary idea being, not *addition* (Alf.), but superposit n. Donalds. *Crat. l.* § 172, *Gramm.* § 483; see notes on ch. iii. 9, and *on Phil.* ii. 20, where (ed. 1) interchange the accidentally transposed 'former' and 'latter.' In Rom. i. 10, and Eph. i. 16 see notes, where ἐπί is used with the gen. in a very similar sentence, a certain amount of temporal force seems fairly recognizable. 'The causal meaning, 'de eo quod vos mei recordamini' Homberg. Michael., al. (comp. 1 Cor i. 4), according to which ὑμῶν is a gen. *subjecti*, is exegetically untenable, as ver. 5 gives the reason for the εὐχαρ., and specifies

ὑμῶν, ⁴ πάντοτε ἐν πάσῃ δεήσει μου ὑπὲρ πάντων ὑμῶν μετὰ χαρᾶς τὴν δέησιν ποιούμενος, ⁵ ἐπὶ τῇ κοινωνίᾳ ὑμῶν εἰς τὸ

something which far more naturally elicited it.   μνείᾳ ὑμῶν] '*remembrance of you,*' 1 Thess. iii. 6, 2 Tim. i. 3; not 'commemorationem vestri' (Van Hengel), — a meaning which, as Meyer rightly observes, it only receives when associated with ποιεῖσθαι; compare Rom. i. 9, Eph. i. 16, 1 Thess. i. 2, Philem. 4.

4. πάντοτε — ποιούμενος] Participial sentence defining and explaining more fully *when* the εὐχαριστῶ κ. τ. λ. takes place, viz., on every occasion that he prayed for them: the εὐχαριστία was based on, and inseparable from the μνεία, and this thankful remembrance ever found an utterance in every prayer. Πάντοτε is clearly not to be joined with εὐχαριστῶ (Wiesing.), — a construction which interferes with the studied and affectionate cumulation πάντοτε, πάσῃ, πάντων (comp. 2 Cor. ix. 8) in the participial clause; compare Col. i. 3, where it also seems best (contr. Meyer, De W.; see notes) to join the adverb with the participle. It may be remarked that no inference can be drawn from the position of πάντοτε (a favorite word with the apostle), it being as often used by him after as before the verb with which it is connected: in the other writers of the N. T. (except John viii. 29, where it is emphatic) it precedes the verb. On the emphatic repetition, πάντοτε, πάσῃ, πάντων, see the copious list of examples in Lobeck, *Paralip.* p. 51 sq.

ὑπὲρ πάντων ὑμῶν] These words may be connected either (*a*) with τὴν δέησιν ποιούμενος, Calv., De Wette, Alf., al., or (*b*) with δεήσει μου, Auth. and all Engl. Vv., Meyer, al. Both are grammatically tenable; the omission of the article before ὑπὲρ πάντων being perfectly justifiable in the first case (see notes on Eph. i. 15), and according to rule in the second; see Winer, *Gr.* § 20. 4, p. 126. The latter, however, seems much more simple and natural; the πάντοτε is defined by πάσῃ δεήσει, and πάσῃ δ. again is limited by ὑπὲρ ὑμῶν, while the article attached to δέησιν (Alf. seems here to argue against himself; compare with Meyer) refers it back to the δέησις thus previously limited: so most of the ancient Vv., Syr., Clarom., Vulg., Coptic. The construction adopted by Est., al., εὐχαρ. — ὑπὲρ πάντ. ὑμ., though elsewhere adopted by St. Paul (Eph. i. 16, comp. Rom. i. 8, 1 Thess. i. 2, 2 Thess. i. 3), seems here very unsatisfactory. On the meaning of δέησις (a special form of προσευχή), see notes on 1 *Tim.* ii. 1.

μετὰ χαρᾶς] These words serve to depict the feelings he bore to his children in the faith at Philippi; he prays for them alway, yea, and he prays *with joy*; διηνεκῶς ὑμῶν μεμνημένος θυμηδίας ἁπάσης ἐμπίμπλαμαι, Theodoret.

5. ἐπὶ τῇ κοινωνίᾳ] '*for your fellowship;*' ἐπὶ correctly marking the *cause* for which the apostle returned thanks, 1 Cor. i. 4, 2 Cor. ix. 15; see Winer, *Gr.* § 48. c, p. 351. This clause is most naturally connected with εὐχαρ. (Beng., al., and apparently Greek commentt.), not with τὴν δέησ. ποιούμ. (Van Heng., De W.; compare Green, *Gr.* p. 292), as there would otherwise be no specific statement of what was the subject of the apostle's εὐχαριστία. De Wette urges as an objection the use of εὐχαρ. ἐπὶ in two different senses, in ver. 3 and 5, but this may be diluted by observing that the first ἐπὶ is not (as with De W.) *temporal*, but *semilocal* (ethico-local), defining the subject on which the thanks rest, and with which they are closely united, the difference between which and the present simply ethical use is but slight. Thus then ver. 3 marks the object *on which* the

εὐαγγέλιον ἀπὸ πρώτης ἡμέρας ἄχρι τοῦ νῦν, ⁶ πεποιθὼς αὐτὰ

εὐχαρ. rests, ver. 4 defines *when* it takes place, ver. 5 *why* it takes place. Such slightly varied and delicate uses of prepositions are certainly not strange to the style of St. Paul.

κοινωνίᾳ εἰς τὸ εὐαγγ.] '*fellowship toward the gospel;*' not '*in the gospel,*' Syr., Vulg. (but not Clarom.), but 'in reference to,' or perhaps more strictly 'toward' (Hamm.), the εἰς marking the object toward which the κοινωνία was directed (Winer, Gr. § 49. a, p. 353),— the fellowship of faith and love which they evinced toward the gospel *primarily* and *generally* in their concordant action in the furtherance of it, and *secondarily* and *specially* in their contribution and assistance to St. Paul. So in effect Chrysostom, ἄρα τὸ συναντιλαμβάνεσθαι κοινωνία ἐστὶ εἰς τὸ εὐαγγέλιον, except that he too much limits the συναντιλαμβ. to the particular assistance rendered to the apostle (so Theophyl., Bisping.), which rather appears *involved in*, than directly conveyed by, the expression. On the other hand, the absence of the article before εἰς τὸ εὐαγγ., which confessedly involves the close connection of κοιν. at ἱ εἰς τὸ εὐαγγ. (Winer, Gr. § 20. 2, p. 123, comp. ch. iv. 15), coupled with the exegetical consideration, that in an epistle which elsewhere so especially commemorates the liberality of the Philippians (ch. iv. 10, 15, 16), such an allusion at the outset would be both natural and probable (comp. De W.), renders it difficult with Mey. and Alf. to restrict κοινωνία merely to 'unanimous action' (Alf.), 'bon accord' (Rilliet), and not to include that particular manifestation of it which so especially marked the liberal and warm-hearted Christians of Philippi; compare Wiesing. *in loc.*, and Neander, *Phil.* p. 25. Κοινωνία is thus absolute (Acts ii. 42, Gal. ii. 9) and abstract,—'fellowship,' not 'contribution'

(Bisp.), a translation which is defensible (see Fritz. on *Rom.* xv. 26, Vol. III. p. 287), but which would mar the studiedly general character of the expression. The interpretation of Theol. (not Chrysost., al., according to which εἰς τὸ εὐαγγ. is a periphrasis for a gen. (κοινωνίαν δὲ τοῦ εὐαγγ. τὴν πίστιν ἐκάλεσε), is grammatically untenable; compare Winer, Gr. § 30. 3, p. 174. ἀπὸ πρώτης ἡμέρας] '*from the first day*,' in which it was preached among them (ἀφ' οὗ ἐπιστεύσατε, Theophyl.), Acts xvi. 13 sq., comp. Col. i. 6. This clause, which seems so obviously in close union with the preceding words, is connected by Lachm. (ed. stereot., but altered in larger ed.) and Meyer with πεποιθὼς κ. τ. λ., on account of the absence of the article. This is hypercriticism, if not error; ἀπὸ πρώτης κ. τ. λ. is a *subordinate* temporal definition so closely joined with the κοινωνία, as both naturally and logically to dispense with the article. The insertion of the article would give the fact of the duration of the κοινωνία a far greater prominence than the apostle seems to have intended, and would in fact suggest two moments of thought. — 'communionem cumque a primâ die,' etc.; comp. Winer, Gr. § 20. 2, and notes on 1 *Tim.* i. 13. Even independently of these grammatical objections, the use of πεποιθώς, which De Wette and Van Heng. remark is usually placed by St. Paul first in the sentence (ch. ii. 24, Rom. ii. 19, 2 Cor. ii. 3, Gal. v. 10, 2 Thess. iii. 4), would certainly seem to suggest for the participle a more prominent position in the sentence. The connection with εὐχαρ. (Œcum., Beza, Beng.) seems equally untenable and unsatisfactory; such a temporal limitation could not suitably be so distant from its finite verb, nor would ἀπὸ πρώτης κ. τ. λ. be in harmony with the pres. εὐχαρ., or the prior temporal

τοῦτο, ὅτι ὁ ἐναρξάμενος ἐν ὑμῖν ἔργον ἀγαθὸν ἐπιτελέσει ἄχρις

clause πάντοτε κ. τ. λ.; compare De Wette.

6. πεποιθὼς αὐτὸ τοῦτο] '*being confident of this very thing*,' viz., that He who,' etc., comp. Col. iv. 8; not 'confident as I am,' Alford (comp. Peile), but with the faint causal force so often couched in the participle, 'seeing I am, etc. ;' ' haec fiducia nervus est gratiarum actionis,' Beng. This clause is thus, grammatically considered, the causal member of the sentence (Donalds. *Gr.* § 615) appended to εὐχαριστῶ κ. τ. λ., standing in parallelism to the temporal member, πάντοτε — ποιούμενος κ. τ. λ., and certainly requires no supplementary καί (Tynd., Flatt, al.), nor any assumption of an asyndeton (Van Heng.). The accus. αὐτὸ τοῦτο is not governed by πεποιθώς (Raphel, Wolf), but is *appended* to it as specially marking the 'content and compass of the action' (Madvig, *Synt.* § 27. a), or, more exactly, 'the object in reference to which the action extends' (Krüger, *Sprachl.* § 46. 4. 1 sq.), which again is more fully defined by the following ὅτι κ. τ. λ.; comp. Winer, *Gr.* § 23. 5, p. 145, where several examples of this construction are cited. It is mainly confined to St. John and St. Paul, and serves to direct the attention somewhat specially to what follows; compare Ellendt, *Lex. Soph.* Vol. II. p. 461. ὁ ἐναρξάμενος] '*He who hath begun*;' obviously God: see ch. ii. 13, and comp. 1 Sam. iii. 12, ἄρξομαι καὶ ἐπιτελέσω; not 'each better one of the Philippians' (Wakef. *Sylv. Crit.* Vol. II. p. 98), — an interpretation to which the following ἔργον ἀγαθὸν (see below) need in no way compel us. The verb ἐνάρχ. occurs again in connection with ἐπιτελ. in Gal. iii. 3, and 2 Cor. viii. 6 (*Lachm.*, but only with B). The compound verb does not appear to mark the ' vim divinam hominum in animis agen-

tem,' Van Heng. (for see Gal. *l. c.*, and comp. Polyb. *Hist.* v. 1. 3, 5), but perhaps only differs from ἄρχεσθαι in this, that it represents the action of the verb as more directly concentrated on the object, whether (as here) expressed, or understood; see Rost u. Palm, *Lex.* s. v. ἐν, E, Vol. I. p. 912.

ἐν ὑμῖν] ' *in you*,' sc. 'in animis vestris,' compare 1 Cor. xii. 6; not 'among you,' Hamm., which would scarcely be in harmony with ὑπὲρ πάντων ὑμῶν, ver. 7. The commencement of the good work was not limited to instances among the Philippian Christians, but was spoken generally in reference to all.

ἔργον ἀγαθόν] '*a good work*,'— not ' the good work,' Luth.: not elsewhere used in ref. to God (yet comp. John x. 32), but only in ref. to man; compare Acts ix. 36, Rom. ii. 7, 2 Cor. ix. 8, Eph. ii. 10, Col. i. 10, Heb xiii. 21, al. Still there is no impropriety in the present use; the ἔργον ἀγαθόν, though here stated indefinitely, does not appear to refer *subjectively* to the good works (Syr. ; τὰ κατορθώματα, Chrys.), the ἔργον τῆς πίστεως (1 Thess. i. 3) of the Philippians generally (Reuss, *Théol. Chrét.* Vol. II. p. 172), but rather *objectively* to the particular κοινωνία εἰς εὐαγγ. previously specified : God had vouchsafed unto them, among other blessings, that of an open hand and heart (ταύτην ὑμῖν δωρησάμενος τὴν προθυμίαν. Theod.); this blessing He will continue. This declaration, however, is expressed in a *general* form; comp. Rom. ii. 7.

ἐπιτελέσει] ' *will accomplish*,' '*will perfect*,' not merely 'will perform it.' Author., but ' will bring it to a complete and perfect end,' Syr. ܢܫܠܡ [explebit] ; see notes *on Gal.* iii. 3. With regard to the dogmatical application of the words, which, owing to their probable

ἡμέρας Χριστοῦ Ἰησοῦ ⁷ καθώς ἐστιν δίκαιον ἐμοὶ τοῦτο φρονεῖν

specific reference cannot safely be pressed, it seems enough to say with Theoph., ἀπὸ τῶν παρελθόντων καὶ περὶ τῶν μελλόντων στοχάζεται: the inference is justly drawn, that God who has thus far blessed them with His grace will also bless them with the gift of perseverance; compare 1 Cor. i. 8: 'Gottes Art ist es ja nicht, etwas halb zu thun,' Neander. The charge of semi-Pelagianism brought against Chrysostom *in loc.* has been satisfactorily disproved by Justiniani, who thus perspicuously sums up that great commentator's doctrinal statements; 'vult Chrysostomus Deum et incipere et perficere; illud excitantis, hoc adjuvantis est gratiæ; illa liberi arbitrii conatum prævenit, hæc comitatur.' On the doctrine of Perseverance generally, see the clear statements of Ebrard, *Christliche Dogmatik,* § 513, 514, Vol. II. p. 534—549. The conclusions arrived at are thus stated: 'Perseverantia est effectus sanctificationis. Sanctificatio est conditio perseverantiæ. Datur apostasia regenitorum, nempe si in sanctificatione inertes sunt,' p. 548; compare also some admirable comments of Jackson, *Creed,* x. 37 4 sq. ἄχρις ἡμέρας Χρ. Ἰησ.] 'unto, or up to the day of Christ Jesus, i.e. ἄχρι τῆς παρουσίας τοῦ Κυρίου, Theoph. That St Paul in these words assumes the nearness of the coming of the Lord (Alf.) cannot be positively asserted. It is certainly evasive to refer this to future generations (τοῖς ἐξ ὑμῶν, Theophyl.), but it may be fairly said that St. Paul is here using language which has not so much a mere historical, as a general and *practical* reference: the day of Christ, whether far off or near, is the decisive day to each individual; it is practically coincident with the day of his death, and becomes, when addressed to the individual, an exaltation and amplification of that term. Death, indeed,

as has been well remarked by Bishop Reynolds, is dwelt upon but little in the N. T.; it is to the resurrection and to the day of Christ that the eyes of the believers are directed; 'semper ad beatam resurrectionem, tanquam ad scopum, referendi sunt oculi,' Calv. To maintain, then, that this is *not* the sense in which the apostle wrote the words (Alf.) seems here unduly and indemonstrably exclusive. See notes on 1 *Tim.* vi. 14, and compare (with caution) Usteri, *Lehrb.* II. 2. 4. n, p. 326 sq. On ἄχρι and μέχρι, see notes on 2 *Tim.* ii. 9.

7. καθώς κ.τ.λ.] 'even as;' explanatory statement of the reason why such a confidence is justly felt; compare 1 Cor. i. 6, Eph. i. 6. On the nature of this particle see notes on *Gal.* iii. 16, and on *Eph. l. c.* δίκαιον] 'right,' 'meet,' scil. 'se unum legem caritatis,' Van Hengel; it is in accordance with the genuine nature of true Love (1 Cor. xiii. 7) to entertain such a confident hope; compare Acts v. 19, Ephes. vi. 1, 2 Pet. i. 13. Alford (with Meyer and De W.) remarks that the two classical constructions are δίκαιον ἐπὶ τοῦτο φρ. (Herod. i. 39), and δίκαιος εἰμί τοῦτο φρ. (Plato, *L. p.* x. 897). The last construction is the most idiomatic comp. Kruger, *Sprachl.* § 55. 3. 10, and perhaps the most usual in the best Greek, but there is nothing unclassical in the present usage; comp. Plato, *Rep.* I. p. 334. δίκαιον τότε τοῖς τοῖς ἐχθροῖς ὠφελεῖν. τοῦτο φρονεῖν] 'to think this,' Auth., Syr.; 'hoc sentire,' Vulg.; *i.e.* to entertain this confidence: 'φρονεῖν hic conducitur animi affectu sed de mentis judicio,' Beza; compare 1 Cor. iv. 6 (R. ?), Gal. v. 10. To refer τοῦτο to the prayer in ver. 4, 'hoc curare pro vobis,' Wolf (comp. Conyb.), or to the expectation in ver. 6, 'hoc omnibus vobis appetere, sed omni

ὑπὲρ πάντων ὑμῶν, διὰ τὸ ἔχειν με ἐν τῇ καρδίᾳ ὑμᾶς, ἔν τε τοῖς
/\

curâ et precibus' (Van Heng.), is unsatisfactory, and is certainly not required by ὑπέρ, which occurs several times in the N. T. (2 Cor. i. 6, 8; 2 Thess. ii. 1, al.), in a sense but little different from περί; see Winer, *Gram.* § 47. l, p. 343. The probable distinction, — 'περὶ solam mentis circumspectionem, ὑπὲρ simul animi propensionem significat' (Weber, *Demosth.* p. 130), is perfectly recognizable in the present case, but cannot be expressed without a periphrasis, *e. g.* 'to entertain this favorable opinion about you,' 'ut ita de vobis sentiam et confidam,' Est. On the uses of ὑπέρ and περί, see notes *on Gal.* i. 4, and on φρονεῖν, see Beck, *Seelenl.* III. 19, p. 61 sq. διὰ τὸ ἔχειν κ. τ. λ.] '*because I have you in my heart,*' ܒܠܒܝ ܣܝܡܝܢ [in corde meo positi] Syr.; not 'because you have me,' Rosenm., Conyb.: the apostle is throughout clearly the subject and agent (comp. ver. 8); the depth of his love warrants the fulness of his confidence. In all cases the context, not the mere position of the accusatives, will be the surest guide; compare John i. 49: see also Winer, *Gr.* § 44. 6, p. 294. The translation of Beza, 'in animo tenere' = 'quasi insculptum habere memoriæ' (ἄσβεστον περιφέρω τὴν μνήμην, Theod.; see especially Justin. *in loc.*), is opposed both to the similar affectionate expressions, 2 Cor. iii. 2, vii. 3, and to the prevailing use of καρδία (comp. Beck, *Bibl. Seelenl.* III. 24, p. 89 sq., notes on ch. iv. 7, and on 1 *Tim.* i. 5) in the N. T. It is the fervent *love* of the apostle that is expressed; and in this *remembrance* is necessarily involved; compare Chrysost. *in loc.* ἔν τε τοῖς δεσμοῖς κ. τ. λ.] It is doubtful whether these words are to be connected with the preceding διὰ τὸ ἔχειν κ. τ. λ. (Chrys., Theoph.), or with the succeeding συγκοι-

νωνούς μου κ. τ. λ. (Calvin, *Lachmann, Tisch.*). Neander and the majority of modern commentators adopt the former; the latter, however, seems more simple and natural. The apostle had his confidence because he cherishes them in his heart; and he cherishes them because their liberality showed that whether in his sufferings (δεσμοῖς), which they alleviated, or in his exertions for the gospel (τῇ ἀπολ. καὶ βεβ.), with which they sympathized, they all were bound up with him in the strictest spiritual fellowship. On τε — καί, which here serves to unite two otherwise separate and distinct notions, slightly enhancing the latter, see Hartung, *Partik.* Vol. II. p. 98, and comp. notes on 1 *Tim.* iv. 10.

ἐν τῇ ἀπολογίᾳ κ. τ. λ.] '*in my defence (of) and confirmation of the gospel.*' These words have been somewhat perversely interpreted. Ἀπολογία and βεβαίωσις are certainly not synonymous (Rheinw), — nor do they form an hendiadys, sc. ἀπολ. εἰς βεβ. (Heinr.; compare Syr. ' defensione quæ est pro veritate [confirmatione] evangelii'), — nor can τῇ ἀπολ. be dissociated from τοῦ εὐαγγ. (Chrys.), both being under the vinculum of a common article (Green, *Gr.* p. 211), — nor, finally, does it seem necessary to restrict the clause to the judicial process which resulted in the apostle's imprisonment (Van Heng.). It seems more natural to give both words their widest reference; to understand by ἀπολογίᾳ St. Paul's defence of the gospel, whether before his heathen judges (compare 2 Tim. iv. 16) or his Jewish opponents (comp. Phil. i. 16, 17), and by βεβαιώσει his confirmation and establishment of its truth (Heb. vi. 16), — not by his sufferings (Chrys., Theod.), but by his teaching and preaching among his own followers and those who resorted to him (compare Acts xxviii. 23, 30): see

δεσμοῖς μου καὶ ἐν τῇ ἀπολογίᾳ καὶ βεβαιώσει τοῦ εὐαγγελίου συγκοινωνούς μου τῆς χάριτος πάντας ὑμᾶς ὄντας. ᵇ μάρτυς γάρ

8. μου ἐστίν] So *Rec.* with ADEKL; great majority of mss.; very many Vv. (but Vv. in such cases can scarcely be depended on for either side) and many Ff. (*Griesb.* [but om.], *Scholz.*). The ἐστίν is omitted by *Tischend.* and bracketed by *Lachm.* with BFG; 17. 67**; Vulg., Claroman.; Chrysost. (ms.), Theod.-Mops. (*Meyer, Alf.*). The external evidence seems too decidedly in favor of the insertion to be overbalanced by the somewhat doubtful internal argument that ἐστίν is a reminiscence of Rom. i. 9 (Mey., Alf.). It does not seem much more probable that the transcriber should have borne in mind a remote reference, than that the apostle should have twice used the same formula.

the good note of Wieseler, *Chronol.* p. 429, 430.

συγκοινωνούς κ. τ. λ.] 'seeing that both in my defence of and, etc., ye are all partakers with me of my grace;' 'ut qui omnes mecum consortes estis gratiae,' Schmid; compare Hamm., and Scholef. *Hints*, p. 104. The preceding ὑμᾶς, further characterized as ἔν τε — συγκοιν., is rhetorically repeated (see Bernhardy, *Synt.* vi. 4, p. 275 sq.) to support πάντας; the whole clause serving to explain the reason for the ἔχειν ἐν τῇ καρδίᾳ. It is doubtful whether μου is to be connected (*a*) with συγκοινωνούς as a second genitive (Syr., Copt.), or (*b*) with τῆς χάριτος (compare Clarom., Vulg.), the pronoun being placed out of its order (Winer, *Gr.* § 22. 7. 1) to mark the reference of the prep. in συγκοιν. As συγκοιν. is found in the N. T. both with persons (1 Cor. ix. 23) and things (Rom. xi. 17), the context alone must decide; this, in consequence of the meaning assigned below to χάρις, seems in favor of (*a*); compare ch. ii. 30: so Hammond, De Wette. τῆς χάριτος] The reference of this subst. has been differently explained: the Greek commentators refer it more specifically ' to the grace of suffering,' comp. ver. 29; Rosenm., al. to the ' munus apostolicum,' scil. ' ye are all assistants to me in my duty,' Storr, Peile; others again to the ' evangelii donatio,'

compare Van Heng.; others to grace in its widest acceptation, Eph. ii. 8, Col. i. 6 (De W. Alf.). Of these the first is too restrictive, the others, especially the last, too vague. The article seems to mark the χάρις as that vouchsafed in both the cases previously contemplated, sufferings for (ver. 29), and exertions in behalf of the gospel. The translation ' gaudii,' Clarom., Vulg., Ambrst., al., is apparently due to the reading χαρᾶς, though no mss. have been adduced in which that variation is found.

8. μάρτυς γάρ κ. τ. λ.] 'For God is my witness;' earnest confirmation of the foregoing verse, more especially of διὰ τὸ ἔχειν με ἐν τῇ καρδίᾳ ὑμᾶς. Chrys. well says, οὐχ ὡς ἀπιστούμενος μάρτυρα καλεῖ τὸν Θεόν, ἀλλ' ἐκ πολλῆς διαθέσεως. The reading μοι [DEFG; al.; Chrys.; Lat Ff.] would scarcely involve any change of sense; it would perhaps only a little more enhance the personal relation. ὡς ἐπιποθῶ] ' how I long after you;' comp. ch ii. 26, Rom. i. 11, 1 Thess. iii. 6, 2 Tim. i. 4. The force of ἐπὶ in this compound does not mark *intension* (' vehementer desidero,' Van Heng.; ' expetam,' Beza), but, as in ἐπιθυμεῖν and similar words, the *direction* of the πόθος; see notes on 2 Tim. ii. 4, and Fritz. *Rom.* i. 9, Vol. i. p. 31. Again, it seems quite unnecessary with Van Heng. to restrict the πόθος to ' ve-

μου ἐστὶν ὁ Θεός, ὡς ἐπιποθῶ πάντας ὑμᾶς ἐν σπλάγχνοις Χριστοῦ Ἰησοῦ. ⁹ Καὶ τοῦτο προσεύχομαι, ἵνα ἡ ἀγάπη ὑμῶν ἔτι

træ consuetudinis desiderium;' the longing and yearning of the apostle was for something more than mere earthly reunion; it was for their eternal welfare and blessedness, and the realization, in its highest form, of the χάρις of which they were now συγκοινωνοί. The context seems clearly to decide that ὡς here, and probably also Rom. i. 9, is not 'quod' (Rosenmuller, De Wette) but 'quomodo' (Syr., Copt.), scil. 'quantopere,' 'quam propense,' Corn. a Lap.; compare Chrysostom, οὐ δυνατὸν εἰπεῖν πῶς ἐκ.ποδῶ.

ἐν σπλάγχνοις X. 'I.] This forcible expression must not be understood merely as qualitative, — 'opponit Christi viscera carnali affectui,' Calv., but as semilocal, 'in the bowels of Christ,' in the bowels of Him with whom the apostle's very being was so united (Gal. ii. 20), that Christ's heart had, as it were, become his, and beat in his bosom: comp. Meyer *in loc.*, who has well maintained this more deep and spiritual interpretation. Ἐν thus retains its natural and usual force (contr. Rilliet), and the gen. is not the gen. *auctoris* or *originis* (Hartung, *Casus*, p. 17), as apparently Chrys. σπλάγχνα γὰρ αὕτη [ἡ συγγένεια ἡ κατὰ Χρ.] ὑμῖν χαρίζεται, but simply *possessiv.* We can hardly term this use of σπλάγχνα (רחמים) completely Hebraistic, as a *similar* use is sufficiently common in classical Greek (see examples in Rost u. Palm, *Lex.* s. v, Vol. II. p. 1504); the verb σπλαγχνίζομαι, however, and the adjectives πολύσπλαγχνος and εὔσπλαγχνος (when not in its medical sense, Hippocr. p. 89) seem purely so, while, on the contrary, the substantive εὐσπλαγχνία occurs in Eurip. *Rhes.* 192. For a list of Hebraisms of the New Test. judiciously classified, see Winer, *Gram.* § 3, p. 27 sq.

9. καὶ τοῦτο προσ.] '*Et hoc precor,*' but not 'propterea precor,' as Wolf, 2: the καί with its simple copulative force introduces the apostle's prayer (ver. 9 - 11) alluded to in ver. 4, while the τοῦτο prepares the reader for the statement of its contents, 'and this which follows is what I pray.' The καί (as Meyer observes) thus coalesces more with τοῦτο than προσεύχομαι; not καὶ προσ. τοῦτο, but καὶ τοῦτο προσ. To connect the clause closely with what precedes (Rilliet) destroys all the force of ver. 8,

ἵνα] The particle has here what has been called its *secondary telic* force (see notes on *Eph.* i. 17); i. e. it does not directly indicate the *purpose* of the prayer, but blends with it also its *subject* and *purport:* Theodorus *in loc.* paraphrases it by a simple infin. It may be again remarked that this secondary and blended use (esp. after verbs of prayer), though not recognized by Meyer and Fritzsche, cannot be safely denied in the N. T.: there are numerous passages (setting aside the disputed use after a prophecy) in which the full *telic* force ('in order that') cannot be sustained in translation without artifice or circumlocution; e. g. comp. Meyer on *John* xv 8. We may observe further, that this use of ἵνα is not confined to the N. T.: it was certainly common in Hellenic Greek (see examples in Winer, *Gr.* § 44. 8, p. 300), and in modern Greek, under the form νὰ with the subj., it lapses (after a large class of verbs) into a mere periphrasis of the infinitive; see Corpe, *Gramm.* pp. 129, 130.

ἡ ἀγάπη ὑμῶν] '*your love,*' not, towards the apostle (Chrys.), — which had been so abundantly shown as to leave a prayer for its increase almost unnecessary; nor again, 'toward God' (Just.), nor even, 'towards one another,' Meyer, Alf. (Theodorus unites the two: comp.

μᾶλλον καὶ μᾶλλον περισσεύῃ ἐν ἐπιγνώσει καὶ πάσῃ αἰσθήσει,

Wiesing.), both of which seem unnecessarily restrictive. It seems rather 'towards all' (comp. De Wette), — a love which, already shown in, and forming an element of, their κοινωνία, ver. 4 (not identical with it, Alf.), the apostle prays may still more and more increase, not so much *per se*, as in the special elements of knowledge and moral perception. Examples of the very intelligible μᾶλλον καὶ μᾶλλον will be found in Kypke, *Obs.* Vol. II. p. 307. περισσεύῃ ἐν κ.τ.λ.] 'may abound in knowledge and all (every form of) perception,' not 'in all knowledge and perception,' Luther, — an attraction for which there seems no authority. The exact force of ἐν is somewhat doubtful; it can scarcely (*a*) approximate in meaning to μετά, Chrys. (who, however, fluctuates between this preposition and ἐξ), Corn. a Lap., al.; for this use, though grammatically defensible (comp. examples in Green, *Gr.* p. 289), is not exegetically satisfactory, as ver. 10 shows that it is not to ἀγάπη together with ἐπιγν. and αἰσθ., but to ἐπιγν. and αἰσθ. more especially, as inspiering and defining that love, that attention is directed; nor (*b*) does it exactly denote the manner of the increase (De W.), as this again seems to give too little prominence to ἐπιγν. and αἰσθ.; nor, lastly, is ἐν here instrumental, Flatt, Heinr., — as love could hardly be said to increase by the agency of knowledge. The prep. is thus not simply equivalent to μετά, κατά, or διά (much less to εἰς, comp. Winer, *Gr.* § 50. 5, p. 370), but with its usual force marks the *sphere*, elements, or particulars, in which the increase was to take place; compare Winer, *Gr.* § 48. a, p. 345. It was not for an increase of their love absolutely that the apostle prayed, for love might become the sport of every impulse (comp. Wiesing.), but it was for its increase in the

important particulars, a sound knowledge of the truth and a right spiritual perception, and of both of which it was to have still more and more. Περισσεύῃ is thus not absolute, but closely in union with ἐν and its dative, and may be considered generally and practically as identical with *abundare* and an ablative, the substantives defining the elements and items in which the increase is realized; compare 2 Cor. vii. 7, Col. ii. 7, al. Lachmann, Tischendorf read περισσεύσῃ with BDE; al., but as two of these mss., DE, adopt the aor. in ver. 26 without critical support, their reading is here suspicious. ἐπιγν. καὶ πάσῃ αἰσθ.] These two substantives may be thus distinguished; ἐπίγνωσις, 'accurata cognitio' (see notes on *Eph.* i. 17), denotes a sound knowledge of theoretical and practical truth (Meyr.), τὴν προσήκουσαν γνῶσιν τῶν εἰς ἀρετὴν συντεινόντων, Theodorus. Αἴσθησις, 'sensus' (Vulg., Clarom.) is more generic, but here, as the context implies, must be limited to right spiritual discernment [intelligentia spiritus] Syr.), a sensitively correct moral perception (νόησις, Hesych.) of the true nature, good or bad, of each circumstance, case, or object which experience may present; compare Prov. i. 4, where it is in connection with ἔννοια, and Exod. xxviii. 3, where it is joined with σοφία. It only occurs here in the N. T.; the instrumental derivative αἰσθητήριον ('organ of feeling,' etc.) is found Heb. v. 14; compare Jer. iv. 19. The adjective πάσῃ is not *intensive* ('plena et solida,' Calv.), but, as apparently always in St. Paul's Epp., *extensive*, 'every form of;' comp. notes on *Eph.* i. 8.

10. εἰς τὸ δοκιμάζειν κ.τ.λ.] '*Ut ye to prove thin s that are excellent;*' purpose of the περισσ. ἐν ἐπιγν. καὶ αἰσθ.

¹⁰ εἰς τὸ δοκιμάζειν ὑμᾶς τὰ διαφέροντα, ἵνα ἦτε εἰλικρινεῖς καὶ

(not result, — a meaning grammatically admissible, but here inapplicable; compare Winer, *Gr.* 44. 5, p. 294, note), to which the further and final purpose ἵνα ἦτε κ. τ. λ. is appended in the next clause. The words δοκ. τὰ διαφ., both here and Rom. ii. 18, may correctly receive two, if not three, different interpretations, varying with the meanings given to διαφέροντα, and the shade of meaning assigned to δοκιμάζειν. Thus they may imply either (*a*) ' *to prove* (*distinguish between*) *things that are different*,' *i. e.* to discriminate (δοκιμάζειν καὶ διακρίνειν, Arrian, *Epict.* 1. 20), — whether simply between what is right and wrong (Theoph. on Rom. ii. 18, De W.), or between different degrees of good and their contraries (εἰδέναι τίνα μὲν καλά, τίνα δὲ κρείττονα, τίνα δὲ παντάπασι τὰ διαφορὰν πρὸς ἄλληλα ἔχοντα, Theod.); so Beza, Van Heng., Alf., al.; (*b*) ' *to approve of things that are excellent*,' ' ut probetis potiora,' Vulg., τὰ διαφέροντα being used in the same sense as in Matth. x. 31, xii. 12, Luke xii. 7, 24 (Meyer adds Xen. *Hier.* 1. 3, τὰ διαφ., Dio Cass XLIV. 25), and δοκιμάζειν in its derivative sense, comp. Rom. xiv. 22, 1 Cor. xvi. 3, and examples in Rost u. Palm, *Lex.* s. v.; so Anthor., Mey., al ; or lastly (*b₁*) ' *to prove, bring to the test, things that are excellent*,' Syr. [ut discernatis convenientia], Æth. [ut perpendatis quæ præstat], the primary meaning of δοκ. being a little more exactly preserved ; see Rom. xii 2, Eph. v. 10. Exegetical considerations must alone decide; these seem slightly in favor of the meaning of διαφέροντα (' præstabilia, sc. in bonis optima,' Beng.) adopted in (*b*) and (*b₁*), — the prayer for the increase of love being more naturally realized in proving or approving what is excellent, what is really worthy of love, than in merely discriminating between what is different. Between (*b*) and (*b₁*) the preceding αἰσθήσει and the prevailing lexical meaning of δοκ. decides us in favor of the *latter* ; so Theophyl. (τὸ σύμφερον δοκιμάσαι καὶ ἐπιγνῶναι τίνας μὲν χρῆ φιλεῖν καὶ τίνας μή), and apparently Chrysostom, Beng. (' *explorare* et amplecti '), al., who appear correctly to hold to the more exact meaning of δοκιμάζειν : comp. notes *on Eph.* v. 10.

εἰλικρινεῖς] '*pure*,' 2 Pet. iii. 1 ; compare 1 Cor. v. 8, 2 Cor. i. 12, ii. 17. The derivation of this adjective, though a word not uncommon either in earlier or later Greek, is somewhat doubtful. The most probable is that adopted by Stallbaum (Plato, *Phæd* 77 A), who derives it from εἶλος [he must mean εἴλη] and κρίνω, with reference to a root εἰλεῖν. As, however, the primary meaning of this root is not quite certain, εἰλικρ. may be either ' what is parcelled off by itself ' (gregatim), with reference to εἴλη (see especially Buttmann, *Lexil.* § 44, and compare Rost u. Palm. *Lex.* s. v.), or more probably, ' volubili agitatione secretum,' with reference to the meaning *volvere*, which has recently been indicated as the primary meaning of εἰλεῖν ; see esp. *Philol. Museum*, Vol. 1. p. 405 sq. So appy. Hesych. εἰλικρινές· τὸ καθαρὸν καὶ ἀμιγὲς ἑτέρου; see Plutarch, *Quæst. Rom.* § 26, εἰλικρινὲς καὶ ἀμιγές ; ib. *Is. et Osir.* § 54, καθαρὸς οὐδ' εἰλικρινής, and esp. § 61, where τὰ εἰλικριν[ῆ] and τὰ μικτὰ are opposed to each other; compare also Max. Tyr. *Diss.* 31. The more usual, but less prob., derivation is from εἵλη, ' splendor ' [' ΕΛ-, cognate with ΣΕΛ,' Benfey, *Wurzellex.* Vol. 1. p. 460], in which case the rough breathing would be more suitable ; compare Schneider on Plato, *Rep.* II. p. 123. Several examples of the use of εἰλικρ. will be found in Loesner, *Obs.* p. 350, Kypke, *Obs.* Vol. II. p. 398, and Elsner, *Obs.* Vol. II. p. 10, of which the most pertinent are

ἀπρόσκοποι εἰς ἡμέραν Χριστοῦ, ¹¹ πεπληρωμένοι καρπὸν δικαιοσύνης τὸν διὰ Ἰησοῦ Χριστοῦ, εἰς δόξαν καὶ ἔπαινον Θεοῦ.

those above.   ἀπρόσκοποι] 'without offence, stumbling;' 'inoffensi o cursu,' Beza; intransitively as in Acts xxiv. 16, Hesych. ἀσκανδάλιστον; compare Suicer, *Thesaur.* s. v. Vol. i. p. 495. Chrys. and others give an active meaning, as in 1 Cor. x. 32, 'giving no offence,' εἴλικρ. marking their relation to God, ἀπρόσκ. th ir relation to men. This hardly accords with the context, in which their inward st e and relations to God form the sole subject of the prayer. It will be best, then, in spite of 1 Cor. l. c., to maintain the intransitive meaning; so apparently Vulg., Syriac, Coptic; but these are cases in which the Vv. scarcely give a definite opinion.

εἰς ἡμέραν Χρ.] 'against the day of Christ;' 'in diem,' Vulg., scil. ἵνα τότε εὑρεθῆτε καθαροί, Chrys.; — not 'till the day,' etc., Anth. Ver. (compare Beza), which would rather have been expressed by ἄχρις ἡμέρας, as in ver 6. The preposition has here not its *temporal*, but its *ethical* force; compare ch. ii. 16, Ephes. iv. 30, and notes on 2 Tim. i. 12. On the expressi n ἡμέρα Χρ. see the notes on ver. 6.

11. πεπληρωμένοι κ. τ. λ.] '*being filled with the fruit of righteousness;*' modal clause defining more fully εἴλικρ. καὶ ἀπρόσκ., and specifying not only on the negative, but also on the positive side the fullest and completest Christian development. The accus. καρπὸν [καρπῶν, *Rec.*, is unsupported by uncial authority] is that of 'the remoter object,' marking that in which the action of the verb has its realization; so Col. i. 9. πληρωθῆτε τὴν ἐπίγνωσιν τοῦ θελήματος; compare Hartung, *Cas s,* p. 62 sq. and notes on 1 *Tim.* vi. 5, where this construction is discussed. If we compare Rom. xv. 14, πεπληρωμένοι πάσης γνώσεως, we may recognize the primary distinction between the cases: the gen., the 'whence-case,' marks the absolute *material* out of which the fullness was realized (compare Krüger, *Sprachl.* § 47. 16); the accus., the 'whither-case,' the o ject towards whi h and along which the a tion tende l, and, as it were, in the *domain* of whi h the fullness was evinced; see Scheuerl., *Synt.* § 9. 1, p. 63. The gen. δικαιοσύνης is the gen. *originis,* that from which the καρπὸς emanates (Hartung, *Casus,* p 63), or perhaps more strictly, that of the *originating cause* (Scheuerl, *Synt.* § 17. 1, p. 125). — a καρπὸς that is the production of δικαιοσύνη; compare Gal. v. 22, Eph. v. 9. James iii. 18, and on the meaning of καρπός, notes on *Gal. l. c.*

With regard to the strict meaning of δικαιοσύνη it may be briefly remark d th at we must in all cases be guided by the context: here ver. 10 and the app. emphasis on καρπὸν point to δικ. as a moral *habitus* (comp Chrys.], as in Rom. vi 13, Eph. v. 9, al., — not 'justification' proper (Rilliet), but the righteousness which results from it and is evinced in good works; so Calv, Meyer, De W. On the distinction between the 'righteousness of sanctification' an l the 'righteousness of justification,' see especi lly the admirable sermon of Hooker, § 6, Vol. iii. p. 611 (ed. Keble), and on the doctrine of justification generally, the short but comprehensive treatise of Waterland, *Works,* Vol vi. pp. 1 - 38.

τὸν διὰ Ἰ. Χ. serves to specify the καρπόν, as being only and solely through Christ; compare notes on 2 *Tim.* i. 13. This fruit is a communication of the Life of Christ to His own (Wiesing.): it results from 'the pure grace of Christ our Lord whereby we were in Him [by the working of the Spirit He s nt, Gal. ii. 20, iii. 22, Mey.] made to do t ose good works that God had appointed for us to

Know that my sufferings have furthered the gospel, for Christ is preached by all. I indeed would fain depart to Christ, but for your sake I shall remain.

¹² Γινώσκειν δὲ ὑμᾶς βούλομαι, ἀδελφοί, ὅτι τὰ κατ' ἐμὲ μᾶλλον εἰς προκοπὴν τοῦ εὐαγγελίου ἐλήλυθεν, ¹³ ὥστε τοὺς δεσμούς μου φανεροὺς

walk in,' *King Edw. VI. Catech.*, cited by Waterland, *Justif.* Vol. vi. p. 31.

εἰς δόξαν καὶ ἔπ. Θεοῦ] 'to the praise and glory of God :' the praise and glory of God is the 'finis primarius' of the πεπληρῶσθαι. Hence 'ad gloriam,' Beza, is more exact than 'in gloriam,' Vulg., Clarom.; see notes *on Eph.* i. 6. Δόξα is here, as Meyer pertinently remarks, the 'majesty' of God *per se*, ἔπαινος, the 'praise and glorification' of the same; compare Eph. i. 6, 12, 14, 1 Pet. i. 7.

12. γινώσκειν δὲ κ. τ. λ.] '*Now I would have you know ;*' the transitional δὲ (Hartung, *Partik.* δέ, 2, 3, Vol. I. p. 165) introduces the fresh subject of the apostle's present condition at Rome, his hopes and fears; compare Rom. i. 13, 1 Cor. xii. 1, 1 Thess. iv. 13, al. It seems rather far-fetched in Meyer, followed by Alf., to refer γινώσκ. to ἐν ἐπιγν. above, 'and as a part of this knowledge I would have you know,' etc. There certainly seems no peculiar emphasis in γινώσκειν; the order is the natural one (comp. Jude 3) when βούλομαι is unemphatic; contrast 1 Tim. ii. 8, v. 14, al. Though few minor points deserve more attention in the study of the N. T. than the collocation of words, we must still be careful not to overpress collocations which arise not so much from design as from a natural and instinctive rhythm; compare 2 Cor. i. 8. τὰ κατ' ἐμέ] 'my circumstances,' 'rerum mearum conditio,' Wolf; comp. Eph. vi. 21, Col. iv. 7, Tobit x. 8, and see illustrations in Elsner, *Obs.* Vol. II. p. 234, Wetst. *in Eph. l. c.* In such cases κατά is *local*, and marks, as it were, an extension along an object; compare Acts xxvi. 3, and see Winer, *Gr.* § 49. d, p 356. In

late writers, κατά with a personal pronoun becomes almost equivalent to a possessive pronoun, and with a substantive almost equivalent to a simple gen. ; comp. 2 Macc. xv. 37.

μᾶλλον] '*rather ;*' not 'maxime' or 'excellenter' (compare Beza), but 'potius,' *rather* than what might have been expected, — viz. hinderance : see Winer, *Gr.* § 35. 4, p. 217, by whom this use of the comparative is well illustrated.

προκοπήν] '*advance,*' '*furtherance ;*' a substantive of later Greek condemned by the Atticists, see notes *on* 1 *Tim.* iv. 15, and compare Triller on Thom. M. s. v. p. 741 (ed. Bernh.), who, though perhaps justly pleading for the word as an intelligible and even elegant form, is unable to cite any instance of its use in any early writer, Attic or otherwise. Numerous examples, especially out of Plutarch, are cited by Wetst. *in loc.*

ἐλήλυθεν] '*have fallen out,*' Author. Ver.; compare Wisdom xv. 5, εἰς ὄνειδος ἔρχεται. Further but doubtful examples are cited by Raphel, *Annot.* Vol II. p. 499; at any rate, from them take out Mark v. 26, Acts xix. 27 (cited even by Meyer), in which ἐλθεῖν certainly implies nothing more than simple (ethical) motion. Alford adduces Herodot. I. 120, ἐς ἀσθενὲς ἔρχεται, which seems fully in point.

13. ὥστε τοὺς δεσμ. κ. τ. λ.] 'so that my bonds have become manifest in Christ ;' illustrations of the above προκοπή; first beneficial result of his imprisonment : 'duos nunc sigillatim apostolus fortunæ suæ adversæ memorat effectus,' Van Heng. The order of the words seems clearly to imply that ἐν Χρ. must be joined, — not with δεσμούς, Author. Ver., al., scil. 'ad provehendum

ἐν Χριστῷ γενέσθαι ἐν ὅλῳ τῷ πραιτωρίῳ καὶ τοῖς λοιποῖς πᾶσιν,

Christi honorem,' Calv., but with φανεροίς, on which, perhaps, there is a slight emphasis; the δεσμοί were not κρυπτοί, but φανεροί; nor φανεροὶ, only, but φανεροὶ ἐν Χρ.] 'manifesta in Christo,' Clarom., manifest — not 'through Christ,' Theoph., Œcum., but 'in Christ,' manifest as borne in fellowship with Him, and in His service. On this important qualitative formula, which must never be vaguely explained away, see notes on Gal. ii. 17, and for a brief explanation of its general force, compare Hooker, Serm. III. Vol. III. p. 763 (ed. Keble). The variation φαν. γενέσθ. (Chrys. adds τοὺς) ἐν Χρ with DEFG; Boern., Vulg., al., shows perhaps that some difficulty has been felt in the connection.

ἐν ὅλῳ τῷ πραιτ.] 'in the whole pretorium.' The meaning of πραιτώριον in this passage has been abundantly discussed. Taken per se, the adjectival substantive 'praetorium' has apparently the following meanings: (a) 'the general's tent,' sc. 'tentorium or tabernaculum' (Livy. VII. 12), and derivatively 'the council of war' held there (Livy XXVI. 15); (b) the palace of a provincial governor' (Cicero, Verr. III. 28; compare Matth. xxvii. 27, Mark xv. 16, al.), sc. 'domicilium,' and thence derivatively, (a) 'the palace of a king' (Juv. x. 161; compare Acts xxiii. 35), and even (β) 'the mansion of a private individual' (compare Suet. Octav. 72); lastly, (c) 'the body-guard of the emperor' (Tacit. Hist. IV. 46); and thence not improbably, (d) 'the guard-house or barracks where they were stationed;' compare Scheller, Lex. s. v., from which this abstract has been compiled. In the present passage Chrys. and the patristic expositors all adopt (b, a) and refer the term to 'the emperor's palace' (τὰ βασίλεια), but since the time of Perizonius (de Prat. et Praetorio, Franeq. 1687)

nearly all modern commentators adopt (d), and refer πραιτ. to the 'castrum Praetorianorum' built and fortified by Sejanus, not far from the 'Porta Viminalis;' compare Suet. Tiber. 37, Tacit. Ann. IV. 2, Dio Cass. LVII. 19. The patristic interpretation, on account of the lax use of 'praetorium,' seems fairly defensible; as, however there is no proof that the imperial palace at Rome was ever so called, and as it is expressly said, Acts xxviii. 16, that St. Paul was delivered τῷ στρατοπεδάρχῃ (one of the two Praefecti Praetorio, perhaps Burrus), and by him assigned to the custody of a (Praetorian) soldier, it seems more probable that the apostle is here referring to the 'castrum Praetorianorum,' — not merely to the smaller portion of it attached to the palace of Nero (Wieseler, Chronol. p. 403, followed by Hows. [Vol. II. p. 510, ed. 2], and Alf. in loc.), but as ὅλῳ and the subsequent generic τοῖς λοιποῖς πᾶσιν seem to imply. — to the whole camp of the Praetorians, whether inside or outside the city, — in which general designation it is not improbable that the οἰκία Καίσαρος (chap. iv. 22) may be included: see notes in loc. The interpr. 'hall of judicature,' Hamm., al. (see Wolf in loc.), does not appear either satisfactory or tenable. The arguments based on this passage by Baur (de Apost. Paul. p. 469 sq.) against the genuineness of this Ep. must be pronounced very hopeless and unconvincing.

καὶ τοῖς λοιποῖς] 'and to all the rest,' beside the Praetorian camp, 'reliquis omnibus Romae versantibus,' comp. Neander, Planting, Vol. I. p. 317 (Bohn): not 'the rest of the Praetorians' (Wieseler, Chronol. p. 457), a meaning too limited; nor, 'hominibus exteris gentilibus quibusennqne,' Van Heng., a meaning which οἱ λοιποί certainly does not necessarily bear. Vulg., Æth, and Author

¹⁴ καὶ τοὺς πλείονας τῶν ἀδελφῶν ἐν Κυρίῳ πεποιθότας τοῖς δεσμοῖς μου περισσοτέρως τολμᾶν ἀφόβως τὸν λόγον λαλεῖν. ¹⁵ Τινὲς

refer τοῖς λοιποῖς to locality, 'in other places' (ἐν τῇ πόλει πάσῃ, Chrys.), the dative being under the vinculum of ἐν: this is grammatically possible, but, as λοιπὸς is not elsewhere applied to places in the N. T., not very probable; comp. 2 Cor. xiii. 2.

14. καὶ τοὺς πλείονας] '*and that the greater part of the brethren:*' second beneficial effect of the apostle's imprisonment. The presence of the article obviously shows that πλείονας must here retain its proper comparative force, — not 'many,' Auth. Ver. ܠܣܘܓܐܐ [multitudo] Syr., but 'the greater portion,' 'the more part,' as Author. in Acts xix. 32, xxvii. 12, 1 Cor. ix. 19, xv. 6. So also 2 Cor. ii. 6, iv. 15, ix. 2, where both Luther and Auth. incorrectly retain the positive.   ἐν Κυρ. πεποιθ.] '*having in the Lord confidence in my bonds;*' not 'in regard of my bonds' (Flatt, Rill.), which vitiates the construction; the dative not being a dative 'of reference to' (comp. Gal. i. 22), but the usual transmissive dative. At first sight it might seem more simple and natural with Syr. to connect ἐν Κυρίῳ with ἀδελφῶν, 'brethren united with, in fellowship with the Lord,' — a construction admissible in point of grammar (Winer, Gr. § 20. 2, p. 123), but open to the serious objection that though the important modal adjunct, ἐν Κυρίῳ, occurs several times in St. Paul's Epistles with substantives or quasi-substantives, e. g. Rom. xvi. 8, 13, Eph. iv. 1, vi. 21, Col. iv. 7, it is never found with ἀδελφός: Eph. vi. 21, cited in opp. by Van Heng., is not in point; see Meyer *in loc.* On the contrary, πεποιθ. is found similarly joined with ἐν Κυρ. chap. ii. 24, Galat. v. 10, 2 Thess. iii. 4, comp. Rom. xiv. 4. The objection that in these and similar cases πεποιθ. stands first in the sentence (Alf.), is not here of any moment; the emphasis rests on ἐν Κυρίῳ, and properly causes its precedence: surely it must have been 'in the Lord,' and in Him only, that confidence could have been felt — when in bonds: so rightly Meyer, and very decidedly Winer, Gr. § 20. 2, p. 124.

περισσοτέρως τολμᾶν] '*are more abundantly bold,*' scil. than when I was not in bonds; not 'are very much emboldened,' Conyb., a needless dilution of the comparative; 'hāc freti plus solito audere debemus, jam in personâ fratrum pignus victoriæ nostræ habentes,' Calv. The construction adopted by Grotius, Baumg., Crus., al., περισσ. ἀφόβως, i. e. ἀφοβωτέρως, is eminently unsatisfactory; each verb naturally takes its own adverb. With ἀφόβως λαλεῖν, comp. Acts iv. 31, ἐλάλουν τὸν λόγον τοῦ Θεοῦ μετὰ παρρησίας, a passage which may have suggested here the insertion of the nearly certain gloss τοῦ Θεοῦ, as in AB; about 20 mss.; majority of Vv. (Lachm.). The variations (see *Tisch.*) serve to confirm the shorter reading.

15. τινὲς μὲν κ. τ. λ.]   '*Some indeed even from envy and strife:*' exceptions to the foregoing; 'this is the case with all; some preach from bad motives.' The previous definition, ἐν Κυρ. πεποιθ., seems to render it impossible that the τινὲς μὲν should be comprised in the ἀδελφοί, ver. 14. The mention of 'speaking the word' brings to the apostle's mind *all* who were doing so; he pauses then to allude to all, specifying under the τινὲς μὲν (obs. not οἱ μὲν as in ver. 16) his *Judaizing* — not his unbelieving (Chrys.) — opponents, while in τινὲς δὲ he reverts to the sounder majority mentioned in ver. 14. Καὶ, with its common contrasting force in such collocations (see notes on chap. iv. 12; comp. Klotz,

μὲν καὶ διὰ φθόνον καὶ ἔριν, τινὲς δὲ καὶ δι' εὐδοκίαν τὸν Χριστὸν κηρύσσουσιν· ¹⁶ οἱ μὲν ἐξ ἀγάπης, εἰδότες ὅτι εἰς ἀπολογίαν τοῦ

Diener. Vol. II. p. 636, and examples in Harmung, *Partik.* Vol. I. pp. 136, 137) marks that there were, alas! other motives beside the good ones that might be inferred from the preceding words. Alford refers καὶ to τινές, 'besides those mentioned ver. 14.' This, however, does not seem tenable. διὰ φθόνον] '*on account of envy*,' or more idiomatically, 'from envy,' 'for envy,' — to gratify that evil feeling; so Matth. xxvii. 18, Mark xv. 10, comp. Winer, *Gr.* § 49. e, p. 355, and notes on *Gal.* iv. 13. Alberti adduces somewhat pertinently Philemon [Major, a comic poet, B. C. 330] πολλά με διδάσκεις ἀφθόνως διὰ φθόνον; see Meineke, *Com. Fragm.* Vol. IV. p. 55. It is scarcely necessary to add that the translation '*amid envy*' (Jowett on *Gal.* iv. 10), is quite untenable: διά with an *accus*. in local or quasi-local references is purely poetical; compare Bernhardy, *Synt.* v. 18, p 236.

δι' εὐδοκίαν] '*on account of, from, good will*,' ἀπὸ προθυμίας ἁπάσης, Chrys.— towards the apostle; not towards others in respect of their salvation (Est.). De W. objects to this meaning of εὐδοκία as not sufficiently confirmed, and adopts the transl. 'good pleasure,' se of me and my affairs. This seems somewhat hypercritical; surely the opposition διὰ φθόνον coupled with ἐξ ἀγάπης, ver. 16, seems sufficient to warrant the current translation; see Fritz. *Rom.* Vol. II. p. 372, whose note, however, is not in all points perfectly exact; comp. notes on *Eph.* i. 5, and the quaint but suggestive comments of Andrewes, *Serm.* XIII. Vol. I. p. 230 (Angl.-Cath. Libr.). The καὶ refers to contrary motives just enunciated; and the party specified under τινὲς δέ, though practically coincident with the πλείονες, are yet, as De Wette rightly observes, put slightly under a different point of view, and as forming the opposite party to those last mentioned. Thus of those who spake the word, τινὲς μέν were factious and envious, τινὲς δέ full of good will and kindly feeling, and the latter were they who constitute the πλείονας τῶν ἀδελφῶν, ver. 14.

16. οἱ μὲν ἐξ ἀγάπης] '*t o e indeed (that are) of* &c (those &c ; *se* ὄντες, comp. Rom. ii. 8, Gal. iii. 7. The two classes mentioned in the last verse are now by οἱ μέν and οἱ δέ a little more exactly specified, the order being inverted. In *Rec.* the more natural order is preserved, but is very insufficiently supported, viz., only by one of the second correctors of D, K (L omits οἱ μὲν ἐξ ἐριθ. to μου), other mss.; Syr.-Philox. and other Vv., and several Greek Ff. The Auth. Ver. and apparently nearly all the older expositors make οἱ μέν the subject, and refer ἐξ ἀγάπης to the supplied clause, τὸν Χρ. κηρ.: so also Matth., Alf., and other modern commentators. This is plausible at first sight, but on a nearer examination can hardly be maintained. For *first*, ἐξ ἀγάπης would thus be only a kind of repetition of δι' εὐδοκίαν, as also ἐξ ἐριθ. of διὰ φθόνον; and *secondly*, the force of the causal participial clause would be much impaired, for the object of the apostle is rather to specify the motives which caused this difference of behavior in the two classes than merely to reiterate the nature of it. See also De Wette *in loc.* by whom the present interpretation is ably maintained; so Meyer, Wies., and (in language perhaps too confident), Van Heng.: where appy. all the ancient versions are on the other side, it is not wise to be too positive. On the expression, οἱ ἐξ ἀγάπης, 'qui ab amore originem ducunt,' see notes on *Gal.* iii. 7, and Fritz. on *Rom.* ii. 8, Vol. I. p. 105. εἰδότες ὅτι κ.τ.λ.]

εὐαγγελίου κεῖμαι, ¹⁷ οἱ δὲ ἐξ ἐριθείας τὸν Χριστὸν καταγγέλλουσιν, οὐχ ἁγνῶς, οἰόμενοι θλίψιν ἐγείρειν τοῖς δεσμοῖς μου.

'as they know that I am appointed for the defence of the gospel,' i. e. 'set to defend the gospel,' Tynd., Cran.; participial clause explaining the motives of the behavior, compare Rom. v. 3, Gal. ii. 6, Eph. vi 8, al. They recognize in me the appointed defender of the gospel,— not the incapacitated preacher, whose position claims their help (Est, Fell 2), but the energetic apostle whose example quickens and evokes their co operation. Κεῖμαι has thus a purely passive reference, not 'jaceo in conditione miserâ,' Van Heng. (a meaning lexically defensible, see examples in Rost u. Palm, Lex. s. v.), but 'constitutus sum,' Æth., 'I am set,' Auth., Θεός με κεχειροτόνηκε, Theodoret: so Luke ii. 34, 1 Thess. iii. 3. The apostle was in confinement, but not, as far as we can gather, either in misery or in suffering; compare Conyb. and Hows. *St. Paul*, Vol. II. p. 515 sq. ἀπολογίαν τοῦ εὐαγγ. is referred by Chrys., Theoph., and Œcum. to the account (τὰς εὐθύνας) of his ministry, which the apostle would have to render up *to God*, and which the co-operation of others might render less heavy. This seems artificial: ἀπολογία is nowhere used in the N T. in reference to God, and can hardly have a different meaning to that which it bears in v. 7 ; see Wieseler, *Chronol.* p. 430 note.

17. οἱ δὲ ἐξ ἐριθείας] 'but they (that are) of party-feeling or dissension;' opposite class to οἱ ἐξ ἀγάπης, ver. 16. On the derivation and true meaning of ἐριθεία,— not exactly 'contention,' Author. (comp. Vulg., Syr., Copt.), followed by many modern commentators, but 'intrigue,' 'party-spirit' (ἀναιδῶς κατὰ τὴν ἀγορὰν περιϊόντες, Theod.), as apparently felt by Clarom. 'dissensio,' and perhaps Æth.,— see notes *on Gal.* v. 20. On the most suitable translation, comp.

notes on *Transl.* καταγγέλλουσιν] 'declare,' 'proclaim;' in effect not different from κηρύσσειν, ver. 16 (καταγγέλλεται· κηρύσσεται, Hesych.), but perhaps presenting a little more distinctly the idea of 'promulgation,' 'making fully known' (Xenoph. *Anab.* II. 5. 11, τινὶ τὴν ἐπιβουλήν); comp. 1 Cor. ix. 14, Coloss. i. 28, and Acts xvii. 3, 23, in which latter book the word occurs about ten times. It is peculiar to St. Paul and St. Luke. In this compound the preposition appears to have an *intensive* force, as in καταλέγειν, καταφαγεῖν κ. τ. λ.; see Rost u. Palm, *Lex.* s. v. IV. 4. Οὐχ ἁγνῶς 'insincerely,' 'with no pure intention,' (οὐκ εἰλικρινῶς οὐδὲ δι' αὐτὸ τὸ πρᾶγμα, Chrysost.), belongs closely to καταγγ., and marks the spirit in which they performed the καταγγελία. On the meaning of ἁγνός ('in quo nihil est impuri') see notes on 1 *Tim.* v. 22, and Tittm. *Synon.* I. p. 22. οἰόμενοι κ. τ. λ.] 'thinking (thus) to raise up, etc.;' not *exactly* parallel to εἰδότες, ver. 16, but explanatory of οὐχ ἁγνῶς. The verb οἴεσθαι seems here to convey a faint idea of intention, though of an intention which was not realized; e. g. Plato, *Apol.* 41 D, οἰόμενοι βλάπτειν (cited by De W.); καὶ καλῶς εἶπε τὸ οἰόμενοι οὐ γὰρ οὕτως ἐξέβαινεν, Chrysost. The reading ἐγείρειν (*Rec.* ἐπιφέρειν) is supported not only by the critical principle, 'proclivi lectioni praestat ardua,' but also by the weight of uncial authority, ABD¹FG; so too, three mss., Vulg., Clarom., Goth., al., and the best modern editors.

τοῖς δεσμοῖς μου] 'unto my bonds,' dat. *incommodi*, Jelf, *Gr.* § 602. 3; endeavoring to make a state already sufficiently full of trouble yet more painful and afflicting. There is some little doubt as to the exact nature of this θλίψις. Is

¹⁹ τί γάρ; πλὴν παντὶ τρόπῳ, εἴτε προφάσει εἴτε ἀληθείᾳ,

it outward, *i.e.* dangers from the inflamed hatred of *heathen* enemies (Chrysost.), or inward, *i.e.* 'trouble of spirit' (Atford)! Not the latter, which is not in harmony with the studiedly objective δεσμοῖς, or with the prevailing use of θλίψις in the N. T.;— nor yet exactly as Chrys., al., which seems too restricted, if not artificial, but, more probably, ill-treatment at the hands of Jews and *Judaizing* Christians, which the false teaching of the οἱ ἐξ ἐριθείας would be sure to call forth. Calvin very prudently observes, 'erant plurimae occasiones [Apostolo nocendi] quae sunt nobis incognitae qui temporum circumstantias non tenemus.'

18. τί γάρ] '*What then;*' 'quid enim,' Vulg., or perhaps more exactly, 'quid ergo;' not 'quid igitur,' Beza, which is not commonly thus used in independent questions. The uses of τί γάρ may be approximately stated as three (*a*) *argumentative,* answering very nearly to the Lat. 'quid enim,' and while confirming or explaining the preceding sentence, often serving to imply tacitly that an opponent has no answer to make; see Hand, *Tursell.* Vol. II. p. 386. It is thus often followed by another interrogation; compare Rom. iii. 3, Job xxi. 4; (*b*) *affirmative;* answering very nearly to 'profecto' or the occasional 'quid ni' of the Latins (Hand, *Tursell.* Vol. IV. p. 186); compare Eurip. *Orest.* 481, Soph. *Œd. Col.* 547, and see Herm. *Viger,* No. 108, and Ellendt, *Lex. Soph.* Vol. I. p. 537, who however has not sufficiently discriminated between the examples adduced; (*c*) *rhetorical,* as apparently here, answering more nearly to 'quid ergo' or 'quid ergo est' (Hand, *Tursell.* Vol. II. p. 456), and marking commonly either a startled question (compare *Œd. Col.* 544, 552), or, as here, and apparently Job xviii. 4, a *brisk* transition ['ubi quis cum alacritate quâdam ad

novam sententiam transgreditur,' Kuhner on Xenoph *Memor.* II. 6. 2 and thus perhaps differing from the calmer τί οὖν. In every one of these cases, however, the proper force of γάρ ('sane pro rebus comparatis') though successively becoming more obscure, may still be recognized, here, for example, the question amounts to, 'things being then as I have described them, what is my state of feeling!' See Klotz, *Devar.* Vol. II. p. 247 sq. All supplements, διαφέρει (Chrys.), μοι μέλει (Theoph., φήσομεν (Van H.), etc., are perfectly unnecessary, if not uncritical.

πλήν] '*notwithstanding,*' '*nevertheless;*' this particle, probably connected with πλέον (Pott, *Etym. Forsch.* Vol. II. pp. 39, 323), not with πέλας (Hartung, *Partik.* Vol. II. p. 30), has properly a comparative force, especially recognizable in the disjunctive comparison πλὴν ἤ, (see Donalds. *Cratyl.* § 160), and its use with the gen. *e. g.* Mark xii. 32, John viii. 10. This might be termed its *prepositional* use. It however soon passed by an intelligible gradation into an *adverbial* use, and came to imply little more than ἀλλά, 'nevertheless,' 'abgesehen davon' (ch. iii 16, iv. 14, 1 Cor. xi, 11, Eph v. 33), with which particle it is not unfrequently joined; see Klotz, *Devar.* Vol. II p. 725. παντὶ τρόπῳ] '*in every way,*' scil. of preaching the gospel, more exactly defined by εἴτε — εἴτε. At first sight there might seem some difficulty in this lenity of St Paul towards false, and perhaps heterodox teachers, — men against whom he warns his converts with such emphasis in ch. iii. 2. The answer seems reasonable, that St. Paul is here contemplating the *personal* motives rather than alluding to the doctrines of the preachers; nay, more, that perverted in many respects as this preaching might be CHRIST is still its subject, and to the

Χριστὸς καταγγέλλεται, καὶ ἐν τούτῳ χαίρω· ἀλλὰ καὶ χαρήσομαι·

large heart of the apostle this is enough; this swallows up every doubt and fear: 'let then the word be preached, and let it be heard; be it sincerely, or be it pretensedly, so it be done, it is to him [St. Paul] and should be to us, matter (not only of contentment, but also) of rejoicing,' Andrewes, *Serm.* IX. Vol. V. p. 191 (A.-C. Libr.); see especially Neander, *Planting,* Vol. I. p. 318 (Bohn), and compare Stier, *Reden Jesu,* Vol. III. p. 29. εἴτε προφάσει κ.τ.λ.] '*whether in pretence or in truth;*' datives expressive of the manner, technically termed, *modal* datt.; see Winer, *Gr.* § 31. 6, p. 193, and especially Jelf, *Gr.* § 603, by whom this use of the dative is well illustrated; compare also Hartung, *Casus,* p. 69. The phraseological annotators, especially Wetstein and Raphel (Vol. II. p 500), adduce numerous instances of a similar opposition between πρόφασις and ἀλήθεια or τἀληθές; these are quite enough, independently of the context, to induce us to reject the translation of προφάσει, adopted by Grot., al., '*occasione,*' *i. e.,* 'be the good not intended but only occasioned by them,' Hammond. On the more general meaning of the here more limited ἀλήθεια, compare Reuss, *Théol. Chrét.* IV. 16, Vol. II. p 169. ἐν τούτῳ] '*therein,*' '*in this state of things,*' scil. that Christ is preached, though from different reasons; comp. Luke X. 20. This use of ἐν τούτῳ, nearly = Germ. '*darüber,*' though apparently not very common in the best prose, is certainly no Hebraism (Rilliet); see Winer, *Gram.* § 48. a, p. 346. Meyer compares Plato, *Republ.* X. p. 603 C, ἐν τούτοις πᾶσιν ἢ λυπουμένους ἢ χαίροντας.

ἀλλὰ καὶ χαρ] '*yea, and I shall rejoice;*' not exactly, ἀεὶ ὑπὲρ τούτων χαρήσομαι, Chrys., Calv., but, in more strict connection with the following fut., *when*

the ἀποβ. εἰς σωτ. is being realized. The punctuation is here not quite certain. *Lachm.*, followed by *Tisch.* and Meyer, places a full stop before ἀλλά, and a colon after χαρ., thus connecting οἶδα γὰρ more immediately with the present clause. This seems right in principle both on grammatical, as well as exegetical, considerations: a colon, however, as in text, seems preferable to a full stop, for there is a kind of sequence in the χαίρω and χαρήσομαι which can hardly be *completely* interrupted. De W., Van Heng., and others who retain the comma (Alford has a comma in text but a colon in translation) suppose an ellipsis of οὐ μόνον before χαίρω. This is very unsatisfactory. Ἀλλὰ καὶ has here its idiomatic meaning '*at etiam,*' the faintly seclusive force of ἀλλά serving specially to confine attention to the new assertion which the καὶ annexes and enhances; see Fritz *Rom.* vi. 5, Vol. I. p. 374. It may be observed that in these words, and also in some uses of the idiomatic ἀλλὰ γάρ, ἀλλὰ μέν, the primary force of ἀλλά ('*aliud jam hoc esse de quo sumus dicturi,*' Klotz, *Devar.* Vol. II. p. 2) is so far obscured that it does practically little more than impart a briskness and emphasis to the declaration; see Klotz, *l. c.,* p. 8, Hartung, *Partik.* Vol. II. p. 35. Lastly, we should be careful to distinguish between the present use of ἀλλὰ καὶ and (*a*) where a hypothetical clause precedes, evoking a more distinct opposition, *e. g.* 1 Cor. iv. 15, 2 Cor. iv. 16; (*b*) where an opposition is involved in the terms themselves, *e. g.* Diod. Sic. v. 84 (Fritz.), ἐν ταῖς νήσοις ἀλλὰ καὶ κατὰ τὴν Ἀσίαν; or (*c*) where ἀλλά occurs in brisk exhortation, *e. g.* Soph. *Philoct.* 796. ἀλλ' ὦ τέκνον καὶ θάρσος ἴσχε; in which passage Hermann's proposed emendation τι θάρσος does not seem either plausible or necessary.

19 οἶδα γαρ ὅτι τοῦτό μοι ἀποβήσεται εἰς σωτηρίαν διὰ τῆς ὑμῶν

19. *οἶδα γάρ*] Confirmation of the words immediately preceding, the γάρ having its simple argumentative force. If with Calv., Beng., al. this clause be referred to ver. 17, γὰρ must have more of an *explanatory* force (comp. notes on *Gal.* ii. 6): such a ref., however, is unduly regressive; τοῦτο here can only mean the same as τούτῳ ver. 19.—the more extended preaching of the gospel of Christ. The words τοῦτο — σωτηρίαν occur in Job xiii. 16, and *may* have been a reminiscence. *εἰς σωτηρίαν*] '*to salvation.*' The exact meaning of σωτηρία has been very differently explained. It has been referred to (*a*) 'salus *corporea*,' scil. 'escape from present danger, ἀπαλλαγήν, Chrys., who however fluctuates; 'preservation in life,' τὸ ὅσον οὐδέ πω μαρτύριον, Œcum., and apparently Syr.; (*b*) 'salus *spiritualis*,' 'Seelenheil,' De Wette, 'his own faithfulness to Christ,' Alford; (*c*) both united, 'for good, whether of soul (Rom. viii. 28) or of body' (Acts xxvii. 34), Peile, Bloomf.; (*d*) 'salus *sempiterna*,' whether (α) in reference to others (Grot., Hamm.), or (β) in ref. to himself, 'suam salutem veram et perennem,' Van Heng. The last of these meanings alone seems to satisfy the future reference (ἀποβ.), and is most in accordance with the prevailing meaning of σωτηρία in St Paul's Epistles; compare ver. 28, ch. ii 12, and *εἰς σωτ.* Rom. i. 16, 2 Thess. ii. 13.

διὰ τῆς κ.τ.λ.] '*through your supplication and the supply of the spirit of J. C.*;' the two means by which the σωτηρία is to be realized, intercessory supplication on the part of man, and supply of the Spirit on the part of God. Meyer and Alford regard the gen. ἐπιχορηγίας as dependent on ὑμῶν, 'your supply to me (by that prayer) of, etc.,' on the ground that διὰ τῆς, or at least τῆς would have been inserted. Independently of the very unsatisfactory meaning in a dogmatical point of view, this is not grammatically exact. No article is required. La b substantive has its own defining genitive, and on this account the use of it may dispense with its article; so Winer, *Gr.* § 19. 5, p. 118 (ed. 6). Meyer is unfortunate in referring to Winer in support of his interpretation, as that scholar will expressly adopts the more natural construction ἐπιχορηγίας τοῦ Πν.] '*supply of the Spirit.*' These words admit of two interpretations according as τοῦ Πν. is considered a gen. *objecti* or *subjecti*; compare Winer, *Gr.* § 30. 1. p. 168. If the former, the meaning will be, 'the supply which is the Spirit,' the genitive being that of *identity* or *apposition* (Scheuerl. *Synt.* § 12. 1. p. 82, 83): so Chrysost., Theoph. Œcum. If the latter, the meaning will be the 'supply which the Spirit gives,' the gen. being that of the *origin* or *agent* (Hartung, *Casus*, p. 17); so Theodoret. De W., Mey. This latter interpretation is on the whole to be preferred, as the parallelism, 'the prayers you offer—the aid the Spirit supplies,' is thus more exactly retained. Wiesing. and Alf. urge Gal. iii. 5, but this can hardly be considered sufficiently in point to fix the interpretation. Still less tenable is the assertion that the gen. *subjecti* would have required the order τοῦ Πν. 'Ι. Χ. ἐπιχορ. as in Eph. iv. 16 Alford]; for in the first place examples of the contrary and indeed, usual) order are most abundant, see Scheuerl. *Synt.* p 126, Winer, *Gr.* p. 167; and in the next place the gen. in Eph. *l. c.* is confessedly of a different grammatical class; see notes *in loc.* The Spirit is here termed τὸ Πν. Ἰησ. Χρ., not merely because Christ gives Himself spiritually in and with the Holy Ghost (Meyer *on Rom.* viii. 9), but because that eternal Spirit proceeds from the Son; so

δεήσεως καὶ ἐπιχορηγίας τοῦ Πνεύματος Ἰησοῦ Χριστοῦ, ²⁰ κατὰ

Pearson, *Creed*, Vol. i. p. 383: in a word the genitive is not so much a definitive or quasi-possess. gen., as a simple genitive *originis*, Hartung, *Casus*, p. 23. Lastly, on ἐπιχορηγία, which perhaps retains a *slight* shade of the primary meaning of χορηγ. in the ampleness and liberality which it seems to hint at on the part of the gift and giver, see notes on Coloss. ii. 19, and Harless on *Ephes.* iv. 16. The ἐπὶ is *directive*, not intensive; see notes on *Eph. l. c.*

20. κατὰ τὴν ἀποκαρ.] '*according to my expectation*,' sc. 'even as I am hoping and expecting,' Syr., 'sicut speravi et confisus sum,' Æth. The curious word ἀποκαραδοκία (Hesych. προσδοκία, ἀπεκδοχή) only here and Rom. viii. 19 in the N. T., is derived from κάρα, and δοκέω [possibly allied to a root *dic*, 'monstrare,' Pott, *Etym. Forsch.* Vol. i. p. 185, 267] and properly denotes 'capitis, scil. oculorum animique ad rem ab aliquo loco expectandam attenta conversio,' and thence derivatively 'patient, persistent, looking for' (Rom. viii. 19), and, with a further weakened force, 'calm expectation,' as in this place; the meaning necessarily varying with that of the simple καραδοκεῖν, which, from the ideas of 'attention' (Eur. *Troad.* 93) and 'observation' (Polyb. *Hist.* x. 42. 6), passes to those of 'suspense' (Eur. *Med.* 1117) and simple 'expectation' (Eur. *Iph. Aul.* 1433). The prep. ἀπὸ is not properly *intensive*, as in ἀποθερίοω, ἀποψεύδομαι, κ. τ. λ. (Tittm. *Synon.* p. 106 sq., and even Meyer on *Rom.* viii. 19), but *local*: it primarily (so to say) localizes the καραδοκεῖν, by marking either (a) the place *from which* the observation is maintained, *e. g.* Joseph. *Bell. Jud.* iii. 7. 26, comp. Polyb. *Hist.* xviii. 31. 4, or (b) the quarter *whence* the thing or issue is looked for, *e. g.* Polyb. *Hist.* xvi. 2. 8,—and comes thence, as in

ἀπεκδέχομαι (Germ. '*abwarten*,' see notes on *Gal.* v. 5), with a gradual, but intelligible, evanescence of the local idea ('quidquid enim expectes alicunde te id expectare oportet,' Fritz.), to imply little more than the *fixedness, permanence*, and *patience* (not 'solicitude,' Tittm.) with which the observation is continued, or the expectation entertained; see Winer, *de Verb. Compos.* iv. p. 14, and especially the excellent discussion of Fritz. *Fritzsch. Opusc.* pp. 150–157.

ὅτι ἐν οὐδενὶ αἰσχ.] '*that in nothing I shall be put to shame.*' These words admit of various possible interpretations; for example (a) ὅτι may be either relatival, 'that,' τὸ ἐλπίζειν ὅτι, Chrys., or argumentative, 'because.' 'quia,' Vulg., Clarom.; (b) οὐδενὶ may be either neuter (Syr., Auth., al.), or masculine in reference to the preachers of the gospel (Hoelem.); again (c) αἰσχυνθ. may be either passive, 'confundar,' Vulg., or with a middle force, 'pudore confusus, ab officio deflectam,' Van Hengel. In this variety of interpretation we must be guided solely by the context: and this seems certainly in favor of the above translation; for (a) ὅτι far more naturally follows ἐλπὶς as defining the subject to which it refers (comp. Rom. viii. 21) than as supplying the reason why it is entertained; the latter interrupts the sequence, vitiates the logic, and leaves the object of hope undefined. Again, (b) οὐδενὶ cannot be masculine; for if so, it would have to be arbitrarily referred *only* to the better class of those mentioned above, whereas if neuter it remains perfectly general and inclusive, not merely οὔτε ἐν τῷ ζῆν οὔτε ἐν θανεῖν, Theoph., —but, 'in no respect, in no particular' (comp. ver. 28), thus forming an antithesis to ἐν πάσῃ παρρ. Lastly, (c) αἰσχ cannot logically be taken with any middle force; St. Paul can scarcely know

τὴν ἀποκαραδοκίαν καὶ ἐλπίδα μου, ὅτι ἐν οὐδενὶ αἰσχυνθήσομαι, ἀλλ' ἐν πάσῃ παρρησίᾳ ὡς πάντοτε καὶ νῦν μεγαλυνθήσεται Χριστὸς ἐν τῷ σώματί μου, εἴτε διὰ ζωῆς εἴτε διὰ θανάτου.

that the preaching will turn out to his salvation, and yet only hope and expect that he shall not fall from his duty. What the apostle does hope and expect is, not merely ὅτι οὐ περισσοῦνται οὗτοι, Chrys., ὅτι κρείσσων ἔσομαι τῶν δυσχερῶν, Theod., but more generally, that he shall not be brought to a state of shame (2 Cor. x. 8, 1 John ii. 28), that he shall not fail in the highest duties and aims of his life; see De Wette *in loc*, who aptly compares the Hebrew גּוֹם Psalm xxxiv. 5 (LXX. καταισχυνθῇ), lxix. 2 (LXX. αἰσχυνθείησαν), and contrasts St. Paul's favorite term καυχᾶσθαι.

ἀλλ' ἐν πάσῃ παρρ.] '*but (on the contrary) in all boldness;*' antithesis to the foregoing clause introduced with the full force of the adversative ἀλλά. Πάσῃ, as has often been remarked (see ver. 9), is not qualitative, 'une pleine liberté,' Rill., but, as usual, quantitative, 'every form and manifestation of boldness,' forming an exact opposition to ἐν οὐδενί above. Ἐν παρρησίᾳ is thus not merely 'in joyfulness' (Wiesing., comp. Eph. iii 12), and certainly not σαφῶς φανερῶς, Œcum., comp. Syr. ܒܓܠܝܐ [revelatâ facie], but, as the contrast and context both imply, 'in fiduciâ,' Vulg., 'in boldness of speech and action;' comp. Eph. vi. 19.

ὡς πάντοτε καὶ νῦν] Temporal clause, following close on the foregoing modal predication (comp. Donalds. *Gr.* § 444). The addition καὶ νῦν gives a dignifying and consoling aspect to the apostle's present condition, cheerless as it might seem, and supplies a retrospective corroboration of ver. 12.

μεγαλυνθήσεται ἐν τῷ σώμ.] '*shall be magnified in my body;*' not ἐν ἐμοί, but, in accordance with the studiedly passive aspect given to the whole declaration (observed by Jer.), — ἐν τῷ σώμ., 'in my body;' 'my body shall be, as it were, the theatre on which Christ's glory shall be displayed,' comp. John xxi. 19, and in illustration of the use of ἐν ('substratum of action') see notes on *Gal.* i. 24, Winer, *Gr.* § 48. a, p. 345, Μεγαλ. is thus not 'shall be extolled,' 'angebitur,' Copt. (comp. Luke i. 58, 2 Cor. x. 15), with reference to the development and growth of Christ within (B.-L.; compare Gal ii. 20, Rom. viii. 10), which here would not harmonize with the modal ἐν παρρ., and still less with the local ἐν σώμ., — but, as in Acts xix 17, 'shall be glorified,' δειχθήσεται ὡς ἐστι Theoph., 'gloriosior apparebit,' Just., the meaning being here appy. a little more forcible than 'be praised' (Alf.; comp. Lk i. 46, Acts v. 13) and pointing more to the general, than to the merely oral spread of the Lord's glory and kingdom among men.

εἴτε διὰ κ. τ. λ.] 'either by life or by death;' two alternatives, suggested by and in explanation of the preceding ἐν σώματι; 'in my body,'—whether that body be preserved alive as an early instrument of my Master's glory, or be given up to martyrdom for His name's sake: διὰ μὲν ζωῆς, ὅτι ἐξελέετο, διὰ θανάτου δέ, ὅτι οὐδὲ θάνατος ἔπεισε με ἀρνήσασθαι αὐτόν, Chrys. Well then might the apostle say οἶδα ὅτι εἰς σωτηρίαν when he could entertain a hope and an expectation so unspeakably blessed. The whole verse, and especially this clause, is strongly confirmatory of the fuller meaning of σωτηρία.

21. ἐμοὶ γάρ] Confirmation and elucidation of the last clause of v. 20. The γάρ has no ref. to any omitted clause (Bl.),

21 Ἐμοὶ γὰρ τὸ ζῆν Χριστὸς καὶ τὸ ἀποθανεῖν κέρδος. 22 εἰ δὲ τὸ

— ever a doubtful and precarious mode of explaining this particle, — but simply confirms the preceding assertion by showing the real nature of ζωή and θάνατος, according to the apostle's present mode of regarding them ; ' in *my* view and definition of the term, *Life* is but another name for Christ,' Peile. The emphatic ἐμοί ('to *me*, in my merely personal capacity,' see Wiesinger) is thus the pronominal dative *judicii* (De W.), or perhaps more correctly and more inclusively, the dative of *ethical relation* (comp. Gal. vi. 14); not merely ' in my estimation,' but ' in my case,' ' life in my realization of it,' — a dative which is allied to, and more fully developed in, the dative *commodi* or *incommodi* ; see Bernhardy, *Synt.* III. 9, p. 85, and especially Krüger, *Sprachl.* § 48. 6. 1 sq., by whom this use of the dative is well illustrated.

τὸ ζῆν Χριστός] ' *to live is Christ*,' i. e. living consists only in union with, and devotion to, Christ ; my whole being and activities are His ; ' quicquid vivo Christum vivo,' Beng. : see Gal. ii. 20, but observe the difference of the application ; there the reference is to faith, here rather to works (De W.), the context showing that Χριστός, beside the idea of union with Him, must also involve that of devotion to His service. So, perhaps too distinctly, Æth. (compare Calv.) ' si vixero, Christo.' Τὸ ζῆν is clearly the subject (' vita mea,' Syriac, Copt.), the *natural* life alluded to in the preceding, and more specifically in the following verse. It cannot refer to *spiritual* life (Rill., comp. Chrys., Theoph.) as the antithesis, ζῆν – ἀποθ., is thus obscured, and the argument impaired : what ζωή is in ver. 20, that must τὸ ζῆν be here.

καὶ τὸ ἀποθ. κέρδος] '*and* [simple copulative] *to die is gain* ;' death is gain, as I shall thus enjoy a still nearer and more blessed union with my Lord ; σα-φέστερον αὐτῷ συνέσομαι, Chrys., Theoph. Κέρδος belongs *only* to this latter clause, the full meaning of which is very easily collected from the context ; compare verse 23. To make Χρ. the subject to both members of the sentence and τὸ ζῆν and τὸ ἀποθ. accusatives of ' reference to ' (Krüger, *Sprachl.* § 46. 4), sc. ' ut tam in vitâ quam in morte lucrum esse prædicetur ' (Calv. ; compare Beza), is to mar the perspicuity, and to introduce a difficulty in point of grammar, as τὸ ἀποθ. could scarcely be ' in moriendo :' such accusatives commonly point to things or actions which may, so to say, be conceived as extensible, and over the whole of which the predication can range ; see Scheuerl. *Synt.* § 9. 3, p. 68, Krüger, *Sprachl.* § 46. 4. 1. Numerous examples of similar expressions are cited by Wetstein *in loc.*, the most pertinent of which is Joseph. *Bell.* VII. 8, 6, συμφορὰ τὸ ζῆν ἐστιν ἀνθρώποις οὐχὶ θάνατος, as it hints at the purely substantival character of τὸ ζῆν (opp. to Alf.) and τὸ ἀποθανεῖν. The practical aspects of the subject will be found in Heber, *Serm.* XVI. XVII.

22. εἰ δὲ τὸ ζῆν κ. τ. λ.] *but if my living in the flesh,* — *if this is to me the* (*the medium of*) *fruit from my labor ;*' so Vulg., Claroman., Goth., and (with obscured τοῦτο) Syr., Copt.: antithetical sentence suggested by the remembrance of his calling as an apostle. There are difficulties in this verse in the individual expressions, as well as in the connection and sequence of thought. We will (1) briefly notice the former : (a) εἰ is not problematical, ' if it chance,' Tyndale, Cranm., but as Meyer correctly observes, *syllogistic*, — and virtually assertory. (β) The addition ἐν σαρκί does not imply any qualitative difference between τὸ ζῆν here and τὸ ζῆν in ver. 21 (Rill.), but guards against it being understood in the

ζῆν ἐν σαρκί, τοῦτό μοι καρπὸς ἔργου· καὶ τί αἱρήσομαι, οὐ γνω-

higher sense, which the preceding τὸ ἀποθ. κέρδος ('to die, *i. e.* to live out of the flesh with Christ, is gain') might otherwise seem naturally to suggest. (γ) Τοῦτο is not a redundancy 'per Hebraismum' (see Glasse, *Phil. Sacr.* p. 738 [219]), but is designed to give special prominence and emphasis to the idea contained in the preceding words; compare Winer, *Gr.* § 44. 4, p. 144. (δ) In καρπὸς ἔργου the genitive is not a gen. of *appositionis*, 'opus pro fructu habet,' Bengel, nor a gen. *objecti*, 'profit for the work' (Rilliet), but a simple gen. *subjecti* [*originis*], 'proventus operis,' De Wette,

ܟܰܦܪܳܐ ܗ̇ܘ ܒܰܥܒ̈ܳܕܰܝ [fructus in operibus meis] Syr., *i. e.* 'conveys with it, is the condition of fruit from apostolical labor,' the ἔργον referring to the *laborious* nature of the apostolic work (Acts xiii. 2, 1 Thess. v. 13, 2 Tim. iv. 5): καρποφορῶ, διδάσκων καὶ φωτίζων πάντας, Theoph.; comp. Raphel, *Obs.* Vol. II. p. 622.

(2) The *connection* then seems to be as follows: in verse 21 the apostle had spoken of life and death from a strictly *personal* point of view (ἐμοί); in this aspect death was gain. The thought, however, of his *official* labors reminds him that his life bears blessings and fruitfulness to others; so he pauses: 'objecti spe conversionis multorum, haeret atque haesitat,' Just: so, in substance, Theophyl. (who has explained this clause briefly and perspicuously), Chrys., Theodoret, Œcumen., and after them, with some variations in detail, De W., Meyer, and the best modern editors. Of the other interpretations the *most* plausible is (*a*) that of Auth., Beng., al., according to which τοῦτο κ. τ. λ. forms the apodosis, ἐστί μοι being supplied after ἐν σαρκί, 'but if I live in the flesh, this is,' etc.; the *least* so (*b*) that of Beza, Genev. (amended by Conyb., but satisfactorily

answered by Alf.), according to which is 'whether,' and καρπὸς ἔργου 'operae pretium' (comp. Grot., Hamm., Scholefield), *Hints*, p. 105,—a modest and doubtful translation), scil. 'and whether to live in the flesh were profitable to me, and what,' etc. The objections to (*a*) is the very harsh and unusual nature of the ellipsis; to (*b*), and perplexity of grammatical objections, the halting and inconsequent nature of the argument; see Alf. *in loc.* καὶ τί αἱρήσομαι κ. τ. λ.] 'then, or why, what I am to choose [observe the middle] I know not:' apodosis to the foregoing. The principal difficulty lies in the use of καί. Though no certain example of an *exactly* similar use of εἰ—καί has been adduced from the N. T. (2 Cor. ii. 2 [De Wette] is not in point, being there the καί of reply, interrogation. Hartung, *Partic.* Vol. 1. p. 147), yet the use of καί at the beginning of the apodosis is so common (see Bruder, *Conc.* s. v. καί, n. I, 455, as to render such a use after εἰ by no means improbable; see examples in Hartung, *Partic.* s. v. καί, 2. 6, Vol. 1. p. 130, and compare the somewhat similar use of 'atque,' Hand, *Tursell.* Vol. 1. p. 484 sq. In such cases the proper force of καί is not wholly lost. Just as, in strict logical sentences, it constantly implies that if one thing be true, then another will be true *also*, *e.g.* εἰ φύσει κινεῖται κἂν βίᾳ κινηθείη, κἂν εἰ βίᾳ καὶ φύσει, Arist. *de Anima*, ch. 3, p. 9 (ed. Bekk.),—so here, if life certainly subserve to apostolic usefulness, there will *also* be a difficulty as to choice. It is thus unnecessary to assume any *aposiopesis* after the first member, scil. 'non repugno,' 'non aegre fero' Müller, Rill. There is only a slight pause, and slight change from the expected, to a more emphatic sequence, which this semi-ratiocinative καί very appropriately introduces. On

ρίζω· ²³ συνέχομαι δὲ ἐκ τῶν δύο, τὴν ἐπιθυμίαν ἔχων εἰς τὸ ἀνα-

the use of the less exact τί for πότερον, see Winer, *Gr.* § 25. 1, p. 153 (ed. 6); and on that of the future in a deliberative clause, Winer, *ib.* § 41. 4. b. p. 267. The strict alliance between the future and the subjunctive renders such an interchange very intelligible.

οὐ γνωρίζω] '*I do not recognize,*' '*I do not clearly perceive,*'— a somewhat exceptional use in the N. T. of γνωρ., which is nearly always 'notum facio.' For examples of the present use, see Ast, *Lex. Plat.* s. v.; comp. Job xxxiv. 25 (LXX), iv. 16 (Symm.).

23. συνέχομαι δὲ κ. τ. λ.] '*yea, I am held in a strait by the two;*' antithetical explanation of the last member of verse 22; the *faintly oppositive* δὲ (not '*metabatic*' [Meyer] on the one hand, nor equivalent to ἀλλὰ on the other) placing the emphatic συνέχομαι in gentle contrast with the preceding οὐ γνωρίζω. The reading γὰρ (*Rec.*) has scarcely any critical support, and is only a correction of the less understood δέ. On the real difference between these two particles in sentences like the present, see especially Klotz, *Devar.* Vol. II. p. 363. The prep. ἐκ is here not used for ἀπό (Bloomf.), nor yet for διά (Heinr.,— instrumentality would have been expressed by a simple dative, *e. g.* Matth. iv. 24, Luke viii. 37, Acts xviii. 5, xxviii. 8), but with its proper force points to the *origin* of the συνοχή, the sources out of which it arises; see notes on *Gal.* ii. 16, where the uses of this preposition in N. T. are briefly noticed. Lastly, the article is not *prospective* (compare Syr.) but *retrospective* (Mey., al.), referring to the two alternatives previously mentioned. This is confirmed by the apparent emphasis on συνέχ., and the illustrative connection with it of the two classes which follow.

τὴν ἐπιθυμίαν ἔχων] '*having my desire;*' not merely '*a desire,*' Author.,

nor '*the desire previously alluded to,*' Hoel.,— as no ἐπιθυμία, strictly speaking, has been alluded to,— but '*the desire which I now feel,*' '*my desire.*' The ἐπιθυμία thus stands absolutely. its direction being defined in the words which follow. A very eloquent and feeling application of this text will be found in Manning, *Serm.* xx. Vol. III p. 370 sq.

εἰς τὸ ἀναλῦσαι] '*towards departing,*' '*turned to departure;*' not '*desiderium solvendi*' (τοῦ ἀναλ., Origen, in a free citation), nor even quite, '*the desire to depart,*' Conyb. (comp. Winer, *Gr.* § 44. 6, p. 294),— both of which would seem to imply the not unusual *definitive* genitive after ἐπιθ. (comp. Thucyd. VII. 84, τοῦ πιεῖν ἐπιθ.), but with the proper force of the preposition εἰς, '*desiderio tendens ad dimissionem;*' compare Winer, *Gr.* § 49. a, p. 354. The preposition is omitted in DEFG; Chrysostom (comm.), apparently by accident, as the construction would not thus be made more easy. Ἀναλῦσαι is not '*dissolvi,*' Vulg, nor even '*liberari,*' Syr. ܡܫܬܪܐ (comp. Schoettg. *in loc.*), but, perhaps with primary reference to breaking up a camp or loosing an anchor, '*migrare,*' Æth. (comp. Judith xiii. 1, Ælian, *Var. Hist.* IV. 23), and thence with a shade of meaning imparted by the context, '*discedere a vita,*' ἡ ἐντεῦθεν ἀπαλλαγή, Theod.; compare notes *on* 2 *Tim.* iv. 6, and see Suicer, *Thesaur.* Vol. I. p. 286 sq., by whom this word is copiously illustrated; add too Perizonius, on Ælian, *Var. Hist. l. c.* The translation adopted by Tertull. '*recipi*' has perhaps reference to the '*receptui canere,*' and is thus virtually the same; comp. Mill., *Prolegom.* p. LXVII.   καὶ σὺν Χρ. εἶναι] From the immediate connection of this clause with ἀναλῦσαι dogmatical deductions have been made in

λῦσαι καὶ σὺν Χριστῷ εἶναι, πολλῷ γὰρ μᾶλλον κρεῖσσον
21 τὸ δὲ ἐπιμένειν ἐν τῇ σαρκὶ ἀναγκαιότερον δι' ὑμᾶς.

reference to the intermediate state; 'clare ostenditur animas sanctorum ex hac vitâ sine peccato migrantium statim post mortem esse cum Christo,' Est.; comp. Cyrill.-Alex cited by Forbes, *Instruct.* XIII. 8. 33, Bull, *Engl Works*, p. 42 (Oxf., 1844), Reuss, *Théol. Chrét.* IV. 21, Vol. II. p. 240. Without presuming to make hasty deductions from isolated passages, we may safely rest on the broad and sound opinion of Bishop Pearson, that life eternal may be regarded as initial, partial, and perfectional, and that the blessed apostle is now in the fruition of that second state, and 'is with Christ who sitteth at the right hand of God,' *Creed*, Art. XII. Vol. I. p 467, and compare Polyc. *ad Phil.* § 9. εἰς τὸν ὀφειλόμενον αὐτοῖς τόπον εἰσὶ παρὰ Κυρίῳ, Clem. Rom. 1 *Cor.* § 5. ἐπορεύθη [Πέτρος] εἰς τὸν ὀφειλ. τόπον τῆς δόξης. For a contrary view, see Burnet, *State of Departed*, ch. III. p. 58; and lastly, for a practical application of the verse, Farindon, *Serm.* XXXVI. Vol. II. p. 1006 (edit. 1672). The meaning involved in the words σὺν Χρ. εἶναι, in reference to the soul's incorporeal state, is explained profoundly, though perhaps somewhat singulary, by Hofmann, *Schriftb.* II. 2, Vol. II. p. 449, 'selbst körperlos, wird er den Leib, in welchem die Fülle der Gottheit wohnt, zu seiner Wohnung haben;' comp. Delitzsch, *Bibl. Psychol.* VI. 6, p. 383 sq.

πολλῷ γάρ κ. τ. λ.] *'for it is very far better,'* scil. being with Christ is so (for me); explanation of the foregoing desire. The comparative strengthened by μᾶλλον gives a force and energy to the assertion that is here very noticeable and appropriate; compare Mark vii. 36, 2 Cor. vii. 13, and Winer, *Gr.* § 35. 1, p. 214. The reading is somewhat doubtful: γάρ is omitted by DEFGKL; great majority of mss., several Vv. and some Ff. (*Rec*, *Griesb.* but om. om.); as, however, it is found in ABC; 31. 67**; Copt; Or. (I), Bas., Aug. (often and explic.— as DEFG show in this passage marks of incertitude in reading πόσῳ for πολλῷ, and lastly, as γάρ might have been thought to interrupt the sequence, we may perhaps safely acquiesce in the insertion with *Lachm.*, *Tisch.*, and even *Elz* and *Scholz*.

21. τὸ δὲ ἐπιμένειν κ. τ. λ.] *'yet to tarry in my flesh.'* In the former verse the apostle stated what is κρεῖσσον, for himself, now he turns to what is ἀναγκαιότερον in regard of his converts. Δέ is thus simply 'but,' 'yet,'—scarcely 'nevertheless,' Auth., which is commonly a more suitable translation of ἀλλά: on the difference between these particles ('verum — sed'), see Klotz, *Devar.* Vol. II. pp. 33, 361. The ἐπί in ἐπιμ. implies *rest* in a place (comp. notes on *Gal.* i. 18), and hints at a more protracted stay; compare Rom. vi 1. The next words ἐν τῇ σαρκί are, as Meyer correctly observes, scarcely quite the same as ἐν σαρκί in ver. 22; there the expression was general, here more specific and individualizing; see Krüger, *Sprachl.* § 50, 2. 3.   ἀναγκαιότερον δι' ὑμᾶς] *'more needful on your account;'* not an inexact comparative (De W.), nor to be diluted into a positive (Clarom., compare Syr.), nor with reference to the apostle's own feelings, scil. 'quam ut meo desiderio satisfiat,' Van Heng., Bengel,—but simply 'more needful,' scil. than the contrary course, than ἀναλῦσαι κ. τ. λ. This latter course St. Paul might have thought ἀναγκαῖον on his own account, a thing to be prayed for and hastened; continuance, however, was ἀναγκαιότερον on account of his converts. The meaning proposed by Loesn., 'praestat,' 'melius est' (comp. Æth.), has

²⁵ καὶ τοῦτο πεποιθὼς οἶδα ὅτι μενῶ καὶ παραμενῶ πᾶσιν ὑμῖν εἰς

25. παραμενῶ] So *Lachm.* with ABCD¹FG; 5 mss.; Vulg., Clarom.; Lat. Ff. (approved by *Griesb., Alf.*). *Tisch.* reads συμπαραμενῶ, appy. only with D³EKL; majority of mss.; Chrys. (expressly), Theod., Dam., Theophyl., al. (*Rec., Scholz, Mey.*). While on the one hand, it is possible that the unusual compound might have been changed into the more simple form, still, on the other hand, the dative πᾶσιν might have suggested the insertion. The uncial authority is moreover far too preponderant to be safely reversed.

no lexical authority, and is not supported by the examples adduced *Obs.* p. 353.

25. καὶ τοῦτο πεποιθώς] '*And being persuaded, being sure, of this;*' scil., that my ἐπιμένειν ἐν τῇ σαρκί is more necessary on your account. Πεποιθώς has thus its natural force and regimen (ver. 6), and is not to be explained away adverbially, πεποιθότως καὶ ἀδιστάκτως

οἶδα, Theoph., [Syriac] [confidenter] Syr., Goth., Copt., or blended with οἶδα (Æth.), but is to be closely connected with τοῦτο, while οἶδα is joined only with ὅτι; 'persuadens mihi vitam meam vobis esse [magis] necessariam, scio quod Deus me vobis adhuc concedet,' Corn. a Lap. οἶδα] '*I know;*' not with any undue emphasis, '*praevideo,*' Van Heng., for see ch. ii. 17, but simply 'I know,' sc. it is my present feeling and conviction; compare Acts xx. 25. For somewhat analogous uses of οἶδα, see the examples adduced by Van Heng., but observe that even in the strongest (Hom. *Il.* VI. 447) οἶδα still refers more to the persuasions of the speaker than to any absolutely prophetic certitude.

παραμενῶ] '*continue here* (on earth),' '*bleiben und dableiben,*' Meyer, who aptly cites Herod. I. 30, τέκνα ἐκγενόμενα καὶ πάντα παραμείναντα; add Plato, *Phædo,* p. 115 D, ἐπειδὰν πίω τὸ φάρμακον, οὐκέτι ὑμῖν παραμενῶ, ib. *Crito,* p. 51, παραμείνῃ, opp. to μετοικεῖν ἄλλοσε. On the reading see critical note. The dative πᾶσιν ὑμῖν may be the dative *of interest,* 'to support and comfort you' (Krüger,

Sprachl. § 48. 4), but is here far more naturally governed by the παρά in the compound; see Plato, *Phæd. l. c, Apol.* p. 39 E, apparently *Protag.* p. 335 D, and contrast 1 Cor. xvi. 6, πρὸς ὑμᾶς παραμενῶ, where the πρὸς gains its force from the intended journey to them just before mentioned; here the apostle is mentally with those he is addressing. This is a somewhat more common regimen than Krüger (*Sprachl.* § 48. 11. 9) seems inclined to admit.

εἰς τὴν ὑμῶν κ. τ. λ.] '*for your furtherance in, and joy of the faith;*' not '*for your furth.,* and for your joy,' etc., Van Heng.,—there being here no reason whatever to depart from the ordinary rule; see Winer. *Gr.* § 19. 4. d, p. 116, and comp. Middleton, *Gr. Art.* p. 368. It is scarcely necessary to say that there is not here any kind of *inversion* ('for your joy and for the increase of your faith') as Syriac, nor any *disjunction* ('for your furth., and for your faith, and for your joy'), as in Æth., nor any *conjunction* ('for the advancement of the joy of your faith'), as Macknight: still the relation of the genitive to the two substantives seems slightly different; in the first case it is a gen. *subjecti,* referrible perhaps to the class of the *possess.* gen; in the latter it is a gen. *originis,* 'quod ex fide promanat,' Zanch., and belongs to the general division of the gen. of *ablation;* compare Schenerl. *Synt.* § 11. 1, p. 79, Donalds. *Gr.* § 448 sq. On χαρά, compare Reuss, *Théol. Chrét.* IV. 18, Vol. II. p. 202, whose definition how-

τὴν ὑμῶν προκοπὴν καὶ χαρὰν τῆς πίστεως, ²⁶ ἵνα τὸ καύχημα ὑμῶν περισσεύῃ ἐν Χριστῷ Ἰησοῦ ἐν ἐμοὶ διὰ τῆς ἐμῆς παρουσίας πάλιν πρὸς ὑμᾶς. ²⁷ Μόνον ἀξίως τοῦ εὐαγγελίου τοῦ Χριστοῦ πολιτεύεσθε, ἵνα εἴτε ἐλθὼν καὶ ἰδὼν ὑμᾶς εἴτε ἀπὼν ἀκούσω τὰ περὶ ὑμῶν, ὅτι στήκετε ἐν ἑνὶ

Live and . . . . gospel, ... the
present . . . . of
you. B . . . . ye
are suff . . . . of Christ.

ever, 'cect se enice d' l'ame qui la p é-
serve de tout de courageme nt dans l'ad-
ver . . .,' imports to χαρά του passive a
ch racter. Χαρά is rat er that active and
operative emanation of love and thankfulness that forms the sort of spiritual
equipoi e to εἰρήνη and ὑπομονή.

26. Ἵνα τὸ καύχημα κ τ λ] 'in
order that your mor er of boast ng many
abound in Jesus Christ in m :' more specific statement of the purpose of the
apostle's continuance with his converts;
the previous abstract εἰς τὴν ὑμῶν προκ.
κ. τ. λ. being expanded into the more
definite and concrete ἵνα κ. τ λ. These
words, simple as they seem, have not been
always clearly understood. In the first
place καύχημα is not the same as καύχησις, not 'gloriatio qua gloriamini.'
Corn. a Lap., but 'gloriandi m teries'
(נתתם, Jere. xvii 14), as it Rom. iv. 2,
1 Co. ix. 15, and anny every w ere i the
N. T. (e notes on G. vi. 4, t is 'ma-
teries' being τὸ ἐστηκέναι ἐν τῇ πίστει,
Chrys., or general y, their possession of
the gospel (Meyer), their cond tion as
Christians. Ag in, ἐν Χριστῷ is not
to be connected, directly or indirectly,
with καύχημα ('l'o ccasion de vons gl ri-
fier d'é re unis à Christ,' Rill. but with
περισσεύῃ, the qualitative ἐν Χρ. defining,
as it were, the blessed sphere in which
the increase takes place, and out of which,
Christianly speaking, it has no existence.
Lastly ἐν ἐμοί is neither—δι' ἐμοῦ. Hein.,
nor 'propter me,' Grot., nor even 'de
me,' Beza, but 'in me,' Vulg.—the
preposition here marking the substratum
of the action, the mirror, as it were
(Zanch.), in which the whole gracious

provid re was displaye d; se otes on
Ga. i 24. It is thus best to be connected with καύχημα direct y or as in Chr s.,
by inversion, ἵνα ἔχω καυχᾶσθαι ἐν ἑαυ
μείζονος, nor even with περισσ. alone
but with the complete idea τὸ καύχ. περισσ. ἐν Χρ. Thus the w ole sense clear:
the καύχημα is their condition as Christians; ἐν Χρ. defines the fulness and
purity of its increase; ἐν ἐμοί. the seat
and substratum of the so a fesat led action. διὰ τῆς κ. τ. λ. is
to be closely connected with ἐμοί as defining the exact means by wa' h the increase of matter of boasting, thus spec fi-
cally Christ'an, is to take place ἐν ἐμοί.
Passages like the present, in which d f-
ferent predications are group d closely
t g ther, will repay careful a alysis.
He e it will be seen ἐν Χρ is the myst-
cal and generic predicat o of proper,
ἐν ἐμοί place, διὰ τῆς παρ. of special instrumentality, involving al o in i s substantive the predication of time; compare
notes on Ephes. i 3, and Donalds. Gr.
§ 444.

27. μόνον] 'Only :' my persuasion
then being as I have to y you, t is is the
sole thing that I specially press upon
you, and exact from you as well persua-
sible; τοῦτο ἐστι ὃ ζητούμενον μόνον καὶ
οὐδὲν ἄλλο. Chrys.: comp re Gal. ii. 10,
v. 13, in which latter passage as here,
'verborum tanquam agmen ab illo ducitur,' Van Heng. In this one requisition
many weighty duties are involved.
τοῦ εὐαγγ. τοῦ Χρ] 'Un sel of
Christ,' i.e. which relates to, we h tells
of Christ; τοῦ Χρ. being the no o .,
not, as Æth. would seem to imp'y, subj.

πνεύματι, μιᾷ ψυχῇ συναθλοῦντες τῇ πίστει τοῦ εὐαγγελίου,

jecti, 'the gospel taught by Him.' In such cases the nature of the gen. is not perfectly certain, but, from the analogy supplied by partially similar use of εὐαγγ., is more probably that *objecti*; see Winer, *Gr.* § 30. 1, p. 168, but observe that the ref. to Rom. i. 3 is of doubtful pertinence.

πολιτεύεσθε] '*have your conversation*,' '*behave yourselves*,' or more exactly, 'lead your life of (Christian) citizenship;' compare Acts xxiii. 1. It can scarcely be doubted that this word, occurring once only in St. Paul's Epistles, though examples of very similar exhortations are not wanting (Eph. iv. 1, Col. i. 10, 1 Thess. ii. 12) has been studiedly used instead of the more common περιπατεῖν, to give force to the idea of fellow-citizenship,—not specially and peculiarly with Christ (Heinr.), but with one another in Him.—joint membership in a heavenly πολίτευμα, comp. ch. iii. 20. Numerous examples of a similar metaphorical use of the word ('vivere, non quoad spiritum et animam, sed quoad mores,' Loesn., 'ad normam institutorum in Republicâ mores vitæque rationem componere,' Krebs.) will be found in Wetstein *in loc.*, Krebs, *Obs.* p. 243, Loesn. *Obs.* p. 226, and especially in Suicer, *Thesaur.* Vol. II. p. 799 sq.

ἵνα εἴτε ἐλθὼν κ. τ. λ.] '*in order that, whether having come and seen you or else remaining absent, I may hear the things concerning you.*' This clause, though perfectly intelligible, is apparently somewhat inexact in structure. It would seem that ἀκούσω (for which Lachmann, with BD[1]; 10 mss.; Basm., reads ἀκούω) really performs a kind of double office; in the one case it stands in antithesis to ἰδὼν (per orat. variat.); in the second place it repeats itself (Van Heng.), or suggests some appropriate verb (εὐφράνδω, Chrys., γνῶ, De Wette) immediately before ὅτι: in a word, *quoad sensum* it seems to belong to ἀπών, *quoad structuram* to ἵνα. Attempts have been made to defend the construction as it stands, either (α) by referring ἀκούσω zeugmatically to both clauses, 'j'apprenne à votre sujet que,' Rill.; or (β) by under-tanding it to imply 'hearing *from themselves*,' in reference to the first clause, 'hearing *from others*,' in the second, Meyer. This last explanation is ingenious, but is apparently precluded by the opposition between ἰδὼν ὑμᾶς and ἀκούσω τὰ περὶ ὑμῶν, which seems too distinct to have been otherwise than specially intended. There must be few, however, who do not prefer the warmhearted *incuria* of such a brevity of expression to restorations like εἴτε ἐλθὼν καὶ ἰδών, εἴτε ἀπὼν ἀκούσω τὰ περὶ ὑμῶν, ἀκούω ὅτι κ. τ. λ., or still worse, ἀπὼν καὶ ἀκούσας τὰ π. ὑμ. γνῶ ὅτι κ. τ. λ., as suggested by modern commentators. ὅτι στήκετε] '*that ye are standing;*' fuller expansion and definition of τὰ περὶ ὑμῶν; the explanatory clause being in structural dependence upon the principal member, according to the ordinary and simplest form of attraction; see especially Winer, *Gr.* § 66. 5, p. 551, where this and other forms of attraction and assimilation are perspicuously discussed. The present form of attraction is especially common after verbs of knowledge, perception, etc., e. g. Mark xii. 34, Acts iii. 10, 1 Cor. xvi. 13, 1 Thess. ii. 1, al. Στήκειν, it may be observed, is not *per se*, 'to stand *fast*,' Author. Ver., 'perstare,' Beza, but simply 'stare,' Vulg., Syriac, Goth., the ideas of readiness (compare Chrys.), persistence, etc., being imparted by the *context*; compare ch. iv. 1, 1 Cor. xvi. 13, Gal. v. 1, 1 Thess. iii. 8, 2 Thess. ii. 15. ἐν ἑνὶ πνεύματι] '*in one spirit;*' in one common higher principle of our nature. The addition

²⁸ καὶ μὴ πτυρόμενοι ἐν μηδενὶ ὑπὸ τῶν ἀντικειμένων, ἥτις

μιᾷ ψυχῇ seems certainly to show that πνεῦμα is here the *human* spirit, the higher part of our immaterial nature (see Schubert, *Gesch. der Seele*, § 48, Vol. II. p. 49 sq.), that in which the agency of the Holy Spirit is especially seen and felt. This common unity of the spirit is, however, so obviously the effect of the inworking of the Holy Spirit, that an indirect reference to τὸ Πνεῦμα (compare Ephes. iv. 4) becomes necessarily involved. Indeed in most cases in the N. T. it may be said that in every mention of the human πνεῦμα some reference to the eternal Spirit may always be recognized; see notes *on 2 Tim.* i. 7, and compare Delitzsch, *Bibl. Psychol.* IV. 5, p. 144 sq.   μιᾷ ψυχῇ] '*with one soul striving together for the faith of the gospel;*' making your united efforts from the common faith from one common centre and seat of interests, affections, and energies. As the higher πνεῦμα which gave direction was to be one and common to them all, so was the lower ψυχή which obeyed those behests to be one, — one common seat of concordant affections and energies. The remark of Bengel is true and deep; 'est interdum inter sanctos naturalis aliqua antipathia: hæc vincitur ubi unitas est non solum spiritus, sed etiam animae.' On the difference between the πνεῦμα ('vis superior, agens, imperans in homine') and the ψυχή, the sphere of the will and affections, the centre of the personality, see Olshausen, *Opuscula*, Art. VI. p 145 sq, Beck, *Bibl. Seelenlehre*, II. 12, 13, p. 30 sq.

συναθλοῦντες must be united with μιᾷ ψυχῇ, thus forming a participial, and indeed psychological, parallel to στήκειν ἐν Πν. It is somewhat singular that the best ancient Vv. (Syr., Vulg., Clar., Æth., Copt.), with Chrys., al., agree in referring μιᾷ ψυχῇ to στήκετε. Such a construction, however, has but little to recommend it in point of grammar, and still less in point of psychology; μιᾷ ψυχῇ stands correctly in prominence after the semi-emphatic ἐν ἑνὶ πν., comp. Jelf, *Gr.* § 902), and forms a modal adjunct to the undefined συναθλοῦντες, especially significant and appropriate; στήκειν ἐν πνεύματι, συναθλεῖν τῇ ψυχῇ. The force of the preposition σὺν has been differently estimated; it is referred by the Greek expositors to the fellowship of the Philipp. (συμπαραλαμβάνετε ἀλλήλους, Chrys.); by Meyer and others to fellowship with St. Paul; the former seems more suitable to the context.

τῇ πίστει] '*for the faith;*' dat. *commodi;* not under the regimen of σύν, 'adjuvantes fidem,' Erasm., — an unexampled prosopopœia; nor a dat. *instrum.* (more precisely termed by Krüger, a 'dynamic' dative, *Sprachl.* § 48. 15), 'fide Ev.,' Calv., 'per fidem Ev.,' Beza, — this construction having previously occurred in the case of μιᾷ ψυχῇ. Πίστις, here, as nearly always in the N. T., has a subjective reference; see notes on *Gal.* i. 23.

28. πτυρόμενοι] '*being terrified;*' ἅπ. λεγόμ. in N. T.; properly used in reference to *scared* horses (Diodor. Sic. XVII. 34, πτυρόμενοι τὰ χαλινὰ διασπῶντο), thence generally, though often with some tinge of its more special meaning, as in Plut. *Mor.* p. 800 e, μήτε ἰδέᾳ μήτε φωνῇ πτυρόμενον, and lastly, as here, in a purely general sense, e.g. [Plato], *Axioch.* § 15, οὐκ ἄν ποτε πτυρείης τὸν θάνατον; comp. Hesych. πτύρεται· σείεται, φοβεῖται. φρ ττει, and Kypke, *Obs.* Vol. II. p. 312. It is not improb. derived from a root ΠΤΥ. — and allied with πτοέω; see Benfey, *Wurzellex.* Vol. II. p. 100. τῶν ἀντικειμένων] '*the opposers,*' '*your adversaries;*' compare 1 Cor. xvi. 9, 2 Thess. ii. 4, Luke xiii. 17, xxi. 15.

ἐστὶν αὐτοῖς ἔνδειξις ἀπωλείας, ὑμῖν δὲ σωτηρίας, καὶ τοῦτο ἀπὸ Θεοῦ· 29 ὅτι ὑμῖν ἐχαρίσθη τὸ ὑπὲρ Χριστοῦ, οὐ μόνον

Who these were is not perfectly certain. The context and general use of the word seem both to point to open and avowed enemies of Christianity; not Judaists, but unbelieving Jews (Usteri, *Lehrb.* p. 332, comp. Acts xvii. 5), or, perhaps even more probably, Gentiles; compare Acts xvi. 19 sq.   ἥτις ἐστίν κ. τ. λ.] '*the which is to them*,' '*seeing it is*,' etc.; viz., when they see, as they cannot fail to do, if they will pause to consider, that they cannot intimidate you; ὅταν γὰρ οἱ διώκοντες τῶν διωκομένων μὴ περιγένωνται, οἱ ἐπιβουλεύοντες τῶν ἐπιβουλευομένων, οἱ κρατοῦντες τῶν κρατουμένων, οὐκ αὐτόθεν ἔσται δῆλον αὐτοῖς, ὅτι ἀπολοῦνται, ὅτι οὐδὲν ἰσχύσουσιν; Chrys. The ὅστις, as in Eph. iii. 13 al., has here a faint *explanatory* force (see especially notes *on Gal.* iv. 23), and is the logical relative to μὴ πτυρόμ. κ. τ. λ., though grammatically connected (by attraction) with the predicate ἔνδειξις; see examples of this species of attraction in Winer, *Gram.* § 24. 3, p. 150; compare also § 66. 5. 2, p. 552, and Madvig, *Synt.* § 98. The dative αὐτοῖς is the dative *incomm.* or, of 'interest' (Krüg., *Sprachl.* § 48. 4), and is dependent on ἔνδειξις, not on ἀπωλείας (Hölem.),—a needlessly involved construction. The reading of *Rec.* αὐτοῖς μὲν ἐστίν has but little critical support [KL; Theodoret, al.], and is properly rejected by all the best editors.   ὑμῖν δὲ σωτηρίας] '*but to you (an evidence) of salvation*;' scil. of final salvation, as opposed to the preceding ἀπώλεια; 'ipsos perdet et ducet in gehennam, vos autem ducet ad salutem et gloriam,' Corn. a Lap.; compare similar antitheses, Rom. ix. 22 sq., 1 Cor. i. 18, al., and on the force of ἀπώλεια, notes *on* 1 *Tim.* vi. 9.   The present reading is somewhat doubtful: ὑμῶν is adopted by *Lachm.* and *Tisch.*

(so Meyer, Alf.) with ABC²; 4 mss.; Clarom., Sangerm.; Chrys. (mss.), Aug., al., and is plausible on account of the possible conformation of ὑμῖν to αὐτοῖς. The text is, however, strongly supported (D³EFKL [ἡμῖν C¹D¹G; 73]; Vulg., Goth., Copt., Basm., Æth. (Platt, Pol.), Syr.-Phil.; Chrys., Theod), and has apparently the diplomatic preponderance plainly in its favor.
καὶ τοῦτο κ. τ. λ.] '*and this from God*,' comp. Eph. ii. 8; *i. e.* not merely 'vos salutem consecuturos esse,' Calvin, which would arbitrarily limit τοῦτο to the latter member; nor even 'illud, adversarios quidem perituros, vos vero salutem,' etc., Grot., but, as the consolatory nature of the context seems to require, with reference to the *whole* preceding (certainly not *succeeding*, Syr. Æth., Clem.-Alexan. *Strom.* iv. p. 604, Pott.) declaration, in fact to ἐπιδείξις (Peile, De W., Alf.); 'et hoc sane non augurium humanum est, sed divinum,' Van Heng., and sim., Michaelis   Whether it be recognized or not as such, there still is this token of the issue for either side, and it is from God; compare Wiesing. *in loc.*

29. ὅτι ὑμῖν κ. τ. λ.] Reason for the declaration immediately preceding, by an appeal to their own cases: not exactly, motives to steadfastness (De W.); as, in the first place, the exhortation to be steadfast is implicit rather than explicit; and, secondly, such motives would have been more naturally introduced by γάρ.   The apostle says, the ἔνδειξις κ. τ. λ. is verily not an 'humanum' but a 'divinum augurium,' because the grace given *to you* (observe the slightly emphatic position,—whatever it may be to others) is such that you are thereby enabled not only to believe in Christ, but also to suffer for him: the double favor

τὸ εἰς αὐτὸν πιστεύειν ἀλλὰ καὶ τὸ ὑπὲρ αὐτοῦ πάσχειν. ¹ τὸν αὐτὸν ἀγῶνα ἔχοντες οἷον εἴδετε ἐν ἐμοὶ καὶ νῦν ἀκούετε ἐν ἐμοί.

Be united in spirit, be lowly in heart as Christ, who humbled Himself unto death, and was exalted with every measure of exaltation.

II. Εἴ τις οὖν παράκλησις ἐν Χριστῷ, εἴ τι

you have received affords the surest proof of the essentiality of the nature of the τὸ αὐτό; see Meyer *in l.*—

ἐχαρίσθη] 'was *freely given*:' τὸ πᾶν ἀνατιθεὶς τῷ Θεῷ, καὶ χάριν εἶναι λέγων καὶ χάρισμα καὶ δωρεὰν τὸ πάσχειν ὑπὲρ Χριστοῦ, Chrys. The aorist is used as referring to the period when the initial grace which has since wrought in the hearts of the Philippians was first given: χαρίζεται would be too present, and indeed prospective (comp. Krüger, *Sprachl.* § 53. 1), to suit the actual circumstances; κεχάρισται would express that the effects of the χάρισμα are remaining, which, though probably really the case, less perfectly harmonizes with the language of implied exhortation than the simple reference to what they once received, and must show that they now possess. The essential character of the tense ('quod praeteriit, se ita ut non definiatur quam late pateat id quod actum est,' Fritz. *de loc. V.* p. 17 sq.) may here be easily traced. τὸ ὑπὲρ Χριστοῦ is not 'in Christi negotio' Beza (comp. Auth.), but is logically dependent on the following πάσχειν, and would have been structurally associated with it if the apostle had not paused to interpolate a clause (οὐ μόνον — ὑπὲρ αὐτοῦ) that serves materially to heighten the assertion and add to its significance: ἐκεῖ μὲν ὀφειλέτης εἰμί, ἐνταῦθα δὲ ὀφειλέτην ἔχω τὸν Χριστόν, Chrys. So expressly Syr., Æth., both of which suppress in translation the prefixed τὸ ὑπὲρ Χρ.

30. ἔχοντες] 'as you have:' further specification of the preceding πάσχειν, with a consolatory turn suggested by the associated example; καὶ τὸ παράδειγμα ἔχετε. πάλιν αὐτοὺς ἐπαίρει, Chrysost. The structure is 'ad sensum' rather than 'ad verbum;' the participle being constructed with the ὑμεῖς which is practically involved in the preceding verse, rather than with the clause immediately preceding, except perhaps 1, II. iv. 2, and notes *in loc.* Such relapses of the participle into the nominative are far too common to render either necessary with Bengel, Bloomf., and what is more singular, Lachm., to enclose ἔ τις — αὐτὸν πάσχων in a parenthesis: see examples in Winer, *Gr.* § 63. 2, p. 505, d. 4, or § 707. The frequent, and almost idiomatic, occurrence of such an anacoluthon is to be referrible to the practically weaker force of the oblique cases of part. ipsos.

οἷον εἴδετε] 'such as you saw in me,' sc. when I was with you at Philippi: compare Acts xvi. 16 sq. ὁ κ. εἶπεν, ἀκηκόατε, ἀλλ', εἴδετε καὶ γὰρ ἐκεῖ ἐλάλησεν ἐν Φιλίπποις, Chrys. In the expression ἐν ἐμοί the prep. marks as it were the *substrat.* of the action; see Winer, *Gr.* § 48. a, p. 345, and compare notes on Gal. i. 24. There is thus no need, with Syr., Æth., etc., to state the second ἐν ἐμοί 'de me' as the Philippians saw the ἀγὼν which was present with them, so low as our of it in his Epistle, in which he as it were personally speaks to them: so also Meyer. The reading ἴδετε (D³ ... F G etc.), though fairly supported [B D¹ E F G K L; very many mss.; Theoph., Œcum.] is apparently only due to the interchange of εἰ and ἰ (itacism): see Scrivener, *Collation*, etc. III. 3, p. LXIX.

CHAPTER II.—1. εἴ τις οὖν] '*If then, etc.*' The οὖν, which has here its *reflexive* rather than collective force, recalls the readers to the consideration of what their duty ought to be under exist-

παραμύθιον ἀγάπης, εἴ τις κοινωνία Πνεύματος, εἴ τινα σπλάγχνα

ing circumstances, with a retrospective ref. to the exhortation in ch. i. 27; 'revocat oὖν lectorem ad rem praesentem, id est, quae nunc enim maxime agitur, eodem prorsus modo, quo Latina particula *igitur*,' Klotz, *Devar*. Vol. II. p. 717. Beza's correction of the Vulg., 'igitur' for 'ergo,' is thus judicious. On the exact difference between these particles, see Hand. *Tursell*. Vol. III. p. 187.

παράκλ. ἐν Χρ.] '*exhortation in Christ*,' i. e. exhortation specified and characterized by being in Him as its sphere and element. This important modal adjunct defines the παράκλησις as being essentially Christian, 'quam [qualem] dat conjunctio cum Christo,' Wahl; it was only 'in Him' that its highest nature was realizable; compare notes on *Eph.* iv. 1. Παράκλησις is apparently here 'exhortation' (comp. 1 Cor. i. 10, Rom. xii. 8, and Fritz. *Rom*. Vol. 1. p. 32), not 'consolatio,' Vulg. ܐܝܟܐ Syriac (compare Goth., Copt.), which, though lexically tenable (see Knapp, *Script. Var. Arg.* Vol. I. p. 132 sq., and comp. notes on 1 *Thess.* v. 11), seems here somewhat tautologous when παραμύθιον so immediately follows. The exact distinction between the clauses is worthy of notice: the first (ἐν Χρ.) and third (Πνεύμ.), as Meyer observes, certainly point to the *objective* principles of Christian life, while the second (ἀγάπης) and fourth (σπλάγχν. κ. οἰκτ.) point to the *subjective* elements: so also Wiesing., who, however, somewhat unsatisfactorily refers the first two members to St. Paul, the last two to the Philippians. Surely the very terms of the exhortation seem to imply that all must be referred to the Philippians. It is the hoped-for, and indirectly assumed, existence of these four elements among his converts that leads the apostle so pressingly to beseech them to fulfil his joy: comp. Chrys., who very well illustrates the force and meaning of the appeal.

παραμύθιον ἀγ.] '*comfort or consolation of love*;' 'solatium caritatis,' Vulg., compare Syr. ܒܘܝܐܐ ܕܚܘܒܐ [loquutio in cor], Æth. and apparently Copt.; not 'winning persuasion,' Wiesing., — a meaning which is defensible (compare Plato, *Legg*. x. p. 880 A, παραμυθίοις εὐπειθὴς γίγνηται), but here apparently precluded by the parallelism σπλάγχνα καὶ οἰκτ. in the fourth clause. The gen. ἀγάπης is the gen. of the *source* or *agent*, 'comfort such as love supplies;' see Scheuerl. *Synt*. § 17, p. 126.

κοινωνία Πν.] '*fellowship of the Spirit*;' gen. *objecti*, communion with, participation in the gifts and influence of the Holy Spirit; τὴν μετοχὴν αὐτοῦ καὶ τὴν μετάληψιν καθ᾽ ἣν ἁγιαζόμεθα, Theoph. on 2 Cor. xiii. 14: so expressly Æth., 'particeps fuit *in* Spiritu;' comp. Chrys. The gen. at first sight might seem a gen. *subjecti* as above, — a construction both lexically and grammatically defensible (compare Fritz. *Rom*. Vol. III. p. 81, 287), but here somewhat at variance with the prevailing use and reference of κοινωνία and κοινωνὸς (comp. 1 Corin. i. 9, 2 Pet. i. 4) in passages of this doctrinal aspect; see Meyer *on* 2 *Cor*. xiii. 14, compare Pearson, *Creed*, Vol. I. p. 419 (edit. Burton), and the good sermon of Waterland, *Works*, Vol. v. p. 351. The Spirit here is not the human spirit, 'animorum conjunctio,' Tirin. (Pol. *Syn*.). De W., al., but the personal Holy Spirit, as the parallelism to the first clause, and the recurrence of the expression in 2 Cor. xiii. 14, seem very distinctly to suggest. So Æthiop. (Polygl., but not Platt), which expressly inserts ἅγιος· εἴ τινα σπλ. κ. τ. λ.] '*if any bowels (heartfelt love) and*

καὶ οἰκτιρμοί. ² πληρώσατέ μου τὴν χαράν, ἵνα τὸ αὐτὸ φρονῆτε, τὴν αὐτὴν ἀγάπην ἔχοντες, σύνψυχοι τὸ ἓν φρονοῦντες, ³ μηδὲν

ro apassions.' By comparing James v. 11, and especially Col. iii. 12, σπλάγχνα οἰκτιρμοῦ, it would seem that there is some distinction between the two words, and that the latter is not a mere explanation of the former (Zanch.). That advanced by Tittmann (*Synon.* 1. p. 69) seems satisfactory, ' σπλ. amorem vehementiorem quem unique denotat (στοργήν, compare Philem. 12); οἰκτ. misericordiam proprie denotat, seu sensum doloris ex malis seu incommodis aliorum;' compare Grot. *in loc.* It is somewhat singular that all the uncial MSS. including א, at least 50 mss., and several Ff. read εἴ τις σπλ. Though adopted by Tisch. (ed. 7) and Lachm., and defended by Green, *Gram.* p. 284, it seems really to have arisen from an erroneous (paradiplomatic) repetition of the preceding τις. The prevalence of such an apparent error need not shake our faith in mere MSS. testimony (Alf.); it rather seems to hint at the general fidelity of the transcribers. They could scarcely have all made the same error; but may very probably have studiously perpetuated it on the authority of two or three more ancient documents. Τινὰ is found in Clem. Alex. *Strom.* IV. p. 604 (ed. Pott.).

2 πληρώσατε] '*fulfil,*' '*make complete;*' οὐκ εἶπε ποιήσατέ μοι, ἀλλὰ, πληρώσατε· τουτέστιν ἤρξασθε φυτεύειν ἐν ἐμοί· ἤδη μοι μετεδώκατε τὸ εἰρηνεύειν, ἀλλ' εἰς τέλος ἐπιθυμῶ ἐλθεῖν, Chrys. The position of μου before χαρὰν does not seem intended to convey any emphasis; see the long list of similar examples in Winer, *Gr.* § 22. 7. 1, p. 140 (ed. 6). ἵνα τὸ αὐτὸ κ. τ. λ.] '*that so ye be likeminded.*' The particle ἵνα does not here denote simple *purpose* (Meyer),—a forced and unsatisfactory interpretation which ignores the usage of later Greek and the analogy of the modern *ed* (see

Corpe, *Gr.* p. 129 sq.),—but, with a weakened force, blends the subject of the entreaty, etc., with the purpose of making it: so rightly Chrys., τί βούλει; ἵνα σε κινδύνων ἀπαλλάξωμεν. ἵνα σοί τι χαρησώμεν; Οὐδὲν τούτων φησίν ἀλλ', ἵνα ὑμεῖς τὸ αὐτὸ φρονῆτε. See notes on *Eph.* i. 17, where this and other uses of ἵνα are briefly investigated. Van Heng. refers ἵνα to an omitted τὰ τήν, sc. χαιρὰν ταύτην ἵνα κ. τ. λ.: this seems very unsatisfactory. Τὸ αὐτὸ φρον. is rightly explained by Tittmann *Synon.* p. 67) as, 'eandem sententiam habere, idem sentire, velle et quaerere,' while the following participial clauses, τὴν αὐτὴν ἀγ. ἔχ. and σύνψ. τὸ ἓν φρ., more nearly define its essence and characteristics. See Fritz. *Rom.* xii. 16, Vol. III. p. 87, who however does not appear quite exact in separating σύνψ. from τὸ ἓν φρον.; see below. τὴν αὐτὴν ἀγ. ἔχ.] '*having the same love;*' closer definition of τὸ αὐτὸ φρονεῖν. ἐστὶ γὰρ καὶ τὸ αὐτὸ φρονεῖν καὶ μὴ ἀγάπην ἔχειν, Chrys. The true nature of such love is well defined by the same able commentator as ὁμοίως καὶ φιλεῖν καὶ φιλεῖσθαι. On the nature of Christian love as delineated in St. Paul's Epistles, the most summary and comprehensive definition of which is in ver. 4, see Usteri, *Lehrb.* II. 1. 4. p. 242 sq., Reuss, *Théo. Chrét.* IV. 19, Vol. II p. 203 sq. σύνψυχοι κ. τ. λ.] '*with accordant souls minding (th) one thing;*' second declining clause, and parallel to τὴν αὐτ. ἀγ. ἔχ. Most of the ancient Vv (Syr., Copt., Aeth., al.), apparently the Greek expositors, and several modern commentators regard σύνψυχοι and τὸ ἓν φρ. as separate predications; it seems however best, with Meyer, to regard them as united, the slightly emphatic σύνψ. forming a quasi-adverbial or secondary predication to τὸ

κατὰ ἐριθείαν μηδὲ κατὰ κενοδοξίαν, ἀλλὰ τῇ ταπεινοφροσύνῃ ἀλλήλους ἡγούμενοι ὑπερέχοντας ἑαυτῶν, ⁴ μὴ τὰ ἑαυτῶν ἕκαστοι

ἐν φρ. There is thus no necessity for any artificial distinctions between τὸ αὐτὸ φρ. and τὸ ἓν φρ. (Tittmann *Synonym.* I. p. 69), nor for the assumption of a studied tautology (comp. Chrys.): σύνψυχοι serves to illustrate the participial clause with which it is associated, while τὸ ἓν φρ. remands the reader to the τὸ αὐτὸ φρ. above, with which it is practically synonymous, and of which it is possibly a more abstract expression; compare Green, *Gram.* p. 201. Middleton (*Gr. Art.* p. 368) following Grotius refers this latter clause to what follows: this is not satisfactory, and mars the symmetry of the sentence. On the distinction between σύνψυχος and ἰσόψυχος, see notes on ver. 20.

3. μηδὲν κατὰ ἐριθ.] '*meditating nothing in the way of dissension*, or *contentiousness;*' not ποιοῦντες, V. Heng., Scholef. (*Hints.* p. 105), or still worse ποιεῖτε, Luth., but simply φρονοῦντες, continued from the preceding verse; see Winer, *Gr.* § 64. 2, p. 618. The prep. κατὰ primarily denotes the *model* or *rule*, and thence, as here, by a very intelligible gradation, the *occasion* or *circumstances* in accordance with it; see notes on *Tit.* iii. 5, and Winer, *Gram.* § 49. d, p. 358. On ἐριθεία see notes on ch. i. 17, and on *Gal.* v. 17; compare too Theophyl. *in loc.*, who appears to have caught the true force and meaning of the word; σπουδάσαι ἔχω, ἵνα μή με νικήσῃ ὁ δεῖνα· τοῦτο ἔστιν ἡ ἐριθεία. μηδὲ κατὰ κενοδοξίαν] '*nor in the way of vainglory.*' Κενοδ. an ἅπ. λεγόμ. in the N. T. (adj. Gal. v. 26) is sufficiently defined by Suidas as, ματαία τις περὶ ἑαυτοῦ οἴησις; compare Polyb. *Hist.* III. 81. 9, x. 33. 6. The reading is here very doubtful, that adopted in the text [ABC; Vulg., Clarom., Sang., Syr. (?) Copt., Æth. (?); Lachm., Tisch.], though not

free from suspicion, has the greatest amount of external evidence, and seems on the whole the most probable and satisfactory. τῇ ταπεινοφροσύνῃ] '*with, under the influence of (due) lowliness;*' *modal* dative (comp. notes on ch. i. 18), or perhaps more precisely dat. of the *subjective cause*, thus falling under the general head of the 'dynamic' dative, see Krüger, *Sprachl.* § 48. 15. 5. On this causal dative, which though allied to, must not be confounded with, the instrumental dat. (as apparently Mey., Alf.), see Bernhardy, *Synt.* III. 14, p. 101, sq., Scheuerl. *Synt.* § 22. e, p. 181, and Krüger, *l. c.* The article here prefixed to the abstract ταπεινοφρ. may have its collective force (Je.f, *Gr.* § 448) and mark 'lowliness' in its most abstract form, 'the virtue of lowliness' (Mey., comp. Middl. *Gram. Art.* p. 90), but more probably only characterizes the ταπειν. as that *due* and befitting lowliness by which each ought to be influenced: comp. Rom. xii. 10 sq., and Fritz. *in loc.* On ταπεινοφροσύνῃ, 'the thinking lowly of ourselves *because we are so*,' and its distinction from πραΰτης, see notes on *Eph.* iv. 2. Trench, *Synon.* § 42, and the more spiritually profound discussion of Neander, *Planting*, Vol. I. p. 483 sq. (Bohn). ὑπερέχοντας ἑαυτῶν] '*superior to themselves;*' compare Rom. xii. 10, Ephes. v. 21, 1 Pet. v. 5. The query of Calvin, how those who really and obviously excel others in certain points can conform to this precept, is satisfactorily answered by considering the true nature of ταπεινοφρ. The ταπεινόφρων is one so conscious of his dependence on God, and of his own imperfections and nothingness, that his own gifts only remind him that others must have gifts also, while his sense of his own utter nothingness suggests to

σκοποῦντες, ἀλλὰ καὶ τὰ ἑτέρων ἕκαστοι. ⁵ Τοῦτο γὰρ φρονεῖτε

5. γάρ] So *Rec.* and now *Tisch.* (ed. 7) with DEFGJK; very many Vv.: Gr. and Lat. Ff. (*Griesb.*, but om. om.; *Va*[*Hort*], *Mey., A*[*f.*]). The particle is omitted by *Lachm.* with ABCℵ, 17. 37; Coptic, Arm., Æth.; Origen, Ath., al. As verse 5 begins an ecclesiastical lection, and as the explicative force of the γάρ might not have been fully understood, and have led to the omission of the particle, the reading of the text seems *slightly* more probable.

φρονεῖτε] So ABCDEFGℵ; 3 mss.; Vulg., Clarom., Syriac, Æth. (Pol. and Platt); Cyr.; Lat. Ff. (*Lachm., Mey.*). The reading of *Tisch* (ed. 2, 7, φρονείσθω, with CKL; nearly all mss.; Copt., Goth., al.; Orig., Ath. (*Rec., Ar.*) is insufficiently attested by uncial authorities, and, on internal grounds, quite as likely to have been a correction of φρονεῖτε (to harmonize with ὃ καὶ ἐν Χρ. Ἰησ.) as vice versâ: compare contra, Fritz. *Fritzsch. Opusc.* p. 49 note, whose judgment, however, seems here hasty and ill-supported. We return, then, to the reading of *Lachm.* at l. *Tisch.* (ed. 1).

him that these gifts may well be superior to his own, and higher in nature and degree: see especially Neander, *Planting*, Vol. 1. p. 485 (Bohn).

4. τὰ ἑαυτῶν σκοπ.] '*regarding, looking to their own interests*:' warning against a selfish regard for themselves, following suitably on the exhortation to ταπεινοφροσύνη. Pride, as Müller well observes, is the most naked form of selfishness: see the excellent remarks on selfishness as the essence of sin, and as specially developing itself in pride and hatred, ib. *Doctr. of Sin*, t. 3. 1 and 2, especially Vol. 1. p. 175 sq. (Clark). Σκοπεῖν is here scarcely different in sense from ζητεῖν, ch. ii 21, 1 Cor. x. 24, 33, xii. 5; compare 2 Macc. iv. 5, τὸ συμφέρον σκοπῶν. Numerous examples of similar forms of expression will be found in Wetstein *in loc.*, the most pertinent of which is from a writer whose diction is said often to reflect that of St. Paul, Plotin. *Enn.* 1. 4. 8, οὐ τὸ ἐκείνων ἔτι σκοπουμένων, ἀλλὰ τὸ ἑαυτῶν. The reading of *Rec.*, ἕκαστος (with CDEKLℵ; al.)—σκοπεῖτε (with L; al.) is rightly rejected by *Lachmann, Tisch.*, and most modern commentators: it may, however, be remarked that in all other cases in the N. T. (Rev. vi. 11 [*Rec.*], is more than doubtful) ἕκαστος is only found in the singular. ἀλλὰ καὶ '*but also:*' a somewhat weakened form of the adversative clause, the καὶ perhaps pointing to the thought that it was natural that a man should look after his own interests; see Winer, *Gr.* § 55. 8, p. 444 sq., Fritz. *Marc.* exc. 11 p. 788. On the difference between οὐκ — ἀλλά, οὐ μόνον — ἀλλά, and οὐ μόνον — ἀλλὰ καί, see the acute remarks of Klotz, *Devar.* Vol. 11. p. 9. It is, perhaps, scarcely necessary to controvert the position of Raphel (*O's.* Vol. 11. p. 503, that τὰ ἑαυτῶν are '*sua domi:*' such an interpretation is less in harmony with the context, and would tend to make καὶ appear redundant. What the apostle condemns is not so much a reasonable regard for their own interests as the selfish exhibition of it; comp. Waterl. *Serm.* v Vol. 11. p. 503.

5. γάρ has here its *ex eventu* force, 'verily,' 'as the case stands,' and serves both to illustrate and confirm the preceding exhortation; see especially notes on *Gal.* ii. 6, where this use of γάρ is briefly illustrated. φρονεῖτε ἐν ὑμῖν] '*entertain this mind or more 'res.,*' sc. 'in animis vestris,' Van H., not 'intra vestrum coetum,' a construction which

ἐν ὑμῖν ὃ καὶ ἐν Χριστῷ Ἰησοῦ, ⁶ ὃς ἐν μορφῇ Θεοῦ ὑπάρχων οὐχ

seems distinctly precluded by the following ἐν Χρ. Meyer compares the Homeric ἐνὶ φρεσί, ἐνὶ θυμῷ, thus similarly combined with φρονεῖν, *Ill.* XXIV. 173, *Odys.* XIV. 82, al.   ὃ καὶ ἐν Χ. Ἰ.] '*which was also in Christ Jesus,*' sc. ἐφρονεῖτο or ἐφρονήθη. The καὶ is not 'cum maxime,' Van. Heng., but simply correlative, indicating the identity of the disposition that is to be between the Philippians and Christ (Wies.): on the insertion of καὶ after relative particles, and the form of comparison it indicates, see Klotz, *Devar.* Vol. II. p. 636. The interpretation of Hofmann (*Schriftb.* Vol. I. p. 130), according to which ὃ is to be referred to φρονεῖν, not ἐφρονήθη, scil. 'welches ein φρονεῖν in ihnen selbst nicht ist, ohne auch in Christo Jesu' (compare Gal. ii. 20), seems artificial and unsatisfactory.

6. ὅς] In this important, and it is to be feared much perverted passage, nearly every word has formed the subject of controversy. In no portion of Scripture is it more necessary to follow the simple and plain grammatical meaning of the words. The first question is, to what does ὅς refer? To Christ as (*a*) the Λόγος ἄσαρκος, Christ in his pre-incarnate state (Chrys. and majority of Ff.), or, as (*b*) the Λόγος ἔνσαρκος, — what is now usually, but not very reverently, termed the 'historical Christ' (Novation, De W., al)? The true answer seems,— to neither *exclusively*, but, as the appropriately chosen antecedent (Χρ. Ἰησ.) suggests, and the profound nature of the subject requires, to (*a*) AND (*b*), to the τέλειος Υἱὸς (Hyppolyt. ap. Routh. *Opusc.* Vol. I. p. 73) in either form of His eternal existence; it being left to the immediate context to define the more immediate reference; compare Col. i. 13, 15, and see Thomasius, *Christi Person,* Vol. II. p. 136. In the present verse the reference seems plainly to (*a*); for as the *tertium comparationis* is manifestly ταπεινοφροσύνη, so this cannot be completely evinced in the case of Christ, unless His prior state be put in clear contrast with that to which He was pleased to condescend; compare 2 Cor. viii. 9, where, while Ἰησ. Χρ. is similarly the subject, πλούσιος ὢν can scarcely admit any other reference than to Christ's pre-incarnate state; so even Usteri, *Lehrb.* II. 2 4, p. 295. In verses 8–12 the reference is as obviously to (*b*): the Λόγος ἄσαρκος, which is the more immediate subject of verse 6, passes into the Λόγος ἔνσαρκος in ver. 7, and as the slight break in the continuity of the sentence, καὶ σχήματι κ.τ.λ., fittingly and significantly indicates, remains so to the end of the clause. Other opinions, especially that of Origen, will be found in the admirable sermon of Waterl. (*Works,* Vol. II. p. 109), in which the whole passage is very clearly discussed. See also Pearson, *Creed,* Art. II. Vol. I. p. 155, Bull, *Prim. Trad.* VI. 21, Jackson, *Creed,* Book VIII. 1, Thomasius, *Chr. Pers.* Vol. II. p. 136 sq. Reference to the older monographs on this subject will be found in Wolf *in loc.*, and to the more recent in Meyer *in loc.* ἐν μορφῇ Θεοῦ ὑπάρ.] '*subsisting in the form of God,*' 'ürstandend u. s. w.,' Thomasius, *l. c.*, scil. from all eternity, in reference to His pre-incarnate existence, the participle not having so much a causal ('inasmuch as he was') as a concessive reference, 'although he was,' a sufficiently common solution of the participle; see Donalds. *Gr.* § 621. The use of ὑπάρχων, not ὤν, is especially noticeable. In the following words, μορφὴ Θεοῦ, there is but little difficulty, if we adhere simply and honestly to the true lexical meaning of μορφή, and properly attend to the subsequent anti-thesis. With respect to μορφή [probably derived from

ἁρπαγμὸν ἡγήσατο τὸ εἶναι ἴσα Θεῷ, ⁷ ἀλλὰ ἑαυτὸν ἐκένωσεν

the Sanscr. *Varpus*, 'form,' comp. Benfey, *Wurzellex.* Vol. II. p. 30 sq., we may first observe, that it is not perfectly identical with φύσις or οὐσία (Chrysost, al., Jackson, *l. c.*), being in fact one of its two essential elements (see especially Aristot. *de Anima*, II. 1), but designates 'form,' 'appearance' (*Eth.*), 'likeness' (Syr.), and may be compared with εἰκών, Col. i. 15, and χαρακτὴρ τῆς ὑποστάσεως, Heb. i. 3; compare Thomasius, *l. c.*, p. 127. As, however, both these allied expressions stand in connection with a reference to the eternal Sonship (Waterl. *l. c.*), as μορφὴ Θεοῦ stands in distinct and undeniable antithesis to μορφὴν δούλου (Bull, *l. c.*), and as this latter expression is referred by the apostle himself to the assumption of human nature, so no candid man can doubt that both ante-Nicene and post-Nicene writers were right in their *deduction* that μορφὴ Θεοῦ has reference to the *divine nature*, and does express as much as Θεὸς ἐκ Θεοῦ (Hippol. Vol. II. p. 29, ed. Fabr.) and υἱὸς Θεοῦ (Dionys.-Alexan. apud Labb. Vol. I. p. 853), and hence, what is truly and essentially divine; see esp. Waterl. *Serm.* v. Vol. II. p 103 sq.

οὐχ ἁρπαγμὸν κ.τ.λ.] '*He did not deem His being on an equality with God a thing to be seized on, or to grasp at.*' On this important clause we must premise the following remarks: (1) the slightly emphatic ἁρπαγμὸν is the predicate, and τὸ εἶναι κ.τ.λ., the immediate object to ἡγήσατο, see Winer, *G.* § 44. 3, p 289; (2) the word ἁρπ., *if considered apart from the context*, does not seem merely = ἅρπαγμα or ἁρπάγιον (Callim. *Hymn. Cer.* 9), but, with the usual force of its termination (Donaldson, *Cratyl.* § 253), would seem to denote 'the act of seizing;' compare Plut. (?) *de Lib. ed.* p. 120 A, τὸν ἐκ Κρήτης καλούμενον ἁρπαγμόν; (3) ἴσα is used adverbially (Winer, *Gr.*

y 27. 3, p. 160, ἔχων ἴσως Θεῷ, 'aequal ter Deo esse,' Thomas., *l. c.*, p. 140, and that no stress can be laid on so bland a use (especially on τὴν πρὸς Deum,' Grote, as the whole force of the assertion of equality lies in the use of the verb. ὑπάρχ., τὸ εἶναι, see Pearson *Creed*, Vol. II p 88, ed. Burton; (II ἐν μορφῇ Θεοῦ ὑπάρχ. and τὸ εἶναι ἴσα Θεῷ are virtually, though not precisely, identical. Both refer to the Divine Nature, the former, however (perhaps with a momentary glance of thought to its ἀλλὰ), points to it in respect of its *form* and *present state*; the latter, with exquisite distinction, to its *state* and *present continuance*, referring the reader, as it were, to the very moment of the ἡγήσατο. On these premises the translation would be, — *a) He thought the being equal to God an act of robbery*, — no usurpation of any dignity which was not His own by right of nature (Jackson, *Creed*, VIII. 1); 'non rapinam existimavit pariari Deo,' Tertullian, see Waterl. *l. c.*, p. 107 sq.: so appy. Syr. [syriac], (reptio), Vulg 'rapinam,' Goth. 'vulva,' and perhaps Copt. *hōlem*' but appy.—ἅρπαγμα a Lev. vi. 4), Authoriz., and many of the other commentators. To this, however, the logical consideration that a collation cannot properly be regarded as a comparison, Hofmann, *Schriftb.* Vol. I. p 151), and the still graver *a-theoretical* considerations, — (α) that the above reading of ἁρπ. ἡγήσ. not only affords no exemplification of μὴ τὰ ἑαυτῶν σκοπεῖν (ver. 4) but really implies the very reverse; β) that the antithesis of ἁρπ. ἡγήσ.—ἀλλὰ ἐκένωσεν is thus wholly destroyed (see below, — present objections so serious, and apparently insurmountable, that we seem justified in reconsidering (2), and in assigning to the *rare* word ἁρπαγμὸς a meaning approaching that of the verbal in -τος

μορφὴν δούλου λαβών, ἐν ὁμοιώματι ἀνθρώπων γενόμενος,

(Hesiod, *Op.* 320) or the substant. in -μα [consider θεσμός, χρησμός, and permutations of -μα and -μος, such as δίωγμα, διωγμός], so that the phrase may be considered closely allied to ἅρπαγμα ἡγεῖσθαι (Heliod. *Æth.* vii. 20) and the similar expressions ἅρπ. ποιεῖσθαι, Euseb. *Const.* ii. 31, ἅρπα θέσθαι, Euseb. *Hist.* viii. 12; compare ἁρπαλέα δόσις, Pind. *Pyth.* viii. 65, and see especially Donalds. *in loc.* The meaning then will be (*b*) *He did not deem the being on an equality with God a thing to be seized on*, a state to be exclusively (so to speak) clutched at, and retained as a prize; the expression οὐχ ἁρπ. ἡγ. being perhaps studiedly used rather than οὐχ ἥρπασε, Æth., 'ut sententiam etiam graviorem redderet, et Christum de illo *ne cogitasse* quidem significaret,' Rübiger, in Thomas. *Christ. Pers.* Vol. ii. p. 139: so in effect Theodoret (οὐ μέγα τοῦτο ὑπέλαβε), and, with some variations in detail, Van Heng., De W., Wiesing., and the majority of modern commentators, except Meyer and Alford), who adopt a *quasi*-active meaning ('ein Verhältniss des Beutemachens,' 'self-enrichment') but somewhat confuse the exegesis. The fuller justification of (*b*) will appear in the following note.

7. ἀλλὰ ἑαυτὸν ἐκέν.] '*but emptied Himself;*' 'He retained not his equality with God, but on the contrary emptied Himself, — *Himself*, with slight emphasis, divine as He was in nature and prerogatives.' The real difficulties of this passage are brought into clear prominence by this adversative clause. We have here two lines of interpretation, perfectly and plainly distinct. (1) If, on the one hand, we adopt (*a*), the first interpretation mentioned ver. 6, then ὑπάρχων will be causal, οὐχ ἁρπ. ἡγ. will refer to the *preceding* account of Christ's greatness (Waterland, *l. c.*, p. 110), and

ἁρπ. will *more nearly* preserve its apparent lexical meaning, but ἀλλὰ will have to be regarded as equivalent to ἀλλ' ὅμως (Waterl., p. 108), and the antithesis as one between whole members, not, as the context seems imperatively to demand, between conterminous clauses; '*He thought the being equal to God no usurpation; yet He emptied Himself;*' so expressly Waterland, and, as far as we can infer from renderings almost perplexingly literal, Auth., and the principal ancient Vv., except Æth. (2) If, on the other hand, we adopt (*b*) as above, then — ὑπαρχ. will be concessive, οὐχ ἁρπ. ἡγ. will refer to the *consequent* account of Christ's humiliation, preserving an exact parallelism to μὴ τὰ ἑαυτῶν σκοπ., ἁρπ. will recede further from its lexical meaning, but ἀλλὰ will retain its usual, proper, and logical force after the negative clause ('aliud jam hoc esse de quo sumus dicturi,' Klotz, *Devar.* Vol. ii. 2), and the sentence will be even, continuous, and in fullest contextual harmony: '*He did not deem His equality to God a prize to be seized, but, etc.;*' in other words, — 'He did not insist on His own eternal prerogatives, but, *on the contrary*, humbled Himself to the condition and sufferings of mortal man.' Of these two interpretations while (1) preserves more nearly the primary lexical meaning of ἁρπαγμός, it so unduly expands that of ἀλλά, and so *completely* mars the regular antithesis (οὐκ — ἀλλά), that we seem bound to adopt confidently and unhesitatingly the latter interpretation: see especially Waterland (*l. c.*, p. 110), who while adopting (1) shows clearly that (2) is a sound and catholic interpretation: compare Middleton, *Gr. Art.* p. 370, Browne, *Articles*, i. 2, p. 41, neither of whom, however, seems to have felt sufficiently the lexical difficulty connected with ἁρπαγμός. All

" καὶ σχήματι εὑρεθεὶς ὡς ἄνθρωπος ἐταπείνωσεν ἑαυτόν, γενόμενος

attempts to preserve both the *exact* meaning of ἁρπ. and the regular grammatical sequence (Meyer, and apparently Alf.), in fact to combine (1) and (2), seem hopeless: the two translations are fundamentally distinct, and most of the confused interpretations of this passage are owing to this distinction and this incompatibility not having been seen and recognized. It is fair to add that of these attempts, the most plausible is the assumed coherence of the negative with ἁρπαγμόν (' non-rapinam '), but to this the form and balance of the sentence, — the appearance of οὐ with an aorist in the first member, followed by ἀλλὰ with a responsive aor. in the second member, — seems, as before, to present a grammatical objection that remains in all its fullest validity. Lastly, it is not correct to say (De Wette) that τὸ εἶναι κ. τ. λ. must refer to something Christ did *not* possess; surely it is logically accurate to say that Christ did not seize for Himself, and covet to retain a state that was then his own. Even though such phrases as τὸν θάνατον ἅρπαγμα θέμενοι (Euseb. *Hist*. VIII. 12) may be found, would it be necessarily incorrect to say of a patriot, οὐχ ἅρπ. (or ἅρπ.), ἡγήσατο τὸν βίον ἀλλ' εἵλετο τὸν θάνατον? ἑαυτὸν ἐκένωσεν] 'emptied *Himself*,' not metaphorically, 'humiliavit,' Æth., but according to the simple and lexical meaning of the word (compare Xenoph. *Œcon*. VIII. 7, al.; 'exinanivit,' Vulg., Claroman.;

[inane reddidit] Syriac, 'effluere fecit,' Copt.; compare 'us-lausida,' Goth. Of what did He empty Himself? Not exactly of the μορφὴ Θεοῦ (Mey., Alf.) unless understood in a sense different to that which it *inferentially* has in the preceding clause, for, as Waterl. truly says, 'He had the same *essential* glory, the

same real dignity He ever had' (αἰῶν ὁ ἦν, ἔλαβεν ὃ οὐκ ἦν (Chrys.), but, as the following clause more expressly shows, of that which he had ere all time (comp. Pearson, *Creed*, Vol. I. p. 178 that Godlike majesty and native glories (comp. Delitzsch, *Ps*. &c. p. 94) which He had from all eternity: τὴν ἀξίαν κατακρύψας τὴν ἀκρὰν ταπεινοφροσύνην εἵλετο, Theodoret. The monetary metaphor which Krebs (*Obs*. p. 329) finds in κενοῦν and even in ἁρπ. ἡγήσ., seems doubtful in the highest degree.

μορφὴν δούλου λαβών] 'taking, or by taking, the form of a servant;' the action of the aor. part. being synchronous with that of the finite verb; see Bernhardy, *Synt.* X. 9, p. 383, notes on *Eph*. i. 9, and serving more fully to explain it: 'si quaeris quomodo Christus seipsum exinanivit? Respondet apostolus, *servi formam accipiens*,' Bull, *Def. Fid. Nic*. VI. 20. The choice of the term δούλου, as the same great writer ably observes, has no reference to any *status* or *Πτωχὴν miseram sortem*,' (Heinr.) but is suggested only by the preceding antithesis μορφῇ Θεοῦ, and marks the relation which our Lord *assumed* towards God; 'ad Deum autem comparata creatura omnis servi formam habet, Deique obedientiam obstricta tenetur,' *ib*. § 24.

ἐν ὁμοιώματι κ. τ. λ.] 'being made in the likeness of men;' modal clause subordinated to the preceding.— 'if any man doubt how Christ emptied Himself, the text will satisfy him, by *taking the form of a servant*; if any still question how he took the form of a servant, he hath the apostle's resolution by being made in the likeness of men,' Pearson, *Creed*, Vol. I. p. 157, ed Burton'. The expression ἐν ὁμοιώμ. is very noticeable; Christ though perfect man was yet not a mere man, a ψιλὸς ἄνθρωπος, but was ὁ Λόγος σὰρξ γενόμενος; compare The-

ὑπήκοος μέχρι θανάτου, θανάτου δὲ σταυροῦ. ⁹ διὸ καὶ ὁ Θεὸς αὐτὸν

ophylact *in loc.*, and Fritz. *Rom.* viii. 3, Vol. 11. p. 97. Lastly, γίνεσθαι does not here imply merely ' to be born,' but, as the context requires, with a greater latitude of meaning, 'apparere,' ' in conspectum venire,' Kühner on Xenophon *Mem.* 111. 3. 6 (Meyer), while ἐν is used with a quasi-local force to mark the envelope or environment; see Bernhardy, *Synt.* v. 7, p 209.

8. καὶ σχήματι κ. τ. λ.] *' and being found in fashion as a man.'* etc. ; dative of reference, Winer, *Gr.* § 31. 6, p. 193, and notes *on Gal.* i. 22 ; οὐ τοῦτο λέγων, ὅτι ἡ φύσις μετέπεσεν οὐδὲ σύγχυσίς τις ἐγένετο, ἀλλὰ σχήματι ἐγένετο, Chrys. This clause is connected by De Wette, Meyer, Tisch. (ed. 2, 7), and others closely with what precedes, a stop being placed after ἄνθρωπος, and ἐταπείνωσεν being left, without any connecting particle, to commence the next clause : so also Copt , and probably Syr. and Æth. To such a punctuation there are two grave objections. On the one hand, such an abrupt separation in a group of clauses which have a close logical and historical coherence is improbable, and apparently unprecedented (the examples cited by De Wette, Gal. iii. 13, v. 25, 2 Cor. v. 21, are not in point): on the other, as was hinted above on ver. 6, the slight break, combined with the somewhat peculiar εὑρεθείς harmonize admirably with the change of subject, and indicate the transition from the pre-incarnate glory to the incarnate humiliation and post-incarnate exaltation of the Eternal Son : so it would seem, expressly, Chrys. *Hom.* vii. 4, init. Εὑρεθείς is thus not for ὤν, but, as always, implies that He was *found*, manifested, acknowledged, to be; see notes *on Gal.* ii. 17, and Winer, *Gram.* § 64. 8, p. 542 sq. On σχῆμα, which, as its derivation [ἔχω] clearly hints, is not = ὁμοίωμα, Heinr., but denotes the *habitus*, 'outward guise, demeanor, and manner of life' (οἰκέτου σχῆμα περιέθηκε, Lucian, *Necyom.* § 16, σχῆμα φρυγανιστῆρος λαβών, Polyæn. *Strategem.* 1. p. 37 [Wetst.]), and its distinction from the more 'intrinsic' and 'essential μορφή,' see *Journ. Class. Phil.* No. vii. p. 115 sq. ; compare notes *on* 2 *Tim.* iii. 5. ὡς ἄνθρωπος] *' as a man ;'* though a perfect man, yet not a mere man ; ἡμεῖς γὰρ ψυχὴ καὶ σῶμα· ἐκεῖνος Θεός, καὶ ψυχή, καὶ σῶμα, Chrys., who, however, would have expressed himself with more psychological exactness if, in both clauses for ψυχή, he had written πνεῦμα καὶ ψυχή ; comp. Luke xxiii. 26. and Delitzsch, *Bibl. Psychol.* v. 1, p. 283 sq.

ἐταπείνωσεν] *' humbled Himself;'* not ἑαυτὸν ἐταπ., the emphasis resting rather on the act, than, as before (ἑαυτ. ἐκέν.) on the subject. Ἐταπείν. is clearly not synonymous with ἐκέν. (Rheinw.), but refers to the acts of condescension and humiliation in that human nature which He emptied Himself to assume : 'non solum, cum Deus esset, naturam assumpsit humanam, verum in eâ se vehementer humiliavit et dejecit,' Bull, *Prim. Trad.* vi. 21. On the meaning of ταπεινὸς [allied with τάπης, and not improbably derived from a root ΣΤΑΠ— 'press,' 'tread,' compare Benfey, *Wurzellex.* Vol. 1. p. 656] in Christian writers in contradistinction to heathen (by whom it is commonly used in a bad sense, *e. g.* ταπεινὴ καὶ ἀνελεύθερος, Plato, *Legg.* iv. p. 774 c.), see Trench. *Synon.* § 42.

γενόμενος κ. τ. λ.] *' by becoming obedient even to death ;'* modal clause appended to and explaining ἐταπείνωσεν, the supplementary words μέχρι κ. τ. λ. not belonging to the finite verb (Beng., Hofm. *Schriftb.* Vol. 11. 1, p. 80), but, as the explanatory nature of the participial clause and the even flow of the

ὑπερύψωσεν καὶ ἐχαρίσατο αὐτῷ ὄνομα τὸ ὑπὲρ πᾶν ὄνομα,

sentence clearly require,—τὸ γενόμενος ὑπήκ. The ὑπακοή here mentioned was not that shown to His earthly parents (Zanch.), or to Jews and Romans (Grotius), but, as the following verse seems distinctly to indicate, to God; compare Matth. xxvi. 39, Rom. v. 19, Heb v. 8. The meaning of the term cannot fairly be pressed, *e. g.* ὑπήκουσεν ὡς υἱός, οὐχ ὡς δοῦλος, Theol., for see Rom. vi. 16, Col. iii. 22. As the derivation suggests, ὑπήκοος and ὑπακούειν involve the idea of 'dicto obtemperare;' πείθεσθαι is rather 'monita sequi,' πειθαρχεῖν 'coactus obsequi;' see Tittm. *Synon.* i. p. 193, and notes *on Tit.* iii. 1. On the apparent futility of distinctions between μέχρι (here not of time but degree) and ἄχρι, see on 2 *Tim.* ii. 9.

θανάτου δὲ στ.] 'yea death on the cross;' not only death, but a death of suffering, shameful and accursed: οὗτος γὰρ [ὁ θάνατος] πάντων ἐπονειδιστικώτερος εἶναι ἐδόκει. οὗτος ὁ αἰσχύνης γέμων, οὗτος ὁ ἐπάρατος, Chrys. On the use of δὲ in repetition, in which however the original oppositive force may just faintly be traced ('similis notio quodam modo opponitur'), see Klotz, *Devar.* Vol. II. p. 361, Hartung, *Partik.* δε, 2. 7, Vol. I. p. 168; and on the genitive (of 'more remote relation'), see exx. in Winer, *Gr.* § 30. 2. p. 168.

9 διὸ καὶ] '*On which account also;*' 'in consequence of this condescension and humiliation on the part of Christ God also, etc.;' the καὶ not being merely consecutive (De W., Mey.), but standing in connection with ὑπερύψ., and serving to place in gentle *contrast* the consequent exaltation with the previous ταπείνωσις; see Klotz, *Devar.* Vol. II p. 635, and notes on ch. iv. 12. The meaning of διὸ, 'quo facto' (comp. Wolf, al.), adopted only, it is to be feared, from dogmatical reasons, is distinctly untena-

ble in grammar, and by no means necessary in point of theology; 'God,'—Bp. Andrewes says, 'not only raised Him, but, *propter hoc*, even "for that cause" exalted Him also to live with Him in glory for ever, *Serm.* I. Vol. II. p. 107, *ib.* p 325: ὅταν τι ς σαρκὸς ἐπιλάβηται ὁ μακάριος Παῦλος πάντα λοιπὸν τὰ ταπεινὰ μετὰ ἀδείας φθέγγεται. Chrys. *in loc.* On the humiliation of the Eternal Son see especially Jackson, *Cred.* VIII. 1. 2, and on the nature and degrees of His exaltation, Andrewes, *Serm.* IX. Vol. I. p 322 sq (A.-C. Lord).

αὐτὸν ὑπερύψωσεν] ܐܰܘܟܺܝܬ ܐܰܣܓܺܝ ܪܰܡܪܡܶܗ [mulum exaltavit eum] Syr.; compare Psalm xcvi. 9. σφόδρα ὑπερυψώθης ὑπὲρ πάντας τοὺς θεοὺς, Dan. iv. 34. The ὑπὲρ is not here temporal, nor even local, though the reference is obviously to the Ascension (Eph. iv. 10) and elevation at the right hand of God, but *ethica*,—'dominate atque imperio supra omnes,' Zanch., 'insigniter extulit,' Just.: so *Æthiopic*. Copt. On St. Paul's favorite use of ὑπὲρ and its compounds, see notes on *Eph.* i i. 20. The exact nature of this exaltation is well discussed in Waterl. *Serm.* II. Vol. II. p. 112; it is to be doubted, however, whether, as Waterl. maintains, the reference is specially to Christ as Son of God, and to 'an exaltation *relative to us*, by a new and real title, viz. that of redemption and salvation;' so also Jack on *Cred.* XI. 3. 4, Bull, *Primit. Tradit.* VI. 23. The accordant opinion of these great writers claims our most serious consideration; still as the aor. seems to point to a definite historical fact,—as in ver. 8 there is apparently almost a marked transition from the pre-incarnate to the incarnate Son,—as in ver. 10 this allusion seems still continued in the name Ἰησοῦ,—so here the

¹⁰ ἵνα ἐν τῷ ὀνόματι Ἰησοῦ πᾶν γόνυ κάμψῃ ἐπουρανίων καὶ

reference is the same; ὑπερυψοῦσθαι λέγεται, καὶ ὡς οὐκ ἔχων, διὰ τὸ ἀνθρώπινον μονονουχί, Hippolyt. *Fragm.* Vol. ii p. 29 (ed. Fabr.). The exaltation is thus not merely relative but proper; an investiture as the Son of Man, with all that full power, glory, and dominion, which as God He never wanted; see Pearson, *Creed*, Vol. i. p. 190 (ed. Burt.). So, distinctly, Chrysost., Theodoret, Cyr.-Alex., some of the ante-Nicene and apparently the bulk of the post-Nicene writers. For the psychological considerations dependent on this exaltation of the God-man, see Delitzsch. *Bibl. Psych.* v. 1, p. 287.   ἐχαρίσατο] '*freely gave;*' chap. i. 29. There is no reason whatever to depart from the simple and proper lexical meaning of the word; εἰ δὲ λέγεται ἐν τάξει χαρίσματος τὸ ὑπὲρ πᾶν ὄνομα δέχεσθαι, εἰς ἐκεῖνο δηλονότι μετὰ σαρκὸς ἐπανάγεται, εἰς ὅπερ ἦν καὶ δίχα σαρκός, Cyr.-Alex. *Thesaur.* p. 130.   ὄνομα κ. τ. λ.] '*a name the which is above every name;*' a name, which, as the context shows, is not to be understood generically (comp. Eph. i. 21, Heb. i. 4), as Κύριος (Mich.), or υἱὸς Θεοῦ, but specifically and expressly as Ἰησοῦς, the name of His humiliation, and henceforth that of His exaltation and glory; a name with which now every highest attribute, grace, power, dominion, and κυριότης (ver. 11) is eternally conjoined. There is thus no reason whatever for modifying the simple meaning of ὄνομα: both here and elsewhere (Mark vi. 14, John xii. 28, Acts iii. 16, Rom. i. 5, al.) the idea of '*dignity*' (Bloomf., Heinr.), is derived solely from the context; see Van Heng. *in loc.* The reading is somewhat doubtful. *Lachm.* and Mey. read τὸ ὄνομα τὸ κ. τ. λ., with ABC; 17; Copt. [a language which has a definite and indefinite article], Dionisius-Alex., Euseb.,

Cyr. (2), al.; but, as the insertion can more plausibly be referred to grammatical correction than the omission to erroneous transcription, — scil. the precedence of τό, we retain with DEFGKL: nearly all mss.; Orig., Ath., Chrys., al., the reading of *Tischendorf.* On the use of the article with the defining clause to characterize more expressly the preceding anarthrous noun, see Winer, § 21. 4, p. 126, who, however, appears to lean to the other reading.

10. ἵνα κ. τ. λ.] '*that in the name of Jesus;*' purpose and intent of the exaltation. Ἐν τῷ ὀνόμ. is not equivalent to εἰς τὸ ὄνομα (Heinr.) as directly specifying that *to* which (-Eth.) the adoration is to be paid, nor yet, 'ad nomen,' Beza (compare Auth.), 'nuncupato nomine,' Grot., — a meaning of ἐν ὀνόμ. wholly without example in the N. T., but, with the full force of the prep., denotes the spiritual sphere, the holy element as it were, *in* which every prayer is to be offered and every knee to bow; see Eph. v. 20, and Harless *in loc.*, who well remarks that τὸ ὄνομα κ. τ. λ. does not imply simply and *per se* the personality ('pro persona positum,' Est.), but that personality as revealed to and acknowledged by man: compare also Winer. *Gr.* § 48. a, p. 345.   πᾶν γόνυ κ. τ. λ.] '*every knee should bow;*' εἰς προσκύνησιν δηλονότι, Œcumen.; genuflection being the external representation of worship and adoration; see Rom. xi. 4, xiv. 11, Eph. iii. 14 and notes *in loc.*, Suicer, *Thesaur.* Vol. 1. p. 777. The subject to whom the adoration is directed, can only be, as Meyer rightly observes, the principal subject of the context, our Lord and Master Jesus Christ. Such an adoration is not, however, as Meyer goes on to say, merely *relative* (comp. ver. 11, εἰς δόξαν Θεοῦ), but, as the whole aspects of the passage, its

ἐπιγείων καὶ καταχθονίων, 11 καὶ πᾶσα γλῶσσα ἐξομολογήσεται ὅτι Κύριος Ἰησοῦς Χριστὸς εἰς δόξαν Θεοῦ πατρός.

clear contrasts, and its concluding theme, — the exaltation of the Son, — seem all plainly to indicate, *positive* and *absolute*. By no one has the distinction between the relative and absolute worship of the Son been more clearly commented than by Bishop Bull; 'si absolute ut Deus spectatur,...idem plane divinus cultus quem Patri extremus omnino debetur. Sin Filium in quantur relate qua Filius est, et ex D o Patre trahit originem; tum cur as certum est cultum et venerationem om ni m quem ipsi deferimus, ad Patrem redundare,' *Fid. Nic.* ix. 15, — a section that for soundness of divinity and clearness of definition deserves attentive perusal; see also Waterl. *Def. of Quer.* xvii. xviii. Vol. ii. p. 421 sq. ἐπουρανίων κ. τ. λ.] '*of things in heaven, and things on earth, and things under the earth;*' 'quae in coelis, et in terrâ, et in abyssis,' Æth. (Platt); comp. Rev. v. 13, and for examples of a similar separation of the noun. from its dependent genitives, Winer, *Gram.* § 30. 2, p. 172. The three classes here mentioned are to be understood not with any ethical reference (καὶ οἱ δίκαιοι [not καὶ οἱ ζῶντες, as cited by Mey. and Alf.] καὶ οἱ ἁμαρτωλοί, Chrys. 2), but simply and plainly, angels and archangels in heaven (comp. Eph. i. 20, Heb. i. 4, 6), men upon earth (compare Plato, *Republ.* viii. p. 548 a, [ib.] *Axioch* 368 a), and the departed under the earth; ἐπουρανίους καλεῖ τὰς ἀοράτους δυνάμεις, ἐπιγείους δὲ τοὺς ἔτι ζῶντας ἀνθρώπους καὶ καταχθονίους τοὺς τεθνεῶτας: c mpare Delitzsch, *Bibl. Psych.* vi. 3, p. 394. The last class is referred by Chrys. 1, Theoph., and Œcum. to δαίμονες, but, as Meyer well observes, such is by no means the locality elsewhere assigned to them by the apostle (comp. Eph. vi. 12), nor is the homage of impotence or subjugated malice (2 Pet. ii. 4, Jude 6) an

also suitable with the precept as with the following clause. The other interpretations that have been proposed are either purely arbitrary (Christ m. J ws, Heathen, or adjusted to doctrinal preconceptions (qui in purgatorio sunt,' Est.) to which the context yields no support. It may be here briefly remarked that the reverential custom of making an outward sign of adoration at the name of Jesus (Canon 18, though certainly not *directly* deduced from this text, may still, as Mede admits, be derived from it ('generali et in ti ā consequentiâ,' *Epist.* 74; see B gh m. *Antiq.* Vol. ix. p. 245 sq., And. *Acs. Serm* ix. Vol. 1. p. 334 sq. (A. C. L. r.).

11. πᾶσα γλῶσσα] 'every tongue;' not metaphorically, πάντα τὰ ἔθνη, Theodoret, but simply and literally in accordance with, and in expansion of, the preceding concrete expression πᾶν γόνυ; 'the knee is but a dumb acknowledgment, but a vocal confession that both utter our mind plainly' Andrewes, *Serm.* ix. Vol. ii. p. 337, who, however, with his characteristic exhaustion of every possible meaning also notices the former, p. 339. ἐξομολογήσεται] '*openly confess,*' 'diserte confiteatur' [confitebitur], Beng.; the prep. not merely pointing to 'ex imo corde,' Van Hengel (comp. Andrewes. *l. c.*), but, as the occurrence of the simple verb in similar but less emphatic passages (John ix. 22, al.), indirectly suggests, the openness and completeness of the ὁμολογία; compare Acts xix. 18, ἐξομολογούμενοι καὶ ἀναγγέλλοντες τὰς πράξεις, Philo, *Leg. Alleg.* § 26, Vol. 1 p. 60 (ed. Mang.), Lucian, *Hermot.* § 75; and see Fritz. on *Matth.* iii. 6, p. 126, who, however, on the other hand, somewhat over-presses the force of the compound; 'lubenter et aperte et vehementer confi-

Work out your salvation; be peaceful and blameless, and give me cause to rejoice, even if I have to be offered up for you.

¹² *Ώστε ἀγαπητοί μου, καθὼς πάντοτε ὑπηκούσατε, μὴ ὡς ἐν τῇ παρουσίᾳ μου μόνον, ἀλλὰ*

teri.' The student must always bear in mind the tendency of later writers to compound forms: see Thiersch, *de Pent.* II. 1, p. 83. The reading is doubtful: on the one hand the fut. [ACDEFGKL; 30 mss.; *Tisch.*] may be due to a change of vowels; on the other hand the subj. [B; *Lachm.* ex errore] is very probably a correction of the anomalous future. On the whole, it seems safer to adhere to the majority of MSS. For examples of ἵνα with a fut. see Winer, *Gr.* § 41. 1. h, p. 258.   Κύριος] Predicate put forward with especial emphasis; the contrary, as Mey. observes, is ἀνάθεμα Ἰησοῦς, 1 Cor. xii. 3. This august title is not to be limited; it does not refer to a κυριότης merely over rational beings (Hoelem.), but assures us that not only hath Jesus Christ 'an absolute, supreme, and universal dominion over all things, as God,' but that as the Son of Man He is invested with all power in heaven and earth; partly economical, for the completing of our redemption; partly consequent unto the union, or due unto the obedience of His passion, Pearson, *Creed,* Art. II. ad fin., Vol. I. p. 196 (ed. Burton).   εἰς δόξαν κ. τ. λ.] '*to the glory of God the Father,*' dependent on ἐξομολ., not on ὅτι κ. τ. λ.; *i. e.* the object contemplated by the act of confession (Mey., De W., Wiesing.), not the subject matter of it, Andrewes (*l. c.*), who, however, notices both. The transl. of Vulg., 'in gloriâ' (Æth., comp. Beng.), is an untenable alteration of the more correct 'in gloriam' [better '*ad* gloriam,' see Hand, *Tursell.* Vol. III. p. 317] of the Old Latin; so correctly Syr., Copt. (?). The confession of Jesus as Lord of all redounds 'to the glory of the Father, whose Son He is; their honor inseparable and their glory one,' Waterl. Vol.

II. p. 118: ὁρᾷς πανταχοῦ ὅταν ὁ Υἱὸς δοξάζηται, τὸν Πατέρα δοξαζόμενον. Οὕτω ὅταν ἀτιμάζηται ὁ Υἱὸς ὁ Πατὴρ ἀτιμάζεται, Chrys.,—true and wise words that it is well to bear in mind. We now pass on to a more easy paragraph.

12. ὥστε] '*So then.*' '*Consequently*;' exhortation directly and definitely flowing, not from all the previous admonitions, ch. i. 27 sq. (De W.), but more especially from the paragraph immediately preceding, εἰς τοῦτο ἀφορῶντες τὸ παράδειγμα, Theodoret. In the union of ὥστε with the imper. the usual force of the particle ('consecutio alicujus rei ex antecedentibus,' Klotz) is somewhat obscured,— the idea of real or logical consequence (see notes on *Gal.* ii. 13) merging into that of inferential exhortation; 'rem faciendam certo documento firmat,' Ellendt, *Lex. Soph.* Vol. II. p. 1013: see also Klotz, *Devar.* Vol. II. p. 776, and for examples, Winer, *Gr.* § 41. 5. 1, p. 269. In such a case the correct translation in Latin is not 'igitur' (Ellendt, *Lex. Soph.* s. v. p. 1013), nor even perhaps 'proinde,' Beza (which according to Heindorf = '*igitur* cum exhortatione quadam'), but 'itaque,' Vulg., this particle being more correctly n·ed of conclusions naturally flowing from what has preceded (*nexus realis*), 'igitur' of conclusions that are the result of pure ratiocination (*nexus logicus*); see especially Hand, *Tursell.* Vol. III. p. 187.

καθὼς πάντοτε κ. τ. λ.] '*as ye were always obedient:*' observe the latent parallelism to ὑπήκοος γενόμ. v. 8. But *to whom* was the obedience shown? Not, as the context might at first sight seem to suggest, '*mihi.*' Æth., Conyb., 'mihi ad salutem vos hortanti,' Beng., but, as the more plausible connection of μὴ ὡς κ. τ. λ. with the last clause seems to in-

νῦν πολλῷ μᾶλλον ἐν τῇ ἀπουσίᾳ μου μετὰ φόβου καὶ τρόμου

dicate, — to the tacit subject of the ὑπακοῇ in ver. 8, i. e. 'to God;' or what is in effect equivalent to it, 'Dei praeceptis ab apostolo traditis,' Estius; so Van Heng., Mey., Alf., and among the older expositors, Crell. and perhaps Justiniani. On the later form καθώς, see notes on Gal. iii. 6.   μὴ ὡς κ. τ. λ.] 'not as if in my presence only, but now much more in my absence.' These words must be connected with the succeeding imperative κατεργ. (Grot., Lachm.), not with the preceding nor. ὑπηκ., — a construction which would certainly seem to require οὐ (see Winer, Gr. § 55. 1, p. 422), and would tend to obliterate the force of νῦν. The ὡς (though omitted by B; a few mss.; Copt., Æth., al.) is certainly genuine, and not to be passed over in translation. The apostle does not content himself with the simple precept, κατεργ. μὴ ἐν παρ. κ. τ. λ. but also specifies the feeling and spirit with which they were to do it; i. e. not with the spirit of men who did it when he was present, but left it undone when he was absent, but who even in the latter case did it in a yet higher degree; see Mey. in loc., who has well explained the force of this particle. The slight difficulty arises from two oppositions — πάντοτε — νῦν, παρουσίᾳ — ἀπουσίᾳ being blended in a single enunciation.   μετὰ φόβου κ. τ. λ.] 'with fear and trembling,' i. e. with anxious solicitude, with a distrust in your powers that you can ever do enough; see especially Eph. vi. 5, and notes in loc.; compare also 1 Cor. ii. 3, 2 Cor. vii. 15, where the meaning is substantially the same. The 'fear' is thus to be referred, not directly to God (κομίζε παρεστάναι τὸν Θεόν, Chrys., Waterland, Works, Vol. v. p. 683), but only indirectly and inferentially; the φόβος arose directly from a sense of the greatness of the work and the possibility of failure; the τρόμος was the anxious solicitude which was naturally associated with it; see Conyb. in loc. An undue exhortation to humility (Neander, p. 475, or warning against false security (Cal.), is not required by the context and is not in accordance with what seems the regular meaning in which the present form of words is used by the apostle; see e. g. the good note of Harmood, who has well investigated the meaning of the expression; comp. Beveridge, Serm. xvi. Vol. 1. p. 294, who, however, is here less precise and discriminating.

τὴν ἑαυτῶν σωτηρ.] 'your own salvation;' the reflexive pronoun not without emphasis, hinting that now they were alone, and must act for themselves; compare Beng. Their salvation was something essentially individual, something between each man and his God. A reference to the example of Christ ('as He obeyed so do you obey,' Alf.) seems very doubtful; the whole exhortation refers to that example, but the individual pronoun more naturally points to the words which immediately precede it. The unsatisfactory interpretation ἑαυτῶν = ἀλλήλων (compare Michaelis) is fairly refuted by Van Heng. in loc. κατεργάζεσθε] 'complete,' 'carry out,' 'peragite,' Grot., 'perficite, perfectum reddite,' Just. 2; compare Rom. vii. 18, Eph. vi. 13, and see notes in loc., where the meanings of this verb are briefly noticed. The compound form does not imply the σπουδή or ἐπιμέλεια (Chrysost.), but the 'perseverantia' that was to be shown, the intensive κατά indicating the carrying through of the ἔργον; see Rost u. Palm, Lex. s. v., and s. v. κατά, iv. Vol. i. p. 1599. On the practical aspects of the doctrine, see the good sermon by Beveridge, Serm. xvi. Vol. i. p. 284 (A.-C. Library), Taylor, Life of Christ iii. 13. 16. Sherlock, Sermon

τὴν ἑαυτῶν σωτηρίαν κατεργάζεσθε· ¹³ Θεὸς γάρ ἐστιν ὁ ἐνεργῶν

XVIII. Vol. I. p. 311 (edit. Hughes).
13. Θεὸς γάρ κ. τ. λ.] '*for God is He who effectually worketh*,' etc.: yea, work and be not disheartened, for verily God is He who worketh within you. The γὰρ is not *argumentative* in reference to a suppressed thought, μὴ φόβου ὅτι εἶπον, μετὰ φόβ. καὶ τρόμου, Chrys., but *explanatory* (see notes *on Gal*. ii. 6), in reference to the preceding command, obviating any objection by demonstrating the vital truth on which it was based, and the great principle on which it was justifiable : ' work anxiously, work solicitously ; *verily* (' sane pro rebus comparatis,' Klotz, *Devar*. Vol. II. p. 232) ' God giveth you the ability ;' compare Lücke *on John* iv. 44. The omission of the article before Θεὸς is justified by ABCD¹ FGK ; al., and is adopted by *Lachm*. and *Tisch*. ὁ ἐνεργῶν] '*He who worketh effectually,*' ܡܚܦܛ [efficiens, sedulam operam navans] Syriac. The full meaning of this word, so frequently used by St. Paul, must not be obscured ; it appears in all cases to point not only to the inward nature of the working, but also to hint at the persistent and effective character of it, scil. ἐνεργὸν εἶναι, ' vim suam exercere ;' comp. Polyb. *Hist*. III. 6. 5, XVII. 14. 18, XXVII. 1. 11. When then Augustine urges in opposition to the Pelagian misinterpretation, ' Deus facit ut faciamus, *praebendo vires efficacissimas* voluntati,' he would seem to be no less verbally exact than doctrinally accurate : compare *de Grat. et Lib. Arb*. 9. 16, *contra Pelag*. 1. 19.

It may be remarked in passing, that ἐνεργεῖν is used several times in Polybius, see Schweigh. *Lex*. s. v. ; there is however this distinction between his use and that of St. Paul, that by the latter it is never used in the passive (see notes on *Gal*. v. 6), and by the former never in the middle; see Fritz. *Rom*. vii. 5, and for a notice of its various constructions, notes *on Gal. l. c*., and *ib*. ii. 8 : see also Suicer, *Thesaur*. Vol. I. p. 1115.

ἐν ὑμῖν] '*in you*,' *i. e*. in your minds, not among you ; this being alike precluded by the prevailing use of the verb (Matth. xiv. 2, 2 Cor. iv. 12, Gal. iii. 5 [see notes], Col. i. 29, al.) and the nature of the context. καὶ τὸ θέλειν κ. τ. λ.] '*both to will and to do*,' as much the one as the other. Observe especially the use of the more emphatic enumeration καὶ—καὶ ; the θέλειν no less than the ἐνεργεῖν is a direct result of the divine ἐνέργεια ; see Winer. *Gr*. § 53. 4; p. 389, notes *on* 1 *Tim*. iv. 10. Of these the first (τὸ θέλειν) is due to the inworking influence of sanctifying grace (Waterl. *Serm*. XXVI. Vol. V. p. 688), or, to speak more precisely, of *gratia praeveniens*, to which the first and feeblest motion of the better will, the first process of the better judgment (2 Cor. iii. 5), is alone to be ascribed ; comp. Andrewes, *Serm*. Vol. V. p. 303 : the second (τὸ ἐνεργεῖν) to the *gratia co-operans*, by the assistance of which *we strive* (' non per vires nativas sed dativas') to perform the will of God ; see Ebrard, *Christl. Dogm*. § 524, Vol. II. p. 566. The language of Chrys. *in loc*., ἂν θελήσῃς, τότε ἐνεργήσει τὸ θέλειν, might thus seem open to exception if the θελήσῃς is to be referred to a ' dispositio praevia ;' this however cannot be certainly inferred from his context. For the diversities of opinion on this text, even among Romanists, see the long and perspicuous note of Justiniani *in loc*., and for the differences among Protestants, and the necessary distinction between *passivity* (' homo convertitur nolens ') and *receptivity* (' ex nolente fit volens '), see Ebrard, *Christl. Dogm*. § 519—522, Vol. II. p. 558 sq. It may be remarked that

ἐν ὑμῖν καὶ τὸ θέλειν καὶ τὸ ἐνεργεῖν ὑπὲρ τῆς εὐδοκίας. 11 πάντα

the repetition of the word ἐνεργεῖν, (preserved correctly by Claroman., Coptic, but not Syr., Vulg.), rather than κατεργάζεσθαι, is due to the fact that it expresses more exactly *the inward ability showing itself in action*, and is thus more suitable in connection with θέλειν. While then this important verse is a conclusive protest against Pelagianism on the one hand, its guarded language as well as its intimate connection with ver. 12 show that it is as conclusive on the other against the Dordracene doctrines of irrevocable election (cap. 1), and all but compelling grace: cap. III. IV. 12, 16. Reject err. 8. ὑπὲρ τῆς εὐδοκ.] '*of His good pleasure*,' *i. e.* in fulfilment of, to carry it out and satisfy it; διὰ τὴν ἀγάπην, διὰ τὴν ἀρεσκείαν αὐτοῦ, Chrys. The prep. ὑπὲρ here seems to approach in meaning κατά (Eph. i. 5), or διά (Eph. ii. 4), but may still be clearly distinguished from either. It does not represent the εὐδοκία as the mere *ratio* of the action, or the mere *norma* according to which it was done, but, as the *interest* or *use* of it; the *commodum* of the εὐδοκία was that which the action was designed to subserve; comp. Rom. xv. 8, John xi. 4, where however the primary meaning of ὑπέρ is less obscured; see Winer, *Gr.* § 47. 1, p. 343, and compare Rost u. Palm, *Lex.* s. v. ὑπέρ, 2, Vol. II. p. 2067. Εὐδοκία is referred by Syr., Æth., Green (*Gram. N. T.* p. 202), to the '*bona voluntas*' of the Philippians: this is grammatically plausible, but owing to the preceding θέλειν (Meyer) not exegetically satisfactory. Still less probable is the connection of the clause with ver. 14 (Conyb.), which, independently of grammatical difficulties (see Alford), has the whole consent of antiquity, Ff. and Vv., opposed to it. On the meaning of εὐδοκία, see notes on *Eph.* i. 5, and compare Andrewes, *Serm.* XIII.

Vol. I. p. 239 (A.-C. Libr.).

14. πάντα] '*all things*,' not as only 'everything you have to do,' or wish of, to ver. 3 (Fell), but, as the context and the last of the two associated substantives seem to suggest, '*everything*' which stands in more immediate connection with the foregoing commands, and in which the malice of the devil might more especially be displayed;' see Chrysost. *in loc*. γογγυσμῶν] '*murmurings*;' compare 1 Pet. iv. 9, ἄνευ γογγυσμοῦ: here apparently against God, ὁ γογγύζων ἀχαριστεῖ τῷ Θεῷ, Chrys.; not, against one another, Wiesinger ('placide se gerant inter homines,' Calv.),—a command which he finds no natural place. Alford urges that in every place in the N. T. (only 4, and only here by St. Paul) γογγυσμ. refers to murmuring against *one*; but of these passages, one (John vi. 43) is not applicable, and another (1 Pet. iv. 9, compare De Wette) not perfectly certain. That it may be applied to God seems demonstrable from 1 Cor. x. 10. The forms γογγίζω and γογγ.-σμός, perhaps derived from the Sanscr. *ganj* 'to murmur,' Benfey, *Wurz.* N. Vol. II. p. 62] are said to be Ionic, the Attic forms being τονθορίζω and τονθ. σμός; see Lobeck, *Phryn.* p. 358, comp. on cum M. p. 856 (ed. Bern.). On the alleged but doubtful distinction between ἄνευ and χωρίς, see notes on *Eph.* i. 12.

διαλογισμῶν] '*doubts*,' 'hæsitationibus,' Vulg., Æthiop. [haesitatione], Copt. [cogitationibus].—not '*detractationibus*,' Clarom., or [Syriac] [divisione], a meaning not found in N. T., and apparently not supported by any good lexical authority; see especially notes on 1 Tim. i. 8, where this word is briefly noticed. Alford urges the use of διαλογίζω [read -ίζομαι] in Mark ix. 33,

ποιεῖτε χωρὶς γογγυσμῶν καὶ διαλογισμῶν, 15 ἵνα γένησθε

34; but even there the idea is 'discussion,' rather than 'dispute' or 'contention:' comp. Xenoph. *Mem.*, III. 5. 1.

15. ἵνα κ. τ. λ.] Object and aim not 'incitamentum' (Van Heng.), contemplated in the foregoing exhortation. They were to fulfil everything connected with the great command, ver. 12 sq., without murmurings and doubtings, that they might both outwardly evince (ἄμεμπτοι) and be inwardly characterized by (ἀκέρ.) rectitude and holiness, and so become examples to an evil world around them. When Alford urges against the internal reference of διαλ. that the object is outward,— blamelessness and good example, he suppresses the direct internal object ἀκέραιοι (suitably answering to χωρὶς διαλ.), and makes the appositionally stated, and more indirect object,— the good example, primary and direct. The reading is very doubtful; *Lachm.* reads ἦτε with AD F¹FG; Vulg., Clarom., al.; Lat. Ff.; but the external authority (BCD²E²KL; appy. all mss.; Chrys., Theod., Dam., al.) combined with the greater probability of correction seems slightly preponderant in favor of the text.   ἀκέραιοι] *'pure,'* simplices,' Vulg., Æth., 'sinceres[i],' Clarom.; not 'harmless,' Auth., Alf., --a meaning not recognized by the best ancient Vv., and neither in harmony with the derivation and lexical meaning of the word (ὁ μὴ κεκραμένος κακοῖς, ἀλλ' ἁπλοῦς καὶ ἀπόικιλος, *Etymol. M.*), nor substantiated by its use in the N. T.: see Matth. x. 16, ἀκέραιοι ὡς αἱ περιστεραί, Rom. xvi. 19, ἀκεραίους εἰς τὸ κακόν; in the former of which passages it stands in a species of antithesis to φρόνιμος, in the latter to σοφός; compare Suicer, *Thesaur.* s. v. Vol. I. p. 154, Krebs. *Obs.* p. 331, and for the distinction between ἀκέρ., ἁπλοῦς, and ἄκακος, Tittm. *Synon.* I. p. 27.   τέκνα Θεοῦ κ. τ. λ.] *'irreproachable, unblamable, children of God* [by virtue of the υἱοθεσία, Rom. viii. 15, 23] *in the midst*,' etc.; not 'irreproachable or blameless in the midst of,' Luth., a position which weakens the climactic force of the epithet, and obscures the apparent allusion to Deut. xxxii. 5, τέκνα μωμητά, γενεὰ σκολιὰ καὶ διεστραμμένη. Ἀμώμητος [*Lachm.* ἄμωμα, with ABC; 2 mss; but an apparent alteration] is a δὶς λεγόμ. in the N. T., here and 2 Pet. iii. 14 (*Lachm., Tisch.*), compare Hom. *Il.* XII. 109; and, as derivation and termination suggest, appears but little different from ἄμεμπτος, except as perhaps approaching nearer to ἄμωμος (Hesych. ἀμώμητος· ἄμωμος), and expressing not merely the unblamed (Xen. *Ages.* VI. 8), but non-blameworthy state of the τέκνα; compare Æsch. *Sept.* 508, and see Tittm. *Synon.* 1. p. 29.   The reading μέσον (adverbially used, Winer, *Gr.* § 54. 6), with ABCD¹FG (*Lachm., Tisch.*), has the weight of uncial authority as well as critical probability in its favor.
σκολιᾶς καὶ διεστρ.] *'crooked and perverted*,' in reference to their moral obliquity and their distorted spiritual growth; compare Deut. xxxii. 5. Σκολιός, allied probably to σκέλος, σκελλός, and σκαίρειν [Pott, *Etym. Forsch.* Vol. I. p. 268, root-form ΣΚ-, 'progression by steps,' Donalds. *Cratyl.* § 387, less probably ΚΡ-, Sanscr. *kri* with prefixed σ, Benfey, *Wurzell.* Vol. II. p. 363], occurs elsewhere in the N. T., once in a proper sense, Luke iii. 5, and twice, as here, in an ethical sense, Acts ii. 40, 1 Peter ii. 18. Διεστρ. is similarly found in Matth. xvii. 17, Luke ix. 41, Acts xx. 30; see also examples from Arrian in Raphel, *Annot.* Vol. II. p. 309.

ἐν οἷς] *'among whom*,'— in reference to the persons of which the γενεά was composed; comp. Winer, *Gr.* § 58. 4. b, p.

ἄμεμπτοι καὶ ἀκέραιοι, τέκνα Θεοῦ ἀμώμητα μέσον γενεᾶς σκολιᾶς
καὶ διεστραμμένης, ἐν οἷς φαίνεσθε ὡς φωστῆρες ἐν κόσμῳ,
¹⁵ λόγον ζωῆς ἐπέχοντες, εἰς καύχημα ἐμοὶ εἰς ἡμέραν Χριστοῦ,

457: so, somewhat similarly, Gal. ii. 2. φαίνεσθε] 'ye appear, are seen;' not 'lucetis,' Vulg., Clarom., Wordsw., al., which would require the active φαίνετε, John i. 5, v. 35, 2 Pet. i. 19, al. Alford objects that the active is not used by St. Paul: but will this justify a departure not only from the simple meaning of the word, but from the special use of the middle in connection with the *appearance* or rising of heavenly bodies? see examples in Rost u. Palm, *Lex.* s. v. 11. 1. b. The verb is indicative (Vulg., Copt., Æth.), not imperat. (Syr., Theophyl.): Christians were not to be, but now actually *were*, as luminaries in a dark, heathen, world; compare Matth. v. 14, Eph. v. 8.

φωστῆρες ἐν κόσμῳ] '*luminaries, heavenly lights in the world;*' ἐν κόσμ. being closely joined with φωστ. as its secondary predicate (Vulg. and all Vv.), not with φαίνεσθε (De W.), which would thus have two prepositional adjuncts. To illustrate the meaning of φωστ. compare Rev. xxi. 11, Gen. i. 14, 16, Ecclus. xliii. 7 (applied to the moon), Wisdom xiii. 2, and for the different uses of κόσμος, here apparently in its ethical sense, see notes *on Gal.* iv. 3. The reference to the use of torches to guide passengers along the narrow and winding streets of a city (Wordsw.) is ingenious, but scarcely in harmony with φαίνεσθε, and the tenor of the context.

16. ἐπέχοντες κ. τ. λ.] '*seeing ye hold forth (are the ministers of) the word of life;*' further and explanatory definition of the preceding, the participle having a slightly *causal* force. The meaning of ἐπέχ. is somewhat doubtful. It certainly cannot be for προσέχοντες, Theod., as this would require a dat.; it may, however, be either (a) *occupants*, comp. Syr.

ܐܝܟ ܕܗܘܝܬܘܢ ܠܗܘܢ ܒܕܘܟܬ ܚܝܐ

[ut sitis illis loco salutis] and thence, with a modification of meaning 'continentes,' Vulg., Claroman, 'tenentes,' Copt. (Æth. paraphrases), κατέχοντες, Chrys., ἔχοντες, Theoph., Œcum.,— a translation that has certainly a lexical basis (see examples in Rost u. Palm, *Lex.* s v. 1. b, Vol. t. p. 1029; and is far too hastily condemned by Van Heng. and Wiesing.; (β) *præcedentes*, Beza, Auth., 'doctrinam spectandam præbentes,' Van Heng., with reference to the preceding image. Of these interpr. (a), has clearly the weight of antiquity on its side; still as no *exactly* opposite example of the modified sense 'continentes' has yet been adduced, and as the meaning 'occupantes' involves an idea foreign to the N. T. (compare Meyer), we seem bound to adhere to (β), a meaning that is lexically accurate and exegetically satisfactory. The objection of Meyer is fully answered by Alford *in loc.*
The λόγος ζωῆς is the gospel. ζωῆς being a species of gen. of the *content*, τὴν αἰώνιον προξενεῖ ζωήν, Theod.: comp. John vi. 68, and notes on *Eph.* i. 13.

εἰς καύχημα] '*to form a ground of boasting for me;*' result, on the side of St. Paul, of his converts becoming ἄμεμπτοι καὶ ἀκέραιοι· τοσαύτη ὑμῶν ἡ ἀρετή, ὡς μὴ ὑμᾶς σώζειν μόνον, ἀλλὰ καὶ ἐμὲ λαμπρὸν ποιεῖν, Chrys.; comp. 2 Cor. i. 14. εἰς ἡμέραν Χρ.] '*against the day of Christ;*' the preposition not so much marking the epoch *to which* (ἕως), as that *for which*, in reference to which, the boasting was to be reserved; compare ch. i. 10, Eph. iv. 30, and notes on *Gal.* iii. 23. On the ex-

ὅτι οὐκ εἰς κενὸν ἔδραμον οὐδὲ εἰς κενὸν ἐκοπίασα. ¹⁷ ἀλλὰ εἰ καὶ σπένδομαι ἐπὶ τῇ θυσίᾳ καὶ λειτουργίᾳ τῆς πίστεως ὑμῶν, χαίρω καὶ συνχαίρω πᾶσιν ὑμῖν· ¹⁸ τὸ δ' αὐτὸ καὶ ὑμεῖς χαίρετε καὶ συνχαίρετέ μοι.

pression ἡμέρα Χρ., see notes on ch. i. 6. ἔδραμον, ἐκοπίασα] The same idea of ministerial activity presented in two different forms of expression, the one figurative, from the stadium (comp. Gal. ii. 2, 2 Tim. iv. 7), the other more general, involving the notion of the toil and suffering undergone in the cause; see notes on 1 Tim. iv. 10. For exx. of the adverbial εἰς κενόν, Heb. לָרִיק, Job xxxix. 16 (comp. εἰς καλόν, εἰς κοινόν, Bernhardy, Synt. v. 11, p. 221), see 2 Cor. vi. 1, Gal. ii. 2, 1 Thess. iii. 5, and Kypke, Obs Vol. i. p. 275.

17. ἀλλὰ κ. τ. λ.] 'Howbeit, if I be even poured out,' contrary hypothesis to that tacitly implied in the preceding verse. In no verse in this epistle is it more necessary to adhere to the exact force of the particles and the strict lexical meaning of the words. Ἀλλά, with its primary and proper force ('aliud jam hoc esse de quo sumus dicturi,' Klotz, Devar. Vol. II. p. 2), has no reference to a suppressed thought (οὐκ ἐκοπ. εἰς κέν., Rill.), but presents the contrary alternative to that already implicitly expressed. The preceding words εἰς καύχημα might seem to imply the expectation, on the part of the apostle, of a living fruition in the Christian progress (ἵνα γεν. ἄμεμπτ.) of his converts; the present verse shows the apostle's joy even in the supposition of his death; compare Bisping. So remote a reference as to ch. i. 26 (De W.) is wholly inconceivable; and even a contrast to an implied hope that the apostle would survive to the ἡμέρα Χρ. (Van Heng.) improbable, as εἰς ἡμ. Χρ. is only a subordinate thought to the general idea implied in εἰς καύχημα ἐμοί. εἰ καί must not be confounded with καὶ εἰ (Scholef. Hints, p. 106), but, in accordance with the position of the ascensive καί, marks a more probable supposition; the καί in the former case being referred to the consequent words (etsi or si etiam), but in the latter merely to the preceding condition (etiam si). Contrast Soph. Œd. Rex, 302, εἰ καὶ μὴ βλέπεις φρονεῖς δ' ὅμως, or ib. 304, εἰ καὶ μὴ κλύεις, with Æsch Choeph. 296, κεἰ μὴ πέποιθα, τοὔργον ἐστ' ἐργαστέον, and see especially Herm. Viger, No. 307, from which these examples are taken; see also Klotz, Devar. Vol. II p. 519, Hartung, Partik. καί, 3. 3, Vol. I. p. 141. Thus, then, in the present case, the apostle in no way seeks to limit the probability of the supposition; his circumstances, though by no means without hope (ch. i. 25), were still such as seemed to preclude any such limitation. It may be remarked, however, that καὶ εἰ is very rare in St. Paul; apparently only in 2 Cor. xiii. 4 (Rec., Tisch.), if indeed the reading be considered genuine; comp. Gal. i. 8.

σπένδομαι] 'am poured out,' am in the act of being so, in reference to the dangers with which he was environed; comp. ch. i. 20. The simple form, which must not be confounded either with ἐπισπένδ. (Herod. II. 39, IV. 62, Plut. Popl. § 4, al), or κατασπένδ. (Plutarch Alex. § 50, ib. Mor. p. 435 B, p. 437 A), both here and in 2 Tim. iv. 5, under the image of the ritual drink-offering which accompanied the sacrifice (Numb. xv. 5, xxviii. 7), alludes to the pouring out of his blood ('libor,'—not 'immolor,' as Vulg., Syriac, Copt.) and the martyr's death by which it might be reserved for the apostle to glorify God; see especially notes on 2 Tim. l. c., Suicer, Thesaur. Vol. II. p. 993, and the good note

I hope to send my unselfish son in the faith, Timothy, and to come myself.

19 Ἐλπίζω δὲ ἐν Κυρίῳ Ἰησοῦ Τιμόθεον ταχέως πέμψαι ὑμῖν, ἵνα κἀγὼ εὐψυχῶ γνοὺς

of Wordsworth *in loc.* ἐπὶ τῇ θυσίᾳ κ. τ. λ.] '*unto the sacrifice and (priestly) service of your faith.*' The exact meaning of θυσίᾳ is somewhat doubtful. There is certainly no ἓν διὰ δυοῖν (comp. Conyb.), but it may be doubted whether the use of the single article does not so connect θυσ and λειτ., that both may specify *acts* of which πίστ. is the common object; see Mey. *in loc.* As, however, θυσία in St. Paul's Epistles, and indeed throughout the N. T., apply. always means the thing sacrificed, not the action, we seem bound with Syriac, Vulg., Copt. [? for comp. John xvi. 2], Æth., and thus far Chrys. and Theod., to retain the simple meaning of θυσ. and to regard πίστεως as a common *gen. objecti* to both, standing in a species of appositional relation to the former (the faith, not the apostle [Chrys., Theod.], was the sacrif.) and of simple relation to the latter. The θυσία, then, is the sacrifice, the λειτ. the act of offering it by the apostle (Bisp.), and the object both of one and the other (in slightly different relations) the πίστις of the Philippians. 'Επὶ will thus be, not simply temporal, '*während*,' Meyer, nor simply ethical, '*propter*,' or '*in sacrificium*,' Æth., but will imply '*addition*,' '*accession to*' (Matth. xxv 20), and will point to the σπένδ. as the concomitant act; see esp. Arrian, *Alex.* vi. 19. 5, σπείσας ἐπὶ τῇ θυσίᾳ, cited by Raphel *in loc.*: so Van Heng. and De Wette. The local meaning is untenable, as with the Jews the libation was *not* poured on (Jahn, *Archaeol.* § 378), but *around* the altar; see Joseph. *Antiq.* III. 9. 4, and notes on 2 Tim. iv. 5. χαίρω καὶ συνχ] '*I rejoice, and jointly rejoice with you all;*' I rejoice absolutely (not ἐπὶ τῇ θυσ. χαίρ. Chrys.), *i. e.* on account of my probable σπένδεσθαι, and do herein

participate in rejoicing with you all; my joy is not altered on the supposition of my death. Συνχαίρω is not '*congratulator*,' Vulg.,—a meaning which the verb apparently may have in classical (Æsch. *d. Fals. Leg.* p. 94 , as well as post-classical writers (Polyb. *Hist.* xxix. 7. 4),—but '*simul gaudeo*,' Copt. [exulto cum] Syr. Æth. (?), the meaning which συνχ. always appears to have in the N. T., and to which the following verse offers no exegetical obstacle (Meyer, Alf.) but is rather confirmatory.

18. τὸ δ' αὐτό] '*you, on the same account;*' not 'in like manner,' Scholef. *Hints*, p. 106, but the simple pronominal accus. after χαίρω; compare Kruger, *Sprachl.* § 46. 5. 9. Meyer reads αὐτὸ τοῦτο, '*hoc ipsum*,' apparently by an oversight, as there is here no difference of reading. χαίρετε καὶ συνχ.] '*rejoice and jointly rejoice;*' not indic. Erasmus, but imper., as Syr and all the best Vv. The apostle had previously said that he rejoiced not only for himself, but associated them with this joy; lest they might think that the probable martyrdom of their loved apostle was not a subject for συνχαίρειν, he emphatically repeats in a reciprocal form (καὶ ὑμ.) what he had implied in the preceding verse,—that they were indeed to rejoice in this seemingly mournful alternative.

19. ἐλπίζω δέ] '*yet I hope;*' the oppositive δέ suggests that the σπένδ above mentioned was not necessarily considered either as certain or immediate. This hope was ἐν Κυρίῳ, it rested and was centred in Him, it arose from no *extraneous* feelings or expectations, and so would doubtless be fulfilled, θαρρῶ ὅτι ἐξαναστήσει μοι ὁ Θεὸς τοῦτο, Chrys.; see notes

τὰ περὶ ὑμῶν. ²⁰ οὐδένα γὰρ ἔχω ἰσόψυχον, ὅστις γνησίως τὰ περὶ ὑμῶν μεριμνήσει· ²¹ οἱ πάντες γὰρ τὰ ἑαυτῶν ζητοῦσιν, οὐ

on *Ephes.* iv. 17, vi. 1.

ὑμῖν] 'to you,' not ' unto you' in the sense of πρὸς ὑμᾶς,—a local usage of the dative too broadly denied by Alf. (see Winer, *Gr.* § 31. 5, p. 192; compare Hartung. *Casus,* p. 81 sq.), nor again the dat. *commodi*, De Wette, but the dative of the recipients (Mey), falling under the general head of what is technically termed the *transmissive* dat. ; compare Jelf, *Gr.* § 587. κἀγὼ εὐψυχῶ] '*I also* (I the sender us well as you the receivers) *may be of good heart.*' Εὐψυχ. is an ἅπ. λεγόμ. in the N. T., but is occasionally found elsewhere, compare Poll. *Onom.* III. 28 : the subst. εὐψυχία (Polyb. I. 57. 2, II. 55. 4, al.) and the adv. εὐψύχως (Polyb. x. 39. 2, al., Joseph. *Ant.* VII. 6. 2) are sufficiently common. The use of the verb in the imperative as a kind of epitaph is noticed by Rost u. Palm, *Lex.* s. v. ; Jacobs, *Anth. Pal.* p. 939.

20. γάρ] Reason for sending Timothy in preference to any one else : Τιμόθεον πέμπεις ; τί δήποτε ; Ναί, φησίν, οὐδένα γὰρ κ. τ. λ., Chrys.
ἰσόψυχον] '*like-minded,*' *i. e.,* with myself, ὁμοίως ἐμοὶ κηδόμενον ὑμῶν καὶ φροντίζοντα, Chrysostom ; compare Syr.

ܐܟܘܬܝ ܕܗܟܢܐ [qui sicut animam meam] : so expressly Copt., Syr. Timothy is not here contrasted with others (Beza), but, in accordance with the natural and logical reference of the ἰσότης to the subject of the sentence, with the apostle. On the distinction between ἰσόψ. 'qui eodem modo est animatus,' and σύμψυχος, 'qui idem sentit, unanimis,' see Tittmann, *Synon.* I. p. 67. The word is an ἅπ. λεγόμ. in the N. T., but is found occasionally elsewhere, both in classical (Æsch. *Agam.* 1479), and post-classical, Greek (Psalm liv. 13) ; comp. ἰσοψύχως,

Eustath. on *Ill.* XI. p. 764.

ὅστις] '*who ;*' not 'quippe qui,' but 'ita comparatus ut,' Mey., 'of that kind, who,' Alf., with reference to the ποιότης of the antecedent (οὐδεὶς τοιοῦτός ἐστιν, Chrys., comp. Hartung, *Casus,* D. 286) ; the relative being here used (to adopt a terminology previously explained) not *explicatively*, but *classifically*, or *qualitatively ;* see notes *on Gal.* iv. 24, and Krüger, *Sprachl.* § 51. 8 sq., where the difference between ὅς and ὅστις is briefly but satisfactorily explained.

γνησίως μεριμνήσει] ' will *genuinely care for,*' '*will have true care for ;*' with that genuineness of feeling which befits the relationship between the apostle and his converts ; γνησίως, τουτέστι πατρικῶς ; compare 1 Tim. i. 2, and see notes *in loc.* Μεριμνᾶν is always thus used with an accusative of the object by St. Paul,— contrast Matth. vi. 25 (dat.), ch. vi. 28, Luke x. 41 (with περί), ch. xii. 25 (absolutely),— and agreeably to its probable derivation and affinities, μεριμηρίζω, μέρμερος [Sanscr. *smri,*—'meminisse,' 'anxium esse,' Benfey, *Wurzellex.* Vol. II. p. 32, Donalds. *Cratyl.* § 410] denotes anxious thought, solicitude, 'ita curare ut solicitus sis' (comp. Luke x. 41), differing in this respect from the simpler φροντίζειν ; see Tittm. *Synon.* I. p. 187. The future is not ethical, but points to the time when Timothy should come to them.

21. οἱ πάντες γάρ] '*for all the rest* (now *with me) ;*' not 'plerique,' Wolf, but 'omnes quos nunc habeo mecum,' Van Heng., the article, apparently specifying the whole number of the others with St. Paul (cuncti), to whom the single one, Timothy, is put in contrast. On this use of the art. with πᾶς, see Krüger, *Sprachl.* § 50. 11. 12, compare Bernhardy, *Synt.* VI. 24, p. 320, and Rose,

τὰ Ἰησοῦ Χριστοῦ. ²² τὴν δὲ δοκιμὴν αὐτοῦ γινώσκετε, ὅτι ὡς πατρὶ τέκνον σὺν ἐμοὶ ἐδούλευσεν εἰς τὸ εὐαγγέλιον· ²³ τοῦτον μὲν οὖν ἐλπίζω πέμψαι, ὡς ἂν ἀφίδω τὰ περὶ ἐμέ, ἐξαυτῆς. ²⁴ πέποιθα δὲ ἐν Κυρίῳ ὅτι καὶ αὐτὸς ταχέως ἐλεύσομαι.

21. Ἰησοῦ Χριστοῦ] So *Lachmann*, with ACDEFG; mss.; many Vv.; Lat. Ff. (*Griesb.*, *Scholz*; *Rec.* inserts τοῦ). The reversed order is adopted by *Tisch.* with BL; great majority of mss.; Demid., Copt., Syr.; Philox.; many Ff. The external authority seems to preponderate decidedly in favor of the text.

in Middl. *Art.* p. 104 note, to whose li t of examples of the art. with πᾶς (plur.), when u ed without a subst., this passage may be added. The attempts to explain away this declaration are very numerous, but all either arbitrary or ungrammatical: this only it seems fair to urge, that the context does necessarily imply *some sort* of limitation, and does apparently warrant our restricting it to all those companions of St. Paul who were available for missionary purposes, who had undertaken, and were now falling back from the hardships of an apostle's life. Who these were, cannot be ascertained; compare Wiesing. *in loc.*

τὰ ἑαυτῶν] '*their own things,*' not specially τὴν οἰκείαν ἀνάπαυσιν καὶ τὸ ἐν ἀσφαλείᾳ εἶναι, Chrys., followed by Theoph. and Œcum., with reference to the difficulties and perils of the journey, but generally, 'sua,' Clarom., 'temporalia commoda consectantes,' Anselm,— considering their own selfish interests, and not the glory and honor of Christ; compare ver. 4.

22. τὴν δὲ δοκιμήν] '*But his tried character;*' contrast of the character of Timothy with that of the οἱ πάντες.

Δοκιμή, ܒܘܩܝܐ [probatio] Syr., 'experimentum,' Vulg., here and Rom. v. 4, 2 Cor. ii. 9, ix. 13, by a very easy gradation of meaning points to the indoles spectata,' Fritz. (*Rom.* v. 4, Vol. 1. p. 259), 'indoles,' Æth. [simply,—almost as we use 'character'], by which Timothy was distinguished, and of which

the Philippians themselves probably had personal experience on a former visit; comp. Acts xvi. 1–4 with ver. 12. The use of δοκιμή in the N. T. is confined to St. Paul's Epistles; compare Reuss, *Théol. Chrét.* iv. 20, Vol. ii. p. 229.

γινώσκετε] '*ye know;*' indicative, as Syr., Clarom., Copt., Æth., not imper., as Vulg., Corn. a Lap.,—a construction almost plainly inconsistent with the following words, which seem specially designed to explain and justify the assertion; καὶ ὅτι οὐχ ἁπλῶς λέγω, φησίν, αὐτοὶ ἐπίστασθε, ὅτι κ.τ.λ. Chrys. ὡς πατρὶ τέκνον] '*as a s n* with a *father*,' 'sicut patri filius,' Vulg., not 'with a father,' Syr., Auth. Ver.; such an omission of the preposition in the first member being apparently confined to poetry; see Jelf, *Gr.* § 650. 1. 2. Krüger, *Sprachl.* § 68. 9. 2. My. and Alf. deny unrestrictedly an omission of the prep. in the first member, but see Esch. *Suppl.* 313, Eurip. *Hel.* 872, and Jelf, *Gr.* § 650. 2. The construction affords an example of what is termed 'oratio variata:' the apostle, feeling that ἐδούλευσεν was scarcely suitable in connection with πατρί and τέκνον, proceeds with the comparison in a slightly changed form; ἐδούλευσεν,— not ἐμοί, as the construction might seem to require (Rom. xvi. 18), but σὺν ἐμοί, as the nature of the relation suggested; see Winer, *Gr.* § 63. 11. 1. p. 509. εἰς τὸ εὐαγγέλιον] '*for the gospel;*' not 'in the gospel,' Auth., Syr., 'in the doctrine of the gospel,' Æth., but 'in evange-

25 Ἀναγκαῖον δὲ ἡγησάμην Ἐπαφρόδιτον τὸν ἀδελφὸν καὶ συνεργὸν καὶ συνστρατιώτην μου, ὑμῶν δὲ ἀπόστολον καὶ λειτουργὸν τῆς

Epaphroditus, your messenger, who has been grievously sick, and has risked his life for me, I send back, that you may rejoice.

lium,' Vulg., i. e. to further the cause of the gospel; the preposition εἰς with its usual force denoting the object and destination of the action; compare Luke v. 4, 2 Cor. ii. 12, and Winer, *Gr.* § 49. a, p. 354.

23. τοῦτον μὲν οὖν] '*Him then;*' the μὲν being antithetical to δέ, ver. 24, and the retrospective οὖν continuing and concluding the subject of the mission of Timothy. On this force of οὖν see notes on Gal. iii. 5. ὡς ἂν ἀφίδω] '*whensoever I shall have seen (the issue of);*' in effect, 'so soon as I shall have, or have seen, etc.,' Auth., ὅταν ἴδω ἐν τίνι ἕστηκα, Chrys., but designedly couched in terms involving more of doubt, the particle ἂν being joined with the temporal ὡς to convey the complete uncertainty when the objectively-possible event specified by the subjunctive will actually take place; compare Jelf, *Gr.* § 841, Herm. *de Partic.* ἄν, II. 11, p. 120, and on the temporal use of ὡς, see Klotz, *Devar.* Vol. II. p. 759. The remark of Eustathius (p. 1214, 40) is very pertinent, ὅτι δέ ἐστί τις καὶ χρονικὴ ποτὲ σημασία, φαίνεται ἐν ἐπιστολῇ τοῦ βασιλέως Ἀντιόχου, οἷον, ὡς ἂν οὖν λάβῃς τὴν ἐπιστολήν, σύνταξον κήρυγμα ποιήσασθαι, ἤγουν ἡνίκα λάβῃς. He would, however, have been more correct if he had said ἡνίκ' ἄν, see Ellendt, *Lex. Sophocl.* Vol. I. p. 773. In the compound form ἀφιδ. the prep. is not intensive, 'see clearly' (Alf.), but local, referring, however, not to the object, but to the observer, 'prospicere,' and perhaps may further involve the idea of a 'terminus' looked to; see Jonah iv. 5 (a pertinent example), Herod. VIII. 37; compare ἀποδεᾶσθαι, ἀποσκοπεῖν, al., and especially Winer, *de Verb. Comp.* IV. p. 11. The change from the tenuis to the aspirate (with ABDFGא; 17, *Lachm.*, *Tisch.*) is ascribed by Winer (*Gr.* § 5. 1, p. 43) to the pronunciation of ἰδεῖν with a digamma; comp. Acts iv. 29 (*Lachm.*, *Tisch.*). τὰ περὶ ἐμέ] '*the things pertaining to me;*' not identical with τὰ κατ' ἐμέ (ch. i. 12), but with a faint idea of motion (occupation about, Acts xix. 25), in ref. to their issue and development; i. e. how they will turn, what issues they will have; ποῖον ἕξει τέλος, Chrys., ἐὰν τέλεον λάβῃ λύσιν τὰ δυσχερῆ, Theod. The form ἐξαυτῆς, sc. τῆς ὥρας, 'illico,' 'e vestigio' (παραυτίκα, Hesych., εὐθέως, Suid.), occurs in Mark vi. 25, Acts x. 33, al.

24. πέποιθ. ἐν Κυρίῳ] '*am confident in the Lord;*' He is the sphere of my confidence; see notes on ver. 19, and on *Eph.* iv. 17, vi. 1.

καὶ αὐτός] '*I myself also;*' the καὶ implying that besides sending Timothy to them, the apostle hoped himself to come in person. The ταχέως, as Meyer remarks, must, as in ver. 19, date from the present time, the time of writing the Epistle. In recurring, however, to the mission of Timothy, ver. 23, he expresses the hope that it would be ἐξαυτῆς, 'forthwith;' his own visit he had good confidence would be ταχέως, i. e. no long interval after.

25. ἀναγκαῖον δὲ ἡγησ.] '*yet I deemed it necessary;*' though probable, the mission of Timothy and the apostle's own visit were both contingent; he deemed it necessary therefore to send (back) one on whom he could rely, and in whom the Philippians had interest and confidence. Wiesinger denies any connection between the sending back Epaphr. and the mission of Timothy; this, however, is surely to overlook the antithesis suggested by δέ. On the use

χρείας μου, πέμψαι πρὸς ὑμᾶς, ²⁶ ἐπειδὴ ἐπιποθῶν ἦν πάντας

of the epistolary aorist (still more expressly ver. 28), see Winer, *Gr.* § 40. 5, b. 2, p. 249. Ἐπαφρόδιτον] Of Epaphroditus, beyond this passage, nothing is known. He has been supposed to be the same with Epaphras, Col. i. 7, iv. 12, Philem 23; but this, though etymologically possible, is certainly not historically demonstrable. As the name appears to have been not uncommon (Sueton. *Nero,* § 49, Joseph *contr. Ap.* I 1, al., see Wetst. *in loc.*),—as Epaphras was a Colossian (Col. iv. 12),—and as the alms of the European city of Philippi would hardly have been committed to the member of a church so remote from it as the Asiatic Colossæ, it seems natural to regard them as different persons. For the necessarily scanty literature on the subject, see Winer, *RWB.* Art. 'Epaphras,' Vol. i. p. 330.
τὸν ἀδελφὸν κ. τ. λ.] Three general but climactic designations of the (spiritual) relation in which Epaphroditus stood to the apostle, under the vinculum of the common article; my brother in the faith, fellow-worker in preaching it, and fellow-soldier in maintaining and defending it; on συνστρατ. compare 2 Tim. ii. 3, and notes *in loc.*
ὑμῶν δὲ κ. τ. λ.] 'but your messenger and minister to my need;' secular and administrative relation in which Epaph. stood to the Philippians. Ἀπόστολον is here used in its simple etymological sense, not 'apostolum,' Vulg., Claroin., τὴν ἐπιμέλειαν ὑμῶν ἐμπεπιστευμένον, Theod., Chrys. 2 (comp. Taylor, *Episc.* § 4. 3). but, as the context seems to require, 'legatum,' Beza, Beng.: comp. 2 Cor. viii. 3, and see notes *on Gal.* i. 1. Λειτουργὸν (Rom. xiii. 6, xv. 16) is used in its general and wider sense of 'minister' in ref. to the office undertaken by Epaphr. ὡς τὰ παρ' αὐτῶν ἀποσταλέντα κομίσαντα χρήματα, Theod. On the various meanings of λειτ. see Suicer, *Thesaur.* s. v. Vol. ii. p. 222. The connection is not perfectly certain, but on the whole it seems most natural to connect ὑμῶν with this as well as with the preceding subst., comp. ver. 30. so Scholef. *Hints,* p. 106; contr. De Wette (comp. Æth.), who, however, urges no satisfactory reason for the separation.
πέμψαι] It was really ἀναπέμψαι, comp. ch. iv. 18: if, however, as does not seem improbable, Epaphr. was sent to stay some little time with the apostle (Beng.), the simple form becomes more appropriate; comp. ver. 28, 30.

26 ἐπειδὴ κ. τ. λ.] Reason for the ἀναγκαῖον ἡγησάμην. The conjunction ἐπειδή, 'quoniam' [quom jam], 'sintemal,' 'since '(sith-then-ee, comp. Tooke, *Div. of Purl.* 1. 8, Vol. i. p. 253). differs thus, and thus only, from ἐπεί, that it also involves the quasi-temporal reference ('affirmatio rerum eventu petita,' Klotz) which is supplied to it by δή, and thus expresses a thing that at once ensues temporally or causally) on the occurrence or realization of another; see Klotz. *Devar.* Vol. ii. p. 518, Hartung, *Partik.* δή, 3. 3, Vol. i. p. 259. It is not of frequent occurrence in the N. T.; in St. Paul only, 1 Cor. i. 21, 22, xiv. 16, xv. 21. ἐπιποθῶν ἦν] '*he was longing after you all.*' On this use of pres. part. with the auxiliary verb, to denote the duration of a state (less commonly in ref. to an action), see Winer, *Gram.* § 45. 5, p. 311, and notes on *Gal.* i. 23. The construction is occasionally found in classical Greek (see examples in Winer, *l. c.*, and Jelf, *Gr.* § 375. 4), but commonly with the limitation that the part. expresses some property inherent in the subject On the (directive) force of ἐπὶ in ἐπιποθ.. see notes on 2 Tim. i. 4. ἀδημονῶν] '*in heaviness;*' see Matth. xxvi. 27, Λυ-

ὑμᾶς, καὶ ἀδημονῶν, διότι ἠκούσατε ὅτι ἠσθένησεν. ²⁷ καὶ γὰρ ἠσθένησεν παραπλήσιον θανάτῳ· ἀλλὰ ὁ Θεὸς ἠλέησεν αὐτόν, οὐκ αὐτὸν δὲ μόνον, ἀλλὰ καὶ ἐμέ, ἵνα μὴ λύπην ἐπὶ λύπην σχῶ. ²⁸ σπουδαιοτέρως οὖν ἔπεμψα αὐτόν, ἵνα ἰδόντες αὐτὸν πάλιν

πεῖσθαι καὶ ἀδημ., Mark xiv. 33, ἐκθαμβεῖσθαι καὶ ἀδημ. This somewhat peculiar verb is explained by Buttmann (*Lexil* § 6. 13) as properly denoting 'great perplexity (*Etym. M.* ἀλύειν καὶ ἀπορεῖν, ἀμηχανεῖν, Hesychius, ἀγωνιᾶν) leading to trouble and distress of mind,' and is to be referred not to a root ἀδέω (Wiesing.), but, as Buttmann plausibly shows, to ἀ, δῆμος; comp. ἀδημεῖν, and see Symm., Eccles. vii. 16, where the LXX. have ἐκπλαγῇς. How the Philippians heard of this, and why Epaphr. was especially so grieved, is not explained.

27. καὶ γὰρ ἠσθ.] 'For he really was sick;' the report you heard was true. In this formula the καί is not otiose, but either with its conjunctive force (comp. notes on ch. iv. 12) annexes sharply and closely the causal member, 'etenim' (comp. Soph. *Antig.* 330), or with its ascensive force throws stress on the predication, 'nam etiam,' as here; see Klotz, *Devar.* Vol. II. p. 642, Hartung, *Partik.* καί, 3. 1, Vol. I. p. 138. The remark of Hartung seems perfectly just that there is no inner and mutually modifying connection between the two particles (contrast καὶ δέ, notes on 1 *Tim.* iii. 10), but that their constant association is really due to the early position which γάρ regularly assumes in the sentence.

παραπλήσιον θανάτῳ] 'like unto death.' There is here neither solecism (Van Heng.) nor brachyology (De W.). Παραπλ. is the adverbial neuter (Polyb. III. 33. 17, with dat.; IV. 40. 10, absolutely; comp. Herod. IV. 99), and like the more usual form παραπλησίως (Plato, *Phædr.* p. 255 E) is associated with the regular dative of 'likeness or similarity;'

see Krüger, *Sprachl.* § 48.13. 8, Jelf, *Gr.* § 594, 2, and the numerous exx. in Rost u. Palm, *Lex.* s. v. The gen. is rare; compare Plato, *Soph.* 217 B, Polyb. *Hist.* I. 23. 6. The meaning is thus in effect the same as μέχρι θανάτου ἤγγισεν, ver. 30, πλήσιον ἀφίκετο θανάτου, Galen in Hippocr. *Epid.* 1. (cited by Wetst.). but the mode of expression is different.

λύπην ἐπὶ λύπην] 'sorrow coming upon sorrow;' λύπη arising from the death of Epaphr. in addition to the λύπη of my own captivity. Bisp.; not as Chrys. τὴν ἀπὸ τῆς τελευτῆς ἐπὶ τῇ διὰ τὴν ἀῤῥωστίαν γενομένην αὐτῷ, for, as Meyer justly observes, this would be clearly inconsistent with ἀλυπότερος, ver. 28. If the second λύπη had arisen from the *sickness* of Epaphr. it would have ceased when he was well enough to be sent away, and the apostle in that respect would have been not comparatively, but positively, ἄλυπος. The reading of the text is supported by ABCDE FGL; major. of mss. (*Lach.*, *Tisch.*), and differs only from the more usual ἐπὶ λύπῃ (*Rec.* with K; Chrys., Theod.) in implying motion in the accumulation; comp. Psalm lxviii. 27, Isaiah xxviii. 10, Ezek. vii. 26.   σχῶ] The subjunctive is here appropriately used after the præterite to mark the abiding character the sorrow would have assumed; see Winer, *Gram.* § 41. 1, p. 257, and especially Klotz, *Devar.* Vol. II. p. 618. This remark, however, must be applied with *great* caution in the N. T. where, in common with later writers, the use of the optative is so noticeably on the decline; see notes on *Gal.* iii. 19.

28. σπουδαιοτέρως] 'more diligently than I should have done if ye had

χαρῆτε κἀγὼ ἀλυπότερος ὦ. ²⁹ προσδέχεσθε οὖν αὐτὸν ἐν Κυρίῳ

30. ἔργον τοῦ Χρ] So *Rec.* with DEKL; al. (*Lachm.* with BFG; al., om. τοῦ Χρ. *Tisch.* omits τοῦ Χρ. only with C,—certainly insufficient authority.

παραβουλευσάμενος] The reading is doubtful. *Rec.* and *Tisch.* read παραβουλευσάμενος with CKL; most mss.; Chrys., Theod., al.; the meaning of which would be 'quum male consuluisset;' comp. Copt., '*paraboulostha*' [cited by *Tisch.* and *Alf.* for the *other* reading]; Syr. ܫܛ [sprevit], Goth. 'ufarmunnonds' [obliviscens], all of which seem in favor of παραβουλ. On the contrary, the form παραβολ. is adopted by *Griesb.*, *Lachm.*, and most modern editors with ABDEFGN; Clarom., Vulg., Aug., Æth. (both), al.; and Lat. Ff.,—and *rightly*, the weight of authority and appy. unique use of the word being in manifest favor of the text.

not heard, and been disquieted by the tidings of his sickness.' In examples of this nature, which are common both to the N. T. and classical Greek, the comp. is not used for the positive, but is to be explained from the context; comp. 1 Tim. iii. 14 (notes), 2 Tim. i. 17 (notes), and see Winer, *Gr.* § 35. 4, p. 247.

πάλιν may be connected with ἰδόντες (Beza, Auth.), but is more naturally referred to χαρῆτε (Vulg., Luth.), it being the habit of St. Paul to place πάλιν before the verb, wherever the structure of the sentence will permit; contrast 2 Cor. x. 7, Gal. iv. 9, v. 3. The same order is regularly adopted by St. Matthew; but St. Mark and St. John, who use the word very frequently, place it nearly as often after, as before, the verb with which it is associated; compare the extremely useful work, Gersdorf, *Beiträge*, p. 491 sq. ἀλυπότερος] '*less sorrowful:*' the joy felt by the Philippians will mitigate the sorrow (in his confinement) of the sympathizing apostle; ἐὰν ὑμεῖς χαίρητε, κἀγὼ χαίρω, Chrysost. The word ἀλυπ. is an ἅπ. λεγόμ. in the N. T.; in classical writers it is occasionally found in a transitive sense; comp. ἄλυπος οἶνος, Athen. 1. 29.

29. προσδέχεσθε οὖν] ' *Receive him then;*' in accordance with my intention in sending him (ἵνα κ. τ. λ.). The οὖν here perhaps slightly differs in meaning from the one immediately preceding. In ver. 28 it is slightly more inferential, here it relapses to its perhaps more usual meaning of 'continuation and retrospect,' Donalds. *Gr.* § 604. On the two uses of οὖν (the *collective* and *reflexive*), see Klotz, *Devar* Vol. ii. p. 717, compared with Hartung, *Partik.* Vol. ii. p. 9 sq., and on its varieties of translation, *Rev. Transl. of St. John*, p. x.

ἐν Κυρίῳ] '*in the Lord*,' almost, 'in a truly Christian mode of reception.' Christ was to be as it were, the element in which the action was to be performed, compare notes on ver. 19 and 24, and the caution in notes on *Eph.* iv. 1.

πάσης χαρᾶς] '*all joy*,' 'every form of it,' not 'summa lætitia,' De Wette (on *James* i. 2); see notes on ch. i. 20, or *Eph.* i. 8, and compare 1 Pet. ii. 1, where this *extensive* force of πᾶς seems made clearly apparent by the plural forms of the associated abstract accusatives. τοὺς τοιούτ. κ. τ. λ.] '*and such hold in honor;*' 'such,' scil. as Epaphroditus, who is the sort of specimen of the class. On the use of the art. with τοιοῦτος to denote a known individual or a whole class of such, see Kühner on Xenoph. *Mem.* 1. 5. 2, and notes on *Gal.* v. 21. The formula ἔντιμον ἔχειν, though not without parallel in classical Greek, *e.g.* ἐντίμ. ἡγεῖσθαι (Plato, *Polit.* p. 64 D), ποιεῖν, al., is more usually ex-

μετὰ πάσης χαρᾶς, καὶ τοὺς τοιούτους ἐντίμους ἔχετε, ³⁰ ὅτι διὰ τὸ ἔργον τοῦ Χριστοῦ μέχρι θανάτου ἤγγισεν παραβολευσάμενος τῇ ψυχῇ, ἵνα ἀναπληρώσῃ τὸ ὑμῶν ὑστέρημα τῆς πρός με λειτουργίας.

pressed with the adverb, *e. g.* ἐντίμως ἔχειν, ἄγειν, compare Plato, *Republ.* VII. p. 528 B, VIII. p. 548 A.

30. διὰ τὸ ἔργον τοῦ Χρ.] 'on account of the work of Christ.' All the Greek commentators refer these and the following words to the danger arising from persecution confronted by Epaphr. at Rome in his endeavor to minister to St. Paul; εἰκὸς οὖν παντὸς καταφρονῆσαι κινδύνου, ὥστε προσελθεῖν καὶ ὑπηρετήσασθαι, Chrys. The foregoing mention, however, of his sickness, and the subsequent statement of the object contemplated by the τὸ παράβολον of his conduct, seem to restrict the reference simply to the service undertaken, and rendered by, Epaphroditus to the apostle, the performance of which exposed him to the danger of an all but mortal sickness. Τὸ ἔργον τοῦ Χρ. is thus not τὸ εὐαγγ. Baumg.-Crus. (compare Rill.), but the service which, by being rendered immediately to the apostle, became immediately rendered to Christ.

μέχρι θανάτου] '*up to death;*' extent of the danger; compare Job XXXII. 2, ἤγγισε εἰς θάνατον ἡ ψυχὴ αὐτοῦ, Isai. XXXVIII. 1, ἐμαλακίσθη ἕως θανάτου; and still more expressly, 4 Macc. 7, μέχρι θανάτου τὰς βασάνους ὑπομεινάντας, and Polyæn. *Stratagem.* p. 666 (Wetstein), μέχρι θανάτου μαχοῦνται. On the force of μέχρι and ἄχρι, see notes *on 2 Tim.* ii. 9. παραβολ. τῇ ψυχῇ] '*having risked, hazarded his life (soul);*' 'tradens,' Vulgate; 'parabolatus de,' Clarom.; 'tradidit,' Æth. The form and meaning of this word has been well investigated by Meyer. It would appear to have been formed from the adj. παράβολος, 'venturesome' (φιλοκίνδυνος καὶ παράβ., Diod. Sic. XIX. 3), like περπερεύεσθαι (1 Cor. xiii. 4), from πέρπερος, and to belong to a class of words in -εύω rightly branded by Lobeck as 'longe maxima pars invecticia,' and designed to express the meaning of the adj. and auxiliary; see Lobeck, *Phryn.* p. 67, 591, and Winer, *Gram.* § 16. 1, p. 85. The meaning will then be παράβολος εἶναι, and thus really but little different in meaning from παραβουλ.,—at any rate as the latter is explained by Theophyl., ἐπέρριψεν ἑαυτὸν τῷ θανάτῳ. Meyer compares παραβάλλομαι τῇ ἐμαυτοῦ κεφαλῇ, Lobeck, *Phryn.* p. 238. The figurative reference to the *stake* (παραβόλιον or παράβολον) which the appellant deposited, and if lost forfeited (Wordsworth), is scarcely so probable as the simpler explanation adopted above. The dative ψυχῇ is the dative 'of reference,' and with the true limiting character of that case expresses the sphere to which the action is confined; see notes *on Gal.* i. 20, and Winer, *Gr.* § 31 6, p. 193. On the relation of the ψυχὴ to animal life, and its intimate connection with the blood, see esp. Delitzsch, *Bibl. Psychol.* IV. 11, p. 195 sq., Beck, *Bibl. Seelenl.* I. 2, p. 4. ἀναπληρώσῃ] '*fill up,*' '*supply;*' compare Col. i. 24 (ἀνταναπλ.), and 1 Cor. xvi. 17. The primary and proper meaning of this compound verb is '*explere,*' '*totum implere*' (1 Thess. ii 16), and thence by an easy gradation of meaning. 'supplere,' the ἀνὰ denoting the addition, or rather making *up*, of what is lacking; comp. Plato, *Conviv.* p. 188 E, εἴ τι ἐξέλιπον σὸν ἔργον ἀναπληρῶσαι. It is thus never merely synonymous with πληροῦν, but has regularly a reference more or less

Rejoice, brethren; beware of Judaizers who trust in the flesh. I have every cause to trust therein, but value nought save Christ, His righteousness, and the power of His resurrection.

III. Τὸ λοιπόν, ἀδελφοί μου, χαίρετε ἐν Κυρίῳ. τὰ αὐτὰ γράφειν ὑμῖν, ἐμοὶ μὲν οὐκ

distinct to a *partial* rather than an entire *vacuum*. Such examples as Thucyd II. 28 (d autoi, belong to another use of the prep.; see especially Winer, *de Verb. Comp.* III. p. 11 sq., and notes on *Gal.* vi. 2. τὸ ὑμῶν ὑστ. κ.τ.λ] 'your lack, i.e. that which you lacked, in your service to me;' ὑμῶν being the gen. of the subj. to ὑμεῖς ὑστερήσατε, Theoph.), and so a kind of gen. *possessivus*, and τῆς λειτουργ., the gen. of the object in reference to which the ὑστέρημα was evinced, and so a gen. of what has been termed 'the point of view;' see Scheuerl. *Synt.* § 17. 2, p. 127 sq., where these double genitives are briefly but clearly discussed; comp. also Winer, *Gr.* § 30. 3. 3, p. 172. There is therefore in the words no call to modesty or humility (Chrys.) on the ground that ὁ πάντες ὀφείλετε μόνος πεποίηκεν (Theod.),—as this would imply a virtual connection of ὑμῶν with λειτουργίας, but only a gentle and affectionate notice of the complete nature of the services of the emissary. All that the Philippians lacked was the joy and privilege of a personal ministration; this Epaphrod. by executing the commission with which he was charged (τῆς πρός με λειτ. comp. verse 25) supplied,—and to the full. It would thus seem probable that the illness of Epaphroditus was connected, not with his journey, but with his anxious attendance on the apostle at Rome. See Meyer *in loc.*, who has well explained the true meaning of this delicate and graceful commendation.

CHAPTER III. 1. τὸ λοιπόν] 'Finally;' preparation for, and transition to, the concluding portion of the Epistle, again repeated yet more specifically ch. iv. 8; compare 2 Cor. xiii. 11, 1 Thess.

iv. 1, 2 Thess. iii. 1, and for the grammatical difference between this and the gen. τοῦ λοιποῦ, see notes on *Gal.* vi. 17. There is perhaps a slight difficulty in the fact, that subjects previously alluded to are again touched on, and that the person l relation of the apostle to the Judaists is so fully stated in a concluding portion of the Epistle. Without having recourse to any arbitrary hypotheses (comp. Van Heng.), it seems enough to say, *first*, that the exhortations all assume a more generic form.— χαίρετε, as Wiesing. remarks, is the key-note, and *secondly*, as Alf. suggests, that the mention of κατατομή leads to one of those digressions, expressively but too familiarly, termed by Paley, 'going off at a word,' which so noticeably characterize the writings of the inspired apostle; see *Horæ Paul.* ch. vi. 3.

χαίρετε ἐν Κυρίῳ] 'rejoice in the Lord;' their joy is to be no joy κατὰ τὸν κόσμον, hollow, earthly, and unreal, but a πνευματικὴ συμηδία (Theod.), a joy in Him; in whom αἱ θλίψεις αὐται ἔχουσι χαράν, Chrys.; compare ch. iv. 10, 24, 29, and notes. τὰ αὐτά] It is very doubtful to what these words refer. Out of the many opinions that have been advanced, three deserve consideration: (*a*) that they refer to exhortations in a lost Epistle (Flatt, Mey.); (*b*) that they refer to oral communications, whether made to the Phil. personally (Calv.), or recently communicated to Timothy and Epaphr. (Wieseler); (*c*) that they refer to the words just preceding, viz. χαίρετε ἐν Κυρίῳ (Wiesing., Alf.). Of these (*a*), whatever may be said of the general question (see notes on *Col.* iv. 16), must *here* be pronounced in a high degree doubtful and precarious, and is expressly rejected by Theodoret

ὀκνηρόν, ὑμῖν δὲ ἀσφαλές. ² βλέπετε τοὺς κύνας, βλέπετε τοὺς

the remark in Polyc. *Phil.* § 3, ὃς καὶ ἅπων ὑμῖν ἔγραψεν ἐπιστόλας, seems fairly neutralized by 'epistolæ ejus,' ch. 11, see Wies. *Chron.* p. 460, and comp. Wordsw. *in loc.* The second (*b*) is well defended by Wieseler, *l. c.*, p. 459 sq., but implies an emphasis on γράφειν, which neither the language nor the order of the words in any way substantiates. The last (*c*) appears on the whole open to least objection, as χαίρειν *does* seem the pervading thought of the Epistle, ch. i. 4, 18, ii. 17, iv. 4, 10, and to have been the more dwelt upon as the actual circumstances of the case might have very naturally suggested the contrary feeling; compare Chrys. *Hom.* x. init., who, however, refers τὰ αὐτὰ to what follows, though admitting the appropriate nature of the precept. The grammatical objection to the plural τὰ αὐτὰ (Van Heng.) is of no weight; the plural idiomatically refers to and generalizes the foregoing precept, hinting at the particulars which it almost necessarily involves; see Jelf, *Gr.* § 383, Kühner on Xenoph. *Mem.* III. 6 6, and the examples collected by Stallbaum on Plato, *Apol.* p. 19 D, and *Gorg.* p. 447 A.

ὀκνηρόν] '*grievous,*' '*irksome;*' compare Soph., *Œd. Rex.* 834, ἡμῖν ταῦτ' ὀκνηρά. The primary idea of ὄκνος and ὀκνηρὸς seems that of 'delay,' or 'loitering,' whether from fear or sloth (Matth. xv. 26, Rom. xii. 11), and thence that which is productive of such feelings in others. The derivation is uncertain; perhaps from Sanscr. *rak*, with the notion of 'bending,' 'stooping,' or 'cowering' (?), see Benfey, *Wurzellex.* Vol. II. p. 22.   ἀσφαλές] '*sure*,' '*safe*;' *i. e.* in effect, as Syr. paraphrases, ܡܛܠ ܕܠܟܘܢ ܡܥܗܕܝܢ [propterea quod vos commonefaciunt]. The word is pressed both by Wieseler (*l. c.*) and De W., though on different sides, and is confessedly somewhat singularly used. It seems, however, suitable on the grounds alleged above, viz, that the Philippians might think they had every reason — not χαίρειν but ἀθυμεῖν. The quasi causative sense is parallel to that in ὀκνηρόν; compare Joseph. *Antiq.* III. 2. 1.

2. βλέπετε] '*look to,*' '*observe;*' '*videte,*' Vulg., Goth., Copt, not 'beware of,' Auth. Ver., with Syr., this being a derived meaning (Winer, *Gram.* § 32. 2, p. 200): Æth (Platt) unites both. This exhortation not unnaturally follows. The remembrance of the many things that wrought against τὸ χαίρ. ἐν Κυρ. rises before the apostle; one of the chief among which,—perhaps immediately suggested by the word ἀσφαλές, — he now enumerates. It was here that a σφάλμα was in some degree to be feared. τοὺς κύνας] '*the dogs,*' not so much, in the *classical* use of the term, in ref to the impudence (Poll. *Onom.* v. 65), or the snarling and reviling spirit (Athen. XIII. § 93), of those so designated,—as in the *Jewish* use, in ref. to the impure (Rev. xxii. 15), and essentially ethnic (Matth. xv. 27, comp. Schoettg. *Hor.* Vol. I. p. 1145), and antichristian character of these spiritual enemies of the Philippians; ὥσπερ οἱ ἐθνικοὶ καὶ τοῦ Θεοῦ καὶ τοῦ Χριστοῦ ἀλλότριοι ἦσαν, Chrys.   τοὺς κακοὺς ἐργ.] '*the evil workers;*' compare 2 Cor. xi. 13, ψευδαπόστολοι, ἐργάται δόλιοι; they were ἐργάται certainly, but the ἐργάζεσθαι was ἐπὶ κακῷ, Chrys. The use of the article seems to show that there were some whom the apostle especially had in his thoughts.   τὴν κατατομήν] '*the concision,*' Auth.; *i. e.* 'the concised' ('curti Judæi,' Hor. *Sat.* 1. 9. 70), 'truncatos in circumcisione,' Æthiop. (Platt) *appy.* [but (?), as

κακοὺς ἐργάτας, βλέπετε τὴν κατατομήν. ³ ἡμεῖς γάρ ἐσμεν ἡ περιτομή, οἱ Πνεύματι Θεοῦ λατρεύοντες καὶ καυχώμενοι ἐν Χριστῷ Ἰησοῦ καὶ οὐκ ἐν σαρκὶ πεποιθότες, ⁴ καίπερ ἐγὼ ἔχων

the word in the original has *also* ref. to excomm unniention; compare Theod.]: a studiedly contemptuous paronomasia, see examples in Winer, *Gr.* § 68. 2, p. 561. The apostle will not say περιτομή, as this, though now abrogated in Christ (1 Cor. vii. 19, Gal. vi. 15), had still its spiritual aspects (ver. 3, Rom. ii. 29, Col. ii. 11),—but κατατομή, a mere hand-wrought, outward mutilation (compare Eph. ii. 11), which these false teachers gloried in and sought to enforce on others; οὐδὲν ἀλλὰ ποιοῦσιν ἢ τὴν σαρκὰ κατατέμνουσιν, Chrys. The reference to excommunication (Theod., Hammond) seems wholly out of place: indeed it is singular that such a very intelligible allusion should have received so many, and some such monstrous interpretations, *e.g.* Baur, *Paulus*, p. 435.

3. ἡμεῖς γὰρ κ. τ. λ.] 'For we are the circumcision;' reason for the designation immediately preceding: 'I say κατατομή, for you and I, whether circumcised in the body or no, are the circumcision, περιτομή in its highest, truest, and spiritual sense,—the circumcised in heart, לב מול (Ezek. xliv. 7);' see Rom. ii. 29, and the good note of Fritz. *in loc.* On the spiritual aspects of περιτομή, see particularly Ebrard, *Abendm.* § 2, Vol. i. p. 23 sq., Kurtz, *Gesch. der Alt. Bund.* § 58. 3, p. 184 sq., where the subject is well discussed.

οἱ Πνεύματι κ. τ. λ.] 'who by the Spirit of God are serving;' apposition by means of the substantival participle (compare Winer, *Gr.* § 45. 7, p. 316), and indirect epexegesis of the preceding collective designation. The sentence might have been expressed by means of ὅσοι or οἵτινες with the indicative, but the former would have too much limited the class, while the latter would have seemed too purely explanatory of the allusion, and so would have weakened the force of the antithesis. The d ive Πνεύμ. is not the dative *usus* (Van Heng., compare notes on *Gal.* v. 16), but, as the context seems to require, the dative *instrumenti*, or what Krüger perhaps more correctly terms, the 'dynamic' dat. (*Sprachl.* § 48. 15), compare Rom. viii. 14, Galat. v. 5, 18. al.; the Holy Spirit was the influence under which the λατρεία was performed; compare John iv. 23. The reading Θεοῦ rests upon the authority of all the uncial MSS. except D¹; more than 60 mss.; Copt., Syr. (Philox), in marg., al., and is adopted by all modern editors. It is to be regretted that Middleton (*Gr. Art.* p. 371) should be led by a doubtful theory to oppose himself to such a preponderance of authority. It seems perfectly reasonable to consider Πνεῦμα Θεοῦ as a proper name, and as having a similar freedom in respect to the article; see Fritz. *Rom.* viii. 4, Vol. ii. p. 105, compare notes on *Gal.* v. 5.

λατρεύοντες] Absolutely, as in Luke ii. 37, Acts xxvi. 7, Heb. ix. 9, x. 2. For a sermon on this and the following verses, more, however, resembling a commentary, see Augustine, *Serm.* CLXIX. Vol. v. p. 915 sq. (ed. Migne).

καὶ οὐκ κ. τ. λ.] '*and not trusting in the flesh;*' opposition to the preceding, though still under the vinculum of a common article: 'we boast in Christ Jesus,—and in the flesh, the bodily and external, far from boasting as they did (Gal. vi. 13), we go not so far even as to put trust.' On the definite negation implied by οὐ with the part., see Winer, *Gr.* § 55. 5, p. 430, Green, *Gr.* p. 120. Σάρξ does not specially and exclusively refer to *circumcision*, but, as the widening

πεποίθησιν καὶ ἐν σαρκί. εἴτις δοκεῖ ἄλλος πεποιθέναι ἐν σαρκί,
ἐγὼ μᾶλλον· ⁵ περιτομῇ ὀκταήμερος, ἐκ γένους Ἰσραήλ, φυλῆς

nature of the context seems to suggest, to the outward, the earthly, and the phenomenal; see Hofmann, *Schriftb*. Vol. 1. p. 541, Müller, *Doctr. of Sin*, II. 2, Vol. I. p 353 (Clark).

4. καίπερ ἐγὼ κ. τ. λ.] '*although myself having*,' etc.; concessive sentence introduced by καίπερ, qualifying the assertion which immediately precedes; see Donalds. *Gr*. § 621. The construction involves but little difficulty. In the preceding ἡμεῖς and οὐ πεποιθ. the apostle is himself included: lest this disavowal of πεποιθ. ἐν σαρκί might on his part be attributed to the absence or forfeiture of claims, rather than the renunciation of them, he passes at once by means of ἐγὼ to *his own* case, and proceeds as if the foregoing clause had been in the singular; 'I put no trust in the flesh, though, as far as externals are concerned, I for my part have an inalienable and *de jure* right (ἔχων) to do so.' Thus, then, καίπερ has its proper construction with the part., and the concessive sentence a simple and perspicuous relation to the foregoing clause. Καίπερ, only used in this place by St. Paul (Heb. v. 8, vii. 5, xii. 17, 2 Pet. i. 12), has its regular meaning, 'even very much' (see Klotz, *Devar*. Vol. II. p. 723), the πὲρ (περὶ) giving to the simple καὶ the idea of 'ambitum rei majorem' (Klotz), or perhaps, more probably, the intensive meaning of 'through-ness' or 'completion;' see Donalds. *Cratyl*. § 178. The meaning 'though,' it need scarcely be said, arises from its combination with the participle. πεποιθ. καὶ ἐν σαρκί] '*confidence even in the flesh*,' 'in it as well as ἐν Χρ.,' the force of καὶ being apparently *descensive;* see notes on *Gal*. iii. 4. There is no reason for modifying the meaning of this word ('gloriandi argumentum,' Calv.), or that of the simple pres. part.

ἔχων ('rem praeteritam facit praesentem,' Van Heng.): πεποιθ. is simply καύχησις, παρρησία, Chrys., and is actually *now* possessed by the apostle; he still has it, though he will not use it; 'habens, non utens,' Beng. δοκεῖ is certainly not pleonastic (see examples in Winer, *Gr*. § 65. 7, p. 540), but may be either (*a*) in the opinion of others, — '*videtur esse*, quam *vere esse* dicere mavult,' Fritz. *Matth*. iii. 9, p. 129, compare 1 Cor. xi. 16, where such a meiosis seems plausible; or (*b*) in his own opinion, — 'opinionem qua quis sibi placeat,' Van Heng., as 1 Cor. iii. 18, viii. 3, al., and appy. in the great majority of cases in the N. T. The latter seems best to suit the presumptuous, subjective πεποίθησις of these Judaists, and does not seem at variance (Mey.) with ἐγὼ μᾶλλον, scil. δοκῶ πεποιθ. ἐν σαρκί, which follows: so Syr., and apparently Copt. Æth. (Platt).

5. περιτομῇ ὀκταήμερος] '*eight days old when circumcised*, lit. *in respect of circumcision*,' dat. of 'reference,' Winer, *Gr*. § 31. 6, p. 193, notes on *Gal*. i. 22. Ritualistic distinction, followed by his natal prerogatives, and (ver. 6) his personal and theological characteristics. Circumcision on the eighth day (Levit. xii. 3) distinguished the native Jew, whether from proselyte or Ishmaelite, the latter of whom was circumcised after the thirteenth year, Joseph. *Antiq*. 1. 12. 2. The nom. περιτομή, which is found in *Steph*. 3, *Elz*. (1624, 1633), with some few mss., and apparently Chrys., Theod., is not correct: the abstract περιτομή is suitably used for the concrete in its collective sense (ver. 3), but apparently never, as assumed here, for a *single* person, Winer, *Gr*. § 31. 3 (ed. 5): so Van Heng., Meyer. ἐκ γένους Ἰσρ.] '*of the race of Israel;*' gen. of

Βενιαμίν, Ἑβραῖος ἐξ Ἑβραίων, κατὰ νόμον Φαρισαῖος, κατὰ

apposition or *identity*, Schenerl. § 12. 1, p. 82, 83: first of the three climaxes the distinctions in regard to race, tribe, and lineage; 'in censum nunc venit splendor natalium,' Van Heng. Ἐκ. γέν. Ἰσρ. is exactly equivalent to Ἰσραηλίτης in the very similar passages, Rom. xi. 3, 2 Cor. xi. 22, and, as the designation Ἰσραὴλ suggests (see Harl. *on Eph.* ii. 12, Meyer *on Cor.* xi. 22), stands in distinction to Idumæan, Ishmaelite, or ethnic origin in a *theocratic* point of view; compare also Trench, *Synon.* § 39. The περιτ. show'd that the apostle was no proselyte; the ἐκ γέν. Ἰσρ. that he was οὐδὲ προσηλύτων γονέων, Chrys. *in loc.* Meyer and Alf. following Theodoret refer Ἰσρ. to the πρόγονον Jacob, but this seems to mar the symmetry of the climax and the parallelism with Rom. xi. 3 and 2 Cor. xi. 22.

φυλῆς Βενιαμίν] '*of the tribe of Benjamin;*' of one of the two most illustrious of the tribes, a true son of the ἀποικία (Ezra iv. 1). Some of the descendants of the other tribes were still existing, and though amalgamated under the common name, Ἰουδαῖοι, could still prove their descent; compare Jost, *Gesch. des Isr. Volks,* Vol. i. p. 407 sq., and Winer, *RWB.* Article 'Sämme,' Vol. ii. p. 515. The assertion of Chrys., ὥστε τοῦ δοκιμωτέρου μέρους, τὰ γὰρ ἱερέων ἐν τῇ κλήρῳ τὰ τῆς ἦν τῆς φυλῆς, is apparently not historically demonstrable. Ἐβραῖος ἐξ Ἑβρ.] '*a Hebrew of Hebrews,*' a Hebrew of Hebrew parentage *and* ancestry, a Hebrew of pure blood; εἰς αὐτὴν τὴν ῥίζαν ἀνέδραμεν, Theodoret: compare Dion.-Hal. iii. p. 163, ἐλεύθεροι ἐξ ἐλευθέρων, Polyb. *Hist.* ii. 59. 1, ἐκ τυράννων πεφυκότα, and other examples in Kypke. *Obs.* Vol. ii. p. 115. It does not seem proper to limit it merely to Hebrew *parents* on both sides (Mey., Alf.). Owing

to the loss of private records in earlier times (comp. Ezra ii. 59, &c.) and the confusions and troubles in later times, there might have been (notwithstanding of the care with which private genealogies were kept, Othon. *Lex. Judg.* p. 76, 324) many a Benjamite, especially among those whose families had left Palestine, who could not prove a pure Hebrew descent. Thus the Jew of Tarsus, the Roman citizen, familiarly speaking and writing Greek, might naturally feel anxious to vindicate his pure descent, and to claim the honorable title of Ἑβραῖος ἐξ ὧν ὤσεν τῶν εὐδοκίμων Ἰουδαίων, Chrys. for himself and his forefathers; compare Winer, *RWB.* Vol. i. p. 472, 473. That Ἑβραῖος may also have reference to language (Chrys.) is for too summarily denied by Meyer and Alford; see Trench, *Synon.* § 39. That it has reference to locality (Palestinian not Hellenist) is every way doubtful: the assertion of Jerome, by which it is supported, that St. Paul was born at Gischala in Palestine, appears only to be (as the writer himself terms it, a 'fabula;' see Neander, *Pflanz.* Vol. i. p. 79 (Bohn).

κατὰ νόμον κ.τ.λ.] 'in respect of the law (of Moses) a Pharisee,' *sc.* in regard of keeping or maintaining it, the prep. κατὰ being used throughout in its more general signification of 'general attitude ad;' compare Winer, *Gr.* § 49. d, p. 357. Νόμος is here the 'Mosaic law;' though it may occasionally have what Reuss calls 'signification générique, tout ce qui tient à l'ancienne dispensation' (*Théol. Chrét.* iv. 7. Vol. ii. p. 66), this would be here out of harmony with the following δίκαιος. ἡ ἐν νόμῳ The present and two following clauses state the theological characteristics of the apostle, arranged perhaps climactically, a Pharisee, a zealous Pharisee, and a blameless Pharisee; comp. Acts xxii.

ζῆλον διώκων τὴν ἐκκλησίαν, κατὰ δικαιοσύνην τὴν ἐν νόμῳ γενόμενος ἄμεμπτος. ⁷ Ἀλλ᾽ ἅτινα ἦν μοι κέρδη, ταῦτα ἥγημαι διὰ

3, xxvi. 5, Gal. i. 14.

6. κατὰ ζῆλον κ.τ.λ.] 'in respect of zeal — persecuting the Church;' comp. Gal. i. 13; said here *perhaps* not without a tinge of sad irony; even in this respect, this mournful exhibition of Judaist zeal, he can, if they will, set himself on a level with them. If they be Judaists he was more so. The present part. is not for the aor. (Grot.), nor used as the historical present (Van Heng.), nor as a substantive (the examples referred to by Mey. and Alf. being all associated with the art.), but is used *adjectivally*, standing in parallelism to the following epithet, ἄμεμπτος, and predicatively in relation to a suppressed verb subst. that pervades the clauses; comp. Winer, *Gr.* § 45. 5, p. 312. The sense is the same, but grammatical propriety seems to require the distinction. δικαιοσ. τὴν ἐν νόμῳ] 'righteousness that is in the law;' righteousness specially so characterized, comp. notes on 1 *Tim.* iii. 14, 2 *Tim.* i. 13. In ver. 9 the same idea is somewhat differently expressed: δικ. ἡ ἐκ νόμου is righteousness that emanates *from* the law, that results from its commands when truly followed; δικ. ἡ ἐν νόμῳ righteousness that resides *in* it, and exists in coincidence with its commands. In the one case the law is the imaginary origin, in the other the imaginary sphere, of the δικαιοσύνη. All limitations of ιόμος, *e. g.* 'specialia instituta,' Grot., 'traditionem patrum,' Vatabl., are completely untenable. On this verse, and on Justification generally, see August. *Serm.* ccxx. Vol. v. p. 926 sq. (edit. Migne). ἄμεμπτος] '*blameless;*' 'proprie est is in quo nihil desiderari potest, ἄμωμος in quo nihil est quod reprehendas.' Tittm. *Synon.* p. 29. The ἀμεμφία here spoken of, in accordance with the clearly external relations

previously enumerated, must be referred to the outward and common judgment of men; 'vitæ meæ rationes ita plane composui ut nihil in me quisquam reprehendere aut damnare posset,' Justiniani *in loc.*

7. ἅτινα] '*the which things;*' scil. the qualities, characteristics, and prerogatives alluded to in the preceding clauses, ὅστις being used in reference to *indefinitely* expressed antecedents; see notes on *Gal.* iv. 24. The general distinction between ὅς and ὅστις has rarely been stated better than by Krüger; 'ὅς is purely objective, ὅστις generic and qualitative,' *Sprachl.* § 51. 8.

ἦν μοι κέρδη] '*were gains to me;*' not, 'in my judgment,' 'non vera sed opinata lucra,' Van Heng., μοι being thus an *ethical* dative (Krüger, *Sprachl.* § 48. 6. 5),— but 'to me,' a simple dat. *commodi*; they were really gains to St. Paul in the state previous to his conversion; compare Schoettg. *in loc.* The plural κέρδη is appropriately used in reference to the different forms and characters of κέρδος involved in the foregoing prerogatives; κέρδος, in fact, considered in the plurality of its parts, Jelf, *Gr.* § 353. 1, Krüger, *Sprachl.* § 44. 3. 5. Meyer compares Herod. III 71, περιβαλλόμενος ἑωυτῷ κέρδεα; add Plato, *Legg.* IX. p. 862 c, βλάβας καὶ κέρδη.

διὰ τὸν Χρ.] '*for Christ's sake,*' more fully explained in ver. 8, 9, and put, for the sake probably of emphasis, between the verb and its accusative. Chrys. here not inappropriately remarks, εἰ διὰ τὸν Χριστόν, οὐ φύσει ζημία.

ἥγημαι ζημίαν] '*I have considered* (and they are now to me) *as loss;*' contrast ἡγοῦμαι, ver. 8, and on the force of the perfect, which here marks 'actionem quæ per effectus suos durat,' see notes on *Eph.* ii. 8. Meyer, followed by Alf.,

τὸν Χριστὸν ζημίαν. ⁸ ἀλλὰ μὲν οὖν καὶ ἡγοῦμαι πάντα ζημίαν εἶναι διὰ τὸ ὑπερέχον τῆς γνώσεως Χριστοῦ Ἰησοῦ τοῦ Κυρίου μου, δι᾽ ὃν τὰ πάντα ἐζημιώθην καὶ ἡγοῦμαι σκύβαλα εἶναι, ἵνα

comments on the use of the sing. ζημίαν as marking 'one loss in all things' of which the apostle is here speaking. This is possible, but it may be doubted whether the singular is not regularly used in this formula (comp. examples in Kypke, Vol. II 315, Elsner, Vol. II p. 252, and especially Wetst. (i. loc.), and whether the use of the plural would not suggest the inappropriate idea of 'punishments,' a prevalent meaning of ζημίαι: see Rost u. Palm, Lex. s. v. The form ζημ. is supposed to be connected with 'damnum,' and perhaps to be referred to the Sanscr. dam, 'domitum esse,' Pott, Etym. Forsch. Vol. 1. p. 261.

8. ἀλλὰ μὲν οὖν κ. τ. λ.] ' Nay more, am indeed also, etc. ;' 'at sane quidem,' Winer, Gr. § 53. 7, p. 392. In this formula, scarcely accurately rendered by 'imo vero,' Wiesinger (after Winer, ed. 5), or 'but moreover,' Alf., each particle has its proper force ; ἀλλὰ contrasts the pres. ἡγοῦμαι with the perf. ἥγημαι, μὲν confirms, while οὖν, with its usual retrospective force, collects and slightly concludes from what has been previously said ; see Klotz, Devar. Vol. II. p. 663, and for the use of μὲν οὖν in adding some emphatic addition or correction, comp. Donalds. Gr. § 567. The continuative force of μὲν οὖν, ' cum quâdam conclusionis significatione,' is noticed by Herm. Viger, No. 342.
The reading of Rec., μενοῦνγε, rests only on A; very many mss.; Theoph., al., and is rightly rejected by Lachm. and Tisch. καὶ ἡγοῦμαι] ' I am also accounting ;' not only ἥγημαι but ἡγοῦμαι, the καί, with its usual ascensive, and indirectly contrasting, force, bringing into prominence the latter verb : it is not with St. Paul merely a past but also a present action.

πάντα] ' all,'—in reference to the preceding ἅτινα ἦν κ. τ. λ., 'illa omnia,' Syr., Copt.; πάντα, as its position shows, having no emphasis, but being used only to include 'qu[a]e cu[m]que antea Apostolo in lucris posita sunt,' V. u Heng. The fuller and regular construction, ζημίαν εἶναι (compare Weller, Posuel. zum Gr. Synt. p. 8,—an ingenious tract), is here adopted on account of the difference in the order of the words.
διὰ τὸ ὑπερ. κ. τ. λ.] ' for the excellency of the knowledge of Christ my Lord,' —' qui mihi super omnia est,' Grotius, 'dominus mihi carissimus,' Van Heng. ; compare Est. in loc. The article with the neuter adjectival participle seems designedly used to bring into prominence the specific characteristic or all il de of the γνῶσις ; it was not merely διὰ τὴν ὑπερέχουσαν γνῶσιν, but διὰ τὸ ὑπερ. τῆς γν., see Bernhardy, Synt. III. 42. d, p. 156, and compare Jelf, Gr. § 436 γ, who notices this use of the neuter part. as very characteristic of Thucydides, I. 142, II. 63, III. 43, al. This nicety of language was not unobserved by Chrysost., who adverts to it to show that the real difference between the γνῶσις and the πάντα (involving the νόμος) with which it was contrasted, lay solely in the ὑπεροχή of the former ; διὰ τὸ ὑπερέχον, οὐ διὰ τὸ ἀλλότριον. τὸ γὰρ ὑπερέχον τοῦ ὁμογενοῦς ὑπερέχει. The deduction, however, is unnecessary if not untenable. The knowledge of Christ admits no homogeneities, and transcends all comparisons. τὰ πάντα ἐζημ.] ' I suffered the loss of them all ;' not with any middle force but purely passive, the retrospective and inclusive τὰ πάντα (καὶ τὰ πάλαι, καὶ τὰ πάροντα, Chrys.) being the regular accus. of the (so termed) quantitative object ; comp

Χριστὸν κερδήσω, ⁹ καὶ εὑρεθῶ ἐν αὐτῷ, μὴ ἔχων ἐμὴν δικαιοσύνην τὴν ἐκ νόμου, ἀλλὰ τὴν διὰ πίστεως Χριστοῦ, τὴν ἐκ Θεοῦ

Matth. xvi. 26, and see Hartung, *Casus*, p. 46, comp. Winer, *Gr.* § 39. 1, p. 223. The verb is designedly stronger than the preceding ἡγοῦμαι ζημίαν, and its object-accus. more comprehensive; both suitably enhancing the climactic sequence of this noble verse. καὶ ἡγοῦμαι σκύβ. εἶναι] 'and count them to be dung;' clearly not a parenthetical clause (Van Heng.), but, as the nature of the verse indicates, joined to, and in sentiment advancing further than what has last been said. The colon in some editions (Oxf. 1836, 1851), is very undesirable; even the comma (*Mill, Griesb., Scholz, Tisch.*) can be dispensed with. The somewhat curious word σκύβαλον appears properly to mean 'dung' (Syr., Clarom., Vulg.), *e. g.* Alex.-Aphrodit. *Probl.* 1. 18, ἐξιᾶσι σκύβ. καὶ οὖρον, and thus is probably to be connected with σκῶρ (not σκώρ), gen. σκατός; see Lobeck, *Pathol.* p. 92, Benfey, *Wurzellex.* Vol. II. p. 172. The old derivation, κυσὶ βαλεῖν, *i. e.* κυσίβαλον (Suid., *Etym. M.*) or ἐς κύνας, is still defended by Pott, *Etym. Forsch.* Vol. II. p. 295. On the various derivative meanings, 'refuse,' 'quisquilias' (Goth., Æth.), etc., see Suicer, *Thesaur.* s. v. Vol. II. p. 978, the numerous exx. collected by Wetst. *in loc.*, and the smaller collections of Kypke, Elsner, and Loesner.
ἵνα Χρ. κερδήσω] 'that I may gain Christ;' purpose of the ἡγ. σκύβ. εἶναι, antithetically expressed with reference to the previous ζημιοῦσθαι. Meyer and Alf. properly object to the bleak interpr. of Grot., 'Christum, *i. e.* Christi favorem:' it is curious that it should have been adopted by so good an expositor as Hammond. To 'gain Christ' is, to use the exquisite language of Bp. Hall, 'to lay fast hold upon Him, to receive Him inwardly into our bosoms, and so to make Him ours and ourselves His, that we may be joined to Him as our Head, espoused to Him as our Husband, incorporated into Him as our Nourishment, engrafted in Him as our Stock, and laid upon Him as a sure Foundation,' *Christ Mystical*, ch. VI. — a treatise of the loftiest spiritual strain.

9. εὑρεθῶ ἐν αὐτῷ] 'be found in Him;' in Him, as the sphere and element of my spiritual being; comp. notes on *Eph.* ii. 6, *Gal.* ii. 17. Εὑρεθῶ must not be regarded as a mere periphrasis for the verb subst., 'existam sive sim,' Grotius (see contra Winer, *Gr.* § 65. 8, p. 542), nor as referring solely to the judgment of God (Beza), nor yet as antithetical to being lost (Bp. Hall), but simply and plainly to the 'judicium universale' (Zanch.), 'the being and being actually found to be ἐν αὐτῷ,' both in the sight of God and his fellow men; see notes on *Gal.* ii 17. μὴ ἔχων] Dependent on the preceding ἵνα, and associated with the preceding εὑρεθῶ as a predication of manner. *Tischend.* and *Lachm.* both remove the comma after ἐν αὐτῷ, thus leaving it doubtful whether μὴ ἔχων may not form a portion of an *objective* sentence (Donalds. *Gr.* § 584 sq.), 'be found in Him not to have, etc.' — a construction that is grammatically defensible (comp. Krüger, *Sprachl.* 56. 7. 2), but certainly not exegetically satisfactory: ἐν αὐτῷ would then be wholly obscured; comp. Meyer *in loc.*
ἐμὴν δικ. κ. τ. λ.] '*my righteousness that is of the law;*' *i. e.* such righteousness as I strove to work out by attempting to obey the behests of the law, τὴν ἰδίαν δικαιοσύνην, Rom. x. 3. The meaning of δικαιοσ. is here slightly different in its two connections. With ἐμὴν it implies an assumed attribute of the apostle, with ἐκ νόμου it implies a righteous-

δικαιοσύνην ἐπὶ τῇ πίστει, ¹⁰ τοῦ γνῶναι αὐτὸν καὶ τὴν δύναμιν

ness reckoned as such, owing to a fulfilment of the claims of the law. On the force of ἐκ in these combinations ('immediate origin,' etc.), see notes on *Gal.* ii. 16. τὴν διὰ πιστ. Χρ] '*that which is through faith in Christ;*' of which faith in Christ is the 'causa medians,' and which, as the following words specify, comes immediately from God as its active source and origin; compare Waterl. *on Justif.* Vol. vi. p. 4 note, Usteri, *Lehrb.* ii. 1. 1, p. 87. On the meaning of πιστ. Χρ. and the dogmatical import of διὰ πιστ., see notes on *Gal.* ii. 16 (comp. notes on *Col.* ii. 12), where both expressions are briefly discussed; and also the short but extremely perspicuous remarks of Hamm., *Pract. Catech.* 1. 4, who well observes that our 'faith itself cannot be regarded, in the strict sense of the term, as a logical instrument of our justification, but as a condition and moral instrument without which we shall not be justified,' p. 73 (A.-C. Libr.); so also with equal perspicuity Forbes, *Instruct.* viii. 23. 22. On the true doctrine of justification see espec. Hooker, *on Justif.* § 6 sq, and for the opposing tenets of the Romanists the clear statements of Möhler, *Symbolik*, § 15, p. 118 sq, § 22, p. 215, 216. ἐπὶ τῇ πίστει] '*based on faith;*' not 'sub hac conditione ut habeas,' Fritz. (*Rom.* Vol. i. p. 46), but 'super fide,' Copt., Beng., πίστις being the foundation on which it firmly and solidly rests. On the force of ἐπί with the dative, which, roughly speaking, denotes a *more* close, while with the gen. it expresses a *less* close connection (Krüger, *Sprachl.* § 68. 41. 1), see notes on ch. i. 3, and esp. on *Eph.* ii. 20,—where, however, observe that (in ed. 1) the words 'former' and 'latter' have become accidentally transposed. Numerous examples of ἐπί with both cases (apparently interchangeably) will be found in [Eratosth.] *Catasterismi*,

ap. Gale, *Mythol.* p. 99-135, but the work is of very doubtful date. The context is not perfectly clear: ἐπὶ τῇ πίστει has been joined, (1) with the preceding τοῦ γνῶναι, Ath. (Pol.), but not Platt, Chrys., and, with a diff. in application, Calv., Beng. (2) which is more remotely preceding ἔχων Mey.; with the immediately preceding δικαιοσύνη, Vulg., Copt., Goth. Of these (2) is not tenable; see below on ver. 10: (1) is improbable and harsh, owing to the distance of ἐπὶ τῇ π from ἔχων; (3) on the other hand is grammatically defensible, and eminently simple and perspicuous. As we may say δικαιοῦσθαι ἐπὶ τῇ πίστει, so δικ. ἐπὶ τῇ πιστ. without the art. is permissible, see Winer, *Gr.* § 20. 2, p. 123, and comp. notes on *Eph.* i. 15.

10. τοῦ γνῶναι] '*that I may know Him,*' Auth. Ver.; infinitive of design dependent on the preceding εἱρέθω, not on μὴ ἔχων (Mey.), which seems to give an undue prominence to the participial clauses. The reference of τοῦ γνῶναι (= ἵνα γνῶ) to ver. 8, as Winer, De W., al., seems to disturb the easy and natural sequence of thought; see Wiesinger and Alf. *in loc.* On the inf. 'of design,' which falls under the general head of the gen. of *adjective relation* (compare Krüger, *Sprachl.* § 47. 22. 2), and is by no means without example in classical Greek (Bernhardy, *Synt.* ix. 2, p. 357, Madvig, *Synt.* § 170 c), see Winer, *Gr.* § 44. 4, p. 291, where other examples are noticed and discussed. The construction of τοῦ γνῶναι with ἐπὶ τῇ πιστ., if (α) as equivalent to ὥστε γνῶναι διὰ τῆς πίστεως (Theod., Chrys.), is opposed to the order of words, and to all rules of grammatical analysis,— if (β) as a definitive gen., 'so as to know Him' (Calv., Beng.), is a construction of πίστις not found in the N. T.; so Meyer and Alf. The knowledge here mentioned, as Meyer rightly observes, is

τῆς ἀναστάσεως αὐτοῦ καὶ τὴν κοινωνίαν τῶν παθημάτων αὐτοῦ, συμμορφιζόμενος τῷ θανάτῳ αὐτοῦ, ¹¹ εἴ πως καταντήσω εἰς τὴν ἐξανάστασιν τὴν ἐκ νεκρῶν.

not merely speculative, but practical and experimental; see especially Beck, *Seelenl.* I. 9, p. 22, comp Andrewes, *Serm.* Vol. II. p. 204 (A.-C. Libr.).

καὶ τὴν δύν. κ. τ. λ.] '*and the power of His resurrection;*' fuller explanation of the preceding αὐτόν, under two different aspects, the Lord's resurrection, and the Lord's sufferings. The δύναμις τῆς ἀναστ. is clearly not 'potentia quâ excitatus fuit,' Vatabl. (ἀναστ. being a gen. objecti), but, 'quâ justos ad immortalitatem revocabit,' Just.,—ἀναστ. being the gen. *originis* (Hartung, *Casus*, p. 23); 'a virtue or power flowing from Christ's resurrection, called by the apostle *vis resurrectionis*,' Andrewes, *Serm.* Vol. II. p. 204 (A.-C. Libr.); compare Theoph. As the resurrection of Christ has at least four spiritual efficacies, viz. (*a*) as quickening our souls, Eph. ii. 5; (*b*) as confirming the hope of our resurrection, Rom. viii. 11, 1 Corinth. xv. 22; (*c*) as assuring us of our present justification, Rom. iv. 24, 25; (*d*) as securing our final justification, our triumph over death, and participation in His glory, 2 Corinth. iv. 10 sq., Colos. iii. 4,—the context can alone determine the immediate reference. Here the general context seems to point to (*c*) or (*d*), the present verse and ver. 11, perhaps more especially to the latter. On the fruits of Christ's resurrection, see Pearson, *Creed*, Art. v. Vol. I. p. 313, Usher, *Body of Div.* ch. xv. ad fin., and on our justification by Christ's resurrection compared with that by His death, the admirable remarks of Jackson, *Creed*, xv. 16. 8.

τὴν κοινωνίαν κ. τ. λ.] '*the fellowship of His sufferings;*' further exemplification of the experimental knowledge of Christ, regarded as *objective* and *present*, suggested by the preceding clause, of which the reference was rather subjective and future. It is only in a participation in His sufferings that there can be one in His resurrection and glory: εἰ τοίνυν μὴ ἐπιστεύομεν ὅτι συμβασιλεύσομεν οὐκ ἂν τοσαῦτα καὶ τὰ τοιαῦτα ἐπάσχομεν, Theoph.; compare Rom. viii. 17, 2 Tim. ii. 11. This partnership in Christ's sufferings is outward and actual (Chrys., al.), not inward and ethical (Zanch.); it is a sharing in the sufferings He suffered, a drinking from the cup He drank; comp. 2 Cor. iv. 10, 1 Pet. iv. 13, notes *on 2 Timothy*, ii. 11, and Reuss, *Théol. Chrét.* IV. 20, Vol. II. p. 224.

συμμορφιζόμ. κ. τ. λ] '*being conformed unto His death,*' *i. e.* 'by being, or while I am, conformed unto His death, even as I now am:' *pres.* participle logically dependent on the preceding γνῶναι; see notes *on Eph.* iii. 18, iv. 2. This conformation, then, is not ethical, 'ut huic mundo emortuus sim quemadmodum Christus mortuus est in cruce.' Van Heng., but, as the connection and tenor of the passage require, *actual*, and as the pres. suggests, even now more especially going on: 'ut cognoscam communicationem passionum ejus, in quam venio, et quæ mihi contigit dum per passiones et mortis pericula quæ pro nomine ejus sustineo, conformis efficior morti ejus,' Estius. The reading is slightly doubtful; *Rec.* has συμμορφούμενος with D³EKL; al.; Chrysost., Theod.: the rarer form in the text is adopted by *Lachmann* and *Tisch.* with ABD¹; 17. 67**71; Orig. (mss.), Bas., Maced., to which the incorrect συνφορτειζόμενος of F and G may lend some slight weight.

11. εἴ πως] '*if by any means,*' '*si quomodo,*' Vulg., Clarom.; an expression, not so much of doubt, as of humility, indicating the object contemplated in

I have not yet obtained, but am eagerly pressing forward: in this imitate me.

12 Οὐχ ὅτι ἤδη ἔλαβον ἢ ἤδη τετελείωμαι,

συμμορφιζ. κ. τ. λ.; οὐ δαρρῶ γάρ, φησίν, οὔπω οὕτως, ἐταπεινοφρόνει, Theoph.: see also Neander, *Phil.* p. 43. In this formula, when thus associated with verbs denoting an action directed to a particular end, the idea of an *attempt* is conveyed ('nixum fidei Paulinae,' Beng.), which may or may not be successful; compare Acts xxvii. 12, Rom. i. 10, xi. 14, and see Fritz. *Rom.* xi. 14, Vol. II. p. 47, Hartung *Partik* ei, 2. 6, Vol. II. p. 206, and for a few examples of the similar use of *si* in Latin, Madvig, *Lat. Gr.* § 451. d. καταντήσω εἰς] 'may attain unto;' not indic. fut., as in Rom. i. 10, and perhaps xi. 14 (Mey.), but aor. subj. (Alf.), as the following words, εἰ καὶ καταλάβω, seem to suggest. On the force of εἰ with the subj. ('ubi nihil nisi conditio ipsa indicetur'), now admitted and acknowledged in the best Attic Greek, see Herm. *de Part.* ἄν, II. 7, p. 97, Klotz, *Devar.* Vol. II. p. 499 sq., comp. Winer, *Gr.* § 41, 2. e, p. 263. The expression καταντᾶν εἰς, 'pervenire ad,' is used in the N. T. in connection with *places* (Acts xvi. 1, xviii. 19, 24, al.), *persons* (1 Cor. x. 11, xiv. 36), and *other relations* (Acts xxvi. 7, Eph. iv. 13), in which last connection it is also found with ἐπί several times in Polyb.; *e. g.* with gen., *Hist.* xiv. 1. 9 (but *l reading*), with accus., III. 11. 4, III. 91. 1, xiv. 1. 9. The ref. of Van Heng. to *time,* 'si perveniam ad tempus hujus eventi,' is thus wholly unnecessary, if indeed not also lexically untenable. ἐξανάστασιν κ. τ. λ] '*the resurrection from the dead:*' i. e., as the context suggests, the *first* resurrection (Rev. xx. 5), when, at the Lord's coming the dead in Him shall rise first (1 Thessalon. iv. 16), and the quick be caught up to meet Him in the clouds (1 Thess. iv. 17); compare Luke xx. 35. The first resurrection will include

only true believers, and will apparently precede the second, that of unbelievers and disbelievers, in point of time; see Ebrard, *Dogmatik*, § 574, and the singular but learned work of Burnet, *de the Departed*, ch. IX. p. 255 (Transl.). Any reference here to a merely ethical resurrection (Coccius) is wholly out of the question. The double compound ἐξανάστασις, an ἅπ. λεγόμ. in N. Test. (comp. Polyb. *Hist.* III. 55. 4, does not appear to have any special force (τὴν ἔνδοξον, τὴν ἐν νεφέλαις ἐξα. σιν, Theophyl.), but seems only an instance of the tendency of later Greek to adopt such forms, without any increase of meaning, see Thiersch, *de Vers. Alex.* II. 1, p. 83, and notes *on Eph.* i. 21: comp. Pearson, *Creed*, Vol. II. p 316 (edit. Burt.). τὴν ἐκ νεκρῶν] Distinct and slightly emphatic specification of the ἐξανάστ.; see notes *on 1 Tim.* iii. 14, 2 Tim. i. 10, where, however, the first art., as being associated with a word of known meaning an ἐ commun occurrence, is omitted after the prep. The reading is slightly doubtful. Meyer finds *Rec.* ἐξαν. τῶν νεκρῶν (Kl., al.), on the ground that elsewhere St Paul regularly omits ἐκ; these internal considerations however must yield to such distinct preponderance of external authority as ABDF; 10 mss.; Syrr., and great majority of Vv.; Bas., Chrysost., al.: so Lachm., Tisch.

12. οὐχ ὅτι] '(*I say*) *not that:*' not so much in confirmation of what precedes (Theoph.), as to avoid misapprehension and by his own example, to confirm his own exhortations, ch. ii. 3, compare iii. 15; 'nolite, inquit, in me falli; plus me ipse novi quam vos. Si nescio quid mihi desit, nescio quid ades,' August. On the use of οὐχ ὅτι scil. οὐκ ἔστι ὅτι, in limiting a preceding assertion or obviating a misapprehension, see Har-

διώκω δὲ εἰ καὶ καταλάβω, ἐφ' ᾧ καὶ κατελήμφθην ὑπὸ Χριστοῦ.

tung, *Partik.* Vol. II. p. 154, compare Herm. *Viger*, No. 253.

ἤδη ἔλαβον] '*I have already attained.*' The object of ἔλαβον is somewhat doubtful. The two most natural supplements are (*a*) Χριστόν, Theod., implied from what precedes; (*b*) βραβεῖον, Chrys., reflected from what follows. Of these (*b*) is to be preferred, as the διώκω immediately following seems to show that the favorite metaphor from the stadium was already occupying the apostle's thoughts. The simple ἔλαβον thus precedes, almost 'generaliter dictum,' to be succeeded by the more specific καταλάβω. On the force of ἤδη and its distinction from νῦν, see *on* 2 *Tim.* iv. 6.

τετελείωμαι] '*have been made perfect:*' more exact explanation of the semi-metaphorical ἔλαβον, and result of it. The preceding aor. is thus not to be regarded as a perfect, but as representing a single action in the past ('ita ut non detiniatur, *quam late pateat* id quod actum est'), Fritz. *de Aoristi* VI, p. 17), which the succeeding perf. explains and expands; comp. Winer, *Gr* § 40. 5, p. 257. That the τελειοῦσθαι has here an ethical reference, 'to be spiritually perfected,' not agonistical (Hamm., Loesner, p. 355), 'to be crowned or receive the reward,' is almost self-evident: compare Reuss, *Théol. Chrét.* IV. 16, Vol. II. p. 182. The verb is only used here by St. Paul (2 Cor. xii. 9 is more than doubtful), though common in Hebrews and elsewhere in the N. T. The ancient gloss ἢ ἤδη δεδικαίωμαι inserted after ἔλαβον DEFG; Clarom.; Iren., al., indirectly shows the meaning here ascribed to τετελείωμαι.   διώκω δέ] '*but I am pressing onward:*' not 'sed persequor,' Beza, but '[per]-sequor autem,' Vulg., with a more just regard to the force of the particle: see Hand, *Tursell.* Vol. I. p. 559. In sentences of

this nature, where a negative has preceded and the regular ἀλλά (sondern) might have been expected (comp. Donalds. *Cratyl.* § 201) it will be nearly always found, that the connection of the two clauses is *oppositive* rather than *adversative*; *i. e.* that in the one case (ἀλλά) the preceding negation is brought into sharp prominence and contrasted with what follows, while in the other (δέ) the negation is almost left unnoticed, and the sentence continued with the (so to say) connective opposition that so regularly characterizes the latter particle; see Klotz, *Devar.* Vol. II. p. 360, and compare Hand, *l. c.*   The metaphor is obviously taken from the stadium (Loesn. *Obs.* p. 355, ἐπαγώνιός εἰμι, Theoph.), and the verb διώκω, as in the examples cited by Loesn., and as also in ver. 14, seems to be here used absolutely, κατὰ σπουδὴν ἐλαύνειν, Phavor.; see examples in Kypke, *Obs.* Vol. II. p. 317, Buttmann, *Lexil.* § 40, p. 232 (Transl.): so, distinctly, Syr., Copt., 'curro,' and apparently Chrys., who regards it as only differing qualitatively (μεθ' ὅσου τόνου) from τρέχω; see also Theophyl. *in loc.* If διώκω be regarded as transitive, the object of διώκω will be the same as that of καταλάβω, scil. the βραβεῖον *implied* in the ἐφ' ᾧ: compare Æth. (Platt). The former construction, however, seems more simple and natural.   εἰ καὶ καταλάβω] '*if I might also lay hold on;*' the καί contrasting καταλάβω not with the more remote ἔλαβον (Mey.), but with the immediately preceding διώκω (Alf): see Ecclus. xi. 10, xxvii. 8, comp. Rom. ix. 30, Lucian, *Hermot.* § 77, Cicero, *Off.* I. 31. 110, in all which passages there seems a contrast more or less defined between the διώκειν and καταλαμβάνειν, the 'sequi' and 'assequi:' compare Fritz. *Rom.* Vol. II. p. 355. On the

13 ἀδελφοί, ἐγὼ ἐμαυτὸν οὐ λογίζομαι κατειληφέναι· 14 ἓν δέ, τὰ

force of εἰ καί see notes on chap. ii. 17. Whether καταλάβω ('assequar,' Rom. ix. 30, 1 Cor. ix. 24) is to be taken absolutely or transitively will depend on the meaning assigned to ἐφ' ᾧ.

ἐφ' ᾧ καὶ κατελ] '*that for which also I we is laid hold on;*' so Syriac ܥܰܠ ܗܳܝ ܕ݁ [i. e. cujus causa], and sim. Æthiopic (Platt), — the only two versions that make their view of this passage perfectly clear. Ἐφ' ᾧ has here received several different interpretations. Taken *per se* it may mean; (a) *quare*, like ἀνθ' ὧν (Luke v. 3), at the beginning of a sentence; comp. Diodor. Sic. XIX. 9, ἐφ' ᾧ τὸν μὲν μείζον καλοῦσι ταῦρον κ. τ. λ.; (β) *eo quod, propterea quod*, scil. ἐπὶ τούτῳ, ὅτι = διότι (apparently Rom. v. 12, 2 Corinth. v. 4), expressed more commonly in the plural ἐφ' οἷς in classical Greek; see Thom. M. p. 400, ed. Bern., and Fritz. *Rom.* Vol. i p. 299; (γ) *sub qua conditione, cujus ea tsâ*, almost 'to which very end,' Hammond (see 1 Thess. iv. 17, Gal. v. 13, and notes, also examples in Lobeck, *Phryn.* p. 475), ᾧ being here regarded as the relative to a suppressed antecedent τοῦτο, the obj. accus. of καταλάβω: comp. Luke v. 25. Of these (β) and (γ) are the only two which here come into consideration. The former is adopted by the Greek commentators, Beng., Meyer, al., and deserves consideration, but introduces a reason where a reason seems hardly appropriate. The latter is adopted by Syriac, Copt., De W., Neand., and apparently the bulk of modern expositors, and seems most in harmony with the context: the apostle was laid hold on by Christ (at his conversion, Horsley, *Serm.* XVII., not necessarily as a fugitive in a race. Chrys., Hamm.) with ref. to that, — to enable him to obtain that, which he was now striving to lay hold of. It may be observed lastly that καί does not refer to a suppressed ἐγώ, nor to κατελ. (Alf.), but to the preceding relative, which it specifies, and tacitly contrasts with other ends which might be conceivable; 'for which, too, for which very salvation, I was apprehended,' etc.; comp. 1 Cor. xiii. 12, καθὼς καὶ ἐπεγνώσθην, and see Klotz, *Devar.* Vol. ii. p. 636.

13. ἀδελφοί] Earnest and emphatic repetition of the preceding statements, under somewhat hortatory aspects, negative and positive: in the first portion of the verse the apostle disavows all self-esteem and self-confidence, — not perhaps without reference to some of his converts (ταῦτα πρὸς τοὺς μεγαλοφρονοῦντας ἐπὶ τοῖς ἤδη κατορθωθεῖσι λέγει, Theod.); in the second portion and verse 14 he declares the persistence and energy of his onward endeavor; ἑνὸς εἰμὶ μόνου, τοῦ τοῖς ἔμπροσθεν ἐπεκτείνεσθαι, Chrys. ἐμαυτὸν οὐ λογίζ. κ. τ. λ.] '*do not esteem MYSELF to have apprehended;*' the juxtaposition of ἐγὼ and the specially added ἐμαυτὸν (see Winer, *Gram.* § 44. 3, p. 287) not only mark the self-ish element which the apostle disavows (Mey.), but declare his own deliberate judgment on his own case; comp. Beng. The verb λογίζομαι is rather a favorite word with St. Paul, being used (ex luding quotations) twenty-nine times in his Epp., and twice only (Mark xi. 31 is very doubtful) in the rest of the N. T.

14 ἓν δέ] '*but one thing I do,*' scil. ποιῶ, the general verb in the first clause being inferred from the special verb that follows; see Winer, *Gr.* § 66. 1. b, p. 546. The ellipsis is variously supplied (ܥܳܒܶܕ݂ [novi] Syriac; φροντίζω or μεριμνῶ, Œcumen. 2; ἐστι, Beza: διώκω, Flatt), evaded (Gothic, passed over (Æthiopic), or left nakedly as it stands

μὲν ὀπίσω ἐπιλανθανόμενος, τοῖς δὲ ἔμπροσθεν ἐπεκτεινόμενος, κατὰ σκοπὸν διώκω ἐπὶ τὸ βραβεῖον τῆς ἄνω κλήσεως τοῦ Θεοῦ

14. ἐπί] So *Rec.*, *Griesb.*, with DEFGKL; majority of mss.; Chrys., Theod. On the other hand, *Lachm.* and *Tisch.* read εἰς with AB; 17. 73. 80; Clem., Ath., al. (*Mey.*, *Alf.*), apparently on the ground of ἐπί being an interpretation of the εἰς of ' destination.' As it can scarcely be said that ἐπί, especially with the meaning anciently assigned to βραβ. (*e. g.* Theod.), is a much easier expression than εἰς, it does not here seem safe to reject the reading of so many uncial MSS.

(Vulg., Copt.). The most simple and natural supplement is that adopted above, as Theoph., Œcum., and most modern expositors; see Jelf, *Gr.* § 895. c. Meyer strongly urges the participial form ποιῶν, but this surely mars the emphasis, and obscures the prominent διώκω, to which the ellipsis seems intended to direct attention. τὰ μὲν ὀπίσω ἐπιλ.] '*forgetting the things behind;*' not the renounced Judaical prerogatives, ver. 5 sq. (Vorst.), nor the deeds done under their influence, but, as the metaphor almost unmistakably suggests, the portions of his Christian course already traversed, ' the things attained and left behind,' Fell ; ἐν ποιῶ, ἑνὸς γίγνομαι μόνου, ὅπως ἀεὶ προκόπτοιμι· ἐπιλανθάνομαι τῶν κατορθωμάτων καὶ ἀφίημι αὐτὰ ὀπίσω, καὶ οὐδὲ μέμνημαι ὅλως αὐτῶν, Theoph. ; compare Chrys. The special reference of Theod. to οἱ περὶ τοῦ κηρύγματος πόνοι is unsatisfactory, as obscuring the general and practical teaching which this vital passage conveys; καὶ ἡμεῖς μὴ ὅσον ἠνύσαμεν τῆς ἀρετῆς ἀναλογιζώμεθα, ἀλλ' ὅσον ἡμῖν λείπει, Chrys. In the verb ἐπιλανθ. (middle, — of the *inward act*, Scheuerl. *Synt.* p. 295 ; act. non occ.) the preposition seems to mark the application of the action to, and perhaps also its extending over (accus.) the object, a little more forcibly than the simple verb (λήθῇ παραδοῦναι, Chrys.); comp. Rost. u. Palm, *Lex.* s. v. ἐπί, C. cc, dd It is occasionally, as here, found with the accus. ; the simple form always with gen. ; compare Jelf, *Gr.* § 512, Thom. M. p. 348 (ed. Bern.). τοῖς δὲ ἔμπροσθεν ἐπεκτ.] '*but stretching out after the things that are in front;*' more distinct emergence of the image of the racer. The τὰ ἔμπροσθεν are the δίαυλοι (to use the language of Chrys.) which are yet to be passed over in the Christian course, and are the successive objects (dat. of *direction*, see Hartung, *Casus*, p. 83) toward which the action of the ἐπεκτειν. is directed : good works done in faith are the successive strides; Andrewes, *Serm.* Vol. III. p. 95 (A.-C. Libr.). In the double compound ἐπεκτ. the ἐπί marks the *direction*, ἐκ the *posture*, in which the racer stretches *out* his body *toward* the objects before him ; ὁ γὰρ ἐπεκτεινόμενος οὗτός ἐστιν ὁ τοὺς πόδας καίτοι τρέχοντας τῷ λοιπῷ σώματι προλαβεῖν σπουδάζων, Chrys. A very similar use of ἐπεκτείνεσθαι is cited in Steph. *Thesaur.* s. v., Strabo, XVII. p. 800. κατὰ σκοπὸν διώκω] ' *I press forward toward the mark.*' The preposition κατά here marks the direction of the διώκειν (see Acts VIII. 26, XVI. 7, and with more geographical reference, II. 10, XXVII. 12), — a direction which, according to the primary meaning of the prep. (κατά = κε-ν -τα) is represented ' beginning near us and proceeding to a point not necessarily distant,' Donalds. *Cratyl.* § 183. On the absolute use of διώκω, see on ver. 12. βραβ. τῆς ἄνω κλήσεως] '*prize of the heavenly calling;*' the gen. not being of apposition (De W.), which would

ἐν Χριστῷ Ἰησοῦ. ¹⁵ Ὅσοι οὖν τέλειοι, τοῦτο φρονῶμεν· καὶ εἴ τι

involve the untenable assumption that κλῆσις = 'superna beatitudo,' Est., compare De W.,—but a species of the gen. *possessivus*, serving to mark the βραβ. as that which the ἄνω κλῆσις has in expectation as its final crown. The βραβεῖον is here, as in 1 Corinth. ix. 24, not 'the goal,' but 'the prize' (τὸ ἆθλον ἐκάλεσεν, Theod.), and is the object which the διώκειν is designed to attain (compare Luke xv. 14, xxii. 52, Acts viii. 36, and see critical note).—'the future eternal glory to which God calls us by the gospel of Christ,' Bull, *Serm.* xiv. p. 268 (Oxf. 1844). The derivation is uncertain; perhaps βρα πρo with reference to the judge sitting forward to award the prize. Benfey, *Wurzell.* Vol. II. p. 105. The κλῆσις, here defined as proceeding from God (gen. *originis*), is still further specified as ἡ ἄνω κλῆσις, the *heavenly* calling (compare Col. iii. 2, Gal iv. 26); not with any *special* reference to the peculiar appointment of St. Paul (Meyer, Alf.), but, as the latitude of the passage seems to require, with *general* reference to its ends and objects; it was a κλῆσις ἐπουράνιος (Heb. i.i. 1). God was its author (1 Thess. ii. 12), heaven the object to which it conducted, and in reference to which it was vouchsafed; compare ver 20. ἐν Χρ. Ἰησ. may be connected (a) with διώκω, as Chrys., app. Theoph., (Œcum., and very emphatically Meyer; or (b) with κλῆσις (Copt., Æth.),—καλεῖν ἐν Χρ., and therefore κλ. ἐν Χρ. without the art. being a permissible formula; see Winer, *Gram.* § 20. 2, p. 123, and notes on *Eph.* i. 18. The latter seems most simple, and most coincident with St. Paul's use of the formula. On the dogmatical significance of this verse, as indicating an effort on our parts through the assistance of grace, compare Reuss, *Théol. Chrét.* iv. 22. Vol. II. p. 255.

15. ὅσοι οὖν] '*As many then as;*' the οὖν with its usual collective and retrospective force gathering into a definite exhortation the statements made in the three preceding verses; compare Klotz, *Devar.* Vol. II. p. 717. Ὅσοι is clearly not synonymous with ἡμεῖς οἱ, Il. Hnr., but is designedly used as leaving to each one's conscience whether he were τέλειος or no.   τέλειοι] '*perfect*,' not absolutely, e.g. τετελειωμένοι (ver. 12), but relatively;—yet not necessarily as opposed to νήπιοι, 'in so i tate Christianâ cum adultis comparati,' Van Heng. (compare 1 Cor. ii. 6, xiv. 20, where, however, the reference seems more to knowledge), but simply as those who had made *some* advance toward the τέλος of Christian life; compare Wiesinger *in loc.*, where this view is elaborately and successfully maintained. τοῦτο φρονῶμεν] '*let us be of this mind*,' 'let us entertain these views with regard to religious practice (Hesly), which I follow, and which I am here inculcating.' Yet what views? Surely not *merely* τὸ ὅτι δεῖ τῶν ὑπισθεν ἐπιλανθάνεσθαι, Chrys.; so that τελειότης in its fullest sense is to consist in τὸ μὴ νομίζειν ἑαυτὸν τέλειον εἶναι (compare Theophyl.), but with a more inclusive reference to the whole great subject which commenced ver. 7, was continued to ver. 12, and was *specially* illustrated in ver. 12-14. That the τοῦτο does refer to what immediately precedes, to the ἐν δὲ of ver. 13, seems required by the rules of perspicuity,—but, that it refers to it only in so far as it forms a sort of example and special statement of the *τέλος ἀποδεί*, in reference to ver. 8 sq., seems required by the evident interdependence of the whole passage.   καὶ εἴ τι κ. τ. λ.] '*and if in any respect ye are differently minded;*' 'if you entertain, as is certainly supposable (εἰ with indic.,

ἑτέρως φρονεῖτε, καὶ τοῦτο ὁ Θεὸς ὑμῖν ἀποκαλύψει. ¹⁶ πλὴν εἰς ὃ ἐφθάσαμεν τῷ αὐτῷ στοιχεῖν.

see Winer, Gr. § 41. 2, notes on Gal. i. 9), upon any point,—not of doctrine or external worship (Horsley), but of moral practice (οὐ περὶ δογμάτων ταῦτα εἴρηται ἀλλὰ περὶ βίου τελειότητος, Chrys.), any different, and so, almost necessarily, less correct sentiments, even this too,—this about which ye are thus differently minded, will God reveal to you in its true relations.' There is thus no need with Horsley, in his able sermon on this passage, to give φρονεῖτε two different references, (a) to religious disposition, (b) to opinion ; nor is it enough to regard ἑτέρως as merely in opposition to 'sameness and uniformity,' when the context seems so clearly to imply an *improper and injurious* diversity ; see examples of this sense of ἕτερος in notes on Gal. i. 6. We may observe (with Wiesinger) that the apostle does not say ἕτερον but ἑτέρως; they did not differ in fundamentals, but in the aspects and relations in which they regarded them and carried them into practice.   καὶ τοῦτο] 'even this,' 'this also,' as well as the other things which God has been pleased to reveal ;' the ascensive καὶ contrasting the present τοῦτο,—the point on which they need revelation, not with the preceding τοῦτο (Flatt), but with the other points (to which εἴ τι is the exception) concerning which they have already received it, and are already in accord with the apostle : compare Hartung, *Partik.* s. v. καί, 2. 8, Vol. 1. p. 135. The τοῦτο is somewhat differently explained, 'justitiam esse ex fide,' Vatabl., 'vos esse deceptos,' Grot., 'quod nos perfecti sentimus,' Beng. ; alii alia. The only natural explanation seems that adopted above, viz., the thing concerning which ἑτέρως φρονεῖτε (Horsley), *i. e.* the true relations of the preceding τί, 'τί in seiner wahrheit,' De Wette ; ὁ Θεὸς ὑμῖν ὡς ἀγνοοῦσιν ὑποδείξει τὸ δέον, Theoph. ἀποκαλύψει] '*will reveal*,' by means of the Πνεῦμα σοφίας καὶ ἀποκαλύψεως, Ephes. i. 17 ; οὐκ εἶπεν. ἐνάξει, ἀλλ' ἀποκαλύψει ἵνα δόξῃ μᾶλλον ἀγνοίας εἶναι τὸ πρᾶγμα, Chrys. The future is not merely expressive of *wish*, but of an assured and predictive *hope;* 'loquitur pro spe quam ex priore ipsorum fide concepeiat ; sic et Gal. v. 10,' Grot. : comp. Winer, *Gr.* § 40. 6, p. 251.

16. πλήν] '*Notwithstanding,*' 'be that as it may,' Horsley ; 'in spite of there being several points in which you will probably need ἀποκάλυψις.' The practically adversative force of πλὴν limits the preceding expression of predictive hope, while its intrinsically comparative force serves also to contrast the aor. ἐφθ. with the fut. ἀποκ. ; see notes on ch. i. 18, and Klotz, *Devar.* Vol. II. p. 724.   εἰς ὃ ἐφθάσαμεν] '*whereto we have attained,*' Matth. xii. 28, Rom. ix. 31. compare Luke xi. 20. The primary and classical meaning of this verb (*prævenire*) appears to have been almost entirely lost sight of in Alexandrian Greek, and to have merged in the general meaning 'venire,' and with εἰς, 'pervenire ;' compare Dan. iv. 19, ἡ μεγαλωσύνη σου ἐμεγαλύνθη καὶ ἔφθασεν εἰς τὸν οὐρανόν: see Fritz. *Rom.* Vol. II. p. 357.   It is doubtful whether ἐφθάσ. denotes advance in moral conduct (Chrys., Theophyl., Mey.), advance in knowledge (De W., Wiesing.), or in both (Alf.) ; the first seems most in accordance with the context and with στοιχεῖν, the last, however, not improbable. Lastly, that ὃ does not indicate a point *common to all*, is almost self-evident : it is a point, in a *common line*, varying in its position according to individual progress.   This common line (produced) the apostle, in the following

Imitate me and my followers, (σ. *οντιç*, alas I must
cast my things. Our country is heaven, whence we
look for our Lord and our
final change.

17 Συμμιμηταί μου γίνεσθε, ἀδελφοί, καὶ σκοπεῖτε τοὺς οὕτω περιπατοῦντας καθὼς ἔχετε τύπον ἡμᾶς. 18 πολλοὶ γὰρ περιπατοῦσιν, οὓς

words, commands all to pursue, and not to diverge from; compare the illustrative diagram of Meyer *in loc.*

τῷ αὐτῷ στοιχεῖν] 'walk onward consentantly with the same,' or 'according to the same;' d. t. *ver. n.*, compare Gal. vi. 16, τῷ κανόνι τούτῳ στοιχεῖν, where see note and references. The infinitive is here imperatival, and in accordance with that usage, conveys a precise and emphatic command, or rather *address* (Krüger, *Sprachl.* § 53. 1. 3), in the second person singular or plural; see Jelf, *Gr.* 671. n, Fritz, *Rom.* Vol. III. p. 86. Hence the hortative translation in the first person, as in Theoph., στοιχῶμεν (comp. Chrys.), and in all the Vv. except Æth. (Platt), seems grammatically doubtful; so rightly Mey., Alf., but not De W. This is perhaps the only certain instance of a pure imperatival infinitive in the N. T.; other instances, *e. g.* Rom. xii 15, pass more into declarations of duty and of what *ought to be done*, and may consequently be joined with all three persons; see Jelf, *Gram.* § 671. b, Winer, *Gr.* § 43. 5, p. 283. The addition in *Rec.*, κανόνι, τὸ αὐτὸ φρονεῖν, which appears, with variations both of words and order, in the majority of uncial MSS (see *Tisch.*), is rejected by AB; 17. 67 *; Copt., Sah., Æth. (Pol., but not Platt), Theodot.-Ancyr.; H.L. Aug., al., and by Luchm., Tisch., and most recent editors. It has been defended by Rinck, Matth., and Wordsw., but, owing to the suspicious variations in words and order, has every appearance of an explanatory gloss; comp. ch. ii. 2, Gal. vi. 16.

17. συμμιμηταί κ. τ. λ.] '*Be imitators together,* scil. with all who imitate me;' 'coimitatores,' Claroin., Copt.:

continuation of the foregoing exhortation with reference to the apostle's own example. The σύν in συμμ is apparently neither otiose on the one hand, as in συμπολῖται, Ephes. ii 19, nor yet on the other does it imply so much as 'omnes uno consensu, et una mente,' Calv., Alford,—a tinge of ethical meaning not suggested or required by the context. It appears simply to mark the common nature of the action in which they all were to share; not merely 'the imitators' (1 Cor. iv. 16), but 'be a company of such; καθάπερ ἐν χορῷ καὶ στρατοπέδῳ τὸν χορηγὸν καὶ στρατηγὸν δεῖ μιμεῖσθαι τοὺς λοιπούς, Chrys. καὶ σκοπεῖτε κ. τ. λ.] 'and mark them which are thus walking;' they were all to imitate the absent apostle and to observe studiously those with them who walked after his example. Who these were cannot be determined; the reference may be to Timothy, Epaphras, and other missionaries of the apostle, but is perhaps more naturally to all those whether holy men among the Philippians, or teachers sent to them, who followed the example of St. Paul; δ. ἄσκει ὡς πολλοῖς ἔχει τοῖδε τοῦ σκοποῦ κοινωνοῦς, Theol.

καθὼς ἔχετε κ. τ. λ.] 'as ye have us for an instance,' καθὼς standing in correlation to the preceding οὕτως, and ἡμᾶς referring to the apostle: so Vulg., Claroin., and all Vv., Chrys and the Greek expositors, and, it may be added, nearly all modern commentators. Meyer and Wiesing. give καθὼς an argumentative force, 'inasmuch as' (see notes on *Eph.* i. 4), but in so doing seem to impair the force, and obscure the perspicuity of the passage; see Alf. *in loc.*, who has satisfactorily refuted this interpretation. The use of the plural ἡμᾶς does

πολλάκις ἔλεγον ὑμῖν, νῦν δὲ καὶ κλαίων λέγω, τοὺς ἐχθροὺς τοῦ σταυροῦ τοῦ Χριστοῦ, ¹⁹ ὧν τὸ τέλος ἀπώλεια, ὧν ὁ Θεὸς ἡ κοιλία

not imply a reference to St. Paul and τοὺς οὕτως περιπ., but seems naturally to point either to the apostle and his fellow-workers (Van Heng., Alf.), or perhaps, more probably, is the apostle's designation of himself viewed less in his personal than his *official* relations : 'be all, in matters of practical religion, imitators of me, Paul, and observe those, etc., who have me their apostle as their ensample;' compare 2 Thess. iii. 7, 9. The singular τύπον yields no support to either interpretation; see Bernhardy, *Synt.* II. 5, p. 61.

18. πολλοὶ γάρ] Reason for the foregoing exhortation arising from the sad nature of the case. Who the πολλοὶ were cannot be exactly determined. It seems, however, clear that they are not the same as those mentioned in ver. 2 sq. The latter were false teachers, and of Judaical tenets; these, on the contrary, were not teachers at all, and were of an Epicurean bias; not, however, Pagans (Rill.), but nominal Christians, baptized sinners (Manning), who disgraced their profession by their sensuality; Χριστιανισμὸν μὲν ὑποκρινόμενοι ἐν τρυφῇ δὲ καὶ ἀνέσει ζῶντες, Theoph., after Chrys. περιπατοῦσιν] 'are walking,' 'are pursuing their course.' There is no need to supply any qualifying adverb (ܐܣܬܢܐܝܬ [aliter] Syr.), or to assume any pause and change of structure (Rill., De W.). Though commonly associated by St. Paul with qualifying adverbs or adv. clauses, whether *in bonam* (Rom. xiii. 13, Eph. iv. 1), or *in malam partem* (2 Cor. iv. 2, 2 Thess iii. 6), the verb itself is of neutral meaning (comp. 1 Thess. iv. 1), and in its metaphorical use seems only to designate a man's course of life *in its practical aspects and manifestations*; it being left to the context to decide whether they are bad or good.

πολλάκις ἔλεγον] '*oftimes used to mention to you;*' most probably by word of mouth; perhaps also in the messages transmitted to them by his emissaries; not by any means necessarily in another Epistle (Flatt). The πολλάκις ('many times') follows the πολλοὶ with a slight rhetorical force not without example in St. Paul's Epistles; see Winer, *Gr.* § 68. 1, p. 560, and compare the large quantity of examples collected by Lobeck, *Paralipom.* p. 56, 57.

καὶ κλαίων] '*even weeping,*' because the evil has so increased; ὄντως δακρύων ἄξιοι οἱ τρυφῶντες, τὸ μὲν περιβόλαιον, τουτέστι, τὸ σῶμα λιπαίνοντες, τῆς δὲ μελλούσης εὐθύνας διδόναι [ψυχῆς?] οὐδένα ποιοῦνται λόγον, Chrys.

τοὺς ἐχθροὺς τοῦ σταυροῦ] '*the (special) enemies of the cross:*' apposition to the preceding relative; compare Winer, *Gr.* § 59. 7, p. 469. The article defines the class sharply and distinctly, and specifies them as enemies κατ' ἐξοχήν. They are so specified, not on account of their doctrinal errors (διδάσκοντας ὅτι δίχα τῆς νομικῆς πολιτείας ἀδύνατον τῆς σωτηρίας τυχεῖν, Theod.), but on account of their sensuality and their practical denial of the great Christian principle, οἱ δὲ τοῦ Χριστοῦ τὴν σάρκα ἐσταύρωσαν σὺν τοῖς παθήμασιν καὶ ταῖς ἐπιθυμίαις, Gal. v. 24. So Chrys., Theoph., Œcumen., and, with a more general ref., Athan. (?) *de Virgin.* § 14. On the practical application of the verse, 'the Cross the measure of sin,' see Manning, *Serm.* XI. Vol. III. p. 201 sq., and compare Bp. Hall, *Serm.* XII. Vol. v. p. 172 sq. (Oxf. 1837).

19 ὧν τὸ τέλος ἀπώλεια] '*whose end is perdition;*' more specific description of their characteristics, and the cer-

καὶ ἡ δόξα ἐν τῇ αἰσχύνῃ αὐτῶν, οἱ τὰ ἐπίγεια φρονοῦντες. ²⁰ ἡμῶν

tain and fearful issues that await them. Τέλος has the article as marking the definite and almost necessary end of such a course (compare 2 Cor. xi 15), while ἀπώλεια marks that end as no merely temporal one, but, as its usage in St. Paul's Eps. (ch. i. 28, Rom. ix. 22, 2 Thess. ii. 3, 1 Tim. vi 9) seems always to indicate, — as *eternal*; compare Fritz. *Romans*, Vol. ii. p. 338, and contrast Rom. vi. 22   ὧν ὁ Θεός] '*whose God is their belly;*' comp. Rom. xvi. 18, τῷ Κυρίῳ ἡμῶν Χριστῷ οὐ δουλεύουσιν ἀλλὰ τῇ ἑαυτῶν κοιλίᾳ (*Tisch.*). That this peculiarly characterizes these renegades as Jews (see Theod.), and esper. Pharisees (Schoettg. *Hor. Hebr.* Vol. i. p. 801), does not seem tenable; see on ver. 18.   Several commentators, B Crus., Alf. (comp. Vulg., Theoph.), regard ὁ Θεός as the predicate; the following clause seems to suggest the contrary.   καὶ ἡ δόξα κ. τ. λ.] '*and (whose) glory is in their shame,*' scil. 'exists in the sphere of it,' 'versatur in,' not 'becomes their shame,' Luther; clause dependent on the preceding ἐν. The δόξα is here, as Meyer rightly suggests, subjective, what they deemed so; αἰσχύνῃ, on the contrary, is objective, what every moral consideration marked to be so. The reference of αἰσχύνῃ to circumcision ('quorum gloria in pudendis,' Aug., Pseudo-Ambr., Anselm), probably suggested by the confusion of those here mentioned with those noticed in verse 2, is alluded to, but rightly not adopted by Chrys. and Theoph.   οἱ τὰ ἐπίγ. φρονοῦντες] '*who mind earthly things;*' relapse into the nominative to give the clause force and emphasis; see Bernhardy, *Synt.* III. 3, p. 68.   This can scarcely be called so much a participial anacoluthon (see examples in Winer, *Gr.* § 63. 2, p. 505), as an emphatic return to the primary construction, πολλοὶ γὰρ περιπ.—οἱ τὰ ἐπίγεια φρονοῦντες. The word φρονεῖν, as Horsley has remarked (on ver. 15), has considerable amplitude of meaning: combined with τὰ ἐπίγεια (contrast ver. 20 it here seems to denote the concentration of all thoughts, feeling, and interest in earthly and earthly things,—τὸ ἐνταῦθα πάντα κεκτῆσθαι, Chrys., who gives special exx.; comp. Alf. *in loc.*

20. ἡμῶν γὰρ τὸ πολ.] '*For our country or commonwealth is in heaven;*' confirmation ('enim,' Clarom, not 'autem,' Vulg.) of the foregoing by means of the contrasted conduct of St. Paul and his followers (ver. 17). ἡμῶν being emphatic, as πολ. ἐν οὐρ. in antithesis to τὰ ἐπίγ φρονεῖν. The word πολίτευμα, an ἅπ. λεγόμ. in the N. T., has received several different explanations. Three deserve consideration; (*a*) *conversation*; 'conversatio,' Vulg., ܕܘܒܪܐ [opus] Syr., 'vita civilis,' Copt., and as far as we can infer, Theodoret, Œcumenius,—the meaning being, 'nostra quam hic sepiamur viventi ratio in cœlis est.' Van Heng., De Wette; (β) *citizenship*, 'municipatus,' Jerome (comp. Tertull. *de Cor. Mil.* § 13), 'jus civitatis nostræ,' Zanch., Luther (earlier ed.),—the meaning being, 'we are freedmen of a heavenly city,' Whichcote, *Serm.* XVIII Vol. II. p. 375, and more recently Manning, *Serm.* x. Vol. III p. 183; (γ) *τὸ πολ. sc. τῶν ἁγίων*, to which we belong as πολῖται; Sanderson, *Serm.* xv. Vol. i. p. 378 (ed. Jacobs.); see 2 Macc. xii. 7, τῶν Ἰοππιτῶν πολίτευμα, Polyb. *Hist.* i. 13. 12. τὰ πολιτεύματα [τῶν Ῥωμ. κ. Καρχ.], and compare Eph. ii. 19, συμπολῖται τῶν ἁγίων; so Theophl. (τὴν πατρίδα), Beng., Mey., Alf., and the majority of modern commentators. Of these (*a*) has this advantage, that being subjective it presents a more exact contrast to τὰ ἐπίγ.

γὰρ τὸ πολίτευμα ἐν οὐρανοῖς ὑπάρχει, ἐξ οὗ καὶ σωτῆρα ἀπεκδεχόμεθα Κύριον Ἰησοῦν Χριστόν, ²¹ ὃς μετασχηματίσει τὸ σῶμα

φρονεῖν; the equiv., however, to ἀναστροφὴ rests only on the use of the verb (comp. Philo, *de Confus.* § 17, χῶρον ἐν ᾧ πολιτεύονται), and is itself not lexically demonstrable. Again in (β) the equivalence of πολίτευμα to πολιτεία (Acts xxii. 28) is equally doubtful, for the passage adduced from Aristot. *Pol.* III. 6, does not prove that the words are used indifferently (Alf.), but indifferently only in regard to a *particular* sense (πόλεως τάξις),—a statement fully confirmed by other passages, Polyb. *Hist.* IV. 23. 9, al., Joseph. *contr. Ap.* II. 17. —a pertinent example; compare Beza *in loc.* We retain then (γ), which appears to yield a pertinent meaning, and was perhaps chosen rather than πόλις (Heb. xi 10), or πατρίς (Heb. xi. 14), as representing our heavenly home, our Ἱερουσαλὴμ ἐπουράνιος (Heb. xii. 22), on the side of its constitution and polity; 'our state, the spiritual constitution to which *we* belong is in heaven:' compare Gal. iv. 26, Rev. xxi. 2, 10, Usteri, *Lehrb.* II. 1. 2, p. 182.   ἐν οὐρανοῖς ὑπάρχ.] '*existeth in heaven,*' 'constituta est,' Clarom.; see Wordsw. *in loc.*, who rightly calls attention to the strong word ὑπάρχει. The various practical aspects of this consolatory declaration are ably stated by Whichcote, *Serm.* XVIII., though somewhat modified by the interpretation assigned to πολίτευμα: our home is in heaven while we are here below, *exemplariter*, as we make it our copy; *finaliter*, as we carry it in our thoughts; *analogice*, in regard to the quality of our actions; *inchoative*, according to the degree of our present station; *intellectualiter*, according to the constitution of our minds; Vol. II. p. 375 sq.
ἐξ οὗ] *from whence,*' 'inde,' Vulgate

ܡܼܢ [exinde] Syr.; not ἐξ οὗ,

scil. πολιτ. (Beng.), a construction permissible, but not necessary, as ἐξ οὗ is purely adverbial; see Winer, *Gr.* § 21. 3, p. 128. The meaning 'ex quo tempore,' is grammatically correct (Krüger, *Sprachl.* § 43. 4. 7) but obviously pointless and unsatisfactory.

καὶ σωτ. ἀπεκδ.] '*we also tarry for as Saviour;*' the καὶ marks the correspondence of the act with the previous declaration, σωτῆρα the capacity in which the Lord was tarried for. The pure ethical meaning of ἀπεκδ. sc. 'constanter, patienter, expectare' (Tittm. *Synon.* I. p. 106), seems here, owing to the preceding ἐξ οὗ, less distinct than in other passages where such local allusions are not present, e. g., Rom. viii. 19, 23, 25, 1 Cor. i. 7, Gal. v. 5, 1 Pet. iii. 20, but is perhaps not wholly lost: see notes *on Gal.* v. 5, Winer, *de Verb. Comp.* IV. p. 14, Fritz. *Fritzsch. Opusc.* p. 156; compare also notes on ch. i. 20. The simple form ἐκδέχεσθαι occurs 1 Cor. xvi. 11, James v. 7; comp. Soph. *Phil.* 123, Dion.-Hal. *Antiq.* VI. 67.

21. μετασχηματίσει] '*shall transform,*' simply;—not 'verklären,' Luth., Neand., a meaning derived only from the context. This peculiar exhibition of our Lord's power at His second coming is brought here into prominence, to enhance the condemnation of sensuality (ver. 19) and to confirm the indirect exhortation to a pure though suffering life. It seems wholly unnecessary to restrict this merely to the living (Mey.); still less can we say with Alf. that 'the words assume, as St. Paul always does when speaking incidentally, the ἡμεῖς surviving to witness the coming of the Lord,' when really every moment of a true Christian's life involves such an ἀπεκδοχήν. On the nature of this μετασχηματισμός, which the following words define to be strictly

τῆς ταπεινώσεως ἡμῶν σύμμορφον τῷ σώματι τῆς δόξης αὐτοῦ, κατὰ τὴν ἐνέργειαν τοῦ δύνασθαι αὐτὸν καὶ ὑποτάξαι αὐτῷ τὰ πάντα.

in accordance with that of the Lord's body, — a change from a natural to a spiritual body (1 Cor. xv. 44), compare Burnet, *State of Dead*, ch VIII. p. 234 (Transl.), Cudworth, *Intell Syst.* v 3, Vol. III. p. 310 sq. (Tegg), Delitzsch, *Psychol.* III. 1, p. 401 sq., and the comments of Words* *in loc.*

τὸ σῶμα κ. τ. λ.] '*the body of our humiliation;*' not 'our vile body,' Auth. Ver., Conyb., a solution of the genitive case which though in some cases admissible (Winer, *Gr.* § 34. 3. b, p. 211) here obscures the full meaning of the words and mars the antithesis. The gen. seems here not so much a gen. of *quality* as of *content*, and to belong to the general category of the genitive *materia* (Scheuerl. *Synt.* § 12. 2. p. 83); the ταπείνωσις was that which the σῶμα contained and involved, that of which it was the receptacle; compare Bernh. *Synt.* III. 45. p. 63. It seems undesirable with Chrys. (comp. Mey., Alf.) to refer ταπείνωσις wholly to the sufferings of the body, 'humil. quae fit per crucem.' Though the more remote context (comp. ver. 18) shows that these must clearly be included, the more immediate antithesis τὸ σῶμα τῆς δόξης seems also to show that the ideas of weakness and fleshly nature (Coloss. i. 22) must not be excluded; compare Fritz. *Rom.* VI. 6, Vol. 2. p. 382. The distinction between ταπείνωσις and ταπεινότης (compare Alf.) cannot safely be pressed; see Luke i. 48, Prov. xvi. 19 al. For examples of a similar connection of the pronoun with the dependent subst., see Green, *Gr.* p. 265. σύμμορφον κ. τ. λ.] '(so as to be) conformed to the body of His glory;' scil. εἰς τὸ γενέσθαι σέμα., — a gloss which *Rec.* with D³D³EKL; many Vv.; Orig., al., retain as a portion of the text. The shorter reading has not only internal, but preponderant external evidence [ABD¹FG; Vuly., Cloom, G th., al.] distinctly in its favor. On this proleptic use of the ἐ γ., see Wine r. *Gr.* § 66. 3, p. 550, Jelf, *Gram.* § 459. 2. The genitival relation τ ς δόξης α τοῦ is exactly similar to that of τ ς ταπ. ἡμ., 'the body which is the receptacle of His glory, in which His glory is manifested.' In respect of this δόξα we are σύμμορφοι, — οὐ κατὰ τὴν ποσότητα ἀλλὰ κατὰ τὴν ποιότητα, Theod. κατὰ τὴν ἐνέργ.] '*according to the working of His ability,*' etc.; compare Eph. i. 19. The object of this clause, as Calvin rightly remarks, is to remove every possible doubt; 'ad intimam Dei potentiam convertere oportet, ut ipsa omnem dubitationem absorbeat. Nec potentiae tantum meminit, sed efficaciae, quae est effectus vel potentia in actum se exserens.' The infin. with τοῦ is dependent on the preceding subst. as a simple (possessive) gen (a construction very common in the N. T., and serves here to express, perhaps a little more forcibly than δύναμις, the enduring nature and latitude of that power; see examples in Winer, *Gr.* § 44. 4. p. 290.

καὶ ὑποτάξαι] '*even to subdue;*' the ascensive καὶ serves to mark the limitless nature of that power; He shall not only transform τὸ σῶμα κ. τ. λ., but shall also subdue τὰ πάντα, all existing things, Death not excluded (1 Cor. xv. 26), to Himself. The Κυριότης of the Eternal Son will then be complete, supreme, and universal; to be resigned unto the Father (1 Cor. xv. 28) in so far as it is economical, to last for ever and for ever in so far as it is 'consequent unto the union, or due unto the obedience of the passion.' Pearson, *Creed*, Art. II. Vol. 1. p. 197

Brethren, stand fast in the Lord.

IV. Ὥστε, ἀδελφοί μου ἀγαπητοὶ καὶ ἐπιπόθητοι, χαρὰ καὶ στέφανός μου, οὕτως στήκετε ἐν Κυρίῳ, ἀγαπητοί.

Let Euodia and Syntyche be of one mind; assist, O yokefellow, the faithful women.

² Εὐοδίαν παρακαλῶ καὶ Συντύχην παρακαλῶ τὸ αὐτὸ φρονεῖν ἐν Κυρίῳ. ³ ναὶ ἐρωτῶ

(ed. Burt.). On the use of αὐτῷ [AB D¹FG], not ἑαυτῷ (*Rec.*), comp. notes on *Eph.* i. 4.

CHAPTER IV. 1. ὥστε] 'So then,' '*Consequently*,' 'itaque,' Vulg.; 'as we have such a heavenly home, and tarry for such a salvation:' concluding exhortation naturally flowing from the preceding paragraph, ch. iii. 17–21, and continued in the same tones of personal entreaty (ἀδελφοί); comp. 1 Cor. xv. 58, where the particle similarly refers to what has immediately preceded. De Wette and Wiesinger refer the particle to ch. iii. 2 sq., but thereby deprive the exhortation of much of its natural and consecutive force. On the force of ὥστε with indic. and inf., see notes on *Gal.* ii. 13, and reff., and with the imper., notes on ch. ii. 12. ἀγαπητοὶ καὶ ἐπιπόθ.] '*beloved and longed after*,'— terms by no means synonymous (Heinr.), but marking both the love the apostle entertained for them (emphatically repeated at the end of the paragraph) and the desire he felt to see them; 'carissimi et desideratissimi,' Vulgate. The word is an ἅπ. λεγόμ. in the N. T., but is occasionally found elsewhere; Appian, *Hisp.* § 43, ἐπιποθήτους ὅρκους (Rost u. Palm, *Lex.*), Clem.-Rom. 1 *Cor.* § 59, εὐκταίαν καὶ ἐπιπόθητον εἰρήνην. On the force of ἐπί, see notes on 2 *Tim.* i. 4. χαρὰ καὶ στέφανός μου] '*my joy and crown*,' scil. ἐφ' οἷς χαρὰν καὶ ἔπαινον ἔχω, Camerar. See especially 1 Thess. ii. 19, in which the words ἐν τῇ αὐτοῦ [Κυρίου] παρουσίᾳ there limit the reference to the Lord's coming,— a reference, however, here

(Alford, comp. Calv.) by no means necessary: the Philippians were a subject of joy and a crown to St. Paul, now as well as hereafter; compare 1 Cor. ix. 2, 3. For examples of this metaphorical use of στέφ., see Isaiah xxviii. 5, Ecclus. i. 11, xxv. 6, Soph. *Ajax*, 460. οὕτως] '*thus*,'—' as I have exhorted you, and as those are acting whose πολίτευμα is in heaven.' A reference to their present state ('sic ut cœpistis, state,' Schmid., Beng.), though suggested by Chrys., seems out of place in this earnest *exhortation*: 1 Cor. ix. 24, cited by Bengel, is not in point. στήκετε ἐν Κυρ.] '*stand (fast) in the Lord*;' not 'per Dominum,' Zanch., but 'in Domino,'— in Him as in the true element of their spiritual life; see 1 Thess. iii. 8, and notes on *Ephes.* iv. 17, vi. 1. al.

2. Εὐοδίαν παρακ.] Special exhortation addressed to two *women*, Euodia and Syntyche; compare ver. 3. The opinion of Grot. that they are the names of two men (Euodias and Syntyches) is untenable; that of Schwegler (*Nachapost. Zeit.* Vol. II. p. 135), that they represent two parties in the Church, monstrous. Of the two persons nothing whatever is known; they may have been deaconesses (Rom. xvi. 1), but were more probably persons of station and influence (Chrys., comp. Acts xvii. 12), whose dissensions, perhaps in matters of religion (τὸ αὐτὸ φρον. ἐν Κυρ.), might have shaken the faith (comp. οὕτως στήκετε immediately preceding) of some of the Philippian converts. Syntyche has a place in the *Acta Sanct.* (July) Vol. v. p. 225. παρακαλῶ] The repetition of this verb is somewhat ne-

καὶ σέ, γνήσιε σύνζυγε, συλλαμβάνου αὐταῖς, αἵτινες ἐν τῷ εὐαγ-
γελίῳ συνήθλησάν μοι, μετὰ καὶ Κλήμεντος καὶ τῶν λοιπῶν συν-
εργῶν μου, ὧν τὰ ὀνόματα ἐν βίβλῳ ζωῆς.

ticeable: it scarcely seems 'ad vehemen-
tiam affectus significandam,' Erasm.,
Mey., but rather to mark that they both
equally needed the exhortation, that they
were in fact both equally to blame. The
ἐν Κυρ. is of course not to be joined with
παρακ., 'obtestor per Dom.,' Beza 2, but
marks the sphere in which the τὸ αὐτὸ
φρον. (see notes on ch. ii. 2) was to be
displayed.

3. ναὶ ἐρωτῶ καὶ σέ] *yea, I beseech even thee*' The particle ναὶ (not
καὶ, Rec., which has scarcely any critical
support) has here its usual and proper
confirmatory force. It is used either (a)
in assent to a direct question, Matth ix.
28, John xi. 27, Rom. iii. 29; (b) in assent to an assertion, Matth. xv. 27,
Mark vii. 28; (c) in graver assertions
as confirmatory of what has preceded,
Matth. xi. 26, Luke xi. 51, xii. 5; (d)
in animated addresses as corroborating
the substance of the petition, Philem. 20
(see Mey. *in loc.*) The simple 'vis ob-
secrandi,'—Heb. נא (Grot., Viger, al.)
cannot be substantiated. For examples
of its use in classical Greek, see Viger,
Idiom. VII. 9. p. 424, Rost u. Palm, *Lex.*
s. v. Vol. II. p. 309. On the
distinction between ἐρωτᾶν ('rogare,'—
equals) and αἰτεῖν ('petere,'—superiors),
see Trench, *Synon.* § 40.

γνήσιε σύνζυγε] 'true yoke-fellow,'
'dilectissime conjunx,' Claroman.—a
translation that may have early been
misunderstood. The explanations of
these words are somewhat numerous.
Setting aside doubtful or untenable
conjectures,—that the person referred
to is the wife of the apostle. Clem. Alex.
Strom. III. 53 [grammatically incorrect
(opp. to Alf.) as the uncertain gender of
σύς (Eur. *Alc.* 315, 343) would cause
γνήσιος to revert to three terminations],

the husband or brother of one of the
women (Chrys., hesitatingly), Timothy
(Estius), Silas (Beng.), Epaphroditus,
though now with the apostle (Grot.,
Hamm.), Christ (Wieseler, *Chronol.* p.
458),—two opinions deserve consideration; (a) that σύνζυγος is a proper name,
and that γνήσιος is used in allusion to
the correspondence between the name of
the man and his relation to the apostle,
'qui vere, et re et nomine, σύνζυγος es,'
Com., Meyer; (b) that the chief of the
ἐπίσκοποι (ch. i. 1) at Philippi is here referred to. Of these (a) harmonizes with
the meaning of γνήσιος (comp. notes on
1 *Tim.* i. 2), and is slightly favored by
the order (Luke i. 3, Galat. iii. 1; but
Kl.; al. *Rec.* reverse it), but is improbable on account of the apparently unique
occurrence of the name. As the only
valid objection to (b),—that St. Paul
never elsewhere so designates any of his
συνεργοί (Mey.), may be diluted by the
fact that the chief Bishop of the place
stood in a somewhat different relation to
such associates, and as the order is probably due to emphasis on γνήσιε (Winer,
Gr. § 59. 2, p. 469), the balance seems
in favor of this latter view: so Luther,
De Wette, and apparently the majority
of modern expositors.

συλλαμβ. αὐταῖς] '*assist them*,' scil.
Euodia and Syntyche, in endeavoring to
bring them to a state of ὁμόνοια; not
'those women which,' Auth. and other
Engl. Vv. (comp. Vulg. 'illas quae').
—an inexact translation of αἵτινες (see
below) which obscures the reference of
αὐταῖς to the preceding substantives.
The middle συλλαμβ. occurs in a similar
construction, Luke v. 7 (βοηθεῖν D),
Gen. xxx. 8 (*Alex.*), Ælian, *Var. Hist.*
II. 4, and with a gen. rei, Soph. *Ph. Oct.*
282. The active is more usual, in this

Rejoice, show forbearance; be not anxious, but tell your wants to God, and His peace shall be with you.

⁴ Χαίρετε ἐν Κυρίῳ πάντοτε· πάλιν ἐρῶ, χαίρετε. ⁵ τὸ ἐπιεικὲς ὑμῶν γνωσθήτω πᾶσιν

sense, in classical Greek; see examples in Rost u Palm, *Lex.* s. v. αἵτινες] '*inasmuch as they*,' 'ut quæ,' Beza, compare Syr. ܩܘ ܗܕܐ [quia ipsæ] and see Scholef. *Hints*, p. 106: a very distinct use of the explicative force of ὅστις: see notes *on Gal.* iv. 24. ἐν τῷ εὐαγγ.] The gospel was the sphere in which the labor was expended; compare Reuss, *Théol. Chrét.* iv. 8, Vol. ii. p. 81. Meyer very appropriately calls attention to the fact that women were apparently the first in whom the gospel took root in Philippi; Acts xvi. 13, ἐλαλοῦμεν ταῖς συνελθούσαις γυναιξίν. 'Women were the first fruits of St. Paul's labors on the continent of Europe,' Baum. *on Acts, l. c.* μετὰ καὶ Κλήμ.] '*in company with Clement also*,' scil. συνήθλησαν: they were associated with Clement and the apostle's other fellow-laborers at Philippi in some efforts to advance the gospel, perhaps, as Beng. suggests, not unattended with danger; Acts xvi. 19 sq., compare Phil. i. 28. It is doubtful whether the Clement here mentioned is identical with the third bp. of Rome, or not. On the one hand we have the very distinct testimony of Origen, *in Joann.* i. 29, Vol. iv. p. 153 (ed. Ben.), Euseb. *Hist. Eccl.* iii. 4, 15, Jerome, *de Vir. Ill.* xv. Vol. ii. p. 839 (ed. Vallars.), Epiphanius, *Hær.* xxvii. 6, *Const. Apost.* vii. 46; see Hammond, *contr. Blond.* p. 254, Lardner, *Credibility*, ii. 38. 23. On the other hand (*a*) the notice of Clem. in Irenæus, *Hær.* iii. 3. 3, ὁ καὶ ἑωρακὼς τοὺς μακαρίους Ἀποστόλους καὶ συμβεβληκὼς αὐτοῖς, — where, however, συμβεβλ. (most unnecessarily queried by Conyb. and Bloomf.) should not be overlooked, — contains no allusion to this special commendation; and (*b*) the present context seems certainly in favor of the supposition that Clement, like Euodia and Syntyche and (appy.) the συνεργοί, was a member of the Church of Philippi. Still, as it is perfectly conceivable that a member of the Church of the Roman city of Philippi might have become 7 or 8 years afterwards (Pearson, *Minor Works*, Vol. ii. p. 465) Bp. of Rome, — as (*b*) is merely negative, and as the early testimony of Origen is positive and distinct, there seems no just ground for summarily rejecting, with De W., Mey., and Alf., this ancient ecclesiastical tradition; compare Winer, *RWB.* Vol. i. p. 232. The position of καί between the prep and the noun is somewhat unusual, such a collocation being in the N. T. apparently confined to γάρ (John iv. 37), γε (Luke xi. 8), δέ (Matth. xi. 12), μέν (Rom. xi 22), μὲν γάρ (Acts xxviii. 22), and τε (Acts x. 39); compare Matth. *Gr.* § 595. 3. In the present case, however, the vinculum of the preposition extends over the whole clause. καὶ — καί (see notes on 1 *Tim.* iv. 10) being correlative. The examples cited by Alf. (compare Mey.), in which only a single καί occurs, are thus not fully in point. ὦν τὰ ὀνόμ. appear only to refer to τῶν λοιπῶν, — 'Clement whom I have mentioned by name, and the rest, who though not named by me, nevertheless have their names in the book of life;' comp. Luke x. 20, Rev. xiii. 8, xvii. 8, xx. 12, xxi. 27. To supply an optative (εἴη, 'existent') and assume that the λοιποί were now dead (Beng.), seems unnecessary and unsatisfactory. The expression is not improbably derived from the Old Test.; compare Exod. xxxii. 32, Psalm lix. 28, Isaiah iv. 3, Ezek. xiii. 9, Dan. xii. 1.

4. χαίρετε] Separate exhortations to the church at large, continued to ver.

ἀνθρώποις. ὁ Κύριος ἐγγύς. ⁶ Μηδὲν μεριμνᾶτε, ἀλλ' ἐν παντὶ

4. They commence with the exhortation, which, as has been already remarked (see notes on ch. iii. 1) pervades the whole Epistle. On the repetition, Chrys. well observes, τοῦτο ϕαρσύνοντος ἐστι καὶ δεικνύντος, ὅτι ὁ ἐν Θεῷ [Κυρίῳ] ὢν ἀεὶ χαίρει· κἂν τε θλίβηται, κἂν ὁτιοῦν πάσχῃ ἀεὶ χαίρει ὁ τοιοῦτος: see the good sermon of Beveridge on this text, *Serm.* cv. Vol. v. p. 62 sq (A.-C. Libr.), and compare August *Serm.* CLXXI. Vol. v. p. 933 (ed Migne).

πάλιν ἐρῶ] '*again I will say*,' not '1 say,' Auth , as ἐρῶ seems regularly and correctly used throughout the N. T. as a future. The traces of a present ἐρέω (Hippocr. *Præcept.* p. 64, *Epidem.* II. p. 691) are few and doubtful; see Buttm. *Irreg. Verbs,* p. 89 (Translation). It is scarcely necessary to do more than notice the very improbable construction of Beng., by which πάντοτε is joined with this clause.

5. τὸ ἐπιεικὲς ὑμῶν] '*your forbearance*,' Conybeare, 'your moderation (Auth.) and readiness to waive all rigor and severity:' compare Joseph. *Arch.* VI. 12. 7, ἐπιεικεῖς καὶ μέτριοι, and Loesn. *Obs* p. 358, where several examples are cited of ἐπιείκεια in connection with πραότης, φιλανθρωπία, and ἡμερότης. See notes on 1 *Tim.* iii. 3, and comp. Trench, *Synon.* § 43. On the use of the abstract neuter (τὸ ἐπιεικὲς = ἐπιείκεια), compare Jelf, *Gr.* § 436. γ, and notes on ch. iii. 8; add Rom. ii. 4, 1 Corinth. i. 25, and Glass-e, *Philol.* III. 1, p. 537.

γνωσθήτω πᾶσιν ἀνθρ.] '*become known to all men*:' 'let the goodness of your principles in this respect be known experimentally by *all* who have dealings with you, be they epicurean enemies of the cross (Chrys., Theoph.), or pagan persecutors' (Theod.). The command is wholly unrestricted.

ὁ Κύριος ἐγγύς] '*the Lord (Jesus) is near.*' The exact meaning and connection of the words is slightly doubtful. The regular meaning of Κύριος in St. Paul's Epistles (compare Winer, *Gram* § 19. 1, p. 113) and the demonstrable temporal meaning of ἐγγύς (Matth. xxiv. 32, Rom xiii. 11, Rev. i. 3 seem clearly to refer this not to a general readiness to help (Manning, *Serm.* XIII. Vol III p. 211), but specially to the Lord's second advent, which the inspired apostle regards as nigh, yet not necessarily as immediate, or to happen in his own Lifetime. That the early church expected a speedy return of Christ,—that they thought that He 'that was to come would come, and would not tarry,' is not to be denied. This general expectation, however, founded on our Master's own declarations, and on the knowledge that the ἔσχαται ἡμέραι (James v. 3, 7) and καιροὶ ὕστεροι were already come, both is and ought to be, separated from any specific and personal anticipations of which the N. Test. presents no certain trace. With regard to the connection, it may be either minatory (Schoettg. *H.* Vol. 1. p. 803) or encouraging (De W.) with regard to what has preceded, or, more probably, consolatory with reference to what follows (Chrys.), or, not unlikely, a bond of union to both (Alf.); on the one hand, the Lord's speedy coming (as Judge) adds a stimulus to our exhibition of forbearance toward others, comp James v 9; on the other, it swallows up all unprofitable anxieties.

6. μηδὲν μεριμν.] '*be careful about nothing*:' 'entertain no disquieting anxieties about anything earthly,' Matth. vi. 25. The accusative is that of the object whereon the μεριμνᾶν is exercised (Jelf, *Gr.* § 551), and stands in emphatic antithesis to the following ἐν παντί. Chrys. and Theophyl. refer μηδὲν mainly to the pressure of calamity or persecution (μήτε

τῇ προσευχῇ καὶ τῇ δεήσει μετὰ εὐχαριστίας τὰ αἰτήματα ὑμῶν γνωριζέσθω πρὸς τὸν Θεόν. ⁷ καὶ ἡ εἰρήνη τοῦ Θεοῦ ἡ ὑπερέχου-

τῆς ἐκείνων ὕβρεως, μήτε τῆς ὑμῶν θλίψεως, Theoph.): it seems better to leave it wholly unrestricted. The practical applications of the text will be found in Beveridge, *Serm.* Vol. v. p. 181 sq. (A.-C. Libr.). ἐν παντί] '*in everything*,' equally unrestricted; not 'in all time,' Syr., Æth., but, 'in omnibus,' Copt., ἐν παντί φησί, τουτέστι πράγματι, Chrys. The translation of Vulg., 'in omni oratione' (so Clarom.), which Meyer, and after him Alford defend as meaning 'in omni (re) oratione,' etc., is certainly rather suspicious.

τῇ προσευχῇ κ.τ.λ.] '*by your prayer and your supplication*,' by the specific prayer offered up when the occasion may require it; compare Middleton, *Art.* v. 1. 3, 4, p. 93 (ed. Rose). The repetition of the article gives an emphasis to the words; each noun is enunciated independently: see Winer, *Gr.* § 19. 5, p. 117. The difference between the more general προσ. (*precatio*) and the more special δέησ. (*rogatio*) is stated in notes on *Eph.* vi. 18, and *on* 1 *Tim.* ii. 1.

μετὰ εὐχαρ.] '*with thanksgiving*,' an adjunct to prayer that should never be wanting, 1 Thess. v. 18, 1 Tim. ii. 2; see Beveridge, *Serm.* CVII. Vol. v. p. 76 sq. (A.-C. Libr.) compare notes *on Col.* iii. 15. Alford remarks on the omission of the article, 'because the matters themselves may not be recognized as grounds of εὐχαριστία.' It seems more simple to say that εὐχαρ., 'thanksgiving for past blessings' (compare Hofm. *Schriftb.* Vol. II. 2, p. 337), is in its nature more general and comprehensive, προσ. and δέησ. almost necessarily more limited and specific. Hence, though εὐχαρ. occurs twelve times in St. Paul's Epistles, it is only twice used with the article, 1 Cor. xiv. 16, 2 Cor. iv. 15. τὰ αἰτήματα]

'*your requests*;' according to termination, 'the things requested' (compare Buttm. *Gr.* § 119. 7), and thence (as the context requires), with a slight modification of meaning, 'the purport or subjects of prayer:' '*petitum*, materia δεήσεως,' Beng.; compare Luke xxiii. 24, 1 John v. 15. There is often, especially in later Greek, a sort of libration of meaning between nouns in σις and -μα; compare 2 Tim. i. 13, al. Meyer quotes Plato, *Rep.* VIII. p. 566 D, where the explanatory clause αἰτεῖν τὸν δῆμον (see Stallb. *in loc.*) seems to show that there is even there also some tinge of such an interchange. πρὸς τὸν Θεόν] '*toward God*,' i. e. 'before and unto God,' the prep. denoting the ethical direction of the prayer; see Winer, *Gr.* § 49. h, p. 371.

7. καὶ ἡ εἰρ. τοῦ Θεοῦ] '*and (so) the peace of God*,' the peace which comes from Him and of which He is the source and origin; gen. *auctoris*, or rather *originis* (Hartung, *Casus*, p. 17, Scheuerl. *Synt.* § 17, p. 125), belonging to the general category of the genitive of *ablation* (Donalds. *Gr.* § 448). On the use of the consecutive καί (Heb. xii. 19, al.), see Winer, *Gram.* § 53. 3, p. 387. The exact meaning of εἰρήνη τοῦ Θεοῦ (see below, ver. 9) is somewhat doubtful. Three meanings have been assigned to εἰρήνη; (a) '*concord*;' '*studium pacis*, unitatis, concordiae, inter homines atque in ecclesiâ' (Pol. *Syn.*), apparently adopted by Theodoret (ὡς ὑπαλλήλων ὄντων τῶν διωγμῶν ἀναγκαίως αὐτοῖς τὴν εἰρ. ἐπηύξατο), and strenuously advocated by Meyer *in loc.*; (β) '*reconciliation*' with God; ἡ καταλλαγή, ἡ ἀγάπη τοῦ Θεοῦ, Chrys. 1; compare Rom. v. 1, and Green, *Gr.* p. 262; (γ) '*peace*,' i. e. the deep tranquillity of a soul resting wholly upon God,—the antithesis

σα πάντα νοῦν φρουρήσει τὰς καρδίας ὑμῶν καὶ τὰ νοήματα ὑμῶν ἐν Χριστῷ Ἰησοῦ.

to the solicitude and anxiety engendered by the world and worldliness; compare John xiv. 27; Chrys. 2, Beza, Beng., al. Of these (a) seems clearly insufficient and not in harmony with the context; (β) points in the right direction, but is unnecessarily restrictive; (γ) i fully in accordance with the context (comp. μηδὲν μεριμν., ver. 6), includes (β), and gives a full and spiritual meaning: so De W., Wiesing., Alf., and most modern commentators; compare notes on Col. iii. 15. ἡ ὑπερ. πάντα νοῦν] 'which overpasseth every understanding;' 'which transcendeth every effort and attempt on the part of the understanding to grasp and realize it.' Νοῦς here, as the context suggests, points to the human πνεῦμα 'quatenus cogitat et intelligit' (Olshaus. Opusc. p. 156),—a meaning, however, in many, perhaps the majority of cases in the N. T., not sufficiently comprehensive; see notes on 1 Tim. vi. 5, and on 2 Tim. iii. 8. It may be observed that the term νοῦς is apparently used by the sacred writers, not to denote any separate essence or quality different from the πνεῦμα, but as a manifestation or outcoming of the same in moral and intellectual action, the human πνεῦμα, 'quatenus cogitat, intelligit, et vult,'—the exact limits of this definition being in all cases best fixed by the immediate context: see especially Beck, Seelenl. II. 18, p. 48 sq., Delitzsch, Bibl. Psych. IV. 5, p. 145, and compare Schubert, Gesch. der Seele, Vol. II. p. 494 sq. On the use of the transitive ὑπερέχειν with an accus. of the object surpassed (contrast chap. ii. 3), see Jelf, Gr. § 504. obs. 2.

φρουρήσει] 'shall guard, keep:' not optative, 'custodiat,' Vulg., Claroman., and in effect Chrys. διαφυλάξει καὶ ἀσφαλίσαιτο, but simply future, as in Goth. 'fastaip' [servabit,—not 'servat,' De Gab.; Goth. pres. commonly supplies place of Greek future], Copt., al.; the event will follow if the exhortation μηδὲν κ. τ. λ. is attended to. We can scarcely say with Conyb. that φρουρ. i . . . . 'shall garrison' (2 Cor. xi 32, Tou vi. 111. 17, Plato, Rep. IV. p. 429 A), as the idea of 'watching over,' 'guarding,' accords with derivation [ς, ο — φρο, and Homeric OP-; Pott, Et. Forsch. Vol. I. p. 122], and appears total in connection with persons and things: Sophocl. Œd. Rex, 1479, Eurip. Cycl. 6-6, Herc. Fur. 399; Hesych. φρουρεῖ· φυλάττει. The nature of the φρούρησις is more nearly defined by ἐν Χρ. Ἰησ. which appears to denote, not so much with a semi-local reference (ὥστε μὴ ἐκπεσεῖν αὐτοῦ τῆς πίστεως, Chrys.) the space in which they were to be kept, as that in which the action was to take place; see Meyer in loc. τὰς καρδίας κ. τ. λ.] 'your hearts and . . . thoughts;' 'corda vestra et cogitationes vestras,' Copt., Æth. The distinction between these two words should not be obscured. Καρδία, properly the (interior) seat of the ψυχή, the 'Lebens-Mitte'—see Beck, Seelenl. III. 20, p. 63), is used with considerable latitude of meaning to denote the centre of feeling, willing, thinking, and even of moral life (see especially Delitzsch, Bibl. Psych. iv. 11, p. 203 sq.), and, to speak roughly, bears much the same relation to the ψυχή that νοῦς bears to πνεῦμα (see above), being in fact the ψυχή in its practical aspects and relations; see Olshaus. Opusc. p. 155 sq., and notes on 1 Tim. i. 5. The νοήματα, on the other hand, are properly (as here) the products of spiritual activity, of thinking, willing, etc. (2 Cor. ii 11), and occasionally and derivatively, the implements or instruments of the same, 2 Cor iii. 14, iv. 4: see Beck, Seelenl. II. 19,

Practise all that is good, and all that you have learned from me.

8 Τὸ λοιπόν, ἀδελφοί, ὅσα ἐστὶν ἀληθῆ, ὅσα σεμνά, ὅσα δίκαια, ὅσα ἁγνά, ὅσα προσφιλῆ, ὅσα

p. 59, Roos, *Psych.* iv. 26. The meaning is thus in effect as stated by Alf., 'your hearts themselves (?) and their fruits;' or as, briefly, by Beng., 'cor sedes cogitationum.' On biblical psychology generally, see the remarks in pref. to *Past. Epist.* p. v., and notes *on* 1 *Tim.* iii. 16.

8. τὸ λοιπόν] '*Finally;*' concluding recapitulation, in an emphatic and comprehensive summary, of the chief subjects for preparatory meditation and (ver. 9) consequent practice. The formula is here more definitely conclusive (πάντα ἡμῖν εἴρηται, Chrys.) than in ch. iii. 1 (see notes), where the nature of the exhortations led to a not unnatural digression. It thus *echoes*, yet, owing to the difference of the exhortations, does not *resume* (Matth.) the preceding τὸ λοιπόν. The sixfold repetition of ὅσα adds much to the vigor and emphasis of the exhortation. On the whole verse see thirteen able sermons by Whichcote, *Works*, Vol. III. p. 368 sq.

ἀ λ η θ ῆ] '*true:*' i. e., as the context requires, in their nature and practical applications, 'genere morum,' Whichcote: so Theoph. (comp. Chrys.) ἀληθῆ· τουτέστιν ἐνάρετα· ἡ γὰρ κακία ψεῦδος ; compare Eph. iv. 21. To restrict the reference to *words* (Beng., Bisp.), or to *doctrine* (Hamm.), seems undesirable; the epithets throughout are general and inclusive. σ ε μ ν ά] '*seemly,*' '*venerable,*' '*deserving of, and receiving, respect,*' Syr. ܟܐܢܐ [verecunda]: compare Hor. *Epist.* 1. 1. 11, 'quid verum atque decens curo et rogo.' The Vulg. '*pudica*' is too special, the Auth. '*honest*' scarcely exact. As the derivation suggests (σέβομαι), the adjective primarily marks whatever calls for 'respect' or 'veneration,' and thence, with a somewhat special application, whatever is so

seemly and grave (ὅσα ἐν σχήμασιν καὶ λόγοις, καὶ βαδίσμασι καὶ πράξεσιν, Œcumen.) as always to secure it ; see Whichcote, p. 399. Τὸ σεμνόν, according to this able writer, consists in 'grave behavior' and 'composure of spirit,' and is briefly characterized by Calvin as 'in hoc situm ut digne vocatione nostra ambulemus :' hence such associations as σεμνὸν καὶ ἅγιον, Plato, *Soph.* p. 249 A, μέτρια καὶ σεμνά, Clem.-Rom. 1 *Cor.* § 1; compare notes *on* 1 *Tim.* ii. 2.

δ ί κ α ι α] '*just ;*' in its widest application, 'quæ talia sunt qualia esse oportet,' Tittm. *Synon.* p. 19: not exactly 'just and equal,' Whichcote, but rather 'just and right,' whether from the proportions of things or constitutions of the law (Whichcote, Vol. iv. p. 10), without any reference to others (Col. iv. 1) : compare Acts x. 22, Rom. v. 7, 1 Tim. i. 9. On the distinction between δίκαιος and the more limited ἀγαθός, see Tittm. *Synon.* p. 19 sq., and on that between δίκ. and ὅσιος notes *on Tit.* i. 8.

ἁ γ ν ά] '*pure ;*' 2 Cor. vii. 11, 1 Tim. v. 22 : not 'chaste,' Grot., Est., al., in the more special and limited meaning of the word. On the use of ἁγνός and its distinction from ἅγιος (with which the Vulgate appears here to have interchanged it), see notes *on* 1 *Tim.* v. 22, and Tittmann, *Synon.* 1. p. 21 sq. Chrys. draws a correct line between this and the preceding σεμνός ; τὸ σεμνὸν τῆς ἔξω ἐστὶ δυνάμεως, τὸ δὲ ἁγνὸν τῆς ψυχῆς. π ρ ο σ φ ι λ ῆ] '*lovely*' (ἅπ. λεγόμ.), not merely in reference to our fellow-men, 'per quæ sitis amabiles hominibus,' Est. (compare Ecclus. iv. 7), nor even with exclusive reference to God (ἅπερ ἐστὶ τῷ Θεῷ προσφ., Theod.) but generally, whatever both in respect of itself, and the disposition of the doer (Whichcote), conciliates love, is generous and noble. See

εὔφημα, εἴ τις ἀρετὴ καὶ εἴ τις ἔπαινος, ταῦτα λογίζεσθα· 9 ἃ καὶ ἐμάθετε καὶ παρελάβετε καὶ ἠκούσατε καὶ εἴδετε ἐν ἐμοί, ταῦτα πράσσετε· καὶ ὁ Θεὸς τῆς εἰρήνης ἔσται μεθ' ὑμῶν.

the good exemplifications of τὸ προσφιλές, in Whichcote, *Serm.* LXXV. Vol. IV. p. 88 sq. — εὔφημα] 'of good report;' not merely 'quæ bonam famam pariunt' (Grot., Calv.), but, in accordance with the more literal meaning of the word, 'well-sounding' (Luth.), 'of auspicious nature when spoken of,' Syriac ܡܫܒܚܐ [laudabilia], — those 'great and bright truths' in relation to God, ourselves, and our fellow-men, which sound well of themselves (loquuntur res), and command belief and entertainment, Whichcote, p. 108 sq. εἴ τις ἀρετή] 'whatever virtue there be,' Scholef. *Hints*, p. 107, or more accurately 'there is,' Alf., it being assumed that there is such; see Latham, *English Lang.* § 614 (ed. 3), and comp. Wordsworth *in loc.*: recapitulation of the foregoing, with ref. perhaps to all the epithets except the last which seems to be generalized by the following ἔπαινος. Ἀρετή [from a root AP- and connected with Sanscr. *vrt*, 'protegere,' Pott, *Etym. Forsch.* Vol. I. p. 221, Donalds. *Crat.* § 285] is only found elsewhere in the N. T. in 2 Pet. i. 5 (in reference to man; compare Wisdom iv. 1) and 1 Pet. ii. 9, 2 Pet. i. 3 (in ref. to God; comp. Hab. iii. 2, Isaiah xliii. 8, al.): it designates, as Meyer observes, 'moral excellence in feeling and action' (ἡ τῶν καλῶν ἑομιζομένων ἐμπειρία, Hesych.), and is opposed to κακία, Plato, *Republ.* IV. 444 D, 445 C: see Whichcote, Vol. IV. p. 120. ἔπαινος] 'praise;' not 'id quod est laudabile,' Calv., or, 'ea quæ laudem apud homines mereantur,' Est., — but 'praise,' in its simple sense, which, as Whichcote observes, 'regularly follows upon virtue, and is a note of it and a piece of the reward thereof,' p. 132. The addition ἐπιστήμης after ἔπαιν. with DEFG; Claram, some mss. of Vulg. al., is an interpolation properly rejected by all modern editors.

λογίζεσθε] 'think on,' 'take account of,' not however merely 'bear them in your thoughts,' 'meditate' (Alf.), but 'use your faculties upon them,' 'horum rationem habete,' Beng.; compare 1 Cor. xiii. 5, and see Whichcote p. 158.

9 ἃ καί] '*which also;*' (ex implication of the foregoing in the apostle himself; τοῦτο διδασκαλίας ἀρίστης, τὸ ἐν πάσαις ταῖς παραινέσεσιν ἑαυτὸν παρέχειν τύπον, Chrysost. The first καί is ascensive ('facit transitionem a generalibus (ὅσα) ad Paulina.' Beng.), — not 'et,' Vulg. (Syr., Copt. omit), but 'etiam,' Luth., the other three simply copulative, the sentence falling into two portions (ἐμάθ. καὶ παρελ. ἠκούσ. καὶ εἴδ.) connected by καί, each of which again is similarly inter-connected: 'duo priora verba ad doctrinam pertinent, duo reliqua ad exemplum,' Estius. compare Theod., καὶ διὰ τῶν λόγων ὑμᾶς ἐδίδαξα, καὶ διὰ τῶν πραγμάτων ἐπέδειξα. So also Van Heng., Mey., Wiesinger, al. παρελάβετε] '*received;*' not, however, in a purely passive (Galat. i. 12, 1 Thess. ii. 13), but, as the climactic order of the words (compare ἠκούσ. καὶ εἴδ.) seems to suggest, with a somewhat active reference (John i. 11, 1 Cor. xv. 1); compare Dion.-Halic. I. p. 44, λέγω δὲ παρὰ τῶν ἐγχωρίων παρέλαβον (quæ ab incolis perceperit), and the somewhat similar ἀναλαβεῖν ἐν καρδίᾳ, Job xxii. 22. The distinction of Grot. '*ἐμάθετε* significat primam institutionem: *παρελάβετε* exactiorem doctrinam' (ἐγγράφως, Theoph., — but qu. reading) seems lexically doubtful: for examples of παραλ. see Kypke, *Obs.* Vol. II. p. 222.

I rejoiced in your renewed aid; yet I am content and want not. Ye have freely supplied my needs, and God shall supply yours.

10 Ἐχάρην δὲ ἐν Κυρίῳ μεγάλως, ὅτι ἤδη ποτὲ ἀνεθάλετε τὸ ὑπὲρ ἐμοῦ φρονεῖν· ἐφ' ᾧ καὶ

ἠκούσατε does not refer to any form of teaching or preaching ('refertur ad familiares sermones,' Grot., Hammond), but, as the division of members, noticed above, seems to require, to the example which the apostle had set them when he was with them;—this they heard from others, and further saw for themselves. Ἐν ἐμοί thus belongs more especially to the two latter verbs, the prep. ἐν denoting the sphere, and as it were *substratum* of the action; see notes *on Galat.* i. 24, and Winer, *Gr.* § 48. a, p. 345.

ταῦτα πράσσετε] Parallel to the preceding ταῦτα λογίζεσθε, without however suggesting any contrast between 'acting' and 'thinking;' λογίζ. (see notes) having a distinctly practical reference; see Meyer *in loc.*

καὶ ὁ Θεὸς κ. τ. λ.] '*and* (so) *the God of peace;*' compare ver. 7, where καί has a similarly consecutive force, and see notes on ver. 12. The expression ὁ Θεὸς τῆς εἰρ. admits of different explanations according to the meaning assigned to εἰρήνη, see Reuss, *Théol. Chrét.* iv. 18, Vol. ii. p. 201. Here there seems no reason to depart from the meaning assigned in ver. 7; the gen. being a form of the gen. *of content*, or (which is nearly allied to it) of the *characterizing attribute;* see Scheuerl. *Synt.* § 16. 3, p. 115, and comp. Andrewes, *Serm.* xviii. Vol. ii. p. 84 (A.-C. Libr.).

10. ἐχάρην δέ] '*Now I rejoiced:*' transition to more special matters, the δέ being μεταβατικόν (Hartung, *Partik.* Vol. i. p. 165), and marking the change to a new subject; εἶτα καὶ περὶ τῶν πεμφθέντων παρ' αὐτῶν γράφει χρημάτων, Theod. The addition ἐν Κυρίῳ serves to define the nature of the joy; it was neither selfish nor earthly, it was *in* his Lord and *without* Him was not; see notes on

ch. iii. 1. ἤδη ποτέ] '*now at length*,' 'tandem aliquando,' Vulg., Rom. i. 10; more fully expressed in Aristoph. *Ran.* 931, ἤδη ποτ' ἐν μακρῷ χρόνῳ, —ἤδη acquiring that meaning from ref. to something long looked for; see Hartung, *Partik.* ἤδη, 2. 4, Vol. i. p. 238. De Wette adopts the translation '*jetzt einmal,*' 'jam aliquando' (comp. Plato, *Symp.* p. 216 E), on the ground that the more usual transl. involves a tacit reproach. This is not the case. The apostle, as the Philippians well knew, in all cases preferred maintaining himself: now, however, his captivity seemed to call for their aid; compare Neand. *Philipp.* p. 25. ἀνεθάλετε κ. τ. λ.] '*put forth new shoots, flourished again, in respect of your solicitude for me;*' '*refloruistis pro me sentire,*' Vulgate, and less literally, Syriac ܚܠܦ ܕܝܢ ܕܬܨܦܘܢ ܕܝܠܝ [ut cœpistis curam habere mei]. There is some little difficulty both in the construction and the exegesis. The verb ἀναθάλλειν may be either *transitive* (Ezek. xvii. 24, Ecclus. i. 18), or *intransitive* (Psalm xxviii. 7, Wisdom iv. 4). In the former case the construction is plain (τὸ ὑπὲρ κ. τ. λ. being a simple accusative after the verb), but the exegesis unsatisfactory, as the ἀναθάλλειν would appear dependent on the will of the Philippians, which the context certainly seems to contradict. In the latter, adopted by Vulg., Copt., Syr., and the Greek commentators the exegesis is less difficult, but the construction somewhat ambiguous. Either (*a*) τὸ ὑπὲρ ἐμοῦ is the accus. object. after φρονεῖν, the verb itself being somewhat laxly appended to ἀνεθάλ., Beng., Mey., Alf.; or (*b*) τὸ ὑπὲρ ἐμοῦ φρονεῖν is the accus. of the

ἐφρονεῖτε, ἠκαιρεῖσθε δέ. ¹¹ οὐχ ὅτι καθ᾽ ὑστέρησιν λέγω ἐγώ

quantitative object (notes on *Eph.* iv. 15) dependent on ἀνεθάλετε, Winer, *Gram.* § 44. 1, p. 284, Wiesing., Bisp., and apparently Chrysost. and Theophyl. (who interpolates *εἰς*). Of these (*α*) is artificial and contrary to the current and sequence of the Greek: (*b*) is simple and intelligible, but certainly involves the difficulty that the following clause (it we retain the proper and obvious reference of ἐφ᾽ ᾧ) will in fact be ἐφρονεῖτε ἐπὶ τῷ ὑπὲρ ἐμοῦ φρονεῖν. As, however, this logical difficulty may be diluted by observing that φρονεῖν is not used exactly in the same sense in the two clauses,— τὸ ὑπὲρ ἐμοῦ φρ. in fact coalescing to form a new idea,—and as (*a*) is not only artificial, but involves an undue emphasis on τὸ ὑπὲρ ἐμοῦ, we somewhat confidently adopt (*b*); so Wiesing. and Bisping. Lastly, ἀνεθάλετε does not involve any censure (ὅτι πρότερον ὄντες ἀπηρθροὶ ἐμαράνθησαν, Chrysost.): the time during which ἠκαιροῦντο was the period of unavoidable torpor; when the suitable time and opportunity came, ἀνέθαλον, comp. Andrewes, *Serm.* XVIII. Vol. III. p. 99 (A.-C. Libr.). The rare aor. ἀνέθ. is noticed by Winer, § 15, Buttm. *Irreg. Verbs*, s. v. θάλλω.

ἐφ᾽ ᾧ] '*for which*,' 'with a view to which,' 'in contemplation of which;' the ἐπὶ marking the object contemplated: not 'sicut,' Vulg., Syr., 'in quo,' Copt., interpretations which obscure the proper force of the prepositions. On the meaning of ἐφ᾽ ᾧ, see the notes on ch. iii. 12. καὶ ἐφρονεῖτε] '*ye also were anxious, careful;*' imperf., marking the continuance of the action, to which the καὶ adds a further emphasis: 'your care for me was of no sudden growth, it did not show itself just when the need came,—far from it, you were *also* anxious long before you ἀνεθάλετε.' The omission of μὲν after ἐφρον. gives, as Meyer observes,

a greater vigor to the antithesis; see Klotz, *Devar.* Vol. II. p. 356, compare notes on *Gal.* ii. 15.

ἠκαιρεῖσθε] '*ye were lack of opportunity;*' i. e. 'it was not from any *barrenness* on your part,' Wordsw. Ἀκαιρ. (ἃπ λεγόμ.) is a word of later Greek, the opposite of which is εὐκαιρεῖν εὐσχολεῖς ἔχειν, a form equally condemned by the Atticists, Lobeck, *Phryn.* p. 125, Thom. M. p. 830. Chrysost. refers the term specially to the temporal meaning of the Phil. οὐκ εἴχετε ἐν χερσί., ὁ δὲ ἑ. ἀραιᾶς ἧτε, and urges the popular use of ἀκαρ. in that sense. It may have been so; it seems, however, safer to preserve the ordinary temporal reference; see above.

11. οὐχ ὅτι] 'not that,' 'I do not mean that;' see notes on ch. iii. 12. Winer, *Gr.* § 64. 6, p. 526. The apostle does not wish his joy at this proof of their sympathy to be misunderstood as mere satisfaction at being relieved from present want or pressure. καθ᾽ ὑστέρησιν] 'in consequence of want,' 'propter penuriam,' Vulg., sim. Syriac [Syriac] [propterea quod defuerit mihi]; see notes on chap. ii. 3, and on *Tit.* iii. 5, where this meaning of κατὰ is briefly investigated. Van Heng., to preserve the more usual meaning of the prep., gives 'ὑστέρησιν a concrete reference, 'ut more receptum est penuriæ;' this is artificial and unnecessary. The meaning is simply οὐ διὰ τὴν ἐμὴν χρείαν, Theodoret; 'notio a eumdem facile transit in notionem *propter*,' Kühner, *Xenoph. Mem.* I. 3. 12. ἐγὼ γὰρ ἔμαθον] '*for I for my part have learned,*' not 'learned,' Alf., which represents the action as too remote to suit the *English* idiom. In the Greek nothing more is said than that the μανθάνειν took place after a given time (see Donalds.

γὰρ ἔμαθον ἐν οἷς εἰμὶ αὐτάρκης εἶναι. ¹² οἶδα καὶ ταπεινοῦσθαι,

Gr. § 432); whether it does or does not last to the present time is left unnoticed; see especially Fritz. *de Aor. Vi*, p. 16 sq. The ἐγώ is emphatic, ' quidquid alii sentiunt aut cupiunt,' and ἔμαθον, as the tenor of the verse seems to indicate, refers to a teaching derived, not 'divinitus,' Beng., but, from the practical experiences of life; διὰ τῶν ἐναντίων ὁδεύων, πεῖραν ἔλαβον ἱκανήν, Theod.
ἐν οἷς εἰμί] '*in what state I am:*' not, on the one hand, with reference merely to his present state, which is too limited, — nor on the other hand, with reference to any possible state, ' in quocunque statu sim,' Raphel (compare Auth.), which would require ἄν, — but with reference to the state in which he is *at the time of consideration*; almost 'in every state that I come into.' The expression ἐν οἷς (no ellipse of χρήμασιν, Wolf, al.), is copiously illustrated by Wetstein *in loc.*; see also Kypke, *Obs.* Vol. II. p. 319.
αὐτάρκης] '*content,*' ' ut sufficiat mihi id quod est mihi,' Syr. (compare Heb. xiii. 5, ἀρκούμενοι τοῖς παροῦσιν), literally self-supporting,' 'independent,' the opposite being, as Meyer observes, προσδεὴς ἄλλων, Plato, *Tim.* 33 D; compare Arist. *Ethic. Nic.* I. 5, τὸ τέλειον ἀγαθὸν αὐτάρκες εἶναι δοκεῖ: see notes *on* 1 *Tim.* vi. 6, and Barrow, *Serm.* XXXVI. Vol. II. p. 404. The practical inferences deducible from this verse are well stated by Sanderson, *Serm.* V. (ad Aul.).

12. οἶδα καὶ ταπειν.] ' *I know (how) also to be abased:* ' second member of the climax (ἔμαθον κ. τ. λ., οἶδα κ. τ. λ., μεμύημαι κ. τ. λ.) explaining more in detail the preceding ἐν οἷς εἰμὶ αὐτάρκ. εἶναι: the apostle, as Andrewes well says, ' had stayed affections.' The first καί thus serves to annex the *special* instance (ταπειν.) to the more *general* statement (see notes *on Eph.* v. 18, Winer, *Gr.* § 53. 3,

p. 388, ed. 6), the second appends to ταπειν. its opposite, and is thus copulative and indirectly contrastive. The use of καί in the N. T., as the Aramaic ‎ו would have led us *à priori* to suppose, is somewhat varied. Though all are really included in the two broad distinctions *et* and *etiam* (see especially Klotz, *Devar.* Vol. II. p. 635), we may perhaps conveniently enumerate the following subdivisions. Under the first (*et*) καί appears as, (α) simply *copulative;* (β) *adjunctive, i. e.* either when the special is annexed to the general as here, Mark i. 5, Eph. vi. 19, al., or conversely the general to the special, Matthew xxvi. 59; (γ) *consecutive,* nearly 'and so,' verse 9, 1 Thessalonians, iv. 1, compare James ii. 23, Matthew xxiii. 32, al. Under the second (*etiam*) καί appears as, (δ) *ascensive,* 'even,' a very common and varied usage (compare notes *on Ephesians,* i. 11), or conversely, *descensive,* Gal. iii. 4, Eph. v. 12, where see notes; (ε) *explanatory,* approaching nearly to 'namely,' 'that is to say,' John i. 16, Gal. ii. 20, vi. 16, where see notes; (ζ) *comparative,* especially in double-membered clauses, see notes *on Eph.* v. 23; to all which we may perhaps add a not uncommon use of καί, which may be termed (η) its *contrasting* force, as here (2ᵈ καί), and more strongly, Mark xii. 12, 1 Thess. ii. 18; compare 1 Cor. ix. 5, 6 (2ᵈ καί). In such a case the particle is not adversative, as often asserted, but copulative and contrasting; the opposition arises merely from the juxtaposition of clauses involving opposing or dissimilar sentiments. These seven heads apparently include all the more common uses of καί in the N. T.; for further examples see the well arranged list in Bruder, *Concord.* s. v. καί, and the much improved notice in the sixth ed. of Winer, *Gr.* § 53. 3. The

οἶδα καὶ περισσεύειν ἐν παντὶ καὶ ἐν πᾶσιν μεμύημαι, καὶ χορτάζεσθαι καὶ πεινῆν, καὶ περισσεύειν καὶ ὑστερεῖσθαι. ¹ πάντα

reading δὲ (οἶδα δὲ) of *Rec.* has scarcely any authority, and is rightly rejected by apparently all modern editors.

περισσεύειν] 'to abound.' The opposition between ταπεινοῦν and περισσ is not exactly perfect (contrast Matth. xxiii. 12, 2 Cor. xi. 7, and above, Phil. ii. 8, 9), but still need not involve a departure from the lexical meaning of either word. The former (ταπεινοῦν) is more general ('to be cast down,'—not expressly, Λιμώττειν, Œcum., and sim. even De W.), but obviously includes the idea of the pressure and dejection arising from want (comp. Æth.); the latter is more specific. The paraphrase of Pelag. (cited by Meyer) is thus perfectly satisfactory, 'ut nec abundantiâ extollar, nec frangar inopiâ.

ἐν παντὶ καὶ ἐν πᾶσιν] 'in everything and in all things,' 'in omni et in omnibus,' Clarom., Goth., not 'ubique et in omnibus,' Vulg., Auth.,— an assumed ellipsis of τόπῳ (Chrys. supplies χρόνῳ) which cannot be substantiated any more than that of ἀνθρώποις (Beng.) after πᾶσιν; compare 2 Cor. ix. 8. The expression seems designed to be perfectly general and inclusive, ἐν παντὶ πρᾶγμ. καὶ ἐν πᾶσι τοῖς παρεμπίπτουσι, Phot. ap. Œcum. μεμύημαι] 'I have been initiated, fully taught,' 'institutus sum,' Vulg., Clarom., Copt.;

ܡܶܬܕܰܒܰܠ ܐܢܳܐ [exercitatus sum] Syr., 'assuetus sum,' Æth.;— climactic, see above. The word is an ἅπ. λεγόμ. in the N. T., and appears used, not in its primary sense, 'disciplinâ arcanâ imbutus sum,' Beng. (μυούμενος· μυσταγωγούμενος, Hesych.), but in its derivative sense, 'I have been fully instructed' (μύησις· μάθησις, κατήχησις, Hesych.), with perhaps some reference to the practical mode in which the knowledge was acquired;

πεῖραν ἁπάντων ἔχω, Phot. ap. Œcum.; see Suicer, *Thesaur.* s. v. Vol. II. p. 379 sq. As μυεῖσθαι is used w. th an accus. of the thing (Plato, *Symp.* p. 209 E, and see exam. Is in Rost u. Palm. *Lex* s. v.), more rarely with a gen. (Hesiod, Æ sop. fr. 17. ee Lobeck, *Ajl oph.* p. 651 note) or dat. (Lucian, *Demon.* 11), some modern commentators (Mey., Alf.) join ἐν παντί κ. τ. λ. with the infinitives. This is harsh and somewhat hypercritical; μυεῖσθαι appears with a prep. (κατὰ) in 3 Macc. ii. 30, and is probably so to be joined here; so Syr., Vulg., Clarom., Goth., and appy. Copt., Æth.

πεινῆν] Later form for πεινῆν, see Winer, *Gram.* § 13. 3, p. 74, Thom. M. p. 699. 'vulgaris horum verborum scriptura cum ingressu Macedoni i ævi, tenuis scaturiginis instar, hic id emicat,' Lobeck, *Paryn.* p. 61. The verb χορτάζω, properly used in ref. to *animals* (Hesiod, *Op.* 454, Aristoph. *Pax*, 175, Plato, *Rep.* II. p. 372 D, comp. ix. p. 586 D), is found always in the N. Test. (except Rev. xix. 21), and very commonly in later writers, in simple ref. to *men*.

13. πάντα ἰσχύω] 'I can do all things,'— not 'all this,' Hammond on 1 Cor. xiii. 7, 'omnia memorata,' Van Heng., but 'all things,' with the most inclusive reference, marking the transition from the special to the general. Bernard (*Serm.* LXXXV.) well says, 'nihil omnipotentiam Verbi clariorem reddit, quam quod omnipotentes facit omnes qui in se [eo] sperant;' see a good sermon on this text by Hammond, *Serm.* xiv. p. 297 (A.-C. Libr.). Πάντα is the accus. of the 'quantitative' object after ἰσχύω (Gal. v. 6, James v. 16, Wisdom xvi. 20), defining the measure and extent of the action; see Madvig, *Synt.* § 27. ἐν τῷ ἐνδυν.] 'in

ἰσχύω ἐν τῷ ἐνδυναμοῦντί με. ¹⁴ πλὴν καλῶς ἐποιήσατε συγκοινωνήσαντές μου τῇ θλίψει. ¹⁵ οἴδατε δὲ καὶ ὑμεῖς, Φιλιππήσιοι, ὅτι ἐν ἀρχῇ τοῦ εὐαγγελίου, ὅτε ἐξῆλθον ἀπὸ Μακεδονίας, οὐδεμία

Him that giveth me inward strength;' not 'per eum,' Beza, but 'in Him,' in vital and living union with Him who is the only source of all spiritual δύναμις; compare 1 Tim. i. 12, 2 Tim. iv. 17, and Ignat. *ad Smyrn.* § 4. The late form ἐνδυναμόω occurs six times in St. Paul's Epistles, in Acts ix. 22, and Heb. xi. 34 (see notes *on* 1 *Tim.* i. 12), Psalm lii. 7, and eccl. writers. The simple form occurs Col. i. 11, Psalm lxviii. 31, and is noticed by Lobeck, *Phryn.* p. 605 note. The interpolation of Χριστῷ after με (*Rec.*) is well supported [D³EFGKL; Boern., Syr. (both), Goth., al.; Gr. Ff.], but seems due to 1 Tim. i. 12, and is rejected by most modern editors.

14. πλὴν κ. τ. λ.] '*Notwithstanding ye did well;'* clearly not 'ye have done well,' Peile, — the event referred to belonged definitely to the past. In this verse and the following, which in fact present the positive side to the negative οὐχ ὅτι, verse 11, the apostle guards against any appearance of slighting the liberality of his converts (Chrys., Calv.), by specifying what peculiarly evoked his joy, — the *sympathy* of the Philippians, τὸ συγκοινωνῆσαί μου τῇ θλίψει. For the explanation of πλὴν see notes on ch. i. 18, iii. 16, and for examples of the idiomatic καλῶς ἐπ. with a part. (Acts x. 33), see Elsner, *Obs* Vol ii. p. 257.

συγκοινων. κ. τ. λ.] '*in that ye communicated, had fellowship, with my affliction,*' see notes *on Eph.* v. 11 : specification of their action viewed in its moral aspects ; ὑμῶν τοῦτο κέρδος· κοινωνοὶ γὰρ τῶν ἐμῶν ἐγένεσθε παθημάτων, Theod. The action of the participle is contemporaneous with that of the finite verb (see Bernhardy, *Synt.* x. 9, p. 383, notes *on Eph.* i. 9, comp. Winer, *Gr.* § 45. 6. b, p. 316), and specifies the act in which

the καλῶς ἐποιήσατε was evinced. It is scarcely necessary to add that θλίψει is not either here or 2 Cor. viii. 13, 'penuriæ' ('necessity,' Peile), but simply 'tribulationis,' Vulg. : the gift of the Philipp. is regarded from a higher point of view, as an act of ministering sympathy.

15. οἴδατε δὲ καὶ ὑμ.] '*Moreover yourselves also know;'* notice of their former liberality in the way of gentle contrast. δὲ here does not merely annex an 'enlargement upon' the preceding verse (Peile, 'and,' Scholef.), but passes to earlier acts, which it puts in juxtaposition with the present; see notes *on Gal.* iii. 8, and Klotz, *Devar.* Vol. ii. p. 356, 362, who has well discussed this particle, with the single exception that he denies any connection between it and the numeral, which seems philologically certain ; Donalds. *Cratyl.* § 155. The καὶ suggests a comparison with the apostle, 'ye too, as well as I;' comp. notes on ver. 12. Φιλιππήσιοι] '*men of Philippi.*' The mention by name is emphatic (compare 2 Corin. vi. 11); it does not mark merely affection ('my Philippians,' Disp.), but specifies them, gratefully and earnestly, as the well remembered and acknowledged doers of the good deed. Beng. goes rather too far when he says, ' innuit antitheton ad alias ecclesias ;' the comparison is instituted in what follows.

ὅτε ἐξῆλθον] '*when I went out,*' 'quando profectus sum,' Vulg., scil. at the time that event took place. It is doubtful whether the apostle alludes (a) to the assistance supplied to him when at Corinth, and especially mentioned 2 Cor. xi. 9; or (b) to that supplied previously to, and possibly at, his departure, Acts xvii. 14. If (a), then ἐξῆλθον must be regarded as having a pluperfect

μοι ἐκκλησία ἐκοινώνησεν εἰς λόγον δόσεως καὶ λήμψεως, εἰ μὴ ὑμεῖς μόνοι. ¹⁶ ὅτι καὶ ἐν Θεσσαλονίκῃ καὶ ἅπαξ καὶ δὶς εἰς τὴν χρείαν μοι

reference (Van Heng., De W., see Paley, *Hor. Paul.* vii. 3), — an interpretation to which no serious grammatical objection can be urged (Jelf, *Gr. gr.* § 404, Winer, *Gram.* § 40. 5; see, however, Fritzsch, *d. Rom.* p. 16), but which seems at variance with ἐν ἀρχῇ τοῦ εὐαγγ., which, as Meyer observes, refers the event to the earliest period of their connection with the apostle. It seems safer, then, to adopt (*b*); so Meyer, Alf., and Bisp. ἐκοινώνησεν κ. τ. λ.] 'communicated with (' dealt with,' Andrewes) me in regard of the account (ver. 17) of giving and receiving;' εἰς λόγον not being taken in the more lax, yet defensible sense, 'ratione habitâ,' Van Heng. (comp. 2 Macc. i. 14, Thucyd. iii. 46), but, as εἰς λόγον below seems to suggest, in the stricter meaning, 'in ratione dati et accepti,' Vulg., Gothic, Copt.; compare Cicero, *Lael.* xvi. (58), 'ratio acceptorum et datorum.' The exact meaning of the words is slightly doubtful. Chrys., Theoph., nearly all the earlier, and the great majority of recent expositors refer the giving and receiving to each party; ὁρᾷς πῶς ἐκοινώνησαν, εἰς λόγον δόσεως τῶν σαρκικῶν καὶ λήψεως τῶν πνευματικῶν, Chrys.; comp. 1 Cor. ix. 11. Grotius and others limit the giving to the Philippians and the receiving to the apostle; 'ego sum in vestris expensi tabulis, vos in meis accepti.' Meyer (followed by Alf.) extends this so far that each party is supposed to open an account with the other, but that the debtor side was vacant in their account, the creditor in his. This last interpr. seems so artificial, and the first so fairly analogous with the spiritual application in ver. 17, that we see no reason for departing from the ordinary interpretation; so recently Wiesing., and Bisping. Examples of the expression λῆψις

καὶ δόσις are cited by Wetstein *in loc.*; compare also Schoettg. *Hor.* Vol. I. p. 801. For the construction of κοινωνέω, see notes on *Gal.* vi. 6.

16. ὅτι] 'because,' — argumentative (not demonstrative, 'that,' Paley, Van Heng., Rilliet, al.), the object of this verse being to justify the statement, ἐν ἀρχῇ τοῦ εὐαγγ. (ver. 15), by noticing a very early period when assistance was sent to the apostle from Philippi. Even before he had left Macedonia they had twice ministered to his necessity; so Goth. ('ante '), and perhaps, Vulg., Clarom., 'quia :' the other Vv. are ambiguous; Æth. omits. The other interpretation of ὅτι reverses the order of time, and disturbs the logical sequence.

καὶ ἐν Θεσσ.] 'even in Thessalonica,' not 'to Thessalonica,' Vulg., Claroman., but, 'when I was in that city.' There is here no ellipse of ὅτι (Beza), nor a direct instance of the preposition of rest in combination with a verb of motion (Mey., Alf.), but only a case of simple and intelligible brachylogy, Winer, *Gr.* § 50. 4, p. 368. The ascensive καὶ is referred by the early commentators to the importance of Thessalonica ; ἐν τῇ μητροπόλει καθήμενος παρὰ τῆς μικρᾶς ἐτρέφετο πόλεως, Chrys. This is doubtful; it seems more naturally ascensive in reference to *time*, 'even at so early a period as when I was at Thessalonica ;' compare Hartung, *Partik.* καί, 2. 8, Vol. I. p. 135. καὶ ἅπαξ καὶ δίς] 'both once and twice,' *i.e.* 'not once only, but twice,' emphatic: see 1 Thessal. i. 18, Nehem. xiii. 30, 1 Macc. iii. 30, and Herod. II. 121. 2, III. 148. Meyer cites as the antithesis οὐχ ἅπαξ οὐδὲ δίς, Plato, *Clitoph.* p. 410 B. On καὶ — καὶ, see notes on 1 *Tim.* iv. 10.

εἰς τὴν χρείαν] 'to supply my necessity ; εἰς marking the ethical desti-

ἐπέμψατε. ¹⁷ οὐχ ὅτι ἐπιζητῶ τὸ δόμα, ἀλλὰ ἐπιζητῶ τὸν καρπὸν τὸν πλεονάζοντα εἰς λόγον ὑμῶν. ¹⁸ ἀπέχω δὲ πάντα καὶ περισ-

nation of the contribution; so εἰς τὸ εὐαγγ., 2 Corinthians ii. 12, 'to preach the gospel;' see examples in Winer, *Gr.* § 49. a, p. 354. The article marks the necessity the apostle then felt, *i. e.* 'my necessity,' Syr., al. Chrysostom calls attention to the absence of the pronoun, οὐκ εἶπε τὰς ἐμὰς [χρείας] ἀλλ' ἁπλῶς, τοῦ σεμνοῦ ἐπιμελόμενος: this is inexact, as the art. fully performs the function of the pronoun; Middl. *Art.* v. 1. 3.

17. οὐχ ὅτι] '*not that;*' added, as before ver. 11, to avoid a misunderstanding; see notes on ch. iii. 12; 'sic laudat Philippensium liberalitatem ut tamen sinistram cupiditatis immodicæ opinionem semper a se rejiciat,' Calvin. ἐπιζητῶ] '*I seek after*,' not 'studiose quæro,' Bretschneid., nor even 'insuper quæro,' Van Heng., who has an elaborate, but not persuasive note on this word: the ἐπί, as in ἐπιποθεῖν κ. τ. λ., only marks the *direction* of the action, see notes on ch. i. 8, and *on* 2 *Tim.* i. 4. In many cases, in this and similar compounds, the directive force is so feebly marked that the difference between the simple and compound is hardly appreciable; compare Winer, *de Verb. Comp.* I. 22. Meyer rightly calls attention to the present,—the 'allzeitiges Präsens' of Krüger (*Sprachl.* § 53. 1), as marking the *regular* and *characteristic* mode of action; see Bernhardy, *Synt.* x. 1, p. 370, and compare the English present, in which, however, habitude is more strongly marked than in the Greek; Latham, *Eng. Lang.* § 507 (ed. 4).

τὸ δόμα] '*the gift*,'— not exactly 'the gift which they had [now] sent him,' Scholef. *Hints,* p. 108, but 'the gift in the particular case in question' (Meyer, Alford), almost in English idiom 'any gift.' The Coptic [*taio*] seems to convey the idea of a recompense, 'honora-

rium.'   ἀλλὰ ἐπιζ] '*but I do seek,*' Alf.: the repetition of the same verb with ἀλλά, as in Rom. viii. 15, Heb. xii. 18, adds force and emphasis, and makes the primary meaning of ἀλλά ('aliud jam hoc esse de quo sumus dicturi,' Klotz, *Devar.* Vol. II. p. 1) still more apparent; compare Fritz. *Rom.* viii. 15.   τὸν καρπὸν κ. τ. λ.] '*the fruit which aboundeth to your account,*' ὑμῶν, οὐκ ἐμοῦ, Chrys.; *i. e.* the future divine recompense, which, on every fresh proof of their love, is represented as being laid up to their account, ὁ καρπὸς ἐκείνοις τίκτεται, Chrys. As πλεονάζειν appears in all other cases in the N. T. to stand alone (2 Thess. i. 3 is doubtful; Alford cites it here as certain, but in his notes *in loc.* takes it differently), Van Heng. and De W. here connect εἰς with ἐπιζητῶ. This seems an unnecessary refinement; there is nothing in πλεονάζω to render its connection with εἰς, as marking the *destination* of the πλεονασμός, either ungrammatical or unnatural: it is joined with ἐν [Plato], *Locr.* p. 103 A.   The u e of λόγος is here the same as in verse 15, not 'habitâ vestrum ratione,' Van Heng., and certainly not = εἰς ὑμᾶς (Rill.; compare Syr.), but 'in rationem vestram,' Vulg., *i. e.*, dropping all metaphor, εἰς τὴν ὑμετέραν σωτηρίαν, Chrys.; compare Calvin *in loc.*

18. ἀπέχω δὲ πάντα] '*But I have all I need;*' 'though I seek not after the gift, I still have all things in abundance; your liberality has left me to want nothing.' The δὲ thus retains its proper oppositive force (not '*and now,*' Peile), and preserves the antithesis between the emphatic ἀπέχω and the foregoing ἐπιζητῶ; ἀπέχω πάντα, οὐδὲν ἐπιζητητέον. 'Απέχω is neither barely 'habeo,' Vulg., nor yet with any special forensic sense (accepti-

σεύω. πεπλήρωμαι δεξάμενος παρὰ Ἐπαφροδίτου τὰ παρ' ὑμῶν, ὀσμὴν εὐωδίας, θυσίαν δεκτήν, εὐάρεστον τῷ Θεῷ. ¹⁹ ὁ δὲ Θεὸς

latio) 'satis habeo.' 'I give you my acquittance,' Hammond on Matt. xiv. 41; compare Cary ; ἴσχων ὅτι ὁ, ἀλλ' ἐστι τὸ πρᾶγμα, but simply 'acceptum teneo,'

[accepi] Syr., Copt., the prep. ἀπὸ apparently having a slightly intensive force ('significat actionis quendam, ut ita dicam, decursum, atque adeo in ngendo persever. utram,' Winer, *Vb. Comp.* vi. p. 7), and marking the complete assent id. ..... of the ἔχων; compare Matth. vi. 2, 5, 16, Luke vi. 24, Philem. 15, Arrian. *Epict.* iii. 24 [p. 228, ed. Buch.] τὸ γὰρ εὐδαιμονεῖν ἀπέχειν δεῖ πάντα ἃ θέλει, and compare Winer, *Gr.* § 40. 4, p. 246.

καὶ περισσεύω] 'and abound;' expansion and amplification of the preceding ἀπέχω. 'I have all I want and more than all,' the following πεπλήρωμαι completing the climax; 'die Fülle und Fülle habe ich,' Meyer. To supply χαρᾶς after πεπλήρ. (Grot.) is to wholly mar the simplicity and climactic force of the sentence. δεξάμενος κ. τ. λ.] Temporal clause, 'now that I have received,' Peile, 'postcaquam accepi,' Eras. m.; compare Donalds. *Gr.* § 573 sq. In the following words there is a slight variation of MSS. [A omits παρὰ Ἐπ: FG, al. supply πεμφθέντα, after ὑμῶν], caused probably by the recurrence of παρά: there is, however, no difficulty ; ὑμεῖς Ἐπαφρόδιτον ἐδώκατε, Ἐπαφρόδιτος ἐμοί, Theodoret.

ὀσμὴν εὐωδίας] 'a sweet-smelling savor;' accus. in apposition to the preceding τὰ παρ' ὑμῶν; compare Eph. v. 2, and notes *in loc*. The reference of A.f. to Kühner, *Gr.* Vol. ii. p. 146, and the examples cited (Hom. *Il.* xxiv. 735, Eurip. *Or. st.* 950) are not quite in point, as the apposition is not to the verbal action contained in the sentence (Jelf, *Gram.*

§ 580. ..... out simply to τὰ παρ' ὑμῶν, which is at most further ..... It is doubtful w... ..... obscure ..... (W., *Gr.* § 54. 2. 1, p. 212 ..... compare Acts i. Pet. i. 11) or a gen. of the *char ..... quality* (see S ..... Guerl. *Synt.* § 16. 3, p. 115) ; the latter is perhaps most simple and most in harmony with the Hebraistic ..... which seems to mark these kinds of gen. in the N. T.; compare Winer, *Gr. l. c.* (text).

θυσίαν κ. τ. λ.] 'a sacrifice acceptable (and) well-pleasing to God;' not an accepted sacrifice such as is,' etc., Peile, (comp. Syr.); both adjectives as well as the preceding ὀσμὴν εὐωδ. (comp. Lev. i. 9, 13) standing in connection with τῷ Θεῷ, which thus falls under the general head of the dative of 'interest;' see Krüger, *Sprachl.* § 48. 4. The good deeds which the Philippians did towards the apostle become, from the spirit in which they were done (comp. Ch. ys.), an accepted sacrifice to God. Hence, it does not seem necessary with Jackson (*Chr. Saer.* ii. 4. Vol. ix. p. 40 (A.-C. L.)], compare Iræneus, *Hær.* iv. 18) to conclude that the alms brought by Epaphr. had been offered by the people at the altar : the sacrifice of alms is one of the spiritual and evangelical sacrifices specially noticed in the N. T., *e.g.* Heb. xiii. 16 ; see the comprehensive list in Waterland, *Doct. of Euch.* ch. xii. Vol. iv. p. 739.

19 ὁ δὲ Θεός μου] Not without emphasis and an expression of hopeful trust, 'qui meam agit causam,' Van Heng.; see notes on chap. i. 3.

πληρώσει κ. τ. λ.] 'shall fulfil' with reciprocating reference to πεπλ. v. 18) 'every need of yours;' not in the form of prayer (ἐπέυχεται αὐτοῖς, Chrys.), but of hopeful promise, the future πληρώσει be-

μου πληρώσει πᾶσαν χρείαν ὑμῶν κατὰ τὸ πλοῦτος αὐτοῦ ἐν δόξῃ ἐν Χριστῷ Ἰησοῦ. ²⁰ τῷ δὲ Θεῷ καὶ πατρὶ ἡμῶν ἡ δόξα εἰς τοὺς αἰῶνας τῶν αἰώνων, ἀμήν.

All here send you greeting. ²¹ Ἀσπάσασθε πάντα ἅγιον ἐν Χριστῷ Ἰησοῦ.

ing distinctly predictive; compare Rom. xvi. 20, 2 Cor. xiii. 11, 2 Tim. iv. 18. The reading πληρώσαι [D¹FG; several mss.; Vulg., Clarom., al.], followed by Theod., Theophylact, seems clearly a gloss. It is doubtful whether χρείαν is to be referred solely to temporal (Chrys.), or solely to spiritual (Theodor.) wants. The use of χρεία and the preceding allusions are in favor of the former; the use of πλοῦτος and the immediate context, of the latter: the inclusive form of the expression seems to justify our uniting both. ἐν δόξῃ] '*in glory;*' not so much an instrumental (Meyer, Alf.) as a *modal* clause, closely in union with ἐν Χρ., the former pointing to the manner in which God will supply their wants, — not, however, merely 'magnifice, splendide,' Calv. (compare Beng.), but with reference to the element or the attribute in which the action will be evinced, — while ἐν Χρ. Ἰησ. specifies the ever-blessed sphere in which alone all is realized; see notes on *Ephes.* ii. 7. So apparently Chrys., οὕτω περισσεύει ὑμῖν ἅπαντα ὥστε ἐν δόξῃ αὐτοῦ ἔχειν. Grotius and others (comp. Æth.) connect ἐν δόξῃ with πλοῦτος; this is grammatically admissible, — the expression πλουτεῖν ἔν τινι (1 Tim. vi. 18) justifying the omission of the article (see notes on *Eph.* i. 18), — and certainly deserves consideration, but the remark of Meyer, that πλοῦτος is always used in the N. T. in such metaphorical expressions with a gen. of the thing (Rom. ii. 4, ix. 23, 2 Cor. viii. 2, Ephes. i. 7, 18, ii. 7, iii. 16, Col. i. 27), and that we should have expected κατὰ τὸ πλοῦτος τῆς δ. αὐτοῦ, seems to strike the balance in favor of πληρ. ἐν δόξῃ: so apparently Syr., but these are cases in which the Vv. cannot safely be adduced on either side. κατὰ τὸ πλ.] '*according to,*' i. e. 'in accordance with the riches He has;' compare notes on *Eph.* i. 5. The clause involves a shade of modal reference, and marks ὅτι εὔκολον αὐτῷ καὶ δυνατόν, καὶ ταχέως ποιεῖν, Chrys.

20. Θεῷ καὶ πατρί] '*to God and our Father;*' anticipatory doxology called forth by the preceding words. On the august title Θεὸς καὶ πατήρ, see notes on *Gal.* i. 4. ἡ δόξα] Scil. εἴη, not ἔστω; see notes on *Ephesians* i. 2. The article seems here to have its 'rhetorical' force (Bernhardy, *Synt.* vi. 22, p. 315), and to mark the δόξα as that 'which especially and peculiarly belongs to God;' see notes on *Gal.* i. 5, where this and the following expression, εἰς τοὺς αἰῶνας τῶν αἰώνων, are briefly investigated. On the two formulæ αἰὼν τῶν αἰώνων, and αἰῶνες τῶν αἰώνων, see Harless on *Eph.* iii. 21, with however the qualifying remarks in notes *in loc.*

21. πάντα ἅγιον] '*every saint:*' not 'omnes sanctos,' Syr., Copt., Æth, but 'omnem sanctum,' Vulg., Clarom: it does not apply to the whole Church, but, as Beng. suggests, *individ. alites:* each one is specially saluted; so Conyb., Wies., Alf. On the term ἅγιος and its application in the N. T., see notes on *Eph.* i. 1. It is doubtful whether ἐν Χρ. is to be joined with ἀσπάσασθε (compare Rom. xvi. 22, 1 Corin xvi. 19) or with ἅγιον (ch. i. 1); the former is adopted by Syr. (plural) and Theod. (ὁ τῷ Κυρίῳ Ἰησοῦ πιστεύων); the latter by Mey. and several modern interpreters. As ἅγιος is connected in this Epistle with ἐν Χρ. (comp. Rom. xvi. 3, 8, 9, 10, 13), and

ἀσπάζονται ὑμᾶς οἱ σὺν ἐμοὶ ἀδελφοί. ²² ἀσπάζονται ὑμᾶς πάντες οἱ ἅγιοι, μάλιστα δὲ οἱ ἐκ τῆς Καίσαρος οἰκίας.

Benediction. ²³ Ἡ χάρις τοῦ Κυρίου Ἰησοῦ Χριστοῦ μετὰ τοῦ πνεύματος ὑμῶν.

as ἀσπάζ does not appear elsewhere used with ἐν Χρ or ἐν Χρ. Ἰησ., but only with ἐν Κυρίῳ, the latter is perhaps slightly the most probable.

οἱ σὺν ἐμοὶ ἀδελφοί] Those who were more immediately in communication with the apostle, suitably and naturally specified before the inclusive πάντες οἱ ἅγιοι in the following verse. The apparent difficulty between this and ch. ii. 20, is simply disposed of by Chrys., οὐ παραιτεῖται καὶ τούτους ἀδελφοὺς καλεῖν.

22. μάλιστα] '*especially*,' they were naturally more in contact with the apostle than the other Christians at Rome, who were not among his immediate associates. The primary force of μάλιστα is alluded to in notes *on* 1 *Tim.* iv. 10.

οἱ ἐκ τῆς Κ. οἰκίας] '*those of Cæsar's household.*' These words have received various interpretations. It seems most natural to regard them as denoting, not on the one hand, merely 'the Prætorian guards' (Matth.), nor on the other, the 'members of Nero's family' (comp. 1 Cor. i. 16), Camer., Van Heng., and more recently, and it is to be feared with obvious reasons, Baur (*Apost. Paulus*, p. 470), — who founds on this interpretation an argument against the genuineness of the Ep., — but simply the οἰκεῖοι (Theod.), the servants and retainers belonging to the emperor's household; see Krebs, *Obs.* p. 332, Loesn *O's.* p. 358. It may thus seem not improbable that St Paul was in confinement in or near to that barrack of the Prætorians which was attached to the palace of Nero (Hows. *St. Paul*, Vol. II p. 510, ed. 2), but it does not necessarily follow that πραιτώριον in ch. i. 13 (see notes) is to be restricted to that smaller portion. The barracks within the walls were probably in constant communication with the camp without. See an interesting paper by Lightfoot, *Journ. Class. Philol.* 1857 (March), p. 58 sq.

23. μετὰ τοῦ πνεύμ.] '*with your spirit:*' the 'potior pars' of our composite nature, the third and highest constituent of man; see notes *on Gal.* vi. 18, and *on* 2 *Tim.* iv. 22. The reading is not very doubtful; the more usual μετὰ πάντων ὑμῶν is not strongly supported [KL; many mss.; Syriac (both), al.; Chrys., Theod.], while the text has decided external evidence [ABDEFG; 17. 67.** 73. 80; Vulg., Clarom., Coptic, Æth. (Plat); many Ff.], and does not seem so likely to have been changed from πάντων ὑμῶν as the converse. The addition of ἡμῶν after Κυρίου [*Rec.* with DE; Coptic, al.] has still less critical support.

THE EPISTLE TO THE COLOSSIANS.

INTRODUCTION.

The profound and difficult Epistle to the Colossians was written by the apostle during his *first* captivity at Rome (Acts xxviii. 16; compare *Introd.* to 1 *Tim.*), and, as far as we can gather from some of the expressions in the concluding chapter (ver. 3, 4), at a period of that captivity, when the apostle's anticipations were not of so grave a character as they appear to us in the Epistle to the Philippians (ch. i. 20, 21, 30, ii. 27; see *Introd. to Philipp.*), and when his restraint was probably less close (comp. Acts xxviii. 16 sq.) and his treatment more merciful (comp. ch. iv. 8 sq.).

We may thus not improbably place it first in the *third* of the four groups (the Epistles of the first captivity) into which St. Paul's Epistles may be conveniently divided, and conceive it to have been written a very short time before the Epistle to the Ephesians, and perhaps about the early part of the year A. D. 62. It was conveyed to the church of Colossæ by Tychicus (ch. iv. 7, 8), who had received a similar commission with reference to the converts at Ephesus (Eph. vi. 21), and it not improbably reached its destination before the Epistle to the last-mentioned Church; comp. Meyer, *Komm. ü. üb. Eph.* p. 17.

The Epistle seems to have been called forth by the information St. Paul had received from Epaphras (ch. iv. 12; Philem. 23), who, if not the actual founder of the Church of Colossæ (Davidson, *Introd.* Vol. II. p. 405), was most certainly one of the very earliest preachers of Christ in that city; compare ch. i. 7 and notes *in loc*. Its *object* transpires very clearly, — an earnest desire on the part of the apostle to warn the Colossians against a system of false teaching, partly Oriental and theosophistic in its character (ch. ii. 18), and partly Judaical and ceremonial (ch. ii. 16), which was tending on the one hand directly to obscure the majesty and glory of Christ (comp. ch. i. 15, ii. 8 sq.), and on the other, to introduce ritualistic observances, especially on the side of bodily austerities (ch. ii. 16 – 23), opposed alike to the simplicity and freedom of the gospel, and to all true and vital union with the risen Lord (ch. ii. 19, iii. 1). For further particulars see Davidson, *Introd.* Vol. II. p.

407 sq., where the sects to which these corrupters of the faith have been supposed to belong, and the peculiar nature of their tenets are very carefully discussed; comp. also Smith, *Dict. of Bible*, Art. ' Ep. to the Colossians,' Vol. I. p. 342.

In reference to the *genuineness* and *authenticity* of this Epistle it may be said briefly that no doubts have been urged that deserve any serious consideration. Even if the external testimonies had been less clear and explicit than we find them to be (Irenæus, *Hær.* III. 14. 1, Clem.-Alex. *Strom.* I. p. 325, ed. Pott, Tertull. *de Præscr.* cap. 7, Origen, *contr. Cels.* V. 8), the internal arguments derived from the peculiarities of style and expression, must have been pronounced by every sagacious critic as final and unanswerable. To class such an Epistle, so marked not only by distinctive peculiarities of style, but by the nerve, force, and originality of its argument, with the vague productions of later Gnosticism (Mayerhoff, Baur, al.) is to bewray such a complete want of critical perception that we can scarcely wonder that such views have been both very generally and very summarily rejected; see Meyer, *Einleitung*, p. 7, Davidson, *Introd.* Vol. II. p. 427 sq. As the latter writer very justly observes, the fabrication of such an Epistle would be ' a phenomenon perfectly inexplicable' (p. 428).

The similarity between many portions of this Epistle and that to the Ephesians has often been noticed, and the claim to priority of composition much debated. With regard to the first point it may be again observed (see *Introd. to Eph.*) that the two Epistles were written closely about the same time, and addressed to two Churches sufficiently near to one another to have had many points of resemblance, and to have needed very similar forms of exhortation, especially in reference to the duties of social and domestic life. With regard to the second point it may be enough to say that the nature of the contents of the two Epistles seems to harmonize best with the opinion that the Epistle to the Colossians was first in order, and that the more directly individualizing and polemical preceded the more directly systematic and doctrinal; see Davidson, *Introd.* Vol. II. p. 346 sq., and compare notes *on Eph.* vi. 21.

THE EPISTLE TO THE COLOSSIANS.

CHAPTER I.

Apostolic address and salutation.

ΠΑΥΛΟΣ ἀπόστολος Χριστοῦ Ἰησοῦ διὰ θελήματος Θεοῦ καὶ Τιμόθεος ὁ

CHAPTER I. 1. ἀπόστ. Χρ. Ἰησ.] 'an apostle of Jesus Christ;' the (possessive) genitive denoting whose minister he was: see notes on *Eph.* i. 1, and for the meanings of ἀπόστολος, here obviously in its higher and more especial sense, see notes on *Gal.* i. 1, and on *Eph.* iv. 11. The form of greeting in this Ep. closely resembles that to the Ephesians; there are, however, as has been previously observed (compare notes on *Eph.* i. 1, and see Ruck. on *Gal.* i. 1), some differences in the addresses of St. Paul's Epistles, especially in the apostle's designation of himself, which, though not in all cases easy to account for, can hardly be deemed accidental. We may thus classify these designations: in 1 Thess. and 2 Thess., simply Παῦλος; in Philemon (very appropriately), δέσμιος Χρ. Ἰ.; in Phil., δοῦλος Θεοῦ (associated with Timothy); in Titus, δοῦλ. Θεοῦ ἀπόστ. δὲ Χ. Ἰ.; in Rom., δοῦλ. Ἰ. Χ (*Tisch.* Χ. Ἰ.) κλητὸς ἀπόστ.; in 1 Cor. (κλητὸς ἀπ. *Tisch.*, *Rec.*, but not certain), 2 Cor., Ephes., Col., 2 Tim. ἀπόστ. Χ. Ἰ. διὰ θελήματος Θεοῦ; in 1 Tim. ἀπόστ. Χ. Ἰ. κατ' ἐπιταγὴν Θ. σωτῆρος ἡμῶν καὶ Χ. Ἰ. κ. τ. λ.; and lastly, with fullest titular distinction, in Galat..

ἀπόστ., οὐκ ἀπ' ἀνθρώπων οὐδὲ δι' ἀνθρ. κ. τ. λ. An interesting paper might be written on these peculiarities of designation διὰ θελήματος Θεοῦ] Added, probably, in thankful remembrance of God's grace, and in feelings of implicit obedience to His will; see notes on *Eph.* i. 1. καὶ Τιμ. ὁ ἀδελφ.] Timothy is similarly associated with the apostle in his greeting in 2 Cor. i. 1, Philem. 1, and, even more conjointly as to form of association, Phil. i. 1, 1 Thess. i. 1, 2 Thess. i. 1; so also Sosthenes, 1 Cor. i. 1, compare Gal. i. 2, and see notes *in loc.* It may be observed, however, that in 1 Cor., Phil., and Philem., the apostle proceeds in the singular, while here, 2 Cor. i. 3 (see Meyer), 1 and 2 Thessalon., he continues the address in the plural; see below, notes on ver. 3. It has been supposed that Timothy was also the transcriber of the Epistle (Steiger, Esp.; compare ch. iv. 18); this is possible, but nothing more. The title ὁ ἀδελφός, as in 1 Cor. i. 1, 2 Cor. i. 1, has no special reference to official (οὐκοῦν καὶ ἀπόστολος, Chrys.), but simply to Christian brotherhood; Timothy was one of οἱ ἀδελφοί, 'der christliche-Mitbruder.' De Wette

ἀδελφὸς ² τοῖς ἐν Κολασσαῖς ἁγίοις καὶ πιστοῖς ἀδελφοῖς ἐν Χριστῷ. χάρις ὑμῖν καὶ εἰρήνη ἀπὸ Θεοῦ πατρὸς ἡμῶν.

2. Κολασσαῖς] So *Rec.* (but not *Elz.*), *Lachm.*, and *Tisch.*, with AB (C in subser.) K; more than 40 mss.; Syr. (both), Copt; Æthiop. (Platt), Slav. (mss.); Origen, Theod., Chrysost. (mss.), Theophyl. (mss.), Suidas, al., to which may be added mss. in Herod. VII. 30 and Xenoph. *Anab.* I. 2. 6. The more usual mode of spelling is found in B²DEFGL; numerous mss.; Vulg., Claroman., al.; Clem., Chrys., Theodoret (mss.), al.; Lat. Ff. (*Rec.*, *Meyer*, al.). It can be proved by coins that the latter was the *correct* form (Eckhel, *Doctr. Num.* III. 147); still the external authority, especially as seen in the Vv., seems so strong, that Κολασσαῖς can hardly be referred to a mere change of vowels in transcription found only in two or three of the leading MSS., but must be regarded as the, not improbably, *provincial* mode of spelling in the time of St. Paul. So too Meyer, who admits that Κολοσσαῖς was an old emendation.

2. Κολασσαῖς] Colossæ or Colassæ (see crit. note) was a city of Phrygia, on the Lycus (an affluent of the Mæander), near to, and nearly equidistant from the more modern cities of Hierapolis and Laodicea. It was anciently a place of considerable importance (πόλις μεγάλη, Herod. VII. 30; πόλις οἰκουμένη, εὐδαίμων καὶ μεγάλη, Xenoph. *Anab.* I. 2. 6), but subsequently so declined in comparison with the commercial city of Apamea on the one side, and the strong, though somewhat shattered city of Laodicea on the other (αἱ μεγίσται τῶν κατὰ τὴν Φρυγίαν πόλεων), as to be classed by Strabo (*Geogr.* XII. 8. 13, ed Kramer) only among the πολίσματα of Phrygia, though still, from past fame, classed by Pliny (*Nat. Hist.* v. 41) among the 'celeberrima oppida' of that country; see Steiger, *Einl.* § 2, p. 17. It afterwards rose again in importance, and under the name of Χῶναι (Theophylact) again received the titles of εὐδαίμων and μεγάλη (Nicetas, *Chon.* p 203, ed. Bonn). It has been supposed to have occupied the site of the modern Chonas or Khonos, but of this there now seem considerable doubts; see Smith, *Dict. Geogr.* s. v., Conyb. and Hows. *St. Paul*, Vol. II. p. 471 note, Pauly, *Real-Encycl.* Vol. II. p. 518, and the very interesting topographical notes of Steiger, *Einl.* p. 1—33. ἁγίοις] '*saints;*' used substantivally, as appy. in all the addresses of St. Paul's Epp., Rom. i. 7, 1 Cor. i. 1, 2 Cor. i. 1, Eph. i. 1, Phil. i. 1; so Copt., Æth. (Platt), and appy. Chrys. De W. and others connect ἁγίοις with ἀδελφ. (so apparently Syriac, Vulg.), but with considerably less plausibility, as in such a case πιστοῖς would far more naturally precede than follow, the more comprehensive ἁγίοις. On the meaning of ἅγιος in such addresses, see Davenant *in loc.*, Beveridge, *Serm.* II. Vol. VI p. 401, and compare notes on *Eph.* i. 1.

πιστοῖς ἀδελφοῖς κ. τ. λ.] '*faithful brethren in Christ;*' more specific, and slightly explanatory, designation of the preceding ἅγιοι. Ἐν Χριστῷ is in close union with ἀδελφοί, and marks the sphere and element in which the brotherhood existed. The omission of the article is perfectly admissible, ἐν Χρ. being associated with ἀδελφοῖς so as to form, as it were, one composite idea; see Winer, *Gr.* § 20. 2, p. 123, and notes on *Eph.* i. 15. The insertion of the article would throw a greater emphasis on ἐν Χρ., 'iisque in Christo,' than is necessary or intended; see notes on 1 *Tim.* iii. 14, *Gal.* iii. 26. Lachm. adds Ἰησοῦ with AD¹E¹FG; 3 mss.; Syriac, Copt

CHAP. I. 3. COLOSSIANS. 123

We thank God for your faith, and love, and progress in the gospel as preached to you by Epaphras.

³ Εὐχαριστοῦμεν τῷ Θεῷ πατρὶ τοῦ Κυρίου ἡμῶν Ἰησοῦ Χριστοῦ, πάντοτε περὶ ὑμῶν προσ-

(not Tahl.), al., but, considering the probability of insertion, not on sufficient authority. It may be observed that here, Rom. i. 7, Eph. i. 1, and Phil. i. 1, the apostle does not write especially to the Church (1 Cor. i. 1, 2 Cor. i. 1, Gal. i. 2 (plural), 1 Thess. i. 1, and 2 Thess. i. 1), but to the Christians collectively. This is perhaps not intentionally significant; at any rate it can hardly be conceived that he only uses the title ἐκκλησία to those churches which he had himself founded: see Meyer *in loc.*

χάρις κ. τ. λ.] On this blended form of the modes of Occidental and Oriental salutation, see notes on *Gal.* i. 3, *Eph.* i. 2. The term χάρις is elaborately explained by Davenant; it seems enough to say with Waterland *Euchar.* x., that χάρις ' in the general signifies ' favor,' ' mercy,' ' indulgence,' ' bounty ;' in particular it signifies a gift, and more especially a 'spiritual gift,' and in a sense yet more restrained, the gift of sanctification, or of such spiritual aids as may enable a man both to will and do according to what God has commanded,' *Works*, Vol. IV. p. 666.

πατρὸς ἡμῶν] The addition καὶ Κυρ. 'I.X. adopted by *Rec.* with ACFG; mss.; Vulg. (ed.), Syr.-Phil.,—but with asterisk, Boern., al.; Gr. Ff. appears rightly rejected by *Lachm., Tisch.*, and most modern editors.

3. εὐχαριστοῦμεν] 'we give thanks;' *i.e.* I and Timothy. In this Ep., as in 2 Cor., the singular and plural are both used (see ch. i. 23, 24, 28, 29; ii. 1; iv. 2, 3 4, 13), and sometimes, as in ch. i. 25, 28, iv. 3, 4, even in juxtaposition: in all cases the context seems fully to account for and justify the appropriateness of the selection; see Meyer on 2 Cor. i. 4. It is doubtful whether πάντοτε is to be joined (*a*) with the finite verb

(1 Cor. i 4, 2 Thess. i. 3, comp. Eph. i. 16), or (*b*) with the participle (comp. are Rom. i. 10, Phil. i. 4). Syr., Æth., and the majority of modern commentators adopt the former; the Greek expositors and apparently Copt. and Vulg. the latter. As περὶ ὑμῶν would seem a very feeble commencement to the principal clause, (*b*) is to be preferred, so Alf. *in loc*, who has well defended this latter construction. On εὐχαριστῶ, see notes on ch. i. 12, and on Phil. i. 3.

The reading is very doubtful. Rec. inserts καὶ before πατρί, with ACD³EKL; al.; *Lachmann* inserts τῷ with DFG; Chrys.; *Tisch.* adopts simply πατρί, with BC¹. As the probability of an insertion, especially of the familiar καί (pl. i. 3, al.), seems very great, we retain, though not with perfect confidence, the reading of *Tisch*. The anarthrous use of πατρί is fully admissible; see the list in Winer, *Gr.* § 19. 1, p. 109 sq.

περὶ ὑμῶν προσ.] 'pro vobis or.' The uncial authorities are here again nearly equally divided between περί [AC D³EKL] and ὑπέρ [BD¹JFG; the former is adopted by *Tisch.*, and on critical grounds is to be preferred, though in grammatical analysis considered the difference is extremely slight, if indeed appreciable; compare Fritz. *Rom.* Vol. I p. 25 sq. The utmost perhaps that can be said is that ὑπέρ seems to direct the attention more to the action itself, περί more to the object or circumstances towards which it is directed, or from which it may be supposed to emanate: see notes on *Gal.* i. 4. On the primary meaning and etymological affinities of περί, see Donalds. *Crat.* l. § 177, 178.

4. ἀκούσαντες] 'having heard,' *i.e.* 'after having heard.' Syriac ܰ‍ܶ‍‍ܩ‍? [a quo audivimus], Æthiop.

εὐχόμενοι, ¹ ἀκούσαντες τὴν πίστιν ὑμῶν ἐν Χριστῷ Ἰησοῦ καὶ
τὴν ἀγάπην ἣν ἔχετε εἰς πάντας τοὺς ἁγίους ⁵ διὰ τὴν ἐλπίδα τὴν

postquam;' *temporal* use of the participle (Donalds. *Gr.* § 575), not causal, 'quoniam audivimus,' Calv. It was not the hearing but the substance of what he heard that caused the apostle to give thanks. For examples of the union of two or more participles with a single finite verb, see Winer, *Gram.* § 45. 3, p. 308. ἐν Χρ. Ἰησ.] '*in Christ Jesus*,'—in Him, as the sphere or substratum of the πίστις, that in which the faith centres itself. The omission of the article gives a more complete unity to the conception, 'Christ-centred faith,' see notes on *Eph.* i. 15, and comp. Fritz. *Rom.* iii. 25, Vol. I. p. 195, note. Πίστις, as usual, has its subjective meaning; not 'externam fidei professionem,' nor both this *and* 'internam et sinceram in corde habitantem fidem' (Davenant), but simply the latter; compare notes on *Gal.* i. 23. ἣν ἔχετε] Further statement of the direction and application of the ἀγάπη. The difference between this and τὴν εἰς (*Rec.*) is slight, but appreciable. The latter simply appends a second moment of thought ('amorem, cumque erga omnes sanctos'), the former draws attention to it, and points to its persistence, ἣν ἐπιδεικνύμενοι διετέλουν, Theodor. The reading of *Rec.* is, however, very feebly supported [D³E'KL; al.] and rejected by all recent editors

5. διὰ τὴν ἐλπίδα is most naturally connected with the preceding relative sentence, not with εὐχαρ., Davenant, Eadie; for, as Meyer justly remarks, this preliminary εὐχαριστία is always, in St. Paul's Epistles (Rom. i. 8, 1 Cor. i. 4, Eph. i. 15, Phil. i. 5, 1 Thess. i. 3, 2 Thessa'on. i. 3, 2 Tim. i. 5, Philem. 4), grounded on the subjective state of his converts, ἀκούσαντες κ. τ. λ. The love they entertained toward the ἅγιοι was evoked and conditioned by no thought of any earthly return (compare Calvin), but by their hope for their μισθὸς in heaven; ἀγαπᾶτέ φησι, τοὺς ἁγίους, οὐ διά τι ἀνθρώπινον, ἀλλὰ διὰ τὸ ἐλπίζειν τὰ μέλλοντα ἀγαθά, Theoph.; so Chrys. and Theodoret. τὴν ἀποκειμένην κ. τ. λ.] '*which is laid up for you in heaven*,' 'propter cœlestem beatitudinem,' Daven. This defining clause, as well as the following words, seem to show that the ἐλπίς must here be regarded, if not as *purely* objective, 'id quod speratur,' Grot., yet certainly as under objective aspects (comp. Rom. viii. 24, ἐλπὶς βλεπομένη, and perhaps Heb. vi. 18), scil. τὴν εὐτρεπισμένην ὑμῖν τῶν οὐρανῶν βασιλείαν, Theod.; compare notes on *Eph.* i. 18. It is characterized as τὴν ἀποκ. κ. τ. λ. partly to mark its security (τὸ ἀσφαλὲς ἔδειξεν, Chrys.), partly its futurity (see notes on 2 *Tim.* iv. 8),'—the ἀπὸ denoting the setting *apart, by itself,* for future purposes or wants; compare Joseph. *Antiq.* xv. 9. 1, καρπῶν ὅσοι ἀπέκειντο δεδαπανημένων, Xen. *Anab.* II. 3. 5, αἱ βάλανοι τῶν φοινίκων τοῖς οἰκέταις ἀπέκειντο, and examples in Kypke, *Obs.* Vol. II. p. 320. προηκούσατε] '*ye heard before:*' before when? Not before its fulfilment, 'respectu spei quæ illis de re futurâ erat facta,' Wolf,—which would leave the compound form very unmeaning; nor yet specifically before this Epistle was written, 'ante quam scriberem,' Beng., but simply and generally, '*formerly*,' Steiger, Alf.,—*i. e.* not before any definite epoch (*e. g.* 'when you received this hope,' Meyer, al.), but merely at some undefined period in the past, 'prius [*sharp*] audistis,' Coptic; compare Herodot. v. 86, οὐ προακηκοόσι τοῖσι Ἀθηναίοισι ἐπιπεσεῖν, VIII. 79, προακήκοε ὅτι; compare Plato, *Legg.* VII. p.

ἀποκειμένην ὑμῖν ἐν τοῖς οὐρανοῖς, ἣν προηκούσατε ἐν τῷ λόγῳ τῆς ἀληθείας τοῦ εὐαγγελίου, ⁶ τοῦ παρόντος εἰς ὑμᾶς καθὼς καὶ ἐν

797 A. The verb is often found with a purely local sense, *e.g.* Xenoph. *Mem.* II. 4. 7, where see Kühner.

τῷ λόγῳ τῆς ἀληθ.] 'The word of Truth;' not the *res*, of *quality* ('verissimum,' Grot.), but the gen. of the *substance* or *contents* (Scheuerlein, *Synt.* § 12. 1, p. 82), τῆς ἀληθείας specifying what was the substance and purport of its teaching; — notes on *Eph.* i. 13. The genitive εὐαγγελίου is usually taken as the genitive of *apposition* to τῷ λόγῳ τῆς ἀληθ. (De Wette, Olsh.); but it seems more simple to regard it as a defining genitive, allied to the genitive *possessionis* (genitive *continentis*), which specifies, and, so to say, localizes the general notion of the governing substantive, — 'the truth which was preached in and was announced in the gospel;' compare notes on *Eph.* i. 13, and see examples in Winer, *Gr.* 30. 2. In Gal. ii. 5, 14, the gen. εὐαγγ. is somewhat different, as ἀλήθεια stands prominent and separate, whereas here it is under the regimen of, and serves to characterize, a preceding substantive.

6. τοῦ παρόντος εἰς ὑμ.] 'which is present with you;' more exactly 'which came to and is present with you,' the εἰς (not ἐν as in the next clause) conveying the idea of the gospel having reached them (Jelf, *Gr.* § 625), while παρόντος implies that it abides there; οὐ παρεγένετο, φησί, καὶ ἀπέστη, ἀλλ᾽ ἔμεινε καὶ ἔστιν ἐκεῖ, Chrys. For examples of this not very uncommon union of verbs of rest with εἰς or πρός (Acts xii. 20), see Winer, *Gr.* § 50. 4, pp. 368, 369. A somewhat extreme case occurs in Jer. xli. 7, ἔσφαξεν αὐτοὺς εἰς τὸ φρέαρ.

καθὼς καὶ κ.τ.λ.] 'even as it also is in the whole world;' πανταχοῦ κρατεῖ, Chrys., — a very natural and intelligible hyperbole; compare Rom. i. 18, x. 18.

It is obviously not necessary either to limit κόσμος to the Roman empire (Michael.), or to understand it with a literal exactness, warranted by the Lord not be substantiated; comp. Orig. *in Matt.* Tract. XXVIII, and Justin *c. Tryph.* § ... καὶ ἔστιν καρποφ. κ.τ.λ.] ... bearing fruit and increasing; or from trees or are *orcines* and plants (Cory, Just.; compare Meyer) depicting the inward and *intensive*, as well as outward and *extensive* progress of the gospel. It may be observed that the *troubled does* not merely append a participle, viz. καὶ καρποφορούμενον, but by a natural change to the finite verb (compare *Eph.* i. 20, Winer, *Gr.* § 63. 2. b, p. 505) throws an emphasis on the fact of the καρποφορία, while by his use of the periphrastic present (not καρποφορεῖ, 'fructificat,' Vulg., but 'est fructificans,' Cassan) he gives further prominence to the idea of its present continuance at Colossae; see Winer, *Gr.* § 45. 5, p. 311. The distinction between the two verbs has been differently explained: on the whole Greek commentators seem right in referring καρποφ. to the inner and spiritual, αὐξ. to the outward and collective increase; καρποφορίαν τῶν ἔργων κέκληκε τὴν πίστιν τῶν ἀκηκοότων καὶ τὴν ἐπαυξανομένην πολιτείαν, αὔξησιν δὲ τῶν πιστευόντων τὸ πλῆθος, Theodoret; compare Acts vi. 7, xii. 24, xix. 20. The middle καρποφ. is an ἅπ. λεγ. in the N.T.; it may perhaps be an instance of the 'dynamic' middle (Donalds. *Gr.* § 432. 2. b', Krüger, *Sprachl.* § 52. 8), and may mark some intensification of the active, 'fructus suos exserit;' compare ἐνεργεῖσθαι, Gal. v. 6, and notes *in loc.* The reading is somewhat doubtful: καὶ αὐξ. with ABCD EFGL, seems to rest on preponderant evidence, but the authorities for the omission [ABCDEFG; Copt.,

παντὶ τῷ κόσμῳ, καὶ ἔστιν καρποφορούμενον καὶ αὐξανόμενον καθὼς καὶ ἐν ὑμῖν, ἀφ' ἧς ἡμέρας ἠκούσατε καὶ ἐπέγνωτε τὴν χάριν τοῦ Θεοῦ ἐν ἀληθείᾳ· ⁷ καθὼς ἐμάθετε ἀπὸ Ἐπαφρᾶ

Sah.], or insertion [D¹D³E²FGKL; Vulg., Claroman., Syr. (both), Æth.] of the first καὶ, owing to the great preponderance of the Vv. on the latter side, are nearly equally balanced. On the whole it seems more likely to have been omitted to modify the hyperbole than inserted to preserve the balance of the sentence; so *Tisch.*, Mey., and De W.

τὴν χάριν τοῦ Θεοῦ] '*the grace of God,*' *i. e.* as evinced and manifested in the gospel: 'amplificat hisce verbis efficaciam evangelii ...... evangelium voluntatem Dei salvantem ostendit, et nobis gratiam in Christo offert,' Daven.; compare Tit. ii. 15. It is doubtful whether this accus. is to be connected (*a*) with both verbs (De Wette), or (*b*) only with ἐπέγνωτε (Mey.). The grammatical sequence appears to suggest the former, and is apparently followed by Chrysost., ᾅμα ἐδέξασθε, ἅμα ἔγνωτε τὴν χάρ. τ. Θ., but the logical connection certainly the latter; for if ἐν ἀληθ. were joined with ἠκούσατε, καθὼς (scil. ἐν ἀληθ., see below) κ. τ. λ. in verse 7 would seem tautologous. On the whole it seems best to adopt (*b*); so Steiger, Mey., al.

ἐν ἀληθείᾳ] '*in truth;*' *i. e.* in no Judaistic or Gnostic form of teaching; ἐν ἀληθ. being (as καθὼς, ver. 7, seems naturally to suggest) an adverbial definition of the manner appended to the preceding ἐπέγνωτε; compare Matth. xxii. 16, and see Winer, *Gr.* § 51. 1, p. 377 (comp. p. 124), Bernhardy, *Synt.* v. 8, p. 211. Alford objects to the adverbial solution, but adopts an interpretation, 'in its truth and with true knowledge,' that does not appreciably differ from it. Both Chrys. and Theoph. (οὐκ ἐν λόγῳ, οὐδὲ ἐν ἀπάτῃ κ. τ. λ.) appear to have given to ἐν more of an instrumental force: this is not grammatically necessary, and has led to the doubtful paraphrase, τουτέστι σημείοις καὶ ἔργοις παραδόξοις, Theophyl.

7. καθώς] 'even as;' not causal 'inasmuch as' (Eph. i. 4), but as usual, simply modal, referring to the preceding ἐν ἀληθείᾳ, and thus serving formally to ratify the preaching of Epaphras: as it was in truth that they had known the grace of God, so was it in truth that they had learnt it. On the later form καθώς, see notes *on Gal.* iii. 6. The *Rec.* adds καὶ after καθὼς: the external authority, however, is weak [D³EKL], and the probability of a mechanical repetition of the preceding καθὼς καὶ far from slight; compare Neander, *Planting,* Vol. I. p. 172 note (Bohn). Ἐπαφρᾶ] A Colossian (ch. iv. 12) who appears from this verse to have been one of the first, if not the first, of the preachers of the gospel in Colossæ: he is again mentioned as being in prison with St. Paul at Rome, Philem. 23. Grotius and others conceive him to have been the Epaphroditus mentioned in Philip. ii. 25; see Thornd. *Right of Ch.* ch. III. 2, Vol. I. p. 462 (A.-C. Libr.): this supposition, however, has nothing in its favor except the possible identity of name; see Winer, *RWB.* Vol. I. p. 330, and notes on ch. ii. 25. The reading καθὼς καὶ ἐμάθ. will not modify the apparent inference that Epaphras was the first preacher at Colossæ; this would have been the case if the order had been καθὼς καὶ ἀπὸ Ἐπ. ἐμάθ.: see Meyer *in loc.* contrasted with Wiggers, *Stud. u. Krit.* for 1838, p. 185. For the arguments that the apostle himself was the founder of this Church, see Lardner, *Credibil.* XIV. Vol. II. p. 472 sq.; for replications and counter-arguments, Davidson, *Introd.* Vol. II. p. 402 sq. συνδούλου]

τοῦ ἀγαπητοῦ συνδούλου ἡμῶν, ὅς ἐστιν πιστὸς ὑπὲρ ὑμῶν διάκονος τοῦ Χριστοῦ, ⁸ ὁ καὶ δηλώσας ἡμῖν τὴν ὑμῶν ἀγάπην ἐν Πνεύματι.

We unceasingly pray that ye may be fruitful in good works, and that khal for your salvation in Christ, who is the creator, ruler, and reconciler of all things.

⁹ Διὰ τοῦτο καὶ ἡμεῖς, ἀφ' ἧς ἡμέρας ἠκούσαμεν, οὐ παυόμεθα ὑπὲρ ὑμῶν προσευχόμενοι καὶ αἰτούμενοι ἵνα πληρωθῆτε τὴν ἐπίγνωσιν

'*fellow-servant*,' i. e. of our common master, Christ : compare ch. iv. 7. This and the further specification in the pronominal clause seem designed to confirm and enhance the authority of Epaphras, τὸ ἀξιόπιστον ἐπιτείνειν δείκνυσι τοῦ ἀνδρός, Theoph., compare Theod.
ὑπὲρ ὑμῶν] '*in your behalf*,' i. e. to advance your spiritual good, ' pro vestrâ salute,' Daven., — not ' in your place,' a translation grammatically (Philem. 13, see notes on *Gal.* ii. 13), but not historically permissible, as this would imply that Epaphr. had been sent to Rome to minister to the apostle (Menoch.), — a supposition which needs confirmation. The reading is slightly doubtful ; *Lachm.* adopts ἡμῶν with ABDFG ; 8 mss.; Boërn., in which case ' vice Apostoli ' (Ambrosiast.) would be the natural translation (opp. to Mey.): the external authority, however, [CD-EFKL ; great majority of mss.; and nearly all Vv.], and the arguments derived from erroneous transcription (compare pref. to *Gal.* p. xvii, ed. 2) seem decidedly in favor of the reading of *Rec.*, as rightly followed by *Tisch.* (ed. 2, 7).

8. ὁ καὶ δηλώσας] '*who also made known ;*' further and accessory statement of the acts of Epaphr. Ἡμῖν, as before, refers to the apostle and Timothy ; see notes on ver. 3. ἀγάπην ἐν Πνεύματι] '*love in the Spirit;*' not merely love towards the apostle (Theoph., Œcum., and appy. Chrys.), but ' brotherly love ' in its most general meaning, in which that towards St. Paul was necessarily included ; ' erga me et omnes Christianos,' Corn. a Lap. This love is characterized .s in ' the (Holy) Spirit ' (compare Rom xiv. 17 χαρὰ ἐν Πν. ἁγίῳ) ; it was from Him that it arose (compare Rom xv. 30, ἀγ. τοῦ Πν.), and it was only in the sphere of His blessed influence (surely not ἐν instrumental, ' a Sp. div. excitatum,' Fritz. *Rom.* Vol III. p. 203) that it was genuine and operative ; αἵ γε ἄλλαι ὄνομα ἀγάπης ἴσχουσι μόνον, Chrys. Œcumenius suggests the the right antithesis (οὐ σαρκικήν, ἀλλὰ πνευματικήν), but dilutes the force by the adjectival solution : the omission of the article before ἐν Πν. is perfectly in accordance with N. Test. usage, and preserves more complete unity of conception : see Winer, *Gram.* § 20. 2. p. 123. On the term ἀγάπη, see Reuss, *Théol. Chrét.* IV. 19, Vol. II. p. 203 sq.

9. διὰ τοῦτο] '*On this account ;*' 'because, as we hear, ye have such faith, and have displayed such love :' καθάπερ ἐν τοῖς ἁγίοισιν ἐκείνους μάλιστα διεγείρομεν τοὺς ἐγγὺς ὄντας τῆς νίκης οὕτω καὶ ὁ Παῦλος τούτους μάλιστα παρακαλεῖ τοὺς τὸ πλέον κατωρθωκότας Chrys.: see esp. Eph. i. 15. Thus the ' causa impulsiva ' (Daven.) of the apostle's prayer is this Christian progress on the part of his converts ; the *mode* of it is warmly expressed by the intensive οὐ παυόμεθα κ. τ. λ.; the *subject* (blended with the purpose of it) by ἵνα πληρωθῆτε κ. τ. λ. καὶ ἡμεῖς] '*we also,*' ' Timothy and I on our parts ;' gentle contrast between the Colossians and their practical display of vital religion, and the reciprocal prayer of the apostle and his helper.

τοῦ θελήματος αὐτοῦ ἐν πάσῃ σοφίᾳ καὶ συνέσει πνευματικῇ,

Καὶ has here its slightly *contrasting* force, and is clearly to be joined with ἡμεῖς, not τοῦτο, as De W.; see notes *on Phil.* iv. 12. ἀφ' ἧς ἡμέρας κ. τ. λ.] '*from the day that we heard;*' incidental definition of the time, with reference to ἀκούσαντες, ver. 4, not ἀφ' ἧς ἡμ. ἠκούσατε, ver. 6 (Huth.), which may be echoed in the present clause, but, from the difference of the subjects of the ἀκούειν, is not directly referred to.

οὐ παυόμεθα κ. τ. λ.] See the exactly similar affectionate hyperbole in Eph. i. 16: οὐ μίαν ἡμέραν ὑπερευχόμεθα, οὐδὲ δύο, οὐ τρεῖς, Chrys. On this idiomatic use of the part., which as usual points to a state supposed to be already in existence, see notes and reff. *on Eph.* i. 16, and for a general investigation of the union of the participle with the finite verb, see the good treatise of Weller, *Bemerk. z. Gr. Synt.* p. 11 sq.

καὶ αἰτούμενοι] '*and making our petition;*' the more special form of the more general προσευχ., see Mark xi. 24, Eph. vi. 18, and notes *in loc.* The present passage seems to confirm the view, expressed Eph. *l. c.*, and *on* 1 Tim. ii. 1, that προσευχή (and προσεύχομαι) is not merely *for good things* (comp. Andrewes, *Serm.* Vol. v. p. 358, A.-C. Libr.), but denotes prayer in its most general aspects. On the exact force of ἵνα, which has here its secondary telic force, and in which the subject of the prayer is blended with the purpose of making it, see notes *on Eph.* i. 16. Meyer, as usual, too strongly presses the latter idea.

τὴν ἐπίγνωσιν κ. τ. λ.] '*the (full) knowledge of His will,*' — of God's will, the subject of αὐτοῦ sufficiently transpiring in προσευχ. κ. τ. λ. The accusative ἐπίγν. is that of the remoter, or, as it is sometimes termed, the 'quantitative' object in which the action of the verb has its realization, see Winer, *Gr.* § 32.

5, p. 205, and notes *on Phil.* i. 11, where this construction is discussed. On the meaning of ἐπίγνωσιν, not barely 'Kenntniss' (compare Rück. *on Rom.* i. 28, Olsh. *on Eph.* i. 17), but 'Erkenntniss,' 'perfecta cognitio,' Daven., see notes *on Eph.* i. 17. The remark of Alf. on ver. 6 is apparently just, that the force of the compound can hardly be expressed in English, but the distinction between γνῶσις and ἐπίγνωσις (opp. to Rück. *on Rom.* i. 28, Olsh. *on Eph.* i. 8) seems no less certain. The former, as De W. rightly suggests, points to a mere unpractical and theoretical, the latter to a full and living, knowledge; see Wordsworth *in loc.* θελήματος] Obviously not with any special reference, διὰ τί τὸν Υἱὸν ἔπεμψεν, but simply and generally, His will, — not only in reference to 'credenda,' but also and perhaps more particularly (Theod.) to 'agenda;' compare ver. 10, and see Davenant *in loc.*

ἐν πάσῃ κ. τ. λ.] '*in all spiritual wisdom and understanding,*' or perhaps more exactly, though less literally, 'in all wisdom and understanding of the Spirit,' πνεύμ. referring to the Holy Spirit,' (Æth.-Pol.), the true source of the σοφία and σύνεσις, see notes *on Ephes.* i. 3; compare Romans i. 11, 1 Cor. ii. 13, al. Thus then πάσῃ (so expressly Syr., Æth. (Platt), Copt.) and πνευματικῇ (opp. to Alf.; compare Chrys.) refer to *both* substantives, the extensive πάσῃ referring to every exhibition or manifestation of the σοφ. καὶ σύν. (see notes *on Eph.* i. 8), while πνευματικῇ points to the characteristics and origin of both. The clause is not purely instrumental, but represents the mode in which, or the concomitant influences under which, the πληρωθῆναι τὴν ἐπίγν. was to take place: this σοφία κ. σύν. was not to be ἀνθρωπίνη (1 Cor. ii. 13) or σαρκική (2 Cor. i. 12), but πνευματική, — inspired by and sent from the

¹⁰ περιπατῆσαι ἀξίως τοῦ Κυρίου εἰς πᾶσαν ἀρέσκειαν, ἐν παντὶ
ἔργῳ ἀγαθῷ καρποφοροῦντες καὶ αὐξανόμενοι τῇ ἐπιγνώσει τοῦ

10. περιπατῆσαι] So *Lachm.* with ABCD¹FG; 10 mss.; Clem. (G*rsb.*, *Scholz*, *Meyer*, *al.*). *Tisch.* (ed. 2, 7) following *Rec.* adds ὑμᾶς with D³EKL; a *c*, majority of mss.; Chrys., Theod., Dam. The addition is deficient in true authority, and somewhat opposed to grammatical usage; compare Winer, Gr. § 44. 3, p. 287 sq.

τῇ ἐπιγνώσει] So *Lachmann* with ABCD¹FG; nearly 10 mss.; Ambr. Tol.; Clem., Syr., Max. (*Griesb.*, *Scholz*, *De W.*, *Alf.*). On the contrary, *Rec.* (ed. 2, 7) reads εἰς τὴν ἐπίγνωσιν with D³E³KL; very great majority of mss.; Tol. 1, Dam., Theoph. (*Rec.*, *Meyer*, *Bisp.*); lastly, ἐν τῇ ἐπιγν. is found in about 4 mss., nearly all the Vv., and Chrys. On reviewing this evidence, the uncial authority is indisputably in favor of the text; the Vv., on the other hand, might seem to be in favor of the insertion of a preposition. As, however, the Vv. may very probably have inserted the prep. to explain the ill-understood instrument dat. τῇ ἐπιγν. as the equally misunderstood εἰς ἐπίγνωσιν, and as internal considerations seem rather in favor of the simple dat., we return to the reading of *Tisch.* (ed. 1).

Holy Spirit; compare Ephes. i. 3, and notes, where however the instrum. force is more distinct. With regard to σοφία and σύνεσις, both appear to have a *practical* reference (see esp. Daven.); the former is, however, a general term, the latter (the opposite of which is ἄγνοια, Plato, *R.* p. 111 p. 376 B) its more special result and application; see Harless on *Eph.* i. 8, and compare Beck, *Seelenl.* II. 19, p. 60. Between σύν. and φρόνησις (Luke i. 17, Eph. i. 8) the difference is very slight; σύνεσις is perhaps seen more in practically embracing a truth (Ephes. iii. 4), φρόν. more in bringing the mind to bear upon it; compare notes on *Eph.* i. 8, and Beck, *l. c.*, p. 61.

10 περιπατῆσαι κ.τ.λ.] 'that ye walk worthily of the Lord;' purpose and object (ἵνα, Theod., compare Theophyl.), not result (steiger, al.) of the πληρωθῆναι, specified by the 'infin. epexegeticus;' see Winer, Gr. § 44. 1, p. 284, Bernhardy, *Synt.* IX. p. 365. For examples of ἀξίως with the genitive, see Eph. iv. 1, Phil. i. 27, 1 Thess. ii. 12, and the examples collected by Raphel, *Annot.* Vol. II. p. 527. Lastly, Κυρίου is not = Θεοῦ (Theod.), but, as appar-ently always in St. Paul's Epistles, refers to our Lord; see Winer, Gr. § 19. 1, p. 113. In the Gospels, 2 Peter, and James, it commonly refers to God, but in 1 Pet ii. 13 (the other example are questioned) to Christ.

εἰς πᾶσαν ἀρέσκ.] 'unto all (every) pleasing,' 'in omne quod placet Deo,' i.e. 'to please Him in all things,' οὕτω ζῆτε ὥστε διὰ πάντα ἀρέσκειν τῷ Θεῷ [Κυρίῳ], Theoph. On the use of ἀρέσκεια, 'studium placendi,' Bengel, *Gn.*, Lösner in the N. Test. see Lösner, *Obs.* p. 361, where the word is found in several illustrative examples from Philo, the most pertinent of which is read *Mund. Opif.* § 30, Vol. 1. p. 25 ed Mangey, πάντα καὶ λέγειν καὶ πράττειν ἐσπούδαζεν εἰς ἀρέσκειαν τοῦ πατρὸς καὶ Βασιλέως, and *de Spec. Leg.* § 8, Vol. II p. 337. διὰ πασῶν ἰέναι τῶν εἰς ἀρέσκειαν ὁδῶν. On the extensive πᾶς, see above, and on *Eph.* i. 8.

ἐν παντὶ ἔργῳ ἀγ.] 'in every good work;' sphere in which the καρποφορία is manifested. This clause is not to be connected with the preceding εἰς ἀρέσκειαν, as Syriac (Pesh.), Chrys., Theoph., but with the following καρποφορ., as Vulg., Gothic,

Θεοῦ, ¹¹ ἐν πάσῃ δυνάμει δυναμούμενοι κατὰ τὸ κράτος τῆς δόξης

Syr. (Philox.), Theod., and the majority of modern commentators. The construction is thus perfectly symmetrical, each participle being associated with a modal or instrumental predication. The participles, it need scarcely be said, do not belong to πληρ. (Beng.), — a construction which Schwartz quaintly terms a 'carnificinam,' but with the infin., the participle having relapsed into the nom.; see Winer, *Gr.* § 63. 2, p. 505, and notes on *Eph.* iii. 18, iv. 2.

καὶ αὐξ. τῇ ἐπιγνώσει] '*and increasing by the (full) knowledge of God.*' The ἐπίγνωσις Θεοῦ was the instrument by which the growth was increased. The reading of *Rec.*, εἰς τὴν ἐπίγν., is not exegetically untenable, as ἐπίγν. may be viewed with a kind of reciprocal reference as the measure of the moral αὔξησις (see Mey. *in loc*, and comp. Ephes. iv. 13), but the weight of external evidence, if not also of internal, preponderates against it; see critical note.

11. ἐν πάσῃ κ. τ. λ.] '*being strengthened with all (every form of) strength;*' third participial clause parallel to, and in co-ordination with, ἐν παντὶ κ. τ. λ. Ἐν here seems purely *instrumental* (contrast ver. 9), the action being considered as involved in the means; see Jelf, *Gr.* § 623. 3: with this may be compared the simple dat. Eph. iii. 16, see notes *in loc.* Alford regards ἐν as denoting the *element*, δύναμις being subjective: this is possible; the instrumental force, however, seems clearly recognized by Theod., τῇ θείᾳ ῥοπῇ κρατυνόμενοι, and appears more simple and natural. The simple form δυναμόω is an ἅπ. λεγόμ. in the N. T. (see Psalm lxvii. 28, Eccles. x. 10, Dan. ix. 27), ἐνδυναμόω being the more usual form.

κατὰ τὸ κράτος τῆς δ.] '*according to the power of His glory;*' not His glorious power,' Anth., Beza, al., but 'the power which is the peculiar characteristic of His glory,' the gen. belonging to the category of the gen. *possessivus*; compare notes *on Eph.* i. 6. The prep. κατὰ represents, not the source (Daven.), nor the motive (Steig.), but, as usual, the *norma*, in accordance with which, and in correspondence with which, the δυνάμωσις would be effected. The power which is the attribute of the glory of God indicates the measure and degree in which the Colossians will be strengthened; οὐχ ἁπλῶς, φησί, δυναμοῦσθε, ἀλλ' ὡς εἰκὸς τοὺς οὕτως ἰσχυρῷ δεσπότῃ δουλεύοντας, Chrysost. On the deriv. of κράτος, see notes *on Eph.* i. 19.

εἰς πᾶσαν κ. τ. λ.] '*unto all patience and longsuffering;*' i. e. 'to insure, to lead you into, every form of patience and longsuffering,' 'ut procreet in nobis [vobis] patientiam,' etc., Davenant,— the prep., as usual, marking the final destination of the δυνάμωσις. The distinction between these words is not very clear: neither that of Chrys. (μακροθυμία πρὸς ἀλλήλους, ὑπομονὴ πρὸς τοὺς ἔξω), nor that quoted, but not adopted by Daven. (ὑπομ. ad illa mala quæ a Deo infliguntur μακροθ. ad illa quæ ab hominibus inferuntur) is quite satisfactory, as both, on different sides, seem too restrictive. Perhaps ὑπομονὴ is more general, designating that '*brave patience*,'—not 'endurance,' with which the Christian ought to bear all trials, whether from God or men, from within or without (see notes *on* 2 Tim. ii. 10, and *on Tit.* ii. 2), while μακροθ. points more to forbearance, whether towards the sinner (see *on Eph.* iv. 2), the gainsayer, or even the persecutor: see *on* 2 *Tim.* iii. 10.   μετὰ χαρᾶς is joined by Theodoret, Olsh., De W., Alf., and others, with the preceding clause; so appy. Vulg., Coptic, Goth., Syriac (Philox.), and Æthiop. Viewed alone, this connection seems

αὐτοῦ εἰς πᾶσαν ὑπομονὴν καὶ μακροθυμίαν, μετὰ χαρᾶς ¹² εὐχαριστοῦντες τῷ Πατρὶ τῷ ἱκανώσαντι ἡμᾶς εἰς τὴν μερίδα τοῦ

very plausible,—the ὑπομ and μακρ. ar to be associated with joy, the resignation is to be genuinely Christian, compare Daven. As, however, each preceding clause commences with a defining prepositional adjunct, and both ὑπομονὴ and μακροθ are perfectly distinct and are commonly used, whether in juxtaposition (2 Cor. vi 4, 6, 2 Tim. iii. 10) or separately (Rom. v. 3, 2 Cor. xii. 12, al ; Gal. v. 22, Col iii 12, al), without any further definition, it seems more natural, with Syr., Chrys., Theoph., Œcumen., and recently Mey., Lachm., and Tisch., to connect the defining words with εὐχαριστοῦντες.

12. εὐχ. τῷ Πατρί] 'giving thanks to the Father,' scil. 'of our Lord Jesus Christ;' participial clause, obviously not dependent on οὐ παυόμ. verse 9 (Chrys., Theoph.), but co-ordinate with the preceding clauses. The meaning of εὐχαρ. is well discussed by Boeckh, Corp. Inser. Vol. 1. p. 524; it is there stated to have four meanings : (a) Attic, 'gratificari,' χάριν διδόναι; (b) non-Attic, 'gratus habere vel referre'; but see Demosth. de Cor. p. 257. 2; (c) gratias agere verbis,' used by Polyb. (xvi. 25. 1, xviii. 26. 4, xxx. 11. 1) and later writers; (d) 'gratias referre simul et agere gratificando' found in certain inscript.: see also notes on Phil. i. 12. The readings τῷ π. καὶ Θεῷ and τῷ Θεῷ κ. π. are obvious interpolations, and rest on no critical authority; see Tisch. in loc. τῷ ἱκανώσαντι κ. τ. λ.] 'who made us meet for the portion of the inheritance of the saints in light.' These words deserve some consideration. In the first place the reading is slightly doubtful : DFG; 17. 80; Claroman., Goth.; Did.; Lat. Ff. read καλέσαντι for ἱκαν., while Lachm., with B, retains both τῷ ἱκαν. καὶ καλ. The critical preponderance is, however, clear-

ly in favor of ἱκαν., for which καλέσ. would have formed a natural gloss. (2) Ἱκαν. is not 'qui dignos fecit,' Vulg., but ܐ̈ܫܘܝ [qui idoneos nos fecit] Syriac, compare Eth.; see 2 Cor. iii. 6, ὃς καὶ ἱκάνωσεν ἡμᾶς, where the meaning is perfectly clear. Again the part. has not here a causal force 'quippe qui,' Meyer (compare Theod., ὅτι κοινωνοὺς ἀπέφηνε), —a meaning which is precluded by the presence of the article (see notes on Eph. i. 12), but is distinctly predicative, and somewhat solemnly descriptive; πολὺ τὸ βάρος ἔδειξεν, Chrys. The principal difficulty is, however, in the construction, as ἐν τῷ φωτὶ may admit of at least four connections, (a) with ἱκανώσαντι, in an instrumental (Meyer) or semi-modal sense,—as apparently Chrys., Œcum., Theoph., who explain φωτὶ as γνώσει; (b) with τὴν μερίδα (Beng.), as having a local force, and defining the position of the μερίς; (c) with ἁγίων,—ἐν φωτὶ designating their abode, compare Grotius, lastly and most probably, (d) with κλήρου, or more exactly κλήρου τῶν ἁγίων, the gen. specifying the possessors, and so indirectly the character of the κλῆρος, the prep. clause its 'situm et conditionem,' Corn. a Lap. Of these (a), though ably defended by Meyer, is harsh and improbable; (b) causes a dislocation in the order, unless μερ. κ. τ. λ. be all taken as one idea (Alford), in which case the omission of the article is not perfectly satisfactory; (c) gives to οἱ ἅγιοι an undue prominence, compare Alford; (d) on the contrary seems to give to the κλῆρος τῶν ἁγ. exactly the qualifying, or possibly localizing definition it requires, and preserves a good antithesis with ἐξ. τοῦ σκότους, v. 13, which (a) especially obscures; compare Acts xxvi 18. The art. before ἐν τῷ φωτὶ is not needed, as

κλήρου τῶν ἁγίων ἐν τῷ φωτί, ¹³ ὃς ἐρρύσατο ἡμᾶς ἐκ τῆς ἐξουσίας τοῦ σκότους, καὶ μετέστησεν εἰς τὴν βασιλείαν τοῦ υἱοῦ τῆς ἀγά-

κλήρ. τῶν ἁγ. ἐν τῷ φ. forms a single idea (Winer, *Gram.* § 20. 2, p. 123) : with the whole clause (Alf.) it could be less easily dispensed with. We retain then (*d*) with De W., perhaps Theod., and apparently the majority of interpreters. There remain only a few details.

κλῆρος] '*inheritance*,' Acts xxvi. 18; properly 'a lot' (Matth. xxvii. 35, Mark xv. 24), thence anything obtained by lot (compare Acts i. 25, *Rec.*), and thence, with a greater latitude, anything assigned or apportioned (τόπος, κτῆμα, οὐσία ἢ λαχμός, Suid.), whether officially (1 Pet. v. 3; 'cleros appellat particulares ecclesias, Calv.), or, as here, a possession and inheritance; comp. Heb. נַחֲלָה. The κλῆρος ἐν φ. is represented as a joint inheritance of the saints, of which each individual has his μερίδα. The derivation is uncertain; perhaps from κλᾶειν, *i. e.* a 'broken-off' portion (Pott, *Etym. Forsch.* Vol. II p. 597), or, less probably, from Sanser. *krī*, with sense of 'casting,' or 'parting off' (Benfey, *Wurzellex.* Vol. II. p. 172). Its more specific use in eccl. writers is well illustrated by Suicer, *Thesaur.* s. v. Vol. II. p. 110 sq.

ἐν τῷ φωτί] It is not necessary to refer this specifically to the heavenly realm : φῶς marks its characteristics on the side, not merely of its glory (Huth., compare Bp. Hall, *Invis. World*, II 5) but, as the antithesis suggests, of i s essential purity and perfections; compare 1 John i. 5. This blessed inheritance may be entered upon in part even here on earth. For a good sermon on this text, see Beveridge, *Serm.* II. Vol. VI. p. 399.

13. ὃς ἐρρύσατο κ. τ. λ.] Appositional relative-sentence (Winer, *Gram.* § 60. 7, p. 479), introducing a contrasted amplification of the preceding clause, and preparing for a transition to the doctrine of the person, the glory, and the redeeming love of Christ, ver. 14–20. The special meanings that have been assigned to ἐρρύσατο ('eripuit; plus hoc est quam liberavit: ..... cripiuntur sæpe inviti,' Zanch.), though in part philologically defensible (see Buttm. *Lexil.* s. v. § 53. 1, 2), cannot be certainly maintained *in the N. T.*, where for the most part the idea of 'dragging from a crowd of enemies' (comp. Luke i. 74, 2 Tim. iii. 11, iv. 17; — surely not unwilling) passes into the more generic idea of 'saving;' see Buttm. *l. c.*, § 3. The remark of Theoph. is much more in point; οὐκ εἶπε δέ, ἐξέβαλεν, ἀλλ' ἐρρύσατο, δεικνὺς ὅτι ὡς αἰχμάλωτοι ἐταλαιπωρούμεθα.

ἐξουσίας τοῦ σκότ.] '*the power of darkness*;' the power which is possessed and exerted by Darkness, — not, however, merely *subjectively*, τῆς πλάνης, Chrys. 1, but evil and sin, viewed *objectively* as the antithesis of φῶς, *i. e.* τοῦ διαβόλου τῆς τυραννίδος, Chrys. 2, Theod. μετέστησεν] '*translated*,' '*removed*;' redemption in its further and positive aspects. The verb clearly involves a local reference, the removing from one place and fixing in another; we were taken out of the realms of darkness and transferred to the kingdom of light : see Joseph. *Antiq.* IX. 11. 1, τοὺς οἰκήτορας μετέστησεν εἰς τὴν αὑτοῦ βασιλείαν. The further idea 'migrare cogit ex *natali solo*,' Daven., though theologically true, is not necessarily involved in the word.

εἰς τὴν βασιλείαν] The term βασιλεία has here a reference neither purely metaphorical (*e. g.* the Church ; comp. Huth.), nor ethical and inward (Olsh. ; Luke xvii. 21), nor yet ideal and proleptic (Mey.), — but, as the image involved in μετέστ. suggests, semilocal and descriptive. Nor is this wholly future; the υἱοὶ τοῦ φωτός, the pure and the holy (comp. Matth. v. 8, Heb. xii. 14), even

πης αὐτοῦ, ¹¹ ἐν ᾧ ἔχομεν τὴν ἀπολύτρωσιν, τὴν ἄφεσιν τῶν ἁμαρ-
τιῶν· ¹⁵ ὅς ἐστιν εἰκὼν τοῦ Θεοῦ τοῦ ἀοράτου, πρωτότοκος πάσης

while tarrying in these lower courts are the subjects of that kingdom the 'denizens' of that πολίτευμα (Phil. iii. 20), the sharers of that υἱοθεσία (Eph. i. 5), just as the υἱοὶ τῆς ἀπειθείας are even here on earth the occupants of the realm of darkness and the vassals of its κοσμοκράτορες. A long and elaborate treatise on the βασιλεία Θεοῦ will be found in Commant. Fim. Vol. ii. p. 107-173. τῆς ἀγάπης αὐτοῦ] 'of His love,' i. e. who is the object of it, whom it embraces. This genitive has received different explanations; it has been regarded as *a*) a genitive of the characterizing quality (compare Winer, Gr. § 34. 3. b, p. 211), in which it differs little from ἀγαπητός, Matthew iii. 17, Mark xii. 6, al., or ἠγαπημένος, Ephes. i. 6, compare Chrys.; (*b*) a species of gen. *originis*, ἀγάπη being considered more as an essence than an attribute; see August. *de Trin*. x. 19 (cited by Est. and Just.), and Olsh. *in loc.*; (*c*) the gen. of the remoter object (comp. Winer, Gr. § 30. 2, p. 169), 'the son who has His love,' Steiger, compare Wordsw.; or, simply and more probably, (*d*) the gen. *subjecti*, ἀγάπης being classed under the general head of the possessive genitive; comp. Krüger, *Sprachl.* § 47. 7. 7; De Wette and Mey. compare Gen. xxxv. 18, υἱὸς ὀδύνης μου. It has been thought that the title is specially selected to imply some reference to the υἱοθεσία (Huth.); this is possible, but the context and a comparison with Ephes. i. 6, 7, do not favor the supposition.

14. ἐν ᾧ] '*in whom :*' certainly not 'by whom,' but '*in*' Him as the living source of redemption : see notes on *Eph.* i. 7, where these and the following words in the clause are commented upon and illustrated.   ἔχομεν τὴν ἀπολ.] '*we are having the redemption,*' not '*our redemption,*' Alford, but '*the red.,*' or with pleonastic omission of the art., 'Redemption,' Auth., — the reference being to the redemption from the wrath and punitive justice of God in its most comprehensive signification, whether special yeons or common to us and to all mankind. The prep. ἀπό is not intensive (οὐκ εἶπε λύτρωσιν, ἀλλ ἀπολ., ὥστε μηδὲ πεσεῖν λοιπόν, Chrys.), but, with its usual force ('*separatio est a actionisque potestas,*' Winer, *Voc. Comp.* iv. 5), points to the punishment at Divine wrath *from* which we were redeemed in Christ and by His blood. On the four degrees of redemption, — viz., (*a*) payment of ransom for all, (*b*) admission into the Church, (*c*) exemption from tyranny of sin here, and (*d*) exemption from hell and death hereafter, — see Jackson, *Creed*, ix. 5, Vol. viii. p. 218 sq. (Oxf. 1844). For other details see notes on *Eph.* i. 7. There is some variation in reading; διὰ τοῦ αἵμ. (Rec.) rests only on cursive mss., and is rightly omitted by nearly all modern editors. Ἔχομεν is more doubtful, as it might be a change in conformity with Eph. i. 7. *Lachm.* reads ἔσχομεν with B (A is doubtful), Copt. [*anse*]; but the diplomatic authority seems insufficient to warrant the change.   τὴν ἄφεσιν τῶν ἁμαρτ.] '*the forgiveness of our sins ;*' apposition to the preceding τὴν ἀπολ., defining more exactly its nature and significance. On the distinction between ἄφεσις and πάρεσις, see Trench, *Synon.* § 33, and on that between ἁμαρτίαι and παραπτώματα, notes on *Eph.* i. 7.

15. ὅς ἐστιν κ. τ. λ.] Detailed description of the person of Christ, His dignity, and His exaltation, for which the preceding verse and the allusion to βασιλεία in ver. 13 form a suitable prep-

κτίσεως, ¹⁶ ὅτι ἐν αὐτῷ ἐκτίσθη τὰ πάντα, τὰ ἐν τοῖς οὐρανοῖς καὶ

aration. As this forms one of the three important passages in St. Paul's Epistles (Ephesians i. 20-23, Phil. ii. 6-11) in which the doctrine of the person of Christ is especially unfolded, both the general divisions and the separate details will require very careful consideration. With regard to the former, it seems scarcely doubtful that there is a *twofold* division, and that, as in Phil. ii. 7, καὶ σχήματι κ τ. λ. seemed to introduce a new portion of the subject, so here the second καὶ αὐτός (v. 18) indicates a similar transition; and further, that, just as in Phil. l. c. the first portion related to the Λόγος ἄσαρκος, the latter to the Λόγος ἔνσαρκος, so here in ver. 15-17, the reference is rather to the *pre-incarnate* Son in His relation to God and to His own creatures, in ver. 18-20 to the *incarnate* and now *glorified* Son in His relations to His Church: so Olsh., hastily condemned by Meyer, but, in effect and inferentially, supported by the principal Greek and majority of Latin Fathers: comp. Pearson, *Creed*, Vol. I. p. 14. See contra, Hofmann, *Schriftb.* Vol. I. p. 135, whose opposition, however, is based on the more than doubtful supposition that καὶ αὐτός (ver. 17) is dependent on the foregoing ὅτι. ʽΟς thus refers to the subject ὁ υἱὸς τῆς ἀγ. αὐτοῦ in its widest and most complex relations, whether as Creator or Redeemer, the immediate context defining the precise nature of the reference: see *on Phil.* ii. 6.

εἰκὼν τοῦ Θεοῦ τ. τ. λ.] ʽthe image of the invisible God;' not 'an image,' Wakef., or ʽimage,' Alf.,—the article is idiomatically omitted after ἐστιν; see Middl. *Gr. Art.* III. 3. 2. With this expression comp. 2 Cor. iv. 4, ὅς ἐστιν εἰκὼν τοῦ Θεοῦ, Heb. i. 3, ἀπαύγασμα τῆς δόξης καὶ χαρακτὴρ τῆς ὑποστάσεως αὐτοῦ: Christ is the original image of God, ʽbearing his figure and resemblance as

truly, fully, and perfectly as a son of man has all the features, lineaments, and perfections belonging to the nature of man,' Waterl. *Serm. Chr. Div.* v. Vol. II. p. 104, see especially Athan. *Nicen. Def.* § 20. Without overpassing the limits of this commentary, we may observe that Christian antiquity has ever regarded the expression ʽimage of God' as denoting the eternal Son's perfect equality with the Father in respect of His substance, nature, and eternity; ʽperfectae aequalitatis significantiam habet similitudo,' Hil. *de Syn.* § 73, ἀπαράλλακτος εἰκὼν τοῦ Πατρὸς [on the subsequent Semi-arian use of this term, see *Oxf. Libr. of Ff.* Vol. VIII. p. 35, 106] καὶ τοῦ πρωτοτύπου ἔκτυπος χαρακτήρ, Alex. ap. Theod. *Hist. Eccl.* I. 4; see Athan. *contr. Arian.* I. 20. The Son is the Father's image in all things save only in being the Father, εἰκὼν φυσικὴ καὶ ἀπαράλλακτος κατὰ πάντα ὁμοία τῷ πατρί, πλὴν τῆς ἀγεννησίας καὶ τῆς πατρότητος, Damasc. *de Imag.* III. 18; comp. Athan. *contr. Arian.* I. 21.

The exact force of the emphatically placed τοῦ ἀοράτου (ʽwho is invisible,' Wordsw.; Winer, *Gram.* § 20. 1. a, p. 120) is somewhat doubtful. Does it point to the primal *invisibility* (Chrys., Orig. ap. Athan. *Nic. Def.* § 27), or, by a tacit antithesis, to the *visibility*, of the εἰκών (Daven., Meyer, al.; compare 2 Cor. iii. 18, Heb. xii. 14)? Apparently to the latter: Christ, as God and as the original image of God, was of course primarily and essentially ἀόρατος (ἐπεὶ οὐδ' ἂν εἰκὼν εἴη, Chrys.); as, however, the Son that declared the Father (John i. 18), as He that was pleased to reveal Himself visibly to the saints in the O. T. (see especially Bull, *Def. Fid. Nic.* I. 1. 1 sq.). He was ὁρατός, the manifester of Him who dwells in φῶς ἀπρόσιτον (1 Tim. vi. 16) and whom no man hath

τὰ ἐπὶ τῆς γῆς, τὰ ὁρατὰ καὶ τὰ ἀόρατα, εἴτε θρόνοι, εἴτε

seen or can see; John i. 18; compare Beng. *in loc*. Whether there is here any approximation to views entertained by Philo (Olsh., Alf., see Usteri, *Lehrb.* II. 2. 4, p. 293), is very doubtful. We must at any rate remember that Philo was the uninspired exponent of the better theosophy of his day, St. Paul the inspired apostle revealing the highest and most transcendent mysteries of the Divine economy. On the meaning of εἰκών, and its distinction from ὁμοίωσις, see Trench, *Synon.* § 15.
πρωτότοκος πάσης κτίσ[εως].] '*the first-born before every creature,*' i. e. 'begotten, and that antecedently to everything that was *created*;' surely not 'the whole creation,' Waterland (Vol. II. p. 57), compare Alf., — an inexact translation which here certainly (contrast *on Eph.* ii. 21) there seems no necessity for maintaining; compare Middleton, *Gr. Art.* p. 373. As verse 17 (πρὸ πάντων) expressly reiterates, our Lord is here solemnly defined as πρωτότοκος in relation to *every* created thing, animate or inanimate, human or superhuman; πρωτότ. τοῦ Θεοῦ, καὶ πρὸ πάντων τῶν κτισμάτων, Just. Martyr, *Dial.* § 100. This notable expression has received every variety of explanation. Grammat. considered, τῆς κτίσεως may perhaps be the *part. gen.*, the *possess. gen.* (Hof. *Schriftb.* Vol. I. 187), or, much more probably, the *gen.* of the *point of view*, 'in reference to,' 'in comparison to,' (Scheuerl. *Synt.* § 18. 1. p. 129), the latent comparative force involved in the πρῶτος rendering this last genitival relation still more intelligible and perspicuous; comp. Fritz. on *Rom.* x. 19, Vol. II p. 421. In the first two cases, πᾶσα κτίσις must be considered as equiv. to a plur. (ܟܠ

ܒܪܝܬܐ [omnium creaturarum] Syr.). *i. e.* every form of creation (comp. Hof-

mann, *l. c.*), the expression compared with πρωτότοκος τῶν νεκρῶν, Rev. i. 5, and (esp. in the last of these cases) the Arian deduction, that Christ is a κτίσις, deemed *grammatically* possible; see Usteri, *Lehrb.* II. 2. 4, and even Reuss, *Théol. Chrét.* IV. 10, Vol. II. p. 100, both which writers use language, which, without the limitation named by Thorndike (*Oec. Gent.* II. 17. 5), must be pronounced simply and plainly Arian. In the last case, πᾶσα κτίσις retains its proper force, πρωτότοκος its comparative reference, and the correction of Athanase, especially when viewed in connection with the context (ὅτι ἐν αὐτῷ ἐκτ., ver. 16), perfectly *inerrable*: ἄλλος ἐστι τῶν κτισμάτων, καὶ κτίσμα μὲν οὐκ ἔστι, κτιστὴς δὲ τῶν κτισμάτων, *contr. Arian.* II. § 62, — a passage of many flows force and perspicuity; see also, both on this and ver. 16, Pearson, *Creed*, Vol. I. p. 148. The term πρωτότοκος (*els.* not πρωτόκτιστος or πρωτόπλαστος) is studiously used to define our Lord's relation to His creatures and His fatherhood with them (comp. Rom viii. 29), and is in this respect distinguished from μονογενὴς which more exactly defines His relation to the Father; μονογενὴς μὲν, διὰ τὴν ἐκ Πατρὸς γέννησιν· πρωτότοκος δὲ, διὰ τὴν εἰς τὴν κτίσιν συγκατάβασιν [condescension] καὶ τὴν τῶν πολλῶν ἀδελφοποίησιν, Athan. *contr. Arian.* II. 62: in a word, He was *begotten*, they were *created*, — the gulf infinite, yet as He stooped to wear their outward form, so He ordains not to institute, by the mouth of His apostle, *temperate* comparison between His own generation from eternity and their creation in time; see Bull, *Def. F. Nic.* III. 9. 9, who however appears to have misunderstood the meaning of συγκατάβασις, compare Newman, in *Oxf. Libr. of F.* Vol. VIII. p. 288.
Lastly, as there seem to be two senses in

κυριότητες, εἴτε ἀρχαί, εἴτε ἐξουσίαι· τὰ πάντα δι' αὐτοῦ καὶ

Scripture in which our Lord is first-born in respect of every creature, viz., in its restoration after the fall as well as in its first origin (see Athan. *l. c.*, § 63), we may possibly admit, as ver. 18 also partially suggests, a secondary and *inferential*, — certainly not a primary (Theod.-Mops.; Æth., '*supra omnia opera*'), nor even co-ordinate, reference to priority in dignity (προτίμησις): see Alf. *in loc.*, who, however, unduly presses this reference, and by referring the whole to Christ in his now glorified state (so Mey., and Hofmann, *Schriftb.* Vol. I. p. 135), certainly seems to impair the theological force and significance of this august passage. For further doctrinal comments see the good note of Wordsworth *in loc.*

16. ὅτι] '*because*,' not 'for,' Alf., a translation better reserved for γάρ, — logical elucidation of the preceding member: He, in the sphere of whose creative power all things were made and on whom all things depend, was truly the προτότ. πάσης κτίσεως, and had an eternal priority in time and dignity. The objections of Schleiermacher (*Stud. u. Krit.* 1832, p. 502) to the logic of this causal explanation are unreasonable and pointless. ἐν αὐτῷ] '*in Him*,' as the creative centre of all things, the causal element of their existence; compare Winer, *Gr.* § 50. 6, p. 372 (ed. 6; here judiciously altered). The preposition has received several different explanations, three of which deserve consideration: ἐν has been referred to Christ as (*a*) the *causa instrumentalis* (ἐν = διά), creation being conceived as existing in the means, Jelf, *Gr.* § 622. 3; (*b*) the *causa exemplaris*, the κόσμος νοητὸς being supposed to be included and to have its essentiality (Olsh.) in Him as the great exemplar; (*c*) the *causa conditionalis*, the act of creation being supposed to rest in Him, and to depend on Him for its completion and realization. Of these (*a*) is adopted by the Greek commentators, but is open to the serious objection that no distinction is preserved between ἐν αὐτῷ here and δι' αὐτοῦ below, which St. Paul's known use of prepositions (see notes *on Gal.* i. 1) would lead us certainly to expect. The second (*b*) is adopted by the schoolmen and recently by Olsh., Neander, Bisp., but is highly artificial, and supported by no analogy of Scripture. We therefore adopt (*c*) which is theologically exact and significant, and in which St. Paul's peculiar, yet somewhat varied, use of ἐν Χριστῷ with verbs (compare 2 Cor. v. 19, Gal. ii. 17, Eph. i. 4, al.) is suitably maintained: compare the similar usage of ἐν, especially with pronouns, to denote the subject in which and on which ('den Haltpunkt') the action depends, *e. g.* ἔν σοι πᾶσ' ἔγωγε σώζομαι, Soph. *Ajax*, 519; see Rost u. Palm, *Lex.* s. v. ἐν, 2. b, Vol 1. p. 509, Bernhardy, *Synt.* v. 8. b, p. 210.

ἐκτίσθη] '*were created*,' with simple physical ref.: observe the *aorist* of the past action, as contrasted with ἔκτισται below, in which the duration and persistence of the act ('per effectus suos durat,' see on *Eph.* ii. 8) is brought into especial prominence; comp. 1 Cor. xv. 27, and Winer, *Gr.* § 40. 4, p. 243. The forced (ethical) meaning 'were arranged, reconstituted' (Schleierm.), though lexically admissible, is fully disproved by Meyer, who observes that κτίζω always in the N. T. (even in Eph. ii. 10, 15, iv. 25) implies the bringing into existence, spiritually or otherwise, of what before was not. For an exposition of this important text see *Conc. Antioch.* ap. Routh, *Reliq. Sacr.* Vol. II. p. 468, referred to by Wordsw. *in loc.* τὰ πάντα] '*all things (that exist)*' — more specifically defined, first in regard of place, sec-

εἰς αὐτὸν ἔκτισται, ¹⁷ καὶ αὐτός ἐστιν πρὸ πάντων, καὶ τὰ πάντα

ondly in regard of *nature* and essential characteristics. On the use of the art ('das All'), see W., *Gr.* § 18. 8, p. 105. τὰ ἐν τοῖς οὐρ. κ τ. λ.] 'the things in the heaven, and the things on the earth;' not in reference merely to intelligent beings (Huther), nor to the exclusion of things under the earth (Phil. ii 10), but, as in Eph. i. 10 (see notes), with the fullest amplitude, — 'all things and beings whatsoever and wheresoever; 'hac distributione universam creaturam complectitur,' Daven. The following clauses carry out the universality of the reference, by specifying the two classes of things, the visible and material, and the invisible and spiritual, — which latter class is still further specified by disjunctive enumerations. τὰ ὁρατὰ καὶ τὰ ἀόρ.] 'the things visible and the things invisible;' amplification — not exclusively of the *former* (διδάσκει σαφέστερον τίνα καλεῖ ὁράτια εἴτε ὁρατά [as sun, moon, and stars] εἴτε ἀόρατα, Theod.), or exclusively of the *latter* member (ἀ ́ρατα τὴν ψυχὴν λέγων, ὁρατὰ πάντας ἀνθρώπους, Chrys.), but of *both*, 'the visible and invisible world;' 'in coelo visibilia sunt sol, luna, stellae; invisibilia, angeli: in terrā visibilia, plantae, elementa, animalia; invisibilia, animae, humanae,' Daven., — unless indeed, as the following enumeration seems to imply, this last class, 'animae humanae,' be grouped with ὁρατά (Mey.). εἴτε θρόνοι κ τ. λ.] '*whether thrones, whether dominions, whether principalities, whether powers:*' disjunctive specification of the preceding ἀόρατα: 'lest in that invisible world, among the many degrees of the celestial hierarchy, any order might seem exempted from an essential dependence upon Him, he nameth those which are of greatest eminence, and in them comprehendeth the rest,' Pearson, *Creed,* Vol I. p. 148. There seems no reason to modify the opinion advanced on Eph. i. 21, that four orders of heavenly intelligence are here enumerated; see notes and references *in loc.,* ii u s, *Theol. Chr̂et.* IV. 20 Vol. II. p. 246 sq., and the extremely good article s.v. Suicer, *Thesaur.* s. v. ἄγγ, Vol. I. p. 30-4. By comparing this passage with Eph. *l. c.,* where the order seems descensive, we may possibly infer that the θρόνοι (not elsewhere in N. T., but noticed by Dionys. Areop. *de Hier.,* and in *Test.* XII *Patr.* p. 532, Fabric.) are the higher order of blessed spirits, those sitting round the eternal throne of God, κυριότητες the fourth, ἀρχαί and ἐξουσίαι the intermediate (Mey.), if indeed, as is observed on *Eph. l. c.,* all such distinctions are not to be deemed precarious and presumptuous; compare Bull, *Serm.* XII. p. 251, and Hofmann, *Schrifw.* Vol. 1 p. 342. This enumeration *may* have been suggested by some known theosophistic speculations of the Colossians (cap. ii. 18, compare Maurice, *Unity of N. T.* p. 566), but more probably, as in Eph. i. 21, was an incidental revelation, which the term ἀόρατα evoked. Of the other numerous interpretations which these words have received (see De Wette *in loc.*), none seem worthy of serious attention. τὰ πάντα κ. τ. λ.] '(*qua*) *all things,*' *etc.;* seems recapitulation of the foregoing. The most natural punctuation seems to be neither a period (*Tisch.*), nor a comma (*Alf.*), least of all a parenthesis (*Lac*), but, as in *Mill,* and in *Buttmann's* recent edition, a colon. δι᾽ αὐτοῦ καὶ εἰς αὐτόν] '*Through Him and for Him;*' resumption of ἐν αὐτῷ ἐκτ. with a change both in tense and prepositions; there the Son was represented as the 'causa conditionalis' of all things, here as the 'causa medians' of creation, and the 'causa finalis' (Daven. or finis ulti-

ἐν αὐτῷ συνέστηκεν ¹⁸ καὶ αὐτός ἐστιν ἡ κεφαλὴ τοῦ σώματος,

mus' (Calov.) to which it is referred. It was to form a portion of His glory, and to be subjected to His dominion (comp. Matth. xxviii. 18) that all things were created; εἰς αὐτὸν κρέμαται ἡ πάντων ὑπόστασις......ὥστε ἂν ἀποσπασθῇ τῆς αὐτοῦ προνοίας, ἀπόλωλε καὶ διέφθαρται, Chrys. We may observe that the mediate creation, and final destination, of the world, here referred to the Son, are in Rom. xi. 36 referred to the Father. Such permutations deserve our serious consideration; if the Son had not been God, such an interchange of important relations would never have seemed possible: compare Waterland *Def.* Qu. xi. Vol. i. p. 383 sq., Vol. ii. p. 54, 56. On the force of the perf. ἔκτισται, see above; and in answer to the attempts to refer this passage to any figurative creation, see Pearson, *Creed*, Vol. i. p. 149, 150 (ed. Burt.).

17. καὶ αὐτός κ.τ.λ.] '*and He Himself*,' etc.; contrast between the creator and the things created; αὐτὸς being emphatic, and καὶ having a *gentle* contrasting force (see notes *on Phil.* iv. 12) by which the tacit antithesis involved in αὐτός ('*ipse* oppositum habet alium,' Hermann, *Dissert.*, αὐτός 1) between the things created (τὰ πάντα) and Him who created them is still more enhanced: *they* were created in time, *He* their creator is and was before all time. It may be observed that though αὐτός appears both in this and the great majority of passages in the N. T. to have its proper classical force ('ut rem ab aliis rebus discernendam esse indicet,' Herm. *Dissert. l. c.*), the Aramaic use of the corresponding pronoun should make us cautious in pressing it *in every case*. The vernacular tongue of the writers of the N. T. must have produced *some* effect on their diction. πρὸ πάντων] '*before all things*,' not 'all

beings' ('omnes,' Vulg., Clarom.), and that too not in *rank*, but, in accordance with the primary meaning of πρωτότοκος and the immediate context, — in *time*; τοῦτο Θεῷ ἅρμοζον, Chrys. Theodoret with reason calls attention to the expression— not ἐγένετο πρὸ πάντων, but ἔστι πρὸ πάντων: contrast John i. 14

ἐν αὐτῷ συνέστ.] '*consist in Him*,' as the causal sphere of their continuing existence: not *exactly* identical with ἐν αὐτῷ above (Mey., Alf.), but, with the very slight change which the change of verb involves, in more of a *causal* ref-; Christ was the conditional element of their *creation*, the causal element of their *persistence*; comp. Heb. i. 3, φέρων τε τὰ πάντα τῷ ῥήματι τῆς δυνάμεως αὐτοῦ. The declaration, as Waterl. observes, is in fact tantamount to 'in Him they live, and move, and have their being' (*Serm.* on *Div.* vii. Vol. ii. p. 164), which is and forms one of the great arguments for the omnipresence and the preserving and sustaining power of Christ; see ib. *Def.* Qu. xviii. Vol. i. p. 430. The verb συνιστάναι is well defined by Reiske, *Ind. Dem.* (quoted by Meyer), as 'corpus unum, integrum, perfectum, secum consentiens esse et permanere,' compare 2 Pet. iii. 5, and [Arist.] *de Mundo*, 6, ἐκ θεοῦ τὰ πάντα, καὶ διὰ θεοῦ ἡμῖν συνέστηκεν; see especially Krebs, *Obs.* p. 334, and Loesner, *Obs.* p. 362, by both of whom this word is copiously illustrated from Josephus and Philo; compare also Elsner, *Obs.* Vol. ii. 239.

18. καὶ αὐτός κ.τ.λ.] Transition to the second part, in which the relation of the incarnate and glorified Son to His *Church* is declared and confirmed, not perhaps without some reference to the erroneous teaching and angel-worship that apparently prevailed in the Church of Colossæ. Αὐτὸς is thus, as before, emphatic, possibly involving an antithe-

τῆς ἐκκλησίας· ὅς ἐστιν ἀρχή, πρωτότοκος ἐκ τῶν νεκρῶν, ἵνα

sis to some falsely imagined κεφαλή or κεφαλαί of the Church; 'He in whom all things consist, He, and no other than He, is the *head* of the Church.' The emphasis, as Meyer observes, rests on κεφαλή rather than ἐκκλησία; it was the headship of the Church, not its imaginary constitution, that formed the undercurrent of the erroneous teaching.

τοῦ σώμ. τῆς ἐκκλ.] '*of His body, the Church,*' τῆς ἐκκλ. being the genitive of *identity* or *apposition*; see Winer, *Gr.* § 59. 8, p. 470, Scheuerl. *Synt.* § 12. 1, p. 82. The apostle does not say merely 'of the Church,' but 'of His body,' etc., to show, — not the φιλανθρωπία of Christ (θέλων ἡμῖν οἰκειότερον δεῖξαι αὐτόν, Chrys.), but the real, vital, and essential union between the Church and its Head; compare Ephes. iv. 15, 16, and notes *in loc.*; see also Rom. xii. 5, 1 Cor. x. 17, Ephes. i. 23, al. ὅς ἐστιν] '*seeing He is;*' the relative having a semi argumentative force, and serving to confirm the previous declaration; see Jelf, *Gram.* § 836. 3. We can scarcely say that in such sentences 'ὅς is for ὅτι' (Jelf, *l. c.*, Matth. *Gr.* § 480. c), but rather that, like the more usual ὅστις, the simple relative force passes into the *explanatory*, which almost necessarily involves some tinge of a causal or argumentative meaning; see notes on *Gal.* ii. 4. ἀρχή] '*the beginning,*' not merely in ref. to the following τῶν νεκρῶν (Meyer, Hofmann, *Schriftb.* Vol. II. 1, p. 241; compare Theod.), nor even to the spiritual resurrection (Daven.), both of which seem too limited; nor yet, with a general and abstract reference, the 'first creative principle' (Steig., Huth.; compare Clem.-Alex. *Strom.* IV. p. 638, ὁ Θεὸς δὲ ἄναρχος ἀρχὴ τῶν ὅλων παντελής), — but, as the more immediate context and the reference to our Lord's Headship of His Church seem certainly to suggest, in ref. to the *new creation* (comp. Calv., Corn. a Lap.; 2 Cor. v. 17, Gal. vi. 15), the following πρωτότοκος ἐκ τῶν νεκρ. serving to define that relation more closely, and to preserve the retrospective allusion to πρωτότ. in ver. 15: our Lord in His glorified humanity is the ἀρχηγὸς τῆς ζωῆς (A. ts ii. 15) to His Church, the beginning, source, origin and leader of the new and spiritual, even as He was of the former and material, creation; see Olsh. at 1 Bisp. *in loc.*, and compare Usteri, *Lehrb.* II. 2, 4, p. 301. The plausible reading ἀπαρχή, adopted by Chrys. and a few mss., is a limiting gloss suggested by the next clause compared with 1 Cor. xv. 23. The omission of the article [inserted in B, 67**] before ἀρχή is due, not to the abstract form of the word (Olshaus.), but simply to the preceding verb ἐστί, Middl. *Gr. Art.* III. 3. 2. πρωτότ. ἐκ τῶν νεκρῶν] '*firstborn from the dead;*' not exactly identical with πρωτότ. τῶν νεκρῶν, Rev. i. 5 (partitive gen.), but with the proper force of the preposition, 'the first, not only *of*, but *out of* the dead;' He left their realm and came again as with a new begetting and new birth into life (see especially Andrewes, *Serm.* Vol. III. p. 57); he was the true ἀπαρχή τῶν κεκοιμημένων, 1 Cor. xv. 23; compare Hofmann, *Schriftb.* Vol. II. 1 p. 241. Others had been translated or had risen to die again, He had risen with glorified humanity to die no more (Rom. vi. 9); hence He is 'not called simply the first that rose, but with a note of generation, πρωτ. ἐκ τῶν νεκρῶν,' Pearson, *Creed,* Vol. I. p. 136 (ed. Burt.).

ἵνα γένηται κ. τ. λ.] '*in order that in all things He might become* (not 'sit,' Vulg.) *pre-eminent, might take the first place,*' 'primas teneat,' Beza, Daven.; πανταχοῦ πρῶτος ἄνω πρῶτος, ἐν τῇ ἐκ-

γένηται ἐν πᾶσιν αὐτὸς πρωτεύων, ¹⁹ ὅτι ἐν αὐτῷ εὐδόκησεν πᾶν

κλησίᾳ πρῶτος, ἐν τῇ ἀναστάσει πρῶτος, Chrys.: divine purpose (ἵνα has here its full telic force, compare *on Eph.* i. 17) of His being the ἀρχὴ of the new creation, and having the priority in the resurrection, — a divine purpose fulfilled in its temporal, and to be fulfilled in all conceivable relations, when all things are put under His feet, and the kingdom of the world is become the kingdom of the Lord and His Christ (Rev. xi. 15). The tense γένηται cannot be safely pressed, as in the subj. the force of the aor. is considerably weakened and modified; see Bernhardy, *Synt.* x. 9, p. 382. The verb πρωτεύειν is an ἅπ. λεγόμ. in the N. T., but is not uncommon elsewhere; compare Zech. iv. 7 (Aquil.), Esth. v. 11, 2 Macc. vi. 18, xiii. 15, in all which passages an idea of προτίμησις seems clearly conveyed. This however does not require a similar meaning to be assigned to πρωτότ. (comp. De W, Alf.): πρωτεύειν was to be the result, πρωτότοκ. κ. τ. λ. was one of the facts which led to it; compare Meyer *in loc.*

ἐν πᾶσιν] '*in all things,*' surely not 'inter omnes,' Beza, — a restricted reference that completely mars the majesty of this passage, and contravenes the force of the neuter τὰ πάντα in the causal sentence which follows. Lastly, αὐτός, as above, must not be left unnoticed; 'si quis alius mortem debellasset, etc., tum Christus non tenuisset primatum in omnibus,' Daven. We may observe that with this clause the predications respecting Christ seem here to reach their acme (comp. 1 Cor. xv. 28), and lead us to admit, if not to expect, a modification of subj. in the causal sentence which follows.

19. ὅτι] '*because;*' confirmation of the divine purpose in reference to Christ's precedence ἐν πᾶσιν: He in whom the whole πλήρωμα (of the Θεότης) was pleased to reside, must needs have had His precedence in all things eternally designed and contemplated.

ἐν αὐτῷ] '*in Him,*' and in Him specially; connected with κατοικεῖν, and put early forward in the sentence to receive full emphasis. The reference, as the context seems to show, is *now* more especially to the *incarnate Son.*

εὐδόκησεν κ. τ. λ.] '*the whole fulness (of the Godhead) was pleased to dwell;*' 'in ipso complacuit omnis plenitudo inhabitare,' Clarom. The first difficulty in this profound verse is to decide on the grammatical subject of εὐδοκεῖν. This verb, a late and probably Macedonian-Greek word (Sturz, *de Dial. Maced.* p. 167), has *four* constructions in the N. T., all personal; with ἐν and a dat. (Matth. iii. 17, xvii. 5, al.: 2 Thessalon. ii. 12 is doubtful), with εἰς and an accus. (2 Pet. i. 17), with a simple accus. (Heb. x. 6, 8), with an infin. referring to the subject (Rom. xv. 12, 1 Corin. i. 21, al., — the principal and prevailing use in St. Paul's Epp.); see Fritz. *Rom.* x. 1, Vol. II. p. 369 sq., where the uses of εὐδοκ. are fully investigated. In the present case three subjects have been proposed; (*a*) Χριστός, the preceding subject, Tertull. *Marc.* v. 19, and recently Conyb., and Hofm. *Schriftb.* Vol. II. 1, p. 242, where it is fairly defended; (*b*) Θεός, supplied from the context; so, it can scarcely be doubted, Syr., Vulg., Goth., Theod., and, by inference, Chrysost., Theoph., and after them the bulk of modern expositors; (*c*) the expressed subject τὸ πᾶν πλήρωμα; Clarom., Copt., apparently Æth., and recently Peile, and, very decidedly, Scholef. *Hints*, p. 108. Of these (*a*) involves indirect opposition to strong analogies of Scripture (*e. g.* 2 Cor. v. 19), and, equally with (*b*), a harsh change of subject to the two infin.: the second (*b*) is dogmatically correct, but involves a very unusual construction of εὐδοκ. (comp.

τὸ πλήρωμα κατοικῆσαι ²⁰ καὶ δἰ αὐτοῦ ἀποκαταλλάξαι τὰ πάντα

Polyb. *Hist.* t. 8. 4. vii. 4. 5, 2 Macc. xiv. 35', a different subject to κατοικ. and ἀποκ., and furt'er an ellipsis of a word, which though not without classical parallel (see Jelf, *Gr.* § 373. 3) would here, in a passage of this doctrinal importance, be in a very high degree unnatural and improbable: the third (*c*) is syntactically simple, it is also in harmony with St. Paul's regular usage of εὐδοκ. when associated with an infin., and, — what is still more important, — both in its causal connection, the nature of the expressions, and the order of the words (Meyer's assertion that it would have been ὅτι πᾶν τὸ πλ. εἰς. κ. τ. λ. falls to the ground; observe also the order in 1 Cor. i. 21, x. 5, Galat. i. 15), stands in closest parallel with the authoritative interpretation in ch. ii. 9, ὅτι ἐν αὐτῷ κατοικεῖ πᾶν τὸ πλ. τῆς θεότητος σωμ. We seem bound then to abide by (*c*). — possibly the interpretat. of the ancient La in Church: it involves, however, as will be seen, some grave, though apparently not insuperable, difficulties. πᾶν τὸ πλήρωμα] 'the whole fulness (*of the Godhead*),' 'omnes divinæ naturæ divitiæ,' Fritz. These words have been very differently explained. Lexically considered, πλήρωμα has three possible meanings, one active, (a) *implendi* etc., and two passives, (β) *id quod impletum est*, Ephes. i. 23 (see notes), and the more common (γ) *id quo res impletur*, Gal. iv. 4, Ephes. iii. 9 (see notes on both passages), which again often passes into the neutral and derivative (γ₁) *affluentia*, *abundantia*, πλοῖτος, — especially in connection with abstract genitives, Rom. xv. 29; see Fritz. *Rom.* xi. 12, Vol. ii. p. 469 sq., Hofmann, *Schriftb.* Vol. ii. 1, p. 26. Of these (γ₁), or perhaps simply (γ), is alone exegetically admissible. The real difficulty is in the supplemental

gen. Setting aside all doubtful and larbitrary explanations, e.g. ἐκκλησία (Heinl., Sever.), 'fulness of the Gentiles' (Sch'eierm.), 'fulness of the universe' (Conyb., Hofm. *l. c.*, p. 26, we have only one authoritative sup. em nt, θεότητος, either exactly in the abstr. sense as in ch. ii. 9, 'plenitudo Deitatis,' or in the more derivative sense, 'plenitudo gratiæ habitualis' (compare Davenant, Mey., al.). The latter of these is adopted by those who advocate construction (*b*) of εὐδοκ., but has this great disadvantage, that it involves two interpretations of πλήρωμα θεότ. (here in ref. to 'divina gratia,' there to 'divina essentia,' so Mey., Alf., al.), whereas on the constr. of εὐδοκ. already adopted, πλήρ. will naturally be the same in both cases, and will imply 'the complete fulness and exhaustless perfection of the Divine Essence,' the plenitudo Deitatis,' — an abstract term of transcendent significance, involving in itself the more concrete Θεός, which, as will less en seems possibly to be the subject of the f'lowing participial clause. When we consider the context in ch. ii. 9, there seem grave reasons for thinking that St. Paul chose this august expression with special reference to some vague or perverted meaning assigned to it by the false teachers and theosophistic speculators at Colossæ; comp. Thorn ike, *Cov. of Gr ace.* ii. 15. 12. κατοικῆσαι] 'to dwell;' a term especially app' d to the indwelling influence of the Father (compare Eph. ii. 22), the Son (Eph. iii. 17), and the Spirit (James iv. 5), enhancing the personal relations involved in the mysterious word πλήρωμα; ἐκεῖ ἔσκην οἷς ἐνέργειά τις ἀλλ' οὐσία, Theoph.yl.]

20. ἀποκατ. τὰ πάντα] 'to reconcile all things;' not 'prorsus reconciliare,' Mey. (compare Chrys., κατηλλαγ-

εἰς αὐτόν, εἰρηνοποιήσας διὰ τοῦ αἵματος τοῦ σταυροῦ αὐτοῦ,

μένοι, ἀλλὰ τελείως ἔδει), but, with the natural force of ἀπὸ in similar compounds (ἀποκαθιστάνειν, ἀπευθύνειν), 'in pristinam conditionem reconciliando reducere;' see Winer, *de Verb. Comp.* IV. p. 7, 8. The subject of the inf. is of course the same as that of κατοικ., *i. e.*, grammatically considered, the πλήρωμα above, but exegetically, — as the following αὐτόν and other scriptural analogies (compare 2 Cor. v. 19, Eph. i. 10) seem to suggest, the more definite Θεός, involved and included in the more mystical and abstract designation. The revelation contained in these words is of the most profound nature, and must be interpreted with the utmost caution and reverence. Without presuming to dilute, or to assign any improper 'elasticity' (Mey.) to, the significant ἀποκατ. (*v. g.* 'reunionem creaturarum inter se invicem,' Dallæus), or to limit the comprehensive and unrestricted τὰ πάντα (*e. g.* 'universam Ecclesiam,' Beza, 'omnes homines,' Corn. a Lap.), we must guard against the irreverence of far-reaching speculations on the reconciliation of the finite and the infinite (Usteri, *Lehrb.* II. 1. 1, p. 129, Marheineke, *Dogm.* § 331 sq.), to which this mighty declaration has been supposed to allude. This, and no less than this, it *does* say,— that the eternal and incarnate Son is the 'causa medians' by which the absolute totality of created things shall be restored into its primal harmony with its Creator, — a declaration more specifically unfolded in the following clause : more than this it *does not* say, and where God is silent it is not for man to speak. See the sober remarks of Hofmann, *Schriftb.* Vol. I. p. 188 sq. The mysterious ἀνακεφαλαιώσασθαι, Ephes. i. 10 (obs. both the prep. and the voice), is a more general and perhaps more developed, while 2 Cor. v. 19, κόσμον καταλλ. is a more limited and more specific, representation of the same eternal truth : see *Destiny of Creature*, p. 85 sq. εἰς αὐτόν] '*unto Himself*,' *i. e.* to God, couched in the foregoing πλήρωμα : a 'prægnans constructio,'— the preposition marking the reconciled access to (comp. Eph. ii. 18), and union with the Creator; compare Winer, *Gr.* § 66. 2, p. 547. The simple dative (Eph. ii. 16 ; compare Rom. v. 10, 2 Cor. v. 19, al.) expresses the object to whom and for whom the action is directed, but leaves the further idea conveyed by the prep. unnoticed. There is no need to read αὐτόν (*Griesb., Scholz*), as the reference to the subject is unemphatic ; see notes on *Eph.* i. 4.   εἰρηνοποιήσας] '*having made peace* ;' *i. e.* God,— a simple and intelligible change of gender suggested by the preceding αὐτὸς and the personal subject involved in the subst. with which the participle is grammatically connected ; in fact, 'a construct. πρὸς τὸ ὑποσημαινόμενον.' The parallel passage Eph. ii. 15, ποιῶν εἰρήνην, would almost seem to justify a reference to the Son (Theod., Œcumen.) by the common participial anacoluthon (Steiger; compare Winer, *Gr.* § 63. 2, p. 505), but as this would seriously dislocate the sentence by separating the modal participial clause from the finite verb, and would introduce confusion among the pronouns, we retain the more simple and direct construction   Thus then the two constructions (*b*) and (*c*) noticed in ver. 19 ultimately coincide in referring verse 20 to God, not Christ; and it is worthy of thought whether the ancient Syr. and Clarom. Vv. may not, by different grammatical processes, exhibit a traditional ref. of ver. 20 to God, of a very remote, and perhaps even authoritative antiquity.   διὰ τοῦ αἵμ. τοῦ σταυρ.] '*by the blood of*

δι' αὐτοῦ, εἴτε τὰ ἐπὶ τῆς γῆς εἴτε τὰ ἐν τοῖς οὐρανοῖς.
²¹ Καὶ ὑμᾶς ποτὲ ὄντας ἀπηλλοτριωμένους

You who were alienated
He reconciled by His death,
If at least ye remain firm in the faith and abide by the hope of the Gospel.

(i. e. *shed upon*) *the cross*;' more specific and circumstantial statement of the 'causa med ans' of the reconciliation. The gen is what is termed of 'remoter reference,' forming in fact a species of *brachylogia*: see especially Winer, *Gr.* § 30. 2, p. 168, where numerous examples are collected. δι' αὐτου] '*by Him*;' it is scarcely necessary to say that δι' αὐτοῦ does not refer to the immediately preceding διὰ τοῦ αἵ., but to the more remote δι' αὐτοῦ of which it is a vivid and emphatic repetition. These words are omitted in some MSS. [BD*FGL; 10 mss], but almost obviously to facilitate the construction. εἴτε τὰ ἐν οὐρ. κ. τ. λ.] '*whether the things upon the earth or the things in the heavens*;' disjunctive enumeration of the 'universitas rerum,' as in ver. 16, with this only difference, that the order is transposed, — possibly from the more close connection of the death of Christ with τὰ ἐπὶ τῆς γῆς. It is hardly necessary to say that the language precludes any idea of reconciliation *between* the occupants of earth and heaven (apparently Cyril.-Hieros. *Catech.* XIV. 3, Chrys. (in part), Theod., al.) or, in reference to the latter, of any reconciliation of only a retrospectively preservative nature (Bramhall, *Disc.* IV. Vol. V. p. 148). *How* the reconciliation of Christ affects the spiritual world — whether by the annihilation of 'posse peccare,' or by the infusion of a more perfect knowledge (Eph. iii. 10), or (less probably) some restorative application to the fallen spiritual world (Orig., Neand. *Planting*, Vol. I. p. 531), — we know not, and we dare not speculate: this, however, we may fearlessly assert, that the efficacy of the sacrifice of the Eternal Son is infinite and limitless, that it extends to all things in earth and heaven, and that it is the blessed medium by which, between God and His creatures, whether angelical, human, animate, or inanimate (Rom. viii. 19 sq.), peace is wrought: see the valuable note of Harless *on Eph.* i. 10, especially p. 52, Hofmann, *Schriftb.* Vol. I. p. 189, and comp. Words-w *in loc.*

21. καὶ ὑμᾶς] '*ad quos sc.*:' new clause, to be separated by a period (not merely by a comma, *Lachm.*, B sp. from ver. 20, descriptive of the application of the universal reconciliation to the special case of the Colossians; compare ch. ii. 13, and see notes on *Eph.* ii. 1. The structure involves a slight anacoluthon: the apostle probably commenced with the intention of placing ὑμᾶς under the *immediate* regimen of ἀποκατήλλ., but was led by ποτὲ ὄντας into the contrasted clause καὶ δὲ before he inserted the verb; compare Winer, *Gr.* II. § 63. 1, p. 504. The reading ἀποκατηλλάγητε adopted by *Lachm.* and Meyer with B [D*FG; Clar., Iren., al., have ἀποκαταλλαγέντες] involves an equally intelligible, though much stronger anacoluthon, but has not sufficient external support.

ὄντας ἀπηλλοτρ.] '*being alienated*,' '*being in a state of alienation*,' scil. 'from God;' compare Eph. iv. 28. The part of the verb subst. is used with the perf. part. to express yet more forcibly the continuing state of the alienation; compare Winer, *Gr.* § 45. 5, p. 511. For illustrations of the emphatic verb ἀπαλλ. ('abalienati,' Beza), see notes *on Eph.* ii. 12, where the application is more expressly restricted. Both there and Eph. iv. 28, the Ephesians were represented as a portion of heathenism, here the Colossians are represented as a portion of the 'universitas rerum,' to whom the redeeming power of Christ extends.

καὶ ἐχθροὺς τῇ διανοίᾳ ἐν τοῖς ἔργοις τοῖς πονηροῖς, νυνὶ δὲ ἀποκατήλλαξεν ²² ἐν τῷ σώματι τῆς σαρκὸς αὐτοῦ διὰ τοῦ θανάτου,

ἐχθροὺς τῇ διαν.] 'enemies in your understanding;' not passive, 'regarded as enemies by God' (Meyer, who compares Rom. v. 10), but, as the subjective tinge given by the limiting dative and the addition ἐν τοῖς ἔργ. seem to imply, αὐτοὺς ἐχθροὶ ἦτε, φησί, καὶ τὰ τῶν ἐχθρῶν ἐπράττετε, Chrysost. The dative διανοίᾳ is what is termed the dat. of reference to (see notes on Gal. i. 22), and represents, as it were, the peculiar spiritual seat of the hostility (comp. notes on Eph. iv. 18), while ἐν τοῖς ἔργοις marks the practical spheres and substrata in which the ἔχθρα was evinced; comp. Huther in loc. On the meaning of διάνοια, the 'higher intellectual nature' (διέξοδος λογική, Orig.), especially as shown in its practical relations (contrast ἔννοια, Heb. iv. 12), see the good remarks of Beck, Seelenl. II. 19. b, p. 58. The addition τοῖς πονηροῖς, not simply ἐν τοῖς πον. ἔργ., serves to give emphasis, and direct attention to the real character of the ἔργα; Winer, Gr. § 20. 1, p. 119.

νυνὶ δὲ ἀποκατ.] 'yet now hath He (God, see next note) reconciled:' antithesis to the preceding ποτὲ ὄντας, the oppositive δὲ in the apodosis being evoked by the latent 'although' (Donalds. Gr. § 621) involved in the participial protasis; compare Xen. Mem. III. 7. 8, ἐκείνους ῥᾳδίως χειρούμενος, τούτοις δὲ μηδένα τρόπον οἴει δυνήσεσθαι προσενεχθῆναι, and see the note and reff. of Kühner, also Buttmann, Mid. Excurs XII. p. 148: add Klotz, Devar. Vol. II. p. 374, Hartung, Partik. δέ, 5. 6, Vol. I. p. 186. Such a construction is not common in Attic writers. In this union of the emphatic particle of absolutely present time with the aor. (comp. Hartung, Partik. Vol. II p. 24) the aor. is not equivalent to a pres. or perf., but marks with the proper force of the tense, that the action followed a given event (here, as the context suggests, the atoning death of Christ), and is now done with; see Donalds. Gr. § 433, compared with Fritz. de Aor. p. 6, 17. Meyer pertinently compares Plato, Symp. p. 193 A, πρὸ τοῦ... ἐν ἦμεν, νυνὶ δὲ διὰ τὴν ἀδικίαν διῳκίσθημεν ὑπὸ τοῦ θεοῦ.

22. ἐν τῷ σώμ. κ. τ. λ.] 'in the body of His flesh,' i. e., as the language and allusion undoubtedly requires,—the flesh of Christ; the prep. ἐν pointing to the substratum of the action; see notes on Gal. i. 24, and comp. especially Andoc. de Myst. p. 33 (ed. Schill.) ὁ μὲν ἀγὼν ἐν τῷ σώματι τῷ ἐμῷ καθέστηκεν. It may justly be considered somewhat doubtful whether the subject of the present clause, and of the verb ἀποκατήλλαξεν is regarded as Christ (Chrysost., Œcum., al.), or God. In favor of the first supposition we have the use of σώματι (which seems to suggest an identity between the subject to which the σῶμα refers and the subject of the verb), perhaps the use of παραστῆσαι (comp. Eph. v. 27, but contrast 2 Cor. iv. 14), and the ready connection of such a purpose with the fact specified by ἀποκατ. (comp. De Wette), and lastly, the semi-parallel passage, Eph. ii. 13. Still the difficulty of a change of subject,—the natural transition from the more general act on the part of God alluded to in ver. 20 to the more particular application of the same to the Colossians,—the fuller amplification which this verse seems to be of the substance of ver. 13,—and the similarity between the circumstantial διὰ τοῦ αἵμ. τοῦ στ. above and the circumstantial ἐν τῷ σώμ. κ. τ. λ. in the present verse, seem to supply distinctly preponderant arguments, and lead us with Bengel, Huth., and others, to refer ἀποκατ. to the subject of ver. 20, i. e. to

παραστῆσαι ὑμᾶς ἁγίους καὶ ἀμώμους καὶ ἀνεγκλήτους κατενώπιον

God. Many reasons have been assigned why St. Paul adds the specifying gen. (*subst. var.* Winer, *Gr.* § 30. 2) τ ς σαρκός. Two opinions deserve consideration; (*a*) that it was to oppose some forms of *Docet c* error which were prevailing at Colossæ, Steiger, Huther, al.; (*b*) that it was directed against a *false spiritualism*, which, from a mistaken asceticism (ch. ii. 23), led to grave error with respect to the efficacy of Christ's atonement in the flesh; so Meyer, followed by Alford. As there are no direct, and appy. no indirect (contrast Ignat. *M rans.* § 9, 11, al.) allusions to Docetic error traceable in this Epistle, the opinion (*b*) is, on the whole, to be preferred. That the addition is used to mark the distinction between this and the Lord's *spiritual* σῶμα, the Church (Olsh.), does not seem natural or probable. διὰ τοῦ θαν.] '*by means of His death;*' added to the preceding ἐν τῷ σώμ. to express the *means* by which the reconciliation was so wrought: it was by means of death, borne in and accomplished in that blessed body, that reconciliation was brought about; compare some valuable remarks in Jackson, *Creed.* VIII. 8. 4.

παραστῆσαι] '*to present;*' infinitive, expressing the actual purpose and intent of the action expressed in ἀποκ.; see Madvig, *Synt.* § 118 where this mood is extremely well discussed. Had ὥστε been inserted, the idea of manner or degree would rather have come into prominence (Madvig, § 166), and the meaning would literally have been ' as with the intention of, etc.,' the finite verb being in fact again tacitly supplied after ὥστε; see especially Weller, *Bemerk. z. Griech. Synt.* p. 14 (Mein. 1843). Meyer calls attention to the tense, but it must be observed that in the infin. the aorist, except after verbs *declarandi vel sentiendi*, is commonly obscure [M. tv , . 172], especially as here in no … space. On παραστῆσαι, which … conveys no sacrificial idea, comp … h v 27. There the reference is more restricted, here more general.

ἁγίους καὶ ἀμ. καὶ ἀνεγκ.] '*holy and blameless and wt …*' designation of their content and … its positive and negative … ἁγίους marking the former, ἀ.. … καὶ ἀνεγκλ. the latter. Strictly considered, the first and second καί are not … coordinate and similar; they do not connect three different ideas … Deum, respectu vestri, respect… Bengel) nor simply aggregate … similar ideas (Daven.); but … first connects the two members of … later antithesis, the second is, as it were, under a vinculum joining the … parts of the second member. On the meaning of ἄμωμος (μώμ… s … s), see notes on *Eph.* i. 4 … less strong than the … ἀνεγκλ.; ἀνεγκλ. γὰρ τότε λέγεται, ὁ … μηδὲ μέχρι καταγινώσκεως μ … ἐγκλήματός ἤ τι πεπραγμένον … (Chrys. Lastly, on the dist … ἀνέγκλητος and ἀνεπίληπτος … sulla justa causa sit reprehen… see Tittmann, *Synon.* t. p. 31.

κατενώπιον αὐτοῦ] '*before Him*' God, — not Christ (M… a reference neither natural nor … suitable with the very similar … Eph. i. 4 There may be here a forward reference to the ' day of Christ's a… .' Alford but it does not seem perfectly certain from the context. With respect to the question whether ' sanctitas *inchoata*' (Huth.), or, perhaps more probably, 'sanctitas *inhærens*,' (Chrys.; compare notes on *Eph.* i. 4) is here alluded to, the remark of Daven at … ms just.— ' cum dicit *ut sistat nos sanctos*, non ut

αὐτοῦ· ²³ εἴγε ἐπιμένετε τῇ πίστει τεθεμελιωμένοι καὶ ἑδραῖοι, καὶ μὴ μετακινούμενοι ἀπὸ τῆς ἐλπίδος τοῦ εὐαγγελίου οὗ ἠκούσατε,

sisteremus nos, manifestum est ipsos reconciliatos et renatos sanctitatem suam a Christo mutuari, sive de actuali, sive de inhaerente, sive de imputatâ loquimur,' p. 113 (ed. 3); 'whensoever we have any of these we have all,— they go together,' Hooker, *Serm. on Justification*, II. 21.

23. εἴγε ἐπιμ. τῇ πίστει] '*if at least ye continue in the faith;*' a tropical use of ἐπιμ. peculiar to St. Paul, Rom. vi. 1, xi. 22, 23, *l* Tim. iv. 16: ἐπιμ., Acts xiii. 43 (*Rec.*), has scarcely any critical support. Like several compounds of ἐπί it has two constructions (see Winer, *Gr.* § 52. 7. p 382), with prepositions ἐπί, πρός, ἐν (Acts xxviii. 14, 1 Cor. xvi. 17, Phil. i. 24), and with the simple dative (Rom. *ll. cc.*, 1 Tim. *l. c.*) which apparently is semilocal (comp. *on Gal.* v. 1), or, perhaps more probably, under the influence of the preposition. The preposition ἐπί is not (per se) intensive (Alf.), but appears to denote *rest* at a place, see notes *on Gal.* i. 18. On the meaning of εἴγε, see notes on *Eph.* iii. 2, and on the distinction between εἴγε (si quidem) and εἴπερ (si omnino), see notes *on Gal.* iii. 4.   τεθεμελ. καὶ ἑδραῖοι] '*grounded and firm;*' specification on the *positive* side of the mode of the ἐπιμονή; compare Eph. iii. 17, ἐῤῥιζωμένοι καὶ τεθεμελιωμένοι, and 1 Cor. xv. 58, ἑδραῖοι, ἀμετακίνητοι. The qualitative termination *-αιος* seems to justify the distinction of Beng., 'τεθεμ. affixi fundamento, ἑδρ. stabiles, firmi intus.' That there is any reference to the metaphor of a temple (Olsh.), seems here very doubtful.   καὶ μὴ μετακιν.] '*and not being moved away;*' nearly identical with ἀμετακίνητοι, 1 Cor. xv. 58, and representing their fixity on its *negative* side: the change to the *present pass.*,— as marking by the tense the process that might be going on, and by the mood (pass., not act., as De Wette), that of which they were now liable to be the victims,— is especially suitable and exact; see the suggestive example cited by Alford, viz. Xenoph. *Rep. Lac.* xv. 1, πολιτείας μετακεκινημένας καὶ ἔτι νῦν μετακινουμένας. On the μὴ with μετακ., which, in a hypothetical sentence like the present, is usual and proper, see, if necessary, Winer, *Gram.* § 55. 1, p. 522.   τῆς ἐλπ. τοῦ εὐαγγ.] ' *the hope of the Gospel*,' i. e. arising from, evoked by, the Gospel, τοῦ εὐαγγ. being the genitive of the *origin* or rather the *originating agent*; see Hartung, *Casus*, p. 17, and comp. notes *on* 1 *Thess.* i. 6. To regard it as a possess. gen. (Alf.) gives an unnecessary vagueness to the expression. Such genitives as those of the *origin* (Hartung, p. 17), *originating agent*, and perhaps a shade stronger, the *causa efficiens* (Scheuerl. *Synt.* § 17), all belong to the general category of the gen. of 'ablation' (Donalds. *Gr.* § 448, 449): the context alone must guide us in our choice. Ἐλπίς can hardly be here, except in a very derivative sense, equivalent to ὁ Χριστός, Chrys.; it seems only to have its usual subjective meaning; compare notes *on Eph.* i. 18.   οὗ ἠκούσατε] ' *which ye heard*,' scil. when it was first preached to you; not ' have heard,' Auth.,— here certainly an unnecessary introduction of the auxiliary. This and the two following clauses serve to give weight to the foregoing μὴ μετακινούμενοι: they had heard the Gospel, the world had heard it (πάλιν αὐτοὺς φέρει μάρτυρας, εἶτα τὴν οἰκουμένην, Chrys.), and he the writer of this Epistle,— who though probably not their founder (see on verse 7), yet stood in close relation to them through Epaphras,— was the

τοῦ κηρυχθέντος ἐν πάσῃ κτίσει τῇ ὑπὸ τὸν οὐρανόν, οὗ ἐγενόμην ἐγὼ Παῦλος διάκονος.

I rejoice in my sufferings for you and the Church; I am preaching the mystery of salvation, and striving to present every man perfect before Christ.

²⁴ Νῦν χαίρω ἐν τοῖς παθήμασιν ὑπὲρ ὑμῶν,

preacher of it: καὶ τοῦτο εἰς τὸ ἀξιόπιστον συντελεῖ, Chrys. The apostle gives weight to his assertions by the special mention of his name, 2 Cor. x. 1, Gal. v. 2, Eph. iii. 1, 1 Thess. ii. 18, Philem. 19. ἐν πάσῃ κτίσει] 'in the hearing of every creature;' surely not 'in the whole of creation,' Alf., — a translation which, even if we concede that πᾶσα κτίσις may be equivalent to 'every form of creation,' i. e. 'all creatures' (Hofm. Schrijth. Vol 1. p. 137), would be needlessly inexact. The art. is inserted in D*EKL (Rec.), but clearly has not sufficient critical support. This noble hyperbole only states in a slightly different form what the Lord had commanded, Mark xvi. 15: the inspired apostle, as Olsh. well says, sees the universal tendency of Christianity already realized. The limitation, τῇ ὑπὸ τὸν οὐρ. characterizes the κτίσις as ἐπίγειος, including however, thereby, all mankind. For the meaning of ἐν, apud, coram, — perhaps here with singular reverting somewhat to the primary idea of sphere of operation, see Winer, Gr. § 48. a. d, p 34. διάκονος] 'a minister;' see notes on Ephes. i. i. 7. The three practical deductions which Davenant draws from this clause are worthy of perusal.

24. νῦν χαίρω] Transition suggested by the preceding clauses, especially by the last, to the apostle's own services in the cause of the Gospel. The νῦν is not merely transitional (compare Klotz, Devar. Vol. ii. p. 677), but, as its position shows, purely temporal and emphatic (2 Corinth. vii. 9), 'now, with the chain round my wrist' (Eadie), forming a contrast with the past time involved in the foregoing κηρυχθέντος and ἐγενόμην.

The reading ὅς ἐν κ. τ. λ. (D*EFG; Vulg., Clarom., al.) seems either due to the preceding letter -ς, or was intended to keep up the supposed connection between ver. 25 and ver. 23. ἐν παθήμασιν] Not exclusively 'de iis quae patior,' Beza, but simply 'in passionibus,' Vulg.; the παθήματα were not only the subject whereupon he rejoiced, but the sphere, the circumstances in which he did so; χαίρω πάσχων, Chry. The brief and semi-adverbial ἐν τούτῳ (Phil. i. 18) is perhaps slightly different. The omission of the article before ὑπὲρ ὑμῶν arises from πάσχειν ὑπὲρ being a legitimate construction; see notes on Eph. i. 15. ὑπὲρ ὑμῶν] 'for you,' not 'in your place,' Steig., nor, with a causal reference, 'on your account,' Eadie, 'vestra causa,' Just. (compare Est. and Corn. a Lap.), but 'vestro fructu et commodo,' Beza, 'zum Vortheil,' Winer, Gr § 47. 1. p. 342, as the more usual meaning of the prep. in the N. T. and its use below both suggest. On the uses of the preposition compare notes on Gal. i. 4, iii. 13, Phil. i. 7. ἀνταναπλ. κ. τ. λ] 'am filling up an the lacking measures of the sufferings of Christ.' The meaning of these words has formed the subject both of exegetical discussion and polemical application; compare Cajet. de Ind.) . Qu. 3. Bellarmine, de Ind.) . Cap 3. Without entering into the latter, we will endeavor briefly to state the grammatical and contextual meaning of the words.

(1) θλίψεις Χριστοῦ is clearly not 'afflictiones propter Christum subeundae,' Elsner (Vol. ii. p. 260). Schoettg., al., nor 'calamitates quas Christus perferendas imposuit,' Fritz. (Rom. Vol. iii. p. 275), — a somewhat artificial gen.

καὶ ἀνταναπληρῶ τὰ ὑστερήματα τῶν θλίψεων τοῦ Χριστοῦ ἐν τῇ σαρκί μου ὑπὲρ τοῦ σώματος αὐτοῦ, ὅ ἐστιν ἡ ἐκκλησία· ²⁵ ἧς

auctoris,—but simply and plainly 'the afflictions of Christ,' *i.e.* which appertain to Christ, not, however, with corporeal reference, ὅσα ὑπέμεινε, Theod., but which are His (Χρ. being a pure *possessive* genit.; compare Winer, *Gr.* § 30. 2, p. 170, note), of which He is the mystical subject; see below. But (2) how are the ὑστερήματα of these afflictions filled up by the apostle? Not (a) by the endurance of afflictions *similar* (ὡσαύτως, Theod.) to those endured (ὑποστατικῶς) by his Master (comp. Heb. xiii. 13, 1 Pet. iv. 13), and by drinking out of the same cup (Matth. xx. 23), as Huth., Mey.,— for, independently of all other considerations, the distinctive feature of the Lord's θλίψεις, vicarious suffering (Olshaus.), was lacking in those of H s apostle (οὐ γὰρ ἴσον τοῦτο οὐδὲ ὅμοιον, πολλοῦ γε καὶ δεῖ, Œcum.),—but, (b), in the deeper sense given to it by Chrys., Theoph., Œcum., and recently adopted by De Wette, Eadie, Alf., al.,—by the endurance of afflictions which Christ endures in His suffering Church (σχετικῶς), and of which the πλήρωμα has not yet come; see Olsh. *in loc.*, who has well defended this vital and consolatory interpretation, and compare August. *in Psalm.* lxi. 4, Vol. IV. p. 731 (edit. Migne). (3) The meaning of ἀνταναπληροῦν has yet to be considered; this is not 'vicissim explere' (Beza, compare Tittmann, *Synon.* II. p. 230), nor 'cum Christo calamitates imponente in malis perferendis æmulans' (Fritz.),—a somewhat artificial interpretation, nor even 'alterius ὑστέρημα de suo explere' (Winer, *de Verb. Comp.* III. 22), but, as Mey. suggests, 'to meet, and fill up the ὑστέρημα with a corresponding πλήρωμα;' the ἀντί contrasting not the actors or their acts (contrast Xenoph. *Hell.* II. 4. 12, ἀντανέπλησαν compared with a previous ἐμπλῆσαι), but the *defect* and the *supply* with which it is met: see the examples cited by Winer, especially Dio Cass. XLIV. 8, ὅσον ἐνέδει τοῦτο ἐκ τῆς παρὰ τῶν ἄλλων συντελείας ἀνταναπληρωθῇ. The simpler ἀναπληρόω [found in FG; mss.: Orig. in allusion] would have expressed nearly the same; the double compound, however, specifies more accurately the intention of the action, and the circumstances (the ὑστερήματα) which it was intended to meet. For a practical sermon on this text, see Donne, *Serm.* XCVII. Vol. IV. p. 261 sq. (ed. Alf.), and compare *Destiny of Creature*, p. 39 sq. ἐν τῇ σαρκί μου clearly belongs to ἀνταναπλ., defining more closely the seat, and thence, inferentially, the mode, of the ἀνταναπλήρωσις (compare 2 Cor. iv. 11, Gal. iv. 14); the word σαρξ, which thus involves the predication of manner, standing, as Meyer acutely observes, in exquisite contrast with the σῶμα, which defines the *object* of the action. Steiger, Huther, al., connect this clause with θλίψεων τοῦ Χρ.: this *may* be grammatically possible (Winer, *Gr.*§ 20. 2, p. 123), but is exegetically untenable, as it would but reiterate what is necessarily involved in the use of the first person of the verb. ὅ ἐστιν ἐκκλ.] As ἐκκλ. might be thought the word of importance, the construction ἥτις ἐστιν ἐκκλ., 1 Tim. iii. 15, might have seemed more natural; compare Winer, *Gr.* § 24. 3, p. 150. The present construction is, however, perfectly correct, as the article and defining gen. associated with σῶμα, as well as the antithetical contrast in which it stands with σάρξ, point to σῶμα as the subst. on which the chief moment of thought really dwells.

25. ἧς ἐγενόμην κ. τ. λ.] '*of which I (Paul) became a minister:*' state-

ἐγενόμην ἐγὼ διάκονος κατὰ τὴν οἰκονομίαν τοῦ Θεοῦ τὴν δοθεῖσαν

ment of the relation in which he stands to the ἐκκλησία just mentioned, the ἧς having a faintly causal, or rather *explanatory* force (see notes on ver. 18, and Ellendt. *Lex. Soph.* s. v. Vol. II. p. 371), and indirectly giving the reason and moving principle of the ἀνταναπληρώσις· 'I fill up the lacking measures of the sufferings of Christ in behalf of His body the Church, being an appointed minister thereof, and having a spiritual function in it committed to me by God.' The ἐγώ continues, in a slightly changed relation, the ἐγὼ Παῦλος of ver. 23; there the διακονία referred to the εὐαγγ., here to the Church by which the εὐαγγ. is preached; 'idem plane est ministrum Ecclesiæ esse et Evangelii,' Just. κατὰ τὴν οἰκον. Θεοῦ] '*in accordance with the dispensation, i.e. the spiritual stewardship, of God;*' τῆς ἐκκλησίας ἐπιστεύθην τὴν σωτηρίαν, καὶ τὴν τοῦ κηρύγματος ἐνεχειρίσθην διακονίαν, Theod. The somewhat difficult word οἰκονομ. seems here, in accordance with τὴν δοθεῖσαν κ. τ. λ. which follows, to refer, not to the '*disposition* of God, Syriac [Syriac] [*gubernationem*], Gothic 'ragina,' Æth. 'ordinationem,' but, as Just., Mey., al., to the 'spiritual function,' the 'office of an οἰκονόμος' (see 1 Cor. ix. 17, compared with 1 Cor. iv. 1), originating from, or assigned by, God; the more remote gen. Θεοῦ denoting either the *origin* of the commission (Hartung, *Casus*, p. 17), or, with more of a possessive force, Him to whom it belonged and in whose service it was borne: see Reuss, *Théol. Chrét.* IV. 9, Vol. II. p. 93, and notes on *Eph.* i. 10, where the meanings of οἰκονομ. in the N. T. are briefly noticed and classified. τὴν δοθεῖσαν κ. τ. λ.] '*which was given me for you;*' further definition of the οἰκον. τοῦ Θεοῦ, the meaning of which, owing to the different meanings of οἰκον., might otherwise have been misunderstood: 'this οἰκονομία was specially assigned to me and you, — you, Gentiles, were to be its object.' The connection of εἰς ὑμᾶς with πληρῶσαι (if. *Huth*, p. 110) does not seem probable: the juxtaposition of the pronoun (μοι εἰς ὑμᾶς) suggests the closer connection. πληρῶσαι τὸν λόγ. τοῦ Θ.] '*to fully the word of God;*' i. e. 'to perform my office in preaching unrestrictedly, to give a full scope to the word of God;' notice of *design* (see notes on ver. 22) dependent either on ἧς ἐγενόμην (Huth., or perhaps more naturally on τὴν δοθεῖσαν κ. τ. λ., thus giving an amplification to the preceding εἰς ὑμᾶς. The glosses on πληρῶσαι are exceedingly numerous: the most probable seem, (*a*) 'ad plene exponendam totam salutis doctrinam,' Daven. 1, compare Olsh., and Tholuck, *Bergpr.* p. 136; (*b*) 'to spread a road,' Huth., — who compares Acts v. 28; (*c*) 'to give its fullest amplitude, to fill up the measures of its fore-ordained universality,' not perhaps without some allusion to the οἰκονομία which would thus be fully discharged; compare Rom. xv. 19, μέχρι τοῦ Ἰλλυρικοῦ πεπληρωκέναι τὸ εὐαγγέλιον τοῦ Χρ. Of these (*b*) has an advantage over (*a*) in implying a πλήρωσις viewed *extensive*ly, in having, in fact a quantitative rather than a qualitative reference, but fails in exhausting the meaning and completely satisfying the context; (*c*) by carrying out the idea further, and pointing to the λόγος as something which was to have a universal application, and not be confined to a single nation (hence the introduction of εἰς ὑμᾶς), seems most in accordance with the spirit of the passage and with the words that follow; compare the somewhat analogous expression, ὁ λόγος τοῦ

μοι εἰς ὑμᾶς πληρῶσαι τὸν λόγον τοῦ Θεοῦ, ²⁶ τὸ μυστήριον τὸ ἀποκεκρυμμένον ἀπὸ τῶν αἰώνων καὶ ἀπὸ τῶν γενεῶν, νυνὶ δὲ ἐφανερώθη τοῖς ἁγίοις αὐτοῦ, ²⁷ οἷς ἠθέλησεν ὁ Θεὸς γνωρίσαι τι

Θεοῦ ηὔξανε, Acts vi. 7, xii. 24. It need hardly be added that the λόγος τοῦ Θεοῦ does not imply the 'promissiones Dei, partim de Christo in genere, partim de vocatione Gentium,' Beza, but simply and plainly τὸ εὐαγγέλιον, as in 1 Cor. xiv. 36, 2 Corinth. ii. 17, 1 Thessal. ii. 13, al.

26. τὸ μυστήριον τὸ ἀποκ.] 'the mystery which hath been hidden;' apposition to the preceding τὸν λόγον τοῦ Θεοῦ. The μυστήριον was the divine purpose of salvation in Christ, and, more especially, as the context seems to show, 'de saivandis Gentibus per gratiam evangelicam,' Daven.; see Ephes. iii. 4 sq., and compare Eph. i. 9. On the meanings of μυστήριον in the N. T., see notes on Eph. v. 32, and Reuss, Théol. Chrét. IV. 9, Vol. II. p. 88, where the applications of the term in the N. T. are briefly elucidated. ἀπὸ τῶν αἰώνων κ. τ. λ.] 'from the ages and from the generations (that have passed);' from the long temporal periods (αἰῶνες) and the successive generations that made them up (γενεαί; see on Eph. iii. 21), which have elapsed (observe the article) since the 'arcanum decretum' was concealed. The expression is not identical with πρὸ τῶν αἰώνων, 1 Cor. ii. 7; the counsel was formed πρὸ τῶν αἰώνων, but concealed ἀπὸ τῶν αἰώνων; comp. Rom. xvi. 25, and see notes on Eph. iii. 9, where the same expression occurs.
νυνὶ δὲ ἐφανερώθη] 'but now has been made manifest;' transition from the participial to the finite construct., suggested by the importance of the predication; see notes on Eph. i. 20, and Winer, Gr. § 63. 2. b, p. 505 sq., where other examples are noticed and discussed. The φανέρωσις, the actual and historical manifestation (De W.), took place, as Meyer observes, in different ways, partly by revelation (Ephes. iii. 5), partly by preaching (ch. iv. 4, Tit. i. 3) and exposition (Rom. xvi. 26), and partly by all combined. On the connection of νυνί [Lachm. νῦν, with BCFG; mss.; Did.] with the aor., see notes on ver. 21, and for a good distinction between νῦν (ἐπὶ τῶν τριῶν χρόνων) and νυνί (ἐπὶ μόνου ἐνεστῶτος), see Ammonius, Voc. Diff. p. 99, ed. Valck. τοῖς ἁγίοις αὐτοῦ] To limit these words to the apostles, from a comparison with Eph. iii. 5 (Steiger, Olsh.: FG; Boern. actually insert ἀποστόλοις), or to the elect, 'quos Deus in Christo consecrandos decrevit' (Daven. 1), is highly unsatisfactory, and quite contrary to St. Paul's regular and unrestricted use of the word; so Theod., who, however, shows that he remembered Eph. iii. 5, τοῖς ἀποστόλοις, καὶ τοῖς διὰ τούτων πεπιστευκόσι. On the meaning of ἅγιος, see notes on ver. 2, and on Eph. i. 1.

27. οἷς ἠθέλησεν ὁ Θ.] 'to whom God did will;' i. e. 'seeing that to them it was God's will,' etc., the relative having probably here, as in ver. 25, an indirectly causal, or explanatory force ('rationem adjungit,' Daven.), and reiterating the subject to introduce more readily the specific purpose γνωρίσαι κ. τ. λ. which was contemplated by God in the φανέρωσις. The most recent commentators, Meyer, Eadie, Alf., rightly reject any reference of ἠθέλησεν to the free grace of God (Eph. i. 9, κατὰ τὴν εὐδοκίαν αὐτοῦ), no such idea being here involved in the context: what ἠθέλησεν here implies is, not on the one hand, that God 'was pleased' (' propensionem voluntatis indicant,' Est.), nor on the other, that He 'was willing,' Hammond, but simply and plainly 'it was God's will'

τὸ πλοῦτος τῆς δόξης τοῦ μυστηρίου τούτου ἐν τοῖς ἔθνεσιν, ὅ

to do so. On the distinction between θέλω and βούλομαι, see notes on 1 Tim. v. 14. γνωρίσαι] 'to make known;' practically little different from φανερῶσαι. The latter perhaps is slightly more restricted, as involving the idea of a previous concealment (see above and compare 2 Tim i. 10), the former more general and unlimited; see Meyer in loc. τί τὸ πλοῦτος κ. τ. λ.] 'what is the riches of the glory of this mystery;' not, exactly, 'how great,' Mey., but with the simple force of τίς, —'what,' referring alike to nature and degree; compare Eph. i. 18, and see notes in loc. The gen. τῆς δόξης is no mere genitive of quality which may be resolved into an adjective, and appended either to πλοῦτος ('herrliche Reichthum,' Luth.) or to μυστήριον ('gloriosi hujus mysterii,' Beza), but, as always in these kinds of accumulated genitives in St. Paul, specially denotes that peculiar attribute of the μυστήριον (gen. subjecti) which more particularly evinces the πλοῦτος; see notes on 1 Tim. on Eph. i. 6, and compare Eph. i. 18. The δόξα its. is not to be limited to the transforming nature of the mystery of the Gospel, in its effects on men (δ. ἡ ἐλευθ. ἡμαδνῶν καὶ πίστεως μόνης, Chrys.), mer y t, on the objective side, to τ. δ δόξα τοῦ Θεοῦ, the grace, glory, and attributes of God which are revealed by it, — but, as the weight of the enunciation requires, to both (see especially De W.), perhaps more particularly to the latter. To make its reference identical with that of the δόξα below (Mey., Alf.), where the preceding words introduce a new shade of thought, does not seem so exegetically satisfactory. The former δόξα gains from its collocation a more general and abstract force; the latter, from its association with ἐλπίς, has a more specific reference. ἐν τοῖς ἔθνεσιν] 'among the Gen-

tiles;' semilocal cause suggested to τί ἐστι τὸ πλοῦτος κ. τ. λ., defining the sphere in which the πλοῦτος τῆς δόξ τοῦ μυστ. is more particularly evinced, φαίνεται δὲ ἐν ἑτέροις, πολλὴ δὲ πλέον ἐν τούτοις ἡ πολλὴ τοῦ μυστηρίου δόξα, Chrys.; see especially 1 Tim. i. 1, where the construction is very similar.

ὅς ἐστιν Χρ.] The reference is here somewhat doubtful. ὅς stands in CDEKL; nearly all mss.; Copt., Theodt. (Fisch., Rec.), and, as being apparently the more difficult reading, is to be preferred to ὅ, adopted by Lachm. (with AB Clem. 17. 67**, and perhaps Vulg., &c.). But to what does it refer? Three interpretations have been suggested; it refers to (a) the complex idea of the entire clause, — Christ in his relation to the Gent., would, De Wette, Eadie; (b) the more immediate τὸ πλοῦτος κ. τ. λ., (Ἐrasm., Dav., Mey.; (c) the more immediate ἐν τοῖς μυστηρίου τούτου, Chrys., Alf., Beng. Of these (a) is defensible (comp. Phil. i. 28), but too vague; (c) is plausible and apparently supported by Eph. iii. 8, but rests too much on the assumption that πλοῦτος is to the filling word (Mey., Wiesing.), whereas it seems clear from ver. 25, that μυστήριον is the really important word in the sentence. We retain therefore the usual reference to μυστήριον; Christ, who was preached, and was working by grace in them, was in Himself the true and real mystery of redemption; compare 1 Tim. iii. 16, Eph. iii. 5. In any case the masc. ὅς results from a simple attraction to the predicate; see Winer, Gr. § 24. 3, p. 150.

ἐν ὑμῖν] 'among you;' not exclusively 'in vobis inhabitans per fidem,' Zanch. (compare Eph. iii. 17), but in parallelism to the preceding ἐν τοῖς ἔθν. As, however, this parallelism is not strictly exact (Alf.). — for ἐν Γαλ. is in close association with the preceding substantive, whereas ἐν τοῖς ἔθνεσιν is not. — we may

ἐστιν Χριστὸς ἐν ὑμῖν, ἡ ἐλπὶς τῆς δόξης· ²⁸ ὃν ἡμεῖς καταγγέλλομεν, νουθετοῦντες πάντα ἄνθρωπον καὶ διδάσκοντες πάντα ἄνθρωπον ἐν πάσῃ σοφίᾳ, ἵνα παραστήσωμεν πάντα ἄνθρωπον

admit that '*in* you' is also virtually and by consequence involved in the present use of the preposition; compare Olsh., Eadie. The connection adopted by Syr. ܣܒܪܐ ܕܒܟܘܢ؟ [qui in vobis est spes] involves an unnecessary and untenable trajection. ἡ ἐλπὶς τῆς δόξης] '*the hope of glory;*' apposition to the preceding Χριστὸς ἐν ὑμῖν; not either the '*spei causa*' (Grot.), or the object of it (Vorst), but its very element and substance; see 1 Tim. i. 1, and notes *in loc.* The *second* gloss of Theoph, ἡ ἐλπὶς ἡμῶν ἔνδοξος, is unusually incorrect; δόξα is a pure substantive, and refers to the future glory and blessedness in heaven, Rom. v. 2, 1 Corin. ii. 7 (apparently), 2 Cor. iv. 17, al. For a list of the various words with which ἐλπὶς is thus joined, see Reuss, *Théol. Chrét.* IV. 20, Vol. II. p. 221.

28. ὃν ἡμεῖς καταγγ.] '*whom we preach;*' whom I and Timothy, with other like-minded teachers (comp. Steiger), do solemnly preach; the ἡμεῖς being emphatic, and instituting a contrast between the accredited and the non-accredited preachers of the Gospel. On the *intensive*, surely not *local* (ἄνωθεν αὐτὸν φέροντες, Chrys.) force of καταγγ., see notes *on Phil.* i. 17.

νουθετοῦντες] '*admonishing,*' '*warning,*' '*corripientes,*' Vulg., Æth.; participial clause defining more nearly the manner or accompaniments of the καταγγελία. The verb νουθετεῖν has its proper force and meaning of '*admonishing with blame*' (νουθετικοὶ λόγοι, Xenoph. *Mem.* 1. 2. 21, compare notes *on Eph.* vi. 4), and, as Meyer (compare De W.) rightly observes, points to the μετανοεῖτε of the evangelical message, while διδάσκ. lays the foundation for the πιστεύετε; so, inferentially, Theophyl., νουθεσία μὲν ἐπὶ τῆς πράξεως, διδασκαλία δὲ ἐπὶ δογμάτων. On the meaning of νουθετεῖν, which implies, primarily, correction by *word*, an appeal to the νοῦς (compare 1 Sam. iii. 12), and derivatively, correction by *act*, Judges viii. 16 (compare Plato, *Leg.* IX. p. 879), see Trench, *Synon.* § 32.

πάντα ἄνθρ.] Thrice repeated and emphatic; apparently not without allusion to the exclusiveness and Judaistic bias of the false teachers at Colossæ. The message was universal; it was addressed to every one, whether in every case it might be received or no: τί λέγεις; πάντα ἄνθρωπον; ναί, φησί, τοῦτο σπουδάζομεν. εἰ δὲ μὴ γένηται οὐδὲν πρὸς ἡμᾶς, Theoph. ἐν πάσῃ σοφίᾳ] '*in all, i. e. in every form of, wisdom;*' see notes *on Eph.* i. 8: mode in which the διδάσκειν was carried out, μετὰ πάσης σοφίας, Chrys. (compare ch. iii. 16), or perhaps, more precisely, the characteristic element in which the διδαχή was always to be, and to which it was to be circumscribed. The meaning is thus really the same, but the manner in which it is expressed slightly different. The lines of demarcation between *sphere of action* (Eph. iv. 17), *accordance with* (Ephes. iv. 16), and *characterizing feature* (Eph. vi. 2), all more or less involving some notion of modality, are not always distinctly recognizable. The influence of the Aramaic ܒ in the various usages of ἐν in the N. T. is by no means inconsiderable. ἵνα παραστήσωμεν] '*in order that we may present,*' exactly as in ver. 22, with implied reference, not to a sacrifice, but to the final appearance of every man before God: '*en metam et scopum Pauli, atque*

τέλειον ἐν Χριστῷ ²⁹ εἰς ὃ καὶ κοπιῶ ἀγωνιζόμενος κατὰ τὴν ἐνέργειαν αὐτοῦ τὴν ἐνεργουμένην ἐν ἐμοὶ ἐν δυνάμει.

adeo omnium verbi ministrorum,' Davenant, — whose remarks on the propriety of the intention, — as coming from one who sat at the Council of Dort, — are not undeserving of perusal. The concluding words ἐν Χρ., as usual, define the sphere in which the τελειότης, 'l'ensemble de toutes les qualités naturelles au Chrétien' (Reuss, *Théol. Chrét.* Vol. II. p 182), i. to consist; compare notes on ch. iv. 12, and *on Eph.* iv. 13. The polemical antithe is which Chrys. here finds, οὐκ ἐν νόμῳ οὐδὲ ἐν ἀγγέλοις, owing to the continual recurrence of ἐν Χρ., is perhaps more than doubtful. The addition of Ἰησοῦ is rightly rejected by *Tisch.* with ABCD FG; mss.; Claromanus; Clem., and Lat. Ff.

29. εἰς ὅ] '*to which end;*' the prep. with its usual and proper force denoting the object contemplated in the κοπιῶν; compare notes *on Gal.* ii. 8.

καὶ κοπιῶ] '*I also toil;*' 'beside preaching with νουθεσία and διδαχή, I also sustain every form of κόπος (2 Cor. vi. 5) in the cause of the Gospel,' the καὶ contrasting (see notes *on Phil.* iv. 12) the κοπιῶ with the previous καταγγ. κ. τ. λ. The relapse into the first person has an individualizing force, and carries on the reader from the general and common labors of preaching the Gospel (ὃν ἡμεῖς καταγγ.), to the struggles of the individual preacher. On the meaning and derivation of κοπιῶ, see notes *on* 1 *Tim.* iv. 10.

ἀγωνιζόμενος] '*striving;*' compare chap. iv. 12, 1 Tim. iv. 10 (*Lachm.*, — a doubtful reading, vi. 12), 2 Tim. iv. 7, and in a more special sense, 1 Cor. ix. 25. It is doubtful whether this is to be referred to an outward, or an inward ἀγών. The former is adopted by Chrys., Theoph., Davanant, al.; the latter by Steig., Olsh., and most modern commentators. The use of κοπιῶ (see *on Tim. l. c.*) perhaps may seem to point to the older interpretation; the immediate context (ch. ii. 1), however, as I t⟨h⟩e use of ἀγωνίζομαι in this Ep. (see ch. iv. 12, ἀγωνιζόμενος ὑπὲρ ὑμῶν ἐν ταῖς προσευχαῖς) seem here rather more in favor of modern exegesis, unless indeed with (Ecum. and De Wette we may not improbably admit both.

κατὰ τὴν ἐνέργ.] '*according to His working which worketh in me;*' measure of the apostle's spiritual κόπος (compare notes *on Eph.* i. 19), viz. not his own ἐνέργεια but, as the context seems to suggest, that of Christ; τὸν αὐτοῦ κόπον καὶ ἀγῶνα τῷ Χριστῷ ἀνατιθείς, (Ecum., who alone of the Greek commentators (Theod. silet) expressly refers the αὐτοῦ to Christ, the others apparently referring it to ὁ Θεός. On the construction of the verb ἐνεργ., see notes *on Gal.* ii. 8, v. 6, and on its meaning, notes *on Phil.* ii. 13. The *passive* interpretation 'quæ agitur, exercetur, perficitur' (Bul., *Ex m. Cons.* II. 3), though lexically defensible, seems certainly at variance with St. Paul's regular use of the verb; see on *Phil. l. c.*

ἐν δυνάμει] '*in power,*' i. e. powerfully; modal adjunct to ὁ ἐνεργουμένην. Though it seems arbitrary to restrict δύναμις to miraculous gifts (Michael.), it still seems equally so (with Meyer and Alf.) summarily to exclude it; compare Gal. iii. 5. The principal reference, as the singular suggests (contrast Rom. i. 4 and Acts ii. 22), seems certainly to inward operations; a secondary reference to outward manifestations of power seems, however, fairly admissible; 'quum res postulat, etiam miraculis,' Calvin, compare Olsh. *in loc.*

I am earnestly striving for you, that you may come to the full knowledge of Christ.

II. Θέλω γὰρ ὑμᾶς εἰδέναι ἡλίκον ἀγῶνα

Let no one deceive you, but as you received Christ, walk in Him.

CHAPTER II. 1. γάρ] Description of the nature and objects of the struggle previously alluded to, introduced by the γάρ *argumentative* (not transitional, ⇌? Syr. [probably not a different reading, see Schaaf, *Lex.* s. v.], and partially even Alf.), which confirms and illustrates,— not merely the foregoing word ἀγωνιζόμενος (Beng.), but the whole current of the verse: 'meminerat in calce superioris capitis suorum laborum et certaminum, eorum nunc causam et materiam explicat,' Just. ἡλίκον ἀγῶνα] '*how great a struggle;*' not 'solicitudinem,' Vulg., but ' certamen,' Clarom., ܒ݁ܐ Syr., 'quantum colluctor,' Æth. The struggle, as the circumstances of the apostle's captivity suggest, was primarily inward,—'intense and painful anxiety,' Eadie (compare ch. iv. 12), yet not perhaps wholly without reference to the outward sufferings which he was enduring for them (ch. i. 24), and for all his converts. The qualitative adj. ἡλίκος (Hesychius ποταπός, μέγας, ὁποῖος; compare Donaldson, *Cratyl.* § 254), occurs only here and James iii. 5. περὶ ὑμῶν] '*for you.*' The reading is somewhat doubtful. *Lachm.* reads ὑπὲρ with ABCD²; 6 mss.; but as this might easily have come from ch. iv. 12 (compare ch. i. 24), it seems best with *Tisch.* to retain περί, which is found in D¹D³EFG KL, and the great majority of mss.: these prepositions are often interchanged. On the distinction between them, see *on Gal.* i. 4, and *on Phil.* i. 7.

καὶ τῶν ἐν Λαοδ.] The Christians in the neighboring city of Laodicea are mentioned with them, as possibly subjected to the same evil influences of heretical teaching. The rich (Rev. iii. 17), commercial (compare Cicero, *Epist. Fam.* III. 5), city of Laodicea, formerly called Diospolis, afterwards Rhoas, and subsequently Laodicea, in honor of Laodice, wife of Antiochus II., was situated on the river Lycus, about eighteen English miles to the west of Colossæ, and about six miles south of Hierapolis, which latter city is not improbably hinted at in καὶ ὅσοι κ. τ. λ.; see Wieseler, *Chronol.* p. 441 note. Close upon the probable date of this Epistle (A. D. 61 or 62), the city suffered severely from an earthquake, but was restored without any assistance from Rome; Tacit. *Ann.* XIV. 27, compare Strabo, *Geogr.* XII. 8. 16 (ed. Kramer): a place bearing the name of Eski-hissar is supposed to mark the site of this once important city. For further notices of Laodicea see Winer, *RWB.* s. v. Vol. II. p. 5, Pauly, *Real-Encycl.* Vol. IV. 1, p. 764, and Arundell, *Seven Churches,* p. 84 sq., ib. *Asia Minor,* Vol. II. p. 180 sq. καὶ ὅσοι κ. τ. λ.] '*and (in a word) as many as, etc.;*' the καὶ probably annexing the general to the special (compare Matth. XXVI. 59, notes *on Eph.* i. 21, *Phil.* iv. 12, and Winer, *Gr.* § 53. 3, p. 388), and including, with perhaps a thought of Hierapolis (see above), all in those parts who had not seen the apostle. The ordinary principles of grammatical perspicuity seem distinctly to imply that the ὑμεῖς and the οἱ ἐν Λαοδ. belong to the general class καὶ ὅσοι κ. τ. λ., and consequently that the Colossians were not personally acquainted with the apostle. Recent attempts have been made either to refer the ὅσοι to a third and different set of persons to the Colossians and Laodiceans (Schulz. *Stud. u. Krit.* 1829, p. 538; so Theodoret and a schol. in Matthæi, p. 168), or to a portion only of those two Churches (Wiggers, *Stud. u.*

ἔχω περὶ ὑμῶν καὶ τῶν ἐν Λαοδικείᾳ, καὶ ὅσοι οὐχ ἑωράκαν τὸ πρόσωπόν μου ἐν σαρκί, ² ἵνα παρακληθῶσιν αἱ καρδίαι αὐτῶν συμβιβασθέντες ἐν ἀγάπῃ καὶ εἰς πᾶν τὸ πλοῦτος τῆς πληροφο-

Krit. 1838, p. 176), but as all the words are, in fact, under the vinculum of a common preposition, and as αὐτῶν, if dissociated from ὑμῶν καὶ τῶν ἐν Λαοδ. (comp. Schulz), would leave the mention of these two former classes most aimless and unnatural, we seem justified in concluding with nearly all modern editors that the Colossians and those of Laodicea had *not* seen the apostle in the flesh; see the good note of Wieseler, *Chronol.* p. 440 sq., and Neander, *Planting*, Vol. 1. p. 171 (Bohn). The form ἑώρακαν adopted by *Lachm., Tisch.* [with ABC (ἑορ.) D¹], is decidedly Alexandrian (see Winer, *Gr.* § 13. 2, p. 71), and probably the true reading. The 'sonstige Gebrauch Pauli' urged against it by Meyer is imaginary, as the third person plur. does not elsewhere occur in St. Paul's Epistles. Ἐν σαρκὶ seems naturally connected with the preceding πρόσωπόν μου (Vulg., Coptic, Æth.), not with ἑώρακαν (Syr., but not Philox., where the order is changed), forming with it one single idea. There is almost obviously here no implied antithesis to πνεύματι (δεικνύσιν ἐνταῦθα ὅτι ἑώρων συνεχῶς ἐν πν., Chrys., Theoph., compare ver. 5): the bodily countenance is not in opposition with 'the spiritual physiognomy,' Olsh., but seems a concrete touch added to enhance the nature of his struggle; it was not for those whom he personally knew and who personally knew him, but for those for whom his interest was purely spiritual and ministerial.

2. ἵνα παρακλ.] '*in order that their hearts may be comforted;*' not 'may be strengthened,' 'inveniant robur,' Copt. [literally, but ? if the derivative meaning 'consol. accipere' is not the most common, e. g. Psalm cxix. 52], De W., Alf.,

al.,—but 'consolentur' (consolationem accipiant), Vulg., ܢܬܒܝܐܐ [consol. accipient], Syr., 'gaudeant,' Æth.,— the fuller meaning who ', in passages of this nature, παρακ. always appears to bear in St. Paul's Epistles, and from which there do *not* here seem sufficient reason to depart (conv. Bisp., Alford): surely those exposed to the sad trial of erroneous teachings needed consolation; compare Davenant in *loc.* For example of παρακαλ. compare ch. iv. 8, Eph. vi. 22, and even 2 Thess. ii. 17, where the associated στηρίξαι is not a repetition, but an amplification, of the preceding παρακαλέσαι. The final ἵνα is obviously dependent on ἀγῶνα ἔχω (comp. Chrys. ἀγ. ἔχω ἵνα τί γένηται), and introduces the *aim* of the struggle,—the consolation and spiritual union of those believers previously mentioned who had not seen the apostle in the flesh.

συμβιβασθέντες ἐν ἀγ.] '*they being knit together in love;*' relapse to the logical subject by the common participial anacoluthon (Eph. iv. 2; see notes on *Eph.* i. 18, and *on Phil.* i. 30), the participle having its modal force, and defining the manner whereby, and circumstances under which, the παράκλησις was to take place; see Madvig, *Synt.* § 176. b. The verb συμβιβ. has not here its derivative sense, 'instructi,' Vulg., Copt., but its primary meaning of *aggregation*, 'knit together,' Auth. (comp. Syr. ܢܬܩܪܒܘܢ [accedant], Æth., 'confirmetur'), as in ch. ii. 19, and Eph iv. 16, where see notes. The reading -ων (*Rec.,* with D¹EKL; al.) seems certainly only a grammatical emendation. Ἐν ἀγάπῃ, with the usual meaning of the preposition, denotes not the instru-

ρίας τῆς συνέσεως, εἰς ἐπίγνωσιν τοῦ μυστηρίου τοῦ Θεοῦ Χριστοῦ,

ment ('per caritatem,' Est.), but the sphere and element in which they were to be knit together, and is associated by means of the copulative καί (not 'etiam,' Beng.) with εἰς πᾶν κ. τ. λ. which defines the object of the union; see next note.

εἰς πᾶν τὸ πλοῦτος] '*unto all the richness:*' prepositional member defining the object and purpose contemplated in the συμβίβασις, and closely connected with the preceding definition of the ethical sphere of the action; deep insight into the mystery of God is the object of the union in love. The connection with παρακληθ. (Baumg.-Crus.) mars the union of the prepositional members, and gains nothing in exegesis. The reading πάντα πλοῦτον, though fairly supported (*Rec.* with DEKL), seems clearly to have had a paradiplomatic origin (see Pref. to *Gal.* p. xvii), the τα being a clerical error for το, and πλοῦτον a corresponding correction. On this neuter form, see notes on *Eph.* i. 7.

τῆς πληροφορίας τῆς συνέσ.] '*of the full assurance of the understanding:*' not 'certo persuasæ intelligentiæ,' Davenant, a resolution of the gen. which is wholly unnecessary: compare notes on ch. i. 27. The word πληροφ. (1 Thess. i. 5, Heb. vi. 11, x. 22) denotes on the qualitative side (πλοῦτ., quantitative, De W.) the completeness of the persuasion which was to be associated with the σύνεσις,—which the σύνεσις was to have and to involve (gen. *possess.*), — and, as Olsh. observes, may denote that the σύνεσις was not to be merely outward, dependent on the intellect, but inward, resting on the testimony of the Spirit; compare Clem.-Rom. 1. *Cor.* § 42. On the meaning of σύνεσις, see notes on ch. i. 9: that it is here Christian σύνεσις, clearly results from the context (Mey.).

εἰς ἐπίγνωσιν κ. τ. λ.] '*unto the full knowledge of the mystery of God, even Christ;*' prepositional member exactly parallel to the preceding εἰς πᾶν τὸ πλ. κ. τ. λ. The construction of the last three words is somewhat doubtful. Three connections present themselves; (α) '*the mystery of the God of Christ,*' Huth., Mey., Χριστοῦ being the possessive gen. of relationship, etc.; see Scheuerl. *Synt.* § 16. 7, p. 123 sq., and comp. *Eph.* i. 17, and notes *in loc.*; (β) '*the mystery of God, even of Christ,*' Χρ. being a gen. in simple apposition to, and more exactly defining Θεοῦ; so in effect, Hil., 'Deus Christus sacramentum est;' (γ) '*the mystery of God, even Christ:*' Χρ. being in apposition, not to Θεοῦ, but to μυστηρίου, and so forming a very close parallel to ch. i. 27. Of these (α) seems hopelessly hard and artificial; (β) though dogmatically true, seems here an unnecessary specification, and exegetically considered, much inferior to (γ), which stands in harmony with the preceding expression μυστηρίου ὅς ἐστι Χριστός (ch i. 27), and has the indirect support of D¹, Clarom., Aug., Vig., and Æth., *zabuenta Chrestos* [quod de Christo]. It seems singular that these words have not given rise to more discussion (South has a doctrinal sermon on the text, Vol. II. p. 174 sq., but does not notice the readings), for (β), though in point of collocation somewhat doubtful, seems still, considered apart from the context, not indefensible, and at any rate is not to be disposed of by Meyer's summary 'entbehrt aller Paulinischen analogie.' We adopt (γ), however, on what seem *decided* exegetical grounds. On the meaning and applications of μυστήριον, see notes on *Ephes.* v. 32, Reuss, *Théol. Chrét.* IV. 9, Vol. II. p. 89; and for the exact force of ἐπίγνωσις ('accurata cognitio') here apparently confirmed by the juxtaposition of the simple γνῶσις, ver. 3, see notes on *Eph.* i. 17.

³ ἐν ᾧ εἰσιν πάντες οἱ θησαυροὶ τῆς σοφίας καὶ τῆς γνώσεως

2. τοῦ Θεοῦ Χριστοῦ] This passage deserves our attentive consideration. The reading of the text is that of B, Hil. (Lachm., Tisch. ed. 1, Mey., Hofm., Bleek, &c.), and has every appearance of being the original reading, and that from which the many perplexing variations have arisen. The other principal readings are (a) τοῦ Θεοῦ, with curs. re mss. 37, 67**, 71, 80*, 116 (Griesb., Scholz, Tisch. ed. 2, 7), followed by O'sh., De W., Alf., and the majority of modern commentators. (b) τοῦ Θεοῦ ὅ ἐστιν Χριστός, with D¹; C. æthm. (Eth., quod de Christo) (c) τοῦ Θεοῦ πατρὸς τοῦ Χριστου with AC³; al.; Vv.; and lastly, (d) τοῦ Θεοῦ καὶ πατρὸς καὶ τοῦ Χρ. with D¹FKL; many mss and Vv.; Theod., Dam., al. (Rec.). Now of these (a) is undoubtedly too weakly supported; (b) seems very like a gloss of the assumed true reading τοῦ Θεοῦ Χρ.; (c) and (d) still more expanded or explanatory readings. As all four may be so simply derived from the text, (a) by omission, the rest by gloss and expansion, we adopt, with considerable confidence, the reading of *Lachm.*, and we believe also, of *Tregelles*.

3. ἐν ᾧ] '*in whom,*' relative sentence explaining the predication involved in the preceding apposition (μυστηρ. — Χριστοῦ), the relative having its explanatory force; see notes on ch. i. 25. To follow the reading of the text, and yet to refer ἐν ᾧ to the μυστήριον (Mey.), seems unusually perplexed, unless (with Mey.) we adopt the unsatisfactory construction (a), previously discussed. De Wette and Mey. urge the implied antithesis between μυστ. and ἀπόκρ., but to this it may be said, — *first*, that what is applicable to μυστ. is equally so to that to which it is equivalent (comp. Bisp.); *secondly*, that the secondary predicate ἀπόκρυφοι (see below) logically elucidates the equivalence of Χριστὸς with the μυστήριον, but would seem otiose if only added to enhance the nature of the μυστήριον or the ἐπίγνωσις thereof: compare Waterl. *Christ's Div.* Serm. VII. Vol. II. p. 156. εἰσὶν πάντες κ. τ. λ.] '*are all the treasures of wisdom and knowledge hidden;*' not '*the secret treasures,* etc.,' Meyer, Alf., which obscures the secondary predication of manner, and in fact confounds it with the usual 'attributive' construction (Krüg., *Sprachl.* § 50. 8). The position of the substantive verb and the order of the words seem to show that ἀπόκρυφοι is not to be joined with εἰσὶν as a direct predication (Syr., Copt., De W., al.), but that it is subjoined to it (Vulgate, Eth.) as the predication of manner, and is in fact equivalent to an adverb, the most distinct type of the secondary predicate; see especially Donaldson, *Crat.* § 304, and comp. Mulder, *Kune Syntax*, Vol. I. p. 310 (Don. Ids.), who is here the credit of first introducing the necessary distinction between 'adjectiva attributa, prædicata, and appositiva;' see also Donaldson, *Gr.* § 436–447. It will be seen that the translation of Meyer and Alf., and especially the explanations based upon it, are unsatisfactory from not having observed these important distinctions. Exegetically considered, the expression seems to convey that all treasures of wisdom and knowledge are in Christ, and are hidden so, 'quo verbo innuitur, quod pretiosum et magnificum est in Christo non prominere, aut protinus in oculos incurrere hominum carnalium, sed ita latere ut conspiciatur tantummodo ab iis quibus Deus oculos dedit aquilinos, id est, spirituales ad vivendum,' Davenant: ὥστε παρ' αὐτοῦ δεῖ πάντα αἰτεῖν, Chrysostom. There is thus no need with Bähr and

ἀπόκρυφοι. ⁴ τοῦτο δὲ λέγω ἵνα μηδεὶς ὑμᾶς παραλογίζηται ἐν πιθανολογίᾳ. ⁵ εἰ γὰρ καὶ τῇ σαρκὶ ἄπειμι, ἀλλὰ τῷ πνεύματι

others to modify the simple meaning of the adjective. σοφίας καὶ γνώσεως] The exact distinction between these words is not perhaps very easy to substantiate. We can hardly say that ' σοφία res credendas, γνῶσις res agendas complectitur ' (Davenant), but rather the contrary. It would seem, as in σοφία and φρόνησις (see notes on *Eph.* i. 9), that σοφία is the more general, ' wisdom,' in its completest sense, κοινῶς ἁπάντων μάθησις, Suid., γνῶσις the more restricted and special, ' knowledge,' as contrasted with the results and applications of it; see Neander, *Planting*, Vol. I. p. 139 (Bohn), Delitzsch, *Bibl. Psychol.* IV. 7, p. 166, and, on the meaning of ' wisdom,' comp. Taylor (II.), *Notes from Life*, p. 95.

4. τοῦτο δὲ λέγω] ' *Now this I say;* ' transition, by means of the δὲ μεταβατικόν (Hartung, *Partik.* Vol. I. p. 165; omitted by *Lachm.* with A¹ (apparently), B; Ambrosiast.), to the warnings which, with some intermixture of exhortation and doctrinal statements, pervade the chapter. The τοῦτο seems clearly to refer not merely to ver. 3, but to the whole introductory paragraph, ver. 1–3. παραλογίζηται] ' *may deceive;* ' only here and James i. 22, though not uncommon in the LXX, *e. g.* Josh. ix. 22, 1 Sam. xii. 28, 2 Sam. xxi. 5, al. The verb παραλογ. is of common occurrence in later Greek, and properly denotes ' to deceive,' either by false reckoning (Demosth. *Aphob.* 1. p. 822), or false reasoning (Isocr. p. 420 c), and thence generally, ἀπατᾶν, ψεύσασθαι (Hesych.); comp. Arrian, *Epict.* II. 20, ἐξαπατῶσιν ὑμᾶς καὶ παραλογίζονται, and examples in Elsner, *Obs.* Vol. II. p. 261, Loesn. *Obs.* p. 335.

ἐν πιθανολογίᾳ] ' *with enticing speech;* ' compare 1 Cor. ii. 4, ἐν πειθοῖς σοφίας λόγοις, the prep. ἐν having that species of instrumental force in which the object is conceived as existing in the means; comp. Jelf, *Gr.* § 622. 3. The subst. occurs in Plato, *Theæt.* p. 162 E, and the verb in Aristot. *Eth. Nic.* I. 1, but with a more special and technical reference to probability as opposed to demonstration or to mathematical certainty.

5. εἰ γὰρ καὶ κ.τ.λ.] ' *for if I am absent verily in the flesh;* ' reason for the foregoing warning, founded on the fact of his spiritual presence with them; εἰ γὰρ καὶ τῇ σαρκὶ ἄπειμι, ἀλλ' ὅμως οἶδα τοὺς ἀπατεῶνας, Chrys. The καὶ does not belong, strictly considered, to the εἰ (compare Raphel *in loc.*), but to σαρκί, on which it throws a slight emphasis, contrasting it with the following πνεύματι: see notes *on Phil.* ii. 17. The dative σαρκί is the dat. ' of reference,' and, with the regular limiting power of that case, marks that to which the ἀπουσία was restricted; see notes *on Gal.* i. 22.

ἀλλά] ' *yet on the contrary,* ' ' *nevertheless;* ' the hypothetical protasis being followed by ἀλλά at the commencement of the apodosis; see examples in Hartung, *Partik.* ἀλλά, 2. 8, Vol. II p. 40. In such cases, which are not uncommon, the ἀλλά preserves its primary and proper force; ' *per istam particulam quasi transitus ad rem novam significatur quæ ei, quæ membro orationis conditionali erat declarata, jam opponatur,*' Klotz, *Devar.* Vol. II. p. 93. τῷ πνεύματι] ' *in the spirit;* ' dative exactly similar to τῇ σαρκί. It need scarcely be said that this is St. Paul's human spirit (Beck, *Seelenl.* II. 11, p. 29 sq.), not any influence of the Holy Spirit, Pseud-Ambr. (compare Grot.; Daven. unites both), which would here violate the obvious antithesis. The deduction of Wig-

σὺν ὑμῖν εἰμί, χαίρων καὶ βλέπων ὑμῶν τὴν τάξιν καὶ τὸ στερίωμα

gers (*Stud. u. Krit.* 1838, p. 181) from this passage and especially from the use of ἄπειμι, that there had been a previous παρουσία with the Col. on the part of St. Paul, is rightly rejected by De Wette and Meyer; the verb itself simply implies *absence* without any reference to a previous *presence*; the accessory thought is supplied by the context. Contrast the other instances in the N. T., 1 Cor. v. 3, 2 Cor. x. 1, 11, xiii 2, 10, Phil i. 27, in all of which πάρειμι is distinctly expressed. σὺν ὑμῖν] 'with you;' 'joined with you,' in a true and close union; compare Gal. iii. 9, where remarks on the difference between σὺν and μετά: compare *on* Eph. vi. 23. χαίρων καὶ βλέπων κ.τ.λ.] 'rejoicing (*with you*), *and seeing your order;*' modal and circumstantial clause defining the feelings with which he was present, and the accessory circumstances. There is some difficulty in the union of these two participles. After rejecting all untenable assumptions, of an ἐν διὰ δυοῖν ('gaudeo dum video,' Wolf), — a zeugmatic construction of the accusative with both verbs ('mit Freuden sehend,' De Wett), — a trajection ('seeing, etc., and rejoicing,' see Winer, *Gram.* § 54. 4, p. 417 note), — a causal use of καί ('gaudens quia cerno,' Daven., compare Syr. ܚܕܐ?), etc., we have three plausible interpretations. (a) '*rejoicing, to wit, seeing,*' etc., καί being used purely explicatively, Olsh., Winer, 2, *l. c.*; (β) '*rejoicing* (*thereat*), *i. e.* at being with you in spirit, *and seeing*, etc.,' the subject of the χαίρων being deduced from the words immediately preceding, and the καί being simply copulative; so Meyer, and after him Eadie and Alf.; (γ) '*rejoicing* (*about you*) *and seeing*,' ἐφ' ὑμῖν being suggested by the preceding σὺν ὑμῖν, Winer 1, *l. c.*, Fritz. *Rom.* Vol. II. p. 425

note. Of the ο (α) seems hard and artificial; (β) imports a somewhat alien thought, for surely it was the state of the Colossians, rather than the being with them in spirit, that made the apostle rejoice; (γ) preserves the practical connection of χαίρ. with the latter part of the sentence, but assumes an ellipse which the context does not very readily supply. It seems best then (δ) so far to modify (γ) as to assume a continuation of σὺν ὑμῖν; the *modal* χαίρων expressing the apostle's general feeling of joyful *sympathy* (suggested by the state in which he found them), while the *circumstantial* βλέπων κ. τ. λ adds a more special, and, in fact, explanatory accessory: for t is use of καί (special after general), comp. notes *on Eph.* v. 18, and *on Phil.* iv. 12. τάξιν] '*order,' i. e.* 'orderly state and conduct;' τὴν τάξιν, τὴν εὐταξίαν φησί, Chrys.; specification of their state *outwardly* considered in reference to church-fellowship, and to the attention and obedience of the good soldier of Christ. ὡς γὰρ ἐπὶ παρατάξεως ἡ εὐταξία τὴν φάλαγγα στερεὰν καθίστησιν οὕτω καὶ ἐπὶ τῆς ἐκκλησίας, ὅταν εὐτάξια ᾖ, τῆς ἀγάπης πάντα καθιστώσης καὶ μὴ ὄντων σχισμάτων, τότε καὶ τὸ στερέωμα γίνεται, Theoph. The allusion may be to a well organized body politic (Meyer, Alford; compare Demosth. *de Rhod. L* 5. p. 200) or, perhaps more probably, in accordance with the apostle's metaphors elsewhere (Up. vi. 11 sq.) to military service; see Wo'f *in loc.* στερέωμα] '*solid foundation,*' '*firm attitude,*' καθάπερ πρὸς στρατιώτας εὐτάκτως ἑστῶτας καὶ βεβαίως, Chrys.; specification of their state inwardly considered: not 'firmitas,' Syr., Æth. [both which languages have another word more exactly answering to the concrete], followed by Huther, De Wette, al., but, 'fundamentum,' Vulg., 'firmamentum,' Copt. — there being no

τῆς εἰς Χριστὸν πίστεως ὑμῶν. ⁶ Ὡς οὖν παρελάβετε τὸν Χριστὸν Ἰησοῦν τὸν Κύριον, ἐν αὐτῷ περιπατεῖτε, ⁷ ἐρριζωμένοι καὶ

lexical ground for regarding the more concrete στερέωμα ('effect of the verb as a concretum,' Buttm. Gr. § 119. 7; nearly = part. in -μενον) as identical in meaning with the purely abstract στερεότης. The wo.d (an ἅπ. λεγόμ. in the N. T.; compare 1 Pet. v. 9, Acts xvi. 5) occurs frequently in the LXX, and nearly always in its proper sense, though occasionally showing the tendency of later Greek in a partial approximation to the verbal in -σις; comp. Esth. ix. 29. The gen. may be a gen. of apposition (comp. notes on Eph. vi. 14), but seems more naturally a gen. subjecti referable to the general category of the possessive genitive. On the construction of πιστ. with εἰς, see notes on 1 Tim. i. 16, and Reuss, Théol. Chrét. iv. 14, Vol. ii. p. 129. After these words we have no reason for doubting that the Church of Colossæ, though tied by heretical teaching, was substantially sound in the faith.

6. ὡς οὖν παρελάβετε] 'As then ye received:' exhortation founded on the words of blended warning and encouragement in the two preceding verses, οὖν having its common retrospective and collective force ('ad ea quæ antea reverâ posita sunt lectorem revocat,' Klotz), and thus answering better to 'then,' Peile, than 'therefore,' Alf.: see Klotz, Devar. Vol. ii. p. 717, compare Donaldson, Gr. § 604. On ὡς see notes on Tit. i. 5. The παρελάβετε can hardly be 'from me,' Alf. (see on ver. 1), but, from Epaphras (ch. i. 7) and your first teachers in Christianity. Though the reference seems mainly to reception by teaching (compare ἐδιδάχθητε, ver. 7), the object is so emphatically specified, τὸν Χρ. Ἰησ. τὸν Κύρ., as apparently to require a more inclusive meaning; they received not merely the ἀκήρατον διδασκαλίαν (Theod.), the 'doctrinam Christi' (Daven.), but Christ Himself, in Himself the sum and substance of all teaching (Olsh., Bisp.); compare Ephes. iv. 20, and notes in loc. τὸν Κύριον] 'The Lord;' not without emphasis; yet not so much as 'for your Lord,' Alf., after Huth. and Mey., — an interpretation which, independently of grammatical difficulties (Κύριον 2 Cor. iv. 5, not τὸν Κύρ., see Middleton, Gr. Art. iii. 3. 4), would make παραλαβεῖν imply rather the recognition of a principle of doctrine, than the spiritual reception of the personal Lord. The title, as both the position and article show, is plainly emphatic, — it marks Him as Lord of all, above all Principality and Power (Eph. i. 20), the Creator of men and angels (Col. i. 16), but cannot be safely regarded as forming a tertiary predication; compare Donalds. Cratyl. § 305. ἐν αὐτῷ περιπατεῖτε] 'walk in Him,' as the sphere and element of your Christian course. Christ is not here represented as an ὁδός (ἡ προσάγουσα εἰς τὸν Πατέρα, Chrys.), but as an ensphering 'Lebens-Element' (Mey.), to which the περιπατεῖν, i. e. life and all its principles and developments, was to be circumscribed; compare Gal. ii. 20, Phil. i. 20. For a practical sermon on this text, see Farindon, Sermon xxxii. Vol. ii. p. 165 (Lond. 1849).

7. ἐρριζωμένοι καὶ ἐποικοδομούμενοι] 'having been rooted and being built up in Him;' modal definitions appended to the preceding περιπατεῖν; the first under the image of a root-fast tree (hence the perf. part.), the second under that of a continually uprising building (hence the pres. part.) marking the stable growth and organic solidity of those who truly walk in Christ. The ἐν αὐτῷ is attached to both: Christ, as Mey

καὶ ἐποικοδομούμενοι ἐν αὐτῷ, καὶ βεβαιούμενοι τῇ πίστει καθὼς ἐδιδάχθητε, περισσεύοντες ἐν αὐτῇ ἐν εὐχαριστίᾳ.

7. ἐν αὐτῇ] So *Rec.*, *Lachm.*, and now *Tisch.* (ed. 7) with BD¹ c.al. gr. t. pr ss of mss.; Vulg. (Clarom., 'am.' 'fu.' as al. o D¹; mss.; and pers s s a r. Vs., to inflexions of which often leave it uncertain whether ἐν αὐτῷ or ἐν αὐτῇ be the original.); Chrys., Theod., al., and Lat. Ff. The two words were read by J ν. (ed. 2) with AC¹; 15 mss.; Am. Tol. (certainly *not* Copt., as Lachm.); Ar-chel., al.,— but are now rightly restored. The authority for the insertion is clearly insufficient, especially when such an omission might so easi'y have been suggested by the difficulty of the construction.

observes, is both the ground *in* which the root is held (Eph. iii. 17), and the solid foundation on which (1 Cor. iii. 11) the building is raised,— the prep. ἐν (not ἐπ' αὐτῷ, Eph. ii. 20) being studiously continued to enhance the idea ἐν Χριστῷ that pervades the passage; comp. Eph. ii. 21, 22. The necessary idea of the *foundation* is admirably conveyed by the ἐπί in the compound verb; comp. 1 Cor. iii. 12, Eph. ii. 20. In a passage of such force and perspicuity we need not pause on the slight mixture or discordance of metaphors; it would be difficult indeed to imagine such fruitful and suggestive thoughts conveyed in so few words.

καὶ βεβαιούμ. τῇ πίστει] 'and being established in your faith;' the idea (τὸ βέβαιον) involved in the preceding participles being still more clearly brought out,— and, as the nature of the case requires, in the *present* tense. The dat. τῇ πίστει is not the instrumental dat. (Mey.), but the dat. 'of reference to' (De Wette), faith being naturally regarded as the principle which needed βεβαίωσιν, and to which it might most appropri tely be restricted: see notes on Gal. i. 22. The prep. ἐν is inserted before πίστει in *Rec.* [with ACD⁴EKL], but is apparently rightly rejected by *Lachm.* and *Tisch.*, though only with BD¹; 4 mss.; Vulg.,— the probability of an insertion being very great.

καθὼς ἐδιδάχθ.] 'even as ye were taught;' scil. to become firmly estab-

lished in faith: this they might have been taught by Epaphras (ch. i. 7) or by some of their early instructors.

περισσ. ἐν αὐτῇ κ. τ. λ.] 'abounding in it with thanksgiv :' part qual. clause subordinate to βεβαιούμ., mainly reiterating with a quantitative, what had been previously expressed with a qualitative reference. Of the two prepositional adjuncts, the first ἐν αὐτῇ is united closely with περισσ., specifying the element and item in which the increase takes place (equivalent to *abundare* with an abl.; see notes on *Phil.* i. 9), the second as the tit l of operation in which (Alf.), or perhaps rather the accompaniment with which (σὺν εὐχαρ., Œcum.), the περισσ. ἐν αὐτῇ was associated and, as it were, environed; compare Luke xiv. 31, 1 pers vs 16, 1 Cor. iv. 21, in which the gradual transition from the more distinct idea of environment to the less defined idea of accompaniment may be easily traced; see Green, *Gr.* p. 289, and notes on ch. iv. 2.

8. βλέπετε μή τις κ.τ.λ.] 'Take heed lest there shall be any one that shall rob you his booty,'— you as well as the others that have been led away: ὑμᾶς, as the order suggests, being slightly emphatic: see critical note. The cautionary imper. βλέπετε is found in at least six combinations in the N. T.; (α) with a simple accus., Mark iv. 24, Phil. iii 2: (β) with ἀπό and a gen., Mark viii 15, xii 38; (c) with πῶς and the indic., Luke

21

Let not worldly wisdom lead you away from Him who is the Head of all, who has quickened you, and for given you, and triumphed over all the powers of evil.

⁸ Βλέπετε μή τις ὑμᾶς ἔσται ὁ συλαγωγῶν διὰ τῆς φιλοσοφίας καὶ κενῆς ἀπάτης κατὰ τὴν

8. *ὑμᾶς ἔσται*] It is curious that apparently no critical editor except Wetst. (and recently *Tisch.* ed. 7) has noticed the doubtful order of these two words. *Tischener* (ed. 2) silently adopted ἔσται ὑμᾶς with ACDE (*Lachmann*), but has now (ed. 7) rightly reversed the position of the words. The order of the text is that of BKL; all mss.; Chr., Theod., al., — and is apparently to be preferred as the less obvious order; so *Rec.* and *Scholz*.

viii. 18, 1 Cor. iii. 10; (*d*) with ἵνα and the subj., 1 Cor. xvi. 10; (*e*) with μή and the subjunctive, — the prevailing construction, Matth. xxiv. 4, Gal. v. 15, al.; (*f*) with μή and the future, only here and Heb iii. 12. The last construction is adopted in the present case as implying the fear that the case contemplated will really occur, 'ne futurus sit qui,' etc.; see Winer, *Gr.* § 56. 2, p. 446, Hartung, *Partik.* μή, 5. 6, Vol. II. p. 140, and compare Herm. Soph. *Elect.* 992. Numerous examples of μή in different constructions after ὅρα κ. τ. λ. will be found in Gayler, *Partik. Neg.* p. 316 sq. συλαγωγῶν] 'bearing away as a booty;' an ἅπ. λεγόμ. in the N. T., found only in later Greek, both directly with an accus. *personæ, e. g.* παρθένον, Heliod. Æth. x. 35, and, in a more derivative sense, with an accus. *rei, e. g.* οἶκον, Aristæn. *Ep.* II. 22. There seems no reason for diluting ὑμᾶς (συλαγωγῶν τὸν νοῦν, Theoph.) or adopting the weaker force of the verb (ἀποσυλῶι τὴν πίστιν, Theod.) : the false teachers sought to lead them away captive, body and mind; the former by ritualistic restrictions (verse 16), the latter by heretical teaching (verse 18). On the use of the art. after the indef. τις, see notes *on Gal.* i. 7. διὰ τῆς φιλοσ. κ. τ. λ.] '*by means of philosophy and vain deceit*,' *i. e.* a philosophy that is essentially and intrinsically so, the absence of both prep. and article before κενῆς ἀπάτης showing that it belongs to the same category as the foregoing φιλοσοφία, and forms with it a joint idea; ἐπειδὴ δοκεῖ σεμνὸν εἶναι τὸ τῆς φιλοσοφίας προσέθηκε, καὶ κενῆς ἀπ., Chrys.: see Winer, *Gram.* § 19. 4, p. 116. Such φιλοσοφία was but a κενὴ ἀπάτη, an empty, puffed-out [comp. Benfey, *Wurzellex.* Vol. II. p. 165] system of deceit and error; compare Eph. v. 6. The term φιλοσοφία in this passage has been abundantly discussed. There seems no sufficient reason for referring it, on the one hand, to Grecian philosophy, whether Epicurean (Clem.-Alex. *Strom.* I. 11 (50), Vol. I. p. 346, ed. Pott.), Stoic and Platonic (Tertull. *Præscr.* § 7), or Pythagorean (Grot.), or on the other, to the 'religio Judaica' (Kypke, *Obs.* Vol. II. p 322; so Loesner and Krebs),— but, as the associated terms and the general contrast seem to suggest, to that hybrid theosophy of Jewish birth and Oriental affinities (τῆς φιλοσ., — the popular, current, philos. of the day), which would be likely to have taken nowhere firmer root than among the speculative and mystery-loving Phrygians of the first century; see Neander, *Planting*, Vol. I. p. 321 sq. (Bohn), and the good note of Wordsw. on this verse. In estimating the errors combated in St. Paul's Epistles which were allied with Judaism, it becomes very necessary to distinguish between, (*a*) Pharisaical Judaism, such as that opposed in the Epistle to the Galatians; (*b*) Christianity tinged with Jewish usages and speculations as condemned in the Pastoral Epistles, — not heresy proper, but an adulterated Chris-

παράδοσιν τῶν ἀνθρώπων, κατὰ τὰ στοιχεῖα τοῦ κόσμου καὶ οὐ κατὰ Χριστόν, ⁹ ὅτι ἐν αὐτῷ κατοικεῖ πᾶν τὸ πλήρωμα τῆς

tianity (see notes on 1 *Tim.* i. 4), which afterwards merged into (c) speculative and heretical Judaism, as noticed in this Epistle; perhaps of a more decided Cabbalistic origin, and associated more intimately with the various forms of Oriental theosophy: see Neander, *l. c.*, Rothe, *Anfänge*, p. 320 sq., Burton, *Lectures*, III. Vol. I. p. 76 (ed. 2), Reuss, *Théol. Chrét.* VI. 13, Vol. II. p. 642 sq.

κατὰ τὴν παράδ. τῶν ἀνθρ.] '*according to the tradition of men;*' a modal predication attached, not to τῆς φιλοσοφίας, κ. τ. λ. (a construction in a high degree grammatically doubtful), but to the part. συλαγωγῶν, defining, first positively and then negatively, the characteristics of the συλαγωγία. Philosophy was the 'causa medians,' παράδ. τῶν ἀνθρ. the 'norma' and 'modus agendi.' The gen. τῶν ἀνθρ. is apparently that of the *origin* (Hartung, *Casus*, p. 23), the παράδοσις took its rise from, and was received from, men; compare Gal. i. 12, 2 Thess. iii. 6. Meyer presses the art. τῶν ἀνθρ. ('τῶν markirt die *Kategorie*, die 'traditio humana' als solche der Offenbarung entgegengesetzt '), but apparently unduly: the article is probably only introduced on the regular principle of correlation; see Middleton, *Gr. Art.* III. 3. 6, p. 48 (ed. Rose). κατὰ τὰ στοιχ. κ. τ. λ.] '*according to the rudiments of the world;*' second modal predication parallel to the foregoing. The antithesis οὐ κατὰ Χρ. seems clearly to show that this expression here includes all rudimental religious teaching of *non-Christian* character, whether heathen or Jewish, or a commixture of both,—the first element *possibly* slightly predominating in thought here, the second in ver. 20. On the various meanings assigned to this difficult expression, see notes on *Gal.* iv. 3.

κατὰ Χριστόν] '*according to Christ;*' clearly not, as Grot., Corn. a Lap., 'secundum doctrinam Christi,' but 'secundum Christum' ὡς τοῦ Χριστοῦ χαριζόντος, Theod. (compare Chrys.). Christ Himself the personal Christ, was the substance, end, and *norma* of all evangelical teaching. A good lecture on the 'ten points of faith' is based on this text by Cyr.-Hieros. *Cat.* ch. IV.

9. ὅτι ἐν αὐτῷ *because in Him;*' reason for the implied exclusion of all other teaching except that κατὰ Χριστόν, ἐν αὐτῷ being prominent and emphatic, and standing in close connection with the preceding Χριστόν, '*in Him,* and in none other than Him.' Mill and Griesb., by placing a period after Χρ. would seem rather to imply a reference to βλέπετε (compare Huth.), to which, however, the emphatic ἐν αὐτῷ seems decidedly opposed. κατοικεῖ] '*doth dwell,*'—now and evermore; observe both the tense and the compound form. The former points to the present, continuing κατοίκησις of the Godhead in the glorified son of God (compare Hofmann, *Schriftb.* Vol. II. 1, p. 24) the latter to the permanent indwelling, the κατοικία, not παροικία, of the πλήρωμα θεότητος, compare Deyling, *Obs.* IV. 1, Vol IV. p. 591, and see notes on ch. i. 19, and on *Eph.* iii. 17.

πᾶν τὸ πλήρ.] '*all the fulness of the Godhead,*' all the exhaustless perfections of the essential being of God: not without emphasis; ἐν ἡμῖν μὲν γὰρ ἀπαρχὴ καὶ ἀρραβὼν θεότητος κατοικεῖ, ἐν Χρ. δὲ πᾶν τὸ πλήρ. τῆς θεότητος, Athan.: see notes on ch. i. 19, where the meaning of πλήρωμα in this connection is briefly investigated. Any reference to the Church (Theod., but with some hesitation) is here wholly out of the question. It is only necessary to add that θεότης must

Θεότητος σωματικῶς, ¹⁰ καὶ ἐστὲ ἐν αὐτῷ πεπληρωμένοι, ὅς ἐστιν

not be confounded with Θειότης (Rom. i. 20), as Copt., Syr., Æth., and, what is more to be wondered at, Vulg., which has certainly two distinct words: the former is *Deitas*, 'die Gottheit,' 'statum [essentiam] ejus qui sit Deus,' August. *Civ. Dei*, vii. 1, and points to the nature of God on the side of the actual *essentia* (τὸ εἶναι Θεόν); the latter '*divinitas*,' 'die Göttlichkeit,' 'conditionem ejus qui sit Θεῖος,' and points to the divine nature on the side of its *qualitas* (τὸ εἶναι Θεῖον); see Fritz. *Rom.* i. 20, Vol. I. p. 62. The real difficulty of the verse is in the next word. σωματικῶς] '*in bodily fashion*,' ܒܐܝܣܪܐ [corporaliter], Syr, 'corporaliter,' Vulg. The meanings assigned to this word are very numerous. If we follow the plain lexical meaning of the word, and the true qualitative force of the termination -ικος ('like what?' Donaldson, *Cratyl.* § 254), we must certainly decide that it signifies neither ἀληθῶς, sc. οὐ τοπικῶς ἢ σκιατικῶς, 'vere, non umbratice' (August., compare Hammond 2), — ὅλως, 'totaliter,' (Capell.), — οὐσιωδῶς sc. οὐ σχετικῶς, essentialiter, non relative' (Œcum., Usteri, *Lehrb.* p. 303), — nor even ὑποστατικῶς, 'personaliter' (compare Cyr.-Alex. *adv. Nest.* I. 8, p. 28), but — with reference, not so much to that which indwells, as to that which is dwelt in (Hofmann, *Schriftb.* Vol. II. 1, p. 25), — '*bodily wise*,' '*in bodily fashion*,' in the once mortal, and now glorified, body of Christ; comp. Phil. iii. 21.

The πλήρωμα Θεότητος, which once dwelt οὐ κατὰ σωματικὸν εἶδος in the Λόγος ἄσαρκος, now dwells forevermore σωματικῶς (Chrys. calls attention to the precision of the language; μὴ νομίσῃς Θεὸν συγκεκλεῖσθαι, ὡς ἐν σώματι) in the Λόγος ἔνσαρκος: compare Meyer *in loc.*, and Hofmann *Schriftb. l. c.* So De Wette, Eadie, Alford, and most modern commentators, and anciently Æthiopic, 'in carne s. corpore hominis,' and apparently Athanasius *contr. Arian.* III. 8, *de Susc. Hum.* Vol. I p. 60, Damasc. *Orthod. Fid.* III. 6, except that the reference is perhaps not sufficiently extended to the present glorified body of our Redeemer: see the copious reff. in Suicer, *Thesaur.* s. v. Vol. II. p. 1216, and compare Wordsw. *in loc.*

10. καὶ ἐστε κ. τ. λ.] '*and* (*because*) *ye are in him filled full;*' not exactly, 'ye are made full in Him' (Eadie), but, as the position of ἐστε and the order of the words seem to require, 'ye are in Him made full,'— there being in fact a double predication, 'ye are united with Christ (do not then seek help of subordinate power), yea and filled with all His plenitude (and so can need nothing supplementary).' There is no necessity to supply any definite genitive, τῆς Θεότητος (Theoph.), τοῦ πληρ. τῆς Θεότ. (De W.), τῆς ζωῆς (Olsh.): all wherewith Christ is full, all His gifts, and graces, and communicable perfections, are included in the πλήρωσις; compare the somewhat parallel text Eph. iii. 19, and see notes *in loc.* Grotius and a few others regard ἐστε as an imper. parallel to βλέπετε, but are rightly opposed by all modern commentators. ὅς ἐστιν κ. τ. λ.] '*who is*, *i. e. seeing He is, the head of all* (*every*) *Principality and Power*,' the ὅς having a slight explanatory force (see notes on ch. i. 25, and *on* 1 *Tim.* ii. 4), and tacitly evincing the folly of seeking a πλήρωσις from any subordinate source, or by any ceremonial agency (compare verse 11). The reading is somewhat doubtful: Lachm. reads ὅ with BDEFG; Clarom., al., and encloses καὶ — ἐν αὐτῷ in a parenthesis, but as the neuter relative would seem to have arisen from a mistaken ref. of ἐν αὐτῷ to πληρ., we seem justified in retaining ὅς with AC KL; nearly all mss.; Chrys., Theod.,

ἡ κεφαλὴ πάσης ἀρχῆς καὶ ἐξουσίας· 11 ἐν ᾧ καὶ περιετμήθητε περιτομῇ ἀχειροποιήτῳ, ἐν τῇ ἀπεκδύσει τοῦ σώματος τῆς σαρκός,

al., followed by *Rev* and *Tisch*. On the use of the abstract terms ἀρχὴ and ἐξουσία to denote orders of *heavenly Intelligences*, see notes and reff. on *Eph*. i. 21, and Suicer, *Thesaur*. s. v. ἄγγελος, Vol. 1. p. 30—48.

11 ἐν ᾧ] 'in whom,' i. e. 'seeing that in Him,' not 'per quem,' Schoettg., ἐν ᾧ being exactly parallel with ἐν αὐτῷ (ver. 10), and the use of the relative similar to that of ὅς in the foregoing clauses: all that the believer can receive in spiritual blessings is already given to him in Christ (Olsh.).

καὶ περιετμήθητε] 'ye were also circumcised,' viz. at your conversion and baptism, 'quum primum facti estis Christiani,' Schoettg.: not ' in whom too, ye, etc.,' Eadie, which tends to separate καὶ from the verb on which it throws emphasis. The Colossians seem to have been exposed to the influence of *two* fundamental errors; *first*, the belief that they were under the influence, or at any rate needed the assistance, of intermediate intelligences; *secondly*, the persuasion that circumcision, the symbol of purification appointed by God, must still be necessary. Both are in fact met by the single clause καὶ ἐστε — πεπληρ. (see above); this, however, is further expanded in two explanatory relatival clauses, ὅς ἐστιν, κ. τ. λ. being directed against the first error, ἐν ᾧ καὶ κ. τ. λ. against the second; see Hofmann, *Schriftb*. Vol. 11. 2, p. 153. ἀχειροποιήτῳ] ' *not hand-wrought*;' they were indeed circumcised — in a spiritual and antitypical manner, as the two characterizing definitions which follow still more clearly show. The epithet ἀχειρ. puts in obvious contrast the spiritual περιτομή [Baptism, see below] with the legal, typical, περιτομὴ χειροποίητος, performed outwardly ἐν σαρκί, Eph. ii. 11. Several references to a spiritual circumcision will be found in Schoettg. *Hor*. Vol. 1. p. 815; compare Deut. x. 16, xxx. 6, al. The form ἀχειρωπ. occurs again Mark xiv. 58 (in expressed contrast), and 2 Cor. v. 1. ἐν τῇ ἀπεκδύσει κ. τ. λ.] ' *in the putting off of the body of the flesh*;' not ' by means of etc.,' Mey., the prep. ἐν not having any quasi-instrumental force, but simply specifying that in which the περιτομὴ consisted (De W.), the external act in which it took place; compare notes on ver. 7, and Winer, *Gr*. § 48. a, p. 315. In all such cases the real use of the preposition is local, but the application ethical. The σῶμα τῆς σαρκός has been somewhat differently explained. Grammatically considered, the expression is exactly the same as in ch. i. 22; σαρκὸς is the gen. of the *material* or specifying element (see notes), but its meaning and application are necessarily different. There it was the material σὰρξ of the Redeemer without any ethical significance; here it is the material σὰρξ quâ the seat of sinful motions, practically synonymous with the more generic σῶμα ἁμαρτίας (Rom. vi. 6), and designedly used in this place to keep up the antithetical allusion to legal circumcision: the περιτ. χειροπ. consisted in the ἀπέκδυσις and περιτομὴ of a part (Exod. iv. 25), the περιτ. Χριστοῦ in the ἀπεκδύσει of the whole σῶμα τῆς σαρκός; see Hofmann, *Schriftb*. Vol. 11. 2, p. 154, and Wordsw. *in loc.*, who pertinently cites the good doctrinal comments of Hilary, *de Trin.* ix. 7. It is somewhat perverse in Müller, *Doctr. of Sin*, Vol. 1. p. 359 (Transl.), p. 435 (Germ.), to salve his general interpretation of σάρξ by here giving to σῶμα a figurative meaning (' massa.' Calv., al.), which, even if lexically admissible, is obviously out of

ἐν τῇ περιτομῇ τοῦ Χριστοῦ, ¹² συνταφέντες αὐτῷ ἐν τῷ βαπτίσ-

harmony with the concrete references (σινταφέντες, συνηγέρθητε) in the context. No writer has more ably vindicated the prevailing meaning of σάρξ (see notes *on Gal.* v. 5), but that there are some passages in the N. T. in which σάρξ has a reference to *sensationalism* generally, to weakness, fleshliness, and sinful motions cannot safely be denied; comp. with this expression, ἀπεκδυσάμενοι τὸν παλαιὸν ἄνθρ. κ. τ. λ. ch. iii. 9, and see especially the excellent article of Tholuck in *Stud. u. Krit.* for 1855, p. 488–492. The reading of *Rec.*, σώμ. τῶν ἁμαρτ. τῆς σ with D²D³E²KL, is rightly rejected by *Tischener* and most modern critics. ἐν τῇ περιτ. τοῦ Χρ.] '*in the circumcision of Christ*,' communicated by, and appertaining unto, Christ; second characterizing definition parallel to ἐν τῇ ἀπεκ. κ. τ. λ. specifying more exactly the nature of the περιτομὴ ἀχειροποίητος. Χριστοῦ is not exactly a gen. *auctoris* (ὁ Χριστὸς περιτέμνει ἐν τῷ βαπτίσματι, Theophyl.), but of the *origin*, or perhaps still more exactly, the *originating cause* (see Hartung, *Casus*, p. 17, and notes on ch. i. 23); τούτων αἴτιος ὁ δεσπότης Χριστός, Theod.: Christ, by union with Himself, brings about the circumcision and imparts it to believers. To give the genitive a strongly *possessive* ref., *e. g.* 'the circumcision undergone by Christ,' Schoettg., seems, exegetically considered, very unsatisfactory; compare Olsh. *in loc.* The reference of ἀπεκ. κ. τ. λ. and περιτ. τοῦ Χρ. to the death of Christ (Schneckenburger, *Theol. Jahrb.* for 1848, p. 286 sq.) is convincingly refuted by Meyer. Even Müller (*on Sin*, Vol. I. p. 359) will take no refuge in such an interpretation.

12. συνταφέντες] '*having been buried together with Him*,' '*when you were*, etc., the action described in the participle being contemporaneous with that of περιετ. (Mey.); compare ch. i. 20, and see Bernhardy, *Synt.* x. 9, p. 383, Stallb. on Plato, *Phædo*, p. 62 D. The temporal force seems, however, here clearly secondary and subordinate, the primary force of the part. being apparently modal, and serving to define the manner in which the περιτομὴ Χρ. was communicated to the believer: compare especially Romans vi. 4. There seems no reason to doubt (with Eadie) that both here and Rom. *l. c.* there is an allusion to the κατάδυσις and ἀνάδυσις in Baptism; see Suicer, *Thesaur.* s. v. ἀνάδ. Vol. I. p. 259, Bingham, *Antiq.* xi. 11. 4, and comp. Jackson, *Creed*, xi. 17. 6. That this burial with Christ is spiritually real and actual (τὸ βάπτισμα κοινωνοὺς ποιεῖ τοῦ θανάτου Χρ. Theod. Mops. *on Rom. l. c.*), not symbolical or commemorative, seems certain from the plain, unrestricted language of the apostle; compare Waterl. *Euchar.* VII. Vol. IV. p. 577. ἐν ᾧ καὶ συνηγ.] '*wherein ye were also raised with Him:*' ἀλλ' οὐ τάφος μόνον ἐστί [τὸ βάπτισμα], ὅρα γὰρ τί φησι, Chrysost. (compare Theoph.), — noticed by Meyer, Alf., and others as referring ᾧ to Χριστός, but apparently without sufficient reason. The reference of ᾧ to Χρ. (Mey., Eadie) is at first sight structurally plausible (ὅς...ἐν ᾧ...ἐν ᾧ), but on a closer consideration certainly not exegetically satisfactory; the two spiritual characteristics, the τὸ συνταφῆναι as shown in the κατάδυσις, the τὸ συνεγερθῆναι as shown in the ἀνάδυσις, must surely stand in close reference and connection with Baptism. The counter-arguments of Meyer founded on the use of the prep. (ἐν ᾧ not ἐξ οὗ), and the parallelism of the prepositional clauses (συνταφ. αὐτῷ ἐν κ. τ. λ., συνηγέρθ. διὰ κ. τ. λ.) are not convincing. In the first place no other preposition would be so appropriate as the semi-local ἐν; and in the second place, διὰ

ματι, ἐν ᾧ καὶ συνηγέρθητε διὰ τῆς πίστεως τῆς ἐνεργείας τοῦ Θεοῦ τοῦ ἐγείραντος αὐτὸν ἐκ τῶν νεκρῶν. ¹³ καὶ ὑμᾶς νεκροὺς ὄντας ἐν τοῖς παραπτώμασιν καὶ τῇ ἀκροβυστίᾳ τῆς σαρκὸς

κ. τ. λ., the statement of the *causa medians*, can scarcely be conceived as forming any logical parallelism with the foregoing semifocal ἐν τῷ βαπτ. Lastly the καὶ seems to keep both συντ. and συνηγ. in close correlative reference to each other. By comparing Rom. vi. 4, it would seem that the primary ref. of συνηγ. is clearly to a *present and spiritual* resurrection, but again by comparing Ephes. ii. 6 (in which the converse seems true; see notes), it would also appear that a secondary ref. to a *future* and *physical* resurrection ought not to be excluded: as Jackson well says, ' of our resurrection unto glory, we receive the pledge or earnest when we receive the grace of regeneration which enables us to walk in newness of life; and this is called the *first resurrection*,' Creed, XI. 17. 7; compare Waterland, *Euchar.* VII. Vol. IV. p 577, Reuss, *Theol. Christ.* IV. 21, Vol. II p. 235.

διὰ τῆς πίστεως] 'through faith;' subjective medium by which the objective grace is received: 'faith is not the mean by which the grace is wrought, effected, or conferred; but it may be and is the mean by which it is *accepted* or *received*,' Waterl. *on Justif.* Vol. VI. p. 23; compare Usteri, *Lehrb.* II. 1. 3, p. 216. The image of Alf., 'the hand which held on, not the plank that saved,' is, in more than one respect, not dogmatically satisfactory. τῆς ἐνεργείας κ. τ. λ.] '(*in) the effectual working of God;*' not gen of the *agent* or *causa efficiens* (De Wette, al.), but more simply and intelligibly the genitive *objecti*: ܕܗܝܡܢܬܘܢ [qui credidistis in] Syr., sim. Æth., 'in fide, in auxilio' (Platt; Pol. invers.). ἐπιστεύσατε ὅτι δύναται ὁ Θεὸς ἐγεῖραι, καὶ οὕτως

ἠγέρθητε Chrys., — as in all cases where πίστις is thus associated with a gen. rei, the gen. appears to denote the object of faith; comp. Acts ii. 16, Phil. i. 27, 2 Thess. ii. 13. The statement of Mey., endorsed by Eadie, and Alf., ut comp. the latter *on Gal.* iii. 2, that this is true in every case except where other refs to the believer, does not seem *prima facie* certain; see notes *on Gal.* ii. 16, iii. 22, and Stier *on Eph.* Vol. I. p. 177.

τοῦ ἐγείραντος κ. τ. λ.] Cause appended, to give us a sure and certain pledge (ἐνέχυρον ἔχοντες τοῦ δεσπότου Χριστοῦ τὴν ἀνάστασιν, Theod.) of the almighty ἐνεργεία of God, both in the present vivification to new life and the future vivification to glory; comp. Eph. i. 20 and notes *in loc.*] — 'Let not anything may be done or suffered by our Saviour in these great transactions but may be acted in our souls and represented in our spirits,' Pearson, *Creed*, Vol. I. p 265 (ed. Burt.).

13. καὶ ὑμᾶς] '*and you also*,' 'et vos etiam,' Copt.; application of the foregoing to the Colossians, especially with reference to their formerly *heathen* state, καὶ being associated with ὑμᾶς and *ascensive*, not with συνεζ. in a merely copulative sense, see notes on *Eph.* ii. 1. The pronoun is repeated after συνεζ. with ACKL (B, al., ἡμᾶς; more than 40 mss.; Copt., Æthiop., al.; Theod. (ms.), Dam, Œcum., and rightly adopted by *Tisch.* and most modern editors; the omission [*Rec.* with DEFG; al.] was obviously suggested by the apparent syntactic difficulty. This, however, is very slight, as a rhetorical pleonasm of the pronoun for the sake of emphasis is not uncommon; see Bernhardy, *Synt.* VI. 4, p. 275.

νεκροὺς ὄντας] '*being dead*,' or 'when

ὑμῶν, συνεζωοποίησεν ὑμᾶς σὺν αὐτῷ, χαρισάμενος ἡμῖν πάντα

you were dead' (not, '*who were dead,*' Alf.), the past sense attributed to ὄντας being justified by the aorists which are associated with it in the sentence (Winer, *Gr.* § 41. 1, p. 305); see also notes on *Ephes.* ii. 1 (*Transl.*). It seems extremely unsatisfactory in Meyer, both here and Ephes. ii. 1, to give νεκροὺς a proleptic reference to *physical* death, scil. ' certo morituri,' ὑπὸ τὴν δίκην ἔκεισθε ἀποθανεῖν, Chrys.: a remote, inferential, reference to physical death may possibly be included (see Alf. on *Eph. l. c.*), but any primary ref. seems wholly irreconcilable with the context.

ἐν τοῖς παραπτ.] ' *in your transgressions ;* ' the prep. as usual marking the element in which the dead state was experienced ; contrast Eph. ii. 1, where the ἐν is omitted and the dat. is instrumental. The prep. is actually omitted in BL; 20 mss.; Goth.; Greek Ff., but appy. either by accident or conformation to Eph. *l. c.* There does not seem reason for receding from the general distinction between παραπτ. and ἀμαρτ. (especially when associated) advanced in notes *on Eph. l. c.* τῇ ἀκροβ. τῆς σαρκός] '*the uncircumcision of your flesh,*' *i. e.* that appertained to, was the distinctive feature of — the gen. not being either of apposition (Storr), or quasi-material (B.-Crus., compare Alf.), but simply *possessive*. The associated words (obs. the omission of the prep.) and the foregoing use of the term (ver. 11) may perhaps justify us in assigning some ethical reference to σάρξ, — not merely your material (Eadie), but your sinful, unpurified flesh, of which the ἀκροβυστία was the visible and external mark ; they were heathens, unconverted, sinful heathens, as their very bodies could attest : this ἀκροβυστία, however, had now lost its significance ; they were περιτετμημένοι in Christ. 'Ακροβυστία is thus not necessarily spiritual (Deut. x. 16, Jerem. iv. 4), but retains its usual and proper sense ; on the derivation (not ἄκρον βύω, but a corruption of ἀκροποσθία) see Fritz. *Rom.* Vol. 1 p. 136.

συνεζωοποίησεν] ' *He together quickened,*' spiritually, — with reference to the life of grace ; a secondary and *inferential* reference to the physical resurrection need not, however, be positively excluded : see above, and notes *on Eph.* ii. 5, where the force of the aorist (what is wrought in Christ is wrought ' ipso facto' in all united with Him) is briefly noticed ; see especially Waterland, *Euchar.* IX. Vol IV. p. 643. The great difficulty in this clause is the subject. On the one hand, a comparison with Rom. viii. 11, and still more Eph. ii. 5, seems to point to the last substant. Θεός, ver. 12 ; so Theod., Theoph., appy. Copt. [' secum,' Wilk., is a mistransl.], and nearly all modern commentators. On the other hand, the logical difficulty of supplying a nom. from the subordinate gen. Θεοῦ, — the obvious prominence given to Christ throughout the preceding portion — the peculiar acts described in the participles (especially ἐξαλ. κ. τ. λ. compared with Eph. ii. 15, and even χαρισ. compared with Col. iii. 13), — the relation of Christ to ἀρχαὶ and ἐξουσίαι (ver. 15, compare i. 16, ii. 10), — and lastly, the extreme difficulty of referring the acts described in ver. 14, 15, to God the Father, are arguments so preponderant, that we can scarcely hesitate to refer συνεζ. and its associated participles to *Christ*, who, as of the same essence and power with the Father and the Holy Ghost, did infallibly quicken Himself (Pearson, *Creed,* Art. v. Vol. I. p. 302, ed. Burt.) : so Chrys. (here, e sil., but elsewhere expressly), apparently Syriac and Goth. (certainly in ver. 15. see below), perhaps Æth. (Platt), and recently

τὰ παραπτώματα, ¹¹ ἐξαλείψας τὸ καθ' ἡμῶν χειρόγραφον τοῖς

Heinr., Baur, *Paulus*, p. 452 note, and very decidedly, Donalds. *Chr. Orthod.* p. 76. It is somewhat singular that the Greek commentators Theod., Theoph., and Œcum., silently adopt Θεὸς as the subject of ver. e 13, and ὁ Θεὸς Λόγος (Theod.), as that of ver. 14, 15; comp. also Wordsw. *in loc.*, who conceives the propositions in this and in the following verses 'to refer to God in Christ, and to Christ as God.' Such an interpretation is dogmatically defensible on the ground of the 'communicatio idiomatum' (compare Ebrard, *Chr. Dogm.* § 385), and certainly deserves consideration, but viewed logically and grammatically seems somewhat artificial and unsatisfactory. We may observe lastly, that if the reference to Christ here advocated is, as it certainly seems to be, correct, it is worthy of serious notice that actions elsewhere ascribed by the apostle to God (Eph. ii. 5, compare Rom viii. 11), are here *unrestrictedly predicated of Christ*. Meyer's objection that the above interpr. is opposed to the 'Lehrtypus,' that God raised Christ, is not very strong; God, it is here said, *did* raise Christ, Christ us, — yet, as God, also Himself.

σὺν αὐτῷ] '*with Himself*.' As this seems a case in which a reference to the subject is somewhat immediate, and in which it is desirable to obviate misunderstanding, the aspirated form may be properly adopted; comp. notes on *Eph.* i. 4.   χαρισάμενος κ. τ. λ.] '*having forgiven us all our transgressions;*' modal participle describing the preliminary act which conditioned the realization of the συζωοποίησις, by removing the true cause of the νεκρότης: πάντα παραπτ. ποῖα; & τὴν νεκρότητα ἐποίει, Chrys.; compare ch iii. 13, 2 Cor. v. 19, Ephes. iv. 32, and observe that in these last two passages Θεὸς is the subject, yet with the noticeable addition, ἐν Χριστῷ. For the reading ὑμῖν (*Elz.* not *Steph.*), there is but little critical authority. Both external and internal arguments suggest the more inclusive ἡμῖν.

14. ἐξαλείψας] '*having blotted out;*' modal participle contemporary with, surely not prior to (Mey.) χαρισάμενος, and detailing it more fully and circumstantially. Christ forgave us our sins when he took them upon Himself and suffered for us; the mode of forgiveness was by cancelling the χειρόγραφον. Surely if this participle be applied to God, arguments might be founded on it not only in support of Patripassian doctrines, but in opposition to the vicarious satisfaction of Christ. If God the Father did all this, what was the precise effect of the expiatory death of Christ? To answer, with Eadie, 'What Christ did, God did by Him,' only evades, but does not meet, the difficulty. The form ἐξαλ. (Acts iii. 19, Rev. iii. 5, vii 17, xxi. 4; compare Psalm l. 9, cviii. 13), as its derivation suggests [ἐ - ἀλά, and Sanscr. *lip*, 'illinere,' Pott, *Etym. Forsch.* Vol. 1. p. 258, Vol. 11. p. 153], properly denotes 'cerâ obducti delere' (compare Krebs, *Obs.* p. 337), and thence, 'to expunge,' 'wipe out,' generally, in opposition to γράφειν, Eurip. ad. ap. Stob. *Floril.* xciii. 10, p. 507 (ed. Gesn.), or ἐγγράφειν, Plato, *Rep.* vi. p. 501 a, compare Xen. *Hell.* ii. 3. 51.

τὸ καθ' ἡμῶν χειρ. κ. τ. λ] '*the handwriting in force against us by its decrees;*' the dative δόγμασιν belonging closely to τὸ καθ' ἡμ. χειρ., and falling under the general head of the dative 'of reference to' (notes *on Gal.* i. 22); the δόγματα were that in which the τὸ καθ' ἡμῶν (the hostile aspect or direction, opposed to ὑπέρ, see Winer, *Gr.* § 47. k, p. 341) of the bond was specially evinced: see Winer, *Gr.* § 31. 10. 1, p. 197. The usual explanation, 'consisting of δόγμα-

22

δόγμασιν ὃ ἦν ὑπεναντίον ἡμῖν, καὶ αὐτὸ ἦρκεν ἐκ τοῦ μέσου, προσ·

τα,' 'rituum chirographo,' Beza, — in which the dat. would be equivalent to a kind of gen. *materiae*, or involve a tacit ellipsis of ἐν (compare Ephes. ii. 15) — seems distinctly ungrammatical, and that of Meyer, Eadie, and Alf., — according to which the dat. is governed by the verbal element in χειρόγρ., — more than doubtful, as χειρ. is a *synthetic* compound (Donalds. *Gr.* § 372), and apparently incapable of such a decomposition; compare Tobit v. 3, ix. 5, Polyb. *Hist.* xxx. 8. 4. The reference of χειρόγραφον has been very differently explained. The context would seem to suggest that χειρογρ. is clearly not the command given to Adam (Theophyl. 2), nor the law of conscience (Luth.), nor even specially, the moral law (Calv.; compare Neand. *Planting*, Vol. I. p. 462), nor yet the ceremonial law (Schoettg., Wordsw.; see especially Deyling, *Obs.* Part. IV. p. 596 sq.), but *the whole law*, 'nam beneficium chirographi ad omnes spectat, tam Gentiles quam Judæos: ergo hujusmodi chirogr. ponere oportet, quo ex aliquâ parte tenentur omnes,' Daven.; compare Andrewes, *Serm.* IV. Vol. I. p. 54 sq. (A.-C. Libr.), and Vol. III. p. 66, where he curiously terms it the 'ragman roll:' so De Wette, Mey., and most modern commentators. The χειρόγρ. was καθ' ἡμῶν, Jews and Gentiles; immediately against the former, mediately and inferentially (as founded on immutable principles of justice and rectitude) against the latter, Rom. ii. 15, compare Rom. iii. 19. It was in the positive commands whether written on stone or in the heart that the τὸ καθ' ἡμῶν was mainly evinced: compare on the prohibitive side, Rom. vii. 7 sq. The law was thus appropriately designated, being a 'bond,' an 'obligatory document' (comp. Plut. *Mor.* p. 829 A, and see exx. in Wetst.), by which all were bound, and which brought penalty in case of non-fulfilment; compare Pearson, *Creed*, Art. IV. Vol. I. p. 248 (ed. Burt.), Usteri, *Lehrb.* II. 1, 2, p. 175, Reuss, *Théol. Chrét.* IV. 17, Vol. II. p. 190.

ὃ ἦν ὑπεναντίον ἡμ.] '*which was against us;*' expansion of the preceding τὸ καθ' ὑμῶν: it was hostile not merely in its direction and aspects, but practically and definitely. The idea of *secret* hostility (ὑπό) is not implied either here, Heb. x. 27, or indeed in the majority of passages where the word occurs: see exx. in Rost u. Palm, *Lex.* s. v. Vol. II. p. 2064. Perhaps the prep. may have primarily involved an idea of locality. local opposition (compare Hesiod, *Scut.* 347, Ἵπποι ὑπεναντίοι ἀλλήλοισιν ὀξεῖα χρέμισαν, 1 Macc. xvi. 7) which in the metaphorical applications of the word necessarily became obliterated. This is further confirmed by the fundamental meaning of ὑπό, which, it may be observed, is not 'under,' but appears to be that of 'motion to the speaker from that which is near to him;' see Donalds. *Cratyl.* § 279. καὶ αὐτὸ κ. τ. λ.]. '*and He hath taken it out of the way;*' change from the participial structure to that of the finite verb to add force and emphasis (see notes on ch. i. 6, 20), and especially to the *perfect* [D¹FG; many mss.; Orig., Theod., al., read ἦρεν, but on insufficient authority] to express the enduring and permanent nature of the act; see Winer, *Gr.* § 40. 4, p. 242, and notes on *Ephes.* ii. 20. The addition ἐκ μέσου expresses still more fully the completeness of the ἦρκεν (ἐποίησε μηδὲ φαίνεσθαι, Theophyl., μὴ ἀφεὶς ἐπὶ χώρας, Œcum.), and perhaps also the impedimental character (Meyer) of the thing taken away; examples of αἴρειν ἐκ μέσου will be found in Kypke, *Obs.* Vol. II. p. 323. προσηλώσας κ. τ. λ.] '*having nailed it to the cross;*' modal

ἡλώσας αὐτὸ τῷ σταυρῷ, ¹⁵ ἀπεκδυσάμενος τὰς ἀρχὰς καὶ τὰς ἐξουσίας ἐδειγμάτισεν ἐν παρρησίᾳ, θριαμβεύσας αὐτοὺς ἐν αὐτῷ.

participle, contemporaneous with the commencement of the ἦρκεν (Alf.) describing the manner in which Christ removed the χειρόγραφον: He nailed the Mosaic law with all its decrees to His cross, and it died with Him; αὐτὸς κολασθεὶς ἔλυσε καὶ τὴν ἁμαρτίαν κα. τὴν κόλασιν, Chrys. The reference to a bond cancelled by striking a nail through it (Pearson, Creed, Art. iv. Vol. ii. p. 248; compare διαρρήξεν, Chrys., κατέσχισεν, Theoph.) seems very doubtful. All that the apostle seems here to imply is, that in Christ's crucifixion, the curse of the law was borne, and its obligatory and condemnatory power, its power as a χειρόγραφον καθ' ἡμῶν, forever extinguished and abrogated; comp. Rom. vii. 6, and see Andrewes, Serm. Vol. i. p. 55 sq. (A.-C. Libr.).

15. ἀπεκδυσ. τὰς ἀρχὰς κ.τ.λ] 'having stripped away from Himself the (hostile) principalities and powers;' neither 'exspolians,' Vulg., silently followed by apparently all modern writers except Deyling (Obs. Vol. ii. p. 609), Donaldson (Chr. Orth. p. 68), Hofmann (Schriftb. Vol. i. p. 305), Alford, and Wordsw., nor even, 'having stripped for Himself,' 'deponere jubens,' Winer, de Verb. Comp. iv. 15,— both interpret. wholly unsupported by the lexical usage of ἀποδύω, ἐκδύω, and ἀπεκδ. (see Rost u. Palm, Lex. s. vv.), and opposed to St. Paul's own use of the word, ch. iii. 9,— but 'exuens se,' Claroman., Copt. [mistransl. by Wilkins], Æth. (Platt), Chrys 2, more distinctly Theoph. 2, and with a special reference, Syriac ܡܶܢ ܢܰܦܫܶܗ per exspoliationem corporis sui]. Goth., 'andhamonds sik leika,' and perhaps Theod. followed by Hil., August., Pacian, and reflected in the ancient gloss

ἀπεκδ. τὴν σάρκα, FG; Boern., al. The rare binary compound ἀπεκδ. was apparently chosen rather than the sim. [ἐκδ.] to express, not only the act of 'divestiture,' but that of 'removal;' see Winer, l. c. It is singular that an interpretation of such antiquity, so well attested, and so lexically certain, should in modern times have been completely, if not contemptuously ignored. The meaning of the expression is, however, somewhat obscure: it appears most probably to imply that, as hinted at by Theod., and apparently all the Greek commentators, our Lord by His death stripped away from Himself all the opposing hostile powers of evil (observe the article) that sought in the nature which He had condescended to assume, to win for themselves a victory, ἀπεκδύσατο τὴν λαβὴν [τὸ ἄνθρωπος εἶναι]. ἀνάληπτος εὑρέθη ταῖς ἀρχαῖς καὶ ταῖς ἐξουσίαις. Theoph. 2, compare Theod. When He died on the cross, when He dissolved that temple in which they, both in earlier Matth. iv. 1 sq., Luke iv. i. sq., obs. πρὸς καιρόν, ver. 13), and later, and perhaps redoubled efforts of temptation (see J. Ln. xv. 30, and especially Luke xxii 53), had vainly endeavored to make sacrilegious entry, He left them away forever, and vindicated His regal power (Pearson, Creed, Vol. i. p. 260, ed. Burt.); yea, the loud voice (Matth. xxvii. 50, Mark xv. 37, Luke xxiii. 46) was the shout of eternal triumph and victory. See Wordsw. in loc., who has adopted the same view, and well explained the peculiar significance of the term. Thus all seems clear, consistent, and theologically profound and significant; while our Saviour bore the curse of the law, He destroyed its condemnatory power forever (περιέπειρεν ἐκεῖ, Chrys.), while He underwent sufferings and death, and the last efforts

172   COLOSSIANS.   Chap. II. 15, 16.

Let no one judge you in ceremonial observances, holding not the Head. Submit not to outward austerities that are inwardly vain and carnal.

16 Μὴ οὖν τις ὑμᾶς κρινέτω ἐν βρώσει ἢ ἐν

of baffled demoniacal malignity, He destroyed τὸν τὸ κράτος ἔχοντα τοῦ θανάτου, τοῦτ' ἔστι τὸν διάβολον, Heb. ii. 14; compare 1 John iii. 8.   τὰς ἀρχὰς καὶ τὰς ἐξ.] '*the Principalities and the Powers (that strove against Him*):' these abstract terms being used, as always in the N. T., with reference to spiritual beings (αὐτοὺς) and Intelligences (see notes on *Eph.* i. 26, vi. 12), the context showing whether the reference is to good (ch. i. 16, see notes), or, as here, to evil angels and spirits; see Usteri, *Lehrb.* II. 1. 2, p. 176, Reuss, *Théol. Chrét.* IV. 20, Vol. II. p. 226 sq. The opinion of Hofmann (*Schriftb.* Vol. 1. p. 305), Alf., al., that good angels only are here referred to, and that ἀπεκδ. refers to God putting aside from Him the *nimbus* of the Powers which shrouded Him from the heathen world (Hofm.), is ingenious, but not satisfactory, and further rests on the assumption that this verse refers to Θεός, not Χριστός.
ἐδειγμάτισεν ἐν παρρ.] '*He made a show of them with boldness;*' not

[diffamavit] Syr., sim. Goth., ἠσχημόνησε, Chrys., compare Æthiopic (Platt) and Theod., — but simply, 'fecit eos manifestos,' Copt., 'ostentui esse fecit,' Hil.: it was an open manifestation, and that too, ἐν παρρησίᾳ, ' with boldness,' — not opp. to ἐν κρυπτῷ (John vii. 4), sc. δημοσίᾳ, πάντων ὁρώντων, Chrysost., but, as the formula seems always used by St. Paul, 'confidenter,' Vulg.; see notes on *Phil.* i. 20. The word δειγματίζειν (Matth. i. 19, *Lachm., Tisch.*), apparently confined to the N. T., does not much differ in meaning from the compound παραδειγματίζειν, except that it confines the idea to an open exhibition (as the *context* shows) in triumph, without any further idea of shame or ignominy (Polybius, *Hist.* XVII. 1. 5,

XXIX. 7. 5). To connect ἐν παρρ. with θριαμβ. (Hofm. *Schriftb.* Vol. I. p. 305) seems very unsatisfactory, but has appy. arisen from the assumption that 'openly' is the correct translation.
θριαμβ. αὐτούς] '*having triumphed over them*;' contemporaneous with ἐδειγμ. (see notes on ver. 12), explaining more fully the circumstances of the action. The expression θριαμβεύειν τινα occurs again 2 Cor. ii. 14, and apparently there (see Mey. *in loc.*) as necessarily here, *not* in a factitive sense, but with an accusative of the object triumphed over, or led in triumph; compare Plut. *Comp Thes. c. Rom.* § 4, βασιλεῖς ἐθριάμβευσε καὶ ἡγεμόνας, and examples cited by Wetst. on 2 *Cor. l. c.* On the derivation of the word [θρι-, cogn. with θυρ-, connected with τρεῖς, and ἴαμβος or ἄμβος, 'procession,' or 'close dance'], see Donaldson, *Cratyl.* § 317, 318, and compare Benfey, *Wurzellex.* Vol. II. p. 260. The varied nature of our blessed Redeemer's meek triumphs is well set forth by Hilary, *de Trin.* x. 48 (cited by Wordsw.).
ἐν αὐτῷ] '*in it*;' not (*a*) 'in the nailed up χειρόγραφον,' Mey., which would give a force to αὐτῷ with which its position and the context seem at variance; nor (*b*) 'in semetipso,' Vulg., Andrewes, *Serm.* Vol. III. p. 66, which would form an almost unnecessary addition; but (*c*) 'in it,' scil. τῷ σταυρῷ (ἐν τῷ ξύλῳ, Orig.) with the Greek commentators and majority of modern expositors; τὸ γὰρ τοῦ κόσμου ὁρῶντος ἄνω ἐν τῷ ξύλῳ τὸν ὄφιν σφαγιασθῆναι, τοῦτό ἐστι τὸ θαυμαστόν, Chrys.; see Pearson, *Creed*, Vol. I. p. 291, and especially notes, Vol. II. p. 217, 218 (ed. Burt.).

16. μὴ οὖν] '*Let not then*,' etc.;' with reference to ver. 14 sq., οὖν having its usual collective force, and recalling the readers to the fact that the Mosaic Law is now abrogated; see notes on

πόσει, ἢ ἐν μέρει ἑορτῆς ἢ νουμηνίας ἢ σαββάτων, ¹⁷ ἅ ἐστιν σκιὰ

16. ἢ ἐν] Tisch. (ed. 2) reads καὶ ἐν only on the authority B; Copt., Syr.(?); Orig. (1); Hier., Theod. (Tisch'l. cit'd times), but now (ed. 7) has rightly returned to the reading of *Rec., Lachm.* The common association of β,ωσις and π.σις would very naturally have suggested the displacement of ἢ for the more usual καί.

ver. 6.   κρινέτω ἐν
βρώσει] 'judge you in eating,' pass a judgment upon what may or may not be eaten; ἐν referring to the item on which the judgment was passed, see Rom. ii. 1, xiv. 22. Βρῶσις is not here 'cibus,' Vulg. (comp. Fritz. Rom. xiv 17, Vol. III. p. 200), but, as apparently always in St. Paul's Epistles (Rom. xiv. 17, 1 Cor. viii. 4, 2 Cor. ix. 10), 'esus,' 'actus cibandi,' Copt., Titt.m. Synon. I. p. 159, the passive verbal being regularly used by the apostle in reference to the thing eaten; comp. 1 Cor. iii. 2, vi. 13, viii. 8, 13. x. 3, 1 Tim. iv. 3. The distinction is, however, not observed in St. John (comp. iv. 32, vi. 27), nor indeed always in classical writers, comp. Hom. Od. i. 191, vi 176; Plato, Legg. vi. p. 783 e, cited by Meyer, does not seem equally certain. The rule of Thom. M., βρώματα πληθυντικῶς, οὐ βρῶμα. οἱ δὲ βρώσις, cannot be substantiated; see notes collected by Bern. in loc., p. 174. ἢ ἐν πόσει] 'or in drinking,' the prep. being repeated to give a slight force to the enumeration. The remarks made in respect to βρῶσις apply exactly to πόσις, contrast 1 Cor. x. 4 with Rom. xiv 17, and compare John vi. 55. As there is no command in the Mosaic law relative to πόσις except in the case of Nazarites (Numb. vi. 3) and priests before going into the tabernacle (Lev. x. 9), and as πόσει seems certainly to form a distinct member (opp. to Alf.), we are driven to the conclusion that the Colossian heretics adopted ascetic practices in respect of wine and strong drinks, perhaps of a Rabbinical origin. The Essenes, we know, only drank water: ποτὸν ὕδωρ ναματιαῖον αὐτοῖς ἐστιν, Philo,

de Vit. Cont. § 4, Vol. II. p. 477 (edit. Mang.)   ἐν μέρει ἑορτῆς] 'in the matter of a joyful feast;' not 'in the partial observance of festivals' (οὐ γὰρ δὴ πάντα κατεῖχον τὰ πρότερα, Chrys.), 'ob partem aliquam festi violatam,' Dav., nor 'in segregatione' (i.e. setting apart one day rather than another), Calv., comp. Syr. ܒܦܠܓܘܬ [in divisionibus s. distinctionibus], nor specifically, 'in the [Talmudical] tract upon,' Hamm. after Casaub. and Scal., — but, simply and plainly, 'in the matter of,' μέρος pointing to the 'class' or 'category' (Mey.); see Plato, Republ. I. p. 348 E, ἐν ἀρετῆς καὶ σοφίας τίθης μέρει τὴν ἀδικίαν, Theæt. p. 1551, al., examples in Loesner Obs. p. 367, and compare 2 Cor. iii. 10. The three objects in the matter of which judgment is forbidden, are enumerated in reference to the frequency of their occurrences, ἑορτῇ referring to one of the greater feasts, νουμηνία to the monthly festival of the new moon (Numb. x. 10; see Jahn, Archæol. § 351, Winer, RWB. s.v. 'Neumonde,' Vol. II. p. 149), and σάββατα to the weekly festival; comp. Gal. iv. 10.

17. ἅ ἐστιν] 'which things are;' relative clause showing the justice of the preceding command, the relative having a slight explanatory force; see notes on ch. i. 25, 27. That ἅ refers not merely to the last three items but to the whole verse, i.e. to all legal or traditionary ceremonies, seems clear from the context. The reading ὅ, with BFG; Clarom., Goth., al. (Lachm.), is not improbable, but is insufficiently attested.

σκιά] 'shadow;' not 'an outline,' in reference to a σκιαγραφία, 'beneficia

τῶν μελλόντων, τὸ δὲ σῶμα Χριστοῦ. ¹⁸ μηδεὶς ὑμᾶς καταβρα-

Christi ac doctrinam evangelicam obscure delineabant,' Daven., — a meaning doubtful even in Heb. x. 1, but, as the antithesis σῶμα obviously requires, ܛܠܢܝܬܐ [umbræ] Syr., shadows opposed to substance (Joseph. *Bell. Jud.* II. 2. 5, σκιὰν αἰτησόμενος βασιλείας, ἧς ἥρπασεν ἑαυτῷ τὸ σῶμα), and with *perhaps* some further reference to the typical character of such institutions, shadows flung forward (' prænunciativæ observationes,' Aug.) from the τὰ μέλλοντα (scil. τὰ τῆς καινῆς διαθήκης, Theoph.), from the future blessings and realities of the Christian covenant; προλαμβάνει δὲ ἡ σκιὰ τὸ σῶμα ἀνίσχοντος τοῦ φωτός, Theod. The use of the present ἐστιν must not be unduly pressed; 'loquitur de illis ut considerantur *in suâ naturâ*, abstractæ a circumstantiis temporis,' Davenant. τὸ δὲ σῶμα Χρ.] ' *but the body (their substance) is Christ's;* ' the σῶμα, sc. τῶν μελλόντων, belongs to Christ in respect of its origin, existence, and realization; ' in Christo habemus illa vera et solida bona quæ erant adumbrata et figurata in prædictis cærimoniis,' Daven. The nom. might at first sight have been expected; the possessive gen. Χριστοῦ [so *Tisch.* rightly, with DEFGKL; not τοῦ Χρ. with ABC; *Lachm.*], however, is of more real force, as marking that the true σῶμα τῶν μελλόντων not merely was Christ, but belonged to, was derived from Him, and so could only be realized by union with Him. A reference of this clause to ver. 18 (comp. August. *Epist.* 59) destroys the obvious antithesis and is wholly untenable. The assertion of Alf. (comp. Olsh.) — that if the ordinance of the Sabbath had been *in any form* of lasting observation in the Christian Church, St. Paul could not have used such language, — cannot be substantiated. The σάββατον of the Jews, as involving other than mere national reminiscences (with Deuteron. v. 15, contrast Exod. xx. 11), was a σκιά of the Lord's day: that a weekly seventh part of our time should be specially given up to God rests on considerations as old as the Creation; that that seventh portion of the week should be the *first* day, rests on apostolical, and perhaps inferentially (as the Lord's appearances on that day seem to show) Divine usage and appointment; see Bramhall, *Lord's Day*, Vol. v p. 32 sq. (A.-C. Libr.), and *Huls. Essay* for 1843, p. 69.

18. κ α τ α β ρ α β ε υ έ τ ω] ' *beguile you of your reward:*' so distinctly, Zonar. on *Conc. Laod.* Can. 35 (Suicer, *Thesaur.* s. v.), καταβραβεύειν ἐστὶ τὸ μὴ νικήσαντα ἀξιοῦν τοῦ βραβείου, ἀλλ' ἑτέρῳ διδόναι αὐτό, ἀδικουμένου τοῦ νικήσαντος, the κατά marking the hostile feeling towards the proper recipient, which dictated the consequent injustice, and τὸ παραβραβεύειν; see Demosth. *Md.* p. 544, ἐπιστάμεθα Στρατῶνα ὑπὸ Μειδίου καταβραβευθέντα καὶ παρὰ πάντα τὰ δίκαια ἀτιμωθέντα, and Buttm. *in loc.* (Index, p. 176), who pertinently remarks, ' verbum in translato sensu aliter usurpari non potuisse quam de eo qui *debitam* alteri victoriam eripit.' The many renderings, either insufficient (κατακρινέτω, Hesych. incorrect (καταπαλαιέτω, Castal. ap. Pol. *Syn.*), or perverted (*e. g.* κατακυριευέτω, Corn. a Lap.), that have been assigned to this word will be found in Pol. *Synops.*, and in Meyer *in loc.* The βραβεῖον, of which the false teachers sought to defraud the Colossians was not their Christian freedom (Grot.), — at first sight a plausible interpretat., — but, as the context and the grave nature of the error it reveals seem certainly to suggest, ' vita æterna,' Gom., τὸ βραβεῖον τῆς ἄνω κλήσεως (Phil. iii. 14), and with a more exact allusion, the ἄφθαρτον στέφανον (1

βενέτω θέλων ἐν ταπεινοφροσύνῃ καὶ θρησκείᾳ τῶν ἀγγέλων, ἃ

Cor. ix. 25), the στέφανον τῆς δικαιοσύνης (2 Tim. iv. 8), τῆς ζωῆς (James i. 12), τῆς δόξης (1 Pet. v. 4), which the Lord, ὁ δίκαιος κριτής (2 Tim. *l. c.*), will give to the Christian victor at the last day. This prize the false teachers sought to obtain, but it was under circumstances of such fatal error, viz., the worship of angels, the introduction, in fact, of fresh mediators, that they would eventually beguile and defraud of the βραβεῖον those who were misled enough to join them: 'nihil aliud moliuntur nisi ut palmam ipsis intercipiant, quia abducunt eos a rectitudine cursus sui,' Calv.,—who, however, does not appear to have felt the precisely correct application of καταβραβεύειν.   θέλων] '*desiring (to do it),*' scil. καταβραβεύειν; θέλων τοῦτο ποιεῖν, (Ecum.; modal participle defining the feelings they evinced, and hinting at the studied nature of the course of action which they followed, and which resulted in the καταβράβευσις; τοῦτο τά νυν συνεβούλευον ἐκείνοι γίγνεσθαι, ταπεινοφροσύνῃ δῆθεν κεχρημένοι, Theodor, who, however, somewhat overpresses θέλων, compare notes on 1 Tim. v. 14. These feelings were not directly, but indirectly, hostile to the καταβραβευθησόμενοι; the purpose was to secure the στέφανος for themselves and their followers; the result, to lose it themselves, and to defraud others of it. Two other interpretations have been proposed; (*a*) the Hebraistic construction, θέλειν ἐν ταπειν., = חָפֵץ בְּ (1 Sam xviii. 22, 2 Sam. xv. 26, 1 Kings xv. 26, 2 Chron. ix. 8, only, however, with a personal pronoun), adopted by Aug., al., and recently by Olshaus., but contrary to all analogy of usage in the N. T.; and, perhaps more plausibly, (*b*) the connection καταβ. θέλων, apparently favored by Syr., and, with varying shades of meaning assigned to the part., by Beza, Zanch., Tittmann

(*Synon.* 1. p. 131), al., and most recently, Alf. The former is distinctly untenable, as contrary to all analogy of usage of θέλειν in the N. Test. The latter is structurally and grammatically defensible, compare 2 Pet. iii. 5, but, even in the translation of Alf., 'of purpose defraud you,' exegetically unsatisfactory, as it would seem to impute to the false teachers a frightful and indeed suicidal malice, which is neither justified by the context, nor in any way credible. They sought to gratify their vanity by gaining adherents, not their malice by compassing, even at their own hazard, their ruin. The καταβράβευσις was perhaps recklessly risked, but not maliciously designed beforehand. The translation of Wordsworth is much more plausible, 'by the exercise of his mere will,' but is perhaps scarcely so simple as that of the Greek commentators proposed above.

ἐν ταπεινοφρ.] '*in lowliness;*' element in which he desires to do it, the prep. ἐν not being so much instrumental (Mey.) as modal, πῶς, ἐν ταπειν.; ἢ πῶς, φυσιούμενος; δείκνυσι κενοδοξίας ὂν τὸ πᾶν, Chrys. It seems clear that ταπεινοφρ. is not here proper Christian humility (see notes on *Phil.* ii 3), but a false and perverted lowliness, which deemed God was so inaccessible that He could only be approached through the mediation of inferior beings; λέγοντες ὡς ἀόρατος ὁ τῶν ὅλων Θεός, ἀνέφικτός τε καὶ ἀκατάληπτος, καὶ προσήκει διὰ τῶν ἀγγέλων τὴν θείαν εὐμένειαν πραγματεύεσθαι, Theod.; see also Zonaras on Can. 35, *Conc. Laod.* (A. D. 363? see Giesel. *Kirchengesch.* Vol. 1. p. 396), where this heresy was expressly condemned; see ap. Bruns, *Concil.* Vol. 1. p. 37.

θρησκείᾳ τῶν ἀγγέλων] '*worship of the angels;*' not gen. *subjecti* (James i. 26), 'quæ angelos deceat,' Wolf, with reference to the ultra-human character of

μὴ ἑόρακεν ἐμβατεύων, εἰκῆ φυσιούμενος ὑπὸ τοῦ νοὸς τῆς σαρκὸς

devotion which the false teachers affected (see Noesselt, *Disput.*, Halæ, 1789), but gen. *objecti* (Wisdom xiv. 21, εἰδώλων θρησκεία, and examples in Krebs, *Obs.* p. 339), worship paid to angels; see Winer, *Gr.* § 20. 1, p. 168, and Suicer, *Thesaur.* Vol. 1. p. 44. Theodoret notices the prevalence of these practices in Phrygia and Pisidia, and the existence of εὐκτήρια to Michael in his own time: even in modern times the worship of the Archangel in that district has not become extinct; see Conyb. notes *in loc.*, and on angel-worship generally, the good note of Wordsw. on ver. 8. Whether this had originally any connection with Essene practices, cannot satisfactorily be determined, as the words of Joseph. *Bell. Jud.* II. 8. 7, are ambiguous; see Whiston *in loc.* That it was practised by Gnostic sects is attested by Tertull. *Præscr.* § 33, Iren. *Hær.* I. 31. 2, Epiph. *Hær.* XX. 2: see further references in Wolf, *in loc.* The evasive interpretation of Θρησκ., talem angelorum cultum qui Christum excludat,' Corn. a Lap., ' *impium* angelorum cultum,' Just , is wholly opposed to the simple and inclusive meaning of the word; compare Browne, *Articles*, Art. xxii. p. 539.

ἃ μὴ ἑόρ. ἐμβ.] '*intruding into the things which he hath not seen;*' μὴ not οὐ, as the dependence of the sentence on μηδεὶς ὑμᾶς καταβρ. leaves the objects naturally indeterminate, and under subjective aspects; see Winer, *Gr.* § 53. 3, p. 426; compare Exod. ix. 21, ὃς μὴ προσέσχε τῇ διανοίᾳ εἰς τὸ ῥῆμα, where the use of the μὴ somewhat similarly results from the indeterminate nature of the subject of the verb. The reading is doubtful. The negative is omitted by *Lachm.* [with ABD¹: 3 mss.; Clarom., Sang., Copt.; Tertull., Ambrst., al.], but rightly retained by *Tisch.* [with CD²D³EKL (FG οὐκ); nearly all mss.; Syr. (both),

Vulg., Boern., Goth., Æth. (Platt), al.; Origen, Chrys., Theod.], as, in the first place, external authority is distinctly preponderant, and secondly, the less usual subjective negative led to correction, and correction to omission. Mey. and Alf. defend the omission, adopting an interpretation ('an inhabitant of the realm of sight, not of faith,' Alf.) which is ingenious, but not very plausible or satisfactory; see Neander, *Planting*, Vol. I. p. 327 note (Bohn).

Ἐμβατεύειν, with an accus. *objecti*, has properly a *local* sense, *e. g.* πόλιν, Eurip. *Electr.* 595, ναόν, ib. *Rhes.* 225 (see further examples in Krebs, *Obs.* p. 3411), and thence by a very intelligible application an ethical reference, the accusative denoting the imaginary *realm* to which the action extended; comp. (but with a dative) Philo, *Plant. Noe*, § 19, Vol. I. p. 341 (ed. Mangey), ἐμβατεύοντες ἐπιστήμαις.   εἰκῆ φυσιούμ.] '*vainly puffed up;*' modal clause, more fully defining ἐμβατεύων. The false teachers were inflated with a sense of their superior knowledge, but it was εἰκῆ (Rom. xiii. 4, 1 Cor. xv. 2, Gal. iii. 4, iv. 11), bootlessly, without ground or reason. On the derivation [from εἴκειν, perhaps Sanscr. *vîcun*, ' recedere '] compare, but with caution, Benfey, *Wurzellex.* Vol. I. p. 349. De W., following Steig., joins εἰκῆ with the preceding clause; this is a possible, but not probable connection, as it would throw an emphasis on the adverb (comp. Gal. iii. 4) which really seems solely confined to ἃ μὴ ἑόρακεν.   ὑπὸ τοῦ νοὸς κ. τ. λ.] '*by the mind of his flesh.*' *i. e.* the higher spiritual principle in its materialized and corrupted form, the genitive probably being simply *possessive* (compare notes *on Eph.* iv. 23), and the contradictory form of the combination being chosen to depict the abnormal

αὐτοῦ. ¹⁹ καὶ οὐ κρατῶν τὴν κεφαλήν, ἐξ οὗ πᾶν τὸ σῶμα διὰ τῶν

condition: the flesh was, as it were endued with a νοῦς (instead of πνεῦμα), and this was the ruling principle; see Olsh. *Opusc.* p. 157, De [Wette?], *P. c. d.* iv. 5, p. 144, and for the normal meaning of νοῦς in the N. T., notes on 1 Tim. vi. 5. The σάρξ apparently stands in latent antithesis to the πνεῦμα (compare Chrys. ὑπὸ σαρκικῆς διανοίας οὐ πνευματικῆς), and seems here clearly to retain its ethical sense, 'his world-mind' (Müller, *Doctr. of Sin*, Vol. 1. p. 355, Clark), his devotion to things phenomenal and material; compare Tholuck, *Stud. u. Krit.* 1855, p. 492, Beck, *Seelenl.* II. 18, p. 59.

19. καὶ οὐ κρατῶν κ. τ. λ.] *'and not holding fast the head;'* οὐ not μή, the negation here becoming direct and objective, and designed to be specially distinct; compare Acts xvii. 27, 1 Cor. ix. 26, and see Winer, *Gr.* § 55. 5, p. 420, and especially Gayler, *Part. Neg.* p. 287 sq., where there is a good collection of examples. Κρατεῖν is here used with an accus. in the same sense as in Acts iii. 11, compare Cant. iii. 4, ἐκ ἄτησα αὐτόν, καὶ οὐκ ἀφῆκα αὐτόν, and Polyb. *Hist.* VIII. 20. 8, and denotes that individual adherence to Christ the Head which alone can constitute life and salvation; τί τοίνυν τὴν κεφαλὴν ἀφεὶς ἔχῃ τῶν μελῶν, Chrysost.; compare the possible physiological reference alluded to in notes on *Eph.* iv. 16.

ἐξ οὗ] *'from which;'* not neut., either in reference to τὸ κρατεῖν, Beng., or under an abstract and generalized aspect (Jelf, *Gr.* § 820. 1, Krüger, *Sprachl.* § 61. 7. 9), to κεφαλήν, Mey., Eadie, Eur.: as the exactly parallel passage Eph. iv. 15 so distinctly suggests, — masc. in ref. to Χριστοῦ, the subject obviously referred to in κεφαλήν. The assertion of Meyer that the reference is not to Christ in His personal relations cannot be substantiated. The followers were not distinctly the contrary. [...] it seem necessary, with [...] mentator, to refer ἐξ οὗ either to [...] triples of [...] iv. 19; the same [...] with a ζεῦγμα [...] some refer [...] notes on Gal. ii. 16.

πᾶν τὸ σῶμα] [...] surely not necessarily 'the body in its every part,' Alf.: between τὸ πᾶν σῶμα (a position of the art. very rarely found in the N. T.) and πᾶν τὸ σῶμα no distinction can safely be drawn. If πᾶς had occupied the position of a secondary predicate (comp. Matth. x. 30, Rom. xii. 4) there would have been some grounds for the distinction.

διὰ τῶν ἀφῶν καὶ συνδ.] *'by means of its joints and bands;'* media of the ἐπιχορήγησις and συμβίβασις. The ἀφαὶ and σύνδεσμοι, as the common article seems to hint, are the same in genus, the former referring, not to the nerves, Mey. (in opp. to Syr., Æth. (Platt), Copt., and all the best Vv.), but to the joints, the 'commissuræ' of the frame; comp. Andrewes, *Serm.* Vol. III p. 96: the latter to the varied ligatures of nerves and muscles and sinews by which the body is bound together. The distinctions adopted by Mey., al. — according to which the ἀφαὶ are specially associated with ἐπιχορ., and referred to Faith; the σύνδ. with συμβ., and referred to Love, — are plausible, but perhaps scarcely to be relied upon. As in Eph. l. c., the passage does not seem so much to involve special metaphors, as to state forcibly and cumulatively a general truth; πᾶσα ἡ ἐκκλησία, ἕως ἂν ἔχῃ τὴν κεφαλήν, αὔξει, Chrys.

ἐπιχορ. καὶ συμβ.] *'being supplied all knit together;'* passive and present: the action was due to communicated influen-

ἀφῶν καὶ συνδέσμων ἐπιχορηγούμενον καὶ συμβιβαζόμενον αὔξει τὴν αὔξησιν τοῦ Θεοῦ. ²⁰ Εἰ ἀπεθάνετε σὺν Χριστῷ ἀπὸ τῶν

ces, and the action was still going on. To give ἐπιχορ. a middle sense (Eadie), 'furnished with reciprocal aid,' seems highly unsatisfactory: the pass. of the simple form is by no means uncommon; see Polyb. *Hist.* III. 75. 3, VI. 15. 4, 3 Macc. vi. 40. The force of ἐπὶ is not *intensive* but *directive*, pointing to the accession of the supply, 'cui, quæ sunt ad incrementum necessaria, sufficiuntur,' Noesselt (see notes *on* Gal. iii. 5); but it does not seem improbable that both in χορηγ. and ἐπιχορ. some trace of the primary meaning, some reference to the *free* and *ample* nature of the supply, is still preserved, compare 2 Pet. i. 5, with ver. 8, and Winer *on* Gal. iii. 5, p. 76. On the meaning of συμβ. see notes *on Eph.* iv. 16 τὴν αὔξ. τοῦ Θεοῦ] '*with the increase of God*,' i. e. the increase which God supplies, τοῦ Θεοῦ being the gen. *auctoris* or *originis*, Hartung, *Casus*, 17, 23; compare 1 Cor. iii. 6, 7, al. To regard the expression as a periphrasis is wholly untenable; see Winer, *Gr.* § 36. 3, p. 221. The accus. αὔξησιν is that of the cognate subst. (not merely 'of reference,' Alf.), and serves to give force to, and develop the meaning of the verb; see Winer, *Gr.* § 32. 2, p. 200, Lobeck, *Paralip.* p. 501 sq., where this etymological figure is elaborately discussed.

20. εἰ ἀπεθ. κ. τ. λ.] '*If ye be dead with Christ;*' warning against false asceticism; see notes on 1 *Tim.* iv. 3, and compare generally Rothe, *Theol. Ethik*, § 878 sq., Vol. III. p. 120 sq. The apostle grounds his gentle expostulation on the acknowledged fact that they were sharers (by baptism, ver. 12) in the death of Christ; in ch. iii. 1, he bases his exhortation on their participation in His resurrection. The collective οὖν, and the art. before Χρ. inserted in *Rec.*, have the authority of *all* the MSS. against them, and are properly rejected by all modern editors. ἀπὸ τῶν στοιχ. τοῦ κόσμου] '*from the rudiments of the world,*' from ritualistic observances and all non-Christian rudiments which in any way resembled them;' see notes on ver. 8. The Law and all its ordinances were wiped out by the death of Christ (ver. 14), they who were united with Him in His death shared with Him all the blessings of the same immunity. There is no brachylogy (Huth.); Christ Himself ἀπέθανεν ἀπὸ νόμου, when He fulfilled all its claims and bore its curse. The 'constructio prægnans' ἀπεθ. ἀπὸ only occurs here in the N. T.; it is probably chosen in preference to the dat. (Rom. vii. 14, Gal. ii. 19), as expressing a more complete severance,—not only death to it, but separation and removal from it; comp. Winer, *Gr.* § 47, p. 331.

ὡς ζῶντες ἐν κόσμῳ] '*as if ye were living in the world,*' i. e. as if ye were in antithetical relations; 'ye are *dead* with *Christ;* why do ye *live* as if in a character exactly the reverse, as in a *non-Christian* realm, from all the rudiments of which ye are really *dead*?' δογματίζεσθε] '*do ye submit to ordinances;*' ὑπόκεισθε τοῖς στοιχείοις, Chrys., τῶν ταῦτα διδασκόντων ἀνέχεσθε, Theod.: *middle,*—certainly not *active*, 'decernitis,' Vulg., 'unrediþ,' Goth. (a meaning here not only inappropriate but lexically incorrect), and appy. not *passive*, 'placitis adstringimini,' Beza; (comp. Syr. ܡܶܬܕܰܢܺܝܢ [judicamini]; Coptic and Æth. paraphrase), as this, though perfectly lexically admissible (observe 2 Macc. x. 8, ἐδογμάτισαν παντὶ τῷ ἔθνει), seems somewhat less in harmony with the tone of this paragraph than the 'do-

στοιχείων τοῦ κόσμου, τί ὡς ζῶντες ἐν κόσμῳ δογματίζεσθε. εἰ Μὴ ἅψῃ, μηδὲ γεύσῃ, μηδὲ θίγῃς = (ἅ ἐστιν πάντα εἰς φθορὰν τῇ

veri vos *sinitis*' (Grot.) of the middle; ὅρα δὲ καὶ πῶς ἠρέμα αὐτοὺς διακωμωδεῖ, δογματίζεσθε εἰπών, Theophyl.: so Winer, *Gr.* § 39. 4, p. 295 (ed. 5), though apparently not in ed. 6. In either case the meaning is practically the same; in the tone of expostulation only is there a slight shade of difference.

21. μὴ ἅψῃ κ. τ. λ.] '*Handle not, nor taste, nor touch;*' examples of the δογματισμὸς to which they allowed themselves to submit; 'recitative have proferuntur ab apostolo,' Daven. With regard to the grammatical association, the coarser ἅψῃ at the beginning, the interposed γεύσῃ, and the more delicate θίγῃς at the end might seem to justify the distinction of Meyer that the first μηδὲ is more adjunctive (see notes on *Gal.* i. 12 and on *Eph.* iv. 27), the second more ascensive, if such a distinction in so regular a sequence as μὴ...μηδὲ...μηδὲ be not somewhat precarious; consider Rom. xiv. 21, and especially Luke xiv. 21, where there is a similar slight disturbance of the climax. The essential character of such quasi-adjunctive enumerations is that the items are not 'apte connexa, sed potius fortuito concursu accedentia,' Klotz, *Devar.* Vol. II. p. 707. With regard to the objects alluded to, the interposed γεύσῃ and the terms of ver. 23 seem certainly to suggest a reference of all three verbs to ceremonial distinctions in βρῶσις and πόσις (verse 16); see especially Xenoph. *Cyr.* I. 3. 5 (cited by Raph.), where all three verbs are used in reference to food, and for examples of ἅπτεσθαι, see Kypke, *Obs.* p. 324, Loesn. *Obs.* p. 372. More minute distinctions, *e. g.* ἅψῃ, women (Olsh.), corpses (Zanch.); θίγῃς, oil (Bochm.; compare Joseph. *Bell.* II. 8. 3), sacred vessels (Zanch.), al., seem very doubtful and uncertain. On the distinction

between the stronger ἅπτεσθαι and the weaker θιγγάνειν [ΘΙΓ, ΤΑΓ, tango, Pott, *Etym. Forsch.* Vol. I. p. 235], compare Trench, *Synon.* § 17.

22. ἅ ἐστιν κ. τ. λ.] '*which things, almost, seeing they are things, which are all to be destroyed in their consumption;*' parenthetical observation of the apostle on the essential character of the meats and drinks which the false teachers invested with such ceremonial characteristics; 'ratio ducitur ab ipsa natura et conditione harum rerum,' Davenant they were ordained to be consumed and enter into fresh physical combinations; compare Matthew xv. 17. To refer this either to the preceding commands, 'quod totum genus praeceptorum,' Aug., Sanderson (*Serm.* VII. ad Pop.), al., or to the preceding clause as the continued statement of the false teachers, Neand. (*Plant.*, Vol. I. p. 328), De W., al., seems to infringe on the meaning of ἀπόχρησις (see Mey.), and certainly gives a less forcible turn to the parenthesis. The objection urged by De Wette, and apparently felt in some measure by Chrysost. and Theoph.—that St Paul would thus be furnishing an argument against restrictions generally, even those sanctioned by divine authority, may be diluted by observing (*a*) that a very similar form of argument occurs in 1 Tim. iv. 3 sq., and (*b*) that these restrictions and observances are not condemned *per se*, but in relation to the new dispensation, in which all ceremonial distinctions were done away, and things remanded (so to say) to their primary conditions. εἰς φθορὰν] '*for destruction, decomposition,*' the prep. marking the destination, and φθορὰ having apparently a simply physical sense; compare Syriac ܡܚܒܠ ܠܚܘܒܠܐ [usus corrupti

ἀποχρήσει), κατὰ τὰ ἐντάλματα καὶ διδασκαλίας τῶν ἀνθρώπων; 23 ἅτινά ἐστιν λόγον μὲν ἔχοντα σοφίας ἐν ἐθελοθρησκείᾳ καὶ

bilis], and very distinctly Theod., εἰς κόπρον γὰρ ἅπαντα μεταβάλλεται, and Œcum. φθορᾷ γάρ, φησιν, ὑπόκειται ἐν τῷ ἀφεδρῶνι. τῇ ἀποχρήσει] '*in their consumption*,' in their being used completely up; οὐ σκοπεῖτε ὡς μόνιμον τούτων οὐδέν, Theod. The compound ἀποχρ. has here a somewhat similar meaning to διαχρ. (comp. Rost u. Palm, *Lex.* s. v.), the prep. ἀπὸ denoting 'non solum separari aliquid ab aliquo, sed ita removeri ut esse prorsus desinat,' Winer, *de Verb. Comp.* IV. p. 5 ; compare Plutarch, *Cæsar*, § 58, καινῆς ἔρωτα δόξης ἀποκεχρημένῳ τῇ παρούσῃ, and see Suicer, *Thesaur.* Vol. I. p. 489, where several pertinent examples are collected from the eccl. writers.
κατὰ τὰ ἐντάλμ.] '*according to the commandments and teachings of men;*' further definition and specification of the preceding δογματίζεσθε; they had died with Christ, they were united with a divine Deliverer, and yet were ready to submit to the ordinances and doctrines of conscience-enslaving men. The διδασκ., as the exceptional omission of the article (Winer, *Gram.* § 19. 3, p. 113) shows, belonged to the same general category as the ἐντάλμ., and are added probably by way of amplification; they were submitting to a δογματισμὸς not only in its preceptive, but even in its doctrinal, aspects; compare Mey. *in loc.* Alford presses τῶν ἀνθρ. as describing the authors 'as generally *human;*' this is doubtful; as ἐντάλμ. has the article, the principle of correlation requires that ἀνθρ. should have it also: see Middleton, *Gr. Art.* III. 3. 6.
23. ἅτινα] '*all which things*,' 'a set of things which;' in reference to the preceding ἐντάλμ. καὶ διδ., and specifying the *class* to which they belonged. On this force of ὅστις, see notes *on Gal.* iv.

24. The difference between ὅς and ὅστις is here very clearly marked; & (ver. 22) points to its antecedents under purely objective, ἅτινα under qualitative and generic aspects; see Krüger, *Sprachl.* § 51. 8. ἐστιν λόγ. ἔχοντα] '*do have the repute of wisdom*,' 'are enjoying the repute of wisdom,' the verb subst. being joined, — not with the concluding clause of the verse (Conyb., Eadie), but, as every rule of perspicuity suggests, with ἔχοντα, and serving to mark the regular normal, *prevailing* character of the ἔχειν; see Winer, *Gr.* § 45. 5, p. 311. The exact meaning of λόγον ἔχειν is somewhat doubtful, as λόγος in this combination admits of at least three different meanings; (α) '*speciem*,' σχῆμα, Theod., Auth. Ver., De W., compare Demosth. *Leptin.* p. 462, λόγον τινὰ ἔχον opp. to ψεῖδος ὂν φανείη, see Elsner. *Obs.* Vol. II. p. 265; (β) '*rationem*,' scil. 'grounds for being considered so,' Vulg., Clarom., and probably Syriac ܐܝܬ ; compare Polyb. *Hist.* XVII. 14. 5, δοκοῦν πανουργότατον εἶναι πολὺν ἔχει λόγον τοῦ φαυλότατον ὑπάρχειν, and other examples in Schweigh. *Lex. Polyb.* s. v.; (γ) '*famam*,' scil. 'has the repute of,' Mey., Alf., and perhaps Chrys., λόγον φησίν, οὐ δύναμιν· ἆρα οὐκ ἀλήθειαν; compare Herod. v 66, ὥσπερ δὴ λόγον ἔχει τὴν Πυθίην ἀναπεῖσαι (cited by Raph.). Of these, though in fact all ultimately coincide, (γ) is perhaps to be preferred ; '*τὰ λόγ. ἔχ.* sunt res ejusmodi quæ quidem vulgo sapientiæ nomen habent, sed a verâ sapientiâ absunt longissime,' Raphel, *Annot.* Vol. II. p. 535. μὲν has here no corresponding δέ, but serves to prepare the reader for a comparison (Klotz, *Devar.* Vol. II. p. 656) which is involved in the phrase λόγον ἔχειν (λόγον οὐ δύναμιν, Chrys.), and is substantiated by the

ταπεινοφροσύνῃ καὶ ἀφειδίᾳ σώματος, οὐκ ἐν τιμῇ τινι, πρὸς πλησμονὴν τῆς σαρκός.

context; see Winer, *Gr.* § 63. 2. e, p. 507, where other omissions of δέ are enumerated and carefully classified.

ἐν ἐθελοθρησκείᾳ] '*in self-imposed worship*,' — ἐν pointing to, not the instrument *by* which (Mey.), but as usually, the ethical domain *in* which, the λόγος σοφίας was acquired, or the substratum on which the τὸ ἔχειν κ. τ. λ. takes place; see Winer, *Gram.* § 48. a, p. 345. The word ἐθελοθρ. is apparently an ἅπ. λεγόμ.; but by a comparison with similar compounds ἐθελοδουλεία, ἐθελοκάκησις, κ. τ. λ. (see Rost u. Palm, *Lex.* Vol. 1. p. 778), and with the verb ἐθελοθρησκεῖν as explained by Suidas (ἰδίῳ θελήματι σέβειν τὸ δοκοῦν) may be clearly assumed to mean, '*an arbitrary self-imposed service*,' — which, as the similar association with ταπειν. in ver. 18 seems to suggest, was evinced in the θρησκεία τῶν ἀγγέλων.

ταπειν. καὶ ἀφειδ. σώμ.] '*lowliness and disregard, or unsparing treatment of the body*:' the two other perverted elements in which the λόγος σοφίας was acquired. On ταπειν., which here also obviously implies a *false*, perverted humility, see notes on verse 18. The ἀφειδ. σώμ. marks the false spirit of asceticism, the unsparing way (compare Diod. Sic. XIII. 60, ἀφειδεῖν σώματος), in which they practised bodily austerities, the σωματικὴ γυμνασία in which Jewish Theosophy so emulously indulged; compare notes on 1 *Tim.* iv 8. The omission of καὶ after ταπειν. and the reading ἀφειδίᾳ (B; [*Lachm.*]. Steig.) is strenuously supported by Hofmann, *Schriftb.* Vol. II. 2, p. 64, who takes it as an adjective (comp. ἀφειδέως, Apoll.-Rhod. III. 897), but seems both unsatisfactory and improbable.

οὐκ ἐν τιμῇ κ. τ. λ.] '*not in any real value serving (only) to the satisfying of the flesh.*' The explanations of this very obscure clause are exceedingly numerous. With regard to the first portion, two only seem to deserve consideration, (*a*) that of the Greek comm., according to which τιμῇ is understood to point antithetically to the preced. ἀφειδ., and to refer to the same gen. (οὐκ ἐν τιμῇ τῷ σώματι χρῶνται, Theophyl.), the clause οὐκ ἐν τιμῇ being regarded as a continuance on the *negative* side of what had previously been expressed in the positive; ἐθελ. κ. τ. λ. were the elements in which the λόγος σοφίας *was*, and τιμῇ τινι the element in which it *was not* acquired; (*b*) that adopted by Syr. and appy. *Æth.* (Platt), according to which τιμῇ approaches to the meaning of 'pretium,' and suggests that there was something which might be a true substratum for the τὸ ἔχειν κ. τ. λ., if properly chosen, — 'a reputation of wisdom evinced in ἐθελ. κ. τ. λ., not in any practices of true value and honor;' so Beza, Beng., al., and, with slight variations in detail, Huther, Meyer, and Neand. *Planting*, Vol. 1. p. 328 (Bohn). Of these, (*a*) has much to recommend it; as however it suggests, if not involves, either a very unsatisfactory meaning of πρὸς πλησμ., 'so that the natural wants of the body are satisfied' (Chrysost., al.), or a retrospective connection of the clause with ἐστιν, or, still less likely, with δογματίζεσθε (Alf.), it seems better to adopt (*b*), to which also the use of τις, almost, 'no value of any kind,' seems decidedly to lean. Πρὸς πλησμονήν, added somewhat closely, then defines gravely and conclusively the real object of all these perverted austerities, — 'the satisfying of the unspiritual element, the fleshly mind;' σαρκὸς having a retrospective reference to νοὸς τῆς σαρκὸς in ver. 18, and contrasting, with great point, the means pursued and the end really in view; they were *unsparing* (ἀφειδ.) with

Mind the things above, for your life is hidden with Christ: when he is manifested so shall ye be also.

III. Εἰ οὖν συνηγέρθητε τῷ Χριστῷ, τὰ ἄνω ζητεῖτε, οὗ ὁ Χριστός ἐστιν ἐν δεξιᾷ τοῦ Θεοῦ καθήμενος· ² τὰ ἄνω φρονεῖτε, μὴ τὰ ἐπὶ

the σῶμα, that they might *satisfy* (πρὸς πλησμ.) — the σάρξ. Syr. and Æth. insert ἀλλὰ before πρὸς πλησ.; this is not necessary; the exposure of the motive is rendered more forcible and emphatic by the omission of all connecting particles.

CHAPTER III. 1. εἰ οὖν] 'If then,' with retrospective reference to εἰ ἀπεθ., chap. ii. 20, οὖν being slightly inferential (resurrection with Christ is implied in death with Him), but still preserving its general meaning of 'continuation and retrospect,' Donalds. *Gr.* § 604. The εἰ is not problematical, but logical (Mey.), introducing in fact the first member of a conditional syllogism; compare Rom. v. 15, and see Fritz. *in loc.* In such cases, instead of diminishing, it really enhances the probability of the truth or justice of the supposition; compare notes *on Phil.* i. 22.   συνηγέρθητε] 'ye were raised together,' scil. in baptism; not merely in a moral sense (De W.), which would render the injunction that follows somewhat superfluous: εἰπών, ὅτι ἀπεθάνετε σὺν Χρ. διὰ τοῦ βαπτίσματος δηλαδή, καὶ κατὰ τὸ σιωπώμενον δοὺς νοεῖν ὅτι καὶ συνηγέρθητε (τὸ γὰρ βάπτισμα, ὥσπερ διὰ τῆς καταδύσεως θάνατον, οὕτω διὰ τῆς ἀναδύσεως τὴν ἀνάστασιν τύποι), νῦν εἰσάγει κ. τ. λ., Theoph.; compare Usteri, *Lehrb.* II. 1. 3, p. 220. On the force and deep reality of these expressions of mystical union with Christ, compare Reuss, *Théol. Chrét.* IV. 16, Vol. II. p. 164.   τὰ ἄνω] 'the things above:' all things pertaining to the πολίτευμα ἐν οὐρανοῖς, Phil. iii. 20, and to the Christian's true home, the ἡ ἄνω Ἰερουσαλήμ, Gal. iv. 26; the contrast being τὰ ἐπὶ τῆς γῆς, ver. 2; comp.

Pearson, *Creed*, Art. VI. Vol. I. p. 322 (ed. Burt.).   οὗ ὁ Χρ. κ.τ.λ.] '*where Christ is, sitting at the right hand of God;*' not exactly, 'where Christ sitteth,' Auth., as there are really two enunciations, 'Christ is there, and in all the glory of His regal and judiciary power;' οὐκ ἠρκέσθη δὲ τῷ ἄνω εἰπεῖν, οὐδέ, οὗ ὁ Χρ. ἐστίν· ἀλλὰ προσέθηκεν, ἐν δεξ. καθημ. τοῦ Θεοῦ, ἵνα πλέον τὶ ἀποστήσῃ τὸν νοῦν ἡμῶν ἀπὸ τῆς γῆς, Theophyl.; comp. Chrys. On the session of Christ at the right hand of God as implying indisturbance, dominion, and judicature, see Pearson, *Creed*, Art. VI. Vol. I. p. 328, and on the real and literal significance, Jackson. *Creed*, Book XI. 1. The student will find a good Sermon on this text by Andrewes, *Sermon* VIII. Vol. II. p 309–322 (A.-C. Libr.), and another by Farindon, *Sermon* XLII. Volume II. p. 359 (London, 1849).

2. τὰ ἄνω φρονεῖτε] '*mind the things above;*' expansion of the preceding command. φρονεῖν having a fuller meaning than ζητεῖν; they were not only *quaerere* but *sapere*. On the force of φρονεῖν, compare notes *on Phil.* iii. 15, Beveridge, *Serm.* CXXXVII. Vol. VI. p. 172 (A.-C. Libr.), and especially the able analysis of Andrewes, *Serm.* VIII. Vol. II. p. 315.   τὰ ἐπὶ τῆς γῆς] '*the things on the earth;*' all things, conditions, and interests that belong to the terrestrial; compare Phil. iii. 19, οἱ τὰ ἐπίγεια φρονοῦντες. There is here certainly not (*a*) any polemical allusion to the earthly rudiments of the false teachers (Theoph., Œcum.), for, as Meyer observes, the remaining portion of the Epistle is not anti-heretical but wholly moral and practical, — nor

τῆς γῆς. ³ ἀπεθάνετε γάρ, καὶ ἡ ζωὴ ὑμῶν κέκρυπται σὺν τῷ Χριστῷ ἐν τῷ Θεῷ· ⁴ ὅταν ὁ Χριστὸς φανερωθῇ, ἡ ζωὴ ἡμῶν, τότε καὶ ὑμεῖς σὺν αὐτῷ φανερωθήσεσθε ἐν δόξῃ.

(b) any special ethical allusion with ref. to ver. 5 (Estius), for the antithesis τὰ ἄνω obviously precludes all such limitation. The command is unrestricted and comprehensive, 'superna curate non terrestria;' see Calv. *in loc*, and the sound sermon by Beveridge, *Serm.* Vol. vi. p. 169 sq. (A. C. Libr.).

3. ἀπεθάνετε γάρ] 'For ye are dead,' Alf., Wordsw., as the reference seems still to the past *act*, ch. 20. Conyb. urges that the associated κέκρυπται shows that the aor. is here used for a perfect. Surely this is inexact; the aor. may, and apparently does, point to the *act*, the perfect to the *state* which ensued thereon and still continues. The nature of θνήσκω, however, is such as to preclude any rigorous translation on either side.   ἡ ζωὴ ὑμῶν] 'your life,' — which succeeded after the ἀπεθάνετε; your real and true life, — not merely your 'resurrection life,' Alf. (τῆς ἡμετέρας ἀναστάσεως τὸ μυστήριον, Theod.), but, with the tinge of ethical meaning which the word ζωή, from its significant antithesis to θάνατος, always seems to involve (compare Reuss, *Théol. Chrét.* IV. 22, Vol. II. p. 252), 'your inward and heavenly life,' of which Christ is the essence, and, so to speak, impersonation (ver. 4), and with whom it will at last receive all its highest developments, expansions, and realizations; comp. notes on 1 *Tim* iv. 8. On the meaning of ζωή, see the good treatise of Olshausen, *Opusc.* Art. VIII. p 187 sq., and on its distinction from βίος, Trench, *Synon.* § 27.
κέκρυπται σὺν τῷ Χρ.] 'hath been (and is) hidden with Christ;' its glory and highest characteristics are concealed from view, — not merely 'laid up,' Alford, but shrouded in the depths of inward experiences and the mystery of its union with the life of Christ. When He is revealed, then the life of which He is the source and element will be revealed in all its proportions and all its blessed characteristics: the manifestation which is now at best only partial and subjective, will then be objective and complete; compare the thoughtful remarks of Delitzsch, *Bibl. Psych.* v. 3, p. 298.   ἐν τῷ Θεῷ] 'in God;' He is the element and sphere in which the ζωή is concealed: in Him, as φῶς οἰκῶν ἀπρόσιτον (1 Tim. vi 6), as the Father in whom is the Eternal Son (John i. 18, xvii. 21), and with whom He forever reigns (ver. 4), the life of which the Son is the essence lies shrouded and concealed. Considered under its *inherent* relations our ζωή is concealed ἐν Θεῷ; considered under its *otherent* relations it is concealed σὺν Χριστῷ; compare Meyer *in loc.*, whose interpretation of ζωή ('das ewige Leben') is, however, narrow and unsatisfactory.

4. φανερωθῇ] 'shall be manifested;' scil. at His second coming, when He shall be seen as He is, and when His present concealment shall cease; οὔτε γὰρ ἐφ' ὑμῶν ὁρᾶται, καὶ ὑπὸ τῶν ἀπίστων παντελῶς ἀγνοεῖται, Theod.: compare 2 Peter iii. 4.   ἡ ζωὴ ἡμῶν] 'our *Life*,' almost, 'being our Life,' the 'praedicatio,' as Daven. acutely observes, being 'causalis non essentialis.' Christ is here termed ἡ ζωὴ ἡμῶν, not, however, as being merely the author of it (Daven.), or the cause of it (Corn. a Lap.), much less 'in the character of it' (Eadie), but as being — our Life *itself*, the essence and the impersonation of it; compare Gal. ii. 20, Phil. i. 21. Thus Christ is termed ἡ ἐλπὶς ἡμῶν, 1 Tim. i. 1; comp

Mortify your members and the evil principles in which ye once walked: put off the old man, and put on the new, in which all are one in Christ.

⁵ Νεκρώσατε οὖν τὰ μέλη ὑμῶν τὰ ἐπὶ τῆς γῆς, πορνείαν, ἀκαθαρσίαν, πάθος, ἐπιθυμίαν

5. τὰ μέλη ὑμῶν] So *Rec.*, *Lachm.*, with AC¹DEFGKL; nearly all mss.; Vulg., Clarom., Syr. (both), Copt., Æth. (Pol. and Platt), Goth., al.; Chrys., Theod., al. (*Meyer, De Wette*). The pronoun is omitted by *Tisch.* (ed. 2, but *not* ed. 7), *Alf.*, with BC¹; 17. 67**. 71; Clem. (1), Orig. (5), al. The great preponderance of MSS., and the accordant testimony of so many Vv. seem to render this otherwise not improbable omission here very doubtful.

Col. i. 27), ἡ εἰρήνη ἡμῶν, Eph. ii. 14, where see notes. The reading is very doubtful: ἡμῶν is adopted by *Rec.*, *Lachm.*, and *Tisch.* with BD²D³E¹KL; great majority of mss.; Syr. (both), al.; Or., Œcum., al. On the other hand, ὑμῶν is supported by CD¹E¹FG; 5 mss.; Vulg., Clarom., Copt. [quoted by *Tisch.* and Alf. for the other reading], Goth., Æth. (Pol. and Platt); many Latin and Greek Ff. As ἡμῶν is far less easy to account for than ὑμῶν, which might have come from ver. 3 or from the ὑμεῖς in the present verse, critical principles seem to decide for the reading of the text.

καὶ ὑμεῖς] '*ye also;*' ye Colossian converts, as well as all other true Christians. The more verbally exact opposition would have been 'your hidden life' (comp. Fell); but this the apostle perhaps designedly neglects, to prevent ζωή being applied, as it has been applied, merely to the resurrection life. Alford urges this clause as fixing that meaning to ζωή; but surely the avoidance of the regular antithesis seems to *hint* the very reverse; ὑμεῖς φανερ. is the natural sequel of your inward and heavenly life, and is its true development.

ἐν δόξῃ] '*in glory;*' compare Rom. viii. 17, εἴπερ συμπάσχομεν ἵνα καὶ συνδοξασθῶμεν. The δόξα will be the issue, development, and crown of the hidden life, and will be displayed both in the material (1 Cor. xv. 43) and immaterial portions of our composite nature: 'hu-

jus æternæ vitæ promissa gloria sita est in duplici stola; in stola animæ et stola corporis,' Daven. The conjunction of body and soul, soul and spirit, will then be complete, harmonious, and indissoluble; ζωή will become ἡ ὄντως ζωή, and will reflect the glories of Him who is its element and essence: comp. Olsh. *Opusc.* p. 195 sq.

5. νεκρώσατε οὖν] '*Make dead then:*' 'as you died, and your true life is hidden with Christ, and hereafter to be developed in glory, act conformably to it, — let nothing live inimical to such a state, kill at once (aor.) the organs and media of a merely earthly life.' Οὖν is thus, as commonly, retrospective and collective ('ad ea quæ antea revera posita lectorem revocat,' Klotz, *Devar.* Vol. II. p. 719), serving to enhance the pertinent reference of νεκρώσατε to the ἀπεθάνετε and ἡ ζωὴ ὑμῶν which have preceded. τὰ μέλη ὑμῶν] '*your members,*' the portions of your bodily organization (compare Rom. vii. 5) *quâ* the instruments and media of sinfulness and lusts; compare with respect to the precept, Rom. viii. 13, Gal. v. 24, and with respect to the image, and form of expression, Matth. v. 29, 30. These are more specifically defined as τὰ ἐπὶ τῆς γῆς (compare ver. 2), as defining the sphere of their activities ('ubi suum habent pabulum,' Beng.), and as justifying the preceding command.

πορνείαν καὶ ἀκαθαρσίαν] '*for-

κακήν, καὶ τὴν πλεονεξίαν ἥτις ἐστὶν εἰδωλολατρεία, ⁶ δι' ἃ

6 ἐπὶ τοὺς υἱοὺς ἀπειθ.] *Tisch.* [*Lachm*], and *Alf.* omit these words with B; Sahid., Æth. (Pol., but not Platt); Clem. (1), Ambro iast. (text). On the one hand, it is certainly possible that they may have been inserted from the parallel passage, Eph. vi. 6; still on the other, the overwhelming weight of external evidence, and the probability, that in two Epistles where so much is alike, even individual expressions might be repeated, seem to render the omission on such evidence more than doubtful.

nication and uncleanness;' specific and generic products of the τὰ ἐπὶ τῆς γῆς μέλη on the side of lust and carnality; compare Eph. v. 3. There is no need to supply mentally νεκρώσατε (Fritz. *Rom.* Vol. 1. p. 379), or to introduce paraphrastically a prep., 'a scortatione,' Æth.; the four accusatives stand in an appositional relation to τὰ μέλη κ. τ. λ., as denoting their evil products and operations; see Winer, *Gr.* § 59. 8, p. 470, and compare Matth. *Gr.* § 432. 3.

πάθος ἐπιθυμ. κακήν] '*lustfulness, evil concupiscence;*' further and more generic manifestation. It does not seem proper, on the one hand, to extend πάθος to 'motus vitiosos, quales sunt ἔχθραι, ἔρεις, ζῆλοι, κ. τ. λ.,' Grot., or, on the other, to limit it to more frightful exhibitions (Rom. i. 26, 27): it points rather, as the evolution of thought seems to require, to 'the disposition toward lust,' Olsh., the 'morbum libidinis,' Beng., — in a word, not merely to lust, but to lustfulness; πάθος ἡ λύσσα τοῦ σώματος, καὶ ὥσπερ πυρετός, ἢ τραῦμα, ἢ ἄλλη νόσος, Theoph. The last, ἐπιθυμία κακή, is still more inclusive and generic; ἰδοὺ γε εἰκὼς τὸ πᾶν εἶπε, Chrys. τὴν πλεονεξίαν] '*Covetousness,*' — with the article, as the notorious form of sin ('die bekannte, hauptsächlich vermeidende Unsittlichkeit,' Winer, *Gr.* § 18. 8, p. 106), that ever preserves so frightful an alliance with the sins of the flesh. There seems no reason whatever to depart from the proper sense of the word; it is neither specially 'base gains derived from uncleanness' (comp. Storr, Flatt, al.), nor generically, '*insatiabil* m cupilitatem voluptatum turpium' E. ius, 'the whole longing of the creature,' Trench (*S. v.* or. § 24. — a very doubtful expansion), but simply 'covetousness,' 'inexplebil m appetitum animi quarens *divitias,*' Daven. (compare Theod., Theoph.), a sin that especially depends on the τὰ ἐπὶ τῆς γῆς ('max me effigit ad terram,' Beng.), and makes, not sensational cravings *per se*, but the *means* of gratifying them, the objects of its interest; see especially Müller, *Doctr. of Sin*, I. 3. 2, Vol. 1 p. 169 (Clark), and notes on *Ephes.* iv. 20.

ἥτις ἐστὶν εἰδωλ.] '*the which is, seeing it is, idolatry;*' explanatory force of ὅστις, see notes on *Gal.* iv. 24. The remark of Theod. is very pertinent, ἐπειδὴ τὸν μαμμωνᾶ κύριον ὁ σωτὴρ προσηγόρευσε διδάσκων, ὡς ὁ τῇ πάσῃ τῆς πλεονεξίας δουλεύων ὡς θεὸν τὸν πλοῦτον τιμᾷ. The very improbable reference of ἥτις to μέλη (Harl. on *Eph.* v. 5), or to all that precedes (Heinr.), is rightly rejected by Winer. *Gr.* § 24. 3, p. 150.

6. δι' ἃ] '*on account of which sins;*' clearly not δι' ἅ, sc. μέλη (Bähr), but in reference to 'peccata praecedentia alia, quae flagitia,' Grot.; compare notes on *Eph.* v. 6. The reading is doubtful: δ is found in CDEFG; Claroman., S. ng.: ἃ in ABC-D-DEKL; al., and apparently rightly adopted by Lachmann and Tisch. after *Rec.* Though an emendation is not improbable, the preponderance of external evidence seems too distinct to be

ἔρχεται ἡ ὀργὴ τοῦ Θεοῦ ἐπὶ τοὺς υἱοὺς τῆς ἀπειθείας· ⁷ ἐν οἷς καὶ ὑμεῖς περιεπατήσατέ ποτε, ὅτε ἐζῆτε ἐν τούτοις· ⁸ νυνὶ δὲ

safely reversed. ἔρχεται] 'doth come;' emphatic, both position and tense. The present hints at the enduring principles of the moral government of God; see notes on *Eph.* v. 5.

ἡ ὀργὴ τοῦ Θεοῦ] Not only here, but hereafter; καὶ ἡ μέλλουσα ὀργὴ καὶ ἡ ἐν τῷ νῦν αἰῶνι πολλάκις καταλαμβάνουσι τοὺς τοιούτους Theoph. Meyer rejects this, but without sufficient reason; see notes on *Eph.* v. 6.

τοὺς υἱοὺς τῆς ἀπειθ.] 'the sons of disobedience;' those who reject and disobey the principles and practice of the Gospel; see notes on *Eph.* v. 6, where the same expression occurs in the same combination, and on the force of the Hebraistic circumlocution, notes on *ib.* ii. 2.

7. ἐν οἷς] 'among whom,' scil. υἱοῖς τῆς ἀπειθείας,—not neuter 'in which,' in reference to the foregoing vices: see Eph. ii. 3, ἐν οἷς καὶ ἡμεῖς ἀνεστράφημεν, which, with the present (longer) reading, seems to leave no room for doubt. The objection of Olsh. that the Colossians were *still* walking among the υἱοῖς τῆς ἀπειθ. as converts, seems easily answered by observing that περιπατεῖν, St. Paul's favorite verb of moral motion (only here and 2 Thess. iii. 11 with persons), seems always used by him to denote an actual participation in a course or manner of life; contrast John xi. 54.

ἐζῆτε ἐν τούτοις] 'ye were *living* in these sins,' 'these things were the sphere of your existence and activities;' the verb ἐζῆτε referring to the preceding ἀπειθ. (ver. 3), and its tense portraying the then continuing state; compare Jelf, *Gr.* § 401. 3. Huther and others regard τούτοις as masc.: this does not seem satisfactory, as ὅτε ἐζ. would be but a weak and tautologous explanation of the preceding ἐν οἷς περιεπ. ποτε, and as ζῆν ἐν (except in its deeper meanings, e. g.

ζῆν ἐν Χρ. κ. τ. λ., Rom. vi. 11, Gal. ii. 20) is always used by St. Paul with *things*; compare Rom. vi. 2, Gal. ii. 20, Phil. i. 22, Col. ii. 20. See the examples collected by Kypke (*Obs.* Vol. II. p. 327), ζῆν ἐν 'Οδυσσείᾳ, ἐν φροντίσιν, ἐν λόγοις, ἐν ἀρετῇ, ἐν φιλοσοφίᾳ κ. τ. λ., in all of which the non-personal substantives similarly define the sphere to which the activities of life were confined; see also examples in Wetst. *in loc.* The reading of *Rec.* αὐτοῖς [D³E²FGKL] has insufficient critical support.

8. νυνὶ δὲ ἀπόθεσθε] 'but NOW lay aside;' emphatic exhortation suggested by their present state, the forcible νυνὶ (Hartung, *Partik.* Vol. II. 24) standing in sharp opposition to the preceding τότε, ὅτε. On the figurative ἀπόθεσθε, opp. to ἐνδύσασθε, compare notes on *Eph.* iv. 22. The translation of Eadie, 'ye too have put off,' perhaps suggested by a misunderstanding of Auth., can only be regarded as an oversight; such mistakes, however, seriously weaken our confidence in this otherwise useful writer as a sound grammatical expositor.

καὶ ὑμεῖς] '*ye also*,' ye as well as other Christians; the καὶ putting them here in *contrast* with their fellow-converts, as in ver. 7 with their fellow-heathens; comp. notes on *Phil.* iv. 12.

τὰ πάντα] '*the whole of them:*' all previously (τούτοις, ver. 7), and hereafter to be mentioned. Winer (*Gr.* § 18. 1, p. 98) refers τὰ πάντα, with an intensive force, only to what had been already adduced: the enumeration which follows seems to require a more comprehensive and prospective reference; see Meyer *in loc.* So similarly Syr., Goth. (Æth. omits), 'hæc omnia' (compare Theod.), except that this is perhaps too exclusively prospective. There is no full stop after this word in *Tisch.*, as is

ἀπόθεσθε καὶ ὑμεῖς τὰ πάντα, ὀργήν, θυμόν, κακίαν, βλασφημίαν, αἰσχρολογίαν, ἐκ τοῦ στόματος ὑμῶν, ⁹ μὴ ψεύδεσθε εἰς ἀλλήλους,

asserted by Alf., nor apparently in any edition. κακίαν] 'malice,' 'badness of heart,' the evil habit of the mind as contrasted with πονηρία, the more definite manifestation of it; comp. Eph. iv. 31, and Trench, Syn. § 11. On the distinction between the preceding ὀργή (the more settled state) and θυμός (the more eruptive and temporary), see notes on Eph. iv. 31, and Trench, Syn. § 37; add also (Eum., who correctly remarks, ἔστι γὰρ θυμὸς .... ἔξαψίς τις καὶ ἀναθύμιασις ὀξεῖα τοῦ πάθους, ὀργὴ δὲ ἔμμονος λύπη. βλασφημίαν may be either against God or against men, according to the context (see notes on 1 Tim. i. 13; here the associated vices seem to limit the reference to the latter; τὰς λοιδορίας οὕτω λέγει, Theoph.; see notes on the very similar passage, Eph. iv. 31. αἰσχρολογίαν] 'coarse (reproachful) speaking.' It is somewhat doubtful whether we are to adopt (a) the more limited meaning 'turpiloquium,' Claroman., sim. Vulg., Syr., 'unglattiaurdein,' Goth., turpi tudo,' Æthiop.: or (b) the more general, 'foul-mouthed abusiveness,' Trench (comp. Copt., where, however, it seems confounded with μωρολογία). 'schandbares Reden,' Meyer. As αἰσχρ. is an ἅπ. λεγόμ. in N. T., and does not occur in LXX., and as both interpretations have good lexical authority,— the former, Xenoph. Lacd. v. 6, Poll. Onomast. iv. 106, Clem.-Alex. Pæd. ii. 6, comp. Suicer, Thesaur. s. v. Vol. i. p. 136; Raphel, Annot. Vol. ii. p. 535; the latter, Polyb. Hist. viii. 13. 8, and xxxi. 10. 4, where it is associated with λοιδορία,—the context alone must decide. As this appy. refers mainly to sins against a neighbor (compare ver. 9), the balance seems in favor of (b), according to which αἰσχρ. will be an extension of βλασφ.,

and will imply all coarse and foulmouthed language, whether in a man or otherwise. ἐκ τοῦ στόματος is not to be referred solely to αἰσχρολ. (Lthr.), but to the two preceding substantives, ἀπωθέσθε being mentally supplied. It seems doubtful whether the edition marks especially to part ii βυθοποιεῖ γὰρ τὸ εἰς βλασφημίαν θεοῦ πεποιημένον στόμα. (Ecum., comp. Chrys.), or the use (Thomas. (Mey.) of the actions which are here described: the latter is perhaps slightly the most probable; comp. James iii. 10.

9. μὴ ψεύδεσθε] 'do not lie;' pres., οὐ; to indulge in the practice. The addition εἰς ἀλλήλους specifies the objects toward whom the practice was forbidden (compare Winer, Gram. § 49. a, p. 353), and stamps it as a social wrong. On the frightful character of untruthfulness, and its evolution from selfishness and lust, see especially Müller, Doctr. of Sin, i. 1. 3. 2, Vol. i. p. 171 sq. (Clark). It seems best with Lachm., Tisch., and apparently most modern editors, to place only a comma between ver. 8 and 9. ἀπεκδυσάμενοι] 'seeing ye have put off,' Auth.; causal participle, giving the reason for the precept, and in point of time being prior to (Meyer), not contemporaneous with ('exspoliantes,' Vulg., Clarom.), the preceding aor. infin. ἀπόθεσθε. Such a reference is not superfluous or inappropriate (De W.); the part. serves suitably to remind them that the condition into which they had now entered rendered a selfish and untruthful life a self-contradiction. To consider ἀπεκδ. as beginning a new period, interrupted and resumed in ver. 12, as Hofmann, Skrift, Vol. ii. 2, p. 268, seems very harsh and improbable. On the double compound ἀπεκδ. see notes on ch. ii. 11. τὸν παλαιὸν

ἀπεκδυσάμενοι τὸν παλαιὸν ἄνθρωπον σὺν ταῖς πράξεσιν αὐτοῦ,
¹⁰ καὶ ἐνδυσάμενοι τὸν νέον τὸν ἀνακαινούμενον εἰς ἐπίγνωσιν κατ'

ἄνθρ.] '*the old man;*' not merely τὴν προτέραν πολιτείαν, Theod., but, with a more individualizing reference, our former unconverted self, our state before regeneration; see notes on *Eph.* iv. 22. Davenant (comp. Calv) refers the term to the '*insita naturæ nostræ corruptio,*' — a special and polemical reference, to which the context, which seems to point simply to their ante-Christian, as contrasted with their present, state (τότε, νυνί), seems to yield no support.
σὺν ταῖς πρ.] '*with his deeds;*' slightly explanatory, marking the practical character of the developments of the παλαιὸς ἄνθρωπος; comp. Gal. v. 24.

10. καὶ ἐνδ. τὸν νέον] '*and have put on the new man;*' closely connected with the preceding clause, and presenting, on the *positive* side, the act succeeding to the ἀπεκδ. on the negative. The νέος ἄνθρ. stands in contrast with the παλαιὸς as specifying the newly-entered and *fresh* state of spiritual conditions after conversion and regeneration. In Eph. iv. 23 the term is καινός, as marking rather the *new* state in respect of quality; compare Tittmann, *Synon.* I. p. 59, notes on *Eph.* iii. 16, iv. 24. It is not improbable that the reference in the two passages is slightly different, there, (Eph.) as the hortatory tone suggests, the reference is primarily to *renovation;* here, as the argumentative allusion seems to imply, primarily to *regeneration*, yet in neither, as the noticeable combinations (ἀνανεοῦσθαι — καινὸν ἄνθρ., νέον ἄνθρ. — τὸν ἀνακαιν.) further suggest, is the reference exclusive. On the distinction, see Waterland, *Regen.* Vol. IV. p. 433 sq., compare Trench, *Synon.* § 18.

τὸν ἀνακαιν.] '*who is being renewed;*' characteristic, not merely of ἀνθρωπον (De W.), but of the νέον ἄνθρωπον: as the prominence of the epithet clearly

requires. This process of ἀνακαίνωσις, of which the *causa instrumentalis* and agent ('Tit. iii. 5, compare Eph. iv. 23) is the Holy Spirit, is represented as continually going on; compare 2 Cor. iv. 16, ὁ ἔσωθεν (ἄνθρ.) ἀνακαινοῦται ἡμέρᾳ καὶ ἡμέρᾳ. The prep ἀνά appears to mark restoration to a former, not necessarily a primal, state; see Winer, *de Verb. Comp.* III. p. 10, compare notes *on Eph.* iv. 23. εἰς ἐπίγνωσιν] '*unto complete knowledge,*' apparently of God, and the mystery of redemption (τοῦ Θεοῦ καὶ τῶν θείων, Theoph); compare ch. i. 9, ii. 2, Ephes. i 17; 'in eo quod ait *qui renov. in agnitionem*, demonstrabat quoniam ipse ille qui ignorantiæ erat homo, id est, ignorans Deum, per (?) eam quæ in eum est agnitionem renovatur,' Iren. *Hær.* v. 12. On the full meaning of ἐπίγν. ('*accurata* cognitio'), see notes on *Eph. l. c.*, and compare on *Col.* ii. 2. This was the object towards which the ἀνακαιν. tended (not the sphere *in* which, Auth., Copt.), — the result which it was designed to attain; comp. Eph. iv. 13. κατ' εἰκόνα κ. τ. λ.] '*after the image of Him that created him.*' By a comparison with the similar and suggestive passage, Eph. iv. 23, there can scarcely be a doubt that this clause is to be connected with ἀνακαιν., not with ἐπίγνωσιν (Meyer, comp. Hofm , *Schriftb.* Vol. I. p. 252), — a construction grammat. admissible (see Win. *Gr.* § 20. 4, p. 126), but not exegetically satisfactory. Κατὰ will thus point ο the '*norma*' or model (notes on *Gal.* iv. 28), and the εἰκὼν τοῦ κτίσ. to the image of God (Theod.), not of Christ (Chrysost.; compare Müller, *Doctr. of Sin*, Vol. II. p. 392, Clark), in which the first man was created, which was lost by sin, but 'is to be restored again by a real though not substantial change,' Pearson, *Creed*,

εἰκόνα τοῦ κτίσαντος αὐτόν· 11 ὅπου οὐκ ἔνι Ἕλλην καὶ Ἰουδαῖος, περιτομὴ καὶ ἀκροβυστία, βάρβαρος, Σκύθης, δοῦλος, ἐλεύθερος, ἀλλὰ τὰ πάντα καὶ ἐν πᾶσιν Χριστός. 12 Ἐνδύσασθε οὖν, ὡς ἐκλεκτοὶ τοῦ Θεοῦ

Put on mercy, by forgiving and loving, and let the peace of God rule in you. Sing aloud, and in your hearts, to God, and give thanks.

Art. 11. Vol. 1. p. 149 (ed. Burt.); 'in. eo quod di it *secundum inter. eo edit is* recapitulationem manifestav't ejus hominis qui in initio secundum Imaginem factus est Dei,' Iren. *Hær.* v. 12, comp. Delitzsch, *Bibl. Psychol.* 11. 2, p. 51, who conceives that with the spiritual, a physical decoration of the image was also included. To assert that a reference to a restoration of the image of God in the first creation involves 'an idea foreign to Scripture' (Alf., comp. Müller, *Doctr. of Sin*, Vol. 11. p. 395, Clark), seems somewhat sweeping; see notes on *Eph.* iv. 24, and the passages collected from the early eccl writers in Bull, *Engl. Works*, Disc. v. p. 478 sq., and especially p. 492. On the meaning of εἰκών, see Trench, *Synon.* 15. αὐτόν] Scil. νέον ἄνδρ.; not merely ἄνδρ. (De W.), which seems opposed to the logical and grammatical connection, and is not required by the preceding interpretation. Whether God be defined as ὁ κτίσας in reference to the *first*, or to the *second* creation (ἀνάκτισις, Pearson, *Creed*, Vol. 11. p. 80, Burt.), does not alter the doctrinal truth involved in the words — 'quod perdidimus in Adam, id est secundum imaginem et similitudinem esse Dei, hoc in Christo Jesu recipimus,' Irenæus, *Hær.* 111. 18.

11. ὅπου] '*where;*' 'quâ in re' ('apud quem,' Æth.), scil. in which condition of ἀπέκδυσις of the old, and ἔνδυσις of the new man; compare Xenophon, *Mem.* 111. 5. 1, and Kühner, *in loc.*, cited (but incorrectly) by Meyer. οὐκ ἔνι] '*there is not;*' see notes on *Gal.* iii. 28, where the grammatical character of this contraction is briefly discussed. Ἕλλην καὶ Ἰουδ] '*Greek and Jew;*' a thr
 involving national distinctions, followed by a second (περιτ. καὶ ἀκρ.) involving ritual characteristics, and by a climax (βάρβ., Σκύθ.) in reference to habits and civilization ('Scythas barbaris barbariores,' Beng., βραχὺ τῶν Σαρμιῶν διαφέροντες, Joseph. *contr. Ap.* 11. 37; see examples in Wetst. *in loc.*), and lastly, by a third unconnected antithesis (δοῦλος, ἐλεύθ.) involving social relations. Between the last two *Lachm.* inserts καὶ, with ADE FG; 3 mss.; Vulg., Clarom., al.: the external authority is fair, but the probability of a conformation to the preceding very great. The addition of καὶ by DEFG after βάρβ. seems a clear interpolation, thus rendering the testimony of the same MSS. of doubtful value in the next pair. To insert 'and' in translation (Scholef. *Hints*, p. 112) seems quite unnecessary. ἀλλὰ τὰ πάντα κ. τ. λ.] '*i.e.* Christ is all and in all;' similar in meaning to πάντες ὑμεῖς εἷς ἐστε ἐν Χ. Ἰησ., Galat. iii. 28, but with a somewhat more comprehensive enunciation: '*Christ*' (place 1 with emphasis at the end, Jelf, *Gram.* § 902, 2) is the aggregation of all things, distinctions, prerogatives, blessings, and moreover is in all, dwelling in all, and so uniting all in the common element of Himself; πάντα ὑμῖν ὁ Χ, ιστὸς ἔσται, καὶ ἀξίωμα καὶ γένος, καὶ ἐν πᾶσιν ὑμῖν αὐτός, Chrys. For examples of εἶναι τὰ πάντα or πάντα [as AC, and many mss. in this place] in ref. to an individual, see the very large collection in Wetstein on 1 *Cor.* xv. 28.

12. ἐνδύσασθε οὖν] '*Put on then;*'

ἅγιοι καὶ ἠγαπημένοι, σπλάγχνα οἰκτιρμοῦ, χρηστότητα, ταπεινοφροσύνην, πραΰτητα, μακροθυμίαν, 13 ἀνεχόμενοι ἀλλήλων καὶ

exhortation naturally following from the fact that the νέος ἄνθρωπος which involved all the above blessings had been put on; 'as you have put on the new man, put on all its characteristic qualities.' The οὖν has thus appy. more of its *reflexive* force; 'it takes up what has been said and continues it,' Donalds. *Cratyl.* § 192; compare notes *on Phil.* ii. 1. ὥς ἐκλ. τοῦ Θεοῦ] '*as chosen ones of God;*' as being men who enjoy and value so great and so singular a blessing as to have been called out of heathen darkness to the knowledge of Christ; compare Tit. i. 1. Meyer acutely calls attention to the fact that ὡς ἐκλεκτοὶ echoes the preceding argumentative ἀπεκδυσ., and thus stands in logical and exegetical connection with what precedes. It is doubtful whether ἅγιοι καὶ ἠγαπημ. are to be regarded as used substantively ('ut sancti et dilecti,' Æth., —Pol., but not Platt), and as co-ordinate to, or as simple predicates to, the preceding ἐκλεκτοὶ τοῦ Θεοῦ. The pure substantival use of the latter expression in St. Paul's Epistles (Rom. viii. 33, Tit. i. 1, compare 2 Tim. ii. 10), coupled with the fact that the force of the exhortation rests on their character as ἐκλεκτοί, not as being ἅγιοι καὶ ἠγαπ., renders the latter connection most plausible; so Beng., and after him Mey., and the majority of modern editors and expositors. Chrysost. and Theoph. *appear* to have regarded them as three attributes; so Daven., Huther, al.

σπλάγχνα οἰκτιρμοῦ] '*bowels of mercy;*' bowels which are characterized by, are the seat of mercy, the gen. being that of the 'predominating quality,' and probably falling under the general head of the genitive *possessivus*; see Scheuerl. *Synt.* § 16. 3, p. 115, and compare Luke i. 78, σπλάγχνα ἐλέους. The expression is probably a little more emphatic than the simple οἰκτιρμούς (Heb. x. 28), or the more common ἔλεος: οὐκ εἶπεν ἔλεον, ἀλλ' ἐμφαντικώτερον διὰ τῶν δύο, Chrys. For exx. of the tropical use of σπλάγχνα, which, however, is here not necessarily required (compare Meyer), see Philippians i. 18, ii. 1, and notes *in loce*. The plur. οἰκτιρμῶν (*Rec.*) has only the support of K; mss.; Theod., al., and is rightly rejected by Lachm. and Tisch.

χρηστότητα] '*kindness;*' 'benevolence and sweetness of disposition as shown in intercourse with one another;' joined in Tit. iii. 4 with φιλανθρωπία, and in Rom. xi. 22 opp. to ἀποτομία; see notes *on Gal.* v. 22.

ταπεινοφροσ.] '*lowliness (of mind),*' the thinking lowly of ourselves because we are so; ἂν ταπεινὸς ᾖς, καὶ ἐννοήσῃς τίς ὢν πῶς ἐσώθης, ἀφορμὴν πρὸς ἀρετὴν λαμβάνεις τὴν μνήμην. Chrys. on *Eph.* iv. 2, here more exact than in his definitions collected in Suicer, *Thesaur.* s. v. On the true meaning of this word see the valuable remarks of Neander, *Planting*, Vol. 1. 483, Trench, *Synon.* § 42, and notes *on Eph.* iv. 2. πραΰτητα] '*meekness,*' in respect of God, *and* toward one another; see notes *on Galat.* v. 23, and *on Eph.* iv. 2, in which latter passage it occurs in exactly the same position with respect to ταπειν. and μακροθυμία. Eadie objects to the primary reference to God, but apparently without sufficient reason: that πραΰτης is frequently used in purely human relations is quite true (compare Titus iii. 2, πραΰτ. πρὸς πάντας ἀνθρώπους), but that its basis is a *meek* acceptance of God's dealings with us seems clearly shown in Matth. xi. 29, where it is an attribute of the Saviour, and in Gal. vi. 1, and perhaps 1 Cor. iv. 21 and 2 Tim. ii. 25, where a sense of dependence on God forms the very

χαριζόμενοι ἑαυτοῖς, ἐάν τις πρός τινα ἔχῃ μομφήν· καθὼς καὶ ὁ Χριστὸς ἐχαρίσατο ὑμῖν οὕτως καὶ ὑμεῖς· ¹⁴ ἐπὶ πᾶσιν δὲ τούτοις

groundwork of the exhortation. In such passages mere gentleness seems quite insufficient. Ὁ. μακροθυμία opp. to ὀξυθυμία (James i. 19), see notes on *Eph.* iv. 2

13. ἀνεχόμενοι ἀλλ.] '*forbearing one another*;' explanation of the last two, and perhaps more particularly of the last, of the above-mentioned virtues; compare Eph. iv. 2, μετὰ μακροθ., ἀνεχόμενοι ἀλλ. ἐν ἀγάπῃ. There does not seem any necessity for enclosing the whole verse (Griesb., Lachm., Battm.), nor even καθὼς καὶ...ὑμεῖς (Winer, Gr. § 64, ed. 5), in a parenthesis. The structure and sequence of thought seem uninterrupted; while the first participial clause expands the preceding substantives, the second is enhanced by an adverbial clause which in its second member carries with it the preceding participle χαριζόμενοι; see Winer, Gr. § 62. 4, p. 499, ed. 6.

χαριζόμενοι ἑαυτοῖς] '*forgiving each other*;' compare Eph. iv. 32. The change to the reflexive pronoun in two members so perfectly similar (Eph. l. c. is a little different) is perhaps not accidental; while ἀλλήλων marks an act to be done by one Christian to his fellow Christian, ἑαυτοῖς may suggest the performance of an act faintly resembling that of Christ's, namely, of each one toward all, — yea even to themselves included ('vobismet ipsis,' Vulg.), Christians being members of one another; ὅσα ἂν ἐν τῷ εὐεργετεῖν ποιῶμεν ἑτέρους, καλῶς ταῦτα, καὶ διὰ τὸ τέλος καὶ διὰ τὸ συσσώμους ἡμᾶς εἶναι, μᾶλλον εἰς ἡμᾶς ἀναφέρεται, Origen on *Eph.* l. c. (Cramer, Cat. Vol. i. p. 311), here perhaps more appropriate. μομφήν] '(ground of) blame.' This form is an ἅπαξ λεγόμ. in the N. T., but, especially in combination with ἔχω, sufficiently common in classical Greek; see examples in Wetstein *in loc.*, and in Rost u. Palm, *Lex.* s. v. The glosses μομφὴν [DEF] and ὀργὴν [FG] are obviously suggested by the non-appearance of the word elsewhere in the N. T. or in the LXX. καθὼς καὶ ὁ Χρ.] '*even as Christ also forgave you*;' comp. ch. ii. 13, where the same doctrine is, as it would there seem, similarly attributed to Christ: contrast Eph. iv. 32, where it is referred to ὁ Θεὸς ἐν Χρ. Καθώς (comp. on Gal. iii. 6), associated with the καὶ of comparison (Klotz, *Devar.* Vol. ii. p. 635) and balanced by the following οὕτως καὶ, here simply introduces an example (μιμεῖσθε τὸν Δεσπότην, Theod.): in Eph. l. c., as the imperatival structure suggests, it has more of an argumentative tinge; see notes *in loc.* The reading is slightly doubtful: Κύριος is adopted by Lachm. with ABD¹FG; 1 mss.; Vulg., Clarom., al.; Aug. al., but is not improbably due to some attempts at conformation to Eph. iv. 32.

καὶ ὑμεῖς] Scil. χαριζόμενοι, the structure remaining participial; see Winer, Gr. § 62. 4, p. 499. The principal Vv.

Syr. (ܘܗܟܢܐ [condonate]), Clarom. ('ita et vos facite'), Goth. ('taujaip'), Æth. ('facite'), and Theod. supply the imperative, which in some MSS. [D¹E¹ FG; al., ποιεῖτε] is actually expressed: this, however, certainly seems at variance with the structure, and interrupts the otherwise easy sequence of clauses; so rightly De Wette and Meyer. On the double καὶ in sentences composed of correlative members, see Klotz, *Devar.* Vol. ii. p. 635, and notes on *Ephes.* v. 23, where the usage is briefly investigated.

14 ἐπὶ πᾶσιν δὲ τούτοις] '*but over all these things*;' not, as in Eph. vi. 14 (see notes *in loc.*), with a simple

τὴν ἀγάπην, ὃ ἐστὶν σύνδεσμος τῆς τελειότητος. ¹⁵ καὶ ἡ εἰρήνη

force of accession or superaddition, Syr. ܟܠܗܝܢ ܗܠܝܢ [cum his omnibus], Æth., but, as the more distinct expression and especially the foregoing image seem to require, with a *semi-local* force ('super,' Vulg., 'ufar,' Goth.), the dative with ἐπί as usual conveying the idea of closer and less separable connections; see notes *on Eph.* ii. 20, but transpose (ed. 1) the accidentally misplaced 'latter' and 'former.' Love toward all (comp. *on Phil.* i. 9) was thus to be the garb that was to be put on over all the other elements in the spiritual ἔνδυσις.

8] '*which (element);*' neuter, the antecedent being viewed under an abstract and generalized aspect; see Jelf, *Gram.* § 820. 1, Krüger, *Sprachl.* § 61. 7. 9. The reading is not perfectly certain; ἥτις (*Rec.*) is fairly supported [D²D³E KL; many Ff.], and is certainly in accordance with St. Paul's (explanatory) use of the indef. relative in similar passages; still the probability of a grammatical gloss seems here so great, that the reading of *Lachm.* and *Tisch.* is to be distinctly preferred.

σύνδεσμος τῆς τελειότητος] '*the bond of perfectness*,' Auth.; not ' of completeness,' Alf., which would be a more suitable translation of ὁλοκληρία; comp. Trench, *Synon.* § 22. The genitival relation has been somewhat differently explained; the abstract gen. may be (*a*) the gen. of *quality*, in which case τελειότ. would be little more than an epithet, 'the most perfect bond,' Hamm., Grot., and even Green, *Gram.* p. 247; (*b*) the gen. of *content*, 'amor complectitur virtutum universitatem,' Bengel, compare Bull, *Exam. Cens.* II. 5, — τῆς τελειότ. marking that which the σύνδ. enclosed within it, De W., Olsh., compare Usteri, *Lehrb.* II. 1. 4, p. 242; or (*c*) the genit. *objecti;* τῆς τελειότ. being that which is held together by it, and on which it exercises its conjunctive power; πάντα ἐκεῖνα αὕτη συσφίγγει, Theophyl.: so Chrys., Theod., apparently Syr. ܙܢܪܐ [cinctorium], and more recently Steig: and Meyer. Of these (*c*) has clearly the advantage, as not involving either a doubtful genitive or an unsatisfactory, if not indemonstrable meaning of σύνδεσμος (comp. Meyer); as, however, it assigns a questionable collective force to τελειότης, scil. τὰ τὴν τελειότητα ποιοῦντα, Chrys., Theoph., it seems more exact to regard the genitive as, (*d*) a gen. *subjecti* belonging to the general category of the gen. *possess.;* love is the bond which belongs to, is the distinctive feature of perfection: contrast Eph. iv. 2, and compare notes *in loc.* The omission of the article may be due to the verb substantive; see Middleton, *Gr. Art.* III. 3. 2, p. 43 (ed. Rose).

15. εἰρήνη τοῦ Χρ.] '*the peace of Christ;*' gen. *auctoris*, or perhaps rather *originis* (Hartung, *Casus*, p. 17, see on ch. i. 23), ' the peace which comes from Him who is our peace (Ephes. ii. 14), and who solemnly left His peace to His church' (John xiv. 27); ἐκείνην (εἰρήνην) ἣν ὁ Χριστὸς ἀφῆκεν αὐτός, Chrys. The peace of Christ must not be restricted merely to ὁμόνοια, though this is apparently the more immediate reference in the present passage, but includes that deep peace and tranquillity which is His blessed gift, and emanates from His Cross; compare εἰρήνη Θεοῦ, Phil. iv. 7, in which the idea is substantially the same, except that perhaps peace is there contemplated as in its antithesis to anxious worldliness (see notes *in loc.*), while here it is rather to the hard, unloving, and unquiet spirit that mars the union of the ἓν σῶμα. The reading τοῦ Θεοῦ (*Rec.*) is fairly supported [C·D³EJK;

τοῦ Χριστοῦ βραβευέτω ἐν ταῖς καρδίαις ὑμῶν, εἰς ἣν καὶ ἐκλή-
θητε ἐν ἑνὶ σώματι· καὶ εὐχάριστοι γίνεσθε. ¹⁶ Ὁ λογος τοῦ

16. ἐν ταῖς καρδίαις] So Griesb., Scholz, Lachm., with ABC*DEFG; 10 mss., apparently all Vv.; Chrysost., Theod (comm.); Lat. Ff. The reading ἐν τῇ καρδία (Rec., Tisch. ed. 2, 7) is too feebly supported,—only by D³EKL (MSS. not of doubtful authority from showing other traces of conformation to Eph. v. 19) great mass of mss.; Comm., Theol. (text), al., and (?) so very probably no good addition to Eph. l. c. (E, however, there reads ἐν ταῖς καρδ.), that it is difficult to conceive what principle, except that of opposition to Lachm., induced Tisch. to retain so very questionable a reading, and to reverse the judgment of his first edition.

nearly all mss.; Goth., al.], but in all probability is a correction.

βραβευέτω] 'rule,' [Syriac] [ducat, regat] Syriac, 'sit gubernatrix,' Beza. The verb βραβεύειν [βρα = προ, see notes on Ph. iii. 14] has here received different explanations, 'exultet,' Vulg., Goth., 'stabilians,' Copt., Æthiop., 'abundet,' Clarom., all perhaps endeavoring to retain some shade of the original meaning (ἀγωνοθετοῦσάν τε καὶ βραβεύουσαν, Theod.), but obscuring rather than elucidating. The later and secondary meaning 'administrare,' 'gubernare,' Hesychius Βυνεσθω Raph., Annot. Vol. II. p. 533 sq. and Schoettg. Lex. Polyb., s. v., seems here the most simple and natural; 'let the peace which comes from Christ order all things in your hearts.' For confirmation of this later meaning, see also the exx. collected by Krebs (Obs. p. 343), and Loesn. (Obs. p. 373), one of the most pertinent of which is Jos. Ant. q. IV. 3. 2, πάντα σῇ προσθέσ. διοικεῖται καὶ .... κατὰ βούλησιν βραβευόμενον τὴν σὴν εἰς τέλος ἔρχεται where the association with διοικεῖσθαι renders the meaning very distinct. On the use of καρδία to denote the subject in its inner relations, see Beck, Seelenl. III. 23, p. 80, compare p. 107. εἰς ἣν καὶ ἐκλήθ.] 'unto which [almost, for unto it (see notes on ch. i. 25, 27)] ye were also called:' unto the enjoyment and participation of

which, the εἰς marking the intermediate (not ultimate) object of the καλεῖν (1 Cor. i. 9, 1 Tim vi. 12, compare notes], and thus differing but little from ἐν τῇ such dat., by which Chryost. here explains it. The latter perhaps involves more the idea of approximation (Donalds. Crat l. § 172), the former of direction. The ascensive καὶ marks the κλῆσις as also having the same object as the apostle's admonition. ἐν ἑνὶ σώματι] 'in one body,' i. e. so as to abide in one body; not marking the object just implied, 'ut unum essetis corpus' (comp. Grotius), nor the matter of the calling (Steig., compare 1 Cor. v. 15), but as the more concrete truth seems to require, simply the result to which it tended; ᾠκονόμησεν ὁ Χρ. τοὺς πάντας ἐν σῶμα ποιῆσαι, (Œcum.; compare Eph. ii 16, and Winer, Gr. § 50. 5, p. 370.

καὶ εὐχάρ. γιν.] 'and be ye (become) thankful,' scil. to God, Chrysost., Theophyl. [as ὁ καλῶν (compare see Gal. i. 6) less probably to Christ, as Theod. and expressly Syr. and Æth. The meaning 'amabiles,' εὐχάριστοι (Olsh. mss., though lexically defensible (comp. Xen. Œc. ix. v. 10), seems here wholly inappropriate. Εὐχαριστία was a duty ever foremost in the thoughts of the great apostle. 1 Thess. v. 18; observe his frequent use of εὐχαριστεῖν (23 times) and εὐχαριστία (12 times), the latter of which only occurs thrice elsewhere (Acts xxiv. 3, Rev.

Χριστοῦ ἐνοικείτω ἐν ὑμῖν πλουσίως, ἐν πάσῃ σοφίᾳ διδάσκοντες καὶ νουθετοῦντες ἑαυτοὺς ψαλμοῖς, ὕμνοις, ᾠδαῖς πνευματικαῖς, ἐν τῇ χάριτι ᾄδοντες ἐν ταῖς καρδίαις ὑμῶν τῷ Θεῷ, [17] καὶ πᾶν ὅ τι

17. Ἰησοῦ Χριστοῦ] So *Lachm.*, with ACD¹FG ; mss. ; very many Vv. ; some Ff. *Rec.*, followed by *Tisch.* and *Alf.*, reads Κυρίου Ἰησοῦ with BD³EK ; great mass of mss. ; Amit., Goth., Syr. (Philox.), al. ; Clem. (?), Theod., al., but appy. with less probability. By a comparison of the variations of this and the preceding verse with those of Eph. v. 19, 20 (Alf.'s remark that there are 'hardly any,' is scantly correct) we may form some interesting *local* comparisons. It will be seen that KL present distinct traces of conformation, E less so, ADFG perhaps still less, and B scarcely any at all ; C has a lacuna at Eph. *l. c.*

iv. 9, vii. 12) in the whole N. T. For a good sermon on the whole of the verse, see Frank, *Serm.* LI. Vol. II. p. 394 (A.-C. Libr.).

16. ὁ λόγος τοῦ Χρ.] '*the word of Christ,*' as delivered in the Gospel, Χριστοῦ being the genitive *subjecti*, the word spoken and proclaimed by Him, 1 Thessalon. i. 8, iv. 15, 2 Thessalon. iii. 1 ; compare Winer, *Gr.* § 30. 1, p. 158. It is perfectly unnecessary, with *Lachm.* (ed. stereot.), to enclose this clause in brackets. The previous more general exhortations to love and peace which conclude with εὐχάρ. γίνεσθε are suitably accompanied by a more special one which shows the efficacy of the Gospel in such respects, and more fully expands the last precept ; παραινέσας εὐχαρίστους εἶναι καὶ τὴν ὁδὸν δείκνυσι, Chrys. ἐνοικείτω ἐν ὑμῖν πλ.] '*dwell within you richly ;*' surely not 'among you,' De W., which would tend to obliterate the force of the compound, nor 'in you as a Church,' Meyer, Alf., which really comes to the same thing, — but, as usual, 'within you' (τὴν τοῦ Χρ. διδασκαλίαν ἐν τῇ ψυχῇ περιφέρειν ἀεί, Theod.), 'in your hearts,' the outcoming and manifestation of which was to be seen in the acts described by the participles. Comp. Rom. viii. 11, 2 Tim. i. 5, 14, the only other passages in St. Paul's Epistles (2 Cor. vi. 16, is a quotation) in which ἐνοικεῖν

ἐν ὑμῖν occurs, and which, though the τὸ ἐνοικοῦν is different, go far to fix the meaning in the present case. The indwelling was to be πλουσίως, 'richly,' 'not with a scanty foothold, but with a large and liberal occupancy,' Eadie. ἐν πάσῃ σοφίᾳ is not to be connected with what precedes (Syr., — but apparently *not* Chrys., as asserted by Meyer, Alf.), but with what follows, as in ch. i. 28. The construction is then perfectly harmonious ; ἐνοικείτω has its single adverb πλουσίως, and is supported and expanded by two *co-ordinate* participial clauses, each of which has its spiritual manner or element of action (ἐν πάσῃ σοφίᾳ, ἐν χάριτι) more exactly defined ; see notes on ch. i. 28.

διδάσκ. καὶ νουθετ. ἑαυτ.] '*teaching and admonishing one another :*' on the meaning and force of νουθετεῖν, see notes on ch. i. 28. On the *possible* force of ἑαυτούς, see notes on ver. 13 : here it is more probably simply for ἀλλήλους ; see Winer, *Gr.* § 22. 5, p. 136. On the very intelligible participial anacoluthon, see Green, *Gr.* p. 313, notes on *Eph.* iii. 18, and on *Phil.* i. 30.

ψαλμοῖς, ὕμνοις, κ. τ. λ.] '*with psalms, hymns, spiritual songs ;*' instrument by which, or vehicle in which (Mey.), the διδαχὴ and νουθέτησις were to be communicated. *Mill* and *Tisch.* connect these datives with the following words, but not with propriety, as ᾄδοντες,

ἐὰν ποιῆτε ἐν λόγῳ ἢ ἐν ἔργῳ, πάντα ἐν ὀνόματι Ἰησοῦ Χριστοῦ
εὐχαριστοῦντες τῷ Θεῷ πατρὶ δι' αὐτοῦ.

has already two defining members associated with it. On the distinction between the terms, and the force of πνεύματι ('such as the Holy Spirit inspires'), see notes on the parallel passage, *Eph.* v. 19. Meyer remarks that the singing, etc., here alluded to, was not necessarily at divine service, but at the ordinary social meetings; see Clem.-Alex. *Pæd.* II. 4, 43, Vol. I. p. 194 (ed. Pott.), where this passage is referred to; compare Suicer, *Thesaur.* Vol. II. p. 1568. On the hymns used by the ancient church in her services, see Bingham, *Antiq.* XIV. 2. 1. The copula καί after ψαλμοῖς [C¹D¹D⁴E KL] and after ὕμνοις [AC¹D¹EKL] seems to have come from the sister passage, and is rightly rejected by *Lachm.*, *Tisch.*, and most modern editors.

ἐν τῇ χάριτι ᾄδ.] '*in Grace singing*;' participial clause co-ordinate to the foregoing, specifying another form of singing, viz., that of the inward heart; see Eph. v. 19, and notes *in loc.* Ἐν τῇ χάρ. [*Rec.* omits τῇ with AD⁴E·KL; al.] is obviously parallel to ἐν πάσῃ σοφίᾳ, and serves to define the characteristic element to which the ᾄδειν was to be circumscribed (see notes on ch. i. 28); it was to be in the element, and with the accompaniment of Divine grace: so Chrys. 2, ἀπὸ τῆς χάριτος τοῦ Πνεύματος, (Œcum., διὰ τῆς παρὰ τοῦ ἁγίου Πνεύματος δοθείσης χάριτος, both of which, however, are rather coarse paraphrases of the preposition. The interpretations 'quod se utilitate commendet,' Beza, 'with becoming thankfulness,' De Wette, etc., are unsatisfactory, and χαριέντως, Grot., 'in dexteritate quâdam gratiosâ,' Davenant 2, untenable, as the singing was not aloud, but in the silence of the heart (Mey.). ἐν ταῖς καρδίαις ὑμῶν] '*in your hearts*;' locality of the ᾄδειν. This ᾄδειν ἐν ταῖς καρδ. is not an expansion of the preceding, defining its proper characteristics or accompaniments (μὴ μόνον τῷ στόματι, Theod.) — in which case the clause would be subordinate, — but specifies another kind of singing, viz., that of the inward heart to God, the former being ἑαυτοῖς; see notes on *Eph.* v. 19. The reading Κυρίῳ [*Rec.* with C¹D EKL] seems clearly to have arisen from the parallel passage.

17. πᾶν ὅ τι... ἔργῳ] An absolute nom., standing out of regimen and placed at the beginning of the sentence with a slight emphatic force; see Jelf, *Gr.* § 477. 1. This seems slightly more correct than to regard it as an accusative reflected from the following πάντα as apparently Steiger and De Wette. πάντα is certainly not adverbial (Storr, compare Kypke, *Obs.* Vol. II. p. 329), nor even a resumption of the preceding πᾶν, but an accus. governed by ποιεῖτε, supplied from the preceding ποιῆτε; compare notes on *Ephes.* v. 22. What had been stated individually in πᾶν ὅ τι κ. τ. λ. is now expressed more fully and collectively by πάντα. It is difficult to understand how the reverse can be the case (Eadie), and the plural 'individualizing.' ἐν ὀνόματι Ἰ Χρ.] '*in the name of Jesus Christ*;' not 'invocato illius adjutorio,' Daven (καλεῖ τὸν Υἱόν, Chrys.), but, as in Eph. v. 20, '*in the name, in that holy and spiritual element which His name betokens*;' see notes on *Ephes.* l. c., on *Phil.* ii. 10, and compare Barrow, *Serm.* XXXIII. 6, Vol. II. p. 323, where every possible meaning is stated and exhausted; see also Whichcote, *Disc.* XLIII. Vol. II. p. 288 sq. (Aberd. 1751), — one of a course of three valuable sermons on this text, and comp. Beveridge, *Serm.* CIX. Vol. V. p. 116 sq. (A.-C. Libr.).

εὐχαρ. τῷ Θεῷ κ. τ. λ.] '*giving thanks*

Wives and husbands, children and parents, observe your duties. Servants, obey your masters and be faithful; masters, be just.

¹⁸ Αἱ γυναῖκες, ὑποτάσσεσθε τοῖς ἀνδράσιν, ὡς ἀνῆκεν ἐν Κυρίῳ. ¹⁹ Οἱ ἄνδρες, ἀγαπᾶτε

to God the Father through Him;' attendant service with which the (ποιεῖτε) πάντα κ.τ.λ. is to be ever associated; comp. Eph. v. 20, and see notes on ver. 15, and *on Phil.* iv. 6; add Hofmann, *Schriftb.* Vol. II. 2, p. 336, who less probably limits the εὐχαρ. to thankfulness for ability thus to do all ἐν ὀνόμ. κ.τ.λ. The reading Θεῷ καὶ πατρὶ (*Rec.*) is well supported [DEFGK; mss.; Vulg., Clar., al.], but opposed to AC and B (an important witness in these verses, see crit. note); some mss.; Goth., Copt., Sah., al.; Clem. and many Ff.; so also *Lachm.* and *Tisch.*

18. αἱ γυναῖκες] This verse and the eight following (iii. 18–iv. 1) contain special precepts, nearly the same as those in the latter part of ch. v. and the beginning of ch. vi. of the Epistle to the Ephesians. Such a similarity, often extending to words and phrases, is noticeable, and not very easy to account for, except on the somewhat obvious supposition that social precepts of this nature addressed, in the first instance, to the Christians of Colossæ and Laodicea, were known and felt by the apostle to be equally necessary and applicable to the church of Ephesus and the Christians of Lydia. The exhortations in the past Epistles are urged under somewhat different aspects. A comparison of the two Epistles will here be found very instructive; it seems to lead to the opinion that the shorter Epistle was written first; compare notes *on Eph.* vi. 21. Alford *in loc.* seems of a contrary opinion, but is in some degree at issue with his *Prolegomena,* p. 42. ὑποτ. τοῖς ἀνδρ.] '*submit yourselves to your husbands;*' see notes *on Eph.* v. 22, where the same precept occurs nearly in the same language. The addition ἰδίοις [*Rec.* with L; many mss.; Vv. and Ff.]

is opposed to the authority of all the other uncial manuscripts.

ὡς ἀνῆκεν] '*as it became fitting*,' '*as it should be,*' as was still more your duty when you entered upon your Christian profession. The imperf. not perf., Huth.) is not for the present (compare Thom. M. s. v., p. 751, ed. Bern.), but, as the associated ἐν Κυρίῳ still more clearly shows, has its proper force, and points to conditions that were *simultaneous* with their entrance into Christianity, but which were still *not completely fulfilled;* see Winer, *Gr.* § 40. 3, p. 242. and Bernhardy, *Synt.* x. 3, p. 373, add also Herodian, s. v., p. 468 (ed. Piers.), where in the similar forms προσῆκε. ἔχρην, ἔδει, the tense is properly recognized. On the frequently recurring ἐν Κυρίῳ, here to be connected with ἀνῆκεν (compare ver. 20), not with ὑποτάσσ. (Chrysost., Theoph.), see notes *on Eph.* iv. 16, vi. 1, *Phil.* ii. 19. al.

19. οἱ ἄνδρες κ.τ.λ.] Repeated in Eph. v. 25, but there enhanced by a comparison of the holy bond between Christ and His Church. The encyclical letter enters into greater and deeper relations. μὴ πικραίνεσθε] '*do not be embittered;*' compare Eph. iv. 31. The verb occurs in its simple sense, Rev. viii. 11, x. 9, 10; here in its metaphorical sense, as occasionally both in classical (e.g. Plato, *Legg.* v. p. 731 D, associated with ἀκραχολεῖν, [Demosth.] *Epist.* p. 1464, joined with μνησικακεῖν), and post-classical, writers, e.g. Exod. xvi. 20, ἐπικράνθη ἐπ' αὐτάς, al., comp. Joseph. *Antiq.* v. 7. 1, ἐπικραινόμενος πρὸς αὐτούς. The form is apparently pass. with a middle force ('medialpass.,' Krüger); compare Theocr. *Idyll.* v. 120, and Schol. *in loc.,* πικραίνεται λυπεῖται, and see Krüger, *Sprachl.* § 52

τὰς γυναῖκας καὶ μὴ πικραίνεσθε πρὸς αὐτάς. ²⁰ Τὰ τέκνα ὑπακούετε τοῖς γονεῦσιν κατὰ πάντα· τοῦτο γὰρ εὐάρεστόν ἐστιν ἐν Κυρίῳ. ²¹ Οἱ πατέρες, μὴ ἐρεθίζετε τὰ τέκνα ὑμῶν, ἵνα μὴ ἀθυ-

20. εὐάρεστόν ἐστιν] So *Tisch.* (ed. 1 *Lachm.*, *Alf.*, al., with ABCD[E]; 3 mss. (Vv. in such cases are hardly to be reckoned). *Tisch.* (ed. 2, 7) adopts the reversed order with FGKL; and great majority of mss.,—apparently very insufficient authority.

6. 1, where a large list of such verbs is given, with examples. On the derivation of πικρός [from a root ΠΙΚ- 'pierce'], see Buttmann, *Lexil.* § 56, comp. Donalds. *Cratyl.* § 266.

20. ὑπακ. τοῖς γον. κ. τ. λ.] '*be obedient to your parents in all things;*' comp. Eph. vi. 1. There the exhortation is accompanied with a special ref. to the fifth commandment; here that reference is applied only, and involved in the argumentative clause. The comprehensive τὰ πάντα is obviously to be regarded as the general rule; exceptional cases (τοῖς γε ἀσεβέσι πατράσιν οὐ κατὰ πάντα δεῖ ὑπακούειν, Theophylact) would be easily recognized; the great apostle was ever more occupied with the rule than with the exceptions to it. On the exceptions in the present case, see Bp. Taylor, *Duct. Dub.* III. 5, Rule 1. and 4 sq. The form ὑπακούετε, if not stronger than ὑποτάσσ. (De W., l. s.) a more inclusive aspect as implying '*datum obtemperare*,'—not merely submission to authority, but obedience to a command; see Tittmann *Synon.* 1. p. 193.
τοῦτο γὰρ κ. τ. λ.] '*for this is well-pleasing to the Lord;*' obviously not 'to the Lord' (Copt., perhaps following a different reading), ἐν not being a 'nota dat.,' nor even 'coram' ܟܕ Syriac, 'apud,' Æth (Pol.), but, as in ver. 18 and elsewhere, 'in Domino,' Vulg., Clarom., Goth, the prep. defining the sphere in which the τὸ εὐάρεστον was especially felt and evinced to be so. The reading of Ἰθ., τῷ Κυρίῳ, has not the support of any uncial MS., and is rejected by all modern editors.

21. μὴ ἐρεθίζετε] '*do not irritate;*' duty of fathers, expressed on the negative side; compare Eph. vi. 4. The command there is μὴ παροργίζετε, between which and the present the difference is perhaps scarcely appreciable. The former verb *perhaps* points to provocation to a deeper feeling, the latter ('irritare') to one more partial and transitory. The derivation of ἐρεθίζω and ἐρέσω is not perfectly certain, it is commonly referred to ἔρις [Lobeck, *Path.* p. 478. Benfey, *Wurzel.* Vol. 1. p. 1024, μὴ φιλονεικοτέρους αὐτοῖς ποιεῖτε, Chrysost.,—but comp. Pott, *Et. Forsch.* Vol. II. p. 182, and Benfey, *Wurzel.* Vol. II. p. 340. Lachmann here, according to his principles, reads παροργίζετε with ACDEFGL; al. Though well-supported, it can scarcely be doubted that it is a conformation to Ephes. l. c.
ἵνα μὴ ἀθυμ.] '*in order that they may not be disheartened;*' that they may not have a broken spirit and pass into apathy and desperation, by seeing their parents so harsh and difficult to please; compare Corn. a Lap. *in loc.* The verb ἀθυμεῖν is an ἅπ. λεγόμ. in the N. T., but sufficiently common both in the LXX. (1 Sam. i. 7, xv. 11, and elsewhere; see examples in Wetst. who cites a pertinent passage from Arrian Tact. [ap. Fabric. III. 30. 10]. *P. ext.* 38. ὀργῇ δὲ μηδένα μέτιοι τῶν τέκνων ἀνθρώπων· ἀθυμότεροι γὰρ εἶεν ἄν.

μῶσιν. ²² Οἱ δοῦλοι, ὑπακούετε κατὰ πάντα τοῖς κατὰ σάρκα κυρίοις, μὴ ἐν ὀφθαλμοδουλείαις ὡς ἀνθρωπάρεσκοι, ἀλλ᾿ ἐν ἁπλότητι καρδίας φοβούμενοι τὸν Κύριον. ²³ ὃ ἐὰν ποιῆτε, ἐκ ψυχῆς

22. *οἱ δοῦλοι*] Duties of slaves, more fully detailed, yet closely sim., both in arguments and language, in the parallel passage in Eph. vi. 5 sq., where see notes. On the general drift and object of these frequently recurring exhortations to slaves, see note *on* 1 *Tim.* vi. 1 sq.   *τοῖς κατὰ σάρκα κυρ*] '*your masters according to the flesh;*' your bodily, earthly masters; you have another Master in heaven: '*οἱ κατὰ σάρκα κύρ.* tacite distinguuntur a Christo,' Fritz. *Rom.* Vol. II. p. 270. There is apparently no consolatory force in the addition (πρόσκαιρος ἡ δουλεία Chrysost., Theoph.; sim. Theod., Œcum.); see notes *on Eph. l. c.* On the neglected distinction between κύριος and δεσπότης, see Trench, *Synon.* § 28, comp. Ammon. *Diff. Voc.* p. 39 (ed. Valck.).
ἐν ὀφθαλμοδουλείαις] '*in acts of eye-service;*' κατ᾿ ὀφθαλμοδουλείαν, Eph. vi. 6; the primary reference to the master's eye (Sanders. *Serm.* VII. 67, ad Pop.), passes into the secondary ref. to falsehearted and hypocritical service generally. For examples of this use of the plural, compare James ii. 1, *ἐν προσωπολημψίαις*, and the long list in Gal. v. 20, where see notes and grammatical references. *Lachm.* here reads ὀφθαλμοδουλείᾳ with ABDEFG; 6 mss.; Dam., Theoph., Chrysost. (varies): in spite of this preponderance of uncial authority we seem justified on *critical* principles in retaining with CKL; great mass of mss.; Clem., Theod., Œcumen. (*Rec.*, *Tisch.*), — the plural, which, even independently of the parallel passage, was so likely to be changed to a reading supposed to be more in harmony with the *ἐν ἁπλότητι καρδίας* in the correlative member which follows.   *ἐν ἁπλότ. καρδίας*] '*in singleness of heart,*' in freedom from all dishonesty, duplicity, and false show of industry; see Eph. vi. 5. where the meaning is slightly more limited by the preceding clause μετὰ φόβου καὶ τρόμου. On the scriptural meaning and application of 'doubleness of heart,' see Beck, *Seelenl.* III. 26, p. 106. *Here*, as Meyer observes, *ἐν ἁπλότ.* in the negative clause answers to *ἐν ὀφθαλμοδ.* in the positive, and the following φοβούμ. τὸν Κύρ. to ὡς ἀνθρωπάρεσκοι. The reading is again *slightly* doubtful. *Rec.* has Θεόν, with D³E²K; mss.; *Lachm.* and *Tisch.* adopt Κύριον, with ABCD¹E¹F GL. — which is certainly to be preferred, as there seems nothing in Eph. *l. c.* to which it could be a conformation.
23. *ὃ ἐὰν ποιῆτε*] More specific explanation and expansion of the preceding positive exhortations. Again, there is a difference of reading; that of the text is found in ABCD¹FG, and adopted by *Lachm.* and *Tisch.* The *Rec.* καὶ πᾶν ὅ τι ἐὰν is feebly supported [D²D³EKL], and possibly a reminiscence of ver. 17. Alford prefixes καί, apparently by an oversight.
ἐκ ψυχῆς] '*from the heart (soul);*' stronger than *ἐν ἁπλότ. καρδ.* above, scil. *ἐξ εὐνοίας καὶ ὅσῃ δύναμις*, Œcum., and as opposed to any outward constraint, Delitzsch, *Psychol.* IV. 7, p. 162: comp. *on Eph.* vi. 7.   *ὡς τῷ Κυρ. κ. τ. λ.*] '*as to the Lord and not to men;*' dat. of 'interest,' Krüger, *Sprachl.* § 48. 4. The *ὡς* serves to mark the mode in which, or the *aspects* under which, the service was to be viewed; see Bernhardy, *Synt.* VII. 1, p. 333, Fritz. *Rom.* Vol. II. p. 360, and notes *on Eph.* v. 22, where this interpretation of *ὡς* is more fully investigated. It is objected to by Eadie (*on Col.* p. 258), but apparently without full reason, being grammatically

ἐργάζεσθε ὡς τῷ Κυρίῳ καὶ οὐκ ἀνθρώποις, ²¹ εἰδότες ὅτι ἀπὸ
Κυρίου ἀπολήμψεσθε τὴν ἀνταπόδοσιν τῆς κληρονομίας. τῷ
Κυρίῳ Χριστῷ δουλεύετε· ²⁵ ὁ γὰρ ἀδικῶν κομίσεται ὃ ἠδίκησεν,
καὶ οὐκ ἔστιν προσωπολημψία.

exact and apparently exegetically satisfactory. The negative οὐκ, as usually in such opposite members, is absolute and objective; they were to work as workers to the Lord and non-workers to men; they were not to serve two masters (Mey.); comp. Winer, Gr. § 55. 1, p. 422, Green, Gr. p. 121 sq.

24. εἰδότες] 'seeing ye know:' causal particle, giving the reason for the preceding command; compare ch. iv. 1, and the parallel passage, Eph. vi. 8. ἀπὸ Κυρίου] 'from the Lord,' not perfectly identical with παρὰ Κυρίου Eph. vi. 8, but, with the proper force of the prep., expressive of procedure from as from the more remote object: see Winer, Gr. 47. b, p. 326, and notes on Gal. i. 11. The remark of Eadie that ἀπὸ marks that the gift 'comes immediately from Christ,' is thus wholly untenable. In παρά (more usual in personal relations) the primary idea of simple motion from the subject passes into the more usual one of motion from the immediate neighborhood of the object: see Donalds. Crat. § 177, Winer, l. c., p. 327. τὴν ἀνταπ. τῆς κληρ.] 'the recompense of the inheritance,' i. e. the recompense which is the inheritance, τῆς κληρον. being the gen. of identity or apposition, Scheuerl. Synt. § 12. 1, pp. 82, 83, Wi. Gr. § 59. 8. a, p. 470. This κληρονομία is obviously the κλῆρον. (ἐν τῇ βασιλείᾳ τοῦ Χρ. καὶ Θεοῦ, Eph. v. 5), which was reserved for them hereafter; compare 1 Pet. i. 4, and on the meaning of the term, Reuss, Theol. Chret. IV. 22, Vol. II. p. 249. The double compound ἀνταπόδοσις in an ἅπ. λεγόμ. in the N. T., but not uncommon elsewhere (1 a lxi. 2, Hosea ix. 7, Polyb. Hist. vi. 5. 3, and with a local reference, iv. 43. 5, al.): the verb is found several times in the

N. T., and the pass. compound, ἀνταπόδομα, twice Luke xiv. 12, Rom. xi. 9 (quotation). The gloss μισθαποδοσίας only occurs in cursive mss.

τῷ Κυρ. Χρ. δουλ.] 'serve ye the Lord Christ:' brief yet comprehensive statement of the duty of δοῦλοι, regarded in its true light, ὡς τῷ Κυρίῳ καὶ οὐκ ἀνθρώποις, ver. 23. So distinctly, imperative, Vulg., Copt. (uri-lók), Æth. (Pol.; mistranslated); Caramanus less probably adopts the present. The reading is scarcely doubtful: Rec. inserts γὰρ with D²D³(E? KL; Syriac (both), Æthopic (Platt), Goth., al., but with very little probability, being weaker than the text in uncial authority [ABC²-DE¹, and suspicious as helping out the seeming want of connection.

25. ὁ γὰρ ἀδικῶν] 'for the wrong-doer.' It is slightly doubtful whether ὁ ἀδικῶν refers to the master (Theoph.), to the slaves (Theoph.), or, more comprehensively, to both (Huther). The prevailing meaning of ἀδικεῖν in the N. T. ('injuriam facere,' Vulg.) is opposed to Rev. xxii. 11, but surely not Philem. 18, as Eadie], and still more the succeeding clause, οὐκ ἔστιν προσωπ., seem conclusively in favor of the former; so that the verse must be regarded as supplying encouragement and consolation to slaves when suffering oppression or injustice at the hands of their masters: ὥστε φησί, κἂν μὴ τύχητε ἀγαθῶν ἀντιδόσεων παρὰ τῶν δεσποτῶν, ἐστὶ δικαιοκριτὴς ὃς οὐκ οἶδε δοῦλον καὶ δεσπότου διαφοράν, ἀλλὰ δικαίαν εἰσφέρει τὴν ψῆφον, Theod. κομίσεται] 'shall receive back,' as it were a deposit: not so much a tautology as a pregnant statement. 'He shall receive back ὃ ἠδίκησε in the form of just retribution,' Winer, Gram. § 66. 1. b, p

IV. Οἱ κύριοι, τὸ δίκαιον καὶ τὴν ἰσότητα τοῖς δούλοις παρέχεσθε, εἰδότες ὅτι καὶ ὑμεῖς ἔχετε Κύριον ἐν οὐρανῷ.

Pray for us and for our success in the Gospel. Walk wisely, speak to the point, and be ready to answer them that ask.
² Τῇ προσευχῇ προσκαρτερεῖτε, γρηγοροῦντες ἐν αὐτῇ ἐν εὐχαριστίᾳ, ³ προσευχόμενοι ἅμα

547. The future refers to the day of final retribution; see *on Eph.* vi. 8. προσωπολημψία] 'respect of persons;' see notes *on Gal.* ii. 6, and on the (Alexandrian) insertion of μ, Tisch. *Prolegom.* p. xlvi. sq. (ed. 7). In the parallel passage, Eph. vi. 9, παρὰ αὐτῷ (Rom. ii. 11. ix. 14) is added [FG παρὰ τῷ Θεῷ], in which case the prep. has its prevailing idea of closeness to (comp. on ver. 24), and marks the ethical presence with the object (Latin *in*) of the quality alluded to; comp. Matt *Gr.* § 588. b.

CHAPTER IV. 1. Οἱ κύριοι] The duties of masters are enunciated on the positive side; in the parallel passage, Ephes. vi. 9, the addition, ἀνιέντες τὴν ἀπειλήν, defines also the negative side. τὴν ἰσότητα] '*equity.*' The association of this word with τὸ δίκαιον and the undoubted occurrence of it in a similar sense elsewhere (see Philo, *de Just.* § 4, Vol. II. p. 363 (ed. Mang.), and esp. § 14, *ib.* p. 374, where it is termed the μήτρη δικαιοσύνης) seem fully to justify the more derivative meaning adopted above: so Syr., Vulg., Æth. (Pol.), apparently Copt., and distinctly Chrysost., and the Greek commentators; ἰσότητα ἐκάλεσε τὴν προσήκουσαν ἐπιμέλειαν, Theod.: so De W., Neander (*Planting*, Vol. I. p. 488), Alf., and the majority of modern expositors. Meyer, and after him Eadie (with modifications), contend for the more literal meaning 'equality' (2 Cor. viii. 13, 14, compare Job xxxvi. 29), *i. e.* the equality of condition in spiritual matters which Christianity brought with it; compare Philem. 16: so perhaps Goth. *ibnassu* [similitudinem;

cognate with '*even*']. This is ingenious and plausible, but, on account of the association with τὸ δίκαιον, not satisfactory. In such a case we may with some profit refer to the ancient Vv. and Greek commentators. παρέχεσθε] '*supply on your side;*' middle, Acts xix. 24, Tit. ii. 7; active elsewhere in the N. T. In this form of the middle voice, called the 'dynamic' (Krüger, *Sprachl.* § 52. 8), or 'intensive' middle, the reference to the powers put forth by the subject is more distinct than in the active, which simply states the action; compare Donalds. *Gram.* § 432. 2. *bb*4. Such delicate shades of meaning can scarcely be expressed in translation, but no less exist; see especially Krüger, *l. c.*, where this verb is particularly noticed, and Kuster, *de Verb. Med.* § 49. The difference appears to have been partially appreciated by Ammonius, in his too narrow distinction, παρέχειν μὲν λέγεται τὰ διὰ χειρὸς διδόμενα, παρέχεσθαι δὲ ἐπὶ τῶν τῆς ψυχῆς διαθέσεων, οἷον προθυμίαν, εὔνοιαν [but see Acts xxviii. 2, al.], *de Diff. Voc.* p. 108 (ed. Valck.).

εἰδότες κ. τ. λ.] '*seeing ye know that ye also;*' causal participle, as in chapter iii. 24. The ascensive καὶ hints that masters and slaves stand really in like conditions of dependence; ὥσπερ ἐκεῖνοι ὑμᾶς, οὕτω καὶ ὑμεῖς ἔχετε Κύριον, Theoph. The reading in the last word of the verse is not quite certain: *Rec.* with good uncial authority [DEFGKL] reads οὐρανοῖς, but not without suspicion, on account of the parallel passage, Eph. vi. 9. The singular is found in ABC; al. (*Lachm., Tisch.*).

2. τῇ προσευχῇ προσκ.] 'con-

καὶ περὶ ἡμῶν, ἵνα ὁ Θεὸς ἀνοίξῃ ἡμῖν θύραν τοῦ λόγου, λαλῆσαι

tinue instant in your prayer;' Rom. xii. 12, Acts i. 14. The verb προσκαρτερεῖν occurs several times in the N. T., and in the majority of cases, as here, with a dat., in which combination it appears to denote an earnest adherence and attention whether to a person (Acts viii. 13) or to a thing; προσκαρ. τῇ προσευχῇ, ὡς περὶ τινος ἐπιπόνου, Chrys. It is found in the LXX. (Num. xiii. 20, absolutely), and in Polyb. (Hist 1. 55. 4, 1. 59. 12, al.) both absolutely and with a dative rei or personae.

γρηγοροῦντες ἐν αὐτῇ] 'being watchful in it;' modal clause to προσκαρτερεῖν: they were not to be dull and heavy in this great duty, but wakeful and active; compare Eph. vi. 18, 1 Pet. iv. 7. Ἐν is here not instrumental (De Wette), but, as usual, denotes the sphere in which the wakefulness and alacrity was to be evinced.

ἐν εὐχαριστίᾳ] 'with thanksgiving.' This clause is not to be connected with the finite verb, but with the participle, and, as in Eph. vi. 18 (see notes), specifies the peculiar accompaniment, or concomitant act with which ἡ προσ. was to be associated; τουτεστι μετὰ εὐχαριστίας ταύτην ποιοῦντες. Theophil. This not uncommon use of ἐν in the N. T. (ἐν adjunctivi) to denote an attendant act, element, or circumstance, has scarcely received from Winer (Gr. § 48 a, p. 344) the notice it deserves; see notes on ch. ii. 7, on Eph. v. 26, and Green, Gr. p. 289. On the duty of εὐχαριστία see notes on ch. iii. 15, and on Phil. iv. 6.

3. καὶ περὶ ἡμῶν] 'for us also;' scil. for the apostle and Timothy, not for the apostle alone (Chrys., Theophil.): the change to the singular in the last clause of the verse (δέδεμαι) would otherwise seem pointless; see notes on ch. i. 3. On the almost interchangeable meanings of περί and ὑπέρ in this and similar

formulæ, see notes on Phil. i. 7, and on Eph. vi. 19. ἵνα κ. τ. λ.] Subject of the prayer blended with the purpose of making it: use of ἵνα in reference to secondary purpose, see notes on Phil. i. 9, and on Eph. i. 17.

ἀνοίξῃ ἡμῖν κ. τ. λ.] 'may open to us a door of the word;' i. e., may remove any obstacle to the preaching of the gospel. The θύρα is thus not exactly εἴσοδος καὶ παρρησία (Chrys., al. mult.), but involves a figurative representation of obstructions and impediments that barred the way to preaching the Gospel, which were removed when the θύρα was opened; compare Acts xiv. 27, 1 Cor. xvi. 9, 2 Cor. ii. 12, Suicer, Thesaur. Vol. t. p. 1415, and examples in Wetstein on 1 Cor. l. c. λαλῆσαι] Infin. of purpose and intention; see notes on ch. i. 23, where this construction is discussed. On the meaning and derivation of λαλεῖν 'vocem ore emittere,' see notes on Tit. ii. 1, and on the distinction between λαλεῖν (τὸ τεταγμένως προφέρεσθαι τὸν λόγον) and λέγειν (τὸ ἀτάκτως ἐκφέρειν τὰ ὑποπίπτοντα ῥήματα).— a distinction, however, which cannot always be maintained in the N. Test., see Ammonius, Diff. Voc. p. 87 (ed. Valck.). μυστήριον τοῦ Χρ.] 'the mystery of Christ;' not 'the mystery relating to Christ,' gen. objecti (De W., comp. Eph. i. 9), but gen. subjecti, 'the mystery of which He is the sum and substance;' see notes on Eph. iii. 4, and compare on Col. ii. 2. On the meaning of μυστήριον, see on Ephes. v. 32, and Reuss, Théol. Chrét. iv. 9, Vol. II. p. 89.

δι' ὃ καὶ δέδεμαι] 'for which I have also been bound;' 'which I have preached even μέχρι δεσμῶν (2 Tim. ii. 9), the ascensive καὶ marking the extreme to which he had proceeded in his evangelical labors: he had endured privations and sufferings, and now beside

τὸ μυστήριον τοῦ Χριστοῦ, δι' ὃ καὶ δέδεμαι, ⁴ ἵνα φανερώσω αὐτὸ ὡς δεῖ με λαλῆσαι. ⁵ Ἐν σοφίᾳ περιπατεῖτε πρὸς τοὺς ἔξω, τὸν

that, bonds. The perf. δέδεμαι ('I have been and am bound') seems clearly to evince that the apostle was now in captivity: that this was at Rome, not at Cæsarea (Mey., *Einl.* p. 5), is satisfactorily shown by Alford, *Prolegom.* p. 20 sq. compared with p. 39. The reading δι' ὅν, adopted by *Lachm.* with BFG; Boern., has not sufficient external support.

4. ἵνα φανερώσω] '*in order that I may make it manifest.*' It is somewhat doubtful whether this clause depends (*a*) on δέδεμαι, Chrys., Beng., al.; compare Phil i. 12, 2 Tim. ii. 9; (*b*) on προσευχόμενοι, De W., Baumg.-Crus., al.; (*c*) on the preceding infinitival clause of purpose, λαλῆσαι τὸ μυστήριον, ver. 3, Mey., al., or more generally, on the whole purpose involved in the verse, viz. unobstructed, unhindered speaking. Of these (*a*) involves a paradoxical assertion, which here, without any further explanation or expansion, seems somewhat ἀπροσδόκητον and out of place: (*b*) impairs the continuity of the sentence, and puts a prayer which thus taken *per se* would naturally be referred to subjunctive capabilities in somewhat awkward parallelism with one which refers to the removal of objective hinderances: (*c*) on the contrary, keeps up the continuity, and carries out with proper modal additions (ὡς δεῖ με λαλῆσαι) the λαλῆσαι which was the object involved in the prayer; οὐχ ὅπως ἀπαλλαγῶ τῶν δεσμῶν, ἀλλ' ὅπως λαλήσω τὰ μυστήριον τοῦ Χριστοῦ, Theoph. ὡς δεῖ με λαλῆσαι] '*as I ought to speak;*' so, but with a slightly different reference, Eph. vi. 20. This was not to be μετὰ πολλῆς τῆς παρρησίας καὶ μηδὲν ὑποστειλάμενον (Chrys.) while in prison (which is apparently the sentiment mainly conveyed in Eph. *l. c.*), nor with any subjective reference to his inward duty (Davenant, Hammond), but, as the previous ἀνοίξῃ θύραν seems to suggest, simply and objectively, 'as I ought to do it (scil. freely and unrestrainedly), so as best to advance and further the gospel.' While δεδεμένος he could not λαλῆσαι ὡς ἔδει αὐτὸν λαλῆσαι; see Meyer *in loc.* Eadie unites both the subjective and objective reference: the phrase is confessedly general, still the context seems to point, mainly and principally, if not exclusively, to the latter. In Eph. *l. c.*, on the contrary, though the language is so very similar, the reference in both members seems to have more of a subjective character, and the construction in consequence to be slightly different.

5. ἐν σοφίᾳ] '*in wisdom;*' element and sphere in which they were to walk, Winer, *Gr.* § 48. a, p. 346: μηδεμίαν αὐτοῖς πρόφασιν δίδοτε βλάβης, πάντα ὑπὲρ τῆς αὐτῶν μηχανᾶσθε σωτηρίας, Theod. On the meaning of σοφία, — not merely 'prudence,' but *practical* Christian wisdom, — compare notes on ch. i. 9, and on *Eph.* i. 8.

πρὸς τοὺς ἔξω] '*toward them that are without,*' τοὺς μηδέπω πεπιστευκότας. Theod.; the regular designation of all who were not Christians, 1 Cor. v. 12, 13, 1 Thessal. iv. 12; see Kypke, *Obs.* Vol. II. p. 198, and notes *on* 1 *Tim.* iii. 7. The prep. πρός, both here and 1 *Thess. l.c.*, marks the social relation (Mey.) in which they were to stand with οἱ ἔξω, the proper meaning of 'ethical direction toward' (Winer, *Gr.* § 49. h, p. 360) being still distinctly apparent. For examples of this use of πρός, see Bernhardy, *Synt.* v. 31, p. 265, Rost u. Palm, *Lex.* s. v. 1. 2, Vol. II. p. 1157, where this prep. is extremely well discussed.

τὸν καιρὸν ἐξαγ.] '*buying up for yourselves the (fitting) season;*' see on *Eph.*

καιρὸν ἐξαγοραζόμενοι. ⁶ ὁ λόγος ὑμῶν πάντοτε ἐν χάριτι, ἅλατι ἠρτυμένος, εἰδέναι πῶς δεῖ ὑμᾶς ἑνὶ ἑκάστῳ ἀποκρίνεσθαι.

You will learn my state and all matters here from Tychicus and Onesimus.

⁷ Τὰ κατ' ἐμὲ πάντα γνωρίσει ὑμῖν Τύχικος ὁ ἀγαπητὸς ἀδελφὸς καὶ πιστὸς διάκονος καὶ

v. 16, where this formula is investigated at length. The exhortation in this verse is extremely similar to that in Ephes. v. 15, 16, except only that the precepts expressed there in a *negative*, are here expressed in a *positive* form. The reason for the present clause is there specifically noticed, ὅτι αἱ ἡμέραι πονηραί εἰσιν: here nothing more is stated than a general precept (ἐν σοφίᾳ περιπατεῖτε) with an adjoined notice of the *manner* in which it was to be carried out: they were to make their own every season for walking in wisdom, and to avail themselves of every opportunity of obeying the command.

6. ὁ λόγος ὑμῶν] '*your speech,*' not only generally, but, as the close of the verse shows, more especially πρὸς τοὺς ἔξω. ἐν χάριτι] '*with grace:*' scil. ἔστω: χάρις was to be the element *in* which, or perhaps the garb *with* which, the λόγος was to be invested; χάρις was to be the 'habitus orationis;' compare notes on 1 Tim. i. 18. ἅλατι ἠρτυμ.] '*seasoned with salt;*' further specification. Their discourse was not to be profitless and insipid, but, as food is seasoned with salt to make it agreeable to the palate, so was it to have a wholesome point and pertinency which might commend itself to, and tend to the edification of the hearers; see Suicer, *Thesaur.* s. v. Vol. ii. p. 181. An indirect caution and antithetical reference to λόγος σαπρός ('ne quid putridi subsit,' Bengel, compare Chrys.) is plausible (compare Eph. iv. 29 sq.), but not in accordance with πῶς δεῖ ἀποκρίνεσθαι, which points to λόγος under forms in which σαπρότης could scarcely have been intruded. The

later classical use of ἅλς, '*sal, sale,*' '*saline,*' seems here out of place. On the later form ἅλας, see Buttm. *Gr.* Vol. i. p. 227. εἰδέναι] '*to know,*' i.e. 'so that you may know;' loosely appended infinitive expressive of consequence; compare Madvig, *Synt.* § 147, rem. For examples of use 'in 3 i. exegeticus,' which is more usually found in clauses expressive of *purpose* or *effect* (see on ch. i. 22), but is also found in laxer combinations (Acts xv. 10, II b. v. 3), see Winer, *Gr.* § 44. 1, p. 2·4.

πῶς δεῖ ἀποκρ.] '*how you ought to return answer;*' the πῶς embracing all the various forms of answer which the occasion might require. The apostle further adds, not without significance, ἑνὶ ἑκάστῳ; each individual, whether putting his questions from malice or ignorance, sincerity or insincerity, was separately to receive the appropriate answer to his inquiry; compare 1 Peter iii. 15. The context, as Meyer observes, seems to limit the present reference to the intercourse of Christians with non-Christians, though the command has obviously an universal application: Chrysost. notices the case of the apostle at Athens; Mey. adds to this his answer before Felix, Festus, and the Jews at Rome.

7. τὰ κατ' ἐμέ] '*my condition,*' '*my circumstances,*' '*res meas,*' Beza: on this formula see reff. on *Eph.* vi. 21, and on the force of κατὰ in this collocation, notes on *Phil.* i. 12.

Τύχικος] not Τυχικός, *Mill, Griesb.*: an Ἀσιανός, mentioned Acts xx. 4, Eph. vi. 21, 2 Tim. iv. 12, Tit. iii. 12; see on *Eph. l. c.* His name is here associated with three titles of esteem and affection; he is an ἀγαπητὸς ἀδελφὸς in reference to

σύνδουλος ἐν Κυρίῳ, ⁸ ὃν ἔπεμψα πρὸς ὑμᾶς εἰς αὐτὸ τοῦτο, ἵνα γνῷ τὰ περὶ ὑμῶν καὶ παρακαλέσῃ τὰς καρδίας ὑμῶν, ⁹ σὺν Ὀνησίμῳ τῷ πιστῷ καὶ ἀγαπητῷ ἀδελφῷ, ὅς ἐστιν ἐξ ὑμῶν· πάντα ὑμῖν γνωριοῦσιν τὰ ὧδε.

the Christian community, a πιστὸς διάκονος in reference to his missionary services to St. Paul (not in the ministry generally, Alford), and further, with a graceful allusion to similarity of duties, a σύνδουλος ἐν Κυρίῳ, a co-operator with, and co-adjutor of, the apostle in the service of the same Master; compare notes on *Eph.* vi. 21.   ἐν Κυρίῳ may be associated with all three designations (De W., compare Eph. *l. c.*), or with the last two (Meyer), or with σύνδουλος Æth.-Pol., and perhaps Syr.). As the two former have defining epithets, perhaps the last connection is slightly the most probable.

8. εἰς αὐτὸ τοῦτο] '*for this very purpose,*' viz. as further defined and expanded in the following clause, ' that he should gain a knowledge of your state, and comfort you.' On the reference of αὐτὸ τοῦτο to what follows, comp. Eph. vi. 22, Phil. i. 6, and notes *in loc.* The reading is doubtful. *Griesb.* and *Lachm.* read γνῶτε and ἡμῶν, with ABD¹FG ; 10 mss.; Clarom., Æth. (both Pol. and Platt) ; Theod. (text), al., to which Mey. adds the argument derived from probable erroneous transcription (comp. Pref. to *Galat.* p. xvii.) ; viz. the accidental omission of the ΤΕ before ΤΑ. The text (*Rec.*, *Tisch.*) is found in CD²D³EKL ; great majority of mss., and (what is very important) Vulg., Syr. (both), Coptic, Goth.; Chrysost., Theod. (comm.), al. The weight of uncial authority is clearly in favor of γνῶτε, still the distinct preponderance of Vv., and the probability of a conformation to Eph. vi. 22, induce us to retain the reading of *Tisch.*; so De Wette and Alf.   παρακαλέσῃ] '*comfort;*' in reference to their own

state; δείκνυσι δὲ αὐτοὺς ἐν πειρασμοῖς ὄντας, καὶ παρακλήσεως δεομένους, Theophyl.: according to the other reading the reference would be to St. Paul; compare on *Eph.* vi. 22.

9. σὺν Ὀνησίμῳ] '*with Onesimus,*' scil. ἔπεμψα. There seems no reason to doubt (Calvin) that the Onesimus here mentioned was the runaway slave of Philemon, whose flight from his master (Philem. 15), and subsequent conversion (at Rome by the apostle, gave rise to the exquisite Epistle to Philemon. Whether he was identical with Onesimus, Bishop of Ephesus, mentioned by Ignatius, *Eph.* § 1, as affirmed by Ado (ap. Usuard. *Martyrology*, p. 272, ed. Soll.), is very doubtful; see Pearson, *Vind. Ign.* II. 8, p. 463 (A.-C. Libr.). The name was not uncommon, added to which the tradition of the Greek Church (*Const. Apost* VII. 46) represents the 'Onesimus Philemonis' to have been Bishop of Beroea in Macedonia; compare Winer, *RWB.* Vol. II. p. 173. There appear to have been two at least of this name in the early martyrologies, the legendary notices of those lives have been mixed up together; see *Acta Sanct.* Feb. 16, Vol. II. p. 855 sq.   ὅς ἐστιν ἐξ ὑμῶν] '*who is of you,*' ' who belongs to your city.' This addition seems to have been made, not to give indirect honor and praise to the Colossians (ἵνα καὶ ἐγκαλλωπίζωνται ὡς τοιοῦτον προενέγκοντες, Theoph.), but to commend the tidings and the joint-bearer of them still more to their attention.

τὰ ὧδε] '*the things here,*' the matters here at Rome, of which τὰ κατ' ἐμέ, ver. 7, would form the principal portion. The addition πραττόμενα [FG; Vulg.

Aristarchus, and others, salute you. Interchange epistles with the church of Laodicea. Tell Archippus to do his work.

¹⁰ Ἀσπάζεται ὑμᾶς Ἀρίσταρχος ὁ συναιχ-

Claroman.; Lat. Vulg.] is a self-evident gloss.

10. Ἀρίσταρχος] A native of Thessalonica (Acts xx. 4), who accompanied St. Paul on his third missionary journey; he was with the apostle in the tumult at Ephesus (Acts xix. 29), and is again noticed as being with him in the voyage to Rome (Acts xxvii. 2). There he shared the apostle's captivity, either as an attendant on him (see below) or a fellow-sufferer. According to some traditions of the Greek Church he is said to have been Bishop of Apamea in Phrygia; according to the Roman martyrologies, Bishop of Thessalonica; see *Martyrol. Rom.* p. 343 (Antwerp, 1589), *Acta Sanct.* Aug. 4, Vol. I. p. 313. In the *Menol. Græc.* (April 15, Vol. III. p. 57) he is said to have been one of the 70 disciples. ὁ συναιχμάλωτός μου] '*my fellow-prisoner.*' It is certainly singular that in the Epistle to Philemon, written so closely at the same time with the present Epistle, Aristarchus should be mentioned not as a συναιχμάλ. but as a συνεργός, while Epaphras, who here indirectly, and still more clearly ch. i. 7, appears in the latter capacity, is there a συναιχμάλωτος. There seem only two probable solutions; either that their positions had become interchanged by the results of some actual trial, or that their captivity was *voluntary*, and that they took their turns in sharing the apostle's captivity, and in ministering to him in his bonds. The latter solution, which is that of Fritz. (*Rom.* Vol. I. p. xxi, followed by Meyer), seems the most natural; compare also Wieseler, *Chronol.* p. 417 note. To regard the term as semititular, and as referring to a bygone captivity (Steiger, compare Rom. xvi. 7), does not seem satisfactory. The term is slightly noticeable ('designat hasta

superatum et captum,' Davers, as carrying out the metaphor of the *αἰχμαλ* Christ, compare Me cross(?).

Μάρκος] Almost certainly the same who holds in Mark the son of Mary (Acts xii. 12), whom St. Paul at St. Barnabas took with them on their first missionary journey, who left them when in Pamphylia, and who was afterwards the cause of the contention between the apostle and St. Barnabas (Acts xv. 39); compare Blunt, *Veracity of Evangelists* 24, where the connection between John Mark and St. Barnabas, and especially the history of the latter, is clearly considered. There seems no reason for doubting (Grot., Kienlen, *Stud. u. Krit.* 1843, p. 423 sq.) that he was identical with St. Mark the Evangelist; see Meyer, *Einl. z. Evang. d. Markus*, p. 2, Fritz. *Prolog. in Marc.* p. 24. According to ecclesiastical tradition, St. Mark was first Bishop of Alexandria, and suffered martyrdom there; see *Acta Sanct.*, April 25. Vol. III. p. 344. ἀνεψιός] 'cousin,' דּוֹדָן. Num. xxxvi. 11; ἀνεψιοι τῶν ἀδελφῶν παῖδες, Ammon. *Voc. Diff.* p. 54 (ed. Val ker); the proper term for what was sometimes designated as ἐξάδελφος by later and rather classical writers; see Lobeck, *Phryn.* p. 306, where the proper meaning of ἀνεψιός is well discussed. St. Mark was thus not the 'nephew' (Auth., but *See remarks in Transl.*), but the 'consobrinus' Vulg., Claroman.), the דּוֹד בֶּן (Syr.) of St. Barnabas; see exx. in Wetst. *in loc.* ἐλάβετε ἐντολάς] '*ye received commands;*' what these were cannot be determined. The conjectural explanations, — messages from Barnabas (Chrysost.), letters of commendation ('literæ formatæ'), either from St. Paul (Daven.) or the Church of Rome (Est.), etc. are very

μάλωτός μου, καὶ Μάρκος ὁ ἀνεψιὸς Βαρνάβα, περὶ οὗ ἐλάβετε ἐντολάς (ἐὰν ἔλθῃ πρὸς ὑμᾶς, δέξασθε αὐτόν), ¹¹ καὶ Ἰησοῦς ὁ λεγόμενος Ἰοῦστος, οἱ ὄντες ἐκ περιτομῆς· οὗτοι μόνοι συνεργοὶ

numerous, but do not any of them seem to deserve particular attention. To find in ἐὰν κ. τ. λ. the 'summa illorum mandatorum,' Beng., is grammatically untenable; the person of the aor. precludes the assumption of its use as an epistolary present. The parenthetical clause, however, so immediately following the ἐλάβετε ἐντολὰς does certainly seem to suggest that these ἐντολαὶ were of a commendatory nature; compare Wieseler, *Chronolog.* p. 452, note. A few MSS. [D₁FG; Syr., Arr.] read δέξασθαι, probably on the same hypothesis as that of Bengel. δέξασθε αὐτόν] 'receive him,' i. e. with hospitality (comp. Matth. x. 14) and friendly feelings (Luke ix. 48, John iv. 45). The historical deduction, founded on the use of the simple δέξασθε (contrast Acts xxi. 17), that St. Mark had not been in the neighborhood of Colossæ, and would not have been recognized as an assistant of St. Paul (Wieseler, *Chronol.* p. 567), seems not only precarious but improbable.

11. Ἰησοῦς ὁ λεγ. Ἰοῦστος] Mentioned only in this place; probably not identical with Justus of Corinth (Acts xviii. 7). Tradition represents him as afterwards bishop of Eleutheropolis. οἱ ὄντες ἐκ περιτ.] 'who are of the circumcision;' participial predication in reference to the three preceding nouns. Meyer, Lachmann, and Buttm. (ed. 1856) remove the stop after περιτομῆς, and regard the clause as in the nom. ('per anacoluthon'), instead of being in the more intelligible partitive genitive. Such an anacoluthon is not uncommon (see Jelf, *Gr.* § 708. 2), but does not seem here necessary as the μόνοι naturally refers the thought to the category last mentioned; 'these only of that class are my helpers:' compare

Philem. 24, where, though Luke and Demas are grouped together with them as συνεργοί, the same general order is still preserved. On the formula εἶναι ἐκ, with abstract substantives, in which ἐκ retains its primary meaning of *origin*, compare notes *on Gal.* iii. 7, and Fritz. *on Rom.* ii. 8, Vol. I. p. 105.
εἰς τὴν βασιλ.] 'unto, towards, the kingdom of God:' 'adjuverunt Paulum ad regnum Messianum qui ei, quum homines idoneos redderet quin in illud regnum aliquando reciperentur, opitulati sunt,' Fritz. *Rom.* xiv. 17, Vol. III. p. 201. On the term βασιλεία Θεοῦ, see an elaborate paper by Bauer (C. G.) in *Comment. Theol.* Part II. p. 107-172, and Reuss, *Théol. Chrét.* IV. 22, Vol. II. p. 244. οἵτινες ἐγεν] 'men who proved;' the indefinite ὅστις being here used in what has been termed its *classific* sense, and pointing to the category to which the antecedents belong; see notes *on Gal.* ii. 4, iv. 24. The passive *form* ἐγενήθ., condemned by Thom. M. p. 189 (ed. Bern.), and rejected by Phrynicus, p 108 (ed. Lobeck), as a Doric inflexion, occurs not uncommonly in the N. T. (noticeably in 1 Thess.), but, as a careful comparison of parallel passages seems to show, without any clearly pronounced passive *meaning*, or any justly appreciable difference from ἐγένετο; comp. Buttm. *Irreg. Verbs*, p. 50. παρηγορία] 'a comfort;' an ἅπαξ λεγόμ in the N. T. but not uncommon elsewhere, see the examples in Kypke, *Obs.* Vol. II. p. 330; add also Æsch. *Agam.* 95, where the term seems to involve a slightly medical allusion. The distinction of Beng. 'παραμυθία in maerore domestico, παρηγορία in forensi periculo,' does not seem substantiated by lexical usage. Perhaps

εἰς τὴν βασιλείαν τοῦ Θεοῦ, οἵτινες ἐγενήθησάν μοι παρηγορία. ¹² ἀσπάζεται ὑμᾶς Ἐπαφρᾶς ὁ ἐξ ὑμῶν, δοῦλος Χριστοῦ Ἰησοῦ, πάντοτε ἀγωνιζόμενος ὑπὲρ ὑμῶν ἐν ταῖς προσευχαῖς, ἵνα στῆτε τέλειοι καὶ πεπληροφορημένοι ἐν παντὶ θελήματι τοῦ Θεοῦ. ¹³ μαρ-

the only real distinction is that παρηγορεῖν and its derivatives admit of physical and quasi-physical references which are not found with the more purely ethical παραμυθεῖσθαι; see the good lists of examples in Rost u. Palm, Lex. s. vv.

12. Ἐπαφρᾶς] See notes on ch. i. 7; he is specified in the same way as Onesimus, as a native of Colossae. For the probable reason of the addition, see notes on ver. 9. δοῦλος Χρ. Ἰησ.] Meyer, and after him Alford, following Griesb. (who, however, reads only Χριστοῦ), join these words with ὁ ἐξ ὑμῶν: this certainly seems unnecessary, the title δοῦλος Χρ. Ἰησ. is of quite sufficient weight and importance to stand alone as a title of honor and distinction; so apparently Copt., as it inserts the def. art. before δοῦλος. In Æth (Polygl.) the position of the pronoun of the 3d pers [appy. here for the verb subst., Ludolph, Gr. p. 135] might seem in favor of the other mode of punctuation; Syr. seems in favor of the text. The insertion of Ἰησοῦ after Χριστοῦ (Lachmann, Tisch.) has good critical support [ABCJ; 10 mss.; Vulg., Copt., Arm.] and is rightly adopted by most modern editors. ἀγωνιζόμενος] 'striving earnestly;' compare Rom. xv. 30, where the compound συναγων. occurs in a similar context; compare ch ii. 1, and notes in loc. ἵνα στῆτε] 'that ye may stand fast;' purpose of the ἀγωνιζόμενος, the more emphatic ἀγωνιζόμ. ἐν προσευχ. (not merely προσευχόμενος) not requiring any dilution of the telic force of ἵνα; comp. notes on Eph. i. 17. Στῆναι has here, as in Eph. vi. 11, 13, al., the meaning of standing firm and unshaken amidst trials and dangers (see notes on Ephes. ll. cc.), and is more nearly defined by the following adjectives and their associated semi-local predication ἐν παντὶ θελήματι.
τέλειοι καὶ πεπληροφ.] 'perfect and fully assured;' secondary predicates of manner (Donalds. Cratyl. § 303), the first referring to their maturity and perfectness (ch. i. 28, Eph. iv. 13), the second to their firm persuasion, and the absence of all doubtfulness or scrupulosity. On the distinction between τέλειος and ὁλόκληρος ('omnibus numeris absolutus') see Trench, Synon. § 22, and between τέλ. and ἄρτιος, notes on 2 Tim. iii. 17. The reading πεπληροφ. is adopted by Lachmann and Tisch. [with ABC D₁FG; 6 mss.], and both on external and on internal grounds is to be preferred to πεπληρωμένοι (Rec.).
ἐν παντὶ θελήματι] 'in every (manifestation of the) will of God,' i. e. 'in everything which God willeth' (Winer, Gr. § 18. 4. p. 101), which, though not grammatically, yet in common usage becomes equivalent to 'in all the will of God,' Auth. It is doubtful whether these words are to be joined with the finite verb (Meyer, Alf.; compare Rom. v. 2, 1 Corinth. xv. 1), or with the secondary predicates τέλειοι καὶ πεπληροφ. (De W.). The latter is most simple, as defining the sphere in which the τελειότης and πληροφορία was to be evinced and find its realization; so Chrys., Theoph., and perhaps Coptic, Gothic, who even with πεπληρωμένοι (comp. on Eph. v. 18) connect ἐν παντὶ θελ. with the secondary predicates. The Vv., however, in such cases cannot be appealed to with confidence, as they commonly preserve the ambiguous order of the original.

13. μαρτυρῶ γάρ] Confirmatory (γὰρ) testimony to the earnestness and activity of Epaphras.   πολὺν

τυρῷ γὰρ αὐτῷ ὅτι ἔχει πολὺν πόνον ὑπὲρ ὑμῶν καὶ τῶν ἐν Λαοδικείᾳ καὶ τῶν ἐν Ἱεραπόλει. ¹⁴ ἀσπάζεται ὑμᾶς Λουκᾶς ὁ ἰατρὸς ὁ ἀγαπητὸς καὶ Δημᾶς. ¹⁵ ἀσπάσασθε τοὺς ἐν Λαοδικείᾳ ἀδελφοὺς

πόνον] 'much labor;' not such as that which attends a combat (Eadie). but, as the etymological affinities of πόνος [connected with πένομαι, and probably derived from ΣΠΑ-, see Benfey, *Wurzellex*. Vol. II. p. 360] seem to suggest, such as implies a putting forth all one's strength (*intentio*); compare Suidas πόνος· σπουδή, ἐπίτασις. The word is rare in the N. T., only here and Rev. xvi. 10, 11, xxi. 4. This may account for the variety of reading; κόπον, D¹FG; ζῆλον D²D³*KL (*Rec.*). The text is supported by ABC; 80; Coptic (*emkah*), and indirectly by D¹FG: so *Lachm., Tisch*.
Λαοδικείᾳ] For a brief notice of this city, see notes on ch. ii. 1.
Ἱεραπόλει] An important city of Phrygia, about twenty English miles NNW. (surely not 'östlich,' Winer) of Colossæ, celebrated for its mineral springs, and a mephitic cavern called Plutonium, which was apparently connected with the worship of the 'Magna Mater;' see Strabo, *Geogr*. XIII. 4. 14 (ed. Kramer), Pliny, *Hist. Nat*. II. 93 (ed. Sillig). The site of Hierapolis appears to have been close to the modern Pambuk-Kalasi, round which extensive ruins are still to be traced; see Forbiger, *Alt. Geograph*. Vol. II. p. 348, 349, Arundell, *Seven Churches*, p. 79 sq., ib. *Asia Minor*, Vol. II. p. 200 sq., and a good article in Kitto's *Bibl. Cyclop*. Vol. II. p. 848. It is curious that this city should apparently have been unnoticed in Pauly, *Real. Encycl*.
14. Λουκᾶς] The Evangelist, who according to ancient tradition (Irenæus, *Hær*. III. 14. 1, 'creditus est referre nobis evangelium') has been regarded as identical with the ἰατρὸς ἀγαπητὸς here mentioned. The tradition that he was a painter (Nicephor. *Hist. Eccl*. II. 13)

is late and untrustworthy. There seems no etymological grounds whatever for identifying him further with the Lucius mentioned in Rom. xvi. 21 (Origen): Lucas may have been a contraction of Lucanus, or possibly even of Lucilius, but not of Lucius. For further notices see notes on 2 *Tim*. iv. 11. The addition ὁ ἰατρὸς ὁ ἀγαπητὸς may possibly have been intended to distinguish the Evangelist from others of the same name (Chrys.), but more probably is only a further designation similar to those given to Tychicus (ver. 7), Onesimus (ver. 9), Aristarchus, Mark (ver. 10), Justus (ver. 11), and Epaphras (ver. 12).
Δημᾶς] Mentioned as one of the apostle's συνεργοί (Philem. 24). but too well remembered as having deserted him in the hour of need; see notes on 2 *Tim*. iv. 10. Whether the omission of a title of honor or affection is accidental, or owing to his having already shown symptoms of the defection of which he was afterwards guilty (Meyer), cannot be determined. The latter does not seem improbable, especially as he here occupies the last place in the enumeration; contrast Philem. 24.
15. καὶ Νυμφᾶν] 'and (among them) Nymphas,' καί being here used to add the special to the general (see notes on *Eph*. v. 18, vi. 19), and to particularize Nymphas, who apparently belonged to Laodicea and, as the following words seem to show, was a person of some importance: ὅρα γοῦν πῶς δείκνυσι μέγαν τὸν ἄνδρα, Chrys.,—who, however, adds too restrictively, εἴ γε ἡ οἰκία αὐτοῦ ἐκκλησία; compare notes on *Philem*. 2. The repetition of the more generic τῇ Λαοδ. ἐκκλ. in ver. 16 would seem to show that the church in the house of Nymphas did not comprehend all the

καὶ Νυμφᾶν καὶ τὴν κατ' οἶκον αὐτοῦ ἐκκλησίαν. ¹⁶ καὶ ὅταν ἀναγνωσθῇ παρ' ὑμῖν ἡ ἐπιστολή, ποιήσατε ἵνα καὶ ἐν τῇ Λαοδικέων ἐκκλησίᾳ ἀναγνωσθῇ, καὶ τὴν ἐκ Λαοδικείας ἵνα καὶ ὑμεῖς ἀναγνῶτε.

Christians of Laodicea. The form Νύμφας (*Lachm.*, *Buttm*., with B²) is not correct; the last syllable is circumflexed, and marks a probable contraction from Nymphodorus (Pliny, *Hist. Nat.* VII. 2), as Ὀλυμπᾶς (Rom. xvi. 15) from Olympiodorus, Ζηνᾶς (Tit. iii. 13) from Zenodorus; compare Fritz. *Rom.* Vol III. p. 309. κατ' οἶκον αὐτοῦ] So Rom. xvi. 5, in reference to Prisca and Aquila, who had also at Corinth (1 Cor. xvi 19) devoted their house to a similar righteous use; compare on *Philem.* 2, and see especially Neand., *Planting*, Vol. I. p. 151, note (Bohn). The reading is somewhat doubtful. The text is supported by DEFGKL; great majority of mss.; Chrys., Theod., al. (*Rec.*, *Tisch.*), and appy. rightly, for though αὐτῶν [AC; 7 mss.; Slav. (ms.)] is not improbable as at first sight a more difficult reading, it may still have easily arisen from the preceding plural, and the desire, even at the expense of the sense, to identify the whole church of Laodicea with that in the house of Nymphas. If αὐτῶν be adopted (Mey., Alf.), then the plural must be referred to 'Nymphas and his family,' involved κατὰ σύνεσιν in the preceding substantive; see Jelf, *Gr.* § 379. b, compare Winer, *Gr.* § 22. 3, p. 132. *Lachm.* reads αὐτῆς, but on authority [B; 67**] manifestly insufficient.

16. ἡ ἐπιστολή] 'the present letter;' compare Rom. xvi. 22, 1 Thess. v. 27. Several cursive mss. add αὐτή, but quite unnecessarily; see Winer, *Gram.* § 18. 1, p. 97.

ποιήσατε ἵνα] 'cause that;' a formula of later Greek (John xi. 37, compare Rev. iii. 9), though not without parallel in the ποιεῖν ὅπως (Jelf, *Gr.* § 666, obs.) of the classical writers. The proper force of ἵνα, though weakened and somewhat approximating to the lax use of τοῦ with the infinitive after ποιεῖν (Acts iii. 12, Josh. xxii. 26, al.), is not wholly lost; see Winer, *Gr.* § 44. s. p. 301.

τὴν ἐκ Λαοδ.] 'that from Laodicea,' not ܕܰܟܬܺܝܒܳܐ ܒܠܰܐܘܕܺܝܩܺܝܰܐ [quae scripta est ex Laodicensibus] Syr., — but corrected in Philox., or 'quam scripsi ex Laod.,' Æth. (compare Theod., but with the usual and proper force of the preposition, 'that out of Laodicea,' 'poei ist us Laud.,' Goth., 'doldon Laod.,' Copt., — two prepositions being really involved in the clause 'the Epistle sent to and to be received from or out of Laod.,' but the latter, by a very intelligible and not uncommon attraction, alone expressed; compare Luke ix. 61, xi. 13, and see Winer, *Gr.* § 66. 6, p. 553, Jelf, *Gr.* § 647. n. The real difficulty is to determine what letter is here referred to. Setting aside attempts to identify it with the 1st Epistle to Tim. (Theophylact), the 1st Ep. of St. John (Lightf.), the Ep. to Philemon — an essentially private letter (Wieseler, *Chronol.* p. 452), two opinions deserve consideration; — (*a*) that it is the Epistle to the Ephesians; (*b*) that it is a lost Epistle. For (*a*) we have the similarity of contents, and the probability, from the absence of greetings and local allusions, that the Ep. to the Ephesians was designed for other readers than those to whom it was primarily addressed. Against it, the great improbability that the apostle should know that his Epist. to the Ephesians would have reached Laodicea at or near the time of the delivery of his Ep. to the Colossians. For (*b*) we may urge the highly probable circumstance that Tychicus might have been the bearer of the two letters

¹⁷ καὶ εἴπατε Ἀρχίππῳ Βλέπε τὴν διακονίαν ἣν παρέλαβες ἐν Κυρίῳ, ἵνα αὐτὴν πληροῖς.

to the two neighboring cities, leaving that to Laodicea first, with orders for the interchange, and then continuing his journey. Against it there is the *à priori* improbability that a letter which, from the present direction given by the apostle, stood apparently in some degree of parallelism to that to the Colossians (we have no right to assume that it was 'of a merely temporary or local nature,' Eadie; see contra Meyer), should have been lost to the Church of Christ. The fact that the *orthodox* early Church (compare Jones *on Canon*, Part III. 6) does not seem to have ever acquiesced in (*b*) makes the decision very difficult; us, however, the Ep. to the Colossians does appear to have been written first, — as the title τοῖς ἐν Ἐφέσῳ (Eph. i. 1) does seem to preclude our assigning to that Epistle a farther destination than to the churches dependent on Ephesus (see crit. note on *Eph.* i. 1), — as there does *seem* a trace of another lost Ep. (1 Cor. v. 9), — as the close neighborhood of Colossæ and Laodicea might prepare us to admit a great similarity in contents, and consequently a very partial loss to the Church, — and lastly, as *à priori* arguments on such subjects are always to be viewed with some suspicion, we decide in favor of (*b*), and believe that an actual Epistle to the Laodiceans is here alluded to, which, possibly from its similarity to its sister-Epistle, it has not pleased God to preserve to us: see Meyer, *Einl. z. Eph.* p. 9 sq., where the question is fairly argued. It may be added in conclusion that the above reasoning rests on the assumption that the Epistle to the Ephesians *was* written to that Church, and that the words ἐν Ἐφέσῳ are genuine. It is right, however, to add that the new-discovered א rejects them, and that thus an important authority has been added to the side of those who deem that a blank was left for the name of the Church, and that the Epistle was purely encyclical. *If* this view (which still seems *very* doubtful) be adopted, the balance will probably lean more to (*a*); at present, however, no more need be said than this, that the title of the Epistle to the Ephesians and the present question may justly be considered as in somewhat close connection. The forged Epistle to the Laodiceans deserves no notice, being a mere cento out of St. Paul's Epistles; see Jones, *on Canon*, Part III. 6.

17. Ἀρχίππῳ] A church-officer of Colossæ, — not of Laodicea (Wieseler, *Chronol.* p. 452, compare *Const. Apost.* VII. 46); possibly an instructor (Theod. *Philem.* 2), but more probably a friend (Chrys., Theophyl. *ib.*) of the household of Philemon, — if, indeed, on account of the position of Arch. in the salutation (Philemon 2), not more nearly related (compare Olsh.). What the διακονία of Archippus was, cannot be determined; that he was a διάκονος in the literal meaning (compare Wordsw.), does not seem improbable. Tradition represents him to have suffered martyrdom at Chonæ; see *Menolog. Græcum*, Nov. 23, Vol. I. p. 206. A brief notice will also be found in the *Acta Sanctorum*, March 20, Vol. III. p. 82. On the somewhat unusual (Ionic) form εἴπατε (Matth. x. 27, xxi. 5], see Winer, *Gr.* § 15, p. 78.

βλέπε τὴν διακονίαν] 'see to, take heed to, the ministry;' somewhat too strongly Syriac, ܚܙܝ [diligens esto], though rightly preserving the construction: for examples of this meaning of βλέπειν see Elsner, *Obs.* Vol. II. p. 272, and comp. *on Eph* v. 15. Grotius and others assume here a Hebraistic inversion

Autograph salutation and benediction.

18 Ὁ ἀσπασμὸς τῇ ἐμῇ χειρὶ Παύλου. μνημονεύετέ μου τῶν δεσμῶν. ἡ χάρις μεθ' ὑμῶν.

for βλέπε ἵνα πληρ.,—a needless violation of the order of the words and of the more usual meaning of ἵνα; the object of the βλέπειν τὴν διακονίαν on the part of Archippus was to be ἵνα αὐτὴν πληροῖ; compare 2 John 8, and notes on *Gal.* iv. 11. The expression πληροῦν διακονίαν occurs again Acts xii. 25; see examples in Raphel, *Annot.* Vol. II. p. 538, Kypke, *Obs.* Vol. II. p. 331, and Wetst. *in loc.* παρελαβες ἐν Κυρίῳ] 'didst receive in the *Lord*;' not 'per Dominum,' Daven., nor 'secundum Domini praecepta,' Grot., but as always, 'in Domino,' Vulg., Clarom., al. The Lord was, as it were, the *sphere* in which he had received his διακονία, and out of which it found no place; see notes on *Eph.* iv. 16, vi. 1, *Phil.* ii. 19, and elsewhere. The addition, as Meyer well observes, still more enhances the obligation of Archippus to fulfil a διακονία so received.

18. ὁ ἀσπασμὸς κ.τ.λ] Autograph salutation of the apostle, to attest the authenticity of the document (2 Thess. iii. 17, contrasted with ib. ch. ii. 2); compare 1 Cor. xvi. 21 and notes on *Gal.* vi. 11. The gen. Παύλου is in apposition to the personal pron. involved in ἐμῇ; see examples in Jelf, *Gr.* § 467. 4. μνημονεύετε μου τῶν δεσμῶν] 'Remember my bonds.' A touching exhortation, speaking vividly to the hearts of his readers, and breathing patience and encouragement; μεγίστη δὲ παράκλησις αὐτοῖς εἰς πᾶσαν θλίψιν τὸ μνημονεύειν Παύλου δεδεμένου, Theoph., compare Chrys. et. The remark of Ladis is just, that as the apostle used his hand to write these words, his bonds yet more keenly, but he should have remembered, that it was (in all probability) not the *left* but the *right* hand that was bound to the soldier that guarded him; see Smith, *Dict. A.* p. s. v. 'Catena,' p. 207.

ἡ χάρις] 'Grace,' κατ' ἐξοχήν; see notes on *Eph.* vi. 24, and on the various meanings of χάρις, Waterl. *Ed* Vol. x. Vol. iv. p. 666. The ἀμήν of *Rec.* is found in DEKL; Vv. and Ff., but is rightly rejected by modern editors on preponderant uncial authority.

THE EPISTLE TO PHILEMON.

INTRODUCTION.

This exquisite and interesting Epistle, alike a master-piece of persuasive tact and delicacy, and an enduring model of truest Christian courtesy, was written by St. Paul to Philemon closely about the same time as the Epistle to the Church of Colossae, and not improbably stands first in the group of Epistles written during the first captivity at Rome; comp. Davidson, *Introd.* Vol. III. p. 158. It would thus have been written about A.D. 61 or 62: see *Introd. to Colossians.*

It was addressed to Philemon, most probably a member of the Church of Colossae (ver. 2, compared with Col. iv. 9, 17), who had originally been converted to Christianity by the apostle (ver. 19), and who, from the honorable title of 'fellow-laborer' (ver. 2; compare ver. 24 and Col. iv. 11), coupled with the notice of 'the church in his house' (ver. 2) and the general tone of the Epistle, appears to have been a person of distinction, worth, and Christian zeal and earnestness (ver. 7). The bearer of the Epistle was Onesimus, a slave who had run away from, and as it would seem robbed Philemon (ver. 18) but who now, after having had the blessing of meeting with St. Paul at Rome, and of being converted to Christianity by him (ver. 10), was returning to the master he had wronged, changed and repentant, especially commended to his love and forgiveness (ver. 17), and mentioned, not without honor (Col. iv. 9), to the Church of which both were now alike to be members. His fellow traveller was Tychicus, the bearer of the Epistles to the Churches of Colossae and Ephesus (Col. iv. 7, Eph. vi. 21), to whose care and good offices he was not improbably further committed, and who might have been instructed by the apostle to induce the Colossian Christians generally to receive the hitherto unprofitable servant (comp. ver. 11) with forbearance and favor.

The *object* of the Epistle is very clearly set before us,— an affectionate desire on the part of the apostle to restore Onesimus to the confidence and love of his master, and to insure for him a reception which he might justly have been considered wholly to have forfeited. The exquisite tact with which his fraudulent conduct towards Philemon is alluded to (ver. 18),— the absence of everything tending to excuse or palliate the misdeed, yet the use of every expression and sentiment calculated to win the fullest measures of Philemon's forgiveness, — has never failed to call forth the reverential admiration of every expositor of this Epistle from the earliest times down to our own day.

The originality with which the Epistle is thus stamped, and the strong external testimonies of antiquity which, short as this Epistle is, are by no means wanting (Tertull. *adv. Marc.* v. 42, Origen, *Hom. xix. in Jerem. ; in Matth.* Tract. XXXIII. XXXIV., Eusebius, *Hist. Eccl.* III. 25), may justly be said to place its *genuineness* and *authenticity* beyond all doubt. It appears, however, to have been carped at in early times (see Jerome, *Proœm. in Philem.*), and has recently been considered by a modern critic (Baur, *Apostel Paulus*, p. 475 sq.) as of doubtful authorship, but on grounds so utterly untenable that we may with justice refuse to notice what the very author of the criticism seems to feel (p. 476) is open to the charge of an undue and unreasonable scepticism.

THE EPISTLE TO PHILEMON.

Apostolic address and salutation.

ΠΑΥΛΟΣ δέσμιος Χριστοῦ Ἰησοῦ καὶ Τιμόθεος ὁ ἀδελφὸς Φιλήμονι τῷ ἀγαπητῷ καὶ συνεργῷ ἡμῶν ² καὶ Ἀπφίᾳ τῇ ἀδελφῇ καὶ Ἀρχίππῳ τῷ

2. ἀδελφῇ] So *Lachm.* and *Tisch.* ed. 1, with AD¹E¹FG; 3 mss.; Claroman., Amit., Tol., Copt., Æth. (Platt); Hes., Hier. (*Meyer*). In his later edd. *Tisch.* reverts to the reading of *Rec.* with D³E²KL; nearly all mss.; Syr. (both,—but Philox with asterisk); Theod.-Mops. (expressly), Chrys., Theod., al. The external authorities are thus very nearly balanced; it does not, however, seem improbable that the supposed connection between Philemon and Apphia might have led to the same title being applied to each.

1. δέσμιος Χρ. Ἰησ.] 'a prisoner of Christ Jesus,' 'whom Christ Jesus and His cause have made a prisoner;' gen. of the author of the captivity; see Winer, *Gram.* § 30. 2, p. 170 (ed. 6), and notes *on Eph.* iii. 1, 2 *Tim.* i. 8. Considering the subject of the Epistle, no title could be more appropriate, or more feelingly prepare Philemon for the request which the apostle is about to make to him. On the titles adopted by St. Paul in his salutations, see notes *on Phil.* i. 1, and especially *on Col.* i. 1.

καὶ Τιμόθεος] Associated with the apostle in the same way as in 2 Cor. i. 1, Col. i. 1, each having a separate, and not, as in Phil. i. 1 (compare 1 and 2 Thess. i. 1), a common title; see notes *on Phil.* i., and *on Col.* i. 1. The association of Timothy in a letter which has the character of a private communication was perhaps, as Chrys. suggests, ὥστε κἀκεῖνον ὑπὸ πολλῶν ἀξιούμενον μᾶλλον εἶξαι καὶ δοῦναι τὴν χάριν.

Φιλήμονι] Philemon was a member of the Church of Colossæ (compare Col. iv. 9), who owed his conversion to St. Paul (verse 19), and who by his zeal in the Christian cause (verse 5), showed himself worthy of the consider t n and regard which the apostle evinces f r him in this Epistle. There does not seem any good ground for the opinion of Wieseler (*Chronol.* p. 452) that Philemon belonged to Laodicea; his house at Colossæ was shown in the time of Theodoret (*Argum. ad Philem.*), and tradition (*Const. Apost.* VII. 46) represents him as having been bishop of that city,—not of Laodicea, as Alford, *Proleg.* I. p. 114. In the *Menol. Græcum*, Nov. 23, Vol. I. p. 206, he is said to have suffered martyrdom with Archippus at Chonæ.

συνεργῷ ἡμῶν] 'our fellow-helper;' more special designation suggested by the zeal of Philemon for the Gospel. The genitive ἡμῶν, as the single article hints, belongs to συνεργῷ and the verbal

συνστρατιώτῃ ἡμῶν, καὶ τῇ κατ οἶκόν σου ἐκκλησίᾳ. ³ χάρις ὑμῖν καὶ εἰρήνη ἀπὸ Θεοῦ πατρὸς ἡμῶν καὶ Κυρίου Ἰησοῦ Χριστοῦ.

I thank God for thy progress in faith, and pray that it may prove beneficial to others: the proofs of thy love to the saints gladdens me.
⁴ Εὐχαριστῶ τῷ Θεῷ μου, πάντοτε μνείαν

ἀγαπητῷ, compare Rom. i. 7. Both titles are dwelt upon by Chrys. and Theophyl.; the latter says, εἰ ἀγαπητός, δώσει τὴν χάριν· εἰ συνεργός, οὐ καθέξει τὸν δοῦλον ἀλλὰ πάλιν ἀποστελεῖ πρὸς ὑπηρεσίαν τοῦ κηρύγματος.

2. Ἀπφίᾳ] Most probably, as suggested by Chrysos. and the Greek commentators, the wife of Philemon. If this be so, it is not improbable that Archippus may have been their son; see notes on *Col.* iv. 17. The name Ἀπφία, which in some mss. appears in the form Ἀππία (see Acts xxviii. 15), is the softened form of the Latin 'Appia' (Grot.).

Ἀρχίππῳ] Supposed by Wieseler (*Chronol.* p. 452), but without sufficient reason, to have been of the Church of Laodicea; see notes *on Col.* iv. 17. He is here distinguished by the honorable title of συνστρατιώτης with the apostle; compare 2 Tim. ii. 3. On the Alexandrian form συνστρ. see Winer, *Gr.* § 5. 4, p. 46. τῇ κατ' οἶκόν σου ἐκκλ.] 'the church in thy house;' not merely the household of Philemon, οὐδὲ δούλους παρῆκεν ἐνταῦθα, Chrys., but, as the expression seems regularly to designate, the assembly of Christians that were accustomed to meet at the house of Philemon, and join with his household in public prayer; compare *on Col.* iv. 15, and Pearson, *Creed*, Art. ix. Vol. i. p. 397.

3. χάρις ὑμῖν κ.τ.λ.] Scil. εἴη, not ἔστω (Koch); see notes *on Eph.* i. 2: the regular form of salutation in St. Paul's Epp. On the spiritual meaning of the blended form of address, see notes on *Gal.* i. 2, *Eph.* i. 2; add also *on Phil.* i. 1. καὶ Κυρίου] Scil. καὶ ἀπὸ Κυρίου κ.τ.λ. as expressly in Syr. ܡܢ ܡܪܢ [et a

Dom. nostro] : the Socinian interpretation καὶ (πατρὸς) Κυρίου seems very improbable; see notes on *Phil.* i. 2.

4. εὐχαριστῶ] Usual eucharistic commencement in reference to the spiritual state of his convert; 'a gratulatione more suo incipit,' Calv.: see Rom. i. 9, 1 Cor. i. 4, and notes *on Phil.* i. 1, where this mode of address is briefly alluded to. For the meaning and uses of εὐχαριστεῖν ('gratias agere') in earlier and later Greek, see notes *on Col.* i. 12. As in Rom. i. 8, 1 Corinth. i. 4, Phil. i. 3, the thanks are returned τῷ Θεῷ μου, to Him 'whose he was and whom he served' (Acts xxvii. 23), a particularizing mode of address called forth from the warm heart of the apostle, by a remembrance of the great mercies vouchsafed to him in having thus been blessed in his labors; comp. *on Phil.* i. 3.

πάντοτε κ.τ.λ.] Participial sentence, defining more closely both when the εὐχαριστία took place, and the circumstances under which it was offered to God; 'nunquam oro quin tui meminerim,' Est. The adverb is here, as also in Phil. i. 4, Col. i. 3, more naturally joined with the participle (Chrysostom, Theod.) than with the preceding εὐχαριστῶ (Syr., Æthiop.), see notes *on Phil.* i. 4, where the reasons for a connection with the participle are more distinct than in the present case.

μνείαν σου] 'mention of thee,' μνεία receiving this meaning when in association with ποιεῖσθαι; see notes *on Phil.* i. 3. The formula is not uncommon in classical Greek (comp. Plato, *Protag.* p. 317 E, and a little more strongly ib. *Phædr.* p. 254 A), and, as Koch remarks, is an expansion of ἔχειν μνείαν τινος (1 Thess. iii. 6, 2 Tim. i. 3), the 'dynamic'

σου ποιούμενος ἐπὶ τῶν προσευχῶν μου, ⁵ ἀκούων σου τὴν ἀγάπην καὶ τὴν πίστιν ἣν ἔχεις πρὸς τὸν Κύριον Ἰησοῦν καὶ εἰς πάντας

middle ποιεῖσθαι not being without its force and significance; comp. Krü⸺r, *Sprchl.* § 52. 8. 1 sq., and notes *Gal.* iv. i. ἐπὶ τῶν προσευχῶν] '*in my prayers*,' not merely 'at the time of making them,' but, with a tinge of local force, 'in orationibus,' Vulg., Syr., Copt., scil. when engaged in offering them; see Bernhardy, *Synt.* v. 23. a, p. 245, and notes on *Eph.* i. 16.

5. ἀκούων] '*as I am hearing*:' causal participle (Donalds. *Gr.* § 616), giving the reason for the εὐχαριστῶ, or, perhaps more exactly, for the circumstances which especially led to its being offered; τὸν τῶν ὅλων Θεὸν ἐπὶ τοῖς σοῖς κατορθώμασιν ἀνυμνῶ, Theod.: contrast Rom. i. 8, where εὐχαρ. is followed by the more definite ὅτι, and the causal sentence is expressed in a passive form.

ἣν ἔχεις] '*which (faith) thou hast toward the Lord Jesus, and dost evince toward all the saints.*' There is some difficulty in these words. In the first place the reading is doubtful; I echois, with ACDE; 17. 137, read εἰς τὸν Κύριον, and with DE; 10 mss.; Syr., al. inverts the order of ἀγάπην and πίστιν. Both, however, seem corrections suggested by the somewhat unusual πίστις πρὸς Κύριον, and the apparently anomalous connection of πίστιν with εἰς πάντας τοὺς ἁγίους. Adopting the present text, we have two explanations: (*a*) that of Meyer, recently adopted by Winer in the *last* edition of his grammar (§ 50. 2, p. 365), according to which πίστις is taken as equivalent to 'fidelity,' and justified by Rom. iii. 3, Gal. v. 22, and Tit. ii. 10, in the first of which passages the meaning occurs in a very different combination, while in the second it is more than doubtful (see notes *in loc.*), and in the third is associated with an adjective; (*b*) that of Grot., al., derived from Theodoret and followed by De Wette, Alf., and most commentators, according to which τὴν ἀγάπην is to be referred by a kind of ζεῦγμα (Jelf, *Gr.* § 901. 3) to εἰς πάντας τοὺς ἁγίους, and τὴν πίστιν alone to τὸν Κύριον. Of these (*a*) does not seem tenable, as it is surely very improbable that in combination with ἀγάπη, πίστις should revert to a meaning so very unusual, and in St. Paul's Epistles so very feebly supported, as that of 'fidelity.' The second (*b*), grammatically considered, is admissible (see Winer, *Gr.* § 50. 2, p. 365), but the distinctive ἣν ἔχεις (see Meyer) and the repetition of the article with both substantives make it very unplausible. In this difficulty a third view seems to deserve consideration, according to which πίστις πρὸς τὸν Κύρ. = 'a faith directed towards the Lord' (comp. 1 Thess. i. 8), in a purely spiritual reference, while πίστις εἰς πάντας κ. τ. λ. = 'a faith evinced towards (ergo) the saints,' with a more practical reference, scil. as shown in contributions to their necessities,—a meaning suggested to the reader by the preceding ἀγάπην, and conveyed by the studied prepositional interchange. The prepositions then substantially preserve the distinction alluded to in notes on *Eph.* iv. 12, *Tit.* i. 1; πρὸς refers to a more *remote*, εἰς to a more *immediate*, application of the specified action, whether (as 2 Corinth. viii. 24, 1 Pet. iv. 9), etc. (Rom. viii. 7), or with a more neutral ref. (2 Cor. x. 1, Col. iii. 9); compare Winer, *Gr.* § 49. a, p. 353. This seems also confirmed by etymology, for while εἰς (ἐς) incorporates the idea of locality, of having reached the place (compare Donaldson *Cratyl.* § 170), πρὸς primarily presents little more than the idea of simple motion forwards; see Donalds. *ib.* § 169, 171. On the various construc-

τοὺς ἁγίους, ⁶ ὅπως ἡ κοινωνία τῆς πίστεώς σου ἐνεργὴς γένηται ἐν ἐπιγνώσει παντὸς ἀγαθοῦ τοῦ ἐν ἡμῖν εἰς Χριστὸν Ἰησοῦν.

tions of πίστις and πιστεύω, see Reuss, *Théol. Chrét.* IV. 13, Vol. II. p. 129.

6. ὅπως] '*in order that;*' dependent on εὐχαριστῶ, or perhaps more immediately on μνείαν σου ποιούμενος ἐπὶ τῶν προσευχῶν, and conveying the object of the prayer (2 Thessalon. i. 12), perhaps *slightly* blended with the subject of it; εὔχομαι, φησίν, ἵνα, ἡ κοινωνία τῆς πίστεώς σου ἐνεργὴς γένηται, Chrysost., and more distinctly Theod., δέομαι καὶ ἀντιβολῶ τὸν κοινὸν εὐεργέτην, τελείαν σοι δοῦναι τὴν κτῆσιν τῶν ἀγαθῶν. To give the particle an exclusive reference to result or consequence (Estius; compare Tittmann, *Synon.* II. p. 55, 58), or to refer it to ver. 5 as giving the 'tendency' of ἣν ἔχεις (Beng., Meyer), is very unsatisfactory. It is singular that two such good commentators as Beng. and Mey. should agree in an interpretation so utterly pointless; see Winer, *Gr.* § 53. 6, p. 410. On the essential meaning of ὅπως, and its distinction from ἵνα, see notes *on 2 Thess.* i. 12.

κοινωνία τῆς πίστεώς σου] '*communication of thy faith;*' scil. 'participation in thy faith enjoyed by others,' πίστεως being not a gen. *subjecti*, but, as more commonly (except with a personal pron.), a gen. *objecti*; comp. Phil. ii. 1, iii. 10, al. The clause thus serves to clear up, and indeed indirectly confirm the interpretation of the preceding πίστιν εἰς πάντας τοὺς ἁγίους. The meaning assigned to κοινωνία by Œcum., ἡ κοινὴ πίστις, ἡ κοινωποιός, 'fides tua, quam communem nobiscum habes' (Bengel), or the more concrete, 'beneficentia ex fide profecta' (Estius, compare Beza), does not seem accordant with the use of κοινωνία in St. Paul's Epistles when associated with a gen. *rei;* compare notes on *Phil.* ii. 1.   ἐνεργὴς γένηται] '*might become operative,*' scil.

ܡܼܥܒܕܐ ܦܐܪ̈ܐ ܒܥܒ̈ܕܐ [reddens fructus in operibus] Syr.; γίνεται ἐνεργὴς ὅταν ἔργα ἔχῃ, Chrys. The translation 'evidens,' Vulg., 'manifesta,' Clarom., appears to have arisen from a mistaken reading ἐναργής.   ἐν ἐπιγνώσει παντὸς ἀγ.] '*in the (complete) knowledge of every good thing;*' sphere and element in which the ἐνέργεια was to be displayed (see notes *on Phil.* i 9), serving also indirectly to define the 'modus operandi;' πῶς δὲ ἔσται ἐνεργής; διὰ τοῦ ἐπιγνῶναί σε καὶ πράττειν πᾶν ἀγαθόν, Œcum, who however unnecessarily introduces καὶ πράττειν, and incorrectly limits it to Philemon, whereas the previous interpretation of κοινωνία shows that the reference is to others, to the κοινωνοὶ τῆς πίστεώς σου; see Meyer *in loc.* On the meaning of ἐπίγνωσις ('accurata cognitio'), see notes on *Eph.* i. 17, *Phil.* i. 9, but observe that this force of ἐπὶ cannot always be conveyed *in translation;* compare *on Col.* i. 9.   τοῦ ἐν ἡμῖν] '*which is in us;*' with special reference to them as Christians, and as recipients of the good gifts and graces of God. The reading is slightly doubtful. *Lachmann* omits τοῦ with AC; 17, but on authority manifestly insufficient. Again *Rec.* reads ὑμῖν with FG; Vulg. (ed.), Syriac (both), Coptic, al., but on weak external, and still weaker internal evidence, as ὑμῖν might have been easily suggested by a desire to conform to the ὑμῖν in ver. 3.   εἰς Χρ. Ἰησ.] '*unto Christ Jesus,*' not merely 'in reference to Him,' but with a closer adherence to the primary force of the preposition, 'for the work of,' 'to the honor of,' 'erga Christum.' Erasm. (compare notes on ver. 5); 'bonum nobis exhibitum redundare debet in Christum,' Bengel. The words obviously belong to

⁷ χαρὰν γὰρ πολλὴν ἔσχον καὶ παράκλησιν ἐπὶ τῇ ἀγάπῃ σου, ὅτι τὰ σπλάγχνα τῶν ἁγίων ἀναπέπαυται διὰ σοῦ ἀδελφέ.

7. χαράν] So *Lachm.* and *Tisch.* ed. 1, with ACDEFG; 10 mss.; apparently all Vv.; Lat. Ff. (*Griesb., Scholz., M.*, g.). In edd. 2 and 7 *Tisch.* reads χάριν with KL; great majority of mss.; Chrys. (ms.), Theod., Dam., Theoph., al. (approved by *Griesb.*, and adopted by *Mll.*). This latter reading has some little claim on our attention, on the principle 'proclivi lectioni praestat ardua,' still as χάριν u. It have been suggested by the εὐχαριστῶ which precedes, it does not appear safe to reverse so great a preponderance of uncial authority.

ἔσχον] So *Lachm.* and *Tisch.* ed. 1, with ACFG, 5 mss.; Vulg., Copt. (al's.), Æth. (Pol. and Platt), al.; Theod.; Lat. Ff. The plur. ἔσχομεν is found 1 in D E; Clarom., Sang.; Hier., al. (*Mey., Alf.*); the pres. ἔχομεν (before πολλ'ῳν) is found 1 in D²JK; great maj. of mss.; Syr. (both); Chrys., Dam., Theoph., al., and adopted by *Tisch.* ed. 2, 7. At first sight the plural (St. Paul and Tim., ver. 1) would seem to be the true reading, of which the text was an alteration. As, however, the change might have been due to the preceding ἡμῖν, we retain the best attested reading.

ἐνεργὴς γένηται, not to what immediately precedes (Syr., Vulg., and more distinctly Æth. (Platt), εἰς being assumed = ἐν), still less to the more remote τῆς πίστεώς σου, as Grotius. *Lachm.* omits Ἰησοῦν with AC; 2 mss.; Copt., Æth. (Polyb., but not Platt); Hier., al., but without sufficient external authority.

7. γάρ] It is somewhat doubtful whether this gives the (subjective) reason for the εὐχαριστία, ver. 4 (Jerome, Mey.), or for the prayer immediately preceding (De W., Alf.). The latter is perhaps the most natural, as the subject of thanksgiving seems insensibly to have passed into that of prayer. The apostle prays that the κοινωνία κ. τ. λ. may prove ἐνεργής, for ('sane rebus ita comparatis,' Klotz) it is at present so great as to cause joy both to himself and to Timothy; σύ μοι παρρησίαν ἔδωκας ἐκ τῶν εἰς ἑτέρους γενομένων, Chrys.

ἔσχον] '*I had;*' scil. when I first heard of your ἀγάπην and πίστιν, ver. 5. The πολλὴν, as Meyer observes, appears to belong to both substantives; compare Jelf, *Gr.* § 39. 1. obs.

ἐπὶ τῇ ἀγάπῃ σου] '*in thy love;*' literally, 'based on thy love,' ἐπὶ with the dat., as usual, marking the basis and foundation upon which the χαρὰ and παράκλ. rested; see notes on *Phil.* i. 3.

ὅτι τὰ σπλάγχνα] 'because the hearts;' explanation of the preceding ἐπὶ τῇ ἀγ.; πολλ῀ης γὰρ ἐμπίμπλαμαι ἡδυμηδίας ὅτι παντοδαπὴν τοῖς ἁγίοις διασπεαν προσφέρεις. Theod. On the semi-Hebraistic σπλάγχνα (ver. 2), 2 Cor vi. 12, al.), see notes on *Phil.* i. 8: there, however, the idea of 'affection' (πνευματικὴ φιλοστοργία, Theod. *in l.c.*) is more predominant; here the term only serves to specify the imaginary seat of it; comp. Lücke on 1 *John* iii. 17. As σπλάγχνα is a somewhat comprehensive term ('proprie sunt viscera ida, nobiliora vocata, cor, pulmones, hepar et lien,' Tittmann, *Synon.* i. p. 68), the ethical applications may obviously be somewhat varied; see Suicer, *Thesaur.* s. v. Vol. II. p. 997. ἀναπέπαυνται] '*have been refreshed;*' so 1 Cor. xvi. 18, 2 Cor. vii. 13. On the distinction between ἀνάπαυσις, 'pause or cessation from labor,' and ἄνεσις, 'relaxation of what had been tightly strained,' see Trench, *Synon.* § 41.

ἀδελφέ] Not '*Bruder* in Wahrheit,' De W., Koch, but as Æth., 'frater mi,' — in tones of earnest affection: 'hoc in

I beseech thee for Onesimus, thy once unprofitable servant, who left thee a servant, to return a brother: receive him as myself. If he be a defaulter, I will repay thee.

⁸ Διὸ πολλὴν ἐν Χριστῷ παρρησίαν ἔχων ἐπιτάσσειν σοι τὸ ἀνῆκον, ⁹ διὰ τὴν ἀγάπην

fine positum multum habet πάθος; conf Virg. Æn. vi. 836,' Scip. Gent. ap. Poli Syn.

8. διό] *'On which account,'* 'as I have so much joy and consolation in thee;' not in connection with παρρ. ἔχων (δυνάμενος, φησί, θαρρεῖν ὡς θερμῶς πεπιστευκότι, Theod.) ,as Syr. and the Greek commentators, but in ref. to the preceding χαρὰν ἔσχον — ἐπὶ τῇ ἀγάπῃ, expressing more fully the motive of the διὰ τὴν ἀγ. μᾶλλον παρακ. which follows; so De Wette, Meyer, Alf. On the use of διό, see notes on *Gal.* iv. 31, and for its distinction from οὖν and ἄρα, see Klotz, *Devar.* Vol. ii. p. 173, but on the two latter particles contrast the more correct remarks of Donalds. *Gram.* § 604, *Cratyl.* § 192. παρρ. ἔχων] '*though I have boldness;*' concessive use of the simple participle, see Donaldson, *Gram.* § 621, and compare the remarks of Winer on the translation of participles, *Gr.* § 46. 12, p. 413, — ed. 5, apparently omitted in ed. 6. On the meaning of παρρ., — here in its derivative sense of ἐξουσία, ἄδεια, Hesych., — see notes on 1 *Tim.* iii. 13. This παρρησία was ἐν Χρ.; He was the element *in* which (not διὰ τὴν πίστιν τὴν εἰς Χρ., Chrys.) it was entertained, and out of which it did not exist: compare on *Eph.* iv. 1. ἐπιτάσσ. σοι τὸ ἀνῆκον] *'to enjoin upon thee that which is fitting;'* explanatory infin. following a phrase expressive of ability or capability; compare Madvig, *Synt.* § 145. 1. The verb ἐπιτάσσ. though not uncommon elsewhere in the N. T. is only found here in St. Paul's Epistles: ἐπιταγή, on the contrary, occurs seven times in these Epistles, but not elsewhere in the N. T. The neuter τὸ ἀνῆκον (comp. Eph. v. 4, Col. iii. 18), not exactly τὸ εἰς χρείαν μου

ἐλθόν, Theoph., but more generically 'quod decet facere,' Coptic ⲉⲙⲡϣⲁ, ⲉϣϣⲉ [illa quæ justa] Syr., τὸ πρέπον, Suid., marks the category (Meyer) to which the receiving back of Onesimus is to be referred.

9. διὰ τὴν ἀγ.] '*on account of love,*' '*for love's sake,*' Auth.; partially explanatory of the preceding διό, but with a more general reference, the ἀγάπη here not being ἣν κἀγὼ ἔχω πρός σε, Theoph., or ἣν ἀγαπῶ τέ σε καὶ ἀγαπῶμαι, Œcum., nor even 'charitas tua in Christum,' Just., but, as the omission of all defining genitives seems to suggest, ' Christian love' in its widest sense (De W., Mey.). The article gives the abstract noun its most generic meaning and application, Middleton, *Gr. Art.* v. 5. 1, p. 89 sq. τοιοῦτος ὤν] '*Being such an one,*' '*As I am such an one,*' scil. who would rather beseech for love's sake, than avail myself of my παρρησίαν ἐπιτάσσειν. There is some little difficulty as to the connection of this participial clause. It is usually regarded as preparatory to the ὡς Παῦλος which follows, and is conceived to more nearly explain it. Meyer, however (whose note on this clause is very persuasive), shows that the undefined τοιοῦτος, though often more nearly explained and defined by οἷος, ὥστε, neither is, nor scarcely can be, associated with ὡς, which naturally presumes a more defined antecedent, and always 'aptius conjungitur cum sequentibus,' Klotz, *Devar.* Vol. ii. p 757. This being apparently the case, τοιοῦτος ὤν must be referred to ver. 8, while ὡς Παῦλος πρεσβύτης, enhanced by νυνὶ δὲ καὶ δέσμιος 'I. X., belongs to the second παρακαλῶ (so Lachm., De Wette, and recently Buttm., Alf.), and states the capacity in

μᾶλλον παρακαλῶ. τοιοῦτος ὢν, ὡς Παῦλος πρεσβύτης, νυνὶ δὲ καὶ δέσμιος Ἰησοῦ Χριστοῦ, ¹¹ παρακαλῶ σε περὶ τοῦ ἐμοῦ τέκνου,

9. Ἰησοῦ Χριστοῦ] So *Rec.* with D¹D³EJGKL; apparently great majority of mss.; Vulg., Clarom., Syr., Æth. (Platt), al.; Chrys., Theod. *Lachm* and *Tisch.* reverse the order with AC; a few mss.; Copt., Æth. (Pol.), Bas., al. The evidence does not seem sufficient to justify the reversed order, especially as the best authorities give Χρ. Ἰησ. in ver. 1, which might easily have suggested the correction.

which the apostle makes his affectionate request. *Lachm* it may be observed encloses ὡς Παῦλος in a parenthesis; *Buttm.* isolates it by commas (so Chrys., ἀπὸ τῆς ποιότητος τοῦ προσώπου· ἀπὸ τῆς ἡλικίας· ἀπὸ τοῦ δικαιοτέρου πάντων ὅτι καὶ δέσμιος κ. τ. λ., compare Æth. [Platt]); both however unsatisfactorily: Παῦλος seems more naturally to stand in immediate union with πρεσβύτης (Syr., Copt.) and to hint at the title he might have assumed, ' Paul the Apostle.'

πρεσβύτης] '*an aged man,*' Auth., '*senex,*' Vulg., ܩܫܝܫܐ Syriac and appy. all Vv. It is quite unnecessary to attempt to explain away the simple meaning of this word ('non ætatem sed officium significat,' Calvin. 'ein Senior der Christenheit,' Koch), or to evade the almost obvious reference to age; see Wolf *in loc.* If with Wieseler we assume as late a year as A. D. 39 for the martyrdom of Stephen, and consider the νεανίας at that time as no more than 25 or 26, the apostle would now (probably A. D. 62) be nearly 50, which, broken as he was with labor, suffering, and anxieties (2 Cor. xii. 24–28), might well entitle him to the appellation of πρεσβύτης. If we follow the tradition in Pseud.-Chrys. Ὄ nt. de Petr. et Paul. (Vol. viii. spur. p. 10, ed. Bened.), that St. Paul's age was 68 when he suffered martyrdom, there will remain no doubt as to the appropriateness of the term. All attempts, however, to fix the year in which St. Paul was born seem hopeless; compare

Winer, *RWB.* Vol. ii. p. 217.

δέσμιος Ἰ. Χ] Not διὰ Χριστὸν δεδεμένος, Chrys., but, as in ver. 1, 'one whom Christ and his cause have bound;' see notes above, and Winer, *Gr.* § 30. 2, p. 170.

10. τοῦ ἐμοῦ τέκνου] '*my own child;*' with tender reference to Philemon as being converted by the apostle, and owing to him his Christian existence; compare 1 Cor. iv. 14, Gal. iv. 19, and Loesner, *Obs.* p. 431, who cites the partially parallel μᾶλλον αὐτὸν ἢ οἱ χ ἧττον τῶν γονέων γεγέννηκα, Philo, *Cai.* § 8, Vol. ii. p. 554 (ed. Mang.). The pronoun ἐμοῦ seems here emphatic. *Lachm.* and Meyer introduce ἐγὼ before ἐγέννησα, but though on internal grounds not improbable, the external authority [A; 2 mss.; Slav. (msl. Chrys. (?)] does not seem nearly sufficient to warrant the insertion. ἐν τοῖς δεσμοῖς] With feeling allusion to the circumstances in which he was when Philemon was converted, and in which he now is again while urging his request; πάλιν οἱ δεσμοὶ δυσωπητικοὶ [exorandi vim habent], Chrys. The addition μου after δεσμοῖς [*Rec.,* Steph., with CDKL; al] seems rightly rejected by *Lachm.* and *Tisch.*

Ὀνήσιμον] Accusative, owing to an inverted form of attraction; the relative which would more usually (compare Winer, *Gr.* § 24. 1, p. 147) have been in the same gender and case as τέκνου here follows the common regimen, passing into the gender of the latter substantive,

ὃν ἐγέννησα ἐν τοῖς δεσμοῖς, Ὀνήσιμον, ¹¹ τόν ποτέ σοι ἄχρηστον, νυνὶ δὲ σοὶ καὶ ἐμοὶ εὔχρηστον, ὃν ἀνέπεμψά σοι. ¹² σὺ δὲ

11. ἀνέπεμψά σοι] So *Lachmann* and *Tischen.* 1, with ACD¹D; 17; Syr., Copt. (*ha-pok*), Æth. (both); Chrys. (πρὸς σέ); Lat. Ff. (*Meyer*). In his second edition *Tisch.* omits σοι with D³FGKL; nearly all mss.; Amit., Fuld., Goth., Syr. (Philox.); many Ff. (*Rec. Alf.*). Independently of external authority which seems to preponderate against the omission, it does not seem improbable that σοι should have been omitted on account of the two preceding repetitions in the same verse, and the σὺ δέ which immediately follows.

and attracting it into its own case; see Winer, *Gram.* § 24. 2, p. 149, § 66. 5, p. 552.

11. τὸν ποτέ σοι ἄχρ.] '*who was once unprofitable,*' '*unserviceable,*' scil. who once did not answer to his name (ὀνήσιμον), but by running away, and apparently also by theft (Chrys. on ver. 18), proved himself ἄχρηστος. The word ἄχρηστ. is an ἅπ. λεγόμ. in the N. Test. (εὔχρηστος, 2 Tim. ii. 21, iv 11), and is defined by Tittm. (*Synon.* II. p. 12) as '*quo uti recte non possumus,*' '*qui nullum usum præbeat.*' The distinction between this and ἀχρεῖος (Matth. xxv. 30, Luke xvii. 10) is not very palpable: perhaps the latter rather implies οὗ οὐκ ἔστι χρεία, '*quo non opus est*' (Tittm.), '*one who could be dispensed with,*' and hence, inferentially, '*worthless,*' ἀχρεῖον καὶ ἀνωφελές, Xen. *Mem.* 1. 2. 54, while ἄχρηστος has less of a negative sense (οὐ χρήσιμον) and more approximates to that of πονηρός. It would seem, however, that ἀχρεῖος belongs mainly to earlier, ἄχρηστος mainly to later Greek. The play on the name, Ὀνήσιμον, τὸν ποτέ ἄχρηστον (not noticed by the Greek commentators), has been recognized by the majority of expositors; see Winer, *Gr.* § 68. 2, p. 561. Any further allusion, χρηστὸς as compared with Χριστιανός (Koch), seems improbable and even untenable, compare Mey. *in loc.*

σοὶ καὶ ἐμοὶ εὔχρ.] '*profitable, serviceable, to thee and to me.*' The εὐχρηστία here alluded to has obviously a higher reference than to merely earthly service (comp. Chrys.): Philemon had now gained in his servant a brother in the faith; St. Paul, one who owed him his hope of future salvation, and was a living proof that he had not run in vain In the delicately added ἐμοί ('Philemonem civiliter præponit sibi,' Beng.) it is somewhat coarse (Theoph., Corn. a Lap.) to find a hint that Philemon was to send him back to the apostle. On the various beauties and persuasive touches in this exquisite Epistle, see Marshall (Nath.), *Serm.* XIII. Vol. II. p. 327 sq. (Lond. 1731). ὃν ἀνέπεμψά σοι] '*I have sent back to thee,*' or even '*I send back, etc.,*'— epistolary aor.; present to the writer, but aoristic to the receiver of the letter; compare ἔπεμψα, Phil. ii. 28, and see examples in Winer, *Gr.* § 40. 5. 2, p. 249.

12. σὺ δὲ αὐτόν] '*But do thou (receive) him.*' The sentence involves an anacoluthon, which, however, affords but little difficulty, as ver. 17, in which the construction is resumed, suggests the natural supplement. The addition προσλαβοῦ [*Rec.* with CDEKL; al.] is well attested, but considering the tendency of St. Paul, esp. in relatival sentences, to pass into anacolutha (see examples in Winer, *Gr.* § 63. 1, p. 500), rightly rejected by *Lachm., Tisch.,* and most modern expositors as an ancient gloss. *Lachmann* also omits σὺ δέ [with AC; 17], but with little probability, as the omission was apparently the result of an at-

αὐτόν, τοῦτ' ἔστιν τὰ ἐμὰ σπλάγχνα, 13 ὃν ἐγὼ ἐβουλόμην πρὸς ἐμαυτὸν κατέχειν, ἵνα ὑπὲρ σοῦ μοι διακονῇ ἐν τοῖς δεσμοῖς τοῦ

tempt to evade the anacoluthon by joining ἀνέπεμψα with αὐτόν; comp. Meyer (crit. note), p. 173. τὰ ἐμὰ σπλάγχνα] 'mine own heart,' 'meinos brusts,' Goth.: οὕτω γὰρ αὐτὸν ἀγαπῶ καὶ ἐν τῇ ψυχῇ περιφέρω, Theoph. The meaning adopted by Syriac [Syriac], Æthiop. (Platt. Polygl. paraphrases), Theod., ἐκ τῶν ἐμῶν γεγέννηται σπλάγχνων, al., though perfectly defensible (see Suicer, *Thesaur.* s. v., and the pertinent examples in Wetstein), does not here seem requisite or indeed satisfactory, as the paternal relation of St. Paul to Onesimus was a purely spiritual one, and as σπλάγχνα appears nearly always in St. Paul to involve some special idea of affection, or, as here, of the seat of it: Meyer (after Groz.) quotes 'meum corculum,' Plaut. *Cas.* iv. 4. 14 (16): compare notes on ver. 7.

13. ἐγὼ ἐβουλόμην] '*I (on my part) was purposing;*' contrast ἠθέλησα, ver. 14, where not only the general distinction between the verbs βούλομαι and θέλω (see notes on 1 *Tim.* v. 14), but, as Meyer remarks, between the *tenses*, is accurately preserved. The imperfect points to the time when the design was formed, and to its non-fulfilment; compare Bernhardy, *Synt.* x. 3, p. 373. The use of ηὐχόμην Rom. ix. 3 (Alf.) though analogous, is not exactly similar, as this belongs to a use of the imperfect where there is a more distinct reference to a suppressed conditional clause; see notes on *Gal.* v. 20. πρὸς ἐμαυτόν] '*with myself;*' the proper and primary meaning of the preposition ('motion toward,' compare Donaldson, *Cratyl.* § 169) is often obscured in con-

nection with persons; see notes on *Gal.* i. 18, and Winer, *Gr.* § 49. h, p. 360. ὑπὲρ σοῦ] '*in thy stead;*' not simply for ἀντί, but with a tinge of the more usual meaning of the preposition 'in the place of, and thereby having tacitly to thee;' compare Eurip. *Alcest.* 700, κατθανεῖν ὑπὲρ σοῦ, and see Green, *Gram.* p. 301. This more derivative meaning of the prep. cannot be denied (see Winer, *Gr.* § 47. l, p. 342), but has been unduly pressed in doctrinal passages; compare notes on *Gal.* iii. 13, and Usteri, *Lehrb.* II. 1. 1, p. 115. The exquisite turn that St. Paul gives to his intention of retaining Onesimus, viz. as a representative of his master (ἵνα τῆς σῆς μοι διακονίας ἐκτίσῃ τὸ χρέος, Theod.), should not be left unnoticed. διακονῇ] '*might minister;*' present, idiomatically referring to the time when the ἐβουλόμην took place, and giving a vividness to the past by representing it as present; see Winer, *Gr.* § 41 b. 1, p. 258, and Klotz, *Devar.* Vol. II. p. 618; compare also Gal. i. 16, but observe that the use of the present is somewhat different; there an event is referred to which was still going on, here the διακονία, in its more direct sense, had now ceased, as Onesimus was all but on his way home to his master. δεσμοῖς τοῦ εὐαγγ.] '*bonds of the gospel;*' scil. 'bonds which the gospel brought with it,—which preaching the gospel entailed on me,' εὐαγγ. being a gen. *auctoris*; see Winer, *Gr.* § 30. 2 β. note, p. 170. Hartung, *Casus*, p. 17. Again a delicate allusion to his sufferings (comp. v. 9), and to a state which could not fail to touch the heart of Philemon.

14. χωρὶς δὲ κ.τ.λ.] '*but without thy own approval;*' comp. Raphel, *Annot.* Vol. II. p. 642, who very appropriately cites Polybius, *Hist.* p. 983 (xv. 18. 4),

εὐαγγελίου· ¹⁴ χωρὶς δὲ τῆς σῆς γνώμης οὐδὲν ἠθέλησα ποιῆσαι, ἵνα μὴ ὡς κατὰ ἀνάγκην τὸ ἀγαθόν σου ᾖ, ἀλλὰ κατὰ ἑκούσιον. ¹⁵ τάχα γὰρ διὰ τοῦτο ἐχωρίσθη πρὸς ὥραν, ἵνα αἰώνιον αὐτὸν

χωρὶς τῆς Ῥωμαίων γνώμης; compare *ib.* III. 21. 7, χωρὶς τῆς αὐτοῦ γνώμης, *ib.* XXI. 8. 7, ἄνευ τῆς ἐκείνου γνώμης (cited in Schweigh. *Lex. Polyb.* p. 89). Γνώμη occurs a few times in the N. T., and in slightly varied senses; comp. Acts xx. 3, where it has apparently the stronger sense of 'design,' and 1 Cor. i. 10, vii. 25, 40, 2 Cor. viii. 20, where it has its more regular meaning of 'sententia' or 'judicium;' compare Meyer *on* 1 *Cor.* i. 10, and Kypke, *Obs,* Vol. II. p. 205. ἠθέλησα] '*was willing;*' nor., see notes on ver. 13.   ὡς κατὰ ἀνάγκην] '*as if by necessity,*' 'compulsion-wise;' the κατὰ marking primarily the *norma* or manner according to which the action was done (see notes *on Titus* iii. 5), and thence the prevailing principle to which it was to be referred (comp. examples in Winer, *Gr.* § 49. d, p. 358), while ὡς marks the *aspect* which the action would have worn; see Bernhardy, *Synt.* VII. 2, p. 333, and notes *on Eph.* v. 22, *Col.* iii. 23. Chrysost., and more fully Theophyl. and Œcum., rightly call attention to this insertion of the particle. τὸ ἀγαθόν σου] '*thy good,*' '*thy beneficence,*' 'the good emanating from or performed by thee,'—the gen. perhaps being not so much a mere possessive gen. as a gen. *auctoris* or *causæ efficientis;* see notes *on Col.* i. 23. The exact meaning of the words is slightly doubtful; there seems certainly no reference to any manumission of Onesimus (Estius, Koch; contrast Maurice, *Unity of N. T.* p. 659), nor merely to the kind reception which Philemon was to give him on his arrival (Hofmann, *Schrifth.* Vol. II. p. 387), nor even to the 'beneficium' which in this *particular* instance Philemon was to confer on the apostle, but, as the more abstract term suggests,

'beneficentia tua' (Calv.), whether as shown in this or in other good and merciful acts generally. If the apostle had retained Onesimus, Philemon would have doubtless consented, but the τὸ ἀγαθὸν in the particular case would have worn the appearance (ὡς) of a kind of constraint; St. Paul, however, wished, as in this so in all other matters, that Philemon's τὸ ἀγαθὸν should be μὴ ὡς κατὰ ἀνάγκην ἀλλὰ κατὰ ἑκούσιον.   On the doubtful distinction in the N. T. between τὸ ἀγαθὸν and τὸ καλόν, see notes *on Gal.* vi. 10.   κατὰ ἑκούσιον] '*voluntarily.*' The more usual periphrasis for the adverb appears in the earlier Greek to have been καθ' ἑκουσίαν, Thucydides VIII. 27, or ἐξ ἑκουσίας, Soph. *Trach.* 724, by an ellipse of γνώμη. In the present case there may have been originally an ellipse of τρόπον (Porphyr. *de Abs.* I. 9, καθ' ἑκούσιον τρόπον); the expression, however, would soon become purely adverbial: comp. Lobeck, *Phryn.* p. 4.

15. τάχα γάρ] '*For perhaps;*' reason that influenced the apostle in sending back Onesimus. The insertion of τάχα (Rom. v. 7; more usually τάχ' ἄν, in classical Greek) gives a softening and suasive turn to the admission of his convert's fault, no less sound in principle ('occulta sunt judicia Dei, et temerarium est quasi de certo pronunciare quod dubium est,' Hieron.) than judicious in its present use; καλῶς τό, τάχα, ἵνα εἴπῃ ὁ δεσπότης, Chrys.; τάχα γὰρ κατὰ θείαν οἰκονομίαν ἔφυγεν, Theoph. Both Chrys. and Jerome admirably illustrate from the history of Joseph the great feature of the providential government of God which these verses disclose,— 'præstabilius ducere Deum de malis bona facere, quam mala nulla facere,' Justin. *in loc.*,

ἀπ᾽ ἐμης, 16 οὐκέτι ὡς δοῦλον, ἀλλ᾽ ὑπὲρ δοῦλον, ἀδελφὸν ἀγαπητόν,

see August. *Enchir.* § 3, Vol. vi. p. 319 (ed. B. n. 1836).

ἐχωρίσθη] 'he departed;' he does not say ἔφυγεν lest he should rouse up any angry remembrances in the mind of Philem.; so Chrys., Œcum., and Theophyl. all of whom have admirably illustrated the delicate touches in this beautiful Ep. For examples of this sort of 'use Calpassive,' in which, however, not only the passive form, but passive meaning, is clearly to be recognized, see Krüger, *Sprachl.* § 52. 6. 1.

πρὸς ὥραν] '*for a season;*' 2 Cor'n. vii. 8, Gal. ii. 5, and more definitely 1 Thess. ii. 17, πρὸς καιρὸν ὥρας. In the present expression the duration of the time is not expressly stated, but it may be inferred from the antithesis to have not been very long; compare Theophyl. *in loc.* The proper force of the prep. ('motion towards') may be easily recognized in the formula, especially when compared with its more appreciable force in such expressions as πρὸς ἑσπέραν (Luke xxiv. 29), al.; compare Bernhardy, *Synt.* v. 31, p. 564. The derivation of ὥρα is uncertain; it has been connected with the Sanscr. *vâra*, 'time' (Benfey, *Wurzellex.* Vol. ii. p. 328), but, perhaps more probably, with the Zend *jâre*, Germ. 'Jahr,' as apparently evinced in the Lat. 'horno;' compare Pott, *Etym. Forsch.* Vol. i. p. 8, 123.

αἰώνιον αὐτὸν ἀπ.] '*mightest receive him eternally, everlastingly,*' not merely 'perpetuum,' Beza (Grot. compares Hor. *Epist.* i. 10. 41, 'serviet æternum'), nor with any allusion to 'perpetua mancipia,' Exodus xxi. 6, Deut. xv. 17 (Beza, Gent.), but 'in æternum.' Clarom., 'aive'nam,' Goth.; οὐκ ἐν τῷ παρόντι μόνον καιρῷ ἀλλὰ καὶ ἐν τῷ μέλλοντι, ἵνα διαπαντὸς ἔχῃς αὐτόν, οὐκέτι δοῦλον ἀλλὰ τιμιώτερον δούλου, Chrys; so pertinently Estius, 'servitus omnis

hac vita finitur, at fraternitas Christiana manet in æternum.' The tertiary pred. cat of title, αἰώνιον, is not an adverb (Meyer), but, as its position suggests, an adverbial adj. 'tive involving a predicate of state and of result; comp. Donalds. *Gr.* § 4. 9 sq., and see examples in Winer, *Gr.* § 54. 2, p. 112. On the compound ἀπέχειν, in which, as ἀπολαμβάνειν κ. τ. λ., the prep. does not apparently so much 'mark the receiving *back*,' as the 'having for one's own' ('sibi habere,' Bengel, 'hinweghaben' Mey.), see notes on *Phil.* iv. 18, comp. Winer, *Gr.* § *C* ap. iv. p. 8.

16. οὐκέτι ὡς δοῦλον] Ch. [...] spiritual relation in which he now would stand to his master; ὥστε καὶ τῇ χρόνῳ κεκέρδακας καὶ τῇ ποιότητι, Chrys. The particle ὡς almost convincingly shews that there is here no reference to manumission (comp. on ver. 14): though actually a slave, he is not to be regarded in the ordinary aspect of one (see verse 14); the inward relation was changed the outward remained the same; comp. Hofmann, *Schriftb.* Vol. ii. 1, p. 318.

ὑπὲρ δοῦλον] 'above a slave,' - rather 'as slave,' 'ufar skalk,' Goth.; [Syriac] [praestantior quam], Syr. sim. .T. h. (Platt). Copt.; not 'pro servo,' Vulg., Clarom., which obscures the force of the preposition; compare Matt. x. 24, 37, Acts xxvi. 13, in which the force of ὑπὲρ is somewhat similar, and see Winer, *Gr.* § 49 e, p. 359. The expression is explained by the following ἀδελφὸν ἀγαπητόν; Onesimus was not now to be regarded in the light of a slave, but in a higher light, viz. as a beloved brother; ἀντὶ δούλου ἀδελφὸν χρηστὸν ἀδελφὸν ἀπείληφας, Œcum. μάλιστα ἐμοί] 'especially to me,' al., to others, to me;' not directly dependent on ἀγαπητόν (Meyer), but, as ἀγαπητὸς in

μάλιστα ἐμοί, πόσῳ δὲ μᾶλλόν σοι καὶ ἐν σαρκὶ καὶ ἐν Κυρίῳ. ¹⁷ εἰ οὖν με ἔχεις κοινωνόν, προσλαβοῦ αὐτὸν ὡς ἐμέ. ¹⁸ εἰ δέ τι

the N. T. has to a great degree lost its verbal character, a dative 'of interest' (Krüger, *Sprachl.* § 48. 4) attached to ἀδελφ. ἀγαπ.; comp. Syr., Bengel. He stood in the light of an ἀδελφ. ἀγαπ. to St. Paul, whom he had now left, but much more so to Philemon, who had formerly known him as a mere δοῦλον, but who was now to have him as his own in a higher and closer relation than before. On the meaning and derivation of μάλιστα, compare notes *on* 1 *Tim.* iv. 10. καὶ ἐν σαρκὶ κ. τ. λ.] '*both in the flesh and in the Lord;*' the two spheres in which Onesimus was to be πόσῳ μᾶλλον an ἀδελφὸς ἀγαπητὸς to Philemon than to the apostle, — 'in the flesh,' *i. e.* in earthly and personal relations (Mey.), as having intercourse and communication with him on a necessarily somewhat altered footing; — 'in the Lord,' as enjoying spiritual communion with him which he had never enjoyed before, — nearly καὶ ἐν ταῖς σωματικαῖς ὑπηρεσίαις καὶ ἐν ταῖς πνευματικαῖς, Schol., except that the idea must not be limited to ὑπηρεσία; compare Theod., Œcum. To define ἐν σαρκὶ more nearly (comp. Grot., al.) is neither here necessary nor in harmony with the general use of the word in St. Paul's Epistles; see notes *on Galat.* v. 16, and the elaborate notes of Koch, p. 99 sq.; 'die Gegensätze, a's *Mensch* und als *Christ* sind in ihrer ganzen Weite zu belassen,' Mey. On the force of καὶ—καί ('as well the one as the other'), see notes *on* 1 *Tim.* iv. 10.

17. εἰ οὖν] '*If then;*' summing up what has been urged, and resuming the request imperfectly expressed in ver. 12. On the 'vis collectiva' of οὖν (Gal. iv. 15, Phil. ii. 29, see notes) and its resumptive force (Galat. iii. 5, see notes), both here united, see Klotz, *Devar.* Vol.

II. pp. 717, 718. κοινωνόν] '*a partner*,' scil. in faith, and love, and Christian principles generally, — not merely in sentiments (εἰ τὰ αὐτά μοι φρονεῖς, ἐπὶ τοῖς αὐτοῖς τρέχεις, εἰ φίλον ἄγῃ, Chrys., Just.), or, still less likely, in community of property ('ut tua sint mea, et mea tua,' Beng., compare Beza, Pagn.), interpretations which here improperly limit what seems purposely left unrestricted. προσλαβοῦ ὡς ἐμέ] '*receive him to thee as myself;*' 'as you would me;' in his spiritual affection towards him he is a part of my very self, compare ver. 12. The form προσλαμβ. occurs in a very similar sense, Rom. xiv. 1, 3, xv. 7, the idea not being so much of a mere kindness of reception (compare Acts xxviii. 2) as of an admission to Christian love and fellowship; see Meyer *on Rom.* xiv. 1, and Fritz. *in loc.*, who, however, in his translation 'in suum contubernium recipere,' somewhat puts out of sight the Christian character of the reception which the context seems to imply.

18. εἰ δέ] '*But if;*' contrasted thought (comp. Alf.), suggested by the remembrance of what might militate against the warmth of the reception. The δέ thus does not seem μεταβατικόν (Mey.), but preserves its usual oppositive force; 'qui loquitur, etiam si nihil positum est in oratione tamen aliquid in mente habet, ad quod respiciens illam oppositionem infert.' Klotz, *Devar.* Vol. II. p. 363. ἠδίκησέν σε] '*wronged thee*,' more specifically explained by the 'mitius synonymon' (Beng.) ἢ ὀφείλει. The Greek commentators draw attention to the tender way in which St. Paul notices that misdeed of the repentant Onesimus which must have tended most to keep up the irritation of Philemon (οὐκ εἶπεν ἔκλεψεν, ἀλλ'

ἠδίκησέν σε ἢ ὀφείλει, τοῦτο ἐμοὶ ἐλλόγα. ¹⁹ ἐγὼ Παῦλος ἔγραψα

εὐφημότερον, ἠδίκησεν ἢ ὀφείλει. Theoph.), and further, the kind and wise way in which he keeps it to the end of his letter; ὅρα πῶς τέθεικε καὶ πότε τὸ ἠδίκημα· ὕστερον μετὰ τὸ πολλὰ ὑπὲρ τούτου προειπεῖν, Chrys.
τοῦτο ἐμοὶ ἐλλόγα] *'Set that to my account,'* scil. ὅ τι ἠδίκησεν σε ἢ ὀφείλει; 'id meis rationibus imputa,' Grot. Though there is no extra-lexical authority for ἐλλογάω (it does not appear in the new ed. of Steph. *Thesaur.*), and though its existence has been somewhat peremptorily denied (Fritz. *Rom.* v. 13, Vol. I. p. 311), yet such as the desiderative λογάω (Lucian, *Lexiph.* 15) is an unknown gl form, and as peculiarities of orthography or errors of transcription cannot be made satisfactorily to account for the assumed permutation of α and ω [Bastius ap. Greg. Cor. p 760 (ed. Schæf.) cited by Fritz. is not in point, as here referring to *curs rec* mss.; see examples and plates referred to] we seem bound to follow the preponderant uncial authority, ACD¹FG; 17. 31. so *Lachm., Tisch.,* and also Meyer, *Alf.*

19. ἐγὼ Παῦλος ἔγρ.] *'I Paul have written;'* scarcely 'I write,' De W., Conyb., Green (*Gr.* p. 17), as this epistolary aorist in the N. Test. does not appear used simply in reference to what *follows*, but always more or less retrospectively, whether in reference to a former letter (2 Cor. ii. 3), to preceding passages in an all but concluded letter (Rom. xv. 15, see Meyer *in loc.*), or to an immediately foregoing portion of one in progress (1 Cor. ix. 15): when the reference is to what is definitely present, the simple γράφω is used in preference to the idiomatic aorist; see Winer, *Gr.* § 40. 5. 2, p. 249, and notes *on Gal.* vi. 11. This would lead us to conclude that St. Paul wrote with his own hand certainly the preceding verse, and not

improbably (Theod., Theron) the whole Epistle. It does not thus seem that He wrote Lατλον and Lotta to mark this ...re the commencement of a new paragraph. ἐγὼ ἀποτίσω] *'I ... pay,' ....* ...ious meaning, as if the apostle sus....ed that Philemon would make a claim, as the Greek comm. state, all observe, χαριέντως (Theoph.), yet, perhaps, as the text words convey, with a graceful, implied exhortation, καὶ ἐπιτρεπτικὰ ἅμα καὶ χαριέντως (Chrys., comp. Theoph., ἀντὶ γραμματίου τόνδε κάτεχε τὴν ἐπιστολὴν πᾶσαν αὐτὴν ἐγὼ γέγραφα. The addition ἐν Κυρίῳ [DEF; Chromatius, Sang.] is an improbable repetition of the Κυρίῳ below. ἵνα μὴ λέγω σοι] *'that I may not say to thee;'* a rhetorical turn, — σχῆμα παρασιωπήσεως Grot., or παραλείψεως, Gicum., 'rhetorica præteritio,' Est., — in w... what might be said is partially suppressed, or only delicately brought to the remembrance of the person addressed. The ἵνα does not seem strictly dependent on ἐγὼ ἀποτίσω, ἀποτίσω (Mey.), nor yet ... supposed imper. 'yield me this request' (Alford), — which would impair the graceful flow of thought, but rather, as Chrys., Theoph., and Œcum. seem to suggest, on a thought tacitly supplied by the ἀποτίσω, — *re pay;* yes I say this, not doubting thee, but not wishing to press on thee the claim I might justly urge: 'it was to be οὐ κατὰ ἀνάγκην ἀλλὰ κατὰ ἑκούσιον.' verse 14. προσοφείλεις] *'thou owest unto me besides;'* Philemon was not only an actual debtor to the apostle of any trifle that he thus (μετὰ χάριτος τῆς πνευματικῆς, Chrysost.) offers to make good, but in addition to it (προσ-, even (καὶ ascensive) his own self, his own Christian existence. Raphel alleges somewhat similar uses of προσοφείλειν in Xen. *Cyr.* iii. p. 59 (iii. 2. 16), *Olum.*

τῇ ἐμῇ χειρί, ἐγὼ ἀποτίσω· ἵνα μὴ λέγω σοι ὅτι καὶ σεαυτόν μοι προσοφείλεις. ²⁰ Ναί, ἀδελφέ, ἐγώ σου ὀναίμην ἐν Κυρίῳ· ἀνάπαυσόν μου τὰ σπλάγχνα ἐν Χριστῷ.

I am confident that thou wilt fully comply with my request. Prepare me a lodging.

²¹ Πεποιθὼς τῇ ὑπακοῇ σου ἔγραψά σοι, εἰδὼς ὅτι καὶ ὑπὲρ ὃ λέγω ποιήσεις

p. 684 (20. 1); the meaning, however, is sufficiently obvious. A curious metaphorical use of προσοφ. ('longe inferiorem esse') will be found in Polyb. *Hist.* xxxix. 2. 6.

20. ναί, ἀδελφέ] '*yea, brother;*' certainly not '*precantis*' (Grot.), nor '*vehementer obsecrantis*' (Gent.), but with the usual force of the particle in the N. Test., 'serio affirmantis' (compare Erasm.), in reference to the request embodied in ver. 12 sq.; ἀφεὶς τὸν χαριεντισμὸν πάλιν ἔχεται τῶν προτέρων τῶν σπουδαίων, Chrys., compare Theoph. and Œcum. On the use of ναί in the N. T., see notes on *Phil.* iv. 3.

ἐγώ σου ὀναίμην] '*may I reap profit from thee;*' — I, not without emphasis; the apostle again (comp. ver. 12, 17) makes it a matter between himself and Philemon, putting for the time Onesimus almost out of sight; it was a favor to himself. The somewhat unusual ὀναίμην [2 aor. opt., see Buttm. *Irreg. Verbs*, p. 189 Transl.], coupled with the significant ἐγώ (*I*, not merely Ones.), seems to confirm the view of most modern commentt., except De W., that there is again a play on the name of Onesimus; see Winer, *Gr.* § 68. 2, p. 561. The form ὀναίμην is similarly used by Ignatius (*Polyc.* 1. 6, *Magn.* 12, al.), — once (*Ephes.* 2) curiously enough, but apparently by mere accident, after a mention of an Onesimus. ἐν Κυρίῳ denotes, as usual, the *sphere* of the ὄνησις, (see on *Ephes.* iv. 17, *Phil.* ii. 19, al.), just as ἐν Χριστῷ, which follows, specifies that of the ἀνάπαυσις; both were to be characterized by being *in* Him, they were to be such as implied His hallowing influences. It may be here observed that ἐν Χρ. has distinctly preponderating authority [ACD₁FGL; al.; Claroman., Syr. (both), Æth (both), Copt., Goth.], and is adopted by nearly all modern eds. τὰ σπλάγχνα] '*my heart;*' not Onesimus, as in v. 12 (Hieron.), which would here be wholly out of place, nor τὴν περὶ σε ἀγάπην (Theoph., Œcum.), but simply the σπλάγχνα of the apostle, — the seat of his love and affections; see notes on ver. 7.

21. πεποιθὼς τῇ ὑπακ.] Concluding allusion to his apostolic authority, but how delicately introduced, how tenderly deferred, and how encouragingly echoing the commendations with which he commenced; ὑπὲρ καὶ ἀρχόμενος εἶπε, παρρησίαν ἔχων τοῦτο καὶ ἐνταῦθα λέγει εἰς τὸ ἐπισφραγίσαι τὴν ἐπιστολήν, Chrys. ἔγραψα] '*I have written,*' not '*I write,*' De W.; see above on ver. 19, and contrast the following present.

ὑπὲρ ὃ λέγω] '*beyond what I am saying;*' compare Eph. iii. 20. It is very doubtful whether this alludes, however faintly, to the manumission of Onesimus (Alf.). The tenor of the Epistle would seem to imply nothing more than encouraging confidence on the part of the apostle (ἅμα καὶ διήγειρεν εἰπὼν τοῦτο, Chrys.), that Philemon would show to the fugitive even greater kindness and a more affectionate reception than he had pleaded for; compare notes on ver. 14 and 16. *Lachm.* here reads ὑπὲρ ἃ with AC; 3 mss.; Coptic, Syr. (Philox.), — not without some reason, as the single request might have suggested the correction (compare Alford); still it is perhaps more safe to retain the text

²² ἅμα δὲ καὶ ἑτοίμαζέ μοι ξενίαν· ἐλπίζω γὰρ ὅτι διὰ τῶν προσευχῶν ὑμῶν χαρισθήσομαι ὑμῖν.

Salutations. ²³ Ἀσπάζεταί σε Ἐπαφρᾶς ὁ συναιχμάλωτός μου ἐν Χριστῷ Ἰησοῦ, ²⁴ Μάρκος, Ἀρίσταρχος, Δημᾶς, Λουκᾶς, οἱ συνεργοί μου.

Benediction. ²⁵ Ἡ χάρις τοῦ Κυρίου ἡμῶν Ἰησοῦ Χριστοῦ μετὰ τοῦ πνεύματος ὑμῶν.

as best supported by external authority.

22 ἅμα δὲ καὶ κ. τ. λ.] 'Moreover at the same time also provide me a lodging;' a commission appended to his request: in addition to complying with the subject of the letter, Philemon was also to make this provision for the expected apostle. Chrys. and Theod. (compare Alf.) find in this message a last thought of Onesimus, and a direction tending to secure him a kind reception; ἵνα προσδοκῶν αὐτοῦ τὴν παρουσίαν αἰδεσθῇ [Φιλ.] καὶ τὰ γράμματα, Theod. It may be doubted, however, whether the *first* view of Theoph. and Œcumen. is not more probable, and more worthy both of Philemon and of the apostle, — viz., that Philemon was not to consider the Epistle a mere petition for Onesimus (εἰ μὴ διὰ Ὀνήσιμον οὐδὲ λόγον με ἠξίου, Theoph.), but as containing special messages on other matters to himself. The word ξενία (II Syh. ὑποδοχή, κατάλυμα) only occurs here and, also in reference to St. Paul, Acts xxviii. 23.

διὰ τῶν προσευχῶν ὑμῶν] *through your prayers;* in reference to Philemon, Apphia, Archippus, and those mentioned in ver. 2. The same expectation of recovering his liberty appears in Phil. i. 25, ii. 24; there, however, the journey contemplated is to the Philippians, and the date when it is formed, according to the general view, a year or two later; comp. Wieseler, *Chronol.* p. 456.

23. ἀσπάζεται] Greetings from the same persons as those mentioned in the Ep. to the Coloss. (ch. iv. 10 sq.), with the exception of Jesus. The order observed is substantially the same. Mark and Aristarchus (οἱ ὄντες ἐκ περιτομῆς, Coloss. iv. 11) preceding Luke and Demas, except that Epaphras is here placed first. The reading ἀσπάζονται [D. with D^dD^bKL] is rightly rejected by most modern editors as a grammatical correction. ὁ συναιχμάλ. μου] '*my fellow-prisoner:*' more specifically defined as ἐν Χριστῷ Ἰησοῦ; see on Eph. iv. 1. The title here given to Epaphras is, in Col. iv. 10, given to Ἀρίσταρχος, while the latter is afterwards named as a συνεργός: for the probable reasons, see notes on *Col. l. c.*

24. Μάρκος] Probably John Mark, and the Evangelist. For a brief notice of him, and those mentioned in this verse, see notes on *Col.* iv. 10 and 14.

25. ἡ χάρις κ. τ. λ.] Precisely the same form of salutation as in Gal. vi. 18, with the exception of the significant conclusion ἀδελφοί. As there, so here (compare also 2 Timothy iv. 22), the apostle prays that the grace of the Lord may be μετὰ τοῦ πνεύματος, 'with the *spirit*' of those whom he is addressing, with the third and highest portion of our composite nature; see notes on *Gal. l. c.*, *Destiny of Creature*, p. 113 sq., and compare Olshaus. *Opusc.* vi. p. 145 sq.

TRANSLATION.

NOTICE.

THE following translation is based on the same principles as those adopted in the portions of this Commentary that have already appeared. The increased and increasing interest in the subject of revision has, however, induced me to be a little fuller in the citations from the eight Versions, which are here compared with the Authorized, and has also suggested the insertion of a few comments on general principles of translation, and of a few brief reasons for changes, which the notes on the original might not fully supply. My humble endeavor has been to avoid everything that might seem arbitrary and capricious, and to cling with all possible tenacity to fixed principles of correction; still there both are and must be many passages in which the context and general tone of the original render one of two apparently synonymous translations not only more appropriate, but even more faithful and correct, than the other. In the present edition a few alterations have been made, but not any of sufficient importance to require here to be separately specified.

Of the older English Vv., the attention of the student may be especially directed to the version of Coverdale, which, considering the time and circumstances under which it was executed, appears remarkably vigorous and faithful. This venerable Version has now become accessible by the reprint of Coverdale's Bible, published by Messrs. Bagster; but a small and cheap edition of the New Testament alone, with perhaps the Version in the 'Duglott' edition [Cov. (Test.)], would, I am confident, be very acceptable to many students who may be deterred by the size and price of the reprint above alluded to. Some interesting remarks on these Versions, and on the subject of Revision generally, will be found in a tract by 'Philalethes,' entitled *The English Bible*, 8vo. Dublin, 1857.

THE EPISTLE TO THE PHILIPPIANS.

CHAPTER I.

PAUL and Timothy, servants of Christ Jesus, to all the saints in Christ Jesus which are at Philippi, with the bishops and deacons: ² grace be unto you, and peace, from God our Father and the Lord Jesus Christ.

³ I thank my God upon all my remembrance of you, ⁴ always, in every supplication of mine for you all, making my supplication with joy, ⁵ for your fellowship shown toward the Gospel from the first day until now ; ⁶ being confident of this very thing, that He

---

CHAPTER I. 1. *Servants*] So *Wicl.*; 'the servants,' *Auth.* and the other Vv. On the designation Timothy ('Timotheus,' *Auth.*), see notes *on Coloss.* i. 1 (*Transl.*). Christ Jesus (1st)] '*Jesus Christ*,' *Auth.*

2. *And the Lord*] So *Cov.* (Test.) : 'and from the Lord,' *Auth.* and the other Vv. except *Wicl.*, 'of.' It is perhaps more exact to omit the preposition in the second member, as in the Greek : here it is unimportant, but in some cases the sense and construction are impaired by the repetition ; comp. Blunt, *Lect. on Par. Priest*, pp. 55, 56.

3. *All my remembrance*] 'Every remembrance,' *Auth.*

4. *Supplication*] 'Prayer,' *Auth.* and all Vv.; it is perhaps better to retain the more special meaning, as evincing the earnest nature of the apostle's prayer; comp. notes *on* 1 *Tim.* ii. 1, and notice below, *Wicl., Cov.* (Test.), in their translation of the second δέησις. It is curious that all the Vv. except *Auth.* change to the plural, 'all my prayers ;' this certainly preserves the παρένχησις (compare on *Eph.* v. 20), but at the expense of accuracy. *My supplication*] 'Request,' *Auth.*; 'biseechynge,' *Wicl.*; 'instaunte prayer,' *Cov.* (Test.); 'prayer,' *Bish.*; 'petition,' *Rhem.*; the remaining Vv. adopt the simple verb 'and praye' (*Tynd., Cov., Cran.*), or 'praying. (*Gen.*).

5. *Shown toward*] 'In,' *Auth.* and all Vv. except *Cran.*, 'of.'

6. *Began*] 'Hath begun,' *Auth.* *In you a good work*] So *Wicl., Cov.* (Test.),

which began in you a good work, will perfect *it* up to the day of Christ Jesus: ⁷ even as it is meet for me to think this of you all, because I have you in my heart; inasmuch as both in my bonds, and in my defence and confirmation of the gospel, ye all are partakers with me of my grace. ⁸ For God is my witness, how I do long after you all in the bowels of Christ Jesus. ⁹ And this I pray, that your love may yet more and more abound in knowledge and *in* all discernment, ¹⁰ to the intent that ye may prove things that are excellent, that ye may be pure and without offence against the day of Christ; ¹¹ being filled with the fruit of righteousness, which is by Jesus Christ, unto the glory and praise of God.

Rhem.: ' a good work (' that g. w.,' *Cov.*, ' the,' *Coverd. Test.*) in you,' *Auth.* and the other Vv.   *Perfect*] So *Rhem.*, and sim. *Cov.* (*Test.*), ' fulende:' ' perform,' *Auth.*, *Wicl.*, *Cranm.*, *Bish.*; ' go forthe with it,' *Tynd.*, *Cov.*, *Gen.* *Up to*] Sim. *Rhem.* ' unto:' ' until,' *Auth.* and remaining Vv. except *Wicl.*, ' til in to.'   *Christ Jesus*] ' *Jesus Christ,' *Auth.*

7. *My defence*] So *Cov.* (*Test.*), *Gen.*: ' the,' *Auth.*, *Cranm.*, *Bish.*, *Rhem.*; ' in defendynge,' *Wicl.*, *Cov.*; ' as I defende,' *Tynd.*   *Partakers with me*] So *Cov.* and sim. *Tynd.*, *Cranm.*, ' companions of grace with me;' ' partakers of my grace,' *Auth.*, *Genev*, *Bish.*, and sim. *Wicl.*, ' felowis of my joie;' ' partakers of my joye,' *Cov.* (*Test.*), *Rhem.*

8. *Witness*] So *Wicl.*, *Rhem.*: ' record,' *Auth.* and the other Vv. except *Tynd.*, *Gen.*, ' beareth me recorde.' *Do long*] So *Cov.* (*Test.*), and sim. *Cov.*; ' greatly long,' *Auth.* and other Vv. except *Wicl.*, *Rhem.*, ' coucite;' *Bish.*, ' hartely I long.' The insertion of the auxiliary seems to throw a slight emphasis on the action expressed by the verb, which is not inappropriate after the solemn adjuration.   *Christ Jesus*] ' *Jesus Christ,' *Auth.*

9. *Yet more and more abound*] Sim. *Rhem.*, ' may more and more abound:' ' abound yet more and more,'*Auth.*, *Bish.*, and, with similar position of the adverbs, the other Vv. The inversion seems a little more closely to preserve the Greek order and the connection of περισσεύειν with the particulars in which the increase takes place.   *All discernment*] More literally 'all manner of,' etc., a translation actually adopted by *Coverd.*, but marred by the untenable attraction, ' in all manner of knowledge and in all experience.'   *Discernment*] ' Judgment,' *Auth.*, *Gen.*; ' wit,' *Wicl.*; ' fealinges,' *Tynd.*; ' experience,' *Cov.*; ' understandyng,' *Cov.* (*Test.*), *Cranm.*, *Bish.*, *Rhem.*

10. *To the intent that*] ' Th..t,' *Auth.* and all other Vv. It seems desirable to make some difference in translation between the more immediate εἰς τὸ κ. τ. λ. and the further and final ἵνα ἦτε κ. τ. λ. *Prove*] So *Wicl.*, *Cov.*: ' approve,' *Auth.*, *Rhem.*; ' accepte,' *Tyndale*, *Cranmer*; ' alowe,' *Cov.* (*Test.*); ' discrne,' *Gen.*, *Bish.*   *Pure*] So *Tynd.* and all Vv. except *Auth.*, *Rhem.*, ' sincere;' *Wicl.*, ' clene.'   *Against*] So *Coverd.* (*Test.*): ' till,' *Auth.*, *Bish.*, and sim. *Tynd.*, *Cran.*, *Gen.*, ' untyll;' ' in,' *Wicl.*; ' unto,' *Cov.*, *Rhem.*

11. *Fruit*] ' *Fruits, *Auth.* *Is*] ' are,' *Auth.*

12. *Now*] ' But,' *Auth.*, *Cov.* (*Test.*),

¹² Now I would have you know, brethren, that matters with me have fallen out rather unto the furtherance of the gospel; ¹³ so that my bonds have become manifest in Christ in the whole prætorium, and to all the rest; ¹⁴ and that the greater part of the brethren having in the Lord confidence in my bonds, are more abundantly bold to speak the word without fear. ¹⁵ Some indeed preach Christ even from envy and strife; and some too from good will: ¹⁶ they that are of love so preach, because they know that I am set for the defence of the gospel: ¹⁷ but they that are of contentiousness pro-

Bish.: 'for,' *W.*; 'and,' *Rhem.*: the rest omit. *Have you know*] So *R*" *n.* and sim. *Cov.* (Test.), 'have you to wite;' 'wute that ye wite,' *Wicl.*; 'ye shuld under stand,' *Auth., Cranm., Bish.,* and sim. *Tynd., Cover d., Genev,* 'wolde ye understode.' *Matters with me*] Somewhat similarly, *Wicl., Cov.* (Test.), 'the thingis that ben aboute me;' 'the things about me,' *Rhem.*; 'the things which happened unto me,' *Author., Cranmer, Genev.* ('have hap.') *Bish.* ('came'); 'my busynes,' *Tynd., Cov.*

13. *Have become*] Sim. *Wicl., Coverd.* (Test.), *Rhem.*, 'weren made;' 'are,' *Auth.* and remaining Vv. The perfect is adopted as perhaps better continuing the tense of the preceding member. *Manifest in Christ*] 'Bonds in Christ,' *Auth. The whol Pretorium*] 'All the palace,' *Auth.*; 'eche moot halle,' *Wicl.*; 'all the judgmen' hall,' *Tynd., Coverd, Cram., Gen., Bish.*; 'every jugement house,' *Coverd.* (Test.); 'at the court,' *Rhem. To all the rest*] Sim. *Rhem.,* 'in all the rest;' *Auth.* (Marg.), 'to all others;' 'in all other places'. *Auth* and remaining Vv.

14. *That the greater part*] 'Many,' *Auth.* and the other Vv. except *Wicl.,* 'mo.' All however except *Auth.* prefix 'that.' *Having in the Lord, etc.*] 'Brethren in the Lord, waxing confident by my bonds,' *Auth.*, and, with some variations, the other Vv. except *Wicl., Coverd.* (Test.), which connect *ἐν Κυρίῳ* with πεποιθότας.

15. *From*] 'Of,' *Auth., Tynd., Cov., Cran., Gen., Bish.*: 'for,' *Wicl., Coverd.* (Test.), *Rhem. Too*] 'Also,' *Auth., Gen., Rhem.*: the rest omit. *From*] 'Of,' *Auth.* and the other Vv. except *Wicl., Cov.* (Test.), *Rhem.*, 'for.'

16. *They that are, etc.*] 'But the other of love,' *Auth,* but with a transposition of ver. 15 and 16. *Because they know*] So *Cran.,* and sim. *Tynd., Cov.*, 'because they se;' 'knowing,' *Auth., Cov.* (Test.), *Gen., Bish., Rhem.*: 'witynge,' *Wicl.*

17. *But they that are, etc.*] 'The one preach Christ of contention, not sincerely, supposing to add affliction to my bonds,' *Auth.,* but with a transposition of ver. 15 and 16. There is some little difficulty in finding a suitable translation for *ἐριθεία*. On the one hand, the older translation, 'strife,' *W.*, *Tynd., Cov., Cran., Gen., Bish.,* is certainly open to the objection of confounding *ἔρις* and *ἐριθεία*, from which that of *Auth., Cov.* (Test.), *Rhem.*, viz., 'contention,' is scarcely free: on the other hand, the more lexically exact, 'a spirit of intrigue,' here certainly presents so inadequate antithesis to *ἀγάπη*. In this difficulty perhaps the term chosen in the text sufficiently maintains the antithesis, while in its etymological formation it approaches lexical accuracy by keeping

claim Christ, not sincerely, thinking *thus* to raise up affliction unto my bonds. ¹⁸ What then! notwithstanding, in every way, whether in pretence or in truth, Christ is proclaimed, and therein I do rejoice; yea, and I shall rejoice; ¹⁹ for I know that this shall issue to me unto salvation, through your supplication and the supply of the Spirit of Jesus Christ, ²⁰ according to my steadfast expectation and hope, that in nothing I shall be put to shame, but *that* with all boldness, as always, so now also, Christ shall be magnified in my body, whether *it be* by life, or by death.   ²¹ For TO ME to live *is* Christ, and to die *is* gain.   ²² But if to live in the flesh, — *if* THIS is to me the fruit of *my* labor, then what I should choose I wot not. ²³ Yea I am held in a strait betwixt the two, having the desire to

in view the *spirit*, the spirit of faction and dissension, that actuated the opponents.   Proclaim] 'Preach,' *Auth.* and the other Vv. except *Wicl.*, *Cov.* (Test.), 'schewen.'
Thinking] 'Supposing,' *Auth.*
To raise up] '*To add,' *Auth.*
18. *In every way*] 'Every way,' *Auth.*; 'on alle maner,' *Wicl.*; 'all maner wayes,' *Tynd.*, *Cov.* ('of wayes'), *Gen.*; 'by every meane,' *Cov.* (Test.); 'anye maner of waye,' *Cran.*, *Bish.*; 'by al meanes,' *Rhem.*   Proclaimed] 'Preached,' *Auth.* and other Vv. except *Wicl.*, 'schewid.'   *Therein I*] 'I therein,' *Auth.*: changed to avoid any false emphasis on the pronoun.
Shall] So *Wicl.* and *Coverd.* (Test.): 'will,' *Auth.* and the remaining Vv.
19. *Issue to me unto sale.*] Sim. *Rhem.*, 'shall fall out to me unto salv.:' 'turn to my salv.,' *Auth.*, *Gen.*, *Bish.*; 'come to me in to helthe,' *Wicl.*; 'shall befal unto me to saluacion,' *Coverd.* (Test.); 'shall chaunce to my salv.,' *Tynd.*, *Cov.*, *Cran.*   Supplication] 'Prayer,' *Auth.* and all the other Vv.
20. *Steadfast expectation*] 'Earnest expectation,' *Auth.*, *Bish.*; 'expectacion,' *Cranm.*, *Rhem.*; 'abidynge,' *Wicl.*; 'as I hertely loke for,' *Tynd.*, *Cov.*, *Gen.*; 'waytynge for,' *Cov.* (Test.).

Hope] So *Wicl.*, *Cov.* (Test.), *Cranm.*, *Rhem.*: 'my hope,' *Auth.*: 'and hope' (verb), *Tynd.*, *Cov.*, *Gen.*, *Bish.*
Put to shame] 'Ashamed,' *Auth.* and all Vv. except *Rhem.*, 'confounded:' it seems desirable to preserve and express the passive αἰσχυνθήσομαι.
22. *But if to live, etc.*] 'But if I live in the flesh, this is the fruit of my labor,' *Auth.*, and somewhat similarly as to construction, *Tynd.*, *Cran.*: the other Vv. are perplexed, except *Cov.*, 'but in as moch as to live in the flesh is fruteful to me for the worke,' and better *Coverd.* (Test.), 'yf to live here in the flesh is frute of my labour, what,' etc., in which though the τοῦτο is overlooked, that division between protasis and apodosis is the preserved which seems, on the whole, most probable: so in this respect similarly *Wicl.*, *Rhem.*   *Then what*] 'Yet what,' *Auth.*; 'lo what,' *Wicl.*; 'and what,' *Tynd.*, *Cranm.*, *Gen.*, *Bish.*; 'I wote not what,' *Cov.*; 'what,' *Cov.* (Test.).   *Should*] 'Shall,' *Auth.* and the other Vv. except *Tynd.*, *Gen.*, 'to chose,'—an idiomatic translation, but tending to obscure the deliberative future.   *Wot not*] So *Auth.*, *Tynd.*, *Cov.*, *Cranm.*, *Gen.*, *Bish.*: scarcely exact, yet forcible and firm in cadence. The translation of *Cov.* (Test.),

depart, and to be with Christ, for it is very far better: ²⁴ yet to abide in the flesh is more needful for your sakes. ²⁵ And being persuaded of this, I know that I shall abide and shall continue here with you all for your furtherance in and joy of Faith, ²⁶ in order that your ground of boasting may abound in Christ Jesus in me through my presence with you again.

²⁷ Only let your conversation be worthy of the gospel of Christ:

'I cannot tel,' is idiomatic, and preferable to 'knowe not,' *Wicl.*, *Rhem.*

23. Ye t] 'For,' *Auth*. *I am held in a strait*] 'I am in a strait,' *Auth.*, *Bish.*; 'I am constreyned,' *Wicl.*, *Tynd.*, *Cran.*; 'both these thinges lye harde upon me,' *Gen.*; 'I am in distresse with two thinges,' *Cov.* (Test.); 'I am greatly in doubte,' *Genev.* 'I am straitened.' *Rhem. The two*] 'Two,' *Auth* and the other Vv. except *Cov.* and *Rhem.*, which (the former somewhat too strongly) express the article. *The desire*] 'A desire,' *Auth.*, *Cov.* (Test.), *Bish.*; 'desire,' *Rhem.*; 'I haue desire,' *Wicl.*; 'I desyre,' *Tynd.*, *Cov.*, *Cranm.*; 'desiring,' *Gen. For it is, etc.*] 'Which is far better,' *Author.*; 'it is myche more better,' *Wiclif*; 'which thinge is best of all,' *Tynd.*, *Genev.*; 'which thinge were moch more better,' *Cov.*; 'the whyche is much more better,' *Cov.* (Test.); 'and to be with Christ is moch better,' *Cran.*; 'which is muche farre better,' *Bish.*; 'a thing much more better,' *Rhem.*

24. Yet] 'Nevertheless,' *Auth.*, *Tynd.*, *Cran.*, *Gen.*, *Bish.*; 'but,' *Wicl.* and the remaining Vv. *For your sakes*] So *Cov.* (Test.); 'for you,' *Auth.* and the other Vv.

25. *Being persuaded of this*] 'Having this confidence,' *Author.*; 'trustynge,' *Wicl.*, *Cov* (Test.), *Rhem.*; 'am I sure of,' *Tynd.*, *Cov.*, *Cran.*, *Gen.*, *Bish.* *Shall continue here with*] 'Continue with,' *Author.*, with a difference of reading, which, however, does not affect the translation. The Vv. are nearly all identical with *Author.*, except *Wicl.*, 'dwelle and perfightli dwelle,' and *Cov.* (Test.), 'continue with you all unto the end.' *Furtherance and joy*] 'Your furtherance and joy,' *Author.*, *Cranmer* ('youre faith'), *Bish.*, *Rhemish* ('the faith'); 'youre profight and joye of faith,' *Wicl.*; 'the furth. and joye of youre f.,' *Tynd.*, *Cov.*; 'to youre profite and rejoyeynge of f.,' *Cov.* (Test.); 'the furtherance and joy of your f.,' *Gen.*

26. *In order that*] 'That,' *Auth.* and all Vv. *Ground of boasting*] 'Rejoicing,' *Auth.*, *Cov.* (Test.), *Cran.*, *Bish.*; 'thanke,' *Wicl.*; 'may moare abundantly rejoyce,' *Tynd.*, *Cov.* (om. 'moare'), *Genev.*; 'your gratulation,' *Rhem. Abound*] So *Wicl.*, *Rhem.*, and sim. *Cov.* (Test.), 'be plenteous'; 'be more abundant,' *Author.*, *Cran.* ('the more'). For *Tynd.*, *Cov.*, *Gen.*, *Bish.*, see above. *In me*] So *Wicl.*, *Cranm.* (but 'thorowe J. C.'), *Rhem.*; 'for me,' *Auth.*, *Gen.*, *Bish.*; 'thorowe me,' *T., L., Cov.*; 'by me,' *Cov.* (Test.). *Through my presence with you*] 'By my coming to you,' *Auth.* and most of the other Vv., — but perhaps less exact than in the text.

27. *Worthy of*] So *Cranm.* (Test.), *Rhem.*, and sim. *Wicl.*, 'worthili to'; 'as it becometh,' *Author.* and remaining Vv. *Remain absent*] 'Be absent,' *Auth.* and the other Vv. except *Wicl.*, 'ethir absent;' *Cov.* (Test.), 'beynge absent.' *Are standing*] Sim. *Wicl.*, *Rhem.*, 'ye stonden:' 'stand fast,' *Author.*, and sim. *Cranmerd.* (Test.),

that whether I come and see you, or remain absent, I may hear of your affairs, that ye are standing in one spirit, with one soul striving together for the faith of the gospel, ²⁸ and not being terrified in anything by your adversaries; the which is to them an evidence of perdition, but to you of salvation, and this from God: ²⁹ because unto you was granted, in behalf of Christ, not only to believe in Him, but also in behalf of Him — to suffer; ³⁰ having the same conflict as ye saw in me, and now hear of in me.

CHAPTER II.

If then *there be* any exhortation in Christ, if any comfort of love, if any fellowship of the Spirit, if any bowels and compassions, ² make

'stande stedfaste;' 'contynue,' *Tynd.*, *Cov.*, *Cran.*, *Gen.*, *Bish.* Soul] So *Tynd.*, *Coverd.*, *Cranm.*, *Bish.*: 'minde,' *Auth.*, *Gen.*, *Rhem.*, and sim. *Cov.* (Test.), 'one mynded;' 'wille,' *Wicl.*

28. *Not being terrified*] 'In nothing terrified,' *Auth.*; 'in no thing be ye aferd,' *Wicl.*, *Cov.* (Test.), 'afraid;' 'in nothynge fearinge,' *Tynd.*, *Cov.*, *Cran.*, *Bish.*; 'in nothing feare,' *Gen.*; 'in nothing be ye terrified,' *Rhem.* The *which*] So *Cov.* (Test.): 'which,' *Auth.* and all remaining Vv. *Evidence*] 'Evident token,' *Author.*; 'cause,' *Wicl.*, *Coverd.* (Test.), *Cranm.*, *Rhem.*; 'token,' *Tynd.*, *Coverd.*, *Genev.*, *Bish.* *This from*] Sim. *Rhem.*, 'this of:' 'that of,' *Auth.* and remaining Vv. except *Wicl.*, 'this thing is of.'

29. *Because*] 'For,' *Auth.* and all Vv. *Was granted*] 'It is given,' *Auth.* and all Vv. *In Him*] So *Wicl.*, *Cov.* (Test.), *Rhem.*: 'on Him,' *Author.* and remaining Vv. It seems very desirable, on account of the etymological affinity of εἰς (ἑνς) and ἐν (Donalds. Cratyl. § 170), to translate πιστεύειν εἰς, 'believe *in*' (where a more literal translation is not possible), and to reserve '*on*' for πιστεύειν ἐπί: for the construction of this verb in the N. T., see notes on 1 Tim. i. 16, Reuss, *Théol. Chrét.* iv. 14, Vol. I. p. 129, and *Rev. Transl.* of St. John, p. x. *In behalf of Him, etc.*] 'Suffer for His sake,' *Author.* and the other Vv. except *Wicl.*, *Coverd.* (Test.), *Rhem.*, 'for Him.' For the reasons for this change, see notes.'

30. *As ye saw*] So *Cov.* (Test.), *Rhem.* ('have seen'), and sim. *Cran.*, 'soch a fyght as ye saw:' 'which ye saw,' *Auth.* and remaining Vv. (*Cov.*, 'have sene'). *Hear of*] 'Hear to be,' *Author.*, *Genev.* ('have heard'); 'han herde of me,' *Wicl.*, *Rhem.*; 'hear of me,' *Tynd.*, *Cov.* (both), *Cran.*; 'heare in me,' *Bish.*

Chapter II. 1. *If then there be*] 'If there be therefore,' *Auth.*, *Cov.* (Test.), *Cran.*, *Gen.*, *Bish.*; 'therfor if ony comfort is,' *Wicl.*; 'if therefore there be,' *Rhem.*; *Tynd.* and *Cov.* omit οὖν. *Exhortation*] 'Consolation,' *Auth.* and the other Vv. except *Wicl.*, *Cov.*, 'comfort.' *Compassions*] 'Mercies,' *Auth.* and sim. *Tynd.*, *Cov.*, *Cran.*, *Gen.*, *Bish.*, 'mercy;' 'inwardnesse of merci doynge,' *Wicl.*; 'entier mocion of pytie,' *Coverd.* (Test.); 'bowels of commiseration,' *Rhem.*

2. *Make ye full*] 'Fulfil ye,' *Auth.*

ye full my joy, that ye mind the same thing, having the same love, with united souls minding the one thing; ³ minding nothing in the way of contentiousness, nor in the way of vain glory, but with due lowliness of mind esteeming other superior to themselves; ⁴ not looking each of you to your own things, but each of you to the things of others also. ⁵ Verily have this mind within you, which was also in Christ Jesus; ⁶ who, though existing in the form of God, esteemed not His being on an equality with God a prize to be seized on, ⁷ but emptied HIMSELF, taking upon Him the form of

Mind the same thing] Sim. *Wicl.*, 'understonde the same thing;' 'be like minded,' *Auth.*, *Cranm.*, *Genev.*, *Bish.*; 'drawe one way,' *Tynd.*, *Cov.*; 'mynde one thing,' *Coverd.* (Test.); 'be of one meaning,' *Rhem.* *With united souls, etc.*] 'Being of one accord, of one mind,' *Auth.*, and sim. *Tynd.*, *Cov.*, *Cranm.* ('and of'), *Bish.*; 'of o wille and felen the same thing,' *Wicl.*; 'of one mynde meanynge one thynge,' *Cov.* (Test.); 'of one accorde and of one judgment,' *Cranm.*; 'of one mind, agreeing in one,' *Rhem.*

3. *Minding, etc.*] 'Let nothing be done through,' *Auth.*, *Cov.* (Test.), *Bish.*, and sim. *Tynd.*, *Cov.* ('there be'), *Cranm.*, *Genev.*; 'that nothinge be done;' 'nothing li,' *Wicl.*, *Rhem.*

Contention] Sim. *Rhem.*, 'contention;' 'strife,' *Auth.* and the remaining Vv.; see notes on ch. i. 17 (*Transl.*).

Nor in the way of] 'Or,' *Auth.*

With due lowliness] 'In lowliness,' *Auth.*; 'in mekness,' *Wicl.*, *Bish.*; 'in mekenesse of mind,' *Tynd.*, *Cranm.*, *Genev.*; 'thorow mekeness,' *Cov.*; 'in humblenesse,' *Coverd.* (Test.); 'in humilitie,' *Rhem.* As the article does not appear merely used to give ταπειν. its more abstract force, but to mark the 'due, befitting' lowliness by which the Philippians were to be influenced, the insertion would seem justifiable. *Esteeming*] So *Coverd.* (Test.); 'let each esteem,' *Auth.*, and sim. the remaining Vv. except *Wicl.* ('demynge'), *Rhem.* ('counting'), which retain the participial construction. *Superior to*] Sim. *Cov.* (Test.), 'the superior of;' 'better than,' *Auth.* and the other Vv. except *Wicl.*, 'higher them.'

4. *Not looking, etc.*] 'Look not "every man on,"' *Auth.*, and sim. in the imperative, *Cranm.*, *Gen.*, *Bish.*; 'not beholdynge,' *Wicl.*; 'and that no man consider,' *Tynd.*; 'and let every man loke not for his awne profit,' *Coverd.*; 'euery one consydering, not,' *Coverd.* (Test.), *Rhem.* *But each of you, etc.*] 'But "every man also on,"' *Auth.*, and sim. *Gen.*, *Bish.*, the only two Vv. that notice in translation the ascensive καί.

5. *Verily*] *Auth.* and all the Vv. omit the translation of γάρ, except *Wicl.*, 'and;' *Rhem.*, 'for.' *Have this, etc.*] 'Let this mind be in you,' *Auth.*, sim. *Tynd.*, *Cov.*, *Cov.*, *Gen.*; 'let the same mind, etc.,' *Cov.* (Test.), *Bish.*; 'that mind, etc.;' 'if ye this thing in you,' *Wicl.*; 'it is think in yourselves.' *Rhem.*

6. *Though existing*] 'Being,' *Auth.*, *Tynd.*, *Gen.*, *Bish.*; 'whanne He was,' *Wicl.* and remaining Vv.

Esteemed not, etc.] 'Thought it not robbery to be equal with God,' *Auth.*, *Tynd.*, *Cov.*, *Bish.*, and sim. *Cov.* (Test.), *Cranm.*, *Gen.*, *Rhem.*, 'no robbery, etc.;' 'demed not raueyn, that him silf were euene to God,' *Wicl.*

a servant, being made in the likeness of men: ⁸ and being found in fashion as a man, He humbled Himself, becoming obedient even unto death, yea unto death on the cross. ⁹ Wherefore God did also highly exalt Him, and bestowed on Him a name which is above every name, ¹⁰ that in the name of Jesus every knee should bow, of *things* in heaven, and *things* on earth, and *things* under the earth; ¹¹ and that every tongue should confess that Jesus Christ *is* LORD, to the glory of God the Father.

¹² So then, my beloved, even as ye were always obedient, not as in my presence only, but now much more in my absence, work out your own salvation with fear and trembling. ¹³ For it is God which worketh in you, both to will and to perform, of His good pleasure.

7. *Emptied* HIMSELF] 'Made Himself of no reputation,' *Author.* and the other Vv. except *Wicl.*, 'lowede Himself;' *Rhem.*, 'exinanited Him self.' *Taking*] So *Wicl.*, *Cov.* (Test.), *Cran.*, *Bish.*, *Rhem.*: 'and took,' *Auth.* and the remaining Vv. There is some little difficulty in the translation of the *modal* (aor.) participle, when, as in the present case, the action of the participle is synchronous with that of the finite verb. On the whole, the pres. part. in English seems the best and most idiomatic equivalent, especially as in practice the tense of the finite verb seems so far reflected on the participle, that though really present in form, it becomes almost aoristic in sense. *Being made*] Sim. *Bish.*, 'and made:' 'was made,' *Auth.*, *Wicl.*, *Cov.* (Test.), *Gen.*; 'became lyke,' *Tynd*, *Coverd.*, *Cranm.*; 'made into,' *Rhem.*

8. *Becoming*] 'And became,' *Author.* and the other Vv. except *Wicl.*, 'and was made;' *Cov.* (Test.), 'was made;' *Bish.*, *Rhem.*, 'made.'
Even unto] 'unto,' *Auth.* *Yea unto death*] Sim. *Wicl*, 'ye to the death:' 'even the death,' *Auth.* and the other Vv. except *Cov.*, which inserts 'unto,' as in text. *On the cross*] 'Of the cross,' *Auth.* and all the other Vv.: the slight change seems to add somewhat to perspicuity, and is compatible with the present use of the gen., which is one of 'more remote relation.'

9. *Did also, etc.*] So *Coverd.* (Test.), 'God also hath,' *Auth.*, *Cranm.*, *Bish.*, *Rhem.*; 'God enhauncid,' *Wicl.*; 'God hath exalted,' *Tynd.*; 'hath God, etc.,' *Cov.*; 'God hath highly exalted,' *Gen.* The change in the text seems to have the advantage of placing the contrasting καὶ in more distinct connection with ὑπερύψωσεν. *Bestowed on*] Sim. *Wicl.*, *Coverd.* (Test.), 'gave:' 'given,' *Author.* and the remaining Vv. except *Rhem.*, 'hath given.'

10. *In the name*] So *Wicl.*, *Tynd.*, *Cov.* (both), *Cran.*, *Gen.*, *Bish.*; 'at the name,' *Auth.*, *Gen.* *On earth*] Sim. *Coverd.*, 'upon erth:' 'in earth,' *Auth.* and remaining Vv. except *Wicl.*, 'erthely thingis;' *Rhem.*, 'terrestrials.'

12. *So then*] 'Wherefore,' *Auth.* and the other Vv. except *Wicl.*, *Cov.* (Test.), *Rhem.*, 'therefore.' *Even as*] 'as,' *Auth.* *Were always ob.*] 'Have always obeyed,' *Auth.* and the other Vv. except *Wicl.*, 'evermore ye han obeischid.'

13. *To perform*] So *Wicl.*, *Coverdale* (Test.), and sim. *Rhem.*, 'accomplish:' 'to do,' *Auth.*, *Bish.*; 'the dede,' *Tynd.*, *Cov.*, *Cran.*, *Gen.*

"Do all things without murmurings and doubtings; 15 that ye may be blameless and pure, children of God without reproach, amidst a crooked and perverse generation, among whom ye appear as heavenly lights in the world, 16 holding forth the word of life; that I may have whereof to boast against the day of Christ, that I did not run in vain nor yet labored in vain. 17 Howbeit if I be even poured out in the sacrifice and service of your faith, I joy, and rejoice with you all. 18 And for the same cause do ye also joy, and rejoice with me.

14. *Doubtings*] So *Wicl.*, *Cov.* (Test.), and sim. *Rhem.*, 'staggerings:' 'disputings,' *Auth.* and, in the sing., *Tynd.*, *Cov.*, *Cran.*, *Bish.*: 'reasonings,' *Gen.*

15. *Pure*] So *Tynd.*, *Cov.*, *Gen.*, *Bish.*: 'harmless,' *Author.* (Marg. 'sincere'); 'simple,' *Wicl.*, *Covrd.* (Test), *Rhem.*; 'unfayned,' *Cran.* ——— *Children of*] So *Cov.* (Test.), *Rhem.*: 'the sons of,' *Author.* and remaining Vv. except *Cran.*, 'unfayned sonnes of.'

Without reproach] 'Without rebuke,' *Auth.* ——— *Amidst*] '* In the midst,' *Auth.* ——— *Generation*] So *Cov.* (Test.), *Rhem.*: 'nation,' *Auth.* and remaining Vv. ——— *Appear*] 'Shine,' *Auth.* and all the other Vv. ——— *Heavenly lights*] 'Lights,' *Auth.* and all the Vv. except *Wicl.*, 'geners of light.'

16. *Have whereof, etc.*] 'Rejoice,' *Author.*, *Cranm.*, *Gen.*; 'to my glorie,' *Wicl.*, *Rhem.*; 'unto my rejoysynge,' *Tynd.*, *Cov.* (both.), *Bish.* ('to'). ——— *Against*] 'In,' *Auth.* and all Vv. ——— *Did not run*] 'Have not run,' *Auth.* and all the Vv. The change to the aoristic form seems in this case clearly proper and necessary: the form with the auxiliary is here chosen for the sake of preserving the rhythm of the *Auth.* Ver., which can rarely be neglected without some loss to the general cadence of the verse. Modern translators have paid far too little attention to this not unimportant element in a good version of the Scriptures. ——— *Nor yet*] 'Neither,'

Author. and all the Vv. except *Rhem.*, 'nor;' *Cov.* (Test.) omits. The change is here made in accordance with the rule generally followed in this revision — to adopt the weaker translation ('nor,' or 'neither') of the disjunctive οὐδέ, where the meanings of the words it disjoins are more similar and accordant, the stronger and *more* emphatic ('nor yet'), where they are *less* so; see notes on 1 Tim. i. 4 (Transl.).

17. *Howbeit*] 'Yea and,' *Auth.* and the other Vv. except *Wicl.*, 'but though;' *Cov.* (Test.) 'but athough;' *Rhem.*, 'but and if,'—an archaic, but not otherwise unsatisfactory transl. ——— *Be even poured out*] 'Be offered,' *Auth.* and sim. *Tynd.* (adds 'or slayn'), *Cov.*, *Cran.*, *Gen.*, *Bish.*, 'be offered up;' 'am off. up,' *Cov.* (Test); 'be immolated,' *Rhem.* ——— *In the*] 'Upon the,' *Author.* and all the Vv (*Wicl.*, 'on the'); it seems, however, desirable to mark in translation that ἐπὶ has here probably not a local but an ethical reference; the more exact 'unto' (see notes) would here be hardly intelligible.

18. *And for*] 'For, etc.,' *Auth.* and the other Vv. except *Wicl.*, 'and the same thing have ye joie;' *Cov.* (Test.), 'be ye glad also of the same;' *Rhem.*, 'and the self same thing do you also rejoice.' The regimen of αὐτὸ is somewhat more exactly expressed by *Covrd.* (Test.) than by *Auth.* and the Text, but there seems scarcely sufficient reason to

¹⁹ Yet I hope in the Lord Jesus shortly to send to you Timothy, that I also may be of good comfort, when I know your state. ²⁰ For I have no man likeminded, who will have a true care for your state. ²¹ For they all seek their own things, not the things of Christ Jesus. ²² But ye know the proof of him, that, as a child to a father, he served with me in furthering the gospel. ²³ Him, then, I hope to send forthwith, so soon as I shall see how it will go with me.

introduce the change, especially as the sense would remain substantially the same, while the rhythm would certainly suffer.

Do ye also] Sim. *Rhem.*, 'do you also:' 'also do ye,' *Auth.*, *Cran.*, *Bish.*; 'also, rejoice ye,' *Tynd.*; 'be ye glad also,' *Cov.* (both); 'also be ye glad,' *Gen.*: *Wicl.* omits 'also.'

19. *Yet I hope*] 'But I trust,' *Author.* (Marg., 'moreover'), *Bish.*; 'and I hope,' *Wicl. Rhem.*; 'I trust,' *Tynd.*, *Cov.* (both), *Cran.*, *Gen.* *Shortly to, etc.*] 'To send Timothy shortly unto you,' *Author.* and the other Vv. except *Wicl.*, 'schal sende Tymothe soone to you;' *Rhem.*, 'to send Tim. unto you quickly.' The change is made to endeavor to show that ὑμῖν is the transmissive dative, and not the same as πρὸς ὑμᾶς, ver. 25; see notes.

20. *Will have a true care*] 'Will naturally care,' *Auth.*, *Bish.*; 'is bisie for you with clene affection;' 'with so pure affeccion careth,' *Tynd.*, *Coverd.*, *Gen.*; 'be careful for you with sincere affeccion,' *Cov.* (Test.); 'with so pure aff. will care,' *Cran.*; 'with sincere affection is careful,' *Rhem.*

21. *They all*] So *Coverd.* (Test.), and somewhat sim. *Tynd.*, *Cov.*, *Cran.*, *Gen.*: 'all,' *Author.*, *Bish.*, *Rhem.*; 'all men,' *Wicl.* *Own things*] 'Own,' *Author.* and the other Vv. except *Wicl.*, *Rhem.* 'the things that ben her owne,' and sim. *Cov.* (Test.). *Of Christ Jesus*] 'Which are *Jesus Christ's,' *Auth.*, *Cran.*, *Cov.* (Test.). ('that be'), *Bish.*, *Rhem.* ('that are'); 'that ben of Crist Jhesus,' *Wicl.*; 'that which is Jesus Christes,' *Tynd.*, *Cov.*, *Gen* The change in the text seems to leave the translation equally uncircumscribed with the Greek: the possessive gen. *in English* seems more limited.

22. *The proof*] So *Auth.* and all the Vv. except *Wicl.*, 'assaie;' *Rhemish*, 'an experiment:' the meaning really amounts to 'proved character' (see notes), but as so many of the Vv. retain the literal meaning of δοκιμή, a change may be deemed unnecessary. *Child to a father*] Sim. *Cov.* (both), 'a chylde unto the father:' 'a son with the father,' *Auth.*, *Bish.*, and the other Vv. except *Wicl.*, 'a sone to the f.;' *Rhem.*, 'a sonne the father.' *Served*] Sim. *Cov.* (Test.), 'dyd he serve,' and sim. as to aoristic form, *Tynd.*, *Cranm.*, *Gen.*: 'hath served,' *Auth.*, *Wicl.*, *Bish.*, *Rhem.*; 'hath he ministred,' *Cov.* *In furthering the gospel*] 'In the gospel,' *Author.* and the other Vv. except *Tynd.*, 'bestowed his labor upon the gospel.'

23. *Then*] 'Therefore,' *Auth.* and the other Vv. except *Tynd.*, *Coverd.*, which omit οὖν in translation. *Forthwith*] 'Presently,' *Auth.*; 'immediately,' *Rhem.*: the rest omit. The concluding words of the verse are due to the version of *Tynd.*, and have been retained by succeeding Vv. except *Bish.*, 'as soone as I knowe my estate;' *Rhem.*, 'that concern me.' The sense is expressed with sufficient accuracy (see notes) to render it undesirable to alter a translation so thoroughly idiomatic.

24. *Myself also*] So *Coverd.* (Test.),

²⁴ But I trust in the Lord that I myself also shall come shortly. ²⁵ Yet I supposed it necessary to send unto you Epaphroditus, my brother, and companion in labor, and fellow-soldier, but your messenger and minister to my need, ²⁶ since he was longing after you all, and was full of heaviness, because that ye heard that he had been sick. ²⁷ For indeed he was sick like unto death: howbeit God had mercy on him; and not on him only, but on me also, that I should not have sorrow upon sorrow. ²⁸ I have sent him

therefore the more diligently, that, when ye see him ye may rejoice again, and that I too may be the less sorrowful. ²⁹ Receive him then in the Lord with all joy, and hold such in honor; ³⁰ because for the work of Christ he went nigh even unto death, having hazarded his life, to supply that which you lacked in your service to me.

CHAPTER III.

FINALLY, my brethren, rejoice in the Lord. To write the same things to you, to me indeed *is* not irksome, while for you *it is* safe.

more consonant with the order of the Greek, and perhaps also with our present modes of expression: as, however, it has a tendency to suggest an undue emphasis on 'again,' and is, perhaps, a modern collocation, we retain the order of the older version. This is one of many minor points that would need careful consideration in any formal revision of our present version.

29. *Then*] 'Therefore,' *Auth.* and all Vv.: see notes *in loc.* *Joy*] So *Wicl., Rhem.*; 'gladness,' *Auth.* and the remaining Vv. It certainly seems undesirable to depart from the usual and almost semi-theological meaning of χαρά. *In honor*] So *Coverd.* (Test.), and sim. *Wicl., Rhem.*: 'in reputation,' *Auth.*; 'make moch of soche,' *Tynd., Coverd., Cran., Gen., Bish.*

30. *Went nigh, etc.*] 'Was nigh unto death,' *Auth., Gen., Bish.*; 'he wente to deeth,' *Wicl.*; 'he went so farre, that he was nye unto deeth,' *Tynd., Cranm.*; came nye unto,' *Coverdale*; 'went to even untyll death,' *Coverdale* (Test.); 'came to the point of death,' *Rhem.*

Having hazarded] 'Not regarding,' *Auth., Bish.*; 'geuynge his liif,' *Wicl.*; 'and regarded not his lyfe,' *Tynd., Coverd., Cran., Gen.*; 'geuyng over his lyfe,' *Coverd.* (Test.); 'yelding his life,' *Rhem.* The translation of the aor. part., when associated with the finite verb, requires very careful consideration. Besides the usual periphrastic translations by means of temporal or causal particles, we have three forms of translation, — (*a*) the present participle; (*b*) the past participle, with the auxiliary 'having;' (*c*) the idiomatic conversion into the finite verb with 'and.' Of these, (*a*) is especially admissible when the part. defines more closely the *manner* of the action expressed by the finite verb, or the circumstances under which it took place (see notes on ch. ii. 7); (*b*) is often useful when it is necessary to mark the *priority* of the action of the part. to that of the finite verb; (*c*) sometimes serves to mark their *contemporaneity*. In the present case the choice seems to be between (*b*) and (*c*), as the παραβολ. may be regarded as partly accompanying, and partly as having preceded, the ἤγγισεν. As, logically considered, the latter idea seems here distinctly more prominent, we adopt the second form of translation.

That which, etc.] So somewhat similarly *Tynd., Cov., Gen.*, 'that service which was lacking on your part to me:' 'your lack of service to me,' *Auth., Bish.*; 'that that falid of you anentis my service,' *Wicl.* — not an incorrect view of the gen. (see notes); 'it that was wantynge unto you toward my willynge ser-

² Look to the dogs, look to the evil-workers, look to the CONCISION.
³ For we are the CIRCUMCISION, which by the Spirit of God serve
Him, and make our boast in Christ Jesus, and put no confidence
in the flesh; ⁴ though myself possessed of confidence even in the
flesh. If any other man deemeth that he can put confidence in the
flesh, I more: ⁵ circumcised the eighth day, of the stock of Israel,

vyce,' *Cov.* (Test.); 'that which was lackynge on youre part toward me,' *Cran.*; 'that which on your part wanted toward my service,' *Rhem.*

CHAPTER III. 1. *Irksome*] 'Grievous,' *Author.*; 'it is not slowe,' *Wicl.*; 'it greveth me not,' *Tynd., Cov., Cran., Gen., Bish.*; 'no grefe,' *Cov.* (Test.); 'tedious,' *Rhem.* *While*] 'But,' *Auth., Cov.* (Test.); 'and,' *Wicl., Cov., Gen., Rhem.*; 'for to you it is, etc.' *Tynd., Cran., Bish.* It would at first sight seem desirable to suppress the μὲν in translation; as, however, the opposition μὲν—δὲ is sparingly used in the N. T., and only when a somewhat decided contrast is intended, it is best to retain *Auth.*

2. *Look to* (3 times)] Sim. *Wicl.*, 'se ye;' *Rhem.*, 'see;' 'beware of,' *Author.* and the remaining Vv.

The dogs] So *Rhem.*; 'dogs,' *Auth.* and the remaining Vv. The presence of the article with the two following substantives seems to show that here the article is not merely generic, but distinctive and definitive; 'indicat enim de certis quibusdam loqui, quos ipsi noverant,' Erasm. *in loc.* *The evil*] So *Rhem.*; *Auth.* and the remaining Vv. omit the article.

3. *By the Spirit of, etc.*] 'Worship *God in the spirit,' *Author.* It seems permissible to add 'Him' to the absolute λατρεύοντες in accordance with *Auth.* in Luke ii. 37, Acts xxvi. 7. The translation of *Cov.*, 'even we that serve, etc.,' by which the appositional character of οἱ Πνεύμ. κ. τ. λ. is fully preserved, is not undeserving of notice: there seems, how-

ever, scarcely sufficient reason for a change. *Make our boast*] Sim. *Wicl., Rhem.*, 'glorie;' 'rejoyce,' *Auth.* and the remaining Vv.

Put] 'Have,' *Auth.* On account of the next clause it seems desirable here to avoid the use of 'have.'

4. *Myself possessed of*] 'Though I might also have,' *Bish., Auth.*, and sim. *Rhem.* ('albeit I also have'); 'though I have trust,' *Wicl.*; 'though I also have confidence,' *Coverd.* (Test.); 'though I have wher of I myght rejoyce,' *Tynd., Cov., Gen.*; 'though I myght also rejoyce,' *Cran.* The change to 'possessed of,' is an endeavor to mark the 'labens, non utens' implied here by ἔχων, and to draw a distinction in translation between πεποιθὼς and ἔχων πεποίθησιν.

Even in the] 'In the flesh,' *Auth.* and all the Vv. except *Wicl.*, 'in flesh.'

Deemeth] 'Thinketh,' *Auth.* and the other Vv. except *Wicl.*, 'is seyn to trist,' *Cov.* (Test.), 'seemeth to have;' *Rhem.*, 'seeme to have.' The slightly stronger 'deemeth,' appears best to coincide with the view of δοκεῖ adopted in the notes.

Can put co f.] 'Hath whereof he might trust,' *Auth., Tynd., Cran., Gen., Bish.*; 'is seyn to trist,' *Wicl.*; 'whereof he might rejoyce,' *Cov.*; 'seemeth to have confidence,' *Coverdale* (Test., Rheims ('seeme'). The literal translation, 'that he hath confidence,' is here slightly ambiguous, and happy warrants our adopting the slight periphrasis in the text.

5. *As regards*] 'As touching,' *Auth.*; 'bi,' *Wicl.*; 'as concernynge,' *Tynd., Cov., Cran.*; 'after,' *Cov.* (Test.), *Bish.*; 'by profession a Ph.,' *Gen.*; 'according

of the tribe of Benjamin, an Hebrew of the Hebrews; as regards the law, a Pharisee; ⁶ as regards zeal, persecuting the church; as regards the righteousness which is in the law, having lived blameless. ⁷ Howbeit what things were gain to me, these for Christ's sake I have counted loss. ⁸ Nay more, and I do also count them all to be loss for the excellency of the knowledge of Christ Jesus my Lord; for whose sake I suffered the loss of all things, and do

to,' *Rhem.* It will be seen (from next verse) that *Wicl.* and *Rhem.* are the only two which preserve the same translation of κατὰ in the three clauses: this certainly seems desirable, as more clearly directing the reader's attention to the three theological characteristics of the apostle, which are not improbably climactic in arrangement.

6. *As regards*] 'Concerning,' *Author., Bish.*; 'as concernynge,' *Tynd., Cov., Cran., Gen.*; 'after,' *Cov.* (*Test.*); 'according to,' *Rhem.*   *As regards the, etc.*] 'Touching,' *Author., Bish.*; 'bi,' *Wicl.*; 'as touchynge,' *Tynd., Cov., Cranm., Gen.*; 'according to,' *Coverd.* (*Test.*), *Rhem.*   *Having lived blameless*] Sim. *Wicl*, 'lyuynge without playnte:' *Cov.* (*Test.*), 'I have walked wythout blame;' *Rhem..* 'conversing without blame;' 'blameless,' *Auth.*; 'I was unrebukeable,' *Tynd., Cov., Cran., Gen.*; 'I was blameless,' *Bish.* The addition of *Wicl.* serves to mark, though not quite adequately, the γενόμενος which *Auth.* leaves unnoticed.

7. *Howbeit*] 'But,' *Auth.* and all the Vv. The adversative ἀλλὰ seems here to require a stronger translation than the merely oppositive 'but.'   *These*] So *Wicl.*: 'those,' *Auth., Cran., Bish., Rhem.*; 'the same,' *Tynd., Cov.* (both), *Gen.*   *For Christ's sake*] So *Tynd., Cov.* (both), *Cranm., Gen., Bish.*, but at the end of the sentence: 'for Christ,' *Auth., Wicl., Rhem.* —also at the end. The change of order perhaps keeps up the antithesis κέρδος

and ζημία with a little more emphasis.   *Have counted*] So sim. *Coverd.* (*Test.*), 'have I counted;' *Wicl.*, 'I have demede;' *Rhemish*, 'have I esteemed;' 'counted,' *Auth.* and the remaining Vv.

8. *Nay more*] '*Yea doubtless,' *Auth., Gen.*; 'netheless,' *Wicl.*; 'ye,' *Tynd., Cor., Cran., Bish.*; 'nevertheless,' *Cov.* (*Test.*); 'yea but,' *Rhem.* The most literal translation would perhaps be 'nay indeed as was said,' but is obviously too heavy for an idiomatic version; comp. notes.   *Do also count them all*] 'I count all things,' *Auth., Cov.* (*Test.*); 'I gesse alle thingis,' *Wicl.*; 'I thinke all thynges,' *Tynd., Cov., Cranm., Gen., Bish.*; 'I esteeme al things,' *Rhem.* The insertion of 'them,' and the change to 'do also count,' seem required to show that the real emphasis does not rest on πάντα, but on ἡγοῦμαι as contrasted with ἥγημαι, while πάντα refers back to the preceding ἅτινα κ. τ. λ.; comp. Meyer *in loc.*   *To be loss*] So *Cov.* (*Test.*), and sim. *Wicl.*, 'to be peirement:' 'but loss,' *Author.* and the remaining Vv.   *For whose sake*] So *Coverd.* (*Test.*), *Bish.*: 'for whom,' *Auth.* and the remaining Vv.: change for the sake of accordance with the translation of διὰ τὸν Χρ., ver. 7.   *Suffered*] 'Have suffered,' *Auth.*, and similarly with the auxiliary 'have,' all Vv. except *Wicl.*, 'I made alle thingis peirement.'   *To be dung*] So *Bish.*: 'but dung,' *Auth., Tynd., Cov., Gen., Bish.*; 'as drit,' *Wicl.*; 'as dounge,' *Cov.* (*Test.*), *Rhem.*: 'but vyle,' *Cran.*

count them to be dung, that I may win Christ, [a] and be found in Him, not having mine own righteousness, which is of the law, but that which is through Faith in Christ, even the righteousness which cometh of God by Faith: [10] that I may know Him, and the power of His resurrection, and the fellowship in His sufferings, being fashioned to the likeness of His death, [11] if by any means I may attain unto the resurrection from the dead.

[12] Not that I have already attained, or am already made perfect; but I am pressing onward if that I may lay hold on that for which

9. *Faith in*] Sim. *Tynd.*, 'the fayth which is in Christ,' 'th· faith of,' *Auth.* and the remaining Vv. *Even*] So *Cranm.*, and sim. *Wicl.*, 'that is:' *Tynd., Gen.*, 'I meane;' *Cov.*, 'namely;' *Auth.* and *Bish.* omit, and *Coverd.* (Test.) and *Rhem.* alter the construction. The insertion, thus sanctioned by six of the Vv., seems to add slightly both to the perspicuity and emphasis.
Cometh of] So *Tynd., Cov., Cram., Gen., Bish.*; 'is of,' *Auth., Wicl., Rhem.*; *Cov.* (Test.) alters the construction. The concluding words, 'by faith,' *Auth.* ('in faith,' *Wicl., Coverd (·· both), Rhem.*; 'thorowe faith,' *Tynd., Cram., Gener., Bish.*), are scarcely an exact translation of ἐπὶ τῇ πίστει (see notes), but are perhaps a sufficiently close approximation to it to be preferable to any periphrasis ('grounded on faith,' 'resting on faith,') which an adhesion to the literal meaning of the prep. would render necessary.

10. *In His*] 'Of His,' *Author* and the remaining Vv. *Fashioned to, etc.*] Somewhat sim. *Wicl.*, 'made lik to;' *Cov.* (Test.). 'lyke fashioned with;' '*made conformable not*,' *Auth.* and the remaining Vv. except *Rhem.* The expression in the original (συμμορ-φίζεσθαι θανάτῳ) though perfectly intelligible, is so far unusual as to require some slight periphrasis in English. The shorter translation, 'being conformed to,' is perhaps open to objection as involving a use of 'conform,' which, though sanctioned by Hooker, is now of rare occurrence. The transl. of *Cony.*, 'sharing the likeness of,' is objectionable as obliterating the passive.

11. *May*] So *Coverd.* (oth·), *Rhem.*; 'might,' *Auth.* and the remaining Vv. except *Wicl.*, 'if......I come.'
From the dead] So *Gen.*; 'of the dead,' *Author.* and the remaining Vv. except *Wicl., Cov.* (Test., *Rhem.*, which follow the reading in the text. These three Vv. all translate τῆς ('that is fro,' *Wicl., Cov.* (Test.); 'which is from,' *Rhem.*); the insertion of the article is certainly intended emphatically to specify, but apply, falls short of the very distinctive force conveyed by the parallel insertion of the relative in English.

12. *Not that*] So *Wicl., Cov.* (both), *Cram., Rhem.*; 'not as though,' *Auth., Tynd., Gen., Bish.* *I hav*] So *Wicl., Coverd.* (both), *Cran., Rhem.*; 'I had,' *Auth., Tynd., Gen., Bish.* On the use of the auxiliary 'have' in the translation of the aor. with ἤδη, see notes o Eph. iii 5 (Trans.), and on 1 Test. i. 20 (Transl.). *Or am perf., etc.*] Sim. *Wicl.*, 'or now am perfect;' *Cov., Cran.*, 'or that I am all ready;' *Cov.* (Test.), 'or that I be now p.;' *Rhem.*, 'or now am p.;' 'either were already perfect,' *Auth., Tynd., Gen., Bish.* On the translation of the perfect, see notes on Col. i. 16 (*Transl.*). *Am pressing*] 'Follow after,' *Auth., Bish.*; 'sue,' *Wicl.*; 'folowe,' *Tynd., Coverd.,*

also I was laid hold on by Christ. ¹³ Brethren, I count not MYSELF to have gotten hold: but one thing *I do*, forgetting the things that are behind, and stretching forth after the things that are before, ¹⁴ I press on toward the mark for the prize of the heavenly calling of God in Christ Jesus. ¹⁵ Let us then, as many as be perfect, be of this mind: and if in any thing ye are differently minded, even this will God reveal unto you. ¹⁶ Nevertheless, whereto we have attained,—in the same direction walk ye onward.

¹⁷ Brethren, be followers together of me, and mark them which

Cran., Gen., Bish.; 'follow upon,' *Cov.* (Test.); 'pursue,' *Rhem.*
Lay hold on — was laid hold on] 'Apprehend — am apprehended of,' *Author*; 'comprehende — am comprehendide of,' *Wicl.* and the remaining Vv.
Christ] '*Christ Jesus,' *Auth.*

13. *Gotten hold*] So *Cov.* (Test.), and sim. *Tynd., Cov., Cranm.*, 'gotten it:' 'apprehended,' *Auth.*; 'comprehendide,' *Wicl., Rhem.*; 'atteyned to the mark,' *Gen.*; 'attained,' *Bish.*
One thing] So *Wicl., Tynd., Cov.* (both), *Gen., Rhem.*: 'this one thing,' *Author., Cran., Bish.* *The things*] So *Wicl., Coverd.* (Test.), *Rhem.*: 'those things,' *Author., Cranm., Bish.*; 'that which,' *Tynd., Cov., Gen.*
That are (twice)] So *Wicl., Cov.* (Test., once), *Rhem.*: 'which,' *Auth.* and the remaining Vv. If the distinction alluded to on *Ephes.* i. 23 be correct, 'that' would seem here slightly more exact than 'which.' *Stretching forth after*] Sim..*Wicl.*, 'strecche forth my silf to;' *Tynd., Cov.*, 'stretche my silfe unto;' *Cov.* (Test.), 'stretchynge myself to:' *Rhem.*, 'stretching forth myself to:' 'reaching forth unto,' *Auth.*; 'endeuore myself unto,' *Cran., Gen., Bish.*

14. *Press on*] 'Press,' *Auth., Tynd., Cov.* (both), *Cranm., Bish.*; 'pursue,' *Wicl., Rhem.*; 'follow hard,' *Gen., Bish.* In this verse the simple English present is more suitable than the auxiliary with the part., as in ver. 12. There the adverb ἤδη and the past tenses ἔλαβον and τετελείωμαι suggested a contrast in point of time; here the iterative force involved in the English present (Latham, *Engl. Lang.* § 573) is more appropriate.
Heavenly] 'High,' *Auth.* and the other Vv. except *Rhem.*, 'supernal.'

15. *Then*] 'Therefore,' *Auth.* and all the Vv. *Of this mind*] 'Thus minded,' *Auth., Coverd.* (Test.), *Bish., Rhem.*; 'feele we this thing,' *Wicl.*; 'thus wyse minded,' *Tynd., Cov., Cran., Gen.* *Are differently*] 'Be otherwise,' *Auth.* and the other Vv. except *Wicl.*, 'understonden in other maner ony thing.' *This will God, etc.*] 'God shall reveal even this unto you,' *Auth.* and, in the same order, with some slight variations of language, the other Vv. except *Wicl.*, 'this thing God schal schewe;' *Rhem.*, 'this also God hath reuealed,'—a singular mistranslation.

16. *Attained*] 'Already attained,' *Author.*; 'han commun,' *Wicl.*; 'are come,' *Tynd., Cov., Gen., Rhem.*; 'attained unto,' *Bish.* *In the same direction, etc.*] '*Let us walk by the same rule, let us mind the same thing,' *Auth.* The verse is obscure from its brevity; the translation 'to what point we have attained,—in the same direction, etc.,' perhaps may slightly clear it up, but is inferior to *Author.* in giving too special a meaning to *εἰς ὅ*.

17. *Are walking*] 'Walk,' *Auth.* and

are walking so as ye have us for an ensample. ¹⁸ For many walk, of whom *many times* I used to tell you and now tell you even weeping, *that they are* the enemies of the cross of Christ: ¹⁹ Whose end is perdition, whose God is their belly, and *whose glory is in their shame*, who are minding earthly things. ²⁰ For our commonwealth is in heaven; from whence we also tarry for a Saviour, the Lord Jesus Christ: ²¹ Who shall transform the body of our humiliation *so that it be* fashioned like unto the body of His glory, according to the working whereby He is able even to subdue all things unto Himself.

CHAPTER IV.

WHEREFORE, my brethren dearly beloved and longed for, my joy and crown, so stand *fast* in the Lord, dearly beloved.

² I exhort Euodia, and I exhort Syntyche, that they be of the same mind in the Lord. ³ Yea I entreat thee also, true yoke-fel-

all the Vv. It seems desirable to make some slight distinction between the pres. participle in this verse and the present indic. in ver. 18.

18. *Many times I us d., &c.*] 'Have told you often,' *Auth.* and the other Vv. except *Wicl.*, 'I have sei le ofte to you,' *Rhem.*, 'often I told you of.' Change to preserve the true force of ἔκλεγον, and the παρήχησις, πολλὰ — πολλάκις.

19. *Perdition*] 'Destruction,' *Author., Rhem.*; 'deeth,' *Wicl., Coverd. (Test.)*; 'dampnacion,' *Tynd., Cov., Cran., Gen., Bish.* Compare on 1 Tim. vi. 9.

Are minding] 'Minde,' *Author., Coverd. (Test.), Bish., Rhem.*; 'saueren.' *Wicl.*; 'are worldely mynded,' *Tynd., Cranm., Gen.*; 'are earthly minded,' *Cov.*

20. *Commonwealth*] 'Conversation,' *Author.* and all the Vv. except *Wicl.*, 'lyuyng.' We also tarry for, etc.] 'Also we look for the Saviour,' *Auth., Gen., Bish.*; 'also we abiden the sanyour,' *Wicl.*; 'we loke for a saveour, even, etc.,' *Tynd., Coverd.* ('the sav. J. C.'); 'we do wayte for the sauconre the Lord J. C.,' *Cov. (Test.)*; 'we loko for

the s., even the Lord J. C.,' *Cran.*; 'wo expect the Saviour our Lord J. C.,' *Rhem.*

21. *Transform*] 'Change,' *Auth.* and the other Vv. except *Wicl., Rhem.*, 'refourme;' *Cov. (Test.)*, 'restore.'

Body of our humiliation] Sim. *Rhem.*, 'body of our humilitie;' *Wicl.*, 'bodi of oure mekenesse;' 'vile body,' *Auth.* and the remaining Vv. *So that it*] 'That it may be,' *Auth.*

Body of His glory] So *Rhem.*, and sim. *Wicl.*, 'bodi of his clereness;' 'glorious body,' *Author.* and the remaining Vv. except *Cov. (Test.)*, 'hys cleare body.'

CHAPTER IV. 1. *Wherefore*] So *Cov.* (both) 'therefore,' *Auth.* and the remaining Vv. The more exact translation, 'so then,' is here somewhat awkward on account of the following 'so.'

Dearly bel. (2nd)] *Auth.* prefixes 'my,' with *Bish., Rhem.*; 'most dere brithern,' *Wicl.*; 'ye beloved,' *Tynd.*, and tho remaining Vv.

2. *Exhort*] 'Beseech,' *Auth., Coverd. (Test.)*; 'preie,' *Wicl.* and the remain-

low, give them aid, since they labored with me in the gospel, in company with Clement also, and the rest of my fellow-laborers whose names are in the book of life.

⁴ Rejoice in the Lord alway: again I will say, Rejoice. ⁵ Let your forbearance be known unto all men. The Lord is at hand. ⁶ Be anxious about nothing; but in every thing by your prayer and your supplication with thanksgiving let your requests be made known before God. ⁷ And the peace of God, which passeth all understandings, shall keep your hearts and your thoughts in Christ Jesus.

⁸ Finally, brethren, whatsoever things are true, whatsoever things

ing Vv. except *Rhem.*, 'desire.' As παρακαλῶ is a word of very frequent occurrence in St. Paul's Epp. (compare notes on 1 *Tim.* i. 3), the translation must vary with the context: here perhaps the slightly stronger 'exhort' is more suitable than the (now) weaker 'beseech.'

3. *Yea*] '*And,' *Auth.* (καὶ ἐρ.)
Give them aid, etc.] 'Help those women which,' *Auth., Cov.* (Test.), *Bish., Rhem.* ('that'); 'the ilke wymmen that,' *Wicl.*; 'the women which,' *Tynd., Cov., Cran., Gen.* *In company with*] 'With,' *Auth.* and all the other Vv.
The rest of] Sim. *Rhem.*, 'the rest my:' 'with other,' *Auth., Tynd., Cov., Cran., Genev., Bish.*; 'and other,' *Wicl.*; 'my other,' *Cov.* (both).

4. *Again*] So *Rhem., Coverd.* (Test.), *Bish.*, and sim. *Wicl.*, 'efte:' 'and again,' *Auth.* and the remaining Vv.
I will say] So *Bish.*: 'I say,' *Auth.* and all the other Vv.

5. *Forbearance*] 'Moderation,' *Auth.*; 'pacience,' *Wicl.*; 'softeness,' *Tynd., Cov.* (both), *Cranm.*; 'patient mynde,' *Gen., Bish.*; 'modestie,' *Rhem.*

6. *Anxious about*] 'Careful for,' *Auth., Cranm., Bish.*; 'no thing bisie,' *Wicl.*; 'not carfull,' *Tynd., Cov., Gen.*; 'nothynge carefull,' *Cov.* (Test.), *Rhem.*
Your (twice)] *Auth.* and the other Vv. simply 'prayer and supplication' (*Wicl.*,

'bisechinge'). The Versions which erroneously connect παντὶ with προσευχῇ are *Wicl., Coverd.* (Test.), and, what is singular, *Cranm.*, as this Version was not from the Vulgate, and was preceded by the correct translations of *Tynd.* and *Cov.* *Before*] So *Coverd.*: 'unto,' *Author.* and the remaining Vv. except *Wicl.*, 'at;' *Rhemish*, 'with.' Though not perfectly exact, the above translation of πρὸς is slightly preferable to 'unto,' as not seeming to imply to the English reader that a dat. is used in the original.

7. *All understandings*] 'All understanding,' *Auth.* and all the Vv. (*Wicl.*, 'witte'). As these words are so familiar to Christian ears, it seems desirable to introduce the slightest possible change consistent with accuracy. This seems to be the change to the plural, as it approximately conveys the meaning of πάντα νοῦν (comp. notes on *Col.* ii. 15), and precludes the ordinary misconception that 'understanding' is a participle. *Your thoughts*] 'Minds,' *Auth.* and the other Vv. except *Wicl., Coverd.* (Test.), 'undirstondingis;' *Rhem.*, 'intelligences.' *In*] So *Wicl., Tynd., Coverd.* (both), *Genev., Bish., Rhemish*: 'through,' *Auth., Cran., Bish.*

8. *Seemly*] 'Honest,' *Author.* and the other Vv. except *Wicl.*, 'chast.'

are seemly, whatsoever things are just, whatsoever things are pure, whatsoever things are lovely, whatsoever things are of good report; if there be any virtue, and if there be any praise, think on these things. ⁹ The things, which ye also learned and received, and heard, and saw in me, the same do: and the God of peace shall be with you.

¹⁰ Now I rejoiced in the Lord greatly, that now at length ye flourished again in respect of your care for me, wherein ye were also careful, but ye lacked opportunity. ¹¹ Not that I speak in consequence of want: for I have learned, in what state I am, *therein* to be content. ¹² I know also how to be abased, I know too how

9. *The things*] So Cov. (Test.), where also it is similarly resumed as in text by 'the same:' 'those things,' *Author*.; 'which,' *Tynd.* and the remaining Vv. except *Wicl.*, 'that.' *Also learned*] Similarly *Wicl.*, 'also ye han lerned:' 'have both learned,' *Auth.* and the remaining Vv. *Sue*] 'Seen,' *Author*. *The same do*] So Cov. (Test.), 'do the same,' and sim. *Tynd., Cov., Cranm., Gen., Bish.*, 'those thynges do;' *Rhemish*, 'these things do ye' (*Wicl.* inverts order): 'do,' *Auth.*

10. *Now*] 'But,' *Auth., Wicl., Cov.* (Test.), *Bish.*; 'and,' *Rhem.*; the rest omit. *At length*] Sim. *Rhem.*, 'at the length:' 'at the last,' *Auth.* and the other Vv. except *Wicl.*, 'sumtyme aftirward.' *Ye flouris-ed again, &c.*] 'Your care of me hath flourished again,' *Auth.*; 'ye flouriden agen to fele for me,' *Wicl.*; 'ye are revived agayne to care for me,' *Tynd., Coverd., Gener., Bish.*; 'ye are flouryshynge agayne to regarde me,' *Coverd.* (Test.); 'your care is renyued againe for me,' *Cran.*; 'you have reflourished to care for me,' *Rhem.*

11. *In consequence of*] 'In respect of,' *Auth.*; 'as for,' *Wicl.*; 'because of,' *Tynd., Cov., Cran., Gen., Bish.*; 'as because of,' *Cov* (Test.); 'as it were for,'

Rhem. The translation in the text is probably a modern form of expression, but is appy. exact: the *Auth.* though not incorrect is somewhat ambiguous. *What state*] Sim. *Coverd* (Test.), 'what cases:' 'whatsoever state,' *A ther.* and the remaining Vv. ('estate') except *Wicl.*, 'to be sufficient in whiche things I am;' *Rhem.*, 'to be content with the things that I have.' *Therein*] 'Therewith.' *Author.* and the other Vv. except *Wicl., Rhem.* (see above), and *Cov.* (Test.), which omits.

12. *Know also*] ' ' Know both,' *Auth., Rhem.*; 'can also,' *Wicl.*; 'can both,' *Tynd., Coverd.* (Test.), *Cov*; 'can,' *Coverd., Gen.*; 'knowe how,' *Bish.* It may here be remarked in passing that the position of και in Greek, and that of 'also,' 'even,' or 'too,' in English, will not always exactly correspond. Here, for instance, και belongs to ταπεινοῦσθαι (see notes), whereas in English the 'also' seems idiomatically to take an earlier place in the sentence and in position to connect itself with 'know:' the translation in the notes, 'know how also to be abased, or to be abased also,' is literal, but scarcely idiomatic. The attention of the student is directed to this point, as it requires some discrimination to perceive when it is positively necessary to retain in translation the position of

to abound: in every thing and in all things I have been fully taught both to be full and to be hungry, both to abound and to suffer need. ¹³ I can do all things in Him that strengtheneth me. ¹⁴ Notwithstanding ye did well that ye bare part with my affliction. ¹⁵ Moreover, Philippians, yourselves also know that in the beginning of the gospel, when I departed from Macedonia, no church communicated with me as touching any account of giving and receiving, but ye only: ¹⁶ since even in Thessalonica ye sent to me both once and again unto my necessity. ¹⁷ Not that I seek after your gift; but

καί, and when to yield to a more usual English collocation. *I know too*] 'And I know,' *Author., Bish.;* 'I can also,' *Wicl., Tynd.;* 'and I can,' *Cov.* (both), *Cranm., Genev.;* 'I know also,' *Rhem. In every thing, etc.*] 'Every where and in all things,' *Auth.* and the other Vv. (*Gen.* omits 'and'). *Have been fully taught*] Sim. *Wicl., Cov.* (Test.), 'I am taughte:' 'am instructed,' *Auth.* and the remaining Vv.

13. *In Him that*] '*Through Christ which,' *Author., Coverd., Cranm., Bish.;* 'thorow the helpe,' *Tynd., Gen. Strengtheneth*] So *Auth.* and all Vv. except *Wicl.* and *Cor.* (Test.), 'coumfortith.' The force of ἐνδυν. cannot be expressed without weakening the emphasis of the verse, and impairing the rhythm.

14. *Did well*] 'Have well done,' *Auth.* and the other Vv. except *Wicl., Coverd.* (both), *Rhem.*, 'han don wel.' *Bare part with*] So *Cov.* (Test.), 'bearynge parte wyth,' and sim. *Tynd., Cov., Cran., Gen.,* 'ye bare part with me in:' 'communicated with,' *Auth.;* 'did communicate to,' *Bish.;* 'communicating to,' *Rhem.*

15. *Moreover, Philippians, etc.*] 'Now ye Phil. know also,' *Auth.*, and sim. *Cov.* (Test.), *Gen.,* 'and ye, etc.;' 'for ye filipensis witen also,' *Wicl.;* 'ye of Philippos knowe that,' *Tynd., Cov., Cranm.,* ('also that'); 'ye Philip. knowe also,' *Bish.;* 'and you also know, O Philipp.,' *Rhem. As touching any, etc.*]

'As concerning giving and receiving,' *Author., Tynd., Cov.* (omits 'as'), *Cran., Gen., Bish.;* 'in resoun of thing gouun and takun,' *Wicl.;* 'in the way of gyfte and receate,' *Coverd.* (Test.); 'in the account of, etc.,' *Rhem.* Perhaps the insertion of the indefinite 'any' may be considered permissible as serving slightly to clear up the meaning; neither 'an account' or 'the account' (*Rhem.*) is free from objections.

16. *Since*] 'For,' *Auth.* and the other Vv. except *Wicl.*, which omits the conjunction. *To me*] So *Wicl.:* *Auth.* and all the other Vv. omit. *Both once*] 'Once,' *Author.* and the other Vv. *Unto*] So *Auth.* and all Vv. (*Wicl.*, 'in to;' *Rhem.*, 'to') except *Coverd.* (Test.), 'to my behofe.' It is a matter of grave consideration whether, in a literal but idiomatic translation like the Authorized Version, we can consistently introduce here and in similar passages such periphrastic yet practically correct translations of εἰς as 'to supply,' 'to meet,' etc. As there might seem to be some difficulty in fixing the limits of such periphrases, and as the older Vv. appear to have but seldom adopted such transl., it is perhaps best in the majority of cases to retain the more literal, though sometimes less intelligible rendering.

17. *That*] So *Tynd., Coverd.* (both), *Cranm., Gen., Bish., Rhem.:* 'because,' *Auth.;* 'for,' *Wicl. Seek after* (twice)] 'Desire,' *Auth.* and the other

I seek after the fruit that multiplieth unto your account. ¹⁸ But I have all things and abound: I am full now that I have received from Epaphroditus the things *which came* from you, a savor of sweet smell, a sacrifice acceptable, well-pleasing to God. ¹⁹ But my God shall supply every need of yours according to His riches, with glory in Christ Jesus. ²⁰ Now unto God and our Father be glory for ever and ever. Amen.

²¹ Salute every saint in Christ Jesus. The brethren which are with me salute you. ²² All the saints salute you, but especially they that are of Caesar's household.

²³ The grace of the Lord Jesus Christ *be* with your spirit.

Vv. except *Wicl., Cov.* (both), *Rhem.* 'seke.' *Your gift*] 'A gift,' *Author.*, *Bish.*; 'giftes,' *Wicl., Covrd.*; 'gyftes,' *Tynd., Cran.*; 'the gifte,' *Cov.* (Test.), *Rhem.*; 'a rewarde' *Gen.* It is doubtful whether the plural translation of *Tynd.* and *Cranm.* does not *practically* convey more clearly than the text the meaning of the present article, 'the gift in the particular case,' *i. e.* 'gifts,' or even 'any gift;' compare notes: such translations, however, involve principles of correction that should be admitted with great caution. *The fruit*] So *Covrd., Gen., Rhem.*; 'fruit,' *Auth., Wicl., Bish.*; 'aboundant frute,' *Tynd., Cran.*; 'plentyfull frute,' *Covrd.* (Test.). *That multiplieth*] 'That may abound,' *Auth.*, and sim. *Gen.*, 'which may forther;' 'abounding,' *Wicl., Bish., Rhem.* The change is of no importance, but made to preserve in the translation the different words used in the original, here and in ver. 18, — πλεονάζειν and περισσεύειν. *Unto*] 'To,' *Auth.*

18. *All things*] So *Wicl., Rhemish*: 'all,' *Auth.* and the remaining Vv. The present translation of ἀπέχω (*Author. Wicl., Cov.* (both), *Bish., Rhem.*) is unduly weak (*Tynd., Cranm., Gen.*, omit 'have'); but the more literal translation, 'I have in full,' 'I have for my own,' seems as unduly strong, and somewhat interferes with the brief and climactic character of the first portion of the verse. *Now that, etc.*] Sim *Tynd., Gen., Bish.*, 'after that I had rec—' *Cov.* 'whan I rec.;' *Cov.* (Test.), 'whan I had received;' *Cranm.*, 'after that I received;' *Rhem.*, 'after I received.' *From*] 'Of,' *Auth.* and all Vv. *Which came*] So *Tynd., Covrd., Gen.*: 'which were sent from,' *Author., Cranm., Bish.*; 'which ye senten,' *Wicl.*, and sim. *Covrd.* (Test.), *Rhem.* *Savor of sweet smell*] Sim. *Cov.* (Test.), 'a savoure of swetnes:' 'of a sweet smell,' *Auth., Cran.*: 'odour of swetnesse,' *Wicl.*; 'an odour that smelleth swete,' *Tynd., Gen.*: 'odour of sweeteness,' *Cov., Rhem.*; 'an odour of a sweete smell,' *Bish.*

19. *With glory*] 'In glory,' *Author, Wicl., Cov.* (both), *Bish., Rhem.*; 'glorious riches,' *Tynd., Cran., Gen.* *In*] So *Wicl., Tynd., Cov.* (both), *Gen., Bish., Rhem.*: 'by,' *Auth., Cran.*

21. *Salute you*] So *Covrd.* (both), *Rhem.*: 'greet,' *Auth.* and the remaining Vv. A change of translation in the same verse does not seem desirable.

22. *But especially*] So *Covrd.* (both), *Rhem.*: 'chiefly,' *Auth.*: 'moost sothli,' *Wicl.*; 'and most of all,' *Tynd., Gen.*; 'most of all,' *Cran., Bish.*

23. *The Lord*] '*Our Lord,' *Auth.* *Your spirit*] '* You all, Amen,' *Auth.*

THE EPISTLE TO THE COLOSSIANS.

CHAPTER I.

PAUL, an apostle of Christ Jesus by the will of God, and Timothy our brother, ² to the saints in Colossæ and faithful brethren in Christ: grace be unto you and peace, from God our Father.

³ We give thanks to God the Father of our Lord Jesus Christ, praying always for you, ⁴ having heard of your faith in Christ Jesus, and of the love which ye have to all the saints, ⁵ because of the hope which is laid up for you in heaven, whereof ye heard be-

---

CHAPTER I. 1. *Christ Jesus*] '*Jesus Christ,' *Auth.* *Timothy*] So *Wicl., Cov.* (Test.), *Rhem.*: 'Timotheus,' *Author.* and the remaining Vv. The principle put forward in the preface to *Auth.*, though apparently not always followed, seems sound and reasonable, — to adopt, in the case of proper names, those forms which are most current, and by which the bearers of the names are most popularly known.

2. *Saints in Colossæ*] Sim. *Tyndal., Cov., Cran.,* 'sayntes which are at Colosse:' 'to the saints and faithful brethren in Christ which are at Colosse,' *Auth.* and, with slight variations in order, the remaining Vv. *God our Father*] *Auth.* adds '*and the Lord Jesus Christ.'

3. *God the Father*] '*God and the Father,' *Auth.*

4. *Having heard*] 'Since we heard,' *Auth., Tynd., Cov., Gen., Bish.* ('have'); 'herynge,' *Wicl., Cov.* (Test.), *Rhem.*;

'for we haue hearde,' *Cran.* The translation of *Auth.*, al. is perhaps somewhat ambiguous, 'since' having as much a causal as a temporal reference. As the latter seems to be the most probable reference in the present case (see notes in *loc.*), it will perhaps be best to adopt what seems a more definitely temporal translation; see notes on *Ph.* ii. 30 (*Transl.*). *To*] So *Auth.* A few of the Vv., *Cov.* (Test.), *Rhem.*, retain the more literal 'toward.'

5. *Because of*] So *Cov.* (Test.); 'for,' *Author., Wicl., Rhem.*; 'for the hope's sake,' *Tynd., Cov., Cran., Gen., Bish. Word of truth, etc.*] So *Cov.* except that *ἐν* (1st) is translated 'by,' and similarly *Gen.,* 'the worde of truth which is in the gospel:' 'word of the truth of the gospel,' *Author., Wicl., Rhem.*: 'true worde of the gospell,' *Tynd., Cran.*; 'worde of truth of the gospel,' *Cov.* (Test.), *Bish.* The true relation of the genitives thus seems expressed by three

fore in the word of Truth in the gospel; ⁶ which is come unto you, as it is also in all the world; and is bringing forth fruit and increasing as it is also in you, since the day ye heard *of it*, and came to know the grace of God in truth: ⁷ even as ye learned of Epaphras our beloved fellow-servant, who is in your behalf a FAITHFUL minister of Christ; ⁸ who also declared unto us your love in the Spirit.

⁹ For this cause we also, since the day we heard *it*, do not cease to pray for you, and to make our petition that ye may be filled with the knowledge of His will in all spiritual wisdom and understanding; ¹⁰ that *ye* may walk worthy of the Lord unto all pleasing, bringing forth fruit in every good work, and increasing by the knowledge of God; ¹¹ being strengthened with all strength, accord-

of the older Vv.; see notes. The article preceding ἀληθείας appears only to mark that ἀληθ. is used in its most abstract sense. This use of the article in the case of abstract nouns is commonly marked in this Revision by a capital letter.

6. *It is also* (1ˢᵗ)] So *Cov.* (Test.), and im. *Wicl.*, 'also it is;' *Rhem.*, 'also in the whole world it is:' 'it is,' *Auth.* and the remaining Vv.

Is bringing forth fruit] 'Bringeth forth fruit,' *Auth.*, *Cor.*, Test. (omits 'forth'); 'makith frute,' *Wicl.*; 'is frutefull,' *Tynd.*, *Cov.*, *Cran.*, *Gen.*, *Bish.*; 'fructifieth,' *Rhem.* *And increasing*] *Auth.* omits. *Is*] 'Doth,' *Auth.* *Came to know*] 'Knew,' *Author.* and the remaining Vv. (*Coverd.* Test., 'haue knowen') except *Tynd.*, *Cran.*, 'had experience '—a translation which similarly with text ἐπέγνωτε (see notes on ver. 9), and deserves consideration.

7. *Even as ye*] *Author.* adds ' *also,' and omits 'even.' The translation of καθώς, whether 'as' or 'even as,' must depend on the general tone of the passage: here the latter seems to connect the present verse a little more closely with the concluding words of ver. 6.

Beloved] 'Dear,' *Auth.*, *Tynd.*, *Coverd.*, *Cran.*, *Gen.*, *Bish.*; 'moost dereworthe,' *Wicl.*; 'mooste beloued,' *Cov.* (Test.); 'deerest,' *Rhem.* *In your behalf*] 'For you,' *Auth.* and the remaining Vv. It seems desirable to select a translation that should prevent ὑπέρ being possibly understood as 'in your place;' see notes.

9. *Make our petition*] 'Desire,' *Auth.* and the other Vv. (*Tynd.*, *Rhem.*, 'desyringe ') except *Wicl.*, 'to axe;' *Cov.* (Test.), 'axing.' *May*] So *Coverd.* (Test.), *Rhem*: 'might,' *Auth.* and the remaining Vv. except *Wicl.*, 'that ye be filled.' *Spiritual wisdom and, etc.*] So *Cov.* (Test.): 'wisdom and spiritual understanding,' *Auth.* and all the remaining Vv.

10. *May*] So *Coverd.* (Test.), *Rhem.*: 'might,' *Author.* and the remaining Vv. except *Wicl.*, 'that ye walke.' *Bringing forth fruit*] So *Cov.* (Test.): 'being fruitful,' *Auth.* It seems desirable to preserve the same translation as in ver. 6. *By the*] ' *In the,' *Auth.*

11. *Being strengthened*] So *Coverdale* (Test.): 'strengthened,' *Author.* and the remaining Vv. except *Wicl.*, 'and be comfortid; ' *Cov.*, 'and to be strong.'

ing to the might of His glory, unto all patience and long-suffering with joy; ¹² giving thanks unto the Father, which made us meet for the portion of the inheritance of the saints in light: ¹³ who delivered us out of the power of darkness, and translated us into the kingdom of the Son of His love; ¹⁴ in whom we have Redemption, even the forgiveness of our sins. ¹⁵ Who is the image of the invisible God, the firstborn before every creature: ¹⁶ because in Him were all things created, the things that are in heaven, and the things that are on earth, the things visible and the things invisible, whether *they be* thrones, or dominions, or principalities, or powers, — all things have been created by Him, and

Strength] 'Might,' *Auth.* and the other Vv. except *Wicl.*, 'vertu;' *Cov.* (both), 'power.' It is perhaps desirable to retain the παντὸς of the original.

The might of His glory] So *Cov.* (both), *Rhem.*, and sim. *Wicl.*, 'migt of Hiiterenesse;' 'glorious power,' *Auth.* and the remaining Vv. *Joy*] So *Wicl.*, *Rhem.*, and, with a different collocation, *Cov.* (Test.); 'joyfulness,' *Author.* and the remaining Vv.: comp. notes on *Phil.* ii. 29 (*Transl.*).

12. *Made*] So *Wicl.*: 'hath made,' *Auth.* and the remaining Vv.

For the portion] 'To be partakers of,' *Auth.*, *Tynd.*, *Cranm.*, *Gen.*, *Bish.*; 'to the part of,' *Wicl.*; 'mete for the inheritance,' *Cov.*; 'worthy of the parte of the enh.,' *Coverd.* (Test.); 'worthy unto the part of the lot,' *Rhem.*

13. *Delivered*] So *Wicl.*: 'hath delivered,' *Auth.* and the remaining Vv. except *Coverd.* (Test.), 'hath drawen us oute.' *Out of*] 'From,' *Auth. Translated*] So *Wicl.*, *Coverd.*: 'hath translated,' *Auth.* and the remaining Vv. *The Son of His love*] So *Rhem.*, and sim. *Wicl.*, 'the sone of His louynge:' 'His dear Son,' *Auth.* and the remaining Vv. except *Cov.* (Test.), 'Hys beloued Sonne.'

14. *Redemption*] *Auth.* adds '*through His blood.' *Our*

sins] 'Sins,' *Auth.* and all the other Vv.

15. *Firstborn*] So *Auth.*, *Cov.* (Test.), *Bish.*, *Rhem.*; 'first begotten,' *Wicl.*, *Tynd.*, *Cov.*, *Cranm.*, *Gen.* It is apparently not of much moment which of these expressions is adopted, as the meaning is substantially the same. In Rom. viii. 29, *Auth.* adopts the former, in Rev. i. 5, the latter: in expressions of this peculiar and mystical nature it seems desirable to preserve a uniform translation. *Before*] So *Cov.* (Test.): 'of,' *Author.* and remaining Vv. This latter translation was retained in ed. 1, as most inclusive; the arguments, however, for the translation in the text (see notes) seem sufficiently strong to justify the alteration.

16. *Because*] 'For,' *Auth.* and all the other Vv. *In*] So *Wicl.*, *Rhem.*; 'by,' *Auth.* and the remaining Vv. *The things that are*] 'That are in heaven and that are in earth, visible and invisible,' *Auth.*, *Cranm.*, *Bish.*, and, with some slight variations, *Wicl.*, *Cov.*, *Gen.*, *Rhem.*: *Tynd.* alone inserts 'things,' four times as in the text. The repetition seems to give emphasis to the enumeration; see notes on *Eph.* i. 10 (*Transl.*). *Have been created*] 'Were created,' *Author.*, *Cran.*, *Gen.*, *Bish.*, *Rhem.*; 'ben made of nought,' *Wicl.*; 'are created,' *Tynd.*,

for Him; [17] and He is before all things, and in Him all things subsist. [18] And He is the head of the body, the church; who is the beginning, the firstborn from the dead, in order that in all *things* He might have the pre-eminence: [19] because in Him it pleased the whole fulness *of the Godhead* to dwell, [20] and by Him to reconcile all things unto Himself, having made peace through the blood of His cross; by Him, *I say*, whether *they be* the things on earth, or the things in heaven.

[21] And you also, though ye were in times past alienated and

Cov. (both). As the Greek perfect expresses both 'have been' *and* 'are;' there is sometimes a difficulty in knowing which of the two to select: perhaps as a general rule (where idiom will permit, and there is no danger of misconception) it is best to adopt the former when *past* time seems to come more in prominence, the latter when *present* effects are more immediately the subject of consideration. To apply this to the present case; as the former part of the verse seems to show that the reference is perhaps more to the past than to present operations of the Divine power, these latter being more alluded to in the following verse,—we may perhaps judiciously change the 'are created' of ed. 1 into the translation now adopted in the text. On the translation of δι' αὐτοῦ, see *Revised Transl. of St. John*, p. xiii.

17. *In*] So *Wicl., Tynd., Cov.* (both), *Gen., Bish., Rhem.*: 'by,' *Auth., Cran.* *Subsist*] 'Consist,' *Auth.*

18. *Who*] So *Auth., Rhem., Wicl.*, and *Cov. Test.* ('whyche'); 'he is the beg.' *Tynd., Cov., Cranm., Gen., Bish.* The relative translation is scarcely sufficient, as it does not fully convey the *explanatory* force in the relative 'being as He is.' As, however, the translation in the commentary 'seeing He is,' though *per se* expressing clearly this force of ὅς, is perhaps somewhat too strong when placed in connection with what precedes and follows, it seems better to leave

Auth. unchanged. *In order that*] 'That,' *Author.* and all the other Vv. The occasional insertion of 'in order' seems useful where it is required to exhibit clearly the purpose involved in the antecedents.

19. *Because in Him, etc.*] So similarly *Wicl.*, 'in Hym it plesid alle plentee to enhabite;' *Coverd.* (Test.), 'it hath pleased alle fulnesse of the Godheade to dwel in Hym;' *Rhem.*, 'it hath wel pleased al fulness to inhabite:' 'for it pleased *the Father* that in Him should all fulness dwell,' *Auth.* and the remaining Vv. (*Coverd.*, 'shuld dwell all f.').

20. *Having made—cross*] *Auth.* places this clause in the first part of the verse, immediately after 'and.' All the other Vv. retain the order of the Greek, but with some variations in the translation of the participle. The things *on earth*] 'Things in earth,' *Auth. The things in*] 'Things in,' *Auth.*

21. *And you also*] 'And you,' *Author.* and all the other Vv. On this translation of καί, see notes *on Eph.* ii. 1. *Though ye were, etc.*] Similarly *Rhem.*, 'whereas you were;' compare *Wicl., Cov.* (Test.), 'whanne ye weren:' 'that were,' *Auth.*; 'whiche were,' *Tynd.* and the remaining Vv. *In times past*] So *Tynd., Cov., Gen.*: 'sometime,' *Auth.* and the remaining Vv. *Understanding*] So *Auth.* in Eph. iv. 18; 'mind,' *Auth.*, and sim. remaining Vv except *Wicl., Coverd.* (Test.), 'witte;'

enemies in *your* understanding in WICKED works, yet now hath He reconciled ²² in the body of His flesh through His death, to present you holy and blameless and without charge in His sight: ²³ if at least ye continue in the faith, grounded and stable, and without being moved away from the hope of the gospel, which ye heard, *and* which was preached in *the hearing of* every creature which is under heaven; whereof I Paul became a minister.

²⁴ Now I rejoice in my sufferings for you, and am filling fully up the lacking measures of the afflictions of Christ in my flesh for His body's sake, which is the church: ²⁵ whereof I became a minister, according to the dispensation of God which was given to me for you, to fulfil the word of God; ²⁶ even the mystery which hath lain hid from the ages and from the generations, but now hath been made manifest to His saints: ²⁷ to whom it was God's will to make

'by cogitation,' *Bish.*: *Rhem.* 'sense.' *In*] So *Wicl.*, *Rhem.*, and, with a different construction, *Tynd.*, *Cov.*, *Cranm.*, *Gen.*, *Bish.*: 'by,' *Author.*: 'geuen to,' etc.' *Cov.* (Test.).

22. *His death*] 'Death,' *Auth.* and all the other Vv. *Blameless and without charge*] 'Unblamable and unreprovable,' *Author.*; 'unwemmed and without repreef,' *Wicl.*; 'unblameable and without faut,' *Tynd.*, *Covrd.*, *Cranm.*, *Gen.*, *Bish.*; 'unspotted and unblameable,' *Covrd.* (Test.); 'immaculate and blameless,' *Rhem.*

23. *If at least*] 'If,' *Auth.* and the remaining Vv. except *Wicl.*, 'if nethelees;' *Rhem.*, 'it yet.' *Stable*] So *Wicl.*, *Rhem.*: 'settled,' *A there*: 'stablysshed,' *Tynd.* and the remaining Vv. *Without being*] 'Be not,' *Auth.* and the other Vv. except *Wicl.*, *Covrd.* (Test.), *Rhem.*, 'unmouable.' *Heard*] 'Have heard,' *Author.* and all the other Vv. *In the hearing of*] 'To,' *Auth.*, *Gener.*, *Bish.*; 'in al creaturis,' *Wicl.*; 'amonge all creatures,' *Tynd.*, *Cov.*, *Cranm.*, *Rhem.*; 'among euery creature,' *Cov.* (Test.).

Became] Similarly *Cov.* (Test.), 'am I Paul become:' 'am made,' *Auth.* and the remaining Vv.

24. *Now I*] '*Who now,' *Auth.* *Am filling fully up*] 'Fill up,' *Author.*; 'fille,' *Wicl.*; 'fulfill,' *Tynd.*, *Covrd.* (both), *Cranm.*, *Gen.*, *Bish.*; 'accomplish,' *Rhem.* *The lacking measures of*] 'That which is behind of,' *Auth.*, *Tynd.*, *Cov.*, *Cranm.*, *Bish.*; 'the thingis that failen of,' *Wicl.*; 'the thynges that are wantynge of,' *Covrd.* (Test.), sim. *Rhem.*; 'the rest of,' *Gen.*

25 *Became*] Similarly *Cov.* (Test.), 'am become:' 'am made,' *Auth.* and the remaining Vv. *Was given*] So *Tynd.*, *Cranm.*: 'is given,' *Auth.* and the remaining Vv.

26. *Lain*] 'Been,' *Author.* Perhaps the slight change may better convey the force of the perf. participle. *From the ages and from the gen.*] 'From ages and from gen.,' *Author.*, *Wicl.*, *Rhem.*; *Tynd.*, *Cov.*, *Cranm.*, *Gen.*, and *Bish.*, paraphrase; 'from euerlastynge and the generacions,' *Cov.* (Test.). *Hath been*] 'Is,' *Auth.* and all the other Vv.

27. *It was God's will*] 'God would,' *Auth.* and all the other Vv.

known what is the riches of the glory of this mystery among the Gentiles; which is Christ among you, the hope of Glory: ²⁸ whom WE proclaim, warning every man, and teaching every man in all wisdom; that we may present every man perfect in Christ: ²⁹ to which end I also toil, striving according to His working, which worketh in me with power.

CHAPTER II.

For I would have you know what great conflict I have for you, and them in Laodicea, and as many as have not seen my face in the flesh; ² that their hearts may be comforted, they being knit together in love and unto all the riches of the full assurance of the understanding, unto the full knowledge of the mystery of God, even Christ; ³ in whom are hiddenly all the treasures of wisdom and knowledge. ⁴ Now this I say, that no one may beguile you with

---

Among (2d)] So *Coverd.* (Test.): 'in,' *Auth.* and the remaining Vv.

Christ] '*Christ Jesus,' *Auth.*

28. *Proclaim*] 'Preach,' *Author.* and the other Vv. except *Wicl.*, 'schewen.'

29. *To which end*] 'Whereunto,' *Auth.*, *Gen.*, *Bish.*; 'in whiche thing,' *Wicl.*; 'wherin,' *Tynd.*, *Coverd.* (both), *Cran.*, *Rhem.* *Toil*] Comp. on 1 Tim. iv. 10: 'labor,' *Auth.* and all Vv. except *Wicl.*, 'traueile.'

With power] Similarly *Cov.* (Test.), 'by power;' *Rhem.*, 'in power:' 'mightily,' *Author.* and the remaining Vv. except *Wicl.*, 'in vertu.'

Chapter II. 1. *Would have you, etc.*] Similarly *Cov.* (Test.), 'would have you to know;' *Rhem.*, 'wil haue you know:' 'would that ye knew,' *Author.*, *Cranm.*, *Bish.*; 'wole that ye wite,' *Wiclif*; 'wolde ye knewe,' *Tynd.*, *Cov.*, *Gen.*

And them] 'And *for* them,' *Auth.*

In] 'At,' *Auth.*, *Wicl.*, *Cranm.*, *Coverd.* (Test.), *Bish.*, *Rhem.*; 'of,' *Tynd.*, *Cov.*, *Gen.* *And as many*] 'And for as many,' *Auth.*

2. *May*] So *Coverd.* (Test.), *Rhem.*; 'might,' *Author.* and the remaining Vv. except *Wicl.*, 'that her hertis counforted.'

They being, etc.] '*Being knit together,' *Author.* *The riches*] So *Wicl.*, *Cov.* (Test.), *Rhem.*; 'riches,' *Auth.* and the remaining Vv. *The understanding*] *Author.* and all the other Vv. omit the article; 'full understondinge,' *Tynd.*, *Cov.*, *Cran.*; 'persuaded underst.,' *Gen.* *Unto*] 'To,' *Auth.*: change to preserve parallelism with the preceding εἰς. *Full knowledge*] 'Acknowledgment,' *Auth.*, 'knowynge,' *Wicl.*; 'for to knowe,' *Tynd.*, *Cranm.*, *Gen.*; 'knowledge,' *Cov.* (both), *Cranm.*; 'to know,' *Bish.* The juxtaposition of ἐπίγνωσις and γνῶσις seems here to justify this translation; comp. notes.

Of God, even Christ] 'Of God *and of the Father, and of Christ,' *Auth.*

3. *Hiddenly*] 'Hid,' *Auth.* and all the other Vv.

4. *Now*] 'And,' *Author.*, *Gen.*; 'for,' *Wicl.*; 'but,' *Coverdale* (Test.), *Rhem.*: *Tynd.*, *Cov.*, *Cran.*, *Bish.* omit.

enticing speech. ⁵ For if I am absent verily in the flesh, yet still I am with you in the spirit, joying *with you* and beholding your order, and the firm foundation of your faith in Christ. ⁶ As then ye received Christ Jesus THE LORD, so walk ye in Him; ⁷ rooted and being built up in Him, and being stablished in your faith, even as ye were taught, abounding therein with thanksgiving.

⁸ Beware lest there shall be any one that maketh you his booty through philosophy and vain deceit, after the tradition of men, after the rudiments of the world, and not after Christ. ⁹ Because IN HIM doth dwell in bodily fashion all the fulness of the Godhead. ¹⁰ And ye are in Him made full; who is the head of every princi-

---

That) *one*] 'Let *any one*,' *Author., May*] 'Should,' *Auth.* and the other Vv. except *Wicl., Cov.* (Test.), *Rhem.*, 'that no man disceyue you.'

Enticing speech] 'Enticing words,' *Auth.* and the other Vv. except *Wicl., Covrd.* (Test.), 'highe of wordis;' *Bish.*, 'persuasion of word;' *Rhem.*, 'loftines of wordes.'

5. *If I am absent verily, etc.*] 'Though I be absent,' *Auth.* and all the other Vv. *Yet still I am*] *Wicl.*, 'Yet am I,' *Author.* and the other Vv. except *Cov.* (Test.), 'but yet am I;' *Rhem.*, 'yet in spirit I am:' *Wicl.* omits. *Joying with you*] 'Joying,' *Author.* and the other Vv. except *Covrd.* (Test.), *Rhem.*, 'rejoyenge.' *Firm foundation*] 'Stedfastness,' *Author., Covrd.* (both); 'sadnesse,' *Wicl.*; 'stedfast fayth,' *Tynd., Cran., Gen., Bish.*; 'constancie.' *Rhem.*

6. *As then ye*] 'As ye have therefore,' *Auth.* and all the other Vv. (*Wicl., Rhem.*, 'therfor as ye han').

7. *Being built up*] *Auth.* and all the other Vv. either omit 'being,' or slightly change the construction. The insertion is an attempt to mark the difference of tense in the two participles. The true force of the tense in each case (as is suggested in notes *in loc.*) is very discernible; they had already been rooted and were now remaining so (pert.); they were being built up (pres.)—the process going on from day to day. What was underneath was firm and was remaining so; what was above was receiving continual increase and accession.

Being stablished] So *Covrd.* (Test.); *Author.* and the remaining Vv. either omit 'being' or slightly change the construction. *Your faith*] 'The faith,' *Author.* and the other Vv. except *Wicl.*, 'the bileue;' *Cov.* (Test.), *Cran.*, 'faith.'

8. *There shall be any one that, etc.*] 'Any man spoil you,' *Auth., Cov., Bish.*; 'that no man disceyue you,' *Wicl., Rhem.*; 'eny man come and spoyle you,' *Tynd., Gen.*; 'ony man deceaue you,' *Cov.* (Test.); 'lest he eny man spoyle you,' *Cran.*

9. *Because*] 'For,' *Auth.* and all the other Vv. *Doth dwell*] 'Dwelleth,' *Auth.* and all the other Vv. The introduction of the auxiliary appears to add a slight force to the important verb κατοικεῖ. The principal emphasis apparently falls on ἐν αὐτῷ; the verb, however, both from meaning and position, is not without prominence.

In bodily fashion] 'Bodily,' *Auth.* and the other Vv. except *Rhem.*, 'corporally.'

10. *In Him made full*] Sim. *Rhem.*, 'in Him replenished;' 'complete in

pality and power : ¹¹ in whom ye were also circumcised with a circumcision not wrought with hand, in the putting off of the body of the flesh, in the circumcision of Christ ; ¹² having been buried with Him in your baptism, wherein ye were also raised with *Him* through your faith in the operation of God, who raised Him from the dead. ¹³ And you also being dead in your trespasses and the

Him,' *Author.* and the other Vv. except *Wicl., Cov.* (Test.), ' filled in Him.'

Who] ' Which,' *Author.* The otherwise unnecessary change adds here to perspicuity. *Every*] ' All,' *Auth.* and the other Vv.

11. *Ye were also circumcised*] ' Also ye are circ.,' *Author.* and the other Vv. except *Rhem.*, ' also you are,' etc.

A circumcision] So *Coverd.* (Test.), and sim. all the other Vv. (except *Author.*), ' circumcision :' *Author.* inserts the definite article. *Not wrought with hand*] ' Made without hands,' *Author., Tynd., Genev., Bish.*; ' not made with hond,' *Wicl., Rhem.* (' by'); ' circum. without hondes,' *Coverd.*; ' not made with handes,' *Cov.* (Test.); ' done without handes,' *Cran. In the putting off, etc.*] ' In putting off,' etc, *Auth.*; ' in dispoilynge of (off),' *Wicl.*; ' by puttinge of (off),' *Tynd., Cov., Gen., Bish.*; ' in robbyng of,' *Cov.* (Test.); ' for asmoch as, etc.,' *Cranm.*; ' in spoiling of,' *Rhem.* The insertion of the articles gives a heaviness to the sentence, but seems required to show that ἐν τῇ ἀπεκδ. is not to be regarded as modal, much less causal, as *Cranm.*

Body of the flesh] ' Body *of the sins of the flesh,' *Auth. In the circumcision*] So *Cov.* (Test.), *Rhem.*, and similarly *Wicl.*, ' in circumcision :' ' by the circumcision,' *Auth., Bish.*; ' thorow the circ.,' *Tynd., Cranm., Gen.*; ' with the circ.,' *Cov.*

12. *Having been buried*] ' Buried,' *Author., Bish., Rhem.*; ' and ye ben biried,' *Wicl.*; ' being buried,' *Coverd.* (Test.); ' in that ye are buried, etc.'

Tynd. and the remaining Vv. Compare notes on *Phil.* ii. 7 (*Transl.*).

Your baptism] ' Baptism,' *Auth.* and all the other Vv. *Ye were also raised*] ' Also ye are risen,' *Auth.*, and with slight variations the other Vv. : the καί, however, is rightly joined in translation with συνηγερθ. by *Tynd., Cov., Cran., Gen., Bish.*

Your faith] ' Faith,' *Author.* and, with some variations in construction, the other Vv. except *Coverd.* (Test.), *Bish., Rhem.*, ' the faith.' The personal address *seems* here to render the translation of the article by the possessive pronoun correct and appropriate; there are, however, many cases in which such attempts at accuracy overload and embarrass the sentence; consider Romans xii. 7 sq., where, as in many other passages, it requires much discrimination to decide when the article has a pronominal force, and when it is merely associated with an abstract noun. *In the operation*] ' Of the operation,' *Auth., Bish., Rhem.*; ' wrought by the operacion of,' *Tynd., Coverd., Cranm., Gen.*; ' of God's workynge,' *Cov.* (Test.). On the translation of this word see notes on 1 *Thess.* ii. 13 : the rendering here adopted by *Author.* may perhaps be allowed to stand; the term ' operation,' though not usually a good translation, here not unsuitably representing the ' potentia in actum se exserens' (Calv. on *Phil.* iii. 21) alluded to and exemplified in the clause which follows.

13. *You also*] *Auth.* and the other Vv. omit ' also :' see, however, notes on *Eph.* ii. 1. *Trespasses*] So

uncircumcision of your flesh, He quickened together with Himself, having forgiven us all our trespasses. ¹⁴ blotting out the handwriting in force against us by its decrees, which was contrary to us; and He hath taken it out of the way, nailing it to His cross; ¹⁵ *and stripping away from Himself principalities and powers, He made a show of them with boldness, triumphing over them in it.*

¹⁶ Let not any man therefore judge you in eating or in drinking, or in the matter of an holy day, or of a new moon, or of a sabbath; ¹⁷ which are a shadow of things to come, but the body is

Auth. in Eph. ii. 1, and in the present verse: 'sins,' *Author.*, *Covrd.* (both), *Bish.*; 'giltes,' *Wicl.*; 'synne,' *Tynd.*, *Cran.*, *Genev.*; 'the offenses,' *Rhem.*

He quickened] So *Wicl.*, *Cov.*, and sim. *Rhem.*, 'did he quicken:' 'hath he, etc.,' *Auth.* and the remaining Vv.

Himself] 'Him,' *Auth.* and all the other Vv. *Us*] 'You,' *Auth.*

Our trespasses] So *Tynd.*, *Cranm.*, *Gen.* ('your'), *Bish.* ('your'): 'trespasses,' *Author.*; 'giltis,' *Wicl.*; 'sins,' *Covrd.* (both); 'offenses,' *Rhem.*

14. *Blotting out*] So *Author.* As this participle seems contemporary with the preceding, and to mark the circumstances under which the preceding act took place, the present participle *in English* may be properly retained; comp. notes on *Phil.* ii. 7 (*Transl.*). The more exact, 'by having, etc.,' is open to the objection of being cumbrous, and perhaps unduly modal. *In force against us, etc.*] 'Of ordinances that was against us,' *Author.*; 'that writynge of decre that was agens us,' *Wicl.*; 'the handwriting that was agaynst us contained in the lawe written,' *Tynd.*, *Cov.*, *Cran.*; 'the hande wrrtynge that was againste us of the decre, *Cov.* (Test.): 'the handwryting of ceremonies that was against us,' *Gen.*, *Bish.* ('ordinances'); 'the handwriting of decrees,' *Rhem.*

Hath taken] So *Tynd.*, *Cov.*, *Cran.*, *Bish.*, *Rhem.*: 'took,' *Auth.* and the remaining Vv. *Auth.* also omits the personal pronoun: the insertion of it, however, coupled with the slight change in punctuation, seems to clear up the construction, and render the connection of clauses somewhat more perspicuous.

15. *Stripping, etc.*] 'Having spoiled,' *Auth.*, *Bish.*, and sim. *Covrd.* (Test.), *Rhem.*, 'spoiling;' 'and hath spoyled,' *Tynd.* and the remaining Vv.

With boldness] Similarly *Cov.* (Test.), 'boldely;' *Rhem.*, 'confidently:' 'openly,' *Authorized* and the remaining Versions.

16. *Let not, etc.*] 'Let no man therefore,' *Author.* and the other Vv. except *Wicl.*, 'therfor no man juge.'

Eating or in drinking] 'Meat or in drink,' *Auth.*, *Wicl.*, *Cov.* (Test.) (omits 'in'), *Bish.*, *Rhem.*: 'meate and drinke,' *Tynd.*, *Cov.* ('or'), *Cran.*, *Gen.*

In the matter of] 'In respect of,' *Author.*; in part of,' *Wicl.*, *Bish.*, *Rhem.*; 'for pece of,' *Tynd.*, *Cov.*, *Cran.*, *Gen.*; 'in a part of,' *Cov.* (Test.). *A new moon*] 'The, etc.,' *Auth.* and the other Vv. except *Wicl.*, 'neomynye.'

A sabbath] 'Sabbath days,' *Auth.* and the other Vv. except *Wicl.*, *Cov.* (Test.); *Rhem.*, 'Sabotis.' As σάββατα is used with the force of a singular (Matth. xii. 1, Luke iv. 16, al.), and as the preceding terms are in the singular, it seems better to revert to that form in translation.

17. *Christ's*] So *Cov.* (Test.), *Rhem.*: 'of Christ,' *Auth.*, *Wicl.*, *Bish.*: 'is in Christ,' *Tynd.*, *Cov.*, *Cran.*, *Gen.*

Christ's. ¹⁸ Let no man beguile you of your reward, desiring *to do it* in *false* lowliness of mind and worshipping of the angels, intruding into the things which he hath not seen, vainly puffed up by the mind of his flesh, ¹⁹ and not holding fast the Head, from which the whole body by means of its joints and bands having nourishment ministered, and being knit together, increaseth with the increase of God. --- ²⁰ If ye be dead with Christ from the rudiments of the world, why, as if ye were living in the world, do ye submit to ordinances, ²¹ Handle not, nor taste, nor touch, ²² (which things are all to be destroyed in their consumption), after the commandments and

18. *Desiring to do it, etc.*] ' In a voluntary humility,' *Auth.*; ' willynge to teche in mekeness,' *Wicl.*; ' which after his awne ymaginacion walketh in the humblenes and holynes of angels,' *Tynd.*, sim. *Cov.*; ' wyllynge in humblynesse,' *Cov.* (Test.), *Rhem.*; ' by the humblenes and holynes of angels,' *Cranm.*; ' by humblenes, and worshipping of angels,' *Gen.*; ' in the humb. and w. of angels,' *Bish.* The insertion of the epithet '*false*,' is only an exegetical gloss to assist the general reader.
The angels] ' Angels,' *Auth.* and all the other Vv. The insertion of the article is perhaps not a certain correction, as it may be used only to specify the genus. It seems however plausible to consider it as referring to the special class to whom this unbecoming adoration was habitually offered. *The things*] So *Wicl.*, *Cov.* (Test.), *Cranm.*, *Rhem.*: ' those things,' *Auth.*, *Bish.*; ' thinges,' *Tynd.*, *Cov.* *The mind of his flesh*] Sim. *Wicl.*, with wit of his fleische :' *Cov.* (Test.), ' in the meanynge of hys flesche :' *Rhem.*, ' by the sense of his flesh :' ' his fleshly mind,' *Auth.* and the remaining Vv. (*Cov.*, ' his owne ').

19. *Holding fast*] ' Holding,' *Wicl.*, *Cov.* (Test.), *Rhem.*; ' holdeth,' *Tynd.* and the remaining Vv. *The whole body*] So *Coverd.* (both), *Rhem.*: ' all the body,' *Auth.* and the remaining Vv. *By means of its joints*]

' By joints,' *Auth.* and the other Vv. except *Coverd.* (Test.), ' by knottes and jointes ;' *Wicl.*, ' bi boondis and joinynges.' ● *Being knit together*] ' Knit together,' *Author.*, *Genev.*, *Bish.*; ' made,' *Wicl.*; ' and is knet together,' *Tynd.*, *Cov.*, *Cran.*; ' fastened together,' *Cov.* (Test.); ' compacted,' *Rhem.*

20. *If*] '*Wherefore if,' *Auth.* *As if ye were living*] ' As though living,' *Auth.*, *Bish.*; *Wicl.* (very exactly), ' as men living ;' ' as though ye yet lived,' *Tynd.*, *Gen.* (*Cov.* omits ' yet. ') *Do ye submit*] ' Are ye subject,' *Auth.*; ' demen ye,' *Wicl.*; ' are ye ledde with tradicions,' *Tynd.*, *Cran.*, *Bish.*; ' holden with soch trad.,' *Coverd.*; ' what do ye yet use decrees,' *Coverd.* (Test.); ' are ye burthened with traditions,' *Gen.*; ' decree,' *Rhem.* The change in the text is intended to express that δογματίζεσθε is here taken as in the middle voice.

21. *Handle not, etc.*] ' Touch not; taste not; handle not,' *Author.* and the other Vv. (*Tynd.* and *Gener.* prefix ' of them that say ') except *Wicl.*, ' that ye touche not, nether taast, nether trete with hondis the thingis ;' *Cov.*, ' as when they say, touch not this, taste not that, handle not that.'

22. *Which things*] ' Which,' *Auth. Are all*] So *Rhem.*, and in a similar collocation *Cov.* (Test.): ' all are,' *Auth.* and the remaining Vv. except *Coverd.*, ' all these things do.' Change made to

doctrines of men?" All which things have indeed the repute of wisdom in voluntary worship, and lowliness of mind, and unsparing treatment of the body, not in any *thing of real* value, serving *only* to satisfy the flesh.

CHAPTER III.

IF then ye were raised together with Christ, seek the things that are above, where Christ is, sitting on the right hand of God.

preserve not only the order but a distinction between the definite and the indefinite relative, see next verse.

To be destroyed, &c.] 'To perish with the using,' *Author.*; 'in to deeth by the ilke use,' *Wicl.*; 'peryssche with the usyng of them,' *Tynd., Com.*; 'do hurt unto men because of the abuse of them,' *Cov.* — an unusually incorrect translation, especially for *Coverd.*; 'do all hurte with the very use,' *Cov. (Test.*); 'peryssche thorow the very a-use,' *Cranm.*; 'be in corruption, in abu-synge,' *Bish.*; 'unto destruction by the very use,' *Rhem.*

23. *All which things*] 'Whi h things,' *Auth.* and the other Vv. except *Wicl., Cov.* (Test.), *Rhem.*, 'which.'

The repute] 'A shew,' *Author., Bish., Gen., Rhem.*; 'a resoun,' *Wicl.*; 'the similitude,' *Tynd., Com.*; 'shyne,' *Cov.* (both). The definite article with 'repute' seems required by usage and ordinary English idiom.

Voluntary worship] Similarly *Gen.*, 'voluntarie worshipping;' *Bish.*, 'voluntarie religion;' 'will worship,' *Author.*; 'veyn relegioun,' *Wicl.*; 'chosen holynes,' *Tynd.*; 'chosen spirituality,' *Cov.*; 'superstricion,' *Cov. (Test.), Gen., Rhem. Lowliness of mind*] 'Humility,' *Author.* Possibly here the epithet 'false' might be inserted as in ver. 18.

Unsparing treatment] 'Neglecting,' *Auth.*: 'not to spare,' *Wicl., Rhem.*; 'in that they spare not,' *Tynd., Coverd.*; 'in not

sparyng,' *Cov d. (Test.), Gen., Bish.* Nothing worthy of.] So we read similarly *Gen.*, 'yet are of no value;' 'in any honour,' *Auth., Bish., Gen., Rhem.*; 'do the flesh no wor-ynp,' *Wicl., Cov d., Cov.*; 'contayning not worthy of ony honoure,' *Cov. (Test.).* It will be observed (see below) that *Gen.* approaches most nearly to the view taken in our text, but that it tacitly assumes a change of construction and an ellipsis of the verb substantive. To avoid this, and to be intelligible, we seem forced to some paraphrase like that in the text

Serving you, &c.] 'To the satisfying of,' *Author.*, and sim. the other Vv. except *Gen.*, which thus paraphrases, '... appertaine to those things wherwith the flesh is crammed.'

CHAPTER III. 1. *If then*] 'If ye then,' *Auth r.* and the other Vv. except *Wicl., Rhem.*, 'therfor if ye;' *Cov. (Test.)*, 'yf ye are therfore.'

Were raised together] 'Be risen,' *Auth., Bish., Rhem.*; 'han rise to gidre,' *Wicl.*; 'be then rysen agayne,' *Tynd., Cranm.*; 'be risen now with,' *Coverd.*; 'are therfore rysen with,' *Coverd. (Test.)*; 'be rys n agayne with,' *Gen. The thi gs that are a ove*] So *Cov. (Test.), Rhem.*; 'those things which are,' *Auth.* and the remaining Vv. except *Wicl.*, 'the thingis that ben.' The lighter relative 'that' seems here more suitable, and

² Set your minds on the things that are above, not on the things that are on the earth. ³ For ye died, and your life hath been hidden with Christ in God. ⁴ When Christ, our Life, shall be manifested, then shall ye also be manifested with Him in glory.

⁵ Make dead then your members which are upon the earth; fornication, uncleanness, lustfulness, evil concupiscence, and covetousness, the which is idolatry: ⁶ for which things' sake the wrath of God doth come on the children of disobedience; ⁷ among whom ye also once walked, when ye were living in these *sins*. ⁸ But

accords with the translation in verse 2. On the supposed distinction between 'that' and 'which,' compare notes on *Eph.* i. 23 (*Transl.*), and Brown, *Gram. of Grammars*, II. 5, p. 293 (ed. 1). Perhaps, as a *very rough* rule, it may be said that 'which' is a little more appropriately used when the clause introduced by the relative tends to form a distinct and separable predication in reference to the antecedent; 'that,' when the relative so coalesces with its concomitants as either to form with them a species of epithet, or to express a predominant and prevailing, rather than an accidental characteristic. *Christ is, sitting*] So *Cov.*: 'sitteth,' *Auth.*, *Tynd.*, *Cran.*, *Gen.*, *Bish.*; 'is sitting at,' *Wicl.*, *Cov.* (Test.), *Rhem.*

2. *Set your minds*] So *Cov.* (Test.), and *Cov.* ('minde'): 'set your affection,' *Auth.* and the remaining Vv. except *Wicl.*, 'sauer tho thingis;' *Bish.*, 'affections' (plural).

The things that are (bis)] So *Rhem.*: 'things' (bis), *Auth.*, *Bish.*; 'tho thingis that ben aboue not tho that ben, etc.,' *Wicl.*, *Coverd.* (Test.); 'thynges that are aboue, and not on thinges which are,' *Tynd.*, *Cov.* (inverts relatives), *Cranm.*, *Gen.* ('which,' bis).

3. *Died*] 'Are dead,' *Author.* and all Vv.; see notes. *Hath been*] 'Is,' *Auth.*

4. *Christ, our Life*] So *Cov.*: *Author.* inserts 'who is;' *Tynd.*, *Cranm.*, *Gen.*,

Bish. insert 'which is;' *Wicl.*, *Coverd.* (Test.), *Rhem.*, 'youre liif.'

Be manifested (bis)] 'Appear' (bis), *Auth.*, *Wicl.*, *Cov.* (Test.), *Bish.*, *Rhem.*; 'shewe him silfe — appeare,' *Tynd.*, *Cov.*, *Cran.*, *Gen.* The change seems necessary to keep up the antithesis between the κέκρυπται and φανερωθῇ.

5. *Make dead then*] 'Mortify therefore,' *Author.* and the other Vv. except *Wicl.*, 'therfor sle ye.' *Which*] So *Auth.* and the other Vv. except *Coverd.* (Test.), *Rhem.*, 'that,' and *Cran.*, 'erthy membres.' Here 'that' seems inexact; the original is τὰ μέλη ὑμῶν τὰ ἐπὶ τῆς γῆς. *Lustfulness*] Similarly *Rhem.*, 'lust;' 'inordinate affection,' *Auth.*, *Bish.*; 'lecherie,' *Wicl.*; 'unnaturall lust,' *Tynd.*, *Cov.* (both), *Cran.*: 'wantonness,' *Gen.* *The which*] 'Which,' *Auth.* and all the other Vv.

6. *Doth come*] So *Coverd.* (Test.), and somewhat similarly *Cranmer*, 'useth to come:' 'cometh,' *Author.*, *Tynd.*, *Cov.*, *Gen.*, *Bish.*, *Rhem.*; 'cam,' *Wicl.*

7. *Among whom*] So *Cran.*: 'in the which,' *Auth.*, *Cov.* (both), *Gen.*, *Bish.*; 'in whiche,' *Wicl.*, *Rhem.*; 'in which thynges,' *Tynd.* *Once*] 'Sometime,' *Auth.* *Were living*] 'Lived,' *Auth.* and the other Vv. except *Cov.* (Test.), 'did live.'

These sins] '*Them,' *Auth.*

8. *Do ye*] 'Ye also,' *Auth.*; the other Vv. adopt the simple imperative form, 'put ye, etc.,' but thereby somewhat ob-

Now do ye also put away from you all these; anger, wrath, malice, railing, coarse speaking out of your mouth; ⁹ do not lie one to another, seeing that ye have put off from you the old man with his deeds; ¹⁰ and have put on the new man, which is being renewed unto knowledge after the image of Him that created him: ¹¹ where there is no Greek and Jew, circumcision and uncircumcision, Barbarian, Scythian, bond-man, free-man; but CHRIST *is* all, and in all.

¹² Put ye on, then, as elect of God, holy and beloved, bowels of mercy, kindness, lowliness of mind, meekness, long-suffering; ¹³ forbearing one another, and forgiving each other, if any man

secure the connection of καὶ with ὑμεῖς. *Put away from you*] So, in slightly varied order, *Tynd.*, *Cov.*, *Cranm.*; *Wicl.*, *Gen.*, and *Bish.* omit 'from you:' 'put off,' *Auth.*; 'lay away,' *Coverd.* (Test.), *Rhem.* It seems desirable to preserve a slight distinction between ἀπόθεσθε and ἀπεκδυσάμενοι ver. 9. *All these*] So *Auth.*, and sim. most of the other Vv. *Bish.* omits 'these,' but is thus very liable to be misunderstood, especially as some edd. leave out the comma that ought to separate 'all' and the subst. that follows.
Railing] 'Blasphemy,' *Author.*, *Wicl.*, *Coverd* (Test.), *Bish.*, *Rhem.*; 'cursed speaking,' *Tynd.*, *Coverd*, *Cran.*, *Gen.* *Coarse speaking*] 'Filthy communication,' *Auth.*, *Cov.* (Test.), *Cran.*, *Bish.*; 'foule word,' *Wicl.*; 'filthy speakynge,' *Tynd.*, *Gen.*; filthy wordes,' *Cov.*; 'filthie talke,' *Rhem.*

9. *Do not li*] 'Lie not,' *Author.* and the other Vv. except *Wicl.*, 'nyle ye lie.' *Off from you*] *Auth.* omits 'from you,' and similarly the other Vv. except *Wicl.*, 'spuyle ye you;' *Cov.* (Test.), 'robbyng yourselves;' *Rhem.*, 'spoiling yourselves of.'

10. *Unto*] So *Rhem.*, and similarly *Wicl.*, *Cov.*, *Bish.*, 'in to:' 'in,' *Auth.* and the remaining Vv.
Is being renewed] 'Is renewed,' *Auth.*

11. *There is no*] 'There is neither,' *Auth.* *And Jew*] So *Wicl.*, *Coverd.* (Test.), *Rhem.*; 'ner,' *Auth.* and the remaining Vv. except *Coverd.*, which omits. *Bond-m., free-man*] Similarly *Wicl.*, 'bonde man and fre man:' 'bond nor free,' *Auth.*; 'or,' *Tynd.*, *Cran.*; 'and,' *Cov.* (Test.), *Rhem.*; *Coverd.*, *Gen.*, *Bish.* omit 'nor.'

12. *Put ye*] So *Cov.* (Test.), *Rhem.*, and similarly *Wicl.*; *Auth.* and the remaining Vv. omit. The insertion of the pronoun is perhaps desirable at the beginning of a new paragraph.
Then] 'Therefore,' *Auth.* and the other Vv. *Elect*] So *Tynd.*, *Cov.* (Test), *Cranm.*, *Gen.*; 'the elect,' *Auth.*, *Cov.*, *Bish.*, *Rhem.*; 'the chosun,' *Wicl.* Perhaps a more exact translation would be 'chosen ones,' as giving to ἐκλεκτοί its substantive force without the inaccuracy of the inserted article.
Mercy] '*Mercies*,' *Auth.*
Lowliness of mind] So *Auth.* in Phil. ii. 3: 'humbleness of mind,' *Auth.* and the other Vv. except *Wicl.*, 'mekenes;' *Cov.* (Test.), 'lowlinesse;' *Rhem.*, 'humilitie.'

13. *Each other*] Similarly *Wicl.*, *Cov.* (Test.), both of which make a difference of translation between ἀλλήλων and ἑαυτοῖς ('ech oon other — you silf,' 'eche other — amonge yourselves'); see notes.

have a complaint against any; as Christ forgave you, even so doing also yourselves. ¹⁴ But over all these *put on* Love, which is the bond of perfectness. ¹⁵ And let the peace of Christ rule in your hearts, to the which ye were also called in one body; and be ye thankful. ¹⁶ Let the word of Christ dwell within you richly, teaching and admonishing one another in all wisdom, with psalms, hymns, *and* spiritual songs, in Grace singing in your hearts to God. ¹⁷ And in every thing, whatsoever ye do in word or deed, *do* all in the name of Jesus Christ, giving thanks to God the Father through Him.

¹⁸ Wives, submit yourselves unto your husbands, as it should be

Auth. and the remaining Vv., 'one another.' Complaint] So *Cov.* (Test.): 'quarrel,' *Author.* and all the remaining Vv. As] 'Even as,' *Auth.* In the attempt to express the true participial structure, idiom seems to require the union of 'even' with the latter member; compare *Tynd., Cran., Gen., Bish.* Even so, *etc.*] 'So also do ye,' *Auth., Bish.*; 'so also ye,' *Wicl.*; 'even so do ye,' *Tynd., Cran., Gen.*; 'so do ye also,' *Coverd.* (both); 'so you also,' *Rhem.*

14. But] So *Coverd., Rhem.*: 'and,' *Auth., Wicl., Cov.* (Test.), *Gen., Bish.*; *Tynd., Cran.* omit. Over] So, with apparently similar local force, *Wicl.,* 'upon:' 'above,' *Auth.* and the remaining Vv., some of which, as *Cov.* (both), 'above all things,' probably here gave to ἐπὶ a decided ethical reference. These] *Auth.* adds 'things,' and so the other Vv. Perhaps the indeterminate 'these,' *i. e.* 'qualities,' 'principles,' 'virtues,' is more exact. Love] So *Tynd., Coverd.* (both), *Cran., Gen.*: 'charity,' *Author., Wicl., Bish., Rhem.* See notes on 1 *Tim.* i. 5 (*Transl.*).

15. Christ] '*God,' *Auth.* Were] 'Are,' *Auth.* and all the other Vv. Also called] Sim. *Coverd.,* 'called also:' *Auth.* ('which also') and *Rhem.* ('wherein also') connect with the pronoun.

16. *Within*] 'In,' *Author.* and all the other Vv. In all wisdom] *Auth.* and all the other Vv. place these words after, and connect them with the adverb. With] So *Cov., Rhem.*: 'in,' *Auth.* and the remaining Vv. Hymns] *Auth.* prefixes '*and;' so also before 'spiritual songs,' but with not much critical probability. In grace] So *Wicl., Rhem.*: 'with grace,' *Auth., Cran., Bish.* The change seems desirable to obviate such misunderstandings as *Tynd., Coverd.,* 'songes which have favour with them;' *Cov.* (Test.), 'graciously;' *Gen.*, 'with a certeyn grace.' Singing in your hearts] So *Wicl., Rhem.*: 'singing with grace in,' *Author.*, and similarly the remaining Vv. It seems especially desirable here to preserve the order of the Greek, as ᾄδειν ἐν ταῖς καρδ. stands in distinct contrast with another and *audible* singing.

17. *And in every thing, whatsoever*] 'And whatsoever,' *Author.* It seems right to preserve the slight irregularity of the original as setting forth the studied inclusiveness of the command. Jesus Christ] '*Lord Jesus,' *Auth.* God the Father] 'God *and the Father,' *Auth.* Through] 'By,' *Auth.* and all the other Vv.

18. Your husbands] 'Your *own hus-

in the Lord. ¹⁹ Husbands, love your wives, and be not embittered towards them. ²⁰ Children, obey your parents in all things; for this is well-pleasing in the Lord. ²¹ Fathers, provoke not your children, lest they be disheartened. ²² Bond-servants, obey in all things your masters according to the flesh; not with acts of eye-service, as men-pleasers, but in singleness of heart, fearing the Lord. ²³ Whatever ye do, do *it* from the heart, as to the Lord and not to men; ²⁴ seeing ye know that of the Lord ye shall receive the recompense of the inheritance. Serve ye the Lord Christ; ²⁵ for the wrong-doer shall receive back that which he did wrongfully; and there is no respect of persons.

CHAPTER IV.

Masters, deal out unto your servants justice and equity; seeing ye know that ye also have a Master in heaven.

bands,' *Auth. It should be*] 'It is fit,' *Auth.*; 'it bihoueth,' *Wicl., Rhem.*; 'it is comly,' *Tynd., Covrd., Cran., Gen., Bish.*; 'it is due,' *Covrd.* (*Test.*).

19. *Embittered*] 'Bitter,' *Auth. Towards*] So *Covrd.* (*Test.*), *Rhem.*; 'against,' *Author., Bish.*; 'to,' *Wicl.*; 'unto,' *Tynd.* and the remaining Vv.

20. *In the Lord*] '*Unto the Lord,' *Auth.*

21. *Provoke*] *Auth., Covrd.* (*Test.*), *Cran., Gen., Bish.* add 'to anger' after 'children.' This seems unnecessary: as in present practice 'provoke,' when used absolutely, nearly always involves the notion of 'anger' or 'indignation.' *Disheartened*] 'Discouraged,' *Author., Bish., Rhem.*; 'be not made febil herted,' *Wicl.*; 'be of a desperate mynde,' *Tynd., Cov., Cranm.*; 'ware not feble mynded,' *Covrd.* (*Test.*); 'cast downe their harts,' *Gen.*

22. *Bond-servants*] 'Servants,' *Auth., Wicl., Tynd., Gen., Bish., Rhem.*; 'ye servants,' *Cov.* (both), *Cran. Acts of eyeservice*] 'Eyeservice,' *Auth.*

and the other Vv. except *Wicl.*, 'scrunynge of the iye;' *Cov.* (*Test.*), *Rhem.* ('to the'). *The Lord*] '*God,' *Auth.*

23. *Whatever*] '*And whatsoever,' *Author. From the heart*] So *Rhem.*; 'heartily,' *Auth.* and the remaining Vv. except *Wicl.*, 'of wille.' *To men*] 'Unto men,' *Auth.*

24. *Seeing ye know*] Similarly *Tynd.*, 'for as moche as ye knowe'; 'knowing,' *Auth., Cov.* (*Test.*), *Gen., Bish., Rhem.*; 'wittynge,' *Wicl.*; 'and ye be sure,' *Cov., Cran.* (omits 'ye'). *Recompense*] 'Reward,' *Author.* and the other Vv. except *Wicl.*, 'gildynge' [giving]; *Rhem.*, 'retribution.' *Serve ye*] '*For ye serve,' *Auth.*

25. *For*] '*But,' *Auth. The wrong-doer*] 'He that doeth wrong,' *Auth., Tynd., Cov., Gen., Bish.*; 'he that doeth injurie,' *Wicl., Rhem.*; 'whoso doth wronge, *Covrd.* (*Test.*); 'he that doth sinne,' *Cran. Receive back*] Sim. *Wicl., Cov.* (*Test.*), *Rhem.*, 'resceyue that, etc.'; 'receive for the wrong which he hath done,' *Auth.*

² Persevere in your prayer, being watchful therein with thanksgiving; ³ withal praying also for us, that God would open unto us a door of the word, to speak the mystery of Christ, for the sake of which I am also in bonds, ⁴ in order that I may make it manifest, as I ought to speak. ⁵ Walk in wisdom toward them which are without, buying up the time. ⁶ Let your speech *be* alway with grace, seasoned with salt, so that ye may know how ye ought to answer every man.

⁷ All my state shall Tychicus declare unto you, our beloved brother, and faithful minister, and fellow-servant in the Lord: ⁸ whom I have sent unto you for this very purpose, that he may

CHAPTER IV. 1. *Deal out*] 'Give,' *Auth.*, *Wicl.*, *Cov.* (Test.); 'do,' *Tynd.* and the remaining Vv.
Justice and equity] 'That which is just and equal,' *Auth.* and all the other Vv. (*Cov.* Test. omits 'which') except *Wicl.*, 'that that is just and euene.'
Seeing ye know] So *Tynd.*: 'knowing,' *Auth.*, *Gen.*, *Bish.*, *Rhem.*; 'witynge,' *Wicl.*; 'and knowe,' *Coverd.*; 'beynge sure,' *Cov.* (Test.); 'and be sure,' *Cran.*

2. *Persevere in*] 'Continue in,' *Auth.* and the other Vv. except *Wicl.*, 'be ye bisie in;' *Rhem.*, 'be instant.'
Your prayer] 'In prayer,' *Author.* and all the other Vv.   *Being watchful*] Sim. *Coverd.* (Test.), *Rhem.*, 'watching:' 'and watch,' *Author.* and the remaining Vv. except *Wicl.*, 'and wake.'   *Therein*] So *Coverd.* (Test.): 'in the same,' *Auth.* and the remaining Vv. except *Wicl.*, *Rhem.*, 'in it.'

3. *Of the word*] So *Cov.* (both), and sim. *Wicl.*, 'of word:' 'of utterance,' *Author.* and the remaining Vv. except *Rhem.*, 'of speech.'   *For the sake of which*] 'For which,' *Auth.*, *Wicl.*; 'wherfore,' *Tynd.*, *Cov.*, *Cranm.*, *Gen.*, *Bish.*; 'for the whyche thynge,' *Coverd.* (Test.); 'for the which,' *Rhem.*

4. *In order that*] 'That,' *Author.* and all the other Vv.

5. *Buying up*] 'Redeeming,' *Auth.*, *Coverd.* (Test.), *Bish.*, *Rhem.*; 'agenbiynge,' *Wicl.*; 'and redeme,' *Tynd.*, *Cov.*, *Cranm.*, *Genev.*; 'lose no opportunite,' *Cran.*

6. *So that*] 'That,' *Auth.* and all the other Vv. The slight change is made to express distinctly the infin. of *consequence*, and to prevent 'that' being regarded as indicative of *purpose*, and as a translation of ἵνα with the subjunctive.

7. *Our beloved*] So *Gen.*, and similarly *Rhemish*, 'our dearest:' 'a beloved,' *Author.*; 'moost dere' (no art.), *Wicl.*; 'the deare,' *Tynd.*, *Cov.*; 'the mooste deare,' *Coverd.* (Test); 'the beloved,' *Cranm.*; 'a dearely beloued,' *Bish.* *Faithful*] So *Wicl.*, *Cov.* (both), *Cran.*, *Bish.*, *Rhem.*; 'a faithful,' *Auth.*, *Tynd.*, *Gen.*

8. *Have sent*] So *Auth.* and the other Vv. except *Wicl.*, *Con.* (Test.), 'sent.' As Tychicus appears certainly to have been the bearer of this letter (compare notes on *Phil.* ii. 28, and on *Philem.* 2), the pres. 'send' was adopted in ed. 1. Our English perfect, however, seems to be used idiomatically with a similar epistolary reference to present time, and may thus be left unchanged.
This very] 'The same,' *Auth.* and the other Vv. except *Wicl.*, *Rhem.*, 'this same;' *Cov.* (Test.), 'therfore.'

know your estate, and comfort your hearts; ⁹ with Onesimus our faithful and beloved brother, who is *one* of you. They shall make known unto you all things which are *done* here.

¹⁰ Aristarchus my fellow-prisoner saluteth you, and Mark, the cousin of Barnabas, touching whom ye received commandments (if he come unto you receive him); ¹¹ and Jesus, which is called Justus, who are of the circumcision. These only are *my* fellow-workers unto the kingdom of God, men who have proved a comfort unto me. ¹² Epaphras, who is *one* of you, a servant of Christ Jesus, saluteth you, always striving earnestly for you in his prayers, that ye may stand *fast*, perfect and fully assured in all the will of God. ¹³ For I bear him witness, that he hath much labor for you, and them that

May] 'Might,' *Auth.* Change to preserve the 'succession' of tenses.

9. *Our faithful*] Sim. *Cor.* (Test.), our mooste beloued and faythfull;' 'a faithful,' *Auth.* and the remaining Vv. except *Wicl.*, moost dere and feithful;' *Rhem.*, 'the most dere and faithful.'

Which are done] So *Auth.*, except that in the more approved editions 'are,' which is necessary for the construction, is in italics, while 'done,' which is a mere exegetical insertion, is in the ordinary character. A better, but now antiquated, translation is that of *Tynd.*, al., 'which are adoynge here.'

10. *Mark*] So *Wicl.*, *Coverd.* (Test.), *Rhem.*; 'Marcus,' *A.C.* and the remaining Vv.; see notes on ch. i. 1.

The cousin of] So *Wic.*, and sim. *Rhem.*, 'the cosin-germain of;' 'sister's son to Barnabas,' *Auth.* and sim. *Tynd.* ('Bartholassis syster sonne') and the other Vv. It seems very doubtful whether this is to be considered a mistake; it is not improbably an archaic mode of expression, equivalent to the 'Geschwisterkind,' of the German. The following words are included by *Auth.* in a parenthesis; this seems hardly correct; see notes.

11. *Men who have proved*] 'Which have been,' *Auth.*, *Cranm.*, *Gish.*, *Rhem.*;

'that when,' *Wic.*; 'which were,' *Tynd.*, *Cov.*, *Gen.*; 'wich comforted,' *Coverd.* (Test.).

12. *Christ Jesus*] "Christ' *Auth. Striving earnestly*] Sim. *Mrg.*, 'striving;' 'laboring fervently,' *Auth.*, *Bish.*, and sim. *Tynd.*, *Cov.*, *Cranm.*, *Gen.*, 'laboreth ferueatly;' 'Iesse for you,' *Wic.*; 'alwaye carefull,' *Cov.* (Test.), *Rhem.* ... *His prayers*] *Auth.* omits 'his' ...

13. *Witness*] Sim. *Wic.*, 'witnesse;' 'record,' *Auth.* and the remaining Vv. except *Rhem.*, 'testimonie.'

Much zeal] 'A great zeal,' *Auth.*

Them that are] So *Auth.*, *Cov.* (Test.); the other Vv. vary; *Wic.* inserts 'tretten' in both clauses; 'them of L. and them of H.,' *Tynd.*, *Gen.*, *Bish.*; 'them at L. and at H.,' *Coverd.*; 'that are of' (in both clauses), *Cranm.*; 'that are in' (in both clauses), *Bish.*; 'that be at L. and that are at H.,' *Rhem.*. In this variety the translation of *Cov.* (Test.) and *Auth.* is, on the whole, most satis-

are in Laodicea, and them in Hierapolis. ¹⁴ Luke, the beloved physician, saluteth you, and Demas. ¹⁵ Salute the brethren that are in Laodicea, and Nymphas, and the church which is in his house. ¹⁶ And when this epistle is read among you, cause that it be read also in the church of the Laodiceans; and that ye likewise read the *epistle* from Laodicea. ¹⁷ And say to Archippus, Take heed to the ministry which thou receivedst in the Lord, that thou fulfil it.

¹⁸ The salutation by the hand of me Paul. REMEMBER MY BONDS. GRACE BE WITH YOU.

factory; the insertion 'that are,' in the first clause, makes the meaning perfectly clear, while its omission, in the second, prevents the sentence being unduly heavy.

14. *Saluteth you*] So *Coverd.* (Test.), *Rhem.*, and, in the same order, *Tynd.*, *Cov.*, *Cranm.*, *Gen.*, 'greteth:' 'greet you' (at the end of the verse), *Author.*, *Wicl.*, *Bish.*

15. *That are*] So *Wicl.*, *Cov.* (Test.), *Rhem.*: 'which are,' *Auth.* and the other Vv Change to preserve a uniform translation with ver. 13.

17. *Receivedst*] 'Hast received,' *Auth.* and the other Vv. except *Wicl.*, 'hast takun.'

18. *With you*] *Auth.* adds '*Amen.'

THE EPISTLE TO PHILEMON.

PAUL, a prisoner of Christ Jesus, and Timothy our brother, unto Philemon our dearly beloved and fellow-laborer, ² and to Apphia our sister and to Archippus our fellow-soldier, and to the church in thy house : ³ grace *be* unto you, and peace, from God our Father and the Lord Jesus Christ. ⁴ I thank my God, always making mention of thee in my prayers, ⁵ hearing, *as I do*, of thy love and the faith, which thou hast toward the Lord, and *dost shew* toward all the saints ; ⁶ that the communication of thy faith may become effectual unto Christ Jesus in the knowledge of every good

---

1. *Beloved and*] 'Beloved, and etc.,' *Auth.* The comma should be removed, as ἡμῶν apparently belongs both to ἀγαπητῷ and συνεργῷ.

2. *Our sister*] '*Our beloved Apphia,' *Auth.* *To Arch.*] So all the Vv. except *Author.* and *Covrd.* (Test.), which omit the 'to.'

3. *Grace be unto you*] 'Grace to you,' *Auth.* The insertion of 'be' with 'to' or 'unto' is the form adopted by *Auth.* elsewhere in St. Paul's Epistles.

4. *Always making mention*] So, in point of order, *Rhem.* The other Vv. differ in their mode of placing the adverb : *Author.* places it after 'of thee ;' *Wicl.* connects it with the foregoing clause ; *Tynd.* and the remaining Vv. insert it directly after 'mention.' It seems best to follow the order of the Greek, and so to retain the slight emphasis which the position implies.

5. *Hearing, as I do*] 'Hearing,' *Auth.*, *Wicl.*, *Covrd.* (Test.), *Bish.*, *Rhem.* 'when I heare,' *Tynd.*, *Cranm.*, *Gen.*: 'for so much as I heare,' *Covrd.* The particle explains the circumstances which led to the prayer being offered.

The faith] So *Covrd.* (Test.) : 'faith,' *Auth.* and the remaining Vv.

Lord] 'Lord *Jesus*,' *Auth.*

Dost shew toward] 'And toward,' *Auth.* and the other Vv. except *Wicl.*, 'and to ;' *Cov.* (Test.), 'and unto.'

The saints] So *Rhem.* : 'saints,' *Auth.* and the remaining Vv. except *Wicl.*, 'holi men.'

6. *Unto Christ Jesus*] 'In Chr. Jesus,' *Author.*, *Wicl.*, *Covrd.* (Test.), *Rhem.*, and at the end of the verse. So, in point of order, *Tynd.*, 'by Jesus Christ ;' *Cranm.*, *Bish.*, 'towarde J. C. ;' 'the good that ye have in J. C.,' *Cov.*; *Gen.*, with a transposed order, 'whatsoever good thing is in you through Christ may be knowen.'

thing which is in us. ⁷ For I had much joy and consolation in thy love, because the hearts of the saints have been refreshed by thee, brother.

⁸ Wherefore, though I have much boldness in Christ to enjoin thee that which is becoming, ⁹ yet for love's sake I rather beseech *thee*. Being such an one as Paul the aged, and now also a prisoner of Jesus Christ, ¹⁰ I beseech thee for my own child Onesimus, whom I begat in my bonds; ¹¹ which in time past was to thee unprofitable, but now profitable to thee and to me; ¹² whom I have sent back to thee. But do thou *receive* him, that is, mine own bowels; ¹³ whom I was purposing to retain with myself, that in thy stead he might minister unto me in the bonds of the gospel: ¹⁴ but without thine approval would I do nothing, that the good thou

In the knowledge] Sim. *Wicl.*, 'in knowinge;' *Coverd.* (Test.), *Cranm., Bish.,* 'in the knowledge;' *Rhem.*, 'in the agnition of:' 'by the acknowledging of,' *Auth.*; 'thorow knowledge,' *Tynd., Cov.; Genev.* changes the construction; see above. *Us*] '*You,' *Auth.*

7. *I had*] '*We have,' *Auth.*

Much] 'Great,' *Auth.*   *Hearts*] So *Tynd., Cran., Gen.*: 'bowels,' *Auth., Bish., Rhem.*; 'entrailis,' *Wicl., Cor.* (Test.); 'are hertely refreszhed,' *Cov.*

Have been] 'Are,' *Auth.* and the other Vv. except *Wicl.*, 'restiden;' *Coverd.* (Test.), 'dyd reste;' *Rhem.*, 'haue rested.'

8. *Have much boldness*] Sim. *Wicl.*, 'hauyng myche trist;' *Rhem.*, 'hauing great confidence:' 'might be bold,' *Auth., Cranm.*; 'be bold,' *Tynd., Gen.*; 'have great boldnes,' *Cov.*; 'I beynge bold,' *Cov.* (Test.); 'be much bolde,' *Bish.*

Enjoin thee] So *Auth.*, following *Tynd.* and *Gen.*; an archaism which it does not seem necessary to remove.

Becoming] Sim. *Tynd., Cov., Gen.*, 'that which becometh the:' 'convenient,' *Auth., Bish.*; 'that that perteyneth to profete,' *Wicl.*; 'that maketh matter,' *Coverd.* (Test.); 'that which was thy dewtye to do,' *Cranmer*; 'that which

perteyneth to the purpose,' *Rhem.*

9. *Thee*] *Auth.* places a comma after 'thee,' and a full stop at the end of the verse; so very similarly all the other Vv.: *Wicl.* ('sithen thou art suche as, etc.') and *Rhem.* ('whereas thou art such an one, etc.') refer the τοιοῦτος ὢν to Philemon.

10. *Own child*] 'Son,' *Auth.* and all the other Vv.   *Begat*] So *Wicl., Tynd., Gen.*: 'have begotten,' *Auth.* and the remaining Vv.

12. *Have sent*] So *Auth.* and the other Vv. except *Wicl, Coverd.*, 'sente:' see notes on Col. iv. 8 (*Transl.*).

Back to thee] *Author* omits '*to thee.'

But do, etc.] 'Thou therefore,' *Auth.*

13. *Was purposing to retain*] 'Would have retained,' *Auth., Rhem.*; 'woold with hoold,' *Wicl.*; 'wolde fayne have retayned,' *Tynd., Cran., Gen.*; 'wolde haue kepte,' *Cov.* (both); 'would have fayne retayned,' *Bish.*

Myself] 'Me,' *Auth.* and all the other Vv.   *Might minister*] So *Rhem.*; 'might have ministered,' *Auth.* and the remaining Vv. except *Wicl.*, 'schulde serve.'

14. *Thine approval*] 'Thy mind,' *Author.* and the other Vv. except *Wicl., Cov.* (Test.), *Rhem.*, 'counceil.'

doest thou. 14 and as it were of necessity, but willingly. 15 For
perhaps he therefore departed for a season, that thou mightest receive him eternally; 16 no longer as a servant, but above a servant,
a brother beloved, specially to me, but how much more to thee,
both in the flesh, and in the Lord? 17 If therefore thou countest
me a partner, receive him as myself. 18 But if he hath wronged
thee, or oweth thee ought, this set down to my account; 19 I Paul
have written with mine own hand, I will repay it: that I may not
say to thee how thou owest unto me even thine own self besides.
20 Yea, brother, may I reap profit from thee in the Lord: refresh
my heart in Christ.

The good thou do] Sim. Cr. (bota;
Cor. Test., 'that thou, etc.'), Croam,
'the good which thou doest;' Tyd.,
'that good which springeth of thee;'
'thy benefit,' Auth., Gen., Bish; 'thy
good,' Wicl., Rhem.

15. *Therefore*] So Auth. and all the
other Vv.; and apparently with good
reason, for the more usual translation,
'for this cause,' seems to fail in connecting the first and second members with
sufficient closeness, unless emphasis is
laid on 'this.' *Mightest*] So
Cor. (Test.), Rhem.; 'shouldest.' Auth.
and the remaining Vv.
Eternally] 'For ever,' Auth.; and the
other Vv. except Wicl., Rhem., 'withouten
ende.'

16. *No longer*] 'Not now,' Auth. and
the other Vv. except Wicl., Rhem., 'now
not.'

17. *If therefore*] So Gen., Rhem., and
sim. Wicl., 'therfor if;' Auth., Croam,
Cor. (Test.), Bish., 'if thou count me
therefore;' Cr. omits. As there is apparently here somewhat of an inferential
tinge (see notes on *Phil.* ii. 28), the
translation 'therefore' may be retained,
and be allowed here to occupy the same
position in the sentence as ουν in the
Greek. *Countest*] So Gen.,
and similarly as to mood, Wicl., 'hast;'
Cor. (Test.), 'boldest;' 'count,' Auth.,

Tynd., Cram, Bish.; 'adde me for,'
Cr d.; 'take me for,' Rhem. On the
frequent use of the infinitive of subjective with 'if,' see Latham, *Eng. Lang.*
§ 614 (ed. 3), and notes on 2 *Tim.* ii.
14 (*Trust*).

18. *But if*] So Coverd. (ort): 'if,'
Auth., and the remaining Vv. except
Wicl., 'for if;' Rhem., 'and if.'

Wronged] So Auth., and in respect
of the assertion of the 'if,' like the
other Vv. This particle may be regarded as one of those cases where, in
our idiom requires the auxiliary to be
inserted. It ought, the overt stress
too far remov'd back is on the past; compare 1 Thess. ii. 16 (Λυσ.).
*Set it down on
mine account*,' Auth.; 'Charge thou
this thing to me,' Wicl. et at; 'put to
my charge,' Tynd., Cr. (Cr. Test.),
'lay that'?, Gen., Gen., Jen.; 'that
impute to me,' Rhem. It will be observed that six out of the eight Vv. retain the emphatic position of ἐμοὶ in a pronoun.

19. *Written*] So Rhem.; 'I have writt.,'
Auth., and the remaining Vv. except
Wicl., 'wroot,' Gen., Jen.; 'written
this.' *That I* — *etc.*]
Very sim. Wicl., 'that I seye to thee
beit, I do not say,' Auth. et al., best;
'so that I do not saye,' Tynd., Coverd.

²¹ Having confidence in thy obedience I have written unto thee, knowing that thou wilt do even above what I say. ²² Moreover at the same time prepare me also a lodging: for I hope that through your prayers I shall be granted unto you.

²³ Epaphras, my fellow-prisoner in Christ Jesus, saluteth thee: ²⁴ Marcus, Aristarchus, Demas, Lucas, my fellow-laborers. ²⁵ The grace of our Lord Jesus Christ *be* with your spirit.

(both), *Cranmer;* 'not to say,' *Rhem.*

20. *May I reap profit from*] 'Let me have joy of,' *Auth.;* 'I schal use thee,' *Wicl.;* 'let me enjoye the,' *Tynd., Cov., Cran., Bish.;* 'thus shall I enjoye thee,' *Cov.* (Test.); 'let me obteyne this fruit,' *Gen.;* 'graunt I may enjoy thee,' *Rhem. Heart*] So *Cov.:* 'bowels,' *Author.* and the other Vv. except *Wicl., Cov.* (Test.), 'entrailis.' *Christ*] '*The Lord,' *Auth.*

21. *Have written*] So *Coverd.* (both), *Rhem.;* 'wrote,' *Auth.* and the remaining Vv. *Do even*] 'Also do,' *Auth., Cranm., Bish.;* 'aboue that also,' *Rhem.;* the rest omit καὶ in translation. *Above what*] Sim. *Coverd.* (Test.), 'above it that;' *Rhem.,* 'above that also which:' 'more than,' *Auth.* and the remaining Vv. except *Wicl.,* 'ouer that that I see.'

22. *Moreover at the same time*] Sim. *Tynd., Cov., Cranm., Gen.,* 'moreover prepare:' 'but withal,' *Author.;* 'also make thou redi,' *Wicl.;* 'and make redy also,' *Cov.* (Test.); 'moreover prep. me also,' *Bish.;* 'and withal,' *Rhem. Granted*] 'Given,' *Auth.* and the other Vv. except *Cov.* (Test.), 'restored.'

23. *Saluteth*] Sim. as to number and position *Wicl.,* 'gretith;' *Cov.* (Test.), 'saluteth the in Christ Jesus:' 'there salute thee,' *Auth.* and the remaining Vv. except *Cov.,* 'saluteth.'

24. *Spirit*] *Auth.* adds '*Amen.'

THE END.

JUST PUBLISHED.

A

HARMONY OF THE FOUR GOSPELS IN GREEK,

ACCORDING TO THE TEXT OF TISCHENDORF, WITH A COLLATION OF THE TEXTUS RECEPTUS, AND OF THE TEXTS OF GRIESBACH, LACHMANN, AND TREGELLES.

BY

FREDERIC GARDINER, D.D.,

PROFESSOR IN THE BERKELEY DIVINITY SCHOOL, AUTHOR OF "A COMMENTARY ON THE EPISTLE OF ST. JUDE," "A HARMONY OF THE GOSPELS IN ENGLISH," ET .

8vo   pp. lvi and 268.   Price, $2.50.

The distinctive features of this Harmony are, —

1. A critical text, viz. the text of Tischendorf's eighth or last edition, embodying the latest results of textual criticism. To obtain the final portions of this edition the publication of this work has been delayed several months. The readings of the *textus receptus*, where they differ from Tischendorf's text, are given in full in the margin; the variations being designated by a different type. The texts of Griesbach, Lachmann, and Tregelles are carefully collated. The relative value of readings as estimated by Griesbach are noted, and original authorities cited in important cases.

2. All distinct quotations from the Old Testament are given in full in the margin, according to Tischendorf's edition of the LXX., together with the *var. lec.* of the Alexandrian text and of the *Codex Sinaiticus*, and of the several other versions named in the title.

3. A choice selection of parallel references has been placed in the margin, chiefly to point out similar language or incidents in other parts of the Gospels, or passages in the Old Testament, on which the language of the Gospels may be founded.

4. Brief notes relating to matters of harmony have been placed at the bottom of the page.

5. Special care has been devoted to the chronological order of the Gospel narratives.

6. The columns are so arranged on the page as to combine the greatest clearness consistent with the least cost. The columns are never interwoven on the page.

7. A synoptical table is given of the arrangement adopted by several harmonists, showing at a glance the general agreement on the main points of chronology, and the points of difference where difference occurs. This is a new feature in this work, and will be found very useful to the student.

WARREN F. DRAPER, Publisher,
Andover, Mass.

A HARMONY OF THE FOUR GOSPELS
IN ENGLISH,

ACCORDING TO THE AUTHORIZED VERSION; CORRECTED BY THE BEST
CRITICAL EDITIONS OF THE ORIGINAL.

By FREDERIC GARDINER, D.D.,

PROFESSOR IN THE BERKELEY DIVINITY SCHOOL; AUTHOR OF "A HARMONY OF THE
GOSPELS IN GREEK," ETC.

8vo.　　pp. xliv and 287.　　Price, $2.00.

This Harmony is a reproduction in English of the author's "Harmony of the Four Gospels" in Greek. Being intended for English readers, so much of the Introduction and of the notes as require a knowledge of Greek, is omitted. Other notes have been abridged in many cases.

DIATESSARON.

THE LIFE OF OUR LORD;
IN
The Words of the Gospels.

By FREDERIC GARDINER, D.D.,

PROFESSOR IN THE BERKELEY DIVINITY SCHOOL, AUTHOR OF "A HARMONY OF THE GOSPELS IN
GREEK," ETC. ETC.

16mo.　　pp. 259.　　Price, $1.00.

This work combines in one continuous narrative the events of the life of Christ as recorded by all the evangelists. His genealogy, conversations, discourses, parables, miracles, his trial, death, resurrection, and ascension, are placed in the order of their occurrence; and in the foot-notes references are made to passages in the Old Testament relating to Christ or quoted by him.

The life of our Lord has been of late years presented in such a multitude of forms, colored with the views and theories of such a multitude of minds, that it is hoped the present effort to present that life in the exact form of the inspired record, without addition or abatement, may tend to the increase of the real knowledge of the life of the Saviour of mankind.

The work is specially adapted for use in the family and' in Sabbath-schools and Bible-classes.

W. F. DRAPER, Publisher,
Andover, Mass.

MISCELLANEOUS WORKS

PUBLISHED BY

WARREN F. DRAPER,

ANDOVER, MASS.

These Books will be sent, post-paid, on receipt of the price affixed.

CLASSICAL STUDY: Its Usefulness illustrated by Selections from the Writings of Eminent Scholars. Edited, with an Introduction, by SAMUEL H. TAYLOR, LL.D., Principal of Phillips Academy. 12mo. pp. 415. Cloth extra. $2.00

This work is designed to present the true objects of Classical Study, and the advantages of it when properly conducted; also to correct the objections which have been raised against the study. It consists of extracts from some of the best critics on classical education in Germany, England, Scotland, and our own country; the writers themselves being presidents of colleges, professors in colleges and theological seminaries, statesmen, lawyers, etc. In the volume therefore will be found the carefully-framed opinions of many of the best minds of the time. No one line of thought has been taken; the subject has been viewed from almost every point. The work therefore contains a fuller discussion of the advantages of classical study than has before been accessible. The need of such a volume is widely felt among the friends of sound learning. Every student as he commences his classical course should understand what he is to aim at and what he is to gain by the study.

ΦΩΚΥΛΙΔΟΥ ΠΟΙΗΜΑ ΝΟΥΘΕΤΙΚΟΝ. PHOCYLIDIS POEMA ADMONITORIUM. Recognovit Brevibusque Notis Instruxit. J. B. FEULING, Ph.D., A.O.S.S., Professor Philologiae Compar. in Univ. Wisconsinensi. Editio Prima Americana. 16mo. pp. 32. Paper, 30 cents; gilt edges, 40 cents.

"Warren F. Draper, of Andover, publishes Prof. J. B. Feuling's *Phocylidis Poema Admonitorium*, with a double introduction and a few notes, all in Latin, the poem itself, however, is in the original Greek, and is a collection of moral sentences after the manner of Phocylides, in hexameter verse, which was probably compiled some eight centuries after the poet's death, though nobody knows when. So argues the right it quite as good as anything the old Milesian ever wrote, and very likely it is; but in language it differs from the genuine hexameter of the Ionian school of poets to which Theognis and Solon belong. The main introduction of the editor relates chiefly to classical studies in America, and the late convention 'in urbe quam vocant Poughkeepsie,' to which by anticipation he dedicates his little book. His notes are valuable for the citations from Theognis, Epictetus, Simplicius, Sophocles, Euripides, Epicharmus, Terence, Cicero, Sallust, Horace, and Ovid; some of which are rare, and all apposite."—*Springfield Republican*.

THE THEOLOGY OF THE GREEK POETS. By W. S. TYLER, Williston Professor of Greek in Amherst College. 12mo. pp. 365. Cloth, beveled. $1.75

"Professor Tyler has here produced a work which is an honor to American Literature. It is well fitted to be a classic in our Colleges and Theological Seminaries. It furnishes admirable illustrations of the truth of both natural and revealed theology, and suggests original methods for the defence of these truths."—*Biblical Repertory*.

"The aim of the author is to detect the analogies between the myths of the Greek drama and epic, and the truths of revelation. The care of the scholar and the enthusiasm of the poet have been given to the work."—*Independent*.

"Prof. Tyler has done good service to the cause of truth in showing that the Iliad and Odyssey, as well as the dramas of Aeschylus and the tragedies of Sophocles, express ideas and sentiments very much like those we find in contemporary Scriptures."—*Hours at Home*.

LECTURES ON PASTORAL THEOLOGY. By ENOCH POND, D.D., Professor in Bangor Theological Seminary. Second Ed. 12mo. pp. 395. $1.75

"This volume is an excellent and practical treatise upon pastoral duty, and is heartily commended to all who are entering upon or engaged in the holy office of the Christian ministry."—*New York Observer*.

"Though especially adapted to Congregational churches and ministers, it will be found of use to all; for they are wise and prudent. All the special matters collated with the ministry are fully and clearly discussed."—*American Presbyterian and Theological Review*.

i

LATELY PUBLISHED.

CLASSICAL STUDY: Its Usefulness illustrated by Selections from the Writings of Eminent Scholars. Edited, with an Introduction, by SAMUEL H. TAYLOR, LL.D., Principal of Phillips Academy. 12mo. pp. 415. Cloth extra, Price, $2.00.

Professor *J. R. Boise, of the University of Chicago,* thus writes in the March number of the *Illinois Teacher:* "The selection of essays made by Dr. Taylor is eminently judicious, and presents the views of many leading writers, both in Europe and in this country. The Introduction, containing about thirty pages, gives, first, a concise and clear sketch of the history of the controversy on the value of classical studies; and then, several reasons why the highest benefits of classical study are seldom reached in this country. On this latter point, we know of no one better qualified by education and long experience as a teacher to speak wisely. This collection of essays reminds us of one feature in the whole controversy with which we have often been struck: the readiness of classical men to concede an honorable position to scientific studies. There have been few exceptions to this rule; whereas, scientific men have not unfrequently demanded for their favorite pursuits the entire field, to the exclusion of everything else; at least, to the entire exclusion of the ancient languages. ..... To all who desire the best collection of essays in our language on classical study, the work of Dr. Taylor will be very welcome. It should have a conspicuous place in every school-library, and in the private library of every educator in our land."

In another connection Prof. Boise adds: "Not the least valuable part of the volume is the Introduction, in which Dr. Taylor so ably, clearly, and fairly balances the arguments on the two sides. The conception of the entire work was a happy thought, and is carried out with that good judgment which I long ago learned to expect from him."

Dr. *McCosh, President of Princeton College* writes: "I value exceedingly your admirable work. The selection seems to me to be judicious, and the general impression left by the perusal is excellent. The work is fitted to do much good. I wish it were known in Great Britain, where there is a strong anti-classical reaction."

Professor Goodwin, of Harvard University, in a note to the Author, thus expresses his appreciation of the work: "You have done an excellent and a most timely service; and I am sure it will do good in counteracting much of the ignorant and nonsensical talk which we hear about the classics. The most ignorant form in which the opposition to the classics appears is when it uses such essays as those of Farrar's as arguments against our system of classical study in America; as if it could be affected by such arguments, even allowing them to be good over against the English system."

Professor George B. Jewett, in a letter to Dr. Taylor, speaks of the work thus: "Most effectually have you, by your own pen and by the writings of others, met and refuted, in this volume the numerous objections to classical study which that groundless prejudice is constantly reiterating; most nobly have you illustrated the value of the pursuit. At first the plan of your work seemed to me to involve much of unavoidable repetition, without securing a corresponding depth of impression. But a careful reading of the book has convinced me of the peculiar excellence of your plan, and, in fact, that it leaves nothing to be regretted, unless, perhaps, that the space occupied by your own pen is so greatly disproportionate to that which you have awarded to others. So far is the book from becoming wearisome by its repetitions, that it is quite kaleidoscopic in the variety and fascination of the views which it presents. It must carry conviction to all who will read it candidly, and who are capable of appreciating its multiform proofs and illustrations. It cannot fail to give a fresh impulse to the cause it so ably advocates. It will serve as a repository of facts and arguments from which inexhaustible supplies may be drawn for the defense and vindication of this sorely abused department of study. For furnishing this storehouse you are entitled to the thanks of all who are striving to promote the interest of sound learning."

President Aiken of Union College says: "It more than meets my expectation, and I am sure will render a valuable and timely service to the cause of good learning. It will prove a rich storehouse of arguments and illustrations for those who believe in the old ways."

"We think Dr. Taylor has made a good fight, and that opponents will have much to do to sustain the onset, if they are not completely unhorsed." — *Philadelphia Paper.*

"We commend the book as a valuable collection of essays on the higher methods of mental training." — *American Presbyterian.*

"We are glad that our friend, Dr. Taylor, the learned and eminent Principal of what we conceive to be, on the whole, the best training school in New England, has thought it wise to bring together into a comely volume, a series of more than twenty testimonies and arguments, from some of the ablest thinkers of the age, in favor of the thorough critical and continuous study of the Greek and Roman classics — prefaced by an apt and convincing discussion of his own. Dr. Taylor thus has gathered together some of the ripest thoughts and most valuable suggestions of Mr. Principal Jones, Prof. Thiersch, Hugh S. Legaré, Dr. Whewell, John Stuart Mill, Prof. Noah Porter, Joseph Payne, Prof. B. B. Edwards, Prof. John Conington, Wm. Howard Gardiner, Esq., Prof Pillans, Dr. Geo. B. Loring, Prof. Sellar, Pres. McCosh, Prof. E. D. Sanborn, Prof Masson, Hon. P. H. Sears, Pres. Felton, Pres. Brown, Prof. D'Arcy W. Thompson, Prof. Goldwin Smith, and Prof. L. Campbell. There is a charm in being able to note so readily the different moving of so many minds upon one such subject as this; as well as great significance and force in the verdict in which such a jury agree." — *Congregationalist.*

WARREN F. DRAPER, Publisher,
ANDOVER, MASS.

RECENT PUBLICATIONS.

Lightfoot. St. Paul's Epistle to the Galatians. A Revised Text, with Introduction, Notes, and Dissertations. By J. B. LIGHTFOOT, D.D., Hulsean Professor of Divinity, and Fellow of Trinity College, Cambridge. 8vo. pp. 402. Uniform in style with Lightfoot Henderson and Murphy.

"This work aims to be, as [in some respects is, more complete than any other] treatise upon the Epistle in the English language. ... Great labor has been expended upon collateral discussions. Indeed the contemporary of the text forms the smaller part of the volume, invested as it is with elaborate dissertations and detached notes before and after and between.

"The commentary is learned without display. It bears marks of original and wide and scholarly research held in strict subordination to the purpose in question. All theories except those which deserve a consideration are left out of the account. Perhaps the collateral dissertations might have been ... pressed. It is independent. Few commentaries bear more character ... freedom from constraint. The author apparently does not worry ... either to agree with or differ from any other writer. He decides for him ... the text, after a revision by Westcott for his use. ... And this leads us to say that it is largely marked by a manly insight. He reaches his results by that process of exclusion which so characterizes Ellicott, and more by a direct apprehension; and he often holds them, perhaps, with more of an instinctive certainty than Alford. ... It is spiritual and evangelical."— *Congregationalist.*

"For a scholar's use Dr. Lightfoot's Commentary is invaluable. He and Lockes Ellicott worthily supplement each other. The Revised Text is one of the best recent contributions to a complete text to the Greek New Testament. ... The criticisms on the text are concise and to the point," etc. — *Am. Presbyterian.*

"Taken as a whole, we venture to say that this is the most complete and exhaustive commentary on the Epistle to the Galatians that has yet appeared, Ellicott's not excepted."— *Christian Intelligencer.*

Reubelt. The Scripture Doctrine of the Person of Christ. By J. A. REUBELT, D.D., Professor in Indiana University, Bloomington, Ind., based on the German of W. F. Gess. 12mo. pp. 456. Cloth. $2.00

"As a whole, this treatise may be briefly characterized as an earnest and ... effort to present the true and consistent doctrine of the Scriptures respecting the person of Christ, and to reconcile the varying confessional statements of the various different denominations, by carefully comparing them with the language of the Scriptures themselves. The investigation is conducted in a devout spirit, and truth-loving spirit, combined with accurate scholarship and thorough study of the subject."— *Lutheran Observer.*

"The translator has executed his task with admirable skill. While preserving the integrity of the original as to its line of thought and argument, he has clothed it in excellent English."— *Christian Intelligencer.*

"Those who hold the doctrine of eternal generation will here find a view calculated in divesting their views of its customary crudeness, and sublimating, as too many be, the inherent contradiction that lies in the two words. We are certain with that view of the phrase, 'only-begotten Son,' which regards it as referring to a human relationship (as usual everywhere significant, but especially so as ..., the unity of nature, possession, peerless interest, and sympathy whether belonging to the Father and the Son.'— *Congregational Review.*

"Though the style of thought is peculiar, and though the opinions often new, and sometimes such as may not command immediate assent or even acquiescence or any assent at all, yet there is an awakening power in the book, and the doctrine at is right."— *Congregationalist.*

WARREN F. DRAPER, Publisher,
Andover, Mass.

Books Published by W. F. Draper.

WINER'S N. T. GRAMMAR. A Grammar of the Idiom of the New Testament: prepared as a Solid Basis for the Interpretation of the New Testament. By Dr. GEORGE BENEDICT WINER. Seventh Edition, enlarged and improved. By Dr. GOTTLIEB LÜNEMANN, Professor of Theology at the University of Göttingen. Revised and authorized Translation. 8vo. pp. 744. Cloth, $5.00; sheep, $6.00; half goat, $6.75.

"Prof. Thayer exhibits the most scholarly and pains-taking accuracy in all his work, especial attention being given to references and indexes, on which the value of such a work so much depends. The indexes alone fill eighty-six pages. The publishers work is handsomely done, and we cannot conceive that a better Winer should be for many years to come accessible to American scholars." — *Princeton Review.*

"Prof. Thayer speaks with great modesty of the work as being 'substantially a revision of Professor Masson's translation.' We have carefully compared many paragraphs and pages, and find that the labor performed by him is by no means hinted in his unpretending preface. The improvement in purity, transparency, and accuracy of style, as well as in fidelity, is very noticeable. This edition has the advantage of being brought down to 1866, embodying the labors of one of the ripest scholars of Germany for a life-time, and containing references in cases of textual criticism to the Codex Sinaiticus. There are three elaborate and exhaustive indexes..... The invaluable contents of the volume are thus at once at the command of the scholar..... We are struck with the appropriateness of an expression on the title-page: 'prepared as a *solid basis* for the interpretation of the New Testament.' Clergymen of scholarly habits will find this Grammar, Robinson's New Test. Lexicon, and a critical edition of the the Greek Testament about all the exegetical apparatus they will need. A clear head, patient study, and sympathy with the Divine Spirit will, with such helps, do the work of a Commentator for them better than Commentaries themselves without them." — *Pacific.*

"We trust that this admirable edition of a justly famous and surpassingly valuable work, will gain extensive circulation, and that the study of it will begin afresh." — *Baptist Quarterly.*

"The seventh edition of Winer, superintended by Lunemann (Leipz. 1867), we have at last, thanks to Prof. Thayer, in a really accurate translation." — *Dr. Ezra Abbott, in Smith's Dictionary of the Bible, American Ed.*

"The translator's preface informs us that after a very considerable portion of the work had been finished, and three hundred pages or more had been stereotyped, the plans which had been formed were largely modified by the publication of the seventh edition of the Grammar in Germany. With a determination to make the work as valuable as possible, the translator resolved to revise the whole in connection with this latest edition. He accordingly retraced his steps to a considerable degree, and prepared his translation in conformity with his modified plan. The result is, that we have before us, in our own language, 'a reproduction of the original work,' in its most perfect form, and with its author's latest additions and improvements. The wisdom, as well as the appreciation of the interests of students of the New Testament, which Professor Thayer has displayed in adopting this course at the cost of long delay and greatly increased labor, entitle him to the favorable regard of the public." — *New Englander.*

"'Without altering the general distribution of matter as it appeared in the sixth edition, he — Winer — constantly improved the book in details, by additions of greater or less extent in more than three hundred and forty places, by erasures and reconstructions, by the multiplication of parallel passages from biblical and from profane literature, by a more precise definition of thoughts and expressions,' etc. Professor Lunemann has added to the seventh edition not only these improvements, but also improvements of his own; and has thus made the seventh edition more full, as well as more accurate, than either of the preceding.... Professor Thayer has introduced numerous and important corrections of Masson's translation, and has made the present edition of the Grammar decidedly superior to any of the preceding translations. He has made it especially convenient for the uses of an English student by noting on the outer margin of the pages the paging of the sixth and seventh German editions, and also of Prof. Masson's translation. Thus the reader of a commentary which refers to the pages of either of those volumes, may easily find the reference by consulting the margin of this volume. Great care has also been bestowed on the indexes of the present volume, which are now very accurate and complete. One of the indexes, that of passages in the New Testament explained or cited occupies sixty pages, and notes distinctively not only the texts which are merely cited, but those also which are commented upon. For this, much credit is due to Prof. G.W. Warren, of the Baptist Theological Seminary in Chicago. The three indexes fill eighty-five pages, and largely augment the value and richness of the volume." — *Bibliotheca Sacra.*

"The work of the American editor is done in a thorough and scholarly manner." — *Congr. Quarterly.*

"The whole appearance of the work as it now stands indicates a careful and thorough scholarship. A critical comparison of several pages with the original confirms the impression made by a general examination of the book. In its present form, this translation may now be recommended as worthy of a place in the library of every minister who desires to study the New Testament with the aid of the best critical helps." — *Theological Eclectic.*

"Great pains also have been taken to secure typographical accuracy, an extremely difficult thing in a work of this kind. We rejoice that so invaluable a work has thus been made as nearly perfect as we can hope ever to have it. It is a work that can hardly fail to facilitate and increase the reverent and accurate study of the Word of God." — *American Presbyterian Review.*

WINER'S CHALDEE GRAMMAR. Translated by PROF. HORATIO B. HACKETT. 8vo. pp. 152. Half cloth, 75 cents.

COMMENTARIES
PUBLISHED BY
WARREN F. DRAPER,
ANDOVER, MASS.

These Books will be sent, post-paid, on receipt of the price affixed.

MURPHY.

Critical and Exegetical Commentaries, by Prof. James G. Murphy, LL.D., T.C.D., viz. on

GENESIS. With a Preface by J. P. Thompson, D.D., New York. 8vo. pp. 545. Cloth, rounded edges.

EXODUS. (Uniform with Genesis.) 8vo. pp. 385.

"Dr. Murphy in his commentaries has a definite plan which he carries out ... text is explained, translated anew, and comments are added at the end ... He is a fair, clear, and candid interpreter. His aim is to reach the sense ... by an impartial examination of the text." — *Amer. Presb. Rev. and Theol. Rev.*

"Thus far nothing has appeared in this country for half a century on the subject of the Pentateuch as valuable as the present two volumes. He is warm-hearted and ... often eloquent. His pages afford golden suggestions and key-thoughts ... laws of interpretation are stated with so fresh and natural a clearness and force that ... will permanently stand." — *Methodist Quarterly.*

"The most valuable contribution that has for a long time been made to ... for the critical study of the Old Testament is Mr. Draper's reproduction in ... on Genesis, in one octavo volume. It is a good deal ... say of a commentary, however ... all sincerity, that this volume furnishes about as fascinating work for ... ing as any volume of the day, in any department of literature ... will be salutary and effective for the truth. . . . . The language and style ... cessible to him who will compare favorably with those ablest in the ... tion of the divine word; while he will, of course, read always with discrimination ... upon the views which find expression." — *Congregationalist.*

STUART.

Critical and Exegetical Commentaries, by Moses Stuart, late Professor in Andover Theological Seminary, viz. on

ROMANS. Third Edition. Edited and revised by Prof. R. D. C. Robbins. 12mo. pp. 544.

HEBREWS. Third Edition. Edited and revised by Prof. R. D. C. Robbins. 12mo. pp. 575.

THE APOCALYPSE. 2 vols. 8vo. pp. 504, 544.

ECCLESIASTES. Second Edition. Edited and revised by Prof. R. D. C. Robbins. 12mo. pp. 346.

BOOK OF PROVERBS. 12mo. pp. 432.

"The first characteristic of Dr. Moses Stuart as a commentator is the exuberant thoroughness of his labors. His exegesis is in a moral skill, and if not unsuccessful in bringing out the meaning of the obscure passages, and adds new and adequate shades of meaning to the more obvious and superficial sense." — *North American Review.*

"The exegetical works of Prof. Stuart have many excellences, and it will be long ... before the student of the Bible in the original will be willing to dispense with them as a part of his critical apparatus." — *Interior Reader.*

"The spirit of the man is so interwined with them as to be a perpetual ... benediction to the reader." — *Cong. Quarterly.*

"In turning over its pages we read with charming the real thoughts ... erasies of one of the most remarkable of the great and good men ... world has produced . . . . This contribution by Prof. Stuart to ... among the Commentaries on the Epistle to the Romans, and, will ... always be held in high estimation by students of the Sacred Scriptures." — *N. Y. Observer.*

Commentaries Published by W. F. Draper.

ELLICOTT.

Commentaries, Critical and Grammatical, by C. J. Ellicott, Bishop of Gloucester and Bristol, viz. on

GALATIANS. With an Introductory Notice by C. E. STOWE, lately Professor in Andover Theological Seminary. 8vo. pp. 183.	$1.75
EPHESIANS. 8vo. pp. 190.	1.75
THESSALONIANS. 8vo. pp. 171.	1.75
THE PASTORAL EPISTLES. 8vo. pp. 265.	2.50
PHILIPPIANS, COLOSSIANS, AND PHILEMON. 8vo. pp. 265.	2.50
THE SET in five volumes, tinted paper, bevelled edges, gilt tops,	12.00
THE SET in two volumes, same style,	10.00
THE SET in two volumes, black cloth, rounded edges,	8.00

"We would recommend all scholars of the original Scriptures who seek directness, luminous brevity, the absence of everything irrelevant to strict grammatical inquiry, with a concise and yet very complete view of the opinions of others, to possess themselves of Ellicott's Commentaries." — *American Presbyterian.*

"His Commentaries are among the best, if not the very best, helps a student can have." — *American Presbyterian and Theological Review.*

"Ellicott is one of the best commentators of this class." — *Princeton Review.*

"I do not know of anything superior to them in their own particular line."—*Dean Alford.*

"We have never met with a learned commentary on any book of the New Testament so nearly perfect in every respect as the Commentary on the Epistle to the Galatians, by Prof. Ellicott, of King's College, London — learned, devout, and orthodox." — *Independent.*

"They fill the scholar with genuine admiration." — *Watchman and Reflector.*

"The Commentaries of Prof. Ellicott belong to the first class of critical writings of the New Testament." — *Boston Recorder.*

"To Bishop Ellicott must be assigned the first rank, if not the first place in the first rank, of English biblical scholarship. The series of Commentaries on the Pauline Epistles are in the highest style of critical exegesis." — *Methodist Quarterly.*

"The best English work of this character."— *New Englander.*

"Strictly grammatical and critical, thorough and fearless, concise yet complete, worthy of all confidence." — *Evangelical Review.*

HENDERSON.

Commentaries, Critical, Philological, and Exegetical, by E. Henderson, D.D., viz. on

THE BOOK OF THE TWELVE MINOR PROPHETS. Translated from the Original Hebrew. With a Biographical Sketch of the Author, by E. P. BARROWS, Hitchcock Professor in Andover Theological Seminary. 8vo. pp. 490.	$4.00
JEREMIAH AND LAMENTATIONS. Translated from the Original Hebrew. 8vo. pp. 315.	$3.00
EZEKIEL. Translated from the Original Hebrew. 8vo. pp. 228.	2.25

"Dr. Henderson's Commentaries are rich in wholesome and true exposition." — *Presbyterian Magazine.*

"The work is invaluable for its philological research and critical acumen..... The notes are replete with the fruits of varied learning." — *The Presbyterian.*

"Dr. Henderson is one of the most eminent of modern biblical critics. One of the leading features of his mode of treating Scripture is his happy blending of textual with exegetical comment. His treatise on Jeremiah is well worthy, by its elevated scholarship, to take a place side by side with the commentaries of Bishop Ellicott and of Professor Murphy, also issued by Mr. Draper." — *Publishers' Circular.*

"He excelled in weighing evidence, and impressing upon it its relative value. His discrimination was clear and his judgment was sound. He dealt with fact, not with fiction. He searched for data, not for opinions. Dr. Henderson was not only well versed in the Hebrew language, but also in its cognates. Few men, either in England or America, have been his equals in Oriental literature. His Commentary on Jeremiah has the same general characteristics which appear in his Commentary on the Minor Prophets." — *Bib. Sacra.*

"The only satisfactory commentary on the Minor Prophets we know of in the English language." — *Episcopal Recorder.*

"The volume before us gives abundant evidence of patient scholarship and clear conceptions of evangelical truth." — *Evangelical Quarterly.*

"We have met with no so satisfactory a commentary on this part of the prophetic scriptures."— *Watchman and Reflector.*

www.ingramcontent.com/pod-product-compliance
Lightning Source LLC
Chambersburg PA
CBHW031337230426
43670CB00006B/361